HISTORIC CARDIGANSHII
AND THEIR FAMILIE

To our Dearest :
Ian & Cidy
from
Hugh & Caroline

Previous publications by Francis Jones

HISTORY OF THE 172 FIELD REGIMENT
HISTORY OF THE SURREY YEOMANRY QMR
THE HOLY WELLS OF WALES
THE PRINCIPALITY AND PRINCES OF WALES
GOD BLESS THE PRINCE OF WALES
AN APPROACH TO WELSH GENEALOGY
AN APPROACH TO WELSH HERALDRY
HISTORIC CARMARTHENSHIRE HOMES AND THEIR FAMILIES
HISTORIC HOUSES OF PEMBROKESHIRE AND THEIR FAMILIES
HISTORIC PEMBROKESHIRE HOMES AND THEIR FAMILIES Extended Edition
HISTORIC CARDIGANSHIRE HOMES AND THEIR FAMILIES
TREASURY OF HISTORIC PEMBROKESHIRE
TREASURY OF HISTORIC CARMARTHENSHIRE

Front Cover Pictures

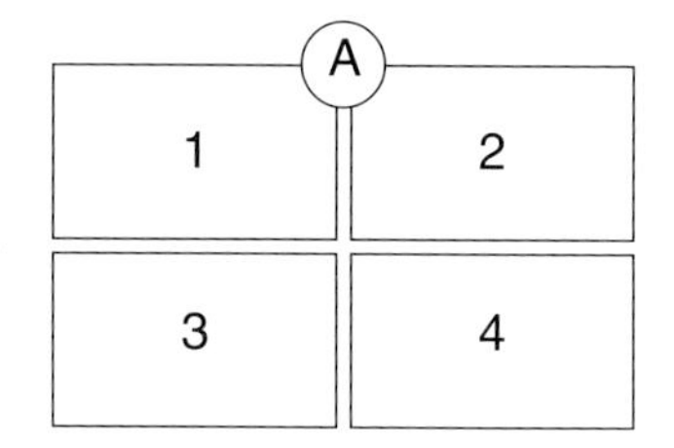

A The Old Welsh Arms
1 Nanteos
2 Parc y gors
3 Bronwydd
4 Ynysgregi

THE FRANCIS JONES

HISTORIC CARDIGANSHIRE HOMES

AND THEIR FAMILIES

From the Archives, articles, manuscripts and researches of the
LATE MAJOR FRANCIS JONES,
C.V.O., T.D., F.S.A., M.A., K.ST.J.,
WALES HERALD AT ARMS

Editor CAROLINE CHARLES-JONES

Compiler LAURIE WIDGERY

Additional Editorial HUGH CHARLES-JONES

Published by
BRAWDY BOOKS
2004

2nd Edition
First published 2000

Published by
Brawdy Books, Plas yr Wregin, Dinas, Newport
Pembrokeshire, SA42 0YH
Telephone: 01348 811450
PlasWregin@aol.com

Web site
www.brawdybooks.com
info@brawdybooks.com

ISBN 0 9528 344 72

Illustrations
The National Library of Wales
Leon Olin, Sylvia Gainsford
Thomas Lloyd

Book Jacket Design
H. Charles-Jones

Design and Make-up
ARTdesigns
Telephone: 01267 290670
artdesigns@hotmail.com

Printed and Bound by
Cambrian Printers
Llanbadarn Road
Aberystwyth
Ceredigion SY23 3TN

Major Francis Jones, Late Wales Herald at Arms, (1908-1993), was one of the most distinguished of Welsh historians. This was recognised by his appointment as Wales Herald at Arms. He was the first man to hold this post for 600 years. He held it with distinction for thirty years.

Many of his happiest, most productive years were spent in Cardiganshire. In the thirties he worked at the National Library of Wales. During this highly creative time he produced research material for this and many other published works. He left Aberystwyth for war service in north Africa, the middle East, Sicily and Italy. This book completes the Dyfed Trilogy, and was compiled from the Francis Jones Archives.

In later life he returned to the National Library of Wales as a Governor where he had once worked as a junior researcher.

Cardiganshire Days 1937-1946
concludes this book. It is a personal account by Francis Jones's son, Hugh Charles Jones of their family life. It is a brief social history of Cardiganshire people; houses such as Gogerddan, Nanteos and Plas Broginan and glimpses of family life during eventful years. Francis Jones's personality emerges from behind his pen and sword as a family man.

Major Francis Jones, Wales Herald at Arms
Inset, as a young man during his Cardiganshire days

CONTENTS

Map of Cardiganshire Tithe Districts viii

Acknowledgements x

Preface by Francis Jones xi

Original Notes of Francis Jones xxii

Foreword by Thomas Lloyd xxiii

Coats of Arms xxvi

Historic Houses 1-281

Cardiganshire Days by Hugh Charles-Jones 282

A Cardiganshire Character 307

Bibliography 314

Bibliographical Abbreviations 318

Glossary of Useful Terms 319

Index 320

The Francis Jones Archives 331

Welsh Historical Societies 332

Cardiganshire Tithe Districts

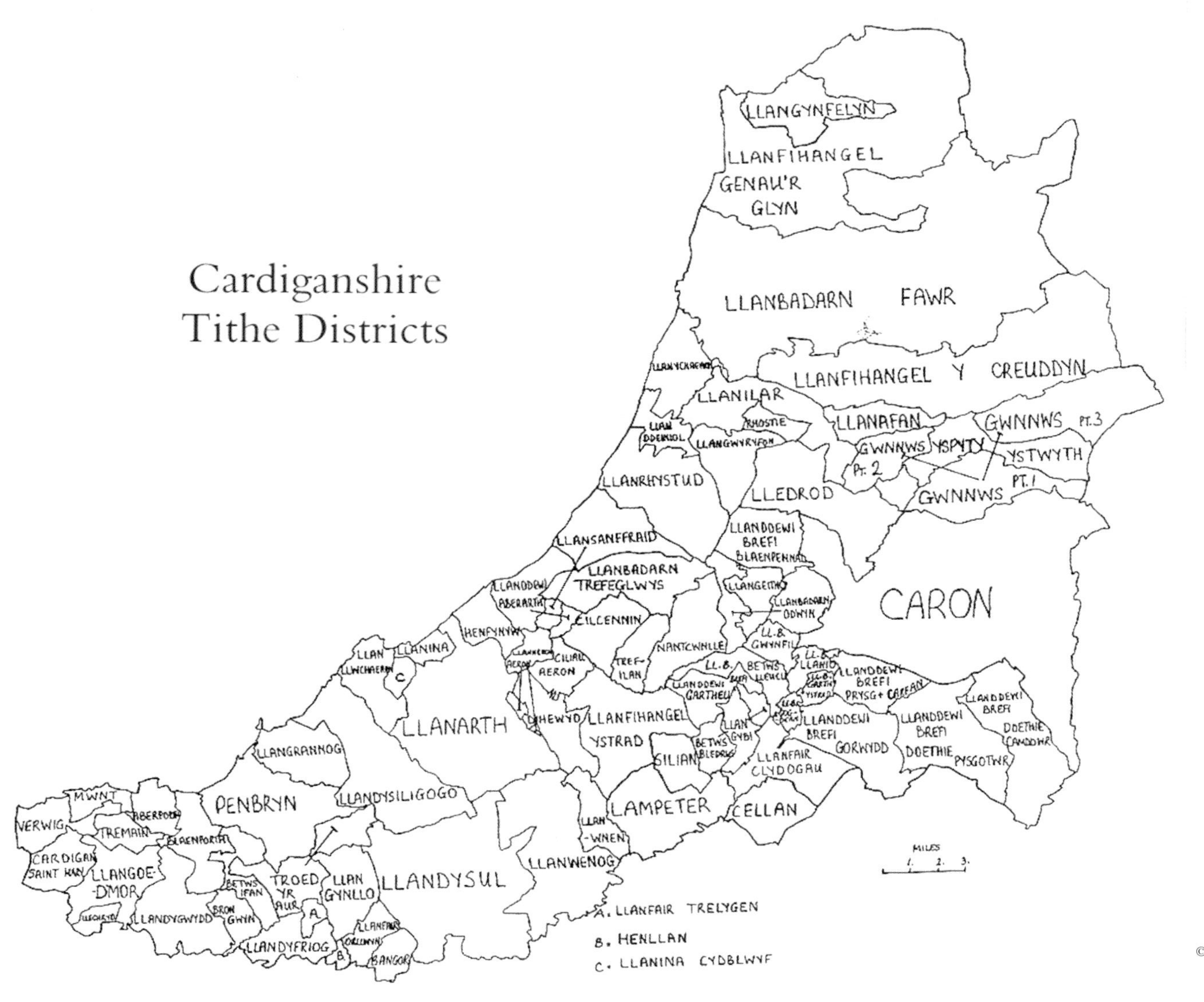

Dedicated to

Francis Jones and his wife Ethel

The inspiration and original research for this volume came about during their happy years in Cardiganshire.

ACKNOWLEDGEMENTS

Our thanks go to the following who gave us their time, expertise, help, advice and illustrations.

To Laurie Widgery who worked tirelessly on this book. Special thanks to Colin Widgery for his support. Laurie Widgery spent countless hours compiling the book from The Francis Jones Archives, and interpreting his hand-written manuscripts.

As always, Pam Davies for being a star supporter, ensuring that our subscribers get their copies of the book.

Leon Olin and Sylvia Gainsford for their enchanting illustrations of the houses.

Tom Lloyd for the loan of photographs, prints of houses, reproductions of Coats of Arms, and encouragement. The National Library of Wales for permission to use prints, maps and other illustrations in this book. The kindly assistance of Mr. Michael Francis and his staff helped smooth the path to publication.

Mrs. M. Madden, for her work on the Index to this book.

For helping with the proof reading our thanks to Dennis Doyle.

Our grateful thanks to the Historical Societies for support, particularly, The Pembrokeshire Historical Society, The Carmarthenshire Antiquarian Society, The Ceredigion Historical Society, The London Pembrokeshire Historical Society and to the Welsh Historic Gardens Trust, the Friends of the National Library and all others who helped and encouraged us.

To Andy Taylor whose professional dedication produced this book ready for the printers. His calm in times of crisis is beyond praise.

To all those unnamed people who helped us along the way; scholars, printers, book-sellers, our thanks.

Brawdy Books was forged by the confidence and support from Patron Subscribers world-wide. To thank them adequately is quite impossible. Especially as without them not a word of Francis Jones's work would have been published. His family salutes your generosity.

PREFACE

Lecture given by Major Francis Jones to the Ceredigion Historical Society at Aberystwyth on Saturday 11th December 1976

There are several reasons that unite to make my visit to this Society an agreeable and gladsome occasion. Some of the happiest years of my life were spent in Ceredigion, particularly in this town, so that my appearance today is in the nature of a home-coming; moreover I can combine the pleasure of meeting old friends, some of them one-time colleagues, with the possibility of making the acquaintance of others who share interests similar to mine; and especially to address an association which has contributed so notably to the encouragement of historical and antiquarian studies and provided a platform for those who devote their time to the bygones of Ceredigion, thus enabling them to present to a wider public the fruits of labours that might otherwise have been consigned to the cobwebbed anonymity of the attic. I have had the pleasure of addressing the Ceredigion Antiquarian Society on previous occasions – the first time being as long ago as 1938 – and that you have invited me once more is surely an indication of the tolerance your humane membership extends to harmless eccentrics.

The Historic Families

The subject of my talk is 'The Historic Homes of Cardiganshire' and it may be appropriate to define in some detail the scope and object of the study. For some time my intention has been to produce a work on the historic homes and families of the thirteen counties of Wales, and to date, I have listed nearly 5,000 of such homes. Of these, 355 are in the old county of Cardigan, Sir Aberteifi. By historic families I mean those who for several generations, many for several centuries, have been involved with local administration, political, social and economic, and who have influenced the development of regional and occasionally national life. It will be appreciated that these families consist of the county gentlefolk and the professional classes, who were almost exclusively enabled to influence local and county affairs, since they were employed by central Government to carry out its dictates, Acts of Parliament, laws and regulations, largely in a voluntary capacity. In other words, they were functionaries, and so long as they had function to perform, so long were they essential for the administration. This state of affairs continued until the new County Councils, and later District and Parish Councils, whose members were popularly elected and professionals who came to be known as Local Government Officials and the Civil Service.

Since several misconceptions have gained currency in modern times, it becomes necessary to review briefly the sort of people these former Governors of Wales were. Often, they are promenaded before us as extremely wealthy folk living in ornate mansions, spending their time on horseback cheering the baying hounds on the trail of the fox, fishing the streams and shooting game fowl, protected by law for their exclusive delectation and pastime; they are represented as hedonists attended by hordes of servitors whose sole concern was ministering to the epicurean tastes of idle masters and mistresses, who at various times of the year continued a butterfly existence at the gaming tables of Bath, the elegant salons of Cheltenham, or the more sybaritic delights of the London season.

Such an idyllic scene is far removed from the reality. In fact, these historical families were hard-working, stay-at-home folk, deeply immersed in the prosaic day-to-day concerns of their homes and estates, all of them practical farmers, often using part of their residences for farming purposes, establishing agricultural societies, introducing innovations and improvements, concerned with local industries and shipping, fulfilling duties of Justices of the Peace (sometimes holding courts in their parlours) acting as Commissioners for implementing Acts of Parliament, assessments, and collection of taxes. In addition they held senior posts, far more burdensome and demanding than in our day, of Lord Lieutenant, Deputy-Lieutenant, High Sheriff and Member of Parliament. The collections of manuscripts and records in our National Library reveal their attachment to, and involvement in, local affairs, while inventories accompanying their wills indicate their personal attachment to commercial matters. They were an intelligent people, aware of what went on around them, in some ways a rustic breed, and until Victorian days largely spoke the ancient language of those ancestors from whom they were proud to claim descent, and of the folk among whom they dwelt. The wicked Squire who was alleged to have lowered an ear-marked sheep down the chimney of an uncooperative tenant to incriminate him in the eyes of the law, is in no way typical of his species, however popular a television play on the affair may have been in recent years. Apart from Leviathans like Vaughan of Crosswood, Pryse of Gogerddan, Lewes of Llanllyr, Lloyd of Peterwell and Gwynne of Mynachty, they were in the main a body of minor gentlefolk, gentlemen farmers and prosperous yeomen.

Neither was entry to their ranks a difficult matter and an individual (or family) whose ability and industry resulted in the acquisition of funds sufficient to enable to undertake the responsibilities and adopt the conventions of the higher class, was readily accepted and quickly absorbed into their ranks; such as Williams of Pantsheriff who derived from yeoman stock, and Jones of Deri Ormond a cattle dealer and drover who had hit the jackpot. By and large, these families consisted of successful people, rejuvenated from time to time by people of similar capacity from the ranks of the people.

Such, briefly, were the families which we can fairly describe as historic, for they formed, influenced and guided, for better or for worse, the events that constituted the history of Wales in bygone days.

The Historic Homes

It is of the homes of these people that I speak today and you may be interested to learn of the route that led me to them. Interest in families involved me in a study of their genealogies, not merely of the main lines but of the many junior branches that stemmed from the parent tree. Old-time genealogists like the deputy herald Lewys Dwnn, George Owen of Henllys, David Edwardes of Rhydygors and William Lewes of Llwynderw appreciated the significance of younger branches – some of whom outstripped the parent line in public service and importance and were careful to include them in their compilations. The most useful of these, especially where Cardiganshire is concerned, are the volumes known as the *Golden Grove MSS* kept in the Public Records Office, a copy of which is available in the National Library, wherein both main and junior lines, even descents from younger daughters, are outlined at length. Accordingly, I noted the dwelling-places of all these families, and as time allowed I visited many of them. Owing to the vicissitude of fortune and changing fashions, many have become ordinary farmhouses, others have been reduced in size, even reduced to ruins, while some have completely disappeared from the face of the earth with but a solitary stone or a grassy mound to indicate their former site. Nevertheless a good number have survived, some still sheltering the old families or their modern successors, while others have been sold and adapted to other purposes. Among the former are Llanllyr, Lovesgrove, Coedmor and Penylan. Among the latter are Gogerddan and Crosswood, now agricultural establishments, Penglais is the official residence of the University Principal, High Mead and Abermad are schools, Cardigan Priory a hospital, Llandyrus a hotel and Falcondale an old folks' home.

Clearly the former status of a number of the homes would not have been apparent had I not approached them through the medium of the pedigrees. In them lived our historic families and so they are historic homes.

You will have noted the title of my talk – Historic *Homes* – not Houses. I believe these buildings have to be examined not only from an architectural stand-point, important as that is, but from their significance in the social and economic life of a district. In other words, you have to ask why were they there at all, who built them, what manner of folk lived in them, how long did the families persist, why did some fall and others survive? Only by considering the human element can we invest them with life and appreciate the style in which they were built, while the architecture itself can indicate changing fashions of bygone centuries. Few have survived in the unchanged guise and purity of the time when they were first built; many are an agglomeration of styles of different periods, internal re-arrangements have been effected, a wing extended, several rooms added, an entrance porch made anew, or remodelled, a chimney discontinued and another erected in another part of the building. They are not always tidy structures fresh from the architects' table, but a huddle of dissonant styles, but nevertheless exciting, often attractive, reflecting changing tastes and fashions, the prosperity or adversity of the owners, an expression of the functions and requirements of a class of people. Examples are found in the mansions of Blaendyffryn and Blaenpant which are an agglomeration of different periods, while on the other hand we have houses like Llanina and Wern which have preserved their style substantially unchanged.

I recall, many years ago, when the owner of a Carmarthenshire mansion applied for a grant for its upkeep to the Historic Buildings Council. This house was, and remains, one of the best examples of a seventeenth century mansion in South Wales, cube-shaped of three storeys with a wing to the rear for domestic offices. However, about 1850, an extension had been made to one of the sides, which contained a dining-room and billiard room, with bedrooms over, but lower than the original cube. A condition of the grant being made, was the total removal of the Victorian extension so that the original fabric remained in its pristine purity. This was done. To me such removal was a violation of the whole ethos and spirit of a residence, for additional growth, be it vulgar or be it in perfect harmony, should be accepted for what it is and not as it should be, provided that structurally it did not impair the original. A Victorian extension is as valid as the Jacobean nucleus.

To me, these were homes not merely houses. An architect's plan, however accurate and meticulous the execution, provides only half of the story. It is like looking at a suit hanging in a wardrobe. A house must not only tell us what the builder's plan had been, but, to be complete, must also tell of the people who lived within it and made it into a home. Accordingly, my notes contain, in addition to a description of the fabric, a précis of the family history associated with it, and any further information relating to a peculiarity or uniqueness relating to both – a form of social history encapsulated within four walls.

Those who have considered the history of Cardiganshire homes in the past – with one notable exception – have concentrated mainly on the major examples, such as Hafod, Gogerddan,

Crosswood, Nanteos, Llanllyr and so on, partly because these have survived to our times; but by far the greater number consisted of minor houses, most of which have undergone many changes. However, some of the latter have survived structurally to a remarkable degree, for example Noyadd [Neuadd-Llanarth], Llanina and Wern Newydd, and this, paradoxically, because their owners were relatively less important. Indeed, obscurity and remoteness have been the salvation of many of these historic houses, have sheltered them from the changing winds of fashion, so that they retain their earlier features to a remarkable degree.

That so many of these homes exist is an expression of the social framework of the Welsh, deriving from medieval systems, and differ radically from the situation across the border. In England these homes are much larger and grander, but relatively fewer in number, while the families are correspondingly fewer than those in Wales, albeit more affluent and powerful. In Wales the opposite was the case. The Welsh governing class mainly descended from the freemen of the Middle Ages, and as emphasis was placed on family relationships, and as younger sons enjoyed the same status as their elder brethren, they tended to proliferate, so that they spread over the land in a vast network of inter-related families. They were the Incas of the Welsh countryside. This is clearly seen in the family trees contained in genealogical collections, and borne out by the number of the historic homes. I have already mentioned there were some 355 of these homes in Cardiganshire alone. Every parish contained at least one, and some parishes contained a formidable number; for instance, in Llandysul there were 30 gentry homes, in Llanbadarnfawr 21, in Llandygwydd 16, in Llangoedmor 15, in Llanfihangel y Creuddyn and Llanfihangel Geneu'r Glyn 12 each, in Llanwenog and Penbryn 11 each, in Llanarth 10, while the other parishes vary between 1 and 9 such homes. Perhaps a detailed list of historic homes in Llandysul parish may be of interest if I enumerate them:

Alltyrodin
Blaen Cerdin
Blaenythan
Bryn Dahawg
Camnant
Castell Hywel
Cefn Gwallter
Coed y Foel
Cwm Huar
Cwm Meudwy
Dinas Cerdin
Dyffryn Llynod
Faerdre Fawr
Faerdre Fach
Ffosesgob
Ffos Helig
Gelli Fraith
Gilfachwen Isaf
Gilfachwen Uchaf
Glan Cletwr
Gwar Coed Einion
Henbant Hall
Llanfair Berth Cyndy
Llwyn Rhydowen
Nant yr ymenin
Pantstreimon
Pant y defaid
Troedrhiw ffenyd
Waunifor
Gelli faharen

This is by no means unusual in Wales. A comparative parish in neighbouring Pembrokeshire, namely Nevern, had 27 such homes. The history and ancestry of the families of the 30 Llandysul homes is known and indicates the care that has to be exercised when considering them. For instance, both the adjoining properties Gilfachwen-Isaf and -Uchaf were once inhabited by families bearing the surname Lloyd – but they derived from entirely different ancestors, the former from Cadifor ap Dinawal of Castell Hywel, the latter from Elystan Glodrudd a mid-Wales prince – so that surnames in Wales can be misleading unless read in their genealogical context.

To understand this remarkable distribution, it is necessary to know something of the social structure that led to it. In other words, we come back to the burden of my gospel – the families. In Wales, family and house must be considered as one unit if the study is to be at all intelligible.

It may be useful at this stage to draw attention to sources providing information about both homes and families. Firstly, manuscript and record sources. In this, Cardiganshire is extremely fortunate in having on its doorstep a veritable Ali Baba's cave of historical treasures. I refer to the National Library, custodian of incomparable collections of the raw materials without which no complete or adequate history of Wales can be written. Among these are the muniments of numerous families, dating from the twelfth century to the present day. Many contain information about the erection of the houses, repairs and alterations made to them, about the lines of the owners, their deeds and misdeeds, and the vicissitudes that beset them. In addition, there are maps, plans, terriers, drawings, paintings and photographs which throw light on the subjects under review. Another important archive in the Library consists of the probate wills and inventories, the latter being particularly helpful as they often reveal how the homes were furnished and the degree of comfort they had to offer. The great pedigree collections, too well-known to require recapitulation, provide us with a framework of the local families whose accuracy can be checked by reference to the deeds and documents contained in the Library's strongrooms.

Then we have printed sources, presenting the labours of bygone antiquaries and historians, the journals of various tourists of the eighteenth and nineteenth centuries and particularly S. R. Meyrick's *Cardiganshire* (1810), a writer who appreciated the link between house and family, and the *Topographical Dictionaries* of Carlisle and Samuel Lewis; parish and regional histories, like those on Llannarth and Llandysul; Eyre Evan's studies on Lampeter; and especially the volumes issued by this learned Society.

Among the more outstanding essays contained in past numbers of *Ceredigion*, are those on the minor county houses by Major H. J. Lloyd-Johnes, the study of Deri Ormond by Miss Inglis-Jones, and the valuable chronicle of Llanllyr from the pen of H.M. Lieutenant, Captain Hext-Lewes. Would that every occupier of a historic home in Cardiganshire followed these worthy examples. The advantage of localised compilations such as these and parish histories, is that they concentrate on a small area which renders it possible to enter into considerable detail, which the fact that they were produced by local men with personal knowledge of the people and places they describe, often produce information that might be denied those unacquainted with the area or who treat subjects in a more generalised manner.

Dineley's account of the *Duke of Beaufort's Progress* through Wales in 1684 contains two of the earliest-known drawings of Cardiganshire houses, namely 'Trawsgoed' and Cardiganshire Priory, which enable us to compare them with the residences as they are today. A volume published in 1904, *Contemporary Biographies of South Wales and Monmouthshire*, contains excellent photographs of Cardigan Priory (then the residence of the Pritchards) and other houses in this county. Further reliable sources of information for the three counties of Dyfed are the photographs made in 1871 by Charles Smith Allen of Tenby, a professional photographer who visited numerous mansions, and afterwards bound the photographs into large, beautifully covered albums which he sold to the proprietors of these houses. One, made for the Lewes family, is still kept at Llanllyr and I am grateful to Captain Hext-Lewes for making it available to me. As the majority of these houses are no longer the seats of their former owners, and have been adapted to other uses, most of them altered and adapted, this Album is now an important historical record, permitting us to learn what they were like in their Victorian heyday, over a hundred years ago.

Likewise, certain maps contain useful evidence, especially those produced in the mid-18th century by Emanuel Bowen and Thomas Kitchin, who, in addition to marking the mansions, includes after them the names of proprietors, e.g. Mabus – Lloyd, Esq., Penybont Tregaron – Johnes Esq., Pant y Gwellt – Griffiths, gent., Abertrinant – Lloyd, Esq., Mynachty – Gwynne Esq., Blaenpenal – Pugh, gent., and so on. Sometimes nominal rolls help to lead us to the houses, such as Blome's *List of Nobility and Gentry*, compiled in 1673, arranged county by county and containing information about Cardiganshire seats and families of that date.

Particularly useful are the Hearth Tax lists compiled in the latter half of the 17th century, when a tax was levied on every fireplace within a house. These are kept in the Public Record Office, London. The lists were compiled under parishes, giving the name of the occupier and the number of hearths his house contained. This provides some indication of the size and importance of the house and although it gives no idea of the size and shape of the rooms, the information is important for comparative purposes. Here are a few examples for this county in 1670 – Gogerddan (Pryse) 16, Plas Cilcennin (Vaughan) 9, Gernos (Lloyd) and Llanfechan (Lloyd) and Noyadd Trefawr (Parry) 7 each, Coedmor (Lewes) and Lodge, Llancynfelin (Pryse) 6 each and Mabws (Lloyd) 3.

The Hearth Tax for Pembrokeshire for 1670, transcribed in toto many years ago by my friend, the late Mr. Francis Green, and published in *West Wales Historical Transactions*, provides us with a complete list of hearths in mansions, farmhouses, cottages and town dwellings of that county. Unfortunately no copy has been made of the Cardiganshire lists. Soon after the last war, when I lived in London, I consulted the lists for Cardiganshire, but made only a few notes of those houses in which I was then interested. This Society would earn the gratitude, not only of its members, but of all antiquaries and historians were it to encourage someone to undertake this project and then to publish the result in the pages of its journal, or, perhaps, the Society might persuade an institution not a hundred miles from this spot, to obtain a photographic copy of the Cardiganshire Hearth Tax lists and so earn additional plaudits to those already generously bestowed and richly deserved, for services to Welsh scholarship.

Heraldry is another guide to those who seek to date buildings and who wish to identify former owners. It is important for those concerned with the study of architecture to master the essentials of this decorative art. The shape of the shield, the style and arrangement of the charges, can often assist in determining the period of a house. The coat-of-arms proclaims the name of the family formerly seated there, and sometimes the marriages alliances, and is often the sole clue to such identification. The lion of the Pryses who trace to Gwaethfoed, the ladders of Lloyds who trace to Cadifor ap Dinawal, the entwined serpents of Lewes who trace to Ednywain ap Bradwen, and the *fleur-de-lis* of Vaughans of Crosswood who trace to Collwyn ap Tangno, the lion and roses of Vaughan of Glanleri who trace to Gwrwared of Dyfed, the ravens of Johnes of Llanfairclydogau who trace to Urien Rheged, are the passports to men and mansions. It is the bearers of these heraldic cognisances, the Welsh gentry, which otherwise might well have dissolved into the mists of oblivion. To family pride, often regarded as the unacceptable face of gentility, I feel much may be forgiven, for its unconscious contribution to the annals of Ceredigion.

Those are some of the main sources essential for the student of the historic homes of Cardiganshire. Of course, there are others, but it would take too long to enumerate and evaluate them in so short a compass as this lecture, but I would emphasise the wide range of information scattered in various places, each incomplete in itself, but when harvested and brought together into the haggard provide an abundant harvest for those with the energy and interest to pursue the subject.

I have said that Ceredigion is fortunate to have at its elbow the vast resources of the National Library, but its good fortune does not end there. In Aberystwyth we have the headquarters of the Royal Commission on Ancient Monuments, whose inspectorate has enriched our knowledge of Welsh bygones to a degree that exceeds all praise, and whose expertise is a guarantee of authenticity, particularly in the sphere of architecture. To Mr. Peter Smith, whose monumental work, *Houses of the Welsh Countryside* continues to delight and instruct us, I am grateful for the generosity he has shown me personally during my foraging in Dimetian pastures. How fortunate we are to possess this co-operative and informed organisation at so convenient a distance.

Equally devoted, and in this case exclusively, to the care of domestic architecture, is the Historical Buildings Council, whose chairman Mr. H. J. Lloyd-Johnes is a descendant of the Johnes of Llanfair Clydogau and Hafod and of the ubiquitous Lloyds. At one time, he too was a member of the staff at the National Library, and his contributions to your journal, particularly on the minor county houses, has pioneered the way for others to follow. To him, both as an old friend and as an expert, I am indebted for encouragement and support.

It is not always essential for the antiquary to possess detailed knowledge of architecture when he concerns himself with these houses. The important point is that he should be sufficiently informed to enable him to recognise a building for what it is, or was, and to know what to look for. Seven matters should command his attention:

1. What is the earliest evidence of occupation on the site or in the near vicinity? This may be a fortification, traces of a moat or early foundation, and also finds of various kinds. Some houses have occupied a site for many centuries, although their form has changed several times, and it is necessary that the dates of early records which mention them, even the briefest reference, should be jotted down, for they are milestones in the biography of a house.

2. Foundations, including cellars and undercrofts, are extremely important in determining the dating of the earlier house, for original foundations are usually retained where a house has been altered or transformed, so that the superstructure may belong to a different period.

3. The framework should be closely examined, for the style and type of construction often enables us to establish an approximate date, and in addition, the stones and woodwork (especially in attics and roofs) must be closely studied.

4. Details of windows, chimney stacks, position of fireplaces, doorways, staircases, all decorative woodwork, plaster work and masonry, both interior and exterior wall decoration, must be taken into account.

5. We must try to establish who were the owners or occupiers, and if possible, determine their standing in the community.

6. The name of the house – Plâs (from the English Place), Ty Mawr, Neuadd, usually suggest gentry status, but not in all cases; the description used in deeds — the 'capital messuage' invariably suggests such a house.

7. Outbuildings, gardens and other buildings near the dwelling house and the names of the fields and meadows in the near vicinity can often provide valuable indications. Some such names known to me include Orchard Park, The Bowling Green and The Butts. Last year I visited an old, fairly-well preserved house that had been a gentry seat for some centuries, but has been a farmhouse from about 1850. The railway has destroyed the lawns that once surrounded it, so that the ornamental grounds have been destroyed. The present owner told me that a number of hop plants grew and flowered annually in one spot near the railway and was at a loss to understand how they came to be there. Later, I examined the Tithe Map for 1836, and was delighted to find the layout of the old lawns, and below them a small enclosure named 'the Hop Field'; so that the persistent hop plants of our times had originated in a period when the dwellers in the plâs provided home-brewed beverage from their own resources. I might add that the Tithe Maps and Schedules contain detailed plans of fields and enclosures, and usually their names are included, so that here again we have a source not to be overlooked.

The question of the original site is often complicated by abandonment of an old home and the erection of a new one some distance away. Several examples of these migratory homesteads exist in the county. For instance, the residence of Abermad (Llanilar) the home of the family of Lloyd (who filled the shrievalty in 1592, 1607 and 1620) which later passed through the hands of the Jones and Pugh families, until abandoned by Lewis Pugh who built a new mansion in 1871-2 on a new site. The farmhouse of Abernantbychan (Penbryn) superseded a much earlier house, the old plâs of the Leweses which had stood in a field to the west of the present house, and where a few traces of the foundations still persist. Alltybwla (Llandygwydd parish) home of a branch of Jenkins of Carrog and Blaenpant, also moved, and in Alltybwla and Alltybwla hen. Among others are Bronwydd (Llangynllo) home of the Lloyds, the present Coedmor (Llangoedmor) home of the Mortimers and Lloyds, stood a considerable distance from the original mansion but the walls of the large garden attached to it still survive. The modern mansion of Cilgwyn was built in the last century by the Fitzwilliam family on the site of a cottage called Emlyn Cottage, but the original mansion of the Lloyds stood some distance away, at the foot of the farmhouse now called Old Cilgwyn, home of Captain Fitzwilliams; and High Mead (Llanwenog) home of the Davies-Evans family migrated from lower ground to its present elevated location.

Sometimes names can be confusing. Take for example Blaendyffryn (Bangor) home, successively, of the families of Morris, Price and Davies; so late as 1783 this house was described in deeds as 'the capital messuage called Blaen Dyffryn alias Blaen Hownant'; and Lovesgrove, not far from this town, which was described in deeds of the early 18th century as 'Lovesgrove otherwise called Bryn Glas'.

There were several reasons why houses were abandoned and allowed to decay or adapted to farming and other purposes. The desire of a more convenient site often provided such reason. Such a change concerned Lanlas, home of the family of Lewis (who traced to Cadwgan Grach o Garrog) abandoned in the eighteenth century by the family who built a new and imposing mansion across on the opposite side of the bank of the Aeron, on which the name Llanaeron, was bestowed.

When families moved away, or became extinct, or whose property was alienated due to financial difficulties or human frailty, some of the houses fell into ruin, some passed to other affluent owners who maintained them, while many were reduced in size and turned into farmhouses. Among those which became farmhouses are Castell Hywel, Parc Rhydderch, Crugbychan, Tywyn, Pantyrodin and Ffosesgob, for example. Among those which illustrate decline and fall are Peterwell, whose gaunt ruins stand in a meadow near Lampeter, where the eccentric Lloyds and their spendthrift heir, John Adams, squandered a fair inheritance, so that family and mansion passed into oblivion; and Bwlchmawr (Llanwenog) home of the Lloyds (who traced to Tewdwr Mawr), the last of whom, so Meyrick tells us in 1810, Charles Lloyd 'spent all his estate and now lives in obscurity in Carmarthen'.

Several families ceased to exist when the male line became extinct and the estate divided between sisters and co-heiresses. Take the case of Dyffryn Llynod (Llandysul), home of the Jenkinses descended from Cadifor ap Dinawal, and so entitled to bear the ladders and castle in their escutcheon. When Thomas Jenkins died without issue in the eighteenth century, the estate passed to his three sisters, all of whom married Bristolians. One of these, Mary, inherited Dyffryn Llynod house, but continued to live at Bristol with her husband Peter Davies, so that the old home was let to tenant farmers, to whose descendants, the Edwardes' of Abermeurig, the property eventually passed. An old ditty recounting what sort of person a suitor had to be in order to obtain the hand of a daughter of Dyffryn Llynod.

He had to be attended by 18 men with 18 shining swords and 18 men in gorgeous livery clad with 18 steeds of speckled hue, before Dyffryn Llynod's maid be had.

Tragedies attended the eclipse of some families. When David Jenkins, tenth of his line at Dolweff in Llanwenog, died without male issue, the estate of 1,640 acres was divided between his three daughters, co-heiresses. Mary, the eldest, inherited Dolwlff mansion and demesne, and married William Lloyd (one of the Cilgwyn family) whose grandson, David Lloyd, then a youth. sole heir of the estate, was attempting to remove a charge from a fowling-piece, when it exploded and killed him. The property was afterwards sold to Herbert Lloyd of Carmarthen and the house let to tenants.

A good example of the changes that have affected residences is provided by Llanllyr and Talsarn. Originally a nunnery, Llanllyr after its dissolution was leased by the Crown in 1537 to a succession of tenants and eventually became the freehold possession of the Lloyds, and from them, through an heiress, briefly to the second Earl of Carbery, who exchanged it with Parry of St. Dogmaels. Parry died in debt in 1642 and the property was sold by mortgagees to the Lloyds of Wernfeilig, the last of whom, William Lloyd, mortgaged it to a William Sumner, an Englishman, who foreclosed on Lloyd's death and placed his son there. But Lloyd's widow came back at the head of a crowd of friends, stormed the house and started to pull down the mansion and did not desist until Sumner fled in terror. Described in 1696 as 'a decayed house' it was eventually sold by the Sumners in 1720 to John Lewes, then living at Carmarthen, and he, at a later date let it to the Revd. Evan Lewis, a pious Nonconformist minister. About 1830 the owners pulled down the old mansion and used its materials to build a new one a short distance away. This has been, ever since, the home of the present line of Lewes.

Just across the stream within a bowshot from Llanllyr, in the hamlet of Talsarn, stood another mansion, far older than its neighbour, called Ty Mawr. This was the seat of one of the oldest of Ceridigion's landowners, who adopted the permanent surname of Evans. However, they gradually descended in the social scale and the last of the family, James Evans went to London, and in 1771 sold 'the capital messuage called Tir y Ty Mawr in Talsarn' and the remainder of his estate in Trefilan, to the Revd. John Allen of Shrewsbury, who later sold it to persons called Preece and Bateman and they, in 1836, sold it to John Lewes of Llanllyr, and it continued to form part of that estate.

Ty Mawr, a two-storeyed house, has survived fairly intact and provides a good example of the traditional minor gentry house. When I visited it last year, I was delighted to find within an interesting doorway with decorative moulding on the frame. Although it has been used as a farmhouse for many generations it still retains an aura of its former status.

Around the Talsarn-Llanllyr area are numerous small gentry homes, Abermeurig, a delightful three-storeyed residence of the old Welsh kind, now home of Mr. Rogers-Lewis and built during the 18th century by his ancestor Peter Edwards, who had married a daughter of Dyffryn Llynod to which I have referred earlier. The Rogers family came from Gelli in nearby Trefilan, another well-kept little mansion; while yet another and much older plâs, Gwasted Gwrda, former home of the Lloyds, but now a farmhouse, is in the vicinity.

In the county there are three mansions built on or near a dissolved religious house. Llanllyr I have mentioned; the others are Cardigan Priory a sketch of which Dineley drew in 1684, and Ystrad Fflur, home of the Stedmans, which is shown in one of Buck's engravings of 1740.

You will have noticed how many of the residences became farmhouses. An interesting example of the opposite trend, that is, a farmhouse graduating into a residence, is provided by Cilbronnen (Llangoedmor). In Elizabethan days this was the home of a freehold farming family whose descendants, by prudence and industry, raised themselves into the ranks of the yeoman, and then of the gentry, improving and extending the home to suit the new circumstances. It became the property of the Jenkins family who improved it further, and in the early part of the present century was completely modernised and remodelled. It contains a very fine heraldic window showing the colourful coat of arms of Sir Laurence Jenkins, descended from Elystan Glodrudd.

Although we can form an idea of what some of the old houses looked like and a general outline plan can often be deduced, we lack the information necessary to complete the picture. Hence the importance of thumb-nail sketches contained in Meyrick's *Cardiganshire*, and although brief, often inadequate, they are useful in providing brief glimpses of the older houses. Among these are: Gelli Fraith (Llandysul), Lloyd and Phillips families, 'a curious ancient building, the roof and pointed arches of the doors and windows . . . ' Llanborth (Penbryn), Lloyd and Morgan families, 'still bears the marks of antiquity. Its pointed doorway, antiquated windows and ivy-mantled roof, bespeak the many centuries it has witnessed'. Lloyd Jack, formerly Lloyd, 'now almost in ruins', Gwernan (Troedyraur) 'the old house stood in a bottom; but John Lloyd Williams, Esq., the present proprietor, has built a handsome one on the summit of the hill. It formerly belonged to a family named Lloyd, long ago extinct'. Ystrad, near Lloyd Jack is described in a sale notice dated 1804 in *The Cambrian* newspaper as: 'lately erected, an elegant modern-built dwelling house, containing on the ground floor two parlours, a dining room, kitchen, outer kitchen, servant's hall, laundry, dairy, pantry and cellar. On the first floor, five good bedchambers and dressing rooms. Attic storey – bedrooms for eight servants.'

There is no particular significance in the distribution of these houses and it is predictable and logical that they tend to be numerous in the fertile river valleys like the Tivyside, the Vale of Aeron, the Ystwyth and in the vicinity of certain towns like Lampeter, Aberystwyth and Cardigan. Wherever there was agricultural land there would be landowners, so that in distant hilly areas historic homes were also found. Indeed, the very remoteness of these areas protected the houses which tended to retain their earlier features, being less susceptible to the changes that occurred in the more prosperous, accessible areas, where affluence influenced fashion and the manner of living of the residents. So it would appear that obscurity has its victories no less than publicity.

Although we do not seem to be aware of it, a notable revolution has taken place in our country since the last war, completely changing the attitudes, beliefs and practices to which we had been long accustomed. It has been a silent revolution. Because no *châteaux* blazed in the Tivyside, because no tumbrils rolled through Aberystwyth streets we have been apt to overlook the significance of the transformation in our economic and social system. All this has had as profound an effect on our architecture and historic homes as they have had on our way of life.

The change in agricultural methods wrought by the introduction of machinery has affected most of the old historic farmhouses, former seats of the ancient families. Milking by hand is no longer necessary, butter and cheese are no longer produced, baking days once a feature of the farmhouse and horses and ploughs, are as remote as medieval times. The days of the milkmaid and the ploughman are over, for machinery has enabled us to dispense with manpower to a remarkable degree. I have known landowners to abandon their mansions for a flat in the town, farmers to abandon ancient farmhouses for a new bungalow or a suburban-type house with all modern conveniences.

Another aspect of change is indicated by the development of the tourist trade, as shown by the Bed and Breakfast signs one observes outside so many farmhouses in the county – a phenomenon unheard of in the days of traditional ways and methods. Another aspect of the threats to ancient homes is the desire for improving and enlarging existing houses, facilitated by what is called an Improvement Grant. However necessary such progress may be, it is sad to reflect that such grants have been responsible for the total destruction of interesting historical features in country houses and farmhouses, which have been ruthlessly swept away and replaced by features, however utilitarian, wholly out of harmony with the styles that gave charm and comfort to these houses. Fashions change and many blanch from being regarded as old-fashioned. The desire to build anew, rather than adapt the old, is another attitude which contributes to the destruction of our historic sites. The tremendous advance in demolition machinery is such that a large house can be totally razed within a day, and I myself have been witness to these unhappy proceedings. Another tendency militating against preservation is the drift towards towns and suburbs and the consequent abandonment of country habitations. For instance, I have a farmer friend who lives with his wife and family in a luxurious house in the town of Carmarthen and he goes daily to attend to his 250 acre farm seven miles away, while the old farmhouse, once one of the oldest mansions in the county, and which contained some attractive features of older times, has been modernised to receive summer visitors and shooting parties in winter.

It would be wrong for us to oppose necessary reform and beneficial change, but should anyone consider it necessary to undertake structural changes in a house with historical associations, then I hope he will get in touch with the Historic Buildings Council or with the Ancient Monuments Commission who are able to make detailed plans and take photographs of the threatened sections, so that, at least, a record can be made of them. I also hope a survey will be undertaken of all the older houses, parish by parish, by enlightened societies, perhaps by senior schools and by the Education Authority, for such exercise is a form of education – history without tears – so that as complete a record as possible can be compiled of our architectural heritage which is subject to steady and relentless erosion by agencies whose threat is not always apparent. I have dwelt on this aspect because time is short and quick action is necessary if we are to safeguard what is left from the past for us to admire and enjoy.

In a talk like this, governed by the limitation of time, I have been able only to attempt a general survey of the Historic Homes. Although I have been able to list some 355 of them, doubtless there are some that have escaped my net.

Mr. Chairman, Her Majesty's Lieutenant, Ladies and Gentlemen, I again thank you for affording me the pleasure of addressing you and for the courteous way you have received me.

Diolch yn fawr.

Aberystwyth Harbour

LLECHWEDD DERI. / Llanwnen Cards

W.W. H.R. i, 41-2, 45. David Evans, H.S. 1641, bought the Peterwell estate, & built the first house of Peterwell.

David Evans of "Llechwedd Dery" traced to Cadifor ap Dinawal according to Wm Lewes: the Evans' were later of Peterwell

Thomas Evans of Ffynnon bedr

— Dale Cas MS, p27. s.n. Llechwedd deri

Ievan ap Ievan of Llechwedd-derry.

Margaret = Walter Price of Dolygwm, Pencarreg, Carm — G G MS I (Tewdwr)

Rebecca = Zaccheus son of John illeg son of Ievan of Parc Rhydderch

John = Judith Jones of Gilfachberthog — G G MS III (Gwaethfoed) fo 34

Hugh ab Evan Gwyn

dr = Evan ab Evan of Llechwedd Deri

David Evans = dr to John Lloyd Jenkin of Moelifor.

Thomas Evans = dr of Evan Gwyn Jenkin of Gilfachwen.

Daniel Evans = Mary dr of Morgan Herbert

— Protheroe MS C. XX (E. Pryse). C/A.

LLECHWEDD DERI. Llanwnen.

Ieuan Coch of Dolau Gwyrddion (to Cantref Hywel)

David Evans of Llechwedd Deri (HS Cards 1641; built Peterwell) = Mary dr of John Lloyd Jenkin of Blaenhirbroch in Ll'geinach, Carms, 2nd son of Jenkin Lloyd David of Gilfachwen

Thomas Evans of Ffynnon Bedr, HS Cards 1653. Parliamentarian

John E. Tregaron, HS Cards 1658

Rees = Anne dr of Fras Lloyd of Llanllyr, Vicar of Llanddewi Brefi

Erasmus E. Vic of Lampeter 1662, Rector of Brechfa, M.A.

Eleanor = Lewis Lloyd of Llygeinach, HS Carms 1654

Sarah = Daniel Lloyd, Laques, 3rd son of Rees Lloyd of Laques.

— Dale Cas p.27. s.n. Peterwell; G.G. MS; NLW 12356E, fo 495.

for good ped. see Arch Camb 1861, p.24 ff. (also GG MS. I. Tydwal)

In 1722 Llechwedd Derry Issa & Ucha, formed part of the Evans of Peterwell estate, & in that year the estate was partitioned betw the coheiresses, & the sd 2 farms given to Walter Lloyd & Eliz uxor.

Llechwedd Deri Uchaf, and -Isaf, 2½ m NW of Llanwnnen village & to the west of the stream — Colby Map 1831

1634 Oct 9. Grant from John Vaughan of Trawscoed, Esq, to Dd Evans of Llechwedd-y-dery, gent of lands in the grange of Havodwen, Cards — NLW Crosswood Deeds, p.63.

1637 Sep 11. Grant from Jas Vn of Trawscoed Esq. to Dd Evans of Llechwedery, Cards, gent. — ib. p 64.

Griffith

Rees ap Griffith of Llechwedd dery Ucha = dr of Ievan Thomas y Saer

dr = Ievan Coch ap Daire

Ievan

Dd Evans of Llechwedd dery — GG MS. I. Tydwal

FOREWORD

OF HERALDIC VISITATIONS AND OLD HOUSE HUNTING

By Thomas Lloyd

One of the memorable pleasures of my younger days fifteen or twenty years ago, was looking at old houses in west Wales with Francis Jones. Working in London my opportunity was limited, but a day with Francis, absolutely in his element, was a privileged occasion for me. I drove; Francis talked; the day, the miles, a riot of anecdotes, characters and centuries of history, all sped by.

It started when I drew up outside his hospitable home, Hendre in Carmarthen. Francis was always ready waiting, keen to start. The ever devoted and dutiful Ethel checked that he had all that was needed – hat, coat and scarf for doubtful weather – waving to us in the distance as we left. The itinerary was revealed but no map was ever needed: old west Wales was F.J.'s fiefdom. All too often our objectives were places I had never heard of, homes of ancient local gentry, long buried and forgotten by all it seemed save Francis, who was acquainted with them as if they had been his friends at school. 'I thought we'd go to . . . (such and such) . . . Have you heard of them? No? Well you should look into them. They're interesting folk, you see.' And then, as if the latch upon a treasure chest was suddenly opened, the jewels of lifelong erudition came spilling out, the achievements, sins and idiosyncrasies of the previous occupants of the house we were on the way to see, all unravelled with absolute precision.

We arrived, unheralded of course, but always expecting to be welcomed. Francis, short and dapper, raising his hat, quietly, smilingly, disarmingly, introducing himself modestly as one interested in local history. As most places on our list were old family farms still, most of those we met seemed to have heard of Francis, so that broad smiles and handshakes quickly followed, together with the invitation to a cup of tea and fresh made cake. The husband was called in from the field and the customary rituals played out, of how each knew the other's second or remote cousins or had other shared connections or experiences, which meant that by the time we came to be offered the hoped-for tour around the house, complete trust had been established and no interesting old nook or corner was hidden from us.

The conversation was, of course, usually carried on in Welsh, which was awkward for me; but Francis took care to excuse my failings to our hosts. Limited though my knowledge was, the discussion generally took familiar lines, which I could roughly comprehend. These were the visits that I treasured most, to comfortable but little modernised old houses, dressers stacked with copper lustre jugs, the huge, dented, blackened kettle simmering in the kitchen. In the rarely used best parlour would be those mind-blowing 1960's swirling patterned carpets, clashing with the stripy wallpaper and equally bold floral curtains, while squatting malevolently in the centre of one wall would be the (now) hideous 'modern' fireplace of shiny beige tiles with central fitted electric fire and little niches for ornaments on each side. I do not at all mean to make fun of this fast disappearing aspect of post-war social history, which brought real colour into drab, often traditionally small windowed rooms, and it did no damage to the historic fabric, unlike much that is done with 'taste' today. Rather, of course, it marked the final turning point, away from local craftsmen and traditions, whereby the character of areas had been defined for centuries, and toward the introduction of mass markets, machine made materials which speak of little save for speed and convenience and cost.

For Francis however, things had been on the slide for much longer than this. Anything after about 1800 was pretty hard to come to terms with and his mind was altogether more at ease when the Welsh Tudors were on the throne. In his magnificent *Historic Carmarthenshire Homes* (1987), the first in the series, he gives a long account of old Iscoed near Ferryside, a good but modest and altered house, and honours it with illustration, whereas the really fine adjacent Iscoed, the Georgian red brick house of Sir William Mansel built in the 1770's, is headed 'modern' and fairly soon disposed of. Indeed Francis had little time for 'proper' architecture. That was an English thing, which Welsh squires got seduced by when they had money. For him it was ecstasy to find a 'simne fawr' still open and in use, with an old settle at right angles to it and the bread oven still open near the back. This, of course, was where his heroes, the old gentry family of the house had cooked and drunk and talked and each in turn become the fabric of his history.

Moreover, it strikes me now, that as we travelled from house to house, I was witness to a remarkable re-incarnation. Here was Francis, the Wales Herald at Arms, conducting himself on a true Heraldic Visitation; such as was carried out by his hero Lewys Dwnn in the years round 1600. Dwnn, 'Deputy Herald at Arms for the three Provinces of Cymru' had gathered in his genealogies from among the living. Francis, who had spent much of his life proving to a sceptical world that Dwnn's work was painstakingly correct, was following Dwnn now, finally checking off the dead before whose hearths he sat, perhaps even the very same hearths that Dwnn had sat by four hundred years before. No wonder Francis hated modern work. He was of course much too polite to express his feelings to such perpetrators face to face, but a rich range of vocabulary enlivened the outward journey down the drive.

The meteoric surge of interest in old buildings in recent times makes it difficult to realise the extent to which trips like those twenty years ago in west Wales were pioneering, and to some surprised owners really quite eccentric. 'Why are you interested in my house?' one might be asked with suspicious overtones. But even my sadly deficient photography captured uniquely valuable details that do not now exist.

Perhaps the most amazing day was one down the Teifi from Llandysul to Cilgerran in summer 1985. The first step was to pick up Dr. Leslie Baker Jones, the hugely knowledgeable antiquary of that area. As I drove, the gentle cross-flow of facts and information grew more intense as we homed in on a target house, each determined to display discoveries about it from more arcanely hidden sources. It was of course a most gentlemanly rivalry, based on a wish to share and learn, but being the first to excavate and announce a fact of value is the lifeblood of academia.

I remember from that day some lovely smaller Cardiganshire houses, Llwyngrawys, Parcygors, Pantgwyn and multi-gabled Noyadd Trefawr, which my great grandfather had rented for some years, long before my time. The Rev. Towyn Jones, Carmarthenshire historian and ghost hunter, and Tony Parkinson, the indefatigable architectural investigator from the Royal Commission on Ancient and Historical Monuments in Aberystwyth, both joined us later and we proceeded finally to Rhosygilwen in Cilgerran, a sad and bewildering sight, as the big and heavy late Victorian house had been substantially gutted by fire just a short time before. The elderly and frail owner, Mrs. Creswell Evans, who had been living there all alone, was shaken but by no means crushed by the disaster and showed us around the debris-strewn, and no doubt dangerous semi-shell. For Tony Parkinson such upsets in a house's history (it having now been happily rebuilt), shed brief and invaluable shafts of light. As plaster crumbles in the heat, long blocked doorways and windows are revealed and indeed the shape and extent of earlier houses, successively altered and enlarged. The day ended in a scene from absurd theatre, with Mrs. Creswell Evans serving tea and cakes to the party in the back courtyard of the blackened and shattered house, seated on such chairs as had been salvaged, the whole affair conducted like the most effête Edwardian Soirée beneath the lovely late afternoon sun and heavy scent of roses and charred wood. By luck I took a photograph to prove it true.

T. L.

Above from left: Major Francis Jones, Dr. Leslie Baker Jones, Tony Parkinson, Mrs. Creswell Evans, the Rev. Towyn Jones at Rhosygilwen, Cilgerran, 1985.

COATS OF ARMS

Bowen of Troedyraur

Brigstocke of Blaenpant

Brenchley of Glaneirw

Chambers of Hafod

Fitzwilliams of Cilgwyn

Griffith of Llwynduris (Llwyndyrys)

Harford of Falcondale

Hope of Pigeonsford

Inglis Jones of Derry Ormond

Johnes of Llanfair Clydogau

Jones of Gwynfryn

Jones of Glandennis

Lewes of Ty Glyn Aeron

Lloyd of Alltyrodin

Lloyd of Bronwydd

Lloyd of Castle Hywell and Ffosybleiddiad

Lloyd of Peterwell

Loxsdale of Castle Hill

Lloyd-Williams of Gwernant

Powell of Nanteos

Pryse of Gogerddan

Saunders-Davies of Pentre

Stewart of Alltyrodin

Vaughan of Trawsgoed
(Earl of Lisburne)

Vaughan of Llangoedmor

Waddingham of Hafod

Webley-Parry of Noyadd Trefawr

Winwood of Ty Glyn Aeron

Brawdy Books are indebted to Thomas Lloyd, Esquire, of Freestone Hall, Pembrokeshire, for his kind permission to reproduce coats of arms from his heraldic collection

BERARTHEN, Penbryn

Located in the south-east of the parish on the outskirts of the hamlet of Glynarthen. Marked on *Colby's Map of 1831* and on modern OS maps. The earliest recorded occupier was Rhys ap Morgan, who married a daughter and co-heiress of Thomas ap Howel ap Llewelyn David Fychan of Aberarthen. Rhys was the son of Morgan Fychan, whose mother was a daughter of Rhys Meredydd ap Owen of Towyn, Ferwig, who, in turn was the son of Adam of Llwyndafydd, who traced to Gwynfardd Dyfed.

James, the heir of Rhys ap Morgan, married Jane, daughter of the powerful Lewes Dafydd Meredydd of Abernantbychan, a neighbouring property, in the middle of the 16th century. They had three children: Elizabeth married Thomas Parry of Cwm-cynon before 1599 and an unnamed daughter married Rhys ab Ievan Prydderch ab Iefan of Pentre-du in Llandyfriog parish. The only son, David James, married Elliw, daughter of Morgan Johns of Penbryn. David and Elliw had two daughters, Fortune and Bridget. Bridget formed a liaison with Robert Lloyd of Cardigan, a member of the Cilrhiwe family in Llanfihangel Penbedw, north Pembrokeshire. Their son, Robert, had a son, John, described as of Emlyn. By 1760 James Lloyd of Cilrhiwe owned Aberarthen-fawr and in 1784 Jonathan Evan, gent., and his wife, Anne, occupied the property. Anne had formerly been married to Simon David of Aberarthen. Nearby was Aberarthen-fach.

Horsfall-Turner tells us, 'at the old farm-house of Aberarthen Vach a century ago lived John Enoch, Captain of the Cardiganshire Militia, the favourite of the barracks and a friend of all the countryside. He was descended from the family which had, for ages untold, possession of the courtly house of Gwernlogws, Carmarthenshire, until it was disposed of by his uncle Hywel Davies. Captain Enoch died in 1833 aged 74. His son, John, entered the regular army when quite young, joining the 23rd Welsh Fusiliers. He was gazetted Colonel in 1854, having served in the Netherlands and Spain – where he lost his horse and was wounded in 1812 at Salamanca – and having participated in the glorious victory of Waterloo, the storming of Cambrai and the taking of Paris. The veteran died in London at the age of 70 in 1855'.

Grid Ref: SN 3140 4870

Ref: Colby Map, 1831; British Museum, Add. MS. 39749 (Wood); CRO, GGMSp; PRO, Dale Castle MS., p. 29 & MS, I (Gwynfardd); WWHR, iii, p. 80; CRO, Aberglasney Papers, p. 129; Horsfall-Turner, *Wanderings,* p. 160.

ABERBRWYNEN, Llanychaearn

Situated between Aberllolwyn and Aber-mad, overlooking the Ystwyth, south of the A485 from Figure Four to Llanilar. Shown on *Colby's Map of 1831* as Aberbrwynen -uchaf and -isaf. Formerly the home of the Lloyds, later of Gwastod, Betws Leucu.

Jane Lloyd, daughter of Thomas Lloyd and Bridget, daughter and co-heiress of John ap Griffith of Glanfrêd, married as her second husband, David Lloyd of Aberbrwynen. Jane was the widow of John Powell of Llechwedd Dyrys. Their daughter Elinor married her cousin, Sir Thomas Powell, Baron of the Exchequer during the reign of James II. In 1643 David Lloyd ap Richard of Llanychaearn and others granted in trust two messuages called Aberbrwynen and Tyddyn Crug-y-fran, both in Llanychaearn to Morris Preignald of Llanbadarn-y-Creuddyn and Richard Morris of Llanychaearn. In 1672 Morris Price of Aberbrwynen mortgaged 'Tyddyn Glanlyllu, Tyddyn Aberbrenan, Cegynan and Llety Powell' all in Llanfihangel-y-Creuddyn to Thomas Powell of Llechwedd Dyrys. By 1690 Aberbrwynen had become part of the estate of Llechwedd Dyrys, later the Nanteos estate by the failure of the mortgagor to repay his loan. Thereafter Aberbrwynen was let to tenants.

A new home was built at Aberbrwynen in 1891 and is now utilised as housing for young bullocks. In the 1890's, Grace Scott, a native of Scotland, and her family, farmed Aberbrwynen and for 30 years following World War II it was the home of Bryn Richards, a popular character, who worked for the NFU. It is now the home of Alwyn and Ann Griffiths and their family.

Grid Ref: SN 5908 7654

Ref: Colby Map, 1831; CRO, GGMS, MS., III; PRO, Dale Castle MS., p. 28; WWHR, i, 45; Protheroe, C, XX, C/A Box 36; NLW, Cwrtmawr Deeds, Nos. 334, 555, 674, 1368, 1625. D and A Griffiths.

ABERCARFAN, Llanddewibrefi

Located near to the confluence of the Teifi and the Carfan adjacent to the B4343 midway between Tregaron and Llanddewibrefi and marked on *Colby's Map of 1831.* The earliest reference to this property is in 1717 when Nathan Griffiths, then of Dol-wen, Llanwenog parish, sold Abercarfan and other lands in Llanddewibrefi to David John of Llansawel, a smith. Nathan Griffiths was the son of the Rev. Thomas Griffiths and Catherine, daughter of Bishop Field of St. Davids. He was a successful lawyer and owner of an estate with properties in seven parishes in Carmarthenshire and Cardiganshire including Cilgwynydd and Pantgilgan, both in Llangeler parish. David John was followed at Abercarfan by Ann Jones possibly his daughter by his wife, Mary. Ann, a devout Christian, married Dafydd Jones (1711-1777), of Caeo, the notable hymn-writer and cattle-drover. When Dafydd and Ann moved to Carmarthenshire, they were succeeded at Abercarfan by Francis Jones and his wife, Mary, who were married on 12 January 1758. Their son, Charles, described in 1796 as a freeholder and drover, the step-son of Dafydd Rowland of Llangeitho, was a drover as well as a jobber. It is interesting to note that R. J. Davies of Cwrt Mawr, Llangeitho, father of Principal J. H. Davies, maintained that Daniel Rowland, the notable Methodist cleric, had a second brother, Dafydd, a tinsmith, who followed the drovers to London and died there at the early age of 45. In 1810 Charles Jones was described as 'late of Abercarfan and now of Giltspur St., London' having sold his home in 1798. In 1850 Abercarfan was owned by Margaret Evans who lived at the 120 acre farm with her daughter, three servants, three maids and six other workers. Some time ago, a memorial stone was unveiled in a field on Abercarfan land, adjoining the Teifi, where Dai Lewis of Tregaron, a fisherman 'without equal' had died.

Grid Ref: SN 6713 5739

Ref: Colby Map, 1831; NLW, Griffith Owen Deeds, 7258, 7259-60, 7261, 7276, 7279; D. Ben Rees, *Hanes Plwyf Llanddewibrefi,* (1984); WWHR, iii, 99.

ABERCEFAIL, Llandysul

Located near the confluence of Nant Cefel and the Cletwr and marked on *Colby's Map of 1831.* Francis Jones gives no other information other than that it was owned at some stage by Ieuan ap Thomas ap Griffith of Abercefail who married Mary, daughter of Thomas David Rhys of Ffosesgob.

Grid Ref: SN 4100 4415

Refs: Colby Map, 1831; PRO, Dale Castle MS., Ped., s.n. Ffos Esgob (113); WWHR, i. 52.

ABERCERI, Brongwyn

Lewis in *TDW* states, 'Abercery, the property of T. Parry Thomas, Esq., is a neat modern villa, beautifully situated, and commanding one of the finest reaches of the Vale of Teivy, including the straggling town of Newcastle Emlyn'. Located on the banks of the Teifi and Ceri rivers near Cwm-cou. The present mansion, built on a wooded slope above the curve of the Teifi is a symmetrical Georgian house with bay windows which were added at the turn of the century, with seven bedrooms, four reception rooms, numerous offices, a coach house and well laid-out gardens and orchard.

Towards the end of the 18th century, Colonel Owen Lloyd, a son of Thomas Lloyd of Bronwydd and Anne, daughter of William Lloyd of Henllys and his wife, Joan, née Ford of Bury, married Elizabeth, daughter and

heiress of Thomas Lloyd of Abertrinant and Elizabeth Vaughan, sister of the 1st Earl of Lisburne. Their daughter, Elizabeth, married Thomas Davies of Nantgwylan, High Sheriff in 1835, and son of the Rev. David Davies, vicar of Llanfihangel-y-Creuddyn and a daughter of Hughes of Nantgwylan. Thomas and Elizabeth had two children: Elen became a devout Roman Catholic, and her brother, Thomas Hughes Ford Davies, inherited Aberceri and the Nantygwylan estate near Newcastle Emlyn in 1866. During his minority Aberceri was occupied by Thomas Parry Thomas, son of John Thomas of Aberduar, Carmarthenshire and his wife, Hester Watkins of Llanllyr who were married in 1790. Thomas Parry Thomas, a surgeon, was succeeded by his son, Thomas, who in 1834 inherited Nantypopty under the terms of the will of Thomas Llewelyn Parry of Gernos. Educated at Magdalen College, Oxford, Thomas Ford Davies assumed the surname Hughes presumably upon inheriting Nantygwylan. On leaving Oxford, Ford Hughes spent some time in London and Paris before returning to live at Penbryn House, Rhydlewis in 1875. Two years later he was High Sheriff. For years he rented or bought vacant houses in the Teifi valley before settling at a modest house in Union Street, Carmarthen where he lived in increasing squalor, his meals brought from an inn in Lammas Street and left outside his door. He was never seen during daylight hours, at night he visited his properties in a horse-drawn fly, staying a few minutes before returning to Union Street before dawn. When the water supply was cut off and his meals were left uneaten, the authorities broke into the property and Ford Hughes was taken to the Workhouse Sanatorium where he died within a few days. His sister, Elen, inherited his estates. Aberceri was later inherited by Dr. John Webb, a retired doctor from Carmarthen who lived there from the 1960's to 1982 when it was put up for sale. Mrs. Webb died in 1983 and her husband in 1987.

Grid Ref: SN 2939 4192

Refs: Colby Map, 1831; Lewis, *TDW;* HM Vaughan, *South Wales Squires*, 1926, pp. 112-5; Nicholas, *County Families,* 1875, i, 192; Charles Allen, Photograph in *South Wales,* 1871; NLW, Morgan Richardson Deeds, i, 211, 863.

ABERLLOLWYN, Llanychaearn

Situated in woodland adjacent to the A487 (T) road near Nant Llolwyn which runs to the Ystwyth near Figure Four. Formerly the residence of Ievan ap Thomas ap Rhys, descended from Ednyfed Fychan who occupied the property in 1609. His son, Hugh, married Margaret, daughter of Thomas Wyn ap Morgan Fychan of Morfa Bychan and their daughter, Jane, married Richard ap Ievan Gwyn. The Lloyds came to Aberllolwyn in the middle of the 17th century. Erasmus Lloyd married Elizabeth Williams, eldest daughter of William Richard of Aberystwyth in 1666. The marriage settlement devised to the couple the capital messuage of Aberllolwyn, Brongelli, Esgair-hir, Sgubor-fawr, Ffynnon-y-march, Melyn and Ffosargaled in the parish of Llanychaearn, Tyddyn y Graig-wen, Tyddyn Graig-wen Ganol and Tyddyn Blaen Gwaun Carrog in Llanddeiniol parish. Erasmus died in September 1688 and is buried at Llanychaearn. He was succeeded by his son, Hugh, High Sheriff in 1714, who died in 1732. Hugh's sister, Elizabeth, had married Charles, second son of Charles Herbert of Pengelli. Hugh Lloyd was followed by his daughter and heiress, Elizabeth, born in 1695, who in 1720 married Thomas Hughes (1697-1771), of Hendrefelin near Ystrad Meurig, a close friend of the powerful Wilmot Vaughan of Trawsgoed. Thomas and Elizabeth had a son, Erasmus, and four daughters, one of whom, Mary, inherited the estate. Mary married Edward Hughes of Dyffryn-gwyn, Meirionydd, described as a solicitor at Aberystwyth in 1761, who died without issue in 1794. Mary remained at Aberllolwyn until her death when the estate passed to her niece, Anna Maria Hughes of Morfa Bychan. On 19 January 1809, Mrs. Johnes of Hafod Uchdryd wrote to her brother, John, of Dolaucothi, 'walked last Monday to Aberllolwyn to see that fine mansion. It is about three miles and a half from here. The heiress of it bestowed her hand and heart on Mr. John Bowen last Saturday, the happy couple attended by her sister . . .'.

Aberllolwyn remained the property of the family throughout the 19th century. In 1878 Mrs. Harriett Vibart Hughes and her daughter, Harriet Stephens granted a lease for 21 years to Mark John Tredwell (1856-1930), son of a wealthy Midlands industrialist whose fortune was made building railways in Britain and India. Tredwell renovated Aberllolwyn and restored the gardens and the home farm. He was also given permission to build a small castle on an islet in the middle of Llyn Eiddwen on Mynydd Bach to entertain his weekend guests at wild parties in the folly. Tredwell entertained lavishly at Aberllolwyn including an extravaganza for members of the Wesleyan Sunday school in Aberystwyth on a very wet afternoon in August 1879.

Having lost an action by a local builder to recover his costs regarding the building of the folly, Tredwell left the area with 17 years of the lease remaining. He died in London in 1930 aged 74 years leaving an estate of just £87.

During the First World War German prisoners-of-war were billeted at Aberllolwyn prior to the ownership of Dr. Edward Roberts, formerly of Pen-wern, New Cross, a retired Manchester eye-specialist.

Francis Jones visited Aberllolwyn in 1979 when it was the residence of Dorothy (née Vickerman) and Denys Evans, a member of a distinguished family of Aberystwyth solicitors and nephew of Ernest Evans, Liberal MP for Cardiganshire, and formerly Private Secretary to David Lloyd George. Mr. and Mrs. Evans are still there.

Grid Ref: SN 5875 7718

Refs: Colby Map, 1831; NLW, Crosswood Deeds, p. 90; NLW, Cwrtmawr Deeds, 203, 1678, 1713; Dale Castle Deeds, MS., ped. 127; Meyrick, *Cardiganshire,* 1810, edn. 1907, p. 283. Phillips, *Dyn a'i Wreiddiau,* 1975; D. Evans.

ABER-MAD, Llanychaearn

The reference given is for the present Aber-mad located on the banks of the Mad, a stream which enters the Ystwyth nearby. Situated in a beautiful valley off the A485 between Figure Four and Llanilar. The earlier *plâs*, now named Henblas, is located a little to the west of the Victorian edifice. Formerly part of the granges of Ystrad Fflur which included a corn water-grist mill on the Mad, to which Jenkin ab Ievan ap Lewis was granted a 99-year-lease by the Abbot in 1533.

The home successively of the Lloyds, Johns and Pughs. The Lloyds of Aber-mad traced to Uchtryd of Tegeingl, grandson of Owain ap Hywel Dda. Ieuan was a son of Lewis Llewelyn Fychan ap Ievan who married Agnes, heiress of Llewelyn ap Dafydd, owner of Aber-mad, who was descended from the Lords of Towyn in Ferwig parish. Their son, Ievan, married Tanglwst, heiress of Gwilym Llewelyn Fychan. They had three sons. The eldest, Dafydd Llwyd ab Ifan, subject of an elegy by Rhisiart Phylip, married Gwerfyl, daughter of Ievan Rhys Goch, and their daughter, Tanglwst married David Llwyd ap Richard of Gogerddan and lived at Rhandir, Llangwyryfon, then part of the Aber-mad estate. The second son was Jenkin. The third son, Lewis ab Ifan, married Eva, daughter and heiress of Rhys David Llewelyn Gwilym and Mawd, daughter of Rhys Llwyd Dafydd Llewelyn of Ffoshelyg. Their son, Ievan Llwyd ap Lewis, who lived at Aber-mad, married Elizabeth, daughter of Jenkin Thomas Howel Fawr of Gilfach-wen, Llandysul. They had two children. Elen married Rhys Fychan ap John Fychan of Glanleri, and David, who adopted Lloyd as his surname, but is also referred to as David Llwyd ab Ievan. He married Mary, daughter of Watkin Thomas of Llwyniorwerth near Capel Bangor and signed for Dwnn in 1588.

Despite serving as High Sheriff in 1592, 1607 and 1620, and being a JP, David Lloyd, helped by his sons, frequently imposed his own kind of justice in their locality, which was far removed from the rightful laws of the kingdom. With a force of local vigilantes he was accused of destroying the existing mill at Aber-mad, leased to Thomas Pryse of Glanfrêd and erecting a replacement mill nearby deploying the existing mill-stones. He was further accused by Richard Lloyd of Llanilar, of bribery, un-lawful imprisonment in irons and other misdemeanours in relation to the Bailwick of Llanilar held by Richard Lloyd. David Lloyd's two sons were Richard and Lewis. The brothers followed in their father's footsteps and at various times were accused of rioting and assault at Aberystwyth and Llanbadarn markets, resisting arrest at Aber-mad and assaulting burgesses and JPs at Llanbadarn-fawr.

In March 1610/11 David Lloyd secured three messuages in Llanychaearn from Reginald Mores of Morfa Bychan on mortgage and in 1620 Ievan Thomas Morris of Lledrod mortgaged in £16.3.4 to David Lloyd a messuage called Tir Pant Camddwr with a cottage or 'somer house' lying adjacent to the Camddwr-fach stream.

Mary, heiress of Lewis Lloyd married James Lewes (1602-1668), of Abernantbychan, High Sheriff of Pembrokeshire in 1641 and 1645 and for Cardiganshire in 1645 and MP for the county from 1624-40 and again in 1656. James sold the Aber-mad estate, consisting of at that time, ten properties in the parishes of Llanychaearn, Llanbadarn, Llanilar and Rhostie, to his cousin, James Jones (Johnes) of Dolaucothi, whose father, Thomas, had married Mary, a daughter of James Lewes. The capital messuage of Aber-mad had previously been tenanted by Evan Thomas who paid an annual rent of £60. James Johnes served as High Sheriff in 1671 and in 1672 he paid tax on three hearths at Aber-mad.

Early in the 18th century Aber-mad was occupied by Thomas, son of James and Eleanor Johnes. Thomas, described by a descendant as 'thoroughly disreputable', acted on behalf of the larger landowners at election times and was involved in many violent disputes in north Cardiganshire. A bachelor with many natural children in the area, he lived at Aber-mad attended by his henchmen, Richard James and Mick Daniel, an Irishman. It was these retainers who shamefully attacked the Rev. Daniel Rowland when he came to Llanilar to preach the Methodist cause. Some years later Rowland returned and Thomas Johnes, High Sheriff in 1737, aided by the Rev. Hughes of Glanyrafon, Llanilar, prepared to mount another disturbance. It was thwarted by Richard James who experienced a religious conversion whilst listening to Rowland.

In the 1740's tension rose in north Cardiganshire regarding claims of local land-

lords and the Crown to the mineral rights. In 1753, Thomas Johnes of Aber-mad was awarded £21 for his part in defending the Crown rights at the Esgair-mwyn mine. The shameful behaviour of the gentry, engaged in plot and counter-plot, resulted in 'Tom Aber-mad', being confined in the Fleet prison for three years from 1757 until he repaid monies owed to Herbert Lloyd of Ffynnon-bedr. Ironically, Thomas is listed as a freeholder of Aber-mad when he was being detained in the filth and squalor of the Fleet. Thomas Johnes sold the estate to Robert Lloyd of Oswestry. By 1813 it was owned by a Mr. Gataker in the right of his wife, daughter of Robert Lloyd.

In 1840 Aber-mad was sold to the Vaughans of Trawsgoed who held it until 1852 when the estate of 1,360 acres was bought by Lewis Pugh, grandson of Humphrey Pugh and Elizabeth, his wife, of Pen-y-graig, Llanychaearn. Lewis Pugh and his wife had two children. Elizabeth married John Evans of Commerce House, Bridge Street, Aberystwyth, who settled at Lovesgrove upon their marriage in 1843. Elizabeth's dowry was her weight in golden sovereigns. Lewis Pugh, a prominent Wesleyan Methodist, was a saddler in Rosemary Lane (later Princess Street), Aberystwyth. In 1834 he bought the lease of the Copa Hill mine in Cwm Ystwyth when the Alderson brothers were declared bankrupt. Almost immediately the price of lead doubled and Lewis Pugh made a fortune estimated at more than a quarter of a million pounds before surrendering the lease in 1844.

Lewis Pugh died in 1868, and the Aber-mad estate of eleven farms in the Ystwyth valley and extensive sheepwalks on Pumlumon passed to his nephew, Lewis Pugh Evans of Lovesgrove on condition that he assumed the name and arms of Pugh, instead of Evans. He became Lewis Pugh Pugh. Born in 1837 he was educated at Winchester and Oxford, was called to the Bar in 1842 and practised for some time at the High Court of Calcutta. In 1864 he married Veronica Harriet, daughter of James Hills of Neechindepore, Bengal. Lewis Pugh Pugh was MP for Cardiganshire from 1880-5. He commissioned J. P. Sneddon, who built the College building at Aberystwyth, to build a new mansion at Aber-mad in 1870. In *County Families* Nicholas tells us 'the mansion of Abermaide is now (1872) in course of erection . . . a sumptuous residence'. Pugh also built another family home at Cymerau, Glandyfi. He died in India in 1908 and was succeeded by his son, Lewis Pugh Evans Pugh, a solicitor, who leased Rhosygilwen, Cilgerran during the First World War. The Roberts family of the Aberystwyth brewers occupied Aber-mad before Prosser Evans, father-in-law of J. E. R. Carson, one-time Clerk of the old Cardiganshire County Council, brought the pupils of his Bognor Regis school to the banks of the Ystwyth as evacuees in 1943, having previously been billeted at Carrog and Lluest. In 1948 Jenkin Alban Davies, a London businessman established a preparatory school at Aber-mad with the Rev. Noel Evans as headmaster, where the boys were taught through the medium of Welsh until they were nine years of age. The school closed in 1970 and in 1985 Aber-mad became a private nursing home owned and run by Donald (who was educated at Aber-mad) and Jane Smyth. In the 1980's Henblas Aber-mad (the earlier *plâs*) became the home of Ian Parrott, formerly Gregynog Professor of Music at the UCW, Aberystwyth.

Grid Ref: SN 6005 7610

Refs: Colby Map, 1831; *Dwnn,* i, 17, 26-7, 51-2; NLW, Griffith Owen List (iv); J. C. Wood, *Principal Rivers of Wales,* 1813, 168; Meyrick, *Cardiganshire,* p. 258; Nicholas, *County Families,* i, p. 210; NLW, Noyadd Trefawr Deeds, No. 282; NLW, Cwrtmawr Deeds, No. 1225; Emyr Gwynne Jones, *Exchequer Proceedings (Equity) Concerning Wales* (Cardiff), 1939, pp. 94-5; *Ceredigion,* vi, 2, pp. 150-67 (1969); *ibid* iii, 1, pp. 1-10 (1956); John Hughes, *Methodistiaeth Cymru II Gwretsan* (1854), pp. 56-7; Bethan Phillips, *Peterwell,* (1997) pp. 67, 125-6, 131, 172; W. J. Lewis, *Born on a Perilous Rock,* Aberystwyth (1980) p. 110; E. G. Bowen, *A History of Llanbadarn Fawr,* (1979), pp. 104-5; D. Smyth.

ABERMAGWR, Llanfihangel-y-Creuddyn

The reference given is for the hamlet of Abermagwr now consisting of some forestry houses, a smithy and a small shop, situated at the confluence of the Magwr and the Ystwyth near Trawsgoed. The precise location of Abermagwr house is unknown. Francis Jones notes that it was the residence of the Lloyd family descended from the Trawsgoed family who settled at Abermagwr and later adopted the surname of Pugh. Reference is given in the *Crosswood Deeds* in 1566 to the messuage and tucking mill of Abermagwr which formed part of the Trawsgoed estate. In the middle of the 16th century, Rhys Lloyd, son of Thomas ap Morus Fychan of Trawsgoed married Elsbeth, daughter of Dafydd Llwyd, son of Morus Goch, who died in 1544/5 and Dyddgu, daughter of Morgan ap Rhys. Her sister, Elliw, married Philip Hywel, son of David Philip Howell later of Llechwedd Dyrys. Rhys Lloyd was succeeded at Abermagwr by his son, Richard, and grandson, Hugh ap Richard who married a daughter of David Philip Howell of Llechwedd Dyrus. They had two sons, Edward and David who adopted the permanent patronymic of Pugh. Edward married a daughter of Jenkins William of Cwmglasffrwd and David married Gwen, daughter of Dafydd Llwyd Meredydd of Cwmbwa, Penrhyn-coch. The *NLW, Cwrtmawr Deeds* record a covenant of 1700 between Benjamin Morgans of Cwmnewidion and Anne, his wife, John Jones of Cruglas, Lledrod and Sarah, his wife, and William Pugh of Abermagwr and Gwen, his wife, and Sir Thomas Powell of Dyffryn Paith, Kt., of lands in Llanbadarn Fawr and Llanfihangel-y-Creuddyn, which included Cwm Magwr. Thereafter the references to Abermagwr are silent. The blacksmith's shop at Abermagwr, at one time the Trawsgoed estate smithy operated by Edward Jenkins, was operated from 1934 by Elias Owens, one of the last to undertake the traditional craft in north Cardiganshire. The hearth at Abermagwr is still glowing.

Grid Ref: SN 6655 7382

Refs: Colby Map, 1831; NLW, Crosswood Deeds, p. 11; *Dwnn,* i, 34; NLW, Cwrtmawr Deeds, Nos. 423, 920; CRO, GGMS, iii (Edwin); *Ceredigion,* Vol. VI, No. 1 (1968), pp. 105-6.

ABERMEURIG, Betws Leucu

The home of the Edwardes, Rogers and Rogers Lewis families and once an estate of 3,000 acres. Located on the banks of the Aeron on the outskirts of the hamlet of the same name. A three-storey house with a range of three windows with an extension on one side which formed part of an earlier residence and was formerly a kitchen. It was built by Peter Davies, formerly of Cae Madog, Nancwnlle, who married Mary, daughter of Thomas Jenkins of Dyffryn Llynod, Llandysul, at the beginning of the 18th century.

The Edwardes family were descended from Gwaethfoed through Rhydderch ab Ieuan Llwyd of Parc Rhydderch and Glyn Aeron. Thomas ap Morgan ab Ieuan ap Gwilym married Margaret, daughter of David Lloyd ap Thomas ab Owen of Cilpyll, Nancwnlle. In 1610 he granted Cae Madog to his son, Edward, who had three children; David, whose will was proved in 1670, Zacheus and Rebecca, who in 1664 married David Morgan ab Ifan Philip of Llanddewibrefi. Their son, Peter Davies, later of Bristol, plays an important part in the fortunes of the Abermeurig family. David, who died in 1670, left his estate to his son, also David, who settled at Abermeurig in 1692 with his wife and three children. David's cousin, Peter Davies, was also brought up at Cae Madog. David Edward (1654-1716), ordained in 1688, became a prominent Dissenter and was assistant minister at Cae'r Onnen, Cellau. His will, proved in 1716, mentions 'ye old cupboard from Gwastod and chair from Llwyn-rhys' and bequests to his second wife, who inherited the 'turff pitt now held by me on Corugam', and 'twenty books of his choice to Phillip Pugh of Llwynpiod'.

Peter, the younger son, succeeded his father, as his brother, John, had pre-deceased his father, David. Peter Edwardes married Diana Thomas of Llanrhian, Pembrokeshire, in 1717 and had three children. Elizabeth married John Davies and lived at Caerllygest, Llangeitho parish and their daughter, Eleanor, married the Rev. Daniel Rowland. One of the trustees of the marriage settlement of Peter Edwardes and Diana was Thomas Jones of Brawdy, an antecedent of Francis Jones. Diana brought £220 to the marriage with the proviso that if she died within three years certain sums of money, on a sliding scale, were to be returned. Peter Edwardes was succeeded by his son, John, who married Anne Thomas of Longhouse, Mathry in 1747 and inherited the Dyffryn Llynod estate in Llandysul following the death of Peter Davies of Bristol brought up at Cae Madog.

John and Anne's daughter, Anne, married Lewis Rogers of Gelli, Trefilan parish, son of Thomas Rogers and his wife, Anne (née Hughes) of Llanychaearn in 1782 and grandson of Henry Rogers, vicar of Ystrad for 45 years. Lewis's sister, Jane, married the Rev. John Williams (*yr hen Syr*) of Ystradmeurig. Lewis Rogers was High Sheriff of Cardiganshire in 1753. His son, John (1786-1864), a notable country physician, who married Anne, daughter of Thomas Jones of Llanio, drowned at Talysarn in 1846 aged 61 years. John and Anne had five children: Margaret (1823-1906), Anne, who died in 1839 aged 18 years, Jane, John and Letitia. John Edwardes Rogers – *'yr hen wr'* – was the senior magistrate for Cardiganshire, 'the most erudite of local antiquaries' and High Sheriff in 1872. He died unmarried at Abermeurig in 1914 aged 88 years. His sister, Letitia, succeeded to the estate. She had married Thomas Lewis, son of the Rev. John Lewis of Rhiwgoch, vicar of Llanrhystud, and a descendant of the Lewis family of Carrog and Tre-faes, Llanilar.

John Felix Rogers Lewis (1858-1890) succeeded to Abermeurig and he married Minnie Whiffen. Their son, John, married

Mary Davies of Park House, Talsarn, in 1900. They had five children: Dorothy Letitia, born in 1902, Margaret Winifred, who married David Thomas, who had a daughter, Jane Margaret, born in 1930. Henry, born in 1904 became a solicitor in London and inherited the estate of 1,300 acres much reduced by death duties. He sold most of the estate to tenants when leases expired. His son, David, lives in Norfolk. The younger brother, John Edwardes Rogers Lewis (1906-1996), lived at Abermeurig throughout his life.

Abermeurig, with 88 acres and 25 acres of woodland, is now a country house offering accommodation to guests. It is run by Nigel Rogers Lewis and his wife, Margaret, who have two children. A beautiful stained glass window in Trefilan church is dedicated to the memory of J. E. Rogers Lewis, great-uncle of the present occupier.

Grid Ref: SN 5638 5655

Refs: Colby Map, 1831; *Dwnn,* i, 39-40, 55; NLW, Bronwydd Deeds, Nos. 2176, 2898; WWHR, ii, 80, 108, 149-160; NLW, Noyadd Trefawr Deeds, 320, 346, 445; Meyrick, *Cardiganshire,* 1810, edn. 1907, p. 211; John Davies, *Annuls and Pedigrees of the Lloyds and Edwards of Crynfryn, and other Families,* Aberystwyth, 1931, p. 11; N. Rogers Lewis.

ABERNANTBYCHAN (PLÂS GLYNARTHEN), Penbryn

The reference given is for the name given to this ancient location on modern OS maps. The *Colby Map of 1831* gives Plâs Abernant Bychan, a name which along with the old house itself has long since disappeared. Over the door of the present farmhouse called Plâs Glynarthen or Plâs-y-glyn is a tablet recording its building in 1835. The old mansion stood in a field adjacent to the present house and faint remains of its foundations can still be traced. Meyrick writes, '. . . [it] is an ancient ediface though not the original one on the estate, that having stood a little to the south-east of the present building. The arch of the door is of the pointed ellipse, and the wainscot within the house, from its carved work and the figures on it, seems about the date of Elizabeth's reign. The mould in the garden is said to have been brought from Ireland, and the vulgar add, on that account no venomous reptile will live on it . . .'.

The first of the family to appear in surviving documents is Lewes Dafydd Meredydd, formerly of the unidentified Gwernygored, who traced to Owen ap Bradwen through Llewelyn Dalran, the first of the family to settle in the south, who married Sioned, daughter and heiress of Gwilym ap Seisyllt, Lord of Abernantbychan. He was also the progenitor of the Lewes of Gellidywyll, Coedmor, Llysnewydd, Gernos, Llanllyr, Dol-haidd, Pantyrodyn, Glasgrug and Llwyndafydd.

In 1542 Lewes Dafydd Meredydd settled all his lands in Cardiganshire on his wife and himself, having married Siwan, heiress of Rhys ap Sion ap Hywel of Gernos. Their son, James, who married firstly Elizabeth Stedman of Ystrad Fflur and secondly Ann, daughter of John Wogan of Wiston, was a man of great influence and power. He served as High Sheriff in 1571 and in 1589, and as one of his five justices in Cardiganshire served in the livery of the Earl of Essex. James became Lord of the manors of Uwch-Cerdin and Is-Hirwen and acquired other lands including Crown leases and the eight properties in the parish of Cenarth bought between 1589 and 1591, which formed the nucleus of the Gellidywyll estate created for James, eldest son of his first marriage. John Lewes, eldest son of the second marriage was educated at Jesus College, Oxford and the Inner Temple. He had five brothers. Nicholas, who settled at Hean Castle, Pembrokeshire. Richard was a 'great and general gamester', Huw, the fifth son, died in Naples aged 21 on his return from Jerusalem having visited the Holy Sepulchre. James's daughter, Sisli, married Rowland Mortimer of Coedmor.

John Lewis succeeded his father in 1598; knighted before his 25th birthday, he became MP for Cardiganshire from 1604-11, succeeding his father-in-law, Sir Richard Pryse of Gogerddan, whose daughter, Bridget, he had married in 1601. In 1617 he bought the Coedmor estate from his brother-in-law, Richard Mortimer. His daughter, Lettice, married David Parry of Noyadd Trefawr, with a portion of £1,000 and his second daughter married George Owen of Henllys, Pembrokeshire, with a portion of £850. Approximately two hundred years later, on 29 June 1801, Sir John's great-great grandson, John Phillips, lawyer of Llandeilo, wrote to tell his brother Dr. Thomas Phillips then serving in India, that he 'had possession of a picture painted [or drawn] of Sir John when a Ranger of Hyde Park in the reign of Charles II'.

Sir John Lewes was High Sheriff in 1609 and 1634 and despite owning a large estate he and his son made several borrowings, on bonds and mortgage in London and when James Lewes inherited upon his father's death in 1656, mounting debts led to the eventual seizure of half of his estates. He married, as his first wife, a daughter and heiress of Lewis Lloyd of Aber-mad, Llanychaearn parish and secondly, in 1638, Mary Lloyd, widow of David Lloyd of Cilciffeth and daughter of John Wogan of Wiston. Their post-nuptial settlement dated 13 October 1641 included the Lordships of Is-Coed, Is-hirwen, the Castle at Cardigan, the Lordship and manor home of Coedmor, other lands in Llangoedmor and Llechryd, Parc Sidan, Parc Mair, Parc yr Arglwydd, Llechryd mill, tenements and lands in the township of Geraldston, otherwise Treferedd, in Tre-main parish.

James Lewes of Coedmor died in 1668 and his son, Col. James Lewes, of Coedmor, High Sheriff in 1664, married firstly, Catherine, daughter of Col. Sir Richard Harrison of Hurst, Berkshire and they had a son, John. Catherine died in 1659 and James married secondly, Ann Rudd. When James died, only a year after his father, he left his only son John, then aged about nine, to be brought up by his mother's eldest brother, Sir Richard Harrison of Hurst, near Reading.

The Aber-mad estate was sold to the Vaughans of Trawsgoed and Abernantbychan became alienated by the Leweses. John Lewes of Hurst, MP for Cardiganshire from 1685-1701, also inherited the Llan-gors estate in Breconshire through his wife, Elizabeth, daughter of Lodwick Lewis, son and heir of Sir William Lewis. Her second husband was Walter Pryse of Painswick whose son, Lewis, later inherited Gogerddan, Llan-gors, Hean Castle and Abernantbychan. Catherine Lewes, John's daughter, or more likely John's sister, married John Langton of Westminster and their son George Lewes Langton was educated at Magdalen College, Oxford and was later of Lincoln's Inn. He had been 'of Abernantbychan' at some time and died unmarried, probably in London, on 22 August 1738 and was buried in an 'English cemetery in a lead coffin'. He left Abernantbychan to the Pryse family of Gogerddan.

In 1672 (whilst the Lewes's were at Coedmor), John Williams paid tax on 7 hearths at Abernantbychan. John was born at Hafod-wen, overlooking the Tywi south of Carmarthen and married Lettice, widow of John Lewes of Coedmor and Abernantbychan and daughter of Rhys Lloyd of Bronwydd, also descended from Lewis Dafydd Meredydd. John Williams died in 1710 and Abernantbychan was occupied by Elizabeth Brigstocke who, when indisposed was, 'in her bed at Abernantbychan House, the place of her then abode'. By 1760, James Thomas is listed as freeholder of the property, probably by lease from the Pryses of Gogerddan, who, between 1838 and 1842, let the Abernantbychan demesne of 63 acres to James Owen.

When the estate was sold, Abernantbychan was bought by the Thomas family, the fourth generation of whom were living there in 1965.

Grid Ref: SN 3149 4947

Refs: Colby Map, 1831; *Dwnn,* i, 39-40, 55; PRO List; Blome List, 1673; Kitchin Map; Meyrick, *Cardiganshire,* 1810, edn. 1907, p. 211; NLW, Bronwydd Deeds, No. 2176, 2898; Exchequer B & A, 13 Geo. I; Noyadd Trefawr Deeds, 37, 335, 418, 1664; NLW, 12356E, 494; Francis Jones, 'Aberglasney and its Families', *NLWJ*, vol. XXXI, No. 1, Summer 1979; CRO, Coedmor Deeds; WWHR, ii, 80, 108; NLW, Noyadd Trefawr Deeds, 320, 346, 445.

ABERPORTH PLÂS, Aberporth

The little cove into which the river Gilwen flows to the sea at Aberporth is called Traeth y Plâs, as it was included in the lands of Plâs farm. The slope on which the Plâs stood is called Banc y Plâs. The house was situated 300 yards from the parish church. When Francis

Jones visited it in 1979 the Plâs was deserted and falling into disrepair. When Meyrick visited Aberporth he noted 'it is now the property of Davis Morgan, Esq. and is a respectable farmhouse'. In *TDW* Lewis wrote, 'The estate of Plâs, belonging to the family of Morgan, has a mansion of great antiquity, built in the form of a cross; and this demesne, as well as that of Pennar-issa, formerly exhibited some fine timber, but it has given place to a few ornamental plantations'.

The first recorded occupier of the Plâs is Hector Morgan, gent., who was married to Bridget, daughter of Thomas Pardo of Cloygin, Llangynderyn, and sister of Thomas Pardo, Principal of Jesus College, Oxford. Hector and Bridget had three sons and three daughters. Hector was buried at Aberporth on 2 October 1734.

The eldest son, David, later became vicar of a church at Coleraine, Northern Ireland. The second son, Hector, was baptised at Cardigan in September 1680. John lived in Cardigan and was High Sheriff in 1750. He was baptised at Aberporth in 1686 and died in 1763. The eldest daughter, Bridget, baptised at Cardigan on 9 July 1678 was buried at Aberporth on 20 July 1760 and Hannah was baptised at Aberporth on 9 September 1691. Mary died in November 1690 aged four weeks. Hector died in 1699 and his will proved on 27 March amounted to £29. The Rev. David Morgan, who succeeded to Plâs Aberporth, married and had four daughters who were his co-heiresses. They were Christiana, Eleanor, Amy and Mary, who on their father's death in 1765, each had one quarter of the estate. The estate being, at this time the capital messuage called Tir Plâs Aberporth, Tythin y Glog isaf and -ucha, Tir y rhos, Tir y Llwyn Du, Llain Ymryson, Clun Gwyn and other messuages in the parish of Aberporth.

Christiana, the eldest daughter, was also the heiress of her uncle John Morgan. She married as his second wife, David Davies, a cousin, later of Oxford, who was a master at the Free School in St. Mary Overy, Southwark. On his marriage to Christiana, David took the name and arms of Morgan; 3 bucks heads couped *sable.* Eleanor married Thomas Pryce, whose sister Bridget married a Mr. Wagner. In 1810 a map of Plâs Aberporth shows it to be the property of John Wagner. His son Thomas Richard Pryce Wagner died 1878, Bridget's grandson then inherited. He left the moiety of Plâs Aberporth to his nephew, John Frederick Mitchell of Cardigan, alive in 1885. Amy, the third daughter of Christiana and David lived in Cardigan and died a spinster in 1766. Mary, the youngest daughter, married William Williams of Cardigan, Esq., in 1779.

Christiana and David Davies Morgan had no children. Christiana was described as a dowager in 1788 and lived in London from 1794 until her death in 1800. David had two sons from his first marriage, Charles Davies, of Fleet St., and the Rev. Hector Davies of Ludgate Hill. Hector married Sophia Blackstone, daughter of John Blackstone, first cousin to Sir William Blackstone, the eminent jurist. They had a son, Hector Davies (1785-1850), a distinguished theological writer of Castle Hedingham, Essex, who on the death of his grandfather assumed the name of Morgan. He married Frances Harrison and succeeded to a half of her share of the estate of Plâs Aberporth on the death of the above Christiana. She also left a moiety to her kinsmen, James Morgan of Llwyn-llwyd and James Phillips a carpenter of Cardigan. They then held a moiety of 1/16th each of the estate. The estate in 1802 amounted to 8 messuages, 8 cottages and 1,300 acres in Aberporth, and in Carmarthenshire, the Pardo lands comprising 15 messuages, 4 water corn-mills and 3,200 acres.

In 1806 David Phillips, the son of James Phillips, released his share to Hector Davies Morgan. Hector retired to Cardigan in 1846 and died there on 23 December 1850. His will was dated 7 March 1846 and was proved on 3 January 1851. His widow died on 27 October 1867. They had three sons, John Blackstone,

Thomas and James David and two daughters. Maria Elizabeth and Anna Sophia Susannah. The eldest son, John became curate of Garsington near Oxford and died in 1832. Thomas became a solicitor, married a daughter of Lewis Evans, solicitor of Cardigan, and succeeded to the estate on the death of his mother in 1867. The lands in Cardiganshire were Capel Gwnda, Pantygronglwyd, Hendraws, Abertyfnant, Penygraig, all in the parish Penbryn with the saleable value of £3,813.15.0 and annual valuation of £152.11.0. A moiety of the farm and lands of Plâs Aberporth was valued at £1,832.10.0 on an annual rental of £91.12.6 from 227 acres. In Carmarthenshire he inherited Gilfach and Clunfelin in the parish Trelech-a'r-Betws valued at £2,750 and rental of £110, the Pentremawr estate, parish Llanpumpsaint worth £5,720 with rental of £228, and a moiety of Gilfach, Cwmmudan, Gwaunyrafar, Rhyd-lydan, Llanygors, Berllan, Rhydyglomen in parishes of Abergwili and St. Peters, Carmarthen worth £2,635 and rental of £131.15.0. Finally there was a moiety of 'Holloway, Parkygwaunrichard, Ffynnaisill, Caerarlish, Emlych, Pistyllgwyn and lands, cottages and gardens', in parishes of Kidwelly and Llanfynydd worth £2,076 and rental of £103.16.0. The whole estate, together with minor properties, had a saleable value of £18,827.5.10 and annual rental of £818.10.6.

Thomas Morgan's only child, Jane Evans Morgan, married Elliott Lloyd Price, attorney of Cardigan, late of Castell Pigyn. The marriage was the subject of a pre-nuptial settlement signed on 4 September 1861. The settled lands in Carmarthenshire and Cardiganshire included the reversion expectant on the death of Frances Morgan of lands in Penbryn parish, and a moiety of the messuage and lands called Plâs Aberporth. Elliott and Jane went to live at Pibwr-wen, Carmarthenshire. They had a son, Morgan Ashby Blackstone Lloyd Price, who died aged three years and two months. Jane died at Pibwr-wen and was buried at Abergwili on 14 December 1874, pre-deceasing her father. Elliott died in 1911 in his 72nd year and was buried with his wife at Abergwili.

On his death in 1879, Thomas Morgan devised all his realty and personal property to his partner, Charles Evans Richardson. On 9 January 1880 the latter changed his name by Deed Poll to Charles Evans Davis Morgan-Richardson and took the arms of Morgan; 3 buck's heads couped s.a. Thomas's youngest son, James, born in 1810 had died in 1846. On 10 June 1872 The *Morgan Richardson Papers* tell us that Thomas Morgan, gent. and Thomas Richard Pryse Wagner of Manereifed, Esq. gave a lease for 21 years 'to Thomas Thomas of Penrallteifed, Llangoedmor, and David Evans of Ffynnon-wen, parish Blaenporth, farmers, of the capital messuage called Place Aberporth, with covenants re. repair of buildings and rent of £100 to each lessor'.

The complications of a split estate continued; Thomas Richard Pryse Wagner, grandson of Bridget Pryse, died in 1878 and his will proved on 26 February 1879. He left a moiety of Plâs Aberporth to his nephew John Frederick Mitchell of Cardigan, alive in 1885. On 26 September 1885 an agreement was drawn up between J. F. Mitchell of Cardigan Esq. and Charles Evans Davis Morgan-Richardson of Noyadd Wilym, solicitor, which included articles of agreement for the purchase of a moiety of six houses and a chapel in Aberporth for £250. By 1918 an Abstract of Title shows C. L. E. Morgan-Richardson to have succeeded to his father's part of the estate.

On 21 December 1918, a little more than one-hundred-and-fifty years after the estate was divided, an agreement between Thomas Thomas, tenant of Plâs Aberporth and Messrs Morgan Richardson, regarding the purchase by the former of the Plâs Estate for £5,100, was drawn up and agreed, and the property became one again.

Francis Jones visited the Plâs on 11 May 1978. He writes, 'the house is at right-angles to the slope and faces east, looking towards the parish church which is about three-hundred-yards away. Here is a large roomy house in ruins. The roof is on but damaged; windows gone, the short wing at rear, roofless and in ruins. The last family there, farmers, was that of Thomas and the last two daughters, Miss Kate Thomas, aged about 85, and Miss Annie Thomas, in her 90's, live at Aberporth and I must call to see them. The Thomas's sold the house to a Dr. Stephens, who died shortly afterwards and Mrs. Stephens sold it to a developer from Cardiff who built some new houses higher up on the slope above the Plâs, and left the Plâs to fall into ruins: this was about six years ago'.

Grid Ref: SN 2537 5112

Refs: Lewis, *TDW;* Horsfall-Turner, *Wanderings,* 140; NLW, Morgan Richardson Deeds, vol ii, 352, 362, 373-4, 375, 385, 1707-8, 1733-4, 1755, 1805, 1822-3, 1824; Map of Plâs Aberporth NLW; Meyrick, *Cardiganshire,* 1810, edn., 1907, p. 208; D. L. Baker-Jones, *Ceredigion,* viii, *2,* 1977, pp. 152-155.

ABERPYLLU, Llanfihangel-y-Creuddyn

The reference given is for the confluence of the Pyllu (now afon Llanfihangel) and the Ystwyth. Aberpyllu no longer exists but the name remains in the farmhouses of Pyllau-isaf and -uchaf on either side of the B4340 between New Cross and Abermagwr. The ancient home of late medieval gentry who traced to Cadifor ap Dinawal and later the Vaughans of Trawsgoed. Rhys ap Dafydd ap Siencyn is the first associated with Aberpyllu. He was a son of Dafydd Siencyn Llwyd who married a daughter of Dafydd Llwyd ap Dafydd ap Rhydderch of Gogerddan. Dafydd's father was Siencyn Llwyd of Llanddwy whose grandfather was Rhys ab Adda Fychan of Trawsgoed. Rhys Dafydd Siencyn, a man of some substance whose estate was worth £150 a year, was High Sheriff in 1573, and is described as of Plâs Newydd in Aberpyllu who signed for Dwnn in 1588. He died in 1589, had no legal heirs but had four natural children by three different ladies. The eldest, Morgan, son of Elen, ferch Rhys, married a daughter of Morgan Glyn, Esq. Gwen married Thomas ap Morus ap Llewelyn and their son, Rhys married a daughter of John Lloyd of Rhandir, Llangwyryfon. Catherine married Thomas ap Morus ap Thomas and Maud became the wife of Ievan Gwyn ap Griffith ap Dafydd. When Morgan died in 1601 he devised most of his estate to his wife, Catrin, but if he should die without legal heirs, the estate would go to Rhys Thomas ap Morus, his natural son and the children of Iefan Gwyn Gruffydd. Rhys Thomas ap Morus brought an action in the Chancery Court claiming ownership of the estate then held by Catrin. The verdict is not known. By 1615 Rhys Vaughan owned Aberpyllu and he was selling parts of the estate to Edward Vaughan of Trawsgoed. A document in the *Crosswood Deeds* state that Rhys Vaughan came to the Aberpyllu estate of Morgan Rhys 'by gift or by stealth'. In his will of 1637, Rhys Vaughan left the remainder of the Aberpyllu estate to his brother, Richard. In the *Crosswood Deeds* between 1652 and 1668, David Vaughan and Anne, his wife, are variously described either as of Aberpyllu, or late of Aberpyllu. Among the last of the family at the property was Richard Vaughan who was living there in 1684. In 1701 Rhys Vaughan owned Pyllu but lived, as a tenant of the Trawsgoed estate, at Glennydd. His son, John, succeeded him but soon Aberpyllu, now divided into Uchaf and Isaf, became the property of the Nanteos and Trawsgoed estates respectively.

Grid Ref: SN 6372 7498.

Refs: Colby Map, 1831; CRO, GGMS; *Dwnn,* i, 48-9; NLW, Crosswood Deeds, pp. 38, 75, 84, 88, 94; Gerald Morgan, *A Welsh Home and its Family: The Vaughans of Trawsgoed* (Llandysul), 1997, pp. 30-2. *Ceredigion,* Vol. XIII, No. 1 (1997), pp. 36-7.

ABERTRINANT, Llanfihangel-y-Creuddyn

Formerly an estate of some consequence which at its zenith in 1792 consisted of some 48 properties in Llanfihangel-y-Creuddyn, Llanbadarn Fawr, Llanfihangel Geneu'r glyn, Aberystwyth and Borth. Located on *Colby's Map of 1831* and on modern OS maps on the outskirts of the village of Llanfihangel-y-Creuddyn off the minor road towards Cnwch-coch. Also marked on *Kitchin's Map of 1754* and *Emanuel Bowen's Map of South Wales,* c. 1760. Meyrick states, 'A seat belonging to a family named Llwyd. The house, which was of the old-fashioned form, has been suffered to fall into decay and is now occupied by a farmer who is its tenant'.

In his will dated 1598, Morgan Dafydd Llwyd of Glasgrug, Llanfihangel-y-Creuddyn, devised Abertrinant and 11 other properties to his son, Rhisiart Morgan Llwyd. However it was Watcyn, the second son who inherited the estate. He died in 1628 and his estate was valued at £288. He was succeeded by his son, Morgan, who married the heiress of Rhiwarthen. In 1632 Morgan failed to answer a summons to the coronation of Charles I and payment of £50 and other subsidies in return for a knighthood, stating erroneously that 'he had noe estate at all'. Morgan died in 1640. His son, another Morgan, High Sheriff in 1713, married Margaret, daughter of Thomas Pryse of Glanfrêd by Margaret, who died in 1689, daughter of Lewis Owen of Peniarth, Meirionnydd.

In 1738/9 Thomas Lloyd of Abertrinant married Jane, of Neuadd Trefechan, Llanbadarn Fawr. He was High Sheriff in 1774. In 1756 their son, Thomas, married the Hon. Elizabeth Vaughan, only daughter of Wilmot Vaughan, Viscount Lisburne, whose portion was £3,000. The house of Abertrinant was decaying and Thomas and his wife moved elsewhere and he died in 1793. Thomas and Elizabeth 'imported' port wine and laver bread from Swansea and in 1784 the Abertrinant and Rhiwarthen estates had an income of £600. Elizabeth is described in 1793 as a widow living in Carmarthen. During their absence at Gogerddan, Abertrinant was occupied by John Ball, later of Grogwynion, an entrepreneur of dubious character in the lead mining industry.

Thomas had a brother, Richard, and three sisters, Anna Maria, Charlotte Jenetta and Bridget. A deed dated 14 February 1792 which describes the estate of 48 properties and included in its assets 'a day's math of hay on Tydre weth in Llanfihangel-y-Creuddyn, the profits of weights, measures and balances in Aberystwyth and £10 per annum issuing from Glanleri and Glanleri mill in Llanfihangel Geneu'r glyn'. Dorothy Elizabeth, eldest daughter of Thomas and Elizabeth Lloyd, married Colonel Owen Lloyd, the second son of Bronwydd, Llangynllo. Their daughter, Elizabeth, married Thomas Davies of Nantgwylan and their children were Thomas Hughes Ford Davies and Elen Lloyd Davies, later of Aberceri. The alienation of the Abertrinant estate began early in the 19th century. Many properties were sold in 1827, some to the Hafod estate. The Lloyds of Abertrinant became the Lloyd Evans concentrated in the south of the county, but Abertrinant itself was still occupied by descendants of the original Lloyds in the 1990's.

Grid Ref: SN 6726 7608

Refs: Colby Map, 1831; Kitchin Map, 1754; Emanuel Bowen Map of South Wales, c. 1760; Morgan Richardson, ii 476; NLW, Crosswood Deeds, pp. 200, 225, 226, 241, 242, 282; NLW, Cwrtmawr Deeds, 1676, 1681, 1694, 1742; Castle Hill Docs., No. 838; CRO, GGMS, III (Gwaethfoed); WWHR, i, 39; *Cambrian Traveller's Guide,* 1813, p. 46; Meyrick, *Cardiganshire,* 287; *Ceredigion,* Vol XIII, No. 1 (1997), p. 36; Gerald Morgan, *Cyfoeth y Cardi,* 1995, pp. 95-6, 161.

ABERYSTWYTH CASTLE HOUSE,
St. Michael, Aberystwyth.

In 1788 Sir Uvedale Price, a prosperous landowner of Foxley, Herefordshire and a close friend of Colonel Thomas Johnes of Hafod, applied to enclose a piece of ground on the town common. It extended from Mrs. Jenkin's garden in Castle Street leading down to Ffynnon Twlc-yr-hwch, a distance of 132 yards, bounded on the north by the sea rock. It was here that he built Castle House in 1795 in the Romantic tradition to an unusual design by John Nash. The house called Lady Caroline's House after Price's wife, was described as 'a strange house resembling a castle with three octagonal towers connected by ranges of apartments having a light and elegant balcony on the side towards the sea'. The house, intended as a summer residence resembled 'a half Gothic castle and half Italian villa . . . said to be patronised by a spiritual resident in the form of a White Lady who is supposed to occupy one of its octagonal towers'.

By 1801 Sir Uvedale was letting his property for three months every year at a rental of 6 guineas a week and by 1824 Castle House had become an annexe of the Talbot hotel. It was then divided into apartments and let to various residents before John Taylor, a lead-mining developer in north Cardiganshire, bought it in 1848. He was followed by A. H. Novelli who extended Castle House before selling it on to Thomas Savin in 1860. Savin, a dashing entrepreneur, who built the railway line from Machynlleth to Aberystwyth, bought Castle House with the intention of creating a huge hotel, 'of which there would not be another like it in the kingdom'. He engaged the well-known architect, J. P. Seddon, to enlarge the original house. The impatient Savin spent £80,000 on Castle House which was opened unfinished in 1865. High interest rates caused him great difficulties and Savin ran out of money. Castle House was put up for sale. The only bid at auction was for £5,000. It was eventually bought by the Committee headed by Hugh Owen who were responsible for the creation of the University of Wales. The Committee had a magnificent building for the very reasonable price of £10,000. It received its first students in October 1872 but the buildings were gutted by fire in 1885 causing damage worth £20,000. The pennies of *y werin* (the common people) came to the rescue again and W. T. Jones, a Melbourne businessman, provided money for the famous Quadrangle to be built over the College Corridor which became a focus for generations of Aber students. Despite developments on the Penglais campus, the old college still houses part of *Y Coleg ger y lli* (the college by the sea).

Grid Ref: SN 5808 8170

Refs: Lewis, *TDW; Cambrian Tourist*, edn., 1814, p 76; NLW, MS. 1340c, 119; *Tour,* 15 Sept. 1801; Lipscomb, *South Wales Tour,* 1802, 163; Thomas Roscoe, *Wanderings and Excursions in South Wales,* London, 1854, p. 12; W. J. Lewis, *Born on a Perilous Rock* (Aberystwyth), 1980, pp. 171-4.

ADPAR HILL (or House), Llandyfriog

Lewis wrote in *TDW,* 'an elegant villa, the seat of John Beynon, Esq.' The house is marked on *Colby's Map of 1831.*

In 1873 Adpar House was the home of E. C. L. H. Fitzwilliams when the *Landowners Return* lists the property as of 904 acres with an annual rental of £934. A letter, written in January 1958 by C. C. L. Fitzwilliams, about his great-grandfather, E. C. L. H Fitzwilliams, JP for Cardigan, Carmarthen and Pembroke, and given to Francis Jones, sheds fascinating light on a colourful personality.

Edward Crompton Lloyd Hall was the first Fitzwilliam, and took a prominent part in local affairs. On reading his grandfather's (C. H. L. Fitzwilliams), family book, C. C. L. Fitzwilliams writes, 'I do not think my grandfather held him in very high esteem, and indeed, two more different characters would be hard to find. One jovial, a radical in politics, a speculator, he left his estate mortgaged and his affairs in the hands of the rascally London solicitor, Mr. Grey. He also left his widow and daughter £40,000 – which my grandfather had a great job to find'.

E. C. L. Hall, later Fitzwilliams, was born on 26 June 1807, at Hill House near Swansea. His grandfather, Admiral Braithwaite, died soon after and left E. C. L. Fitzwilliams's mother two-thirds of the Cilgwyn estate. The other third went to the Lloyds. It is said that the Admiral had never come down to Cardiganshire, for, 'Wales was a long way from London, and the coaches and Inns uncomfortable'. When the family did at last visit Adpar Hill House, which had been left to them, it had 'been looted by the Lloyd relations'. Apparently even the main staircase had been removed. C. C. L. Fitzwilliams writes, 'all that was left was an oak box, which I now have, and the picture of Capt. Thomas Lloyd. The oak box was too valueless and heavy to remove, and the picture of the man who had left much of his estate to an outsider, too hated to carry away'.

E. C. L. Fitzwilliam's mother, known in the family as Granny Campbell, appears to have been a very hard woman. When E. C. L. Fitzwilliams was a boy she had held his hand up against the bars of the fire 'to teach him not to play with fire.' He was privately educated, graduated from the University of London, practiced at the Bar, went to the South Wales Circuit and possessed a first-class legal mind. He was known to take on cases for nothing if he thought an injustice was being done. In Cardiganshire, however, he was disliked by his own class, 'the family were looked on as interlopers, he was not . . . a sportsman, he was ultra-radical in politics . . . had a good opinion of himself and a sharp tongue. There is a story about him sitting on the bench with two other magistrates. He was Chairman of the Bench and thought the prisoner guilty, but the other two did not . . . he told the prisoner 'You have been found not guilty, but you would not have been if I had not had a fool on one side of me and a drunkard on the other'.

He is remembered with gratitude by those in the village for saving 80 'half-starved men, one winter of distress' by giving them employment herringboning the walls around the Cilgwyn estate (which are still in evidence) and allowing them to gather wood on the estate. He drove himself about with four, 'and in time of snow, six ponies', and used harnesses with 'jingling chains'.

In June 1833 he married Mary Alexina, second daughter of Duncan and Harriet Campbell by whom he had three sons and five daughters. He lived at Kilrhue and Adpar, and in 1853 on the death of his mother he succeeded to Cilgwyn. On 13 December 1849 he changed the family surname to Fitzwilliams.

In 1855, as director of the Great Western Railway he was liable for the huge debts of the company while it waited for a bill to be put through Parliament and so everything was sold up and when the bailiffs came to call, the family escaped along the Upper Carmarthenshire Road. 'The family had intended to go to the Balearic Islands but when they got as far as Poitiers money had run out and they were in a starving condition . . . Mary, his wife, refused to go further.' The family appear to have stayed on the Continent for many years, possibly as long as ten. When the Bill at last went through Parliament, E. C. L. Fitzwilliams was repaid and once more lived at Adpar Hill House.

He took up the threads of his life at Adpar, drove around with a team of cream-coloured ponies, ploughed with oxen, 'not the last to do so in Wales but was the last round here'. His working oxen are said to have won prizes at Smithfield, due, he said to the muscle turning to fat. Many people had stories to tell about him. He once sacked a look-out, posted to watch out for him while they took a break, for not spotting him, saying, 'if you can't look after your fellow-workmates' interests better than that, you can't look after mine'.

Another story concerns shareholders bemoaning the falling revenue from the shares taken out for the building of New Quay; his answer to them was to take them round the graveyard and to point out that 'there will be less widows and orphans [which] recompenses . . . for the loss of money'. A memory recalled in Newcastle Emlyn was about his coachman who had 'borrowed' his master's ponies to take one of the maids to the races. Needing transport, E. C. L. Fitzwilliams was reduced to utilizing the wicker governess cart and a donkey. He was a large man and must have looked rather strange and not a little funny in the tiny cart. When John Rees, the coachman returned and presented himself to his master who asked him if he had enjoyed himself. 'Yes, Sir' came the reply, to which his master responded 'So did I', and that was the last John heard of the matter.

He must have been a man with a ripe sense of humour for when castigated by a client for 'overcharging' her for a will, he set about turning it into one of the longest wills ever made and was thus the scourge of every local lawyer involved in its intricacies for five generations.

E. C. L. Fitzwilliams was also something of an archaeologist: 'he is said to have removed Allt Cunedda's skull from the burial ground on the farm of that name which we owned near Ferryside, and sold about 1900.'

C. C. L. Fitzwilliams ends his letter, 'I hope a man of flesh and blood arises, no doubt vain of his legal knowledge and original in outlook, good humoured, kind, always willing to help the poor, and a keen freemason, one of the founders of St. Peter's Lodge'. He also comments that 'I have his wig and it fits me'. E. C. L. Fitzwilliams died on 17 April 1880 and was interred in the Cilgwyn burying place at Llandyfriog churchyard on 22 April 1880.

His only surviving son, Charles Home Lloyd Fitzwilliams succeeded to all his estates, subject to a settlement of £40,000 for his widow and younger children and certain legacies to relatives, friends, servants and work people.

C. H. L. Fitzwilliams's son was (Col.) Edward C. L. Fitzwilliams, CMG, DL of Cilgwyn, Newcastle Emlyn. His obituary in the *Western Mail* of 11 July 1936, describes him as having fought in the Great War along with his seven brothers, four of whom were killed. E. C. L. Fitzwilliams served for three years with the 1st Battalion Welch Regiment before he transferred to the Army Service Corps and served with distinction in many countries including China and South Africa, where he was wounded, and was mentioned five times in dispatches. In civilian life he was Commissioner of Boy Scouts, an active churchman and a member of the Governing Body of the Church in Wales. He was 'revered in Cardiganshire for his great solicitude to men who had served and had fallen on evil days'. He was a JP for Cardiganshire and Carmarthenshire and died on 10 July 1936.

The square three-bay, three-storey regency house was demolished c. 1910 by Charles Fitzwilliams, as 'not fit for a gentleman to live in'.

Grid Ref: SN 3095 4114

Refs: Colby Map, 1831; Lewis, *TDW;* Landowners Return, 1840; Thomas Lloyd, *The Lost Houses of Wales,* 1986; Letter, C. C. L. Fitzwilliams, 1958.

ALDERBROOK HALL, see GWERNAN

ALLT-DDU, Tregaron

Shown on *Colby's Map of 1831,* halfway between Tregaron and Pontrhydfendigaid. It was the home in 1670 of Edward Evans, gent., son of Rees Evans who married Mary, reputed daughter of Lewis Gwyn of Jordanston, gent., of Pembrokeshire. Under the terms of the marriage settlement, the following lands were settled on her marriage: Moeldy Ucha, Tir yr Hook, Skyoog and other lands in the parishes of St. Nicholas, Granston, St. David's and Llanhywel and two messuages in Llangurig parish. On 3 June 1670, Edward Evans granted the Pembrokeshire lands to Jenkin Vaughan of Jordanston, who, in turn, granted the Llangurig lands to Edward Evans. Mary Evans was described as Edward's late wife in 1670. In 1678 a deed of release from Edward Evans of Allt-ddu was given to Evan Jones, of Little Hern, Montgomeryshire, gent. of the equity of redemption to Allt-ddu in the parish of Caron which Edward Evans and his father Rees Evans had mortgaged to the said Evan Jones, then of Llanafan. In 1687 Edward Vaughan of Trawsgoed leased Allt-ddu to Llewelyn Jenkins, of Caron parish, yeoman, for ten years. There is a photograph of Allt-ddu showing its proximity to Cors Caron in *Crwydro Ceredigion.* Mr. Daniel of Allt-ddu was a member of the committee formed in Tregaron in 1857 to establish a school in the town.

Grid Ref: SN 7020 6375

Refs: Colby Map, 1831; NLW, Cwrtmawr Deeds, No. 1139; NLW, Crosswood Deeds, p. 110, 117.

ALLT FADOG, Llanbadarn Fawr

Situated in woodland near the source of the Peithyll north of Capel Bangor and south-west of Trefeurig and marked on *Colby's Map of 1831.* The home, in the 18th century of the scholar, poet and map-maker Lewis Morris (Llewelyn Ddu o Fon, 1701-65), later at Penbryn, Goginan, who had many interests in the lead-mining industry in north Cardiganshire. Allt Fadog was formerly the home of a Richard Lewis, High Sheriff of Cardiganshire in 1701 also described as of Cefn-gwyn. Bont-goch. In earlier days Elizabeth, daughter of Edward William of Allt Fadog, married Meredith Lloyd of Cwmbwa, and John Edward married Dorothy, a daughter of David Lloyd of Cwmbwa. Dates are lacking.

Grid Ref: SN 6605 8198

Refs: Colby Map, 1831; Phillips, *Sheriffs of Cardiganshire;* CRO, GGMS, III (Gwaethfoed).

ALLT-GOCH, Llanwenog

Situated near Cwrtnewydd on a slope north of Court Farm. Allt-goch is an old farmhouse in the upper part of Llanwenog parish. Nearby is an old fortification called Castell Allt-goch. Marked on *Colby's Map of 1831.* The present house was built in 1802 and the ruins of the older house are on the slope below the farmyard. Llewelin Parry, of Llanerchaeron, married the widow of John Hughes, clerk and on 20 May 1635 granted a lease to Samuel Hughes of Allt-goch of all the messuages and lands of the late John Hughes to which Llewelin was entitled in the right of his wife: 'namely one-third of two messuages and land, three parcels, four messuages and land, Tir ffynnon ddewi, Dol y buart, Tir ffynnon Vair of Tir llwyn kellin, and a cottage and garden, all being in the parish of Bangor, Llanbedrpont Stephan and Kellan, west Cardiganshire; and a messuage and land called Yr Erw Benfraith in Abergwili parish, Carmarthenshire, for fifty-one years if the said Llewelin Parry and his wife Jane should so long live, at a yearly rent of £10'.

From 1640-1700 Morgan Rhydderch lived at Allt-goch. Samuel Hughes was a JP in 1705 and had a daughter, Rachel, who married David Lloyd, eldest son of Thomas Lloyd of Gwastod Gwrda. She died without issue and her will was proved in 1696. This property provided the county with two other High Sheriffs; John Martin in 1787 and William Skyrme in 1809. In 1882 a pre-nuptial settlement was agreed between Evan Evans of Allt-goch and Lettice, daughter of Evan Davies of Faerdre, in the parish of Caeo, Carmarthenshire.

Grid Ref: SN4945 4865

Refs: Colby Map, 1831; Davies, *Hanes Plwyf Llanwenog,* 1929, p. 73; Griffith Owen Deeds, No. 666; PRO List; Cardiff Central Library Deeds; CRO, GGMS, I (Tydwal Gloff); WWHR, i, 47; NLW, 12356E, 392.

ALLT-LWYD, Llansanffraid

Shown on *Colby's Map of 1831,* lying south-west of Llanrhystyd. The home of the Hughes family descended from William Hughes of Rhos Tyddn, Devil's Bridge. William's son, also William, was vicar of Llanilar and married Dorothy, daughter of Thomas Evans of Ty Mawr, Talsarn. Their son, John Hughes of Glanrafon (1768-1821), married Jane Edwards, the widow of Thomas Evans of Llanilar. They had a son and two daughters. John, the heir, Jane, who married the Rev. John Jones and Elizabeth, who married John Sime of Edinburgh. John, born on 15 July 1805, described as of Allt-lwyd, was a JP and Deputy-Lieutenant for the county. In 1837 he presented a silver cup and paten to Llanrhystud church. He married Mary Anne, eldest daughter of Alban T. J. Gwynne of Mynachdy on 6 March 1833; they had an only daughter who died in infancy. After Mary's death, John married secondly, on 10 August 1836, Elizabeth, the second daughter of George William Parry of Llidiardau. By his second wife he had two sons: John, the heir, born in 1837 and William Thomas, born on 5 November 1839 and three daughters, Annie who died unmarried in 1857, Elizabeth Georgeana, who married, in 1874, David Brown, MD of Winchester, Hampshire, and Jane Maria who married Col. Anthony Lennon Brown, AMD, also in 1874.

The eldest son, John George Parry Hughes, born on 20 October 1837 was High Sheriff of Cardiganshire in 1864 a JP and Deputy-Lieutenant. On 27 May 1869 he married Elizabeth Charlotte Mary, elder daughter and co-heiress of Col. J. A. Lloyd-Philipps of Mabws and Dale Castle in Pembrokeshire. He was a Captain and honorary Major of the Royal Carmarthenshire County Militia from 1867-85. The *Landowners Return of 1873* lists John George Parry Hughes of Alltlwyd who owned 1,317 acres with an annual rental of £1,238. He died in 1906. Their son, John Lloyd Hughes JP, born on 5 October 1871, followed his father into the military and served firstly as a Captain and later promoted to Major of the Cardigan RGA (Militia). He married twice; firstly on 3 September 1910 to Margaret, only surviving daughter of John Richards of Llanarth, and secondly, Nellie Rees of Aberystwyth, the manageress of a ladies' dress shop in Aberystwyth called 'Sonia'. They had no children but were breeders of pedigree Large White Yorkshire pigs. In 1898, John Lloyd Hughes's sister, Dorothy Edith married Captain (later Lt.-Colonel) John Prescott Law, DSO, of the Devonshire Regiment. Dorothy died in September 1929.

By 1986 Allt-lwyd was an hotel and its name had been changed to Post-gwyn.

Grid Ref: SN 5275 6835

Refs: Colby Map, 1831; Burke, *LG,* 1850; Landowners Return, 1873; Meyrick, *Cardiganshire,* 367.

ALLTYBEILI

Site unknown but possibly Llanbadarn Fawr. An unknown location probably east of Llanbadarn Fawr village. The place name suggests a property located on a wooded slope in the vicinity of an unidentified medieval fortification. The earliest recorded owner of Alltybeili is Morgan Lloyd, gent. On 8 June 1642, with David Lloyd of Cwmnewidion and Rees Morgan, a post-nuptial settlement, dated 8 June 1642, was agreed between Morgan Lloyd and Elizabeth, one of the daughters of Morgan Richard late of Cwmnewidion, deceased. The lands of 'Tythin Allt y Baili, Tyddin y Wayn wen and Tythin Keyro ycha all in the parish of Llanbadarn fawr, and a burgage and garden in the town of Aberystwyth' were settled on the couple.

The NLW, Cwrtmawr Deeds state that on 25 June 1672 Morgan Lloyd and his son and heir, David, agreed the terms of a mortgage with Thomas Powell of Llechwedd Dyrys, Esq. of 'a tenement called Tythyn y wein wenne in Llanbadarn y Croythyn which was taken as part of the tenement of Allt y Baily, together with 2 closes and parcels on both sides of the river Paith and extending to the pinfold or common pound adjoining a smith's forge in Llanbadarn y Croythyn, all in Llanbadarn y Croythyn in the parish of Llanbadarn Vawr and now late part of Allt y Baily and all lands he owns in the parish'. In 1673 Morgan Lloyd 'of Allt y Baily granted Tythyn Allt y Baily and all his other properties to his son and heir apparent David Lloyd'. The same deeds record that in 1674 and 1675 Morgan, gent., his wife Elizabeth and David Lloyd their son gave further mortgages on Alltybeili to Thomas Powell of Llechwedd Dyrys. In 1678 David Lloyd, described as late of Eurglawdd, Cardiganshire and Morgan Lloyd of Alltybeili obtained a General Release on the property.

Refs: NLW, Cwrtmawr Deeds, Nos. 30, 48, 127, 249, 258, 484, 1370.

ALLTYBWLA, Llandygwydd

Marked on *Colby's Map of 1831* as Alltybwla with another farm Allt y bwla hen. Meyrick described it as a farm near Cenarth located on the bank of the meandering Teifi. This was the home of the Jenkins, a cadet line of Blaen-pant. Jenkin Thomas of Alltybwla had a daughter, Joan who married David ap David ap Evan of Dyffryn Hoynant, also Jenkin Thomas David who had a son, John Jenkins, who married Dyddgu, the daughter of David Parry of Noyadd Trefawr. Dates are not given.

The *Edwinsford Deeds* state that 'in 1640 Michael Williams of Rhydodyn, Esq., Thomas Jenkins of Allty Bwla, Cardiganshire, gent., Rice Thomas, citizen and innholder of London and Edward Bracewell, citizen and merchant tailor of London gave a bond to Richard Fittz of London, gent., for payment of £52'.

By 1760, Rowland Philipps Laugharne of Pontfaen, Pembrokeshire owned Allt y bwla. He was High Sheriff of Cardiganshire in 1762.

Grid Ref: SN 2605 4213

Refs: Colby Map, 1831; Meyrick, *Cardiganshire,* 355; C/A Protheroe, C, VI; CRO, GGMS, II (Gwyddno); WWHR, iii, 79; NLW Edwinsford Deeds, No. 775.

ALLTYCORDDE, Penbryn

Marked on *Colby's Map of 1831* as Allt y Gorde, just north-west of Abernantbychan, near Penrallt Gordde. The house stands near the confluence of the Dulas and a small stream between Rhipyn-llwyd and Glynarthen.

In 1571/2 an agreement was made between Meredydd Vaughan of Penbryn, Cardiganshire, gent., Thomas ap Mores Phillippe of Cardigan gent., and John ap Ievan ap Jenkyn of Penbryn, yeoman for the settlement of the capital messuage called 'Place Allt y Kordde with lands called Tir y Khinnie gwunion, tenements called Tythin pant y main gwunion, Tythin y krug koy and Ruovelen (lately the gift to 1, of Hoell Gitto Mowr and Elene verch Ivan ap Jenkin) and Tythin Kastell yn dolig, all in Penbryn parish, to the use of 1 for his life, with contingent uses to Jenkin, 3rd son of 1, and his bodily heirs begotten on Mary verch James, finally to the right heirs of 1'.

By 1684, James Lewes is shown as of Allt-y-Cordde. He was the eldest son and heir of John Lewes who had married Lettice, daughter of Hugh Bowen of Upton, the widow of Vaughan of Penbryn. His younger brother, George, described as of Hendre in Cemaes, Pembrokeshire, married Sarah, daughter of Captain William Owen of Cwmeog. Mary died unmarried and Ann, the youngest, married Alban Thomas of Aberporth. James, of Alltycordde, married Grace, daughter of John Lewes and had four sons, Thomas, David, James and William, and two daughters, Elizabeth and Lettice. Thomas married Eleanor, daughter of John Lloyd of Llangennech, Carmarthenshire; David was unmarried, James married Elenor, daughter of Rees Evans, William and Elizabeth were unmarried and Lettice married William Evans.

In 1760 Griffiths Evans held the lease of 'AllteyGordde' and by 1807, the property of 220 acres was tenanted by William Davies and Evan

John. The lease was held for three lives and formed part of the Peterwell estate and was listed as thus in its Sale Catalogue of August 1807.

Grid Ref: SN 3078 4986

Refs: Colby Map, 1831; Noyadd Trefawr Deeds, Nos. 974, 1008; NLW, Cwrtmawr Deeds; WWHR, iii, 80; Sale Catalogue Peterwell Estate, August 1807; CRO, GGMS, III (Owen ap Bradwen), fo. 3.

ALLTYRODYN, Llandysul

Lewis in *TDW* tells us 'Galltyrodin, the seat of the family of Lloyd, is an elegant mansion, built on the declivity of a steep hill . . . the library is enriched with a valuable collection of genealogical manuscripts'. Marked on *Kitchin's Map of 1754* as Allt yr Odin Place and on *Colby's Map of 1831* as to the east of Afon Cletwr, four miles north-east of Llandysul.

The Lloyds were descended from Rees David Llewelyn Lloyd of Castell Hywel. Ievan Lloyd of Alltyrodin married Maud, daughter and co-heiress of Richard Lewis of Caeo. Their son, David, High Sheriff in 1667/8, Deputy-Lieutenant and described as a Royalist, married Mary, daughter of Henry Price of Abergorlech, Carmarthen. They had five sons and two daughters:

1. Ievan, who succeeded to the estate.

2. Thomas, a tanner living in Carmarthen, who married a daughter of Thomas Jones, the widow of Walter Thomas David Lloyd.

3. Harry, who married a daughter of David Lloyd of Bwlchmawr, in the parish of Llanwenog.

4. David, who died unmarried at Oxford.

5. Rhys was of Cilyblaidd, one of the 5 JP's for Carmarthenshire in the reign of James II. He married Jane, the daughter and co-heiress of David Jenkins of Dol-wlff. They had two sons and two daughters. The elder son, David Lloyd of Clun-y-march, Llansawel who married firstly, Dorothy, daughter of the Rev. Evan Jones, and secondly, Jane, the daughter and heiress of J. Davies of Dôle Gwynddion (Dolaugwyrddion). There were no children from either marriage. The younger son, John died unmarried. The daughters, both co-heiresses were Jane, and Rachel, who married David Pugh of Coedmor in Pencarreg. The daughters of David and Mary were Jane, who married Thomas ab Owen of Bwlchbychan and Mary, who married firstly, Hugh Lloyd of Lloyd Jack and secondly, a Mr. Phillips.

David Lloyd's will, dated 20 May 1679 and proved on 10 October of that year, detailed the estate as: 'Alltyrodin and water mill called Melin y Pandy, messuages and land in the parish of Llansawel, Carmarthenshire called Tir Byarth y Blaydd and Tir Kilwenne with six unnamed messuages, a water corn mill called Melin Kilwerne and another unnamed message. A messuage in the parish of Llanfynydd, Carmarthenshire called Esker Grynddy, otherwise Eskall grynddy, an unnamed messuage, a messuage and land in the parish of Cynma Gaeo called Tir Glaydythe. 2 messuages and land in the parish of Llanfihangel Year'th called Tir y pant Mawr and Tir Blodoyen. 2 messuages and land in the parish of Talley, one called Tir Kilwoor. Messuages and land in the parish of Llandysul called Tir Dol Walker and Tir Penn bont of Lanrhyd Llanfihangel, and messuages and land in the parish of Llanfihangel Year'th'. With the will was an attached inventory.

Ievan Lloyd, who succeeded to the estate was High Sheriff of Cardiganshire in 1685 and had three sons and two daughters. David, the heir, who married his cousin, and the aforementioned Jane, daughter of Rhys Lloyd of Cilyblaidd. John died unmarried. Evan, described as 'at Oxford' in 1752, died unmarried. Anne married John Rice, son of Jenkin Rice of Gellyfergam and Mary married twice; firstly to Morgan Lloyd of Ffoshelyg and secondly, to Thomas Phillips of Trewinsor.

Hanes Plwyf Llandysul tells us that, '*circa* 1735 the Baptists started to hold meetings at a house near the bridge of Llandysul, home of Rhys Thomas William. The congregations were so large that they were held in the open outside the house. This offended some local people who went to complain to Mr. Lloyd of Alltyrodin, the landowner, that the congregations were destroying his land by tramping over it. At one meeting, Mr. Lloyd arrived, then climbed to the preaching place. He looked around, and asked "What destruction has been done?" and immediately answered his own question – "Nothing except envy." He called Thomas

Rhys William before him and told him the things he had heard and then asked him to tell all preachers who came there to pray for him (Mr. Lloyd). He then said "Things are not satisfactory like this, you must raise a meeting-house (ty cwrdd) and you are welcome to raise one on my land". Accordingly the chapel of Pen-y-bont, Llandysul was built. For many years afterwards the preachers included Mr. Lloyd in their prayers'. Further information tells us that 'the Lloyds of Alltryodin were helpful to the Unitarians . . . David Lloyd gave them a lease for 99 years at a yearly rental of 1/- of the land on which the chapel was built'.

David Lloyd, of Alltyrodin, elder brother to John Lloyd, vicar of Llanarth, was High Sheriff in 1742 and married as his first wife, Alicia, the daughter of Thomas Lloyd of Berllandywyll and secondly Justinia, daughter and co-heiress of John Pryse of Blaendyffryn. David and Justinia had three sons. David, the heir was born in 1748, John, who married Elizabeth, daughter of Charles Lloyd of Heol-ddu, Aberglasney; they had 21 children. The third son was Thomas, who died unmarried in 1768.

David Lloyd, High Sheriff in 1780, married Elizabeth, daughter of Herbert Evans of Highmead. In *Tours in Wales*, Fenton tells us, 'Mr Lloyd of Alltyrodin received me very civilly. Shewed me several fragments and books of his genealogical collection relating to Pembrokeshire, which he has kindly promised me the use of. Had some refreshment and then, accompanied by the Gentlemen of the house, was shewn a most beautiful Tumulus situated on the south side of the River near a fordable place called Tommen Rhyd Owen. Mr. Lloyd has planted it with silver fir. I longed to have had Mr. Cunnington there to have got into its Bowels'.

Malkin states in *South Wales* 'There are at Alltyrodin some valuable manuscripts chiefly genealogical, which their owner, a gentleman of more intelligence than most in the country, has furnished for the use of the *Cambrian Register;* and it is probable that the next volume will be enriched with a part of their content'.

David and Elizabeth had two sons and three daughters, David, John, Anne, Justinia and Elizabeth. Elizabeth, wife of David, died in 1805 aged 36 and David died in 1822 aged 74. John, known as *Lloyd Coch*, succeeded to Alltyrodin when his older brother, David died. John died unmarried and the estate passed to his cousin, Mrs. John Lloyd Davies, formerly Anne Stewart from Carmarthen, (the only one of the 21 children to have survived her mother) and her husband, John Lloyd Davies. He therefore succeeded, *iure uxoris,* to the estate, which comprised of Alltyrodin, and 46 other properties amounting to 5,294 acres.

John Lloyd Davies (1801-60) was born in the Black Lion Fach in Bridge Street, a small inn in Aberystwyth. He was a 'boots' in the pub and later became bound-servant to John Walters, lawyer of Newcastle Emlyn who later inherited Aberglasney. John studied law and eventually qualified as a solicitor. He was a JP, was Deputy-Lieutenant of Cardiganshire and Carmarthenshire and Conservative MP for Cardigan Borough. He was a supporter of the Church of England and was a strong opponent of the Rebecca Riots. He married Anne in 1825 and after her death he married Elizabeth, a rich Englishwoman, the only child of Thomas Bluett Hardwicke, of Tytherington Grange, Gloucestershire. The house was rebuilt in 1827, with a three-storeyed residential block at the front and a lower servants' courtyard at the rear.

In 1837 'The Society of Gentlemen, Husbandmen and others, living in Llandysul parish and district, Cardiganshire', was founded in Llandysul. It met in the house of John Mathias called The Lion Rampant. John was one of the trustees along with the Rev. Thomas Bowen of Waunifor.

By John's first marriage to Anne he had a son, Arthur Lloyd Davies (1827-1852) who was killed following a fall from his horse. Arthur's son, John (1850-1878), was described as the heir in 1876. John's death in April 1878 at the age of 28 caused considerable excitement in Llandysul and further afield. John had left the bulk of his estate to James Allen, clerk to a London solicitor. Mrs. Massey, John's sister took action in the Chancery Court and the matter was eventually settled amicably with the family remaining on the estate and James Allen awarded £5,000. John's early death was not helped by his addiction to drink and it is stated that his hands shook so much that he could no long put out a candle with a duelling pistol. John's sister, lived at Alltyrodin for a few years after the death of her brother, then sold the Alltyrodin, Blaendyffryn and Heol-ddu estates. Captain James Stewart bought the mansion of Alltyrodin and some of the farms. He was a JP and was High Sheriff of Cardiganshire in 1896.

The *Bronwydd Deeds* of 3 November 1881 list the fixtures and fittings purchased by James Stewart. In 1929, when Alltyrodin was again offered for sale, this time by Douglas Dormer Stewart. The Sale Catalogue describes the property as an 'early Georgian residence, with, on the ground floor, a stone entrance portico, lounge hall, dining room with a marble fire-place, smoking room, drawing room, gun room, store room, and on the first floor, reached by a primary and secondary staircase, a large library with a small museum room adjoining, two double bedrooms with dressing rooms, a single bedroom, double servants bedroom, bathroom, w.c. and boxroom. On the second floor, a double bedroom with dressing room, three bedrooms, four servants bedrooms and a bathroom. The domestic offices comprised kitchen, larder, washing room, serving room, and servant's hall, outbuildings and cellars.' There was also a walled garden, a home farm and two entrance lodges. The estate at that time comprised of three farms, Bryngolen, Penwern and Rhyd-cynydd. Carved over an old stable door at Alltyrodin were the words *Sic siti laetantur equi- Yn y fath sefyllfa y ceffylau lawenhant.*

Grid Ref: SN 4493 4425

Refs: Colby Map, 1831; Kitchin Map, 1754; Blome List, 1673; WWHR, i, 50-1; Meyrick, *Cardiganshire,* 1818 (edn. 1907) 195-6; Lewis, *TDW*, 1840; Malkin, *South Wales,* ii, 148-9 (1807 edn.); W. J. Davies, *Hanes Plwyf Llandysul,* 1896, pp. 23, 61, 72, 112-3, 230, 337; *Carmarthen Studies,* 1974, pp. 74-5, 97, plan, pl. XV; P. Smith, *Houses,* p. 326, fig. 187; *Arch. Cam.* 1898, p. 352; BLG, 1898, ii, 1409; NLW, Bronwydd Deeds, 4265; Lloyd Family Records, p. 46; Landowners Return, 1873; Fenton, *Tours in Wales,* 1804-1813, p. 8; TM Schedule of Llandysul parish, 1841; CRO, GGMS, I (Tydwal Gloff), fo. 20; Carmarthen RO, SC53.

ARGOED HALL, Tregaron

Marked on *Colby's Map of 1831* together with Argoed-fach, lying south of Tregaron village.

In 1760 Thomas Jones, an author of the Exchequer, London, owned Argoed. He was a prominent member of the Cymmrodorion Society in London.

The present house was built in 1874 for a surgeon, Rowland Rowland, who was born in Llangeitho. It is a six-bedroom, three-storeyed residential block at the front with a lower service courtyard at the rear. By 1930 Argoed Hall was owned by D. D. Williams, a farmer and one of the founder members of the Royal Welsh Show. Argoed Hall boasted 15 acres and 500 yards of fishing rights on the Teifi. The house was renovated in the 1970's by a local businessman and his wife. Since which the house often changed hands.

Sculptor Herta Keller and her husband John Wilson, writer and publisher, have further up-graded the property.

Grid Ref: SN 6760 5855

Refs: Colby Map, 1831; WWHR, iii, 99, 113; CRO, GGMS (Gwynfardd) 29.

BEILI (BAYLY), Llandygwydd
Marked as Baili on *Colby's Map of 1831* and modern OS maps and situated south-east of Llandygwydd church. Little is known of Beili except that it belonged to Ieuan Ddu, father of Llewelyn and then to his son Ieuan. Ieuan's son, Griffith, married Sage, daughter of Owen ap Howel who traced to Gwynfardd and they had a daughter, Isabel. The *Golden Grove Manuscripts* tell us that Maud, daughter and heiress of Llewelyn Goch ap Dafydd of Blaen-pant, Llandygwydd married David Parry of Noyadd Trefawr. Her mother was Dyddgu, daughter of Rhydderch ab Evan ap Llewelyn ab Evan Ddu of Beili.

Grid Ref: SN 2495 4355

Refs: Colby Map, 1831; CRO, GGMS, (Gwyddno).

BERTH-RHYS, Llanychaearn
Situated between Llanddeiniol and Blaen-plwyf, adjacent to Pencwm-mawr flats, and marked on *Colby's Map of 1831* and modern OS maps. It was owned by four generations of Lloyds, David, Ieuan, then David, whose son, Ieuan ap David, married Elsbeth, daughter of Ieuan ap Thomas of Aberllolwyn at the beginning of the 17th century who signed for Dwnn.

Grid Ref: SN 5670 7413

Refs: Colby Map, 1831; *Dwnn,* i, 16 (G.M. Aberllolwyn).

BIRCHGROVE (ALLTFEDW), Llanilar
Located in woodland named Alltfedw on the south bank of the Ystwyth adjacent to Trawsgoed bridge and opposite the former home of Lord Lisburne. The present building is late Georgian, built as the dower house of the Trawsgoed estate. However, Evans in his *Cardiganshire* writes, 'This old homestead was a former residence of the Powell's of Nanteos. On all sides remain traces of the taste displayed in its surroundings, the avenue, the masses of rhododendron bushes, the circular eel pond, the quaint stabling – which tell of past days'. Nicholas describes Birchgrove as, 'the embowered residence of the heir of the Crosswood estate, Lord Vaughan, and usually appropriated to a cadet of the family'. In 1848 it was the home of the Hon. William Mallet Vaughan, who was still in residence in 1860. Later Birchgrove became the home of the estate agent of Trawsgoed and was occupied in the 1880's by the loyal Scot, Robert Gardiner and his family. In 1888 the sixth Earl of Lisburne's marriage to his father's sister-in-law was celebrated with a sumptuous party for the tenants at Birchgrove. The next recorded occupier was a retired colonel, Crawley-Bovey, who rented the home from the Trawsgoed estate before Birchgrove was sold in 1921. During World War II it was the base for 25 land-army girls who worked on local farms and for whom Trawsgoed bridge became an important rendezvous for local boys after working hours. Capt J. J. Lloyd-Williams, M.C., formerly Chief Constable of Cardiganshire never lived at Birchgrove. He died in 1949. Major J. A. Lloyd-Williams, M.C. of the 2nd King Edward's Own Goorkas, bought Birchgrove in 1960. He sold it in 1976. The present occupiers, Tony and Gwen Burgess, who run a wholesale egg business, bought the property in 1981 from the owner of Walkers Electronics of Aberystwyth. In the drawing room is a handsome fireplace rescued from Hafod mansion and in the well-maintained grounds is a magnificent *Wellingtonia*, a giant 130 foot redwood. Mrs. Burgess, the daughter of Reuben Morgan, formerly of Galloway and Morgan, booksellers of Aberystwyth, states that living at Birchgrove is, as for other owners of large country houses, 'a labour of love'.

Grid Ref: SN 6650 7305

Refs: Colby *Map,* 1831; Lewis, *TDW,* 1840; Murray, *Handbook of South Wales,* 1860, 117; Nicholas, *County Families,* 1872 & 1875; Evans, *Cardiganshire,* 1903, pp. 32-3; 1881 Census Returns, Mrs. G. Burgess.

BLAENAU GWENOG, Llanwenog
Located north of Cwrtnewydd and south of Moeddyn-fach and marked on *Colby's Map of 1831* and modern OS maps. This house belonged to a branch of Saer-y-cwm and was a farm of over 400 acres. In 1760, Thomas Evans was the owner-occupier. He served as High Sheriff of Cardiganshire in 1765. By 1831, Blaenau Gwenog was owned by the Davies family who were zealous Baptists. The family remained in occupation for nearly a century. A grandson of Evan Davies (1809-85), John Evans of Llys-wen, Sheffield, was High Sheriff of Cardiganshire in 1926, as was his grandson, Josiah Jones of Garthowen in 1937. Two other grandsons were the doctors E. and A. Evans of Lampeter. Another descendant, John Davies, farmed Crug-y-whyl in Bro Gwenog.

Grid Ref: SN 4787 5138

Refs: Colby Map, 1831; WWHR, i, 54; Davies, *Hanes Llanwenog,* 1939, pp. 75, 149.

BLAENCERDIN, Llandysul
Standing on a slope above the Cerdin river south of Capel Cynon. Blaencerdin Fach is nearby. Abercerdin is at the confluence of the Cerdin and the Teifi rivers. Marked on *Colby's Map of 1831.*

John Lewis, descended from Morydd, king of Ceredigion, owned and occupied Blaencerdin in 1760. The estate was assessed for tax in 1758-9 at £6. John Lewis had three sons and a daughter, John of Cwmdulas, James, Nicholas and a daughter, Rachel who married David Parry of Esgergraig. Meyrick wrote 'Dinas Cerdin and Blaencerdin are still in possession of descendants of the family' The *Llandysul Tithe Map of 1841* listed Blaencerdin-fawr as a holding of 165 acres, and Blaencerdin-fach as of 107 acres and were owned by Alban Thomas Jones Gwynne and tenanted by Evan Lloyd and David Llwyd.

Grid Ref: SN 3865 4895

Refs: Colby Map, 1831; WWHR 1760; NLW, Morgan Richardson Deeds, No. 2697; Llandysul Tithe Map, 1841.

BLAENDYFFRYN, Bangor Teifi
Located south of the A475 near Horeb and described as the only house of consequence in the parish and formerly owned by a family of the name of Price. A photograph taken between 1860-70 shows a large double-pile house of three-storeys, with another large extension built on to one end. Blaendyffryn was the home of three High Sheriffs; Rhys David Morris in 1712, John Price in 1732 and John Lloyd Davies in 1845. John Price, JP, married Mary, daughter and sole heiress of Rees Davies of Bangor Teifi and had four children; Justinia, Mary, Anne and Jane. Mary married Lewis James of Tre-haidd, Nevern in 1785. Anne died unmarried, and Jane married Thomas James, Tre-faes from the parish of Moylgrove. John's sister married a son of David Lewis of Cefn-crwth, Carmarthenshire and they had a son in 1768. John's eldest daughter, Justinia, married David Lloyd of Alltyrodin and they had two sons, David and John. John Lloyd, gent of Carmarthen, the younger son, was awarded the Blaendyffryn estate when his grandmother's estate was partitioned. 'In 1785 the partition of the estate of Mary Price includes land in Conwyl Elfet, Llanfihangel Yorath, Llandysul, Lampeter, Abergwili, Bangor and Llangeler – includes the capital messuage called Blaen Dyffryn alias Tyr Blaen Hownant, and other lands in the parish of Bangor awarded to John Lloyd, younger son.'

The next known owner was William Williams, grandson of Rees and Joan Williams, who had three sons and two daughters; William, David, Lewis Elizabeth and Mary. David married Esther Lloyd of Caeo, Carmarthenshire, who in turn had two sons, William and John. William William's will is at Carmarthen. John Williams 'migrated across the border' and had issue.

Blaendyffryn was described as 'the property of John Lloyd Davies, Esq., to whom it passed by marriage with Miss Price, niece of the late proprietor, is pleasantly situated within this parish.' The entry in the *Landowners Return of 1873* shows Blaendyffryn to be in the ownership of Lloyd Davies, being of 159 acres, with a rental of £41 p.a. John Davies Lloyd of Alltyrodin owned Blaendyffryn until his death and the property was offered for sale in 1881. The catalogue describes the mansion: 'in the basement, a dairy or larder and salting room, coal cellar, large wine and beer cellars: on the ground floor, a massive stone porte-cochere leading from carriage sweep to vestibule or inner hall, whence a wide oak staircase ascends to the first floor; dining room, drawing room, library, house-keeper's room, w.c., door to garden, secondary staircase, lobby leading to wing in which are stone-paved hall and back porch entrance with small conservatory over; housemaid's cupboard, stone-paved kitchen with linen-cupboard in chimney recess, two large store cupboards, servant's hall, butler's pantry, glass cupboard, scullery. On the first floor, 4 bedrooms, 2 dressing rooms, landing, wc., lobby leading to wing in which is a drawing room or ballroom with statuary marble mantelpiece, and communicating by French casement with conservatories and vineries, and thence with pleasure gardens; also a small ante-room, cupboards: on second floor, 2 bedrooms, a bedroom with dressing room, another bedroom; attic and lumber room in roof; in the wing approached by a winding staircase leading from the secondary staircase to the first floor, are 3 attics, box-room and cistern cupboard. The residence is capable of considerable improvement, having been for some time unoccupied: there are some well-timbered grounds, croquet and tennis lawn, pleasure and kitchen gardens, numerous outbuildings and a farmhouse and buildings; about one and a half miles away is Allt y Cafan bridge, built some 50 years ago by John Lloyd Davies, a former owner of Blaen Dyffryn'.

Blaendyffryn was bought for £4,150 by Rees Thomas of Dol-llan, later of Gwynionydd, Llandysul. Later it was converted into an hotel and is now a residential home.

Grid Ref: SN 3928 4165

Refs: Meyrick, *Cardiganshire,* 189; CRO Sc; *The Tivyside Photographic Souvenir: Pen-y-lan* (in the possession of Miss Gwynedd Taylor, Manorbier, 1975); Griffith Owen Deeds, No. 6029; Colby Map, 1831; NLW, BRA Schedule, p. 89 No. 365-6; Lewis, *TDW,* 1840; Landowners Return 1873.

BLAENHOFFNANT,
(Blaen Hownant), Penbryn

This house is near the source of the river Hoffnant which enters the sea near Penbryn, west of New Inn and now named Blaenhoffnant-uchaf. In *TDW* Lewis states 'At Blaenhoznant, another farm in this parish, is a large *carnedd* and there are two others in the immediate neighbourhood'. The *Protheroe Deeds* tell us that Thomas Price was of 'Blaenhoynant Issa' and married Catherine daughter of Philip ap Mereydd, by his wife a daughter of Castell Hywel.

Five successive generations of the Llwyd family lived at Blaenhoffnant although the dates are obscure. David Llwyd was father of Evan David. His son David ap Evan was followed by Evan ap David, then David ap Evan. In 1760 the Davies's sold Blaen Hoffnant to Griffith Rice, an officer of Shropshire and a freeholder.

Grid Ref: SN 3280 5175

Refs: Colby Map, 1831; Protheroe Deeds, c, vi; WWHR, iii, 80; Lewis, *TDW,* 1840.

BLAEN-NANT, Llandyfriog

Situated north-east of Old Cilgwyn and marked on *Colby's Map of 1831* and modern OS maps, the home to the Rees and Prydderch families. The earliest owner was Ieuan Ddu, followed by his son David, and his grandson, Rhydderch, whose daughter Lleucu, married Rhys ap Richard ap Rhys of Llwyncadfor in Llandyfriog. Their son, John ap Rhys, married Jane, daughter of Thomas Davies, vicar of Llandysul commonly called *y ficer coch.* They had a son, Rhys ap John who married Joan, daughter of Rhys Thomas ab Rhydderch of Pentre-du in Llandyfriog and Gerddi-bach. Their son, David Rees married Angharad, the daughter of Morgan Thomas Prydderch of Blaen-nant in Llandyfriog, who was, in turn, the son of Rhys Thomas ap Rhydderch. Thus the two families who had owned Blaen-nant were joined.

David and Angharad had five children, two sons and three daughters. Methusalem became vicar of Pencarreg, Carmarthenshire, and Richard was vicar of Cenarth and married Margaret Rees, a drover's daughter. They named their son Methusalem after his paternal uncle. He was described as living at Llwyn-cadfor and married Grace, daughter of James Williams of Cil-y-cwm. Another daughter married Evan Griffith of Twr-gwyn who was described as 'ye Welsh poet.' Methusalem and Richard took the surname Davies. The only date attributable is that relating to their son, James Davies, described as a minor in 1739 who, following family tradition became a clergyman.

Grid Ref: SN 3220 4238

Refs: Colby Map, 1831; Dale Castle MSS., p. 29 (110); WWHR, i, 48; CRO, GGMS, i, p. 33.

BLAEN-PANT, Llandygwydd

A large handsome mansion surrounded by thriving plantations situated north-east of Llandygwydd village and marked on both *Kitchin's Map of 1754* and *Colby's Map of 1831,* and on modern OS maps. The home of the Parry, Jenkins and Brigstocke families. The earliest known owner at Blaen-pant was John Parry, High Sheriff of Cardiganshire in 1621. His son, Llewelyn Charles Lloyd Parry, succeeded to the property and his daughter, Sage, married Charles Lloyd of Alltycadno.

The second family of note to live at Blaen-Pant were the Jenkins. Reynald Jenkins was the son of William Jenkins and his wife, Elizabeth Lloyd, of Carrog, Llanddeiniol, who died in 1688. Reynald was married twice, firstly to Eleanor, daughter and heiress of David Parry of Noyadd Trefawr and they had a son, Parry who died unmarried. It is unclear which of the other children are of Reynald's first or second marriage, for he married secondly, Lettice Jenkins, who was living in 1676. By that date Reynald's second son, William, had married Bridget, daughter of James Lewes and Joan, his wife, of Gellidywyll, Carmarthenshire, whilst he was still a minor. Reynald's other children were Morgan, who died in 1687, John, alive in 1683, David, living in 1683, who had a natural daughter, Anne, Druscilla, Penelope who married a Woolley, Lettice and Margaret, who married Henry Lewis of Laugharne.

Blaen-pant was described as 'commodious' and in 1672, William Jenkins was assessed at 7 hearths. He was buried on 29 January 1704/5. William and Bridget had a daughter and heiress, Elizabeth, who married William Brigstocke. Elizabeth was buried in January 1739, aged 52 and her will was proved in the same year. The Brigstocke association with the house, during the 18th and 19th centuries was to last for 160 years. William and Elizabeth's son, also William, succeeded to the estate on the death of his father in 1732, with the following exceptions which were granted to his mother: 'Whereas the said Elizabeth enjoys for life the following properties; in Llandygwydd parish – the capital messuage of Blaen-pant. Messuages called Pen Allt Gibbie and Nant Gwgn (both now late in tenancy of James Lewis, gent.), Pengwern vach and Tir Blaen Gwrrog, Pengwern vawr, Tyr Blaen Nawmore, Park Pengwern vach, Tyr Coed y Cwm alias Place Coed y Cym and Try hene velin alias Try dan Alt gydd, Troedrhiw, Tyr Lodrgan and Tyr Cwd yth, Pentre Gwynne vach, Baily and Park ffynnon Dewy; a field or close called Baily field; a messuage called Pen y Vay alias Tyr yr forwr; 2 pieces or parcels of meadow being part of 2 meadows called Pwll y gelod and Ddolran; a messuage called Kill Llwch, messuages called Knwch y fedwen, Henbant alias Pistyll Llanddwr du, Glan hir wen and a parcel thereto belonging; a water cornmill called Blaenypant mill. In Llangoedmore parish and Chapelry of Llechryd, Co. Cards.: messuages called Tyr Powell Mawr alias Penyrallt issa, Tyr Alt y Glwchell alias Park y

Gweningoed, Tyr Dyffryn Llechryd, and Tyr pen pont Llechryd ; a field or close called Ddole pen yr allt. In Brongwynne parish, a messuage called Tyre y gore. In Blaenporth parish a messuage called Vid race ycha alias Carn Tree person. In Penbryn parish, messuages called Cwm barre and Ffoeslas. In Troedyroyr parish a messuage called Tyr pen y gare.'

William and Elizabeth's son Owen, (1741-1778), succeeded to Blaen-pant and married a daughter of Sir Thomas Brown. One of William's greatest achievements was his library. 'In the house is an extensive and valuable library, principally collected by Colonel Owen Brigstocke.' His son, William Owen Brigstocke (1761-1831), succeeded to his father's lands. He was High Sheriff in 1794 and had also inherited Gellidywyll in Cenarth parish. The Land Tax of 1800 shows 48 properties in total in 8 different parishes and singly taxed between 1/3d. and 14 shillings, with a total payment due of £15.16.1. The Brigstockes added considerable lands to the estate. Carlisle wrote, 'This is a very extensive, well-cultivated and wooded parish; especially the demesne of Blaen-pant, belonging to William Owen Brigstocke Esq. whose extensive plantations add greatly to the beauty of the neighbouring country, and whose system of agriculture is uniformly good.'

An inventory of goods at Blaen-pant, 'property of the late William Owen Brigstocke 1832,' lists: the large hall, drawing room, dining room, study, kitchen, servant's hall, house-keeper's room, housekeeper's pantry, butler's Pantry, scullery, storeroom, lumber room, cellar, 14 bedrooms, small sitting room, and outbuildings comprising, coach house, cart house, dairy, laundry and granary. Details were also given of furniture, silver, cattle and stock, grain, china and glass, valued at £1,837.16.0.

Augustus Brigstocke succeeded to Blaen-pant and married Jane Davies of Pentre, Maenordeifi. William Owen Brigstocke quickly succeeded him in 1832 and sold Gellidywyll to Lord Cawdor. A photograph in the *Tivyside Photographic Souvenir* in 1860 shows that Blaent-pant had been considerably enlarged and was a large 18th century house of 2 storeys, and attic storey, a range of six windows on ground and first floor, with a jumble of domestic buildings behind the main block. The Brigstockes continued to own Blaen-pant during the early years of the 20th century. Gwilym Owen Brigstocke was born there in 1905 and Augustus Brigstock died there in 1930. By 1974 the house had been converted to an hotel.

Grid Ref: SN 2532 4438

Refs: Colby Map, 1831; Kitchin Map, 1754; Noy-add Trefawr Deeds, 474; PRO List; Meyrick, *Cardiganshire,* 1810 (ed. 1907), 184; Carlisle, *TDW,* 1811; NLW, Morgan Richardson Deeds, No. 2364; Blome List, 1673; *Dwnn,* i, 56; Lewis, *TDW*; CRO, GGMS, I (Gwyddas); ibid. Brigstocke Docs. A.C. 5991.

BLAENPISTYLL, Llangoedmor

Located on a minor road off the A487 (T) road between Llwyngrawys and Tre-main in the parish of Llangoedmor, and marked on *Colby's Map of 1831* and on modern OS maps, Blaen-pistyll was the home of David Evans, gent., who owned the freehold in 1760. He was an Independent minister and died in 1773, aged 66. Little is known about the next owner, Thomas Probert except that he mortgaged for £600 a messuage called 'Cytyr Ucha and Crygwynne in the parish of Tremaine and Aberporth' to David Harries of Dinas Island, Pembrokeshire. His son, also Thomas, headed a large and prosperous family. An only son, born in 1793, he studied medicine and became a doctor. He married Julia, only daughter of Robert Ross, a solicitor of Cork. Thomas Probert became High Sheriff in 1857 and was an acknowledged authority on miniatures and Wedgewood china. He is better known, however, for founding Epsom College in 1855. He had seven children, three of whom made 'most advantageous marriages' His eldest son, John Lumsden Probert, MB, MRCS, JP, became a surgeon in London and married Jessica May Hughes, daughter of a solicitor from Powick, Worcestershire, in 1864. The second son, William, entered the Indian Civil Service. In 1852 Sophia, Thomas's eldest daughter married E. Norton Clifton, of Harley Street, architect, and Mary, the youngest daughter became the wife of Wharton P. Hood, MP, of Upper Berkeley Street.

Grid Ref: SN 2312 4796

Refs: Colby Map, 1831; Morgan. Richardson, ii, 474; WWHR, iii, 78.

BLAEN-Y-RHAW. Site unknown

Formerly an important house at an unknown location in the Tregaron/Llanddewibrefi area and owned for four generations by the Llwyd family. John, Howell his son, Ieuan coch, whose daughter and heiress married Gruffydd, known as 'The Cantors', whose father Rees ap Cantor was directly descended from Rhys ap Ieuan ap Gruffydd, ap Thomas ap Sir Rhys Hen, Kt., Lord of Llansadwrn and Abermarlais, ap Gruffydd ap Howel ap Ednyfed Fychan.

The arms of Sir Rhys Hen are: *azure* 3 falcons volant *or*, sed q. His son Thomas ap Rhys was chanter of 'Ye Collegiate Church of Llanddewy brevy.' It was his son Rhys ap Cantor of Tyglyn who was the aforesaid Griffith's father. Dates are lacking.

Ref: C/A Copy by Wh from DE.

BLAENYTHAN, Llandysul

Standing on a plateau in hilly land two-and-a-half miles north-west of Llandysul village near Croes-fan. A farm called Aberythan, is situated near a confluence of this stream and the Cerdin.

Blaenythan was the home of three generations of Lloyds; John, descended from Jenkin Llwyd of Cemaes, whose second son Evan had a son, Griffith, the first known owner of Blaenythan. According to the *Dale Castle Manuscripts* Griffith's son, John Llwyd Griffith married a daughter of John Lloyd ab David Llewelyn. They had a son, Howell, whose son Philip Howell married Elen, daughter of Lewis David Meredydd of Abernantbychan, descended from Owen ap Bradwen, and they had at least four children.

James took the surname Phillip and married Jane, daughter of Gwyon Llewelyn Lloyd of Llanfechan. Their son Philip James, married Joan, daughter of David Lloyd Thomas of Gellifraich and had a son John Phillips, who lived at his maternal grandparents' property Gelli-fraich. He married Anne, daughter of Hugh Bowen of Upton, the son-in-law of Anne Wogan whose will was made in 1700-1. Their son, Thomas married Gwen Philip of Tremain.

A daughter, Elen married Thomas ap Evan ap Thomas ap Saer y Cwm and their son Evan married a daughter of Thomas ap Owen of Bwlchbychan. Their other son was Lewis, who was later knighted and an MA. The second daughter, Lleucu married Thomas Ievan of Cwrtnewydd. Mary married David ap Meredydd ap Jenkin Meredydd.

By 1841 Blaenythan was owned by David Arthur Saunders Davies Esq., of Pentre, Maenordeifi with James Davies as tenant. The families of Pontgilgan in Llangeler and the Philipps of Dol-haidd, near Henllan are descended from Blaenythan.

Grid Ref: SN 3925 4438

Refs: Colby Map, 1831; CRO, GGMS.; PRO, Dale Castle MS., pp. 16, 26, 44, 59; CRO, GGMS, i (Tydwal Gloff), fo. 25, 45; Word MSS., BM; WWHR, i, 37; ibid, ii 7 &21; Protheroe, C, VI & XX; Llandysul Tithe Map, 1841; *Cambrian Journal,* 1864, 109.

BODFRIGAN, see LODGE PARK

BODYRYCHAIN (BOD-RYCHEN). Site unknown

There is no information on the location of this house but it was probably situated in the south-west of the county. Bodyrychain is very closely associated with Cadifor ap Dinawal of Castell Hywel and Gilfach-wen. His grandson, Rhys ap Rhydderch, married Catherine, daughter of Sir Elidir Ddu, Kt. Their son, Griffith Goch married Dyddgu of Caeo. They had a son, Gwilym, who married Gwenllian, daughter of Llewelyn ap Owain ap Owain, Lord of Iscoed. Their son lived at Castell Hywel. The daughter of Griffith Goch married Ievan Griffith David Llewelyn Foel Moreiddig Blegwyryd ap Dinawal. They had a son, Griffith ap Ievan, who married Elen, daughter of Meredydd Thomas Llewelyn Owen who traced to Tewdwr of Penrallt Gwerchydd.

Refs: Lloyd Ped. p. 22; Lloyd Fam., Rees (Peo., p. 23; Davies, *Hanes Plwyf Llandysul,* p. 225; CRO, GGMS, I (Tydwal Gloff), fo. 42; HS *Cardiganshire,* 1567. Pedigree belonging to Mr. Lucas, Long House, Reynoldston, Gower, 1981.

BROGYNIN PLÂS, Llanbadarn Fawr

Now called Plâs Brogynin, described by Francis Jones as being in a remote little vale near Penrhyncoch, shown on *Colby's Map of 1831* as -fach and -fawr.

Inhabited in 1771 by Shadrach Jones, gent., and by John Richards in 1806, gent., of Brogynin-fawr. The house itself is the subject of much conjecture. Francis Jones lived at Brogynin-fawr in 1936-37 and wrote, 'The poet Dafydd ap Gwilym is said to have lived here for some time at the workman's cottage, now ruined, but without any evidence whatsoever. Dafydd was an *uchelwr,* descended from Gwynfardd, and if he had been associated with this area, it would undoubtedly have been at Plâs Brogynin on the slope high above this ruined cottage'.

Brogynin was demolished during the 1914-18 war, its stones used to repair roads, and a modern bungalow built in its place. The owner built a larger property opposite the old ruin and called it Plâs Brogynin (now Brogynin-fawr). David Jenkins, former Librarian of the National Library of Wales who lived at the house in his youth with his grandparents, wrote that Dafydd's house was the size of a small country house. It was more substantial than other farmhouses in the area and contained plaster dating from the 16th century.

Grid Refs: SN 6624 8446

Refs: NLW Gwynfryn Deeds, No. 204; Glanpaith Deeds, 93, 218; *Arch. Cam.* 1907, p. 262; *Ceredigion,* ii, 1952-55, p. 277-8; *Genhinen,* 11, 1961, 180-4; *Cymru,* 43, 1912, 153-4; Fenton, *Tours in Wales,* 1804-1813, pp. 268, 271-2. David Jenkins *Bro Dafydd ap Gwilym* (Aberystwyth) 1992, pp. 27-32.

BRONGEST, Llanbedr Pont Steffan (Lampeter)

Situated east of Lampeter bridge, and shown on *Colby's Map of 1831* and on modern OS maps. The first known owner was Oakley Leigh, the son of a Carmarthen family, who was a JP and churchwarden of Lampeter in 1753 and Portreeve in 1758-8 and 1767-8. He was also steward of the Manor of Peterwell, Lampeter and agent to 'the wicked' Sir Herbert Lloyd. He had two natural children, David and Jemima, by Mary Price, both of whom were baptised at Lampeter in 1766. From a second liaison, with Anne, daughter of David Thomas Lewis, another daughter, Bridget was also baptised at Lampeter in 1778. He had seven other natural children, John, Watkin, George, John the younger, Charlotte, Thomas and Charlton. He recognised and gave his name to all ten of his children and they were all were named in his will as beneficiaries. He was buried at Lampeter in December 1788. John Leigh, his eldest natural son, received a farm and was elected a warden and overseer in 1793. Charlotte and Thomas were awarded £20 each and Charlton, landlord of the Swan Inn, Lampeter from 1777-1800, had a guinea. Charlton was appointed 'to serve out as churchwarden' from September 1780 until Easter 1781 following the death in office of Thomas Morgan of the Green Dragon. The precise portions of the other children are not known. Watkin, of Tyn-yr-heol, the second eldest natural son, was a yeoman and admitted a burgess in 1813. Misfortune hit the family when 28-year-old John Leigh, the younger, perished in the snow on Llancrwys mountain, when travelling from Cil-y-cwm to his mother's house at Cellan. His body, which was not found for five weeks, was laid to rest in the parish churchyard on 13 February 1832.

Grid Ref: SN 5833 4788

Refs: Colby Map, 1831; G. E. Evans, *Lampeter,* pp. 12, 15, 17, 24- 25, 34, 37, 40-44, 51-2, 57, 60-61, 68-69, 102, 204

BRONWYDD, Llangynllo

Situated north of Aber-banc off the B4334 towards Penrhiw-pal and built on a slope with a steep drop overlooking a wooded vale through which flows a stream. In 1853, Burke's *Visitation of Seats* states, 'the original house was built about three hundred years ago; since then there have been many additions; castellated with a "Norman" tower at the west front, 60 feet high, and stands on a hill'. Bronwydd is marked on *Kitchin's Map of 1754.*

Philip Bryne (of Ffoshelyg in 1552), bought Bronwydd on 14 July 1562 and was living there in 1589. He married Mary, daughter of Jenkin Lloyd of Ffoshelyg. Mary had a natural son by Francis Read, called David Read and it was this David who inherited Ffoshelyg from his mother. The *Bronwydd Deeds* record that Philip Bryne of Ffoshelyg released a tenement of land in 1562 'called Tythyn y bronwydd, a parcel annexed to the said tenement called Tir ffynnon wladys in the parish of Llangunllo and a tenement called Tir Dyffryn Llech in the parish of Llanfair Trelygen'.

The first of the Lloyd family to live at Bronwydd, was the Rev. Thomas Lloyd, son of David ap Rhys ap Howel ap Rhys of Crynfryn, descended from Selyf, King of Dyfed, who bore the arms: *azure* a wolf salient *argent*, and who traced to Tydwal Gloff, son of Rhodri Mawr. The *NLW, Cwrtmawr Deeds* describes the estate of the Rev. Thomas Lloyd in 1613/14 as consisting of the capital messuage called Bronwydd, and 31 other properties in the parishes of Llangynllo, Nancwnlle, Llangeitho, Caron, Betws Bledrws, Llangybi, Llanfair Clydogau, Llandysul, Llanfair Orllwyn and Llanddewibrefi.

Rhys ap Howell ap Rhys Griffith Lloyd had a son, David ap Rees. David had four sons and one daughter. The eldest son Morgan became Vicar of Llanboidy and had two daughters. The second son, David, is described as of Crynfryn and the third son was Thomas. The youngest son was Richard. The only daughter, Joan, was married twice; firstly to Rees David of Glan-y-wern and secondly to John Thomas who traced to 'ye Cantors'.

The Rev. Thomas Lloyd, the third son, (will proved in 1630), married Sage, daughter of George Bryne of Pant Dafydd in Llanfair Treflygen. Thomas Lloyd was the rector of Llangynllo and vicar of Penbryn. He bought Bronwydd from his in-laws. Thomas and Sage Lloyd had four sons and three daughters. The *Golden Grove MSS* record that David, the eldest, was disinherited 'for his profane way of living and had but a small part of his father's inheritance'. David had married *'in nolente patre'* Catherine, daughter of John Morgan, mercer of Carmarthen. Thomas and Sage's other children were Rees, James, who died without issue and John, born 1610, was educated at Oxford. In 1619, Joan married Lewis Bevan of Pen-y-coed, Carmarthen, High Sheriff in 1634. Anne Lloyd married Francis Bowen of Bwlchbychan and Mary married Thomas Lloyd of Gwastod, (Betws Leucu). Thomas and Sage's second son, Rees, succeeded to most of his father's estates.

Rhys Lloyd, High Sheriff in 1632 (d. 1646), was married twice; firstly to Mary, daughter of John Parry of Blaen-nant and secondly to Elizabeth, daughter of Thomas Birt of Llwyndyrys. By his first marriage he had a son and a daughter, Thomas and Sage, and two daughters, Lettice and Charity by his second marriage. Sage Lloyd married her first cousin, Col. John Robinson of Gwersyllt in 1642 and died without issue. Lettice Lloyd married twice; firstly, John Lewis of Coedmor and Abernantbychan and secondly, John Williams of Hafod-wen, High Sheriff of Cardiganshire in 1666. Charity Lloyd married Daniel Jones. Thomas Lloyd, eldest son of Thomas and Sage Lloyd succeeded to Bronwydd and was married in 1642 to Magdalen Robinson, daughter of William Robinson of Gwersyllt, Denbigh. The marriage was subject to a pre-nuptial settlement dated 1642. Thomas died in 1663 and on his death, his widow, Magdalen, lived with her sister at Lodge Park, (Bodfrigan), leased from the Pryses of Gogerddan, and paid tax on 8 hearths.

TCAS details the 1663 'Inventory of goods and chattels of Thomas Lloyd of Bronwydd taken and apprized 14 May 1663 by Thomas Parry of Llangunllo, Cardiganshire and John David of Llangeler, Carmarthenshire, gt.:

	£ s d
13 kine	15 6 8
13 kine more & 3 yokes of oxyen	31 6 8
25 young beasts	11 10 8
27 young beasts more	18 3 4
5 mares, 6 horses, 10 colts	23 10 0
200 sheep	25 0 0
1 silver beer bowl	1 0 0
5 silver spoons	16 8 0
4 rugs, 9 old coverlets & 12 prs blankets	5 1 8
All linen in the house	5 5 0
9 old feather beds, 10 bolsters & 4 pillows	9 0 0
12 cushions	12 0
6 brass pots, 6 brass pans & 1 brass couldron	3 14 0
Barrels, hogsheads & other wooden vessels	1 0 0
All pewter in the house	3 12 0
Chairs, tables, bed heads	5 2 0
Spits, racks and tongs	6 8
Ploughs, harrows, & other implts of husbandry	15 0
Corn in the ground	5 0 0
His wearing apparel	5 0 0
In ready money	600 0 0
Due by bond from Thomas Parry of St Dogmael's, Pembs, gt.	40 0 0
Due by bond from David Lloyd of Gwastod, Cards, gent.,	40 0 0
TOTAL	£851 2 4

(Endorsed) an Inventory of the goods of Thos. Lloyd of Bronwydd taken in 1669.

Thomas and Magdalen Lloyd had two sons and three daughters. Thomas, the eldest, of whom more later. The second son, John, lived with his mother at Lodge Park. His daughters were Magdalen, Jane and Sage. Magdalen married David Lewis of Dol-haidd Uchaf, High Sheriff in 1706. Jane married John Blome of Penybanc Uchaf, Carmarthenshire; her will was proved in 1737. Thomas Lloyd, (will proved 1692), the eldest son, described by Carlisle as the 'patriotic Thomas Lloyd of Bronwydd' served as a colonel in the Tivyside Volunteers and the Fishguard and Newport Fencibles. He married Bridget Johnes, daughter of James Johnes of Dolaucothi. In 1693, after Thomas Lloyd's death, she married John Williams of Talley and they lived at Deri Ormond.

Thomas and Bridget's son, Thomas, born in 1679, sold Bronwydd to his uncle, John Lloyd of Cilrhiwe and lived with his mother at Lodge Park. Thomas married Anne, heir to her mother, who was a daughter of Lewis Wogan of Wiston who came to live at Cilrhiwe. Thomas died at Faenor and his will was proved in 1737. His eldest son, James Lloyd, inherited Cilrhiwe and in 1727 married Elizabeth, the daughter of James Ladd, MD, of London. Her brother, John Ladd of Cilgerran, was Steward of the Barony of Cemaes in 1744. Thomas Lloyd, the second son, succeeded to Bronwydd which was willed to him by his uncle, John Lloyd, who had died without issue. Thomas and Anne's other children were: Anna Louisa who had married William Wogan of Wiston, (High Sheriff in 1724, and buried at Wiston in 1730), lived as a widow at Faenor, and in 1736, Letters of Administration were granted to her brother, James. John Lloyd, of Cardigan alive in 1742, married Mary, widow of Thomas Lloyd of Coedmor, and of Robinson Lloyd who was himself married twice, firstly to Ursula Davies, daughter of Thomas Davies of Dyffryn and secondly to Margaret, widow of David Harries and of Peter Watts of Hayscastle who was alive in 1750.

Thomas Lloyd (1703-1775), succeeded to Bronwydd in 1730 and married Anne Lloyd, daughter and heiress of William Lloyd of Henllys, Penpedwast and Monkton Hadley in Essex. He prospered and became High Sheriff in 1733. He was a barrister and purchased a moiety of the barony of Cemaes from John Laugharne of Llanrheithan in 1750. He called himself Lord of Cemaes.

Thomas and Anne Lloyd had four children:

1. Thomas, who succeeded to Bronwydd.

2. Owen Lloyd of Abertrinant later Colonel, who married Dorothy Elizabeth Mary, daughter and heiress of Thomas Lloyd of Abertrinant and Elizabeth Dorothea, grand-daughter of Wilmot, 3rd Lord Lisburne. Their son, Owen, of Abertrinant, was nephew and devisee of his aunt, Beatrice in 1796 and their daughters were Elizabeth, Anna Louisa, Bridget and Jane.

3. Joan married William Lewes of Llys-newydd, Dyffryn and Llanllyr.

4. Beatrice, a spinster in 1775, died before December 1796, naming her nephew Owen as her beneficiary.

Thomas Lloyd, the eldest son, born in 1736, succeeded to Bronwydd and married Mary Jones, daughter of John Jones, MD, of Haverfordwest, who built the first sea-water baths in Tenby. Thomas Lloyd served as a Captain in the 11th Foot and was Colonel commanding Fishguard and Newport Volunteers in 1797. He died on 13 July 1807, and his will was proved in 1812. Thomas and Mary's marriage was very fruitful, they had nine children; five sons and four daughters: Thomas was born in 1788, James, born in 1795 was educated at Brasenose College, Oxford. The other children were Sarah, Mary, Owen, Richard, William, Anna, Elizabeth, Louisa and Amelia. The Rev. Maurice Evans, 1765-1831, vicar of Llangeler, wrote an elegy on the death of Mrs Lloyd of Bronwydd who died suddenly on 9 July 1830.

The eldest son of Thomas and Mary Lloyd, Thomas Lloyd of Bronwydd and Cilrhiwe (1788-1845), JP, DL, was High Sheriff in 1814 and served with the 3rd Buffs and the 87th Regiment. In 1819, he married Anne, the daughter of John Thomas of Llwyd-coed and Llety-mawr, Carmarthenshire. They had four sons;

1. Thomas Davies Lloyd of Bronwydd.

2. George Martin Lloyd, died 1849.

3. Owen, born 1831 – a Captain in the 3rd Battalion, Warwickshire Regiment, who took the name Treherne in 1890 and married firstly, Elizabeth Caroline Anne, only child of Commander T. Mitchell, RN, who died in 1888 and secondly in 1899, Emma, daughter of S. Careless of Springfield, Broadway, Worcester.

4. James John Lloyd of the 13th Horse married Susan Maria Anne, daughter of David Arthur Saunders Davies of Pentre, and the Rev. Rhys Jones Lloyd, BA, 1827-1904, rector of Troed-yr-aur. In 1853 he married Anne, daughter of Lewis Lloyd of Nant-gwyllt, Radnorshire.

Between 1850 and 1853 a new house was built at Bronwydd, described by Horsfall-Turner in *Wanderings* as 'a modern mansion of an ancient family. The mansion of Bronwydd commands a beautiful prospect of the valley. The older seat was in the hollow below, where the trees are so thickly clustered . . . but the present building is upon the hill-slopes' A photograph of the exterior in 1860 in *The Tivyside Photographic Souvenir* shows 'a large, particularly ugly house of "gothic" style, two circular towers with turrets and a large square turret in castellated style'. A photograph of the exterior can also be found in *Contemporary Biographies of South Wales and Monmouthshire* which describes Bronwydd as 'a hideous castellated house with pepper-pot towers'.

Thomas Davies Lloyd who succeeded to Bronwydd was created a baronet in 1863 and became an MP. He owned 1,974 acres with a rental of £1,287 p.a. In 1846 he married Henrietta Mary, daughter of Geoffrey Reid of Watknighton, and Louisa, the daughter of Sir Charles Oakley, Bt. Sir Thomas made a gift to Llangynllo church of one of only two jewelled sets of plate in Cardiganshire. The oaken chest which contains the plate was made from an oak beam from the old church of Llangynllo pulled down in 1868 when a new one was built and consecrated in 1870. Placed inside this chest is a vellum scroll, carefully mounted, which reads: 'To the honour and glory of God. The plate for the Holy Communion was presented to Llangynllo church by the Houses of Bronwydd and Mount Gernos, AD 1870'. The jewels in the chalice represent the initials of the christian and surnames of the two families. On the base was written:

1. Lapis Lazuli – Sir Thomas Davies Lloyd
2. Hyacinth – Henrietta M. Lloyd
3. Malachite – Marteine O. M. Lloyd
4. Topaz – Gwinnett Tyler
5. Jasper – Judith Tyler
6. Garnet – Gwinnett George Tyler

and on the bosses are the names of the youngest children of the 'House of Mount Gernos', six in all, together with jewels representing their initials.

By 1881, the Lloyd estate had prospered and grown considerably to 7,946 acres, with an annual rental of £6,597. By 1879, when Sir Thomas's son, Sir Marteine Owen Lloyd, 2nd and last baronet, succeeded, the estate which included lands in Cardiganshire, Pembrokeshire, Carmarthenshire and Glamorgan and rights over 30,000 acres in the Lordship of Cemaes, Pembrokeshire, was worth £7000. p.a. Sir Marteine, born in 1851, was JP, DL, and High Sheriff of Cardiganshire in 1881 and served as a Captain in the Pembroke Yeoman Cavalry. In 1878 he married Katherine Helena Denniston, the third daughter of Alexander Denniston of Golfhill, Lanarkshire. Their son, Marteine Kemes Arundel Lloyd, born 1890, served as a Captain in the Special Reserves, Grenadier Guards, and was killed in action in France in 1916 during the First World War. Their daughter Nesta Constance Muriel, was born in 1879 and married Frederick Edward Withington of Bicester, son of the Rev. Edward Withington, JP. Their youngest daughter, Joan Henllys Lloyd, born in 1897, married Philip Saxon Gregson Ellis, of the Grenadier Guards, the son of Col. William Saxon Gregson Ellis of Co. Denbighshire who became a Major-General. Joan and Philip's granddaughter, Hyacinth, became Lady Marcher, and married John Hawksworth. They own Newport Castle, Pembrokeshire which is currently tenanted.

On 5 August 1937 the Bronwydd estate of 2,072 acres was advertised for sale in 98 lots and describes the mansion, 'which for centuries has been the home of the Lord Marchers of Kemes' as follows: 'basement, 3 wine-cellars; ground floor, main hall, staircase hall, dining room, drawing room, morning room, smoke room; lavatory, W.C., housekeeper's room, servants hall and lavatory, kitchen, scullery, larder, pantry, boot room, 2 footmen's rooms, back kitchen, dairy, laundry, chauffeur's room, coal and wash houses, lavatory, meat larder. On the first floor, 9 principal bedrooms, dressing rooms, 2 bathrooms and W.C.'s, store room; on second floor, 8 servant's bedrooms; there are outbuildings and walled gardens; farm buildings and farm (90 acres)'.

Among the properties sold as part of the Bronwydd estate were 'Ffynnon Fair (138a), Llanfair Trelygen, Penllwyn Cwrws (12a), Llandyfriog, Querchyr, Henllan Nantypobty, Penbeili Mawr (136a) and Ffynnon Wen (128a) in the parish of Llangunllo, Penbeili Mawr (136a), Homestead, stone, slated dwelling house, parlour, living room, kitchen, dairy, 4 bed-rooms, boxroom, storeroom. The outbuildings consist of the old farm house with corrugated-iron roof, cowshed, tenant Mr. J. Evans'.

The Bronwydd house itself was bought by a contractor who stripped it of all its doors, windows and fittings and left it to decay. Francis Jones visited Bronwydd with Thomas Lloyd of Cwrt Henry on 5 November 1983. He noted that the house was by then a complete ruin, the roof and floors had fallen and it was dangerous to enter. The arches of windows and doors were still there and over the doorways could still be seen inscriptions of 'a pious nature'.

Grid Ref: SN 3538 4330

Refs: Kitchin Map, 1754; WWHR, i, 21, 28; PRO, Dale Castle MS., p. 23; Burke, *LG,* 1850; *Dwnn*, i, 41; Meyrick, *Cardiganshire,* 1810 (edn. 1907, p. 201); Burke, *Visitation of Seats,* 1853, i, 70; *Contemporary Biographies of South Wales and Monmouthshire,* 1907, 153; Horsfall-Turner, *Wanderings,* 157; NLW, Bronwydd Deeds, Nos. 2038, 2331, 2826, 4251-4254 & 5822-5881 (Blue schedule, Blue Nos. 534, 675, 679, 7300, 7301, 7305); *The Tivyside Photographic Souvenir,* C. Allen (Tenby), Album in the possession of Miss Gwynedd Taylor, Manorbier, 1975; Carlisle, *TDW,* 1811. *Who's Who in Wales,* 1st ed., 1921.

BRYNEITHIN, Llanychaearn

Marked on *Colby's Map of 1831* as Bron yr Eithin and modern maps as Bryneithin (Hall), north-west of Llanfarian village three miles from Aberystwyth. The home of the Richardes family during the middle of the 19th century. William Eardley Richardes, who died 1874, was the owner of Bryneithin during the Napoleonic Wars. Bryneithin estate was of 62 acres valued at £172 p.a. in 1873. Originally from Penglais, he was the son of William Richardes (born 1792), and his wife, Anna Arabella, daughter of Thomas Rivett of Derby. William Eardley Richardes was the brother of Roderick, who married Anne Corbetta, daughter of William E. Powell of Nanteos, who succeeded to Penglais. His other siblings were Col. Charles Eardley Richardes of Hon. East India Company, of Aberllolwyn, Anna Maria, who married her cousin Sir James Rivett, Bart. from Carnac, MP for Lymington, and Francis of Milford, Hampshire.

William Eardley Richardes entered Woolwich Royal Artillery and served at the Battle of Waterloo as a Lieutenant. He was a JP for Cardiganshire and married Marianne, the daughter of Hugh Stephens JP, High Sheriff of Radnorshire. They had four sons and one daughter. Charles served in the Indian Army during the mutiny and died in 1867 without issue. William served as a Captain in the 21st Horse and died in 1865 and Frank was an Ensign in the Indian Army who died in 1855. In his *County Families,* Nicholas states that the eldest son, Hugh given as of Rushmoor, succeeded to Bryneithin in 1872 and left the estate to the son and heir of his sister Francis Anne, who was married to the Rev. Charles Marriott Leir of Charlton Musgrove, Somerset. In 1879, Edward Methuen Leir, (1854-1919), JP, married Elizabeth Jane, daughter of John Geoffrey William Bonsall of Fronfraith.

Capt. J. J. Lloyd-Williams, M.C. lived at Bryneithin from 1939 to 1944 when he was Chief Constable of Cardiganshire.

In April 1944, Bryneithin became the home of Ifan (later Sir), ab Owen Edwards, his wife Eirlys and their sons, Owen and Prys. Sir Ifan founded Urdd Goboith Cymru in 1922. It is now headquarters of the National Geological Survey.

Grid Ref: SN 5825 7812

Refs: Colby Map, 1831; Nicholas, *County Families,* 1875, 210; HS, 1698, 1770, 1813; BLG, 1898, ii, 1254; Landowners Return, 1873; R. E. Griffith, *Urdd Gobaith Cymru*, I, p. 345 (1971).

BRYNELE, Nancwnlle

Marked on *Colby's Map of 1831* north-west of Nancwnlle church. The *Golden Grove Manuscripts* tell us that David Lloyd, elder son of the Rev. Thomas Lloyd of Bronwydd, Rector of Llangynllo and vicar of Penbryn, was disinherited by his father (see Bronwydd), for his 'profane way of living and had but a small portion of his father's estate'. It is thought that Brynele was part of David Lloyd's small inheritance. He married *nolente patre,* Catherine, daughter of John Morgan, a mercer from Carmarthen' descended from Cadifor Fawr. The younger son, Rees Lloyd of Bronwydd, inherited the main part of his father's estate. David and Catherine had two sons and three daughters. Thomas, the eldest son, married Elinor, daughter of Griffith Lloyd of Gwernmacwy. John Lloyd, the second son of Newcastle Emlyn, whose will was proved on 30 April 1706, married Mary, daughter of David Philips of Llether Neuadd and they had two sons, Samuel and David. David and Catherine's three daughters were; Sara, married twice, firstly to Thomas Evans of Achaeth whose will was proved in 1677, and secondly to Charles Powell, the son of Morgan Powell of Aberduar, but described as of Llanegwad in 1693. Catherine, whose will was proved in 1693. Lettice, who married Daniel Jones of Llanio.

On 7/8 March 1669/70 the *NLW, Cwrtmawr Deeds* give details of a 'Lease and Release of a moiety of the town and manor of Aberystwyth, moiety of the castle and of all their messuages, within the town and liberties, also of rents of assize, tolls of buying and selling, between Thomas Lloyd of Brinele, Walter Pryse of Glan y Wern, gent., John Lloyd of Gwern Mackwy, gent. and Thomas Powell of Llechwedd Dyrus, Esq.' Thomas Lloyd of Brynele, paid tax on three hearths in 1672.

Thomas and Elinor Lloyd had one son and three daughters. Thomas Lloyd, gent., dsp whose will was dated 1702 and proved in 1706. Catherine, married Griffith Richard of Glanceulan, Cardiganshire, alive in 1702, Elinor, married David Jones of Llanio, and they had three sons, Thomas, John and David.

Thomas and Elinor's youngest daughter was Jane. The eldest son, Thomas Lloyd, had two daughters, Catherine and Elinor named after their aunts. It is not clear whether either of his daughters had issue, but the house passed into the ownership of Thomas Jones, a nephew, son of David Jones of Llanio, who married Gwen, daughter of David Thomas alias Davies of Fairdrefach. They had a son and heir Walter Jones of Llanio who married Lettice, who died in 1798 aged 83.

By 1798 Brynele was owned by Lewis Rogers. The *Mynachty Deeds* give details showing that 'Lewis Rogers of Brinele, Nantcwnlle parish, gent.,' was 'the son and heir of Thomas Rogers, late of Gelly, in the parish of Trefilan, dec.' and that his brother, the Rev. Henry

Rogers of Essex, clerk, the youngest son was a legatee under the will of the late Thomas Rogers.

The Williams family bought Brynele in the 19th century. In 1902 Mr. J. J. Lloyd-Williams (grandfather of Major J. A. Lloyd-Williams) built Brynele house as a holiday house for his family. After the death of Mr. J. J. Lloyd-Williams, his widow, Lilian, sold Gelli and two other farms in the Aeron Valley, to enable her to purchase Moreton Hall, near Oswestry, where she started a girls' school. On her death she left Brynele to three of her daughters, and on the death of the last of these, the property passed to Major J. A. Lloyd-Williams. His wife sold it in 1978.

Grid Ref: SN 5665 6034

Refs: Colby Map, 1831; Blome List, 1673; CRO, GGMS, iii, fo. 33; CRO, GGMS, II (Gwaethfoed), fo. 33; NLW, Cwrtmawr Deeds Nos. 197-8, 1032, 176-7; Mynachty Deeds.

BRYN-HAWG (BRYNDAHAWG), Llanwenog

Marked as Bryn-da-Hawg on *Colby's Map of 1831,* lying about a mile north-east of Waunifor mansion, just across the River Teifi, and opposite Llanllwni church.

Formerly the home of the Lloyd family, a branch of the Lloyds of Faerdre. Griffith Lloyd of Rhuddlan, in the parish of Llanwenog, owned 'Brindahawk' and was succeeded by his son, David Lloyd Griffith of Faerdre. David had four sons who succeeded to various properties; Ieuan, the eldest, to Faerdref, Thomas to Cwm Meudwy, Griffith Lloyd to Bwlch-mawr and David, the youngest son succeeded to Bryndahawg. This David's son, also named David, married the daughter of Thomas Bowen of Bwlchbychan and had a son, Griffith Lloyd, alive in 1709. He married Elizabeth, daughter of Rees Thomas of Bryn yr Eglwys, and a daughter, Eleri, who married David Thomas of Gellifaharen.

Grid Ref: SN 4775 4174

Refs: Colby Map, 1831; NLW, Alcwyn Evans, 12356 E; WWHR, iii, 87; CRO, GGMS, i (Tewdwr), fo. 40.

BRYNLLEFRITH, Llanwenog

An old farmhouse south-west of Cwrtnewydd and marked on *Colby's Map of 1831* and modern OS maps. An inscribed stone over the door says that Brynllefrith was built in 1748 by John Davies at the cost of David Hughes, Esq. John Davies died in 1750 and was buried at Llanwenog. Shortly afterwards, the Rev. David Lloyd, son of Richard Lloyd of 'Coed Lannell' born in 1724 and descended from Cadifor ap Dinawal, Lord of Castell Hywel, and minister of Llwynrhydowen and Alltyblaca, lived at Brynllefrith and remained there until his death in 1779. He was a talented man, a Unitarian minister, scholar, poet and hymn-writer. He was married twice, firstly to Jane, the daughter of another Unitarian minister, the Rev. Jenkin Jones, and then to Letitia, *'merch yr uchelwr o Lanfechan'* (daughter of the Squire of Llanfechan). Thomas and Letitia had five children. The eldest son was the Rev. Richard Lloyd (d. 1797); the youngest son was the Rev. Charles Lloyd, Ll.D (1766-1829), described as a 'Quantity Doctor' in about 1801. From about 1814 until 1939, descendants of Griffith Jones, who came from the family of Gwarbrestygwinwydd have lived at Brynllefrith. In 1910 a Celtic cross was placed on the Rev. David Lloyd's grave in Llanwenog churchyard by Lucy Lloyd Theakstone, his great-niece. The fourth generation still lived there in 1939. Extensive alterations were made to the house in 1935.

Grid Ref: SN 4877 4749

Refs: D. R. & L. S. Cledlyn Davies, *Hanes Llanwenog,* 1939, 63-4, 74.

BRYNLLYS, Llanfihangel Genau'r-glyn

This property lies near Glan-y-wern, west of Borth in the north of the county, across the river Leri and is marked on *Colby's Map of 1831* and modern OS maps. Brynllys was the home of the family of James (to Brochwel Ysgythrog), in the 18th century. In 1754 Richard James married Anne, daughter of James Daniel of Cyfoeth y Brenin – who bore the arms; *argent* a pale lozengy *sable*. Their son James James of Llety llwyd also bore a coat of arms; *sable* a chevron between 3 horse heads erased *argent*, followed by 7 quarterings.

Grid Ref: SN 6201 8878

Refs: Colby Map, 1831; NLW, MS. 8717.

BRYNOG (BRAENOG), Trefilan

Also known as Braenog or Brainog and lies about one-and-a-quarter miles north of Llanllyr overlooking the Aeron and marked on *Colby's Map of 1831* and on modern OS maps. Francis Jones states that the house is always pronounced locally as Brainog.

The *Llanllyr Deeds* detail in 1667 the estate of William Lloyd of Llanllyr and showed that among the properties owned by him was a messuage and land called Y Braynog in the parish of Trefilan. Little is known of successive generations at Brynog until John Lloyd of Lloyd Jack succeeded to the estate. His eldest son, Hugh, inherited Lloyd Jack; his second son, David succeeded to Brynog and the youngest son, Thomas, inherited Gwernfeilig.

In 1762 Dorothy, Lady Viscountess Dowager Lisburn granted to David Lloyd of Brynog an annuity charged on the estate in Cardiganshire. David died without issue, and under the terms of his will dated 1769, John Vaughan, the youngest of Lady Lisburn's three natural sons by Edward Vaughan of Greengrove (Edward and David having died without issue), succeeded to Brynog. The will specified that John should assume the name Lloyd on inheriting the Brynog estate from his uncle and it contained instructions concerning improvements to be made to the house. Meyrick tells us that the family pedigree was recorded at this time. John's brothers also took the Lloyd name and his eldest brother, Edward Vaughan Lloyd, succeeded to the Greengrove estate. John and his wife Anne, daughter of Hugh Pugh, had a large family of eight children, all of whom continued using the Lloyd name.

A mural tablet in Llanfihangel Ystrad church is dedicated to 'John Crosby Vaughan of Brynog and Greengrove, Esq. Captain 38th Regiment, who served from the commencement of the Crimean War and died 16th June 1855 of wounds, before Sebastopol, aged 25'. His arms and motto were *Non revertar inultus*. An elegy of 15 verses *Marwnad Capten Vaughan* to John Crosby Vaughan, was composed by the prolific poet John Jenkins (1825-94), a farmer of Penbryn mawr on Llanllyr estate, about half a mile north-east of Temple Bar. John Jenkins wrote under the names of *Cerngoch* and *Siaci*

Pen-bryn. Over 150 of his poems were published in *Cerddi Cerngoch*. The elegy, with the old notation score, was published in *Ceredigion* in 1971 with a photograph of the memorial.

By 1873 the house was in the possession of his brother, Captain H. Vaughan at which time the Brynog estate was of 3,561 acres, with an annual rental of £1,927. Captain Vaughan was succeeded by his son, Lieut.-Col. John Lewis Vaughan, born in 1863, who served in the Boer and Great War. Shortly afterwards the estate was sold and the Davieses, three brothers, bought the house of Brynog, the home farm and Ty Newydd respectively. A son of one of the brothers, Mr. J. Davies and his wife now run a guesthouse at Brynog.

Grid Ref: SN 5995 5743

Refs: Colby Map, 1831; Meyrick, *Cardiganshire,* 374; M. Richardson, ii, 408; Castle Hill Docs, 633-5; Morgan Llanllyr Deeds, 5 BLG, 1898, ii, 1516; Landowners Return, 1873; CRO, GGMS, III (Gwaethfoed), fo. 30; NLW, Llanllyr Deeds, No. 5; *Ceredigion*, VI, 197, pp. 423-35.

BRYSGAGA (PRYSGAGA), Llanbadarn Fawr

Situated a little to the east of Bow Street and shown on *Colby's Map of 1831* and modern OS maps. This house was owned by the Lloyd family throughout the 16th and 17th centuries and by the Jones family in the 18th century.

During the reign of James I (VI of Scotland), Hugh ap John Lloyd of 'Geneu'r glyn Llancastell Gwallter' lived there, signed his pedigree for the herald, Dwnn. A John Lloyd was living at Brysgaga as early as 1593. More is known of Hugh Lloyd, grandson of Hugh ap John Lloyd. A deed dated 1615 describes Hugh Lloyd, gent., as living in the capital messuage of Prysgaga 'wherein Hugh ap John Lloyd, gent, deceased grandfather of the said Hugh Lloyd, had lived'. Hugh's estate consisted of lands in the parishes of Llanbadarn Fawr, Llanfihangel Castell Gwallter, Llanfihangel Geneu'r-glyn, Bryngwyn and Llangynfelyn. In 1615 he married Mary, daughter of Edward Pryse of Kynfal, Montgomeryshire, gent. Their pre-nuptial settlement settled the capital messuage of Prysgaga in the parish of Llanbadarn Fawr, a messuage and meadows in Dyffryn Clarach, messuages in the parish of Llanfihangel Geneu'r glyn, including Blaen Eynon and a 'sommer or dayry house' called Nant Bryntirion, messuages in Broncastellan in the parish of Llanbadarn Fawr, messuages in Bryngwyn and a house in Tre'r-ddol in the parish of Llangynfelyn, all in Cardiganshire. Mary's portion was £170, of which '£70 was to be bestowed for the education of the three brothers of the said Hugh Lloyd'.

The Lloyds left Brysgaga and the estate was bought by William Jones, formerly of Dôl-cletwr who died in 1736, aged 36. His son, also William, was High Sheriff in 1766 and is described as of Brysgaga in 1780. His will, dated 1779, and proved on 3 February 1780, mentions 'my uncle Lewis Nanney Esq. of Llwyn, Merionethshire, my sisters Jane and Mary Gilbertson, both of London'. He left all his lands to his natural daughter, Jane Jones, by his housekeeper Ann Jones. To his natural daughter by Margaret Evans of Cefn Llwydyart, (Cefnllidiart), he left £30. Jane Jones married Thomas Watkins, son of Enoch Watkin, veterinary surgeon of Bryn-gwyn Mawr, and died at Brysgaga in 1845 when she was 72. W. J. Watkins lived at Brysgaga but later sold it to Sir Pryse Pryse of Gogerddan. In 1793 a Methodist chapel called the Garn was built at Nantafallen on land given by John Watkin of Brysgaga.

Jane and Thomas's daughter, Jane (1795-1873), married David Humphreys (1791-1860), Methodist minister of Nant-llan, in Llandyfaelog, Carmarthenshire. Their daughter, Frances, married Robert Joseph Davies of Cwrtmawr, Cardiganshire, and their son was John Humphreys Davies, former Principal of UCW, Aberystwyth. Brysgaga is now farmed by the Rees family who breed award winning Welsh Black cattle.

Grid Ref: SN 6265 8475

Refs: Colby Map, 1831; *Dwnn,* i, 29; NLW, Noyadd Trefawr Deeds, No. 486 (p. 142, Schedule).

BWLCHBYCHAN, Llanwenog

Marked on *Kitchin's Map of 1754*, *Colby's Map of 1831* and modern OS maps, south of Llanwenog with views of the Teifi. Formerly the estate of Owain, natural son of David ap Rhydderch of Pantstreimon, a descendant of Cadifor ap Dinawal, who signed his pedigree for the herald Dwnn. He was succeeded by Thomas ap Owain, attorney in sessions, who married Catherine, daughter of Sion ap Gwion ap Llewelyn Lloyd. They had eight children. Francis Thomas, the heir and eldest son, succeeded to Bwlchbychan and took the name Bowen. His son, Thomas, married a daughter

of Lodwick Lewis of Brenhinlle. The family were in residence for over a hundred years. John Bowen, living in 1709, was the last of the family to live at Bwlchbychan. His brother Daniel, married Mary, daughter of Thomas Davies Troedrhiwffenyd and had two sons, Thomas of Waunifor and John, who married Margaret, daughter of Thomas Thomas of Maesycrugiau.

The house became part of the estate of Pryse Pryse of Gogerddan. His third son, John Pugh Vaughan Pryse, born in 1818, lived at Bwlchbychan and was married twice; firstly, in 1844, to Mary Anne, daughter of J. W. Philipps of Aberglasney, who died in 1851, and secondly in 1853, to Decima Dorothea, daughter of Walter Rice of Llwynybrain, who succeeded to Bwlchbychan.

The house was rebuilt in 1850 'in the plain domestic style of architecture'. Pryse chased the fox as often as he could. In *The South Wales Squires,* Herbert Vaughan writes 'A rather dismal home . . . His residence reflected clearly his own tastes . . . in the dining-room alone were to be seen some thirty foxes' masks, varied by a few heads of hares and otters' poles. On the hearth-rug lay a footstool composed of a complete stuffed fox'. He died at a ripe old age in 1903. John Vaughan Pryse was succeeded by his only surviving daughter, Mary Ann Emily Jane, who married Lieut.-Col. Charles George Adams Mayhew of the Royal Welsh Fusiliers in 1872.

Grid Ref: SN 4811 4338

Refs: Kitchin Map, 1754; Colby Map, 1831; *Dwnn,* i, 239; WWHR, i, 50; Meyrick, *Cardiganshire,* 216 (pedigree); Nicholas, *County Families,* i, 1875, 209; *South Wales Squires,* 1926 p. 5; CRO, Aberglasney, iii; PRO, Dale Castle MS., p. 29; CRO, GGMS, i (Tydwal Gloff), p. 37; Protheroe, I (Long) 3, fo. 70; CRO, GGMS, III (Owen ap Bradwen), fo. 7.

BWLCH EINION (EYNON), Eglwys-fach

Situated in Cwm Einion on high land overlooking the village of Furnace in the north of the county. Little is known about this house except that Llewelyn, descended from David ap Rhydderch ap Ievan Lloyd of Glyn Aeron, Griffith of Pantydwn, and then Llewelyn's son, Jenkin, lived here. Jenkin's grandson was Griffith of Llanfread (Glanfrêd). He had a son, John and two daughters, Jane and Elizabeth. John had a daughter, Bridget who married twice, firstly to Thomas Pryse, secondly to John Pugh. Jane married Morris Vaughan of Glanleri and Elizabeth married David Llwyd of Ynys -hir and had a son, John.

Grid Ref: SN 6960 9470

Ref: CRO, GGMS, iv (Gwaethfoed), fo. 27.

BWLCH-MAWR, Llanwenog

Situated near Bwlchbychan west of Highmead. The first known owners were Griffith Lloyd, (descended from Ieuan of Faerdre, who in turn was descended from Tewdwr Mawr), and his wife Lettice, the daughter of John Lewes of Gernos. He was succeeded by his son, David, who had five children, four sons and one daughter; Ieuan, of Faerdref, married Elen, daughter of David Lewis David Meredydd of Gernos, Thomas was of Cwm Meudwy and had a son John Thomas. Griffith succeeded to Bwlch-mawr and David had a son, David Lloyd of Bryndahawg, who married a daughter of Thomas Bowen of Bwlchbychan. Gwenllian married Harry Lloyd, a younger son of Alltyrodyn.

Griffith Lloyd, who succeeded to Bwlch-mawr, had a son David and a grandson, also Griffith, who lived at Bwlch-mawr in 1709. He married Elizabeth, a daughter of Rhys Thomas of Brynyreglwys. In *Cardiganshire* Meyrick writes, 'Now the property of Herbert Lloyd, Esq. Attorney, of Carmarthen, which formerly belonged to a branch of the Vandref family; the last of whom, Charles Lloyd, spent all the estate and now lives in obscurity in Carmarthen'.

Grid Ref: SN 4870 4329

Refs: Colby Map, 1831; WWHR, i, 52-3; Meyrick, *Cardiganshire,* 217; CRO, GGMS, III (Owen ap Bradwen), fo. 7; PRO, Dale Castle MS., p. 30; Edwinsford DW, No. 2573; CRO, GGMS, (Tewdr), fo. 40.

BWLCHNEWYDD. Site unknown

The location and even the county of this house is uncertain. Thought to be in Cardiganshire, it has been included in the hope that someone may identify it, and find the information given of use. Evan Williams of Gelliddewi was descended from Bledri of Cilsant and John ap Richard of Blaen-tren. Ill-fortune hit the family and Evan's son, David, went to London in early life in a bid to repair his fortune as 'his father had sold the inheritance'. He appears to have prospered as Evan's second son Thomas, married to Sarah Walters of Llanfairclydogau, succeeded to Bwlchnewydd after his elder brother, the Rev. David Williams, rector of Bridport, Dorset, died unmarried.

Thomas and Sarah's son, John, became Vicar of Cilycwm. He married Margaret, daughter of Lewis Powell of Maescarnog, Breconshire and died in 1859. Their son, the Rev. Morgan Powell Williams became Rector of Llansantffraid in 1842. He married Elizabeth Sarah, daughter of Lewis Watkins of Glasbury.

Ref: Jones, Brec., iv, 143, ed.

AE MADOC (G).

Site unknown, thought to be Llangeitho

The location of this house is unknown. Thomas ap Morgan ap Ieuan ap Gwilym ap Ieuan ap Philip ap Rhydderch ap Ieuan Llwyd (descended from Gwaethfoed) signed for Dwnn. His son, Edward ap Thomas, was 'grantee of Cae Madock' from his father in 1610, witness to a deed in 1620 and was living at Cae Madock in 1632. He had two sons and a daughter: David, of whom more later; Zaccheus, of whom little is known and Rebecca, who married twice, firstly to David Morgan in 1664 and secondly to Harry John. Rebecca and David had a son, Peter Davies, who married Mary Jenkins (co-heiress of Dyffryn Llynod).

David Edwards, aforesaid, of Cae Madoc died in 1670. His will was proved in the same year and mentions the furniture in Cae Madoc, which included 'ye old cupboard from Gwastod'.

He had one son, also David Edwards, who was 'brought up as a lad together with his cousin Peter Davies at Cae Madoc'. Peter Davies went to Bristol and died in 1746 leaving the Dyffryn Llynod estate (which he inherited from his mother) to his nephew, John Edwards. David Edwards, who lived at Abermeurig, married twice. His first wife is unknown and his second wife was Jane Brown and they had two sons and a daughter; John Edwards died without issue; Peter Edwards married Diana Thomas of Llanrhian, Pembrokeshire, in 1717, of whom more later; Elizabeth Edwards married John Davies of Caerllygest, whose father was from Llysfaen, Llanwnen, but who bought Caerllygest farm in 1712 for John and Elizabeth when they married. Their daughter, Elizabeth, married the Rev. Daniel Rowland of Llangeitho.

Peter and Diana Edwards had a son, John Edwards, who married Anne Thomas of Laugharne, Pembrokeshire, in 1747. Their daughter, Anne, married Lewis Rogers of Gelli in 1782 from whom the Rogers of Gelli and Abermeurig descend.

Refs: CRO, GGMS (Cardiganshire), 22, 26, 32; Dwnn, *Heraldic Visitations,* I, 15, 44; WWHR, ii, pp. 152-3, 159.

CAERAU, Llanwenog

Located on *Colby's Map of 1831* and on modern OS maps south of Cwmsychpant on the banks of the Einon. The place name Caerau (fort) suggests a location of great antiquity. The home of Lloyds of Caerau, a branch of the Alltyrodyn family.

David ap Rees ap David ap Llewelyn Lloyd of Castell Hywel had three sons: 1. Ieuan Lloyd of Alltyrodyn; 2. Rees ap Llewelyn of Llwynrhydowen; 3. David of Bayref in Llanwenog, who married a daughter of Roger Prys of Caerau. David was the son of David ap Rees ap David ap David ap Llewelyn Lloyd of Castell Hywel. Their son Rees David (1704-60) is shown as of Henbant in Llandysul, who married a daughter of John Evan of Pant-cou.

Evan Thomas of Beili bach owned 'Caire alias Beily bach' in 1760.

Grid Ref: SN 4777 4481

Refs: WWHR, iii, 85; Meyrick, *Cardiganshire,* 1810 (ed. 1907), 199; CRO, GGMS, I (Tydwal Gloff), fo. 20, A.E. 12356 E.

CAERLLYGEST, Llangeitho

Situated about one mile north of Llangeitho village near Cwrt Mawr and shown on *Colby's Map of 1831.* The home of John Davies, who lived there in 1712, and his wife Elizabeth, daughter of David Edwards (1654-1716) of Cae Madog in Nancwnlle. They had a son, Peter, and a daughter Eleanor. Eleanor married the Rev. Daniel Rowland (1713-1790) the famous Methodist cleric of Pantybeudy in Nancwnlle parish. She died in 1792. They had two sons – the Rev. John and the Rev. Nathaniel Rowland.

Peter Davies married Magdalen Jones (d. 1755), daughter and co-heiress of John Jones (d. 1725), of Llwyn-rhys. Their son John Davies is shown as of Glyn, but his son and his grandson, both named Peter, are both shown as of Caerllygest.

Refs: Colby Map, 1831; WWHR, ii, 159.

CAMNANT, Llandysul

Situated in the north of the parish and shown on *Colby's Map of 1831* and located on modern OS maps as west of Rhydowen, north of the A475. Meyrick notes 'It stands near a little meandering brook, from which it takes its name and which falls into the Cletwr'. Rhys David, described as of Llwynrhydowen, son of David ap Rhys, traced to Castell Hywel, married Jane Bowen, daughter of Thomas Bowen of Bwlchbychan and had a son, David Rhys (d. 1709), who married Jane, the daughter of David Lloyd John of Camnant.

In 1709, their son, Thomas David of Camnant married Gwenllian Thomas, daughter and heiress of David Thomas of Pantydefaid, and was living at his wife's home in 1709. Gwenllian's father was David Thomas David ap Aron and her grandfather John David John of Pant-y-moch, the poet.

Rees Thomas of Fadva then owned Camnant, but by 1760 Thomas Davies owned it and lived there with his wife, Elizabeth. Nothing is known of their first daughter, but in 1774 their second daughter, Mary, married Evan Evans of Penrhiwgaled, gent, who was buried at Llanina.

By 1841, David Evans owned Camnant, tenanted by Elizabeth Morgan and shown on the *Llandysul Tithe Map* as 162 acres 30 p. In 1869, the house was owned by David Morgan, then aged 60, who was a descendant of Evan Evans.

The house descended through a female line to Edward Walter David Evans, JP and High Sheriff in 1901. Meyrick tells us, in *Cardiganshire*, that 'the estate is still in the possession of his (David ap Rhys) descendant, a respectable freeholder'.

Grid Ref: SN 4465 4562

Refs: Colby Map, 1831; WWHR, i, 52; ibid, iii, 85; Meyrick, *Cardiganshire,* 200, 357; NLW, BRA 898, No. 85; PRO, Dale Castle MS., p. 30; Llandysul Tithe Map, 1841.

CAPEL CYNON, Troed-yr-aur (Tredroyr)

Shown on *Colby's Map of 1831* as on the border with the parish of Llandysilio'gogo, north of Ffostrasol on the banks of the Afon Cerdin, south of Wstrws. Now a hamlet on A486. The location of the house is unknown.

The property was owned by Meredydd Jenkins of Capel Cynon and Dinas Cerdin, in Llandysul parish, although it is unclear whether he lived there. His daughter married Morris ap David of Bronhydden (traced to Lloyd of Fforest and Pontgilgan), the natural son of David Lloyd of Gilfachwen. Their daughter, Margaret, married twice: firstly to David Havard of Dolhaidd, and after his death she married John Philip Hywel John Lloyd. Dates are unclear.

In 1873 the *Landowners Return* shows that Captain Castle of Capel Cynon owned 297 acres with a rental of £58 p.a.

Grid Ref: 3820 4950

Refs: Colby Map, 1831; CRO, GGMS, I (Elystan Glodrudd); Landowners Return, 1873;. WWHR, i, 18.

CAPEL DEWI, Llandysul

Little is known of the occupants of this house except that Rees ap Jenkins was the first known owner. His son, Evan, succeeded to the property, followed by his son, John, then his son, David Lloyd, who married Sage, the daughter of Rees Read, son of Nicholas Read. Dates are not given.

Grid Ref: SN 4523 4249

Refs: CRO, GGMS, II (Adv. Carms.), fo. 204.

CAPEL GWNDA, Penbryn

Situated to the east of Rhydlewis, north of Troed-yr-aur church, south-east of Betws Ifan church and shown on modern OS maps. *Colby's Map of 1831* shows that Felin Wnda, on Afon Ceri, is alongside Capel Gwnda.

Mary Parry, daughter of John Parry of Panteynon and Noyadd Trefawr married, before 1715, Charles Evans of Capelgwnda (of Llwyndyrus in 1721). Mary was the sister of Stephen Parry, whose will was proved in 1721. Charles Evans died at Gwernan and left two daughters and four sons. Little is known of one of the daughters, but the eldest, Dorothy Evans, married William Jones, younger son of John Jones of Tyglyn by Bridget Parry of Noyadd Trefawr. Of the sons, James and Caesar Evans dsp., David Evans married and had a son, Stephen Evans, who died unmarried and intestate, and Rees Evans, of Llanarth, who married and had two sons, John Evans of Gelli in Llanarth a farmer. The other son, William Evans became a minister, was of Towy (Tywi) Castle and whose will was proved in 1883. He married

Mary Lewis, daughter of Rees Lewis and had six children. Between 1838 and 1842 Capel Gwnda was a holding of 82 acres.

Grid Ref: SN 3226 4721

Refs: Francis Jones Archives; Colby Map 1831.

CARDIGAN, THE PRIORY, St. Mary's
Formerly the home of the Philipps, Pryse, Johnes and the Marquess of Lansdowne [see also Tregybi]. Situated at the eastern fringe of the town and originally founded as a Benedictine Priory by Gilbert de Clare in 1108 – called 'Colledg' on *Speed's Map* and later rebuilt as a private house.

Horsfall-Turner writes in his *Wanderings*, 'The Priory is a modern residence close to the chancel of the church and is built upon the side of a former Benedictine house' and in *Journeys of Sir R. C. Hoare 1793-1810,* 'A modern Gothic house which has been built on the ground adjoining the Old Priory, the eastern front of which, with part of the church annexed, still remains.'

The *Noyadd Trefawr Deeds* show an agreement dated 18 December 1584 between John Nicholas gent. of Cardigan Town and Einion Phillipps Esq., of a grant in fee form of a toft, garden and half a tenement on the street leading from The High Cross towards the Dark Gate, in the town of Cardigan. Einion Philipps, of Cardigan Priory, was High Sheriff in 1588. George Philipps was High Sheriff in 1606 and acquired in 1616 by Letters Patent from James I, the late Priory of Cardigan and the rectories and churches of Ferwig and Tre-main which had been exchanged by Sir William Cavendish with Edward VI.

By 1672, James Philipps owned the manors of Cardigan and the Priory of Cardigan. The *Griffith Owen Deeds* show 'the manor or mansion house and lands called Tregibby otherwise Gibby, in Cardigan parish; the mansion house called the Priory of Cardigan, the capital messuage and other messuages in Co. Cardigan, called the Priory Estate'. The house was substantial and was assessed at 11 hearths in 1672. James was High Sheriff in 1649 and MP between 1653-5.

James Philipps' wife was the poetess 'the matchless Orinda.' Lewis says 'The Priory was afterwards the residence of the celebrated Katherine Philipps, daughter of Mr. John Fowler, a London merchant, and wife of James Philipps, Esq. better known by her poetical name of Orinda, and as the author of some pleasing poems, and a small work entitled "*Letters from Orinda to Poliarchus*", by which name was designated her early friend and patron, Sir Charles Cottrell'.

Malkin, in *South Wales* tells us 'This place was her favourite residence, before she went to Ireland: though anxiety made it appear to her as a melancholy retirement after her return'. Aylwin Sampson notes in *Aberteifi, Cardiganshire* that the 'Matchless Orinda presented the maces to the town'. These were reputed to have been drinking goblets dating from Charles I.

By 1685-6, the Priory had passed to Hector Philipps, High Sheriff in 1688. The house then passed from the ownership of the Philipps family.

In 1717, Walter Lloyd, gent., was in residence. and by 1744 the Priory mansion was created on the site of the small Benedictine Priory. The Priory and estate was then owned by Thomas Pryse of Gogerddan. He died in 1745 and devised his estates to trustees to sell to pay debts, subject to his son John Pugh Price for life, and afterwards to his issue.

In 1770 the Priory was sold to Albany Wallis, a London solicitor, in trust for £15,000 for John Pugh Pryse, who died in 1774 and made his mother, Maria Charlotte Lloyd, his sole executor. She claimed the Priory estate and sold it to Thomas Johnes for £21,200 in October 1774, the father of Colonel Johnes of Hafod.

Between 1793 and 1803 the Priory was rebuilt from a design by John Nash for a Bowen of Troed-yr-aur. *The Journeys of Sir R. C. Hoare 1793-1810* states – 'a modern Gothic house has been built on the ground adjoining the old priory, the eastern front of which, with part of the church annexed still remains'. Mr. Bowen is described by Malkin as 'a very respectable gentleman, brother to the most assiduous agriculturalist in the county, the Rev. Mr. Bowen of Troedyraur'.

The design is described by Meyrick as 'an elegant fabric was erected on the site of the old ruins, when the grounds belonging to it, which formerly lay exposed, were surrounded by a handsome wall, with neat doors, in what is generally termed the gothic taste, to correspond with the house'.

In 1807, John Philipps, of Llandeilo, a solicitor, wrote to his brother Thomas Philipps of Aberglasney 'I hear that the Marquis of Lansdowne has purchased the Priory of Cardigan for £60,000'.

In 1815 the *NLW Cwrtmawr Deeds* show an Abstract Title of Richard Hart Davies Esq. to an estate called the Priory in Co. Cardigan, previously owned by Thomas Johnes, but by 1828 the house was owned by George Woolgar Griffith Esq., JP for Pembrokeshire, and later of Pant-gwyn.

In 1840, T. D. W. Lewis wrote 'On the site of the ancient mansion is now a handsome villa, which, with the whole of the Priory estate, is the property of Philip John Miles, Esq. of Leigh Court, in the county of Somerset'. He was a London banker and a millionaire. When he died in 1845 his will comprised over 300 files. The estate passed in turn to Canon Miles of Lincoln Cathedral, then to George Miles and eventually to Colonel Napier Miles who served in the Egyptian Campaign of 1862.

In 1861 a Richard David Jenkins, a member of the celebrated Cilbronnau family in Llangoedmor lived there. Thirty years later in 1891 the mansion was advertised to be let by William Picton Evans who had married Margarette, daughter of R. D. Jenkins of Cilbronnau in 1868, who later lived at Treforgan, Llangoedmor. The Priory consisted mainly of a dining room, a drawing room, morning room, study and nine bedrooms. It was purchased in 1897 by Dr. John Pritchard of Rochester, New York, who served in the Civil War. His wife Emily was an author of books on the Priory and St. Dogmael's Abbey. Dr. Pritchard died in 1911.

After World War I, the mansion was bought for £4,250 and was converted into a Cottage Hospital, which was opened in July 1922. During its conversion the Priory underwent many changes. It remains a hospital.

Grid Ref: SN 1812 4605

Refs: Blome List, 1673; Horsfall-Turner, *Wanderings,* 181-8; *Dwnn,* i, 43, 84-5; WWHR, i, 14-15; Dinely, *Progress,* fo. 247; Meyrick, *Cardiganshire,* 172; Lewis, *TDW*; *Contemporary Biographies of South Wales & Monmouth,* 1907, 165-6; Aylwin Sampson, *Aberteifi, Cardigan,* 197; Carlisle TDW, 1811, 11-20; CRO, Aberglasney Papers; Malkin, *South Wales,* 1804 (repub. 1970), p. 410; Griffith Owen Deeds, No. 6280; Chanc. p. 5, 1758-1800, Lloyd and Johnes; NLW, Cwrtmawr Deeds, Nos. 1172 & 295; NLW, Noyadd Trefawr Deeds, No. 57; *Journeys of Sir R. C. Hoare 1793-1810,* (Ed) Thompson, p. 42.

CARDIGAN TOWN

There were two residences in the town, which cannot be identified and have clearly been long demolished or converted; namely the home of the Gwynn family and of the Folk family (the herald Dwnn wrote both family's pedigrees). Rees Gwyn of Cardigan, descended from Sir Thomas Philipps of Picton Castle in Pembrokeshire, gent., married Margaret, daughter of David Scurlock, gent. The marriage was the subject of a pre-nuptial settlement on 17 May 1666. Their son, George, living there in 1715, married and his eldest son and heir apparent, Rice Gwyn (the elder), married Gwen Pugh, only daughter of . . . Pugh and his wife Anne. Anne is described as of Coedmor, Pencarreg, Carmarthenshire in 1715, by then a widow, still living in 1774. Rice Gwyn (the younger) was as of Cardigan, will dated 1760. His brother Daniel married Joan, and was living in 1774. Daniel and Joan had a son Rice Gwyn, living in 1769 and a daughter Rachel, living in 1769 and described as of Llanwennog in 1774.

Refs: GS, Cards (Protheroe), 14 Charles II, challenge ped.; J. F. Collection, Carmarthen RO.

CARREG-LWYD, Llanychaearn

Near the village of Blaenplwyf, west of the A487 by the television transmitter.

Hywel ap Rhys, descended from Meurig Goch of Cil-y-cwm, Carmarthenshire, had issue, Rhys of Crynfryn, Nancwnlle and David, the younger son. Rhys had a son, Lloyd of Crynfryn and David's son, Rees ap David, was of Garreg-llwyd. He had five children, Morgan, David, Thomas, Margaret and Mary. The family signed for Dwnn. Dates are lacking.

Grid Ref: SN 5665 7505

Refs: Dwnn, i, 41 (1613).

CARROG, Llanddeiniol

Situated a quarter of a mile north of Llanddeiniol church and shown on the 14th century *Rees Map, Kitchin's Map of 1754, Colby's Map of 1831*, and modern OS maps.

Reynald Jenkins, son of 'Jenkin of Carrog' a descendant of Rees ap Philip ap Rees and his wife, daughter and co-heiress of Evan Coch David ap Llewelyn of Cefn-melgoed, had one son and two daughters. Catherine married Morgan David Bowen of Pencarreg and another daughter who married Hercules Lewes.

In 1622, William Jenkins, the only son of Reynald Jenkins of Carrog, married Elizabeth Llwyd, daughter of Morgan Llwyd of Llwyd Jack. In the same year *Powis Castle Deeds* show us that 'William Jenkins of Carrogge otherwise Llanddeniol, Cards, gent., and Ellen Gwynne of Morvamaure, widow, and Dorytye Gwne of same assigned a mortgage in £14.13.4 of three parcels of land in Llansantffraid parish'.

William and Elizabeth Jenkins had three sons and five daughters. Of their daughters, one married a Captain Price, Drusilla married David Oliver, Penelope married James Woolley of Knighton and Margaret married Harry Lewis of Trehir. Lettice remained unmarried. Of their sons, little is known of Morgan, William was killed in a duel 'engaged twixt the Duke of Buckingham and the Earl of Shrewsbury'.

Reynald Jenkins, the eldest son succeeded to Carrog in 1655 and married Elenor, daughter and heiress of David Parry of Neuadd Trefawr at about the same time. They had one son, William Jenkins of Blaen-pant, who married Bridget Lewes of Gellidywyll, Carmarthenshire. Their daughter, Elizabeth Jenkins, married William Brigstocke and was co-heiress to Blaen-pant. The family signed for Dwnn.

William Brigstocke of Blaen-pant succeeded to Carrog on his marriage to Elizabeth, and mortgaged the capital messuage called Carrog and Cwm-bach to John Corrie of Carmarthen in 1720. William died in 1725.

The estate next passed to the Morris's. A Dr. John Morris of Carrog, third son of Morris Thomas ap Ievan Llwyd by Catherine Owen, his wife, (described in *CRO, GGMS* as 'chisurgeon in ye Carnary Islands'), married Mary, daughter of Morgan Llwyd. They had a daughter and two sons. Their daughter Mary (1681-1727) married twice, firstly to William Hughes of Plâs Cilcennin, will proved in 1719, and secondly to John Jones of Tyglyn and Plâs Cilcennin who died in 1756. Of the two sons, the youngest was Captain John Morris of whom little is known.

The *Trefaes Deeds* show on 1-2 October 1723, 'Richard Morris of Carrog, Esq., son and heir and executor of John Morris, gt. of same place, deceased. Richard Morris married Mary Lewes, the eldest daughter of John Lewes of Gernos, (sister and co-heiress with David Lewes of Gernos). Their eldest son and heir, John Morris was a JP, appointed in 1748. His daughter, Elizabeth was married to the Rev. Philip Pugh of Blaenpenal (1679-1760).

By 1760, Carrog was owned by Richard Morris and passed to James Morris, gent, who was appointed churchwarden on 7 April 1806 and was still of Carrog in 1825.

Meyrick tells us 'From the Jenkins, the estate came into possession of the Morris's, the male line of which family became extinct about fifty years ago. Miss Morris, the daughter and heiress, marrying the Rev. Thomas Richards of Serygog, carried the estate to him, whose son is now the possessor'.

The Rev. Thomas Richards, a philanthropist, did much to establish the National School and a Savings Bank in Aberystwyth. He contributed £100 to the school and is said to have contributed more than any individual to the management of the school even promising to meet any financial deficiencies from his own resources. Carrog House, his town house in Bridge Street, Aberystwyth (now the RAFA branch headquarters), was a haven for visiting authors, clergy and academics. Thomas's former colleagues at Cambridge such as William Wilberforce, Thomas Clarkson and others including John Keble who composed the hymn *Sun of my soul, thou Saviour dear* after witnessing the sun setting over Cardigan Bay, stayed in Bridge Street.

After the 1868 election some tenants of the Carrog estate were evicted for voting against the wishes of their landlord. Much later Plâs Carrog became the home of Geoffrey Williams, a gynaecologist at Bronglais Hospital.

It is now occupied by Drs. J. and G. Davies, both GPs in Aberystwyth.

Grid Ref: SN 8625 7250

Refs: Meyrick, *Cardiganshire,* p. 28, 282; NLW, BRA 906, No. 29; ; *Chanc. Pros.* 1714-58; WWHR, i, 15-16; ibid, ii, 154-5; ibid, iii, 95; NLW, Griffith Owen Deeds, No. 1179; *Pembs.*, iv, 397 n 1; *Dwnn,* i, 28; ibid, i, 219, 222; Rees Map 14th C; NLW, Morgan Richardson Deeds, i, 177; CRO, GGMS, I (Tydwal Gloff); CRO, GGMS, III (Edwinsford); PRO List; Powis Castle Deeds, 16226; NLW, Trefaes Deeds; PRO, Dale Castle MS., p. 24 (95). W. S. Lewis, *Born on a Perilous Rock*, 1980, p. 255; *Ceredigion,* Vol. 2, No. 2 (1953), pp. 66-71

CASTELL BIGYN, Llanrhystud

The *Tithe Apportionment Schedule of 1839* shows that there was a 28 acre farm called 'Castell Piggin' and a 63 acre farm called 'Blaenpigin or Tynymyndd', in Llanrhystud parish.

A daughter and co-heiress of Jenkin ap Rhys David of Gilfachwen married Rhys David Thomas of the Gilfachwen and Cilgwyn family. Their son Robert ap Rhys had a son Rhys ap Robert Esq. of Castell Bigin, who married Jonet, daughter and heiress of Jenkin ap Rhydderch ap Ievan Lloyd. They had a daughter, Gwenllian,, who married Jenkin ap Rhys David Thomas of Blaentren. Dates are lacking.

Refs: WWHR, i, 29; Tithe Apportionment Schedule 1839.

CASTELL CEFEL, Llangoedmor

The old mansion of the Mortimers, which stood above the Teifi between the present Coedmor and the old Coedmor. The remains of the old garden are still there. Of the element 'cefel' there is also a farm Gwarcefel in the Faedref division of Llandysul parish noted in 1758 and a Trecevel in Caron parish.

Rhydderch ap Rees ap Meredith, Lord of Towyn, (Tywyn), married the daughter of Sir John Lingen of Co. Hereford and his wife, a daughter of Sir John Burgh. Their daughter, Elizabeth, married James Mortimer of Castle Kefael. They had at least two sons; David Mortimer of Castell Maelgwn and John Mortimer of Coedmor. *CRO GGMS* tell us that 'this John lived at Castle Cefel in Coedmor where Sir Preder ap Efrog, one of King Arthyr's knights dwelt'. John had a son Richard Mortimer of whom little is known.

Grid Ref: SN 1926 4361

Refs: O Pemb., iv, p. 495, n 18; CRO, GGMS (Gwynfardd) p. 28 & CRO, GGMS, II Adv. Cards., fo. 188.

CASTELL DU, Llanwnnen

A large farmhouse built on a slope just east of and above Llanwnen hamlet and shown on *Colby's Map of 1831* as on high ground just above Llanwnen village. Lewis tells us 'on the banks of the Granell is a moated mound called Castell Du . . . which gives its name to the farm on which it is situated'.

The eldest daughter of Evan Watkin of Kynnillmawr (Cynnull-mawr), was co-heiress of the estate, with her sister, Jane. She married William Jones of Gwynfryn in 1749 and Jane married a son of Hughes of Castell du. In 1746, Llowtre House alias Chamber, on the land of Castell du was registered as a place of 'dissenting worship'.

In the chancel of Llanwnen church, lies the body of John Hughes (d. 1806, aged 66) of Llysfaen Isa and family. The Castell Du family graves are railed in close to the church tower.

Thomas R. H. J. Hughes of Castell Du, was listed in the *Landowners Return of 1873* as having 2,249 acres with an estimated rental of £1,331, and Thomas Hughes, also of Castell Du who married Margaret, second daughter of Thomas Jones of Neuadd Fawr, also holding 291 acres, with an estimated rental of £102.

Castell Du became part of the Neuadd Fawr estate and in the Catalogue of that estate, sold on 17 June 1931, it is described as of 135 acres. The farmhouse had two front rooms, two back rooms, back kitchen, dairy, six bedrooms and outbuildings.

Grid Ref: SN 5350 4713

Refs: Colby Map, 1831; Landowners Return, 1873; Lewis, *TDW,* 1840; Horsfall-Turner, *Wanderings,* 225.

CASTLE GREEN, St. Mary's, Cardigan

Located in the grounds of the medieval fortress built by Gilbert de Clare in 1110 on a bluff overlooking the Teifi and the site of the first Eisteddfod in 1176.

In 1673 the home of Abel Griffiths of Cardigan, who, according to Pritchard held Manaian Fawr and other lands in St. Dogmaels rented from the Parry family. He had two sons, James Griffiths, gent., aged sixty in 1691 and Mathew, who succeeded his father as tenant of the above properties. In his *Guide to Cardigan and District*, W. E. James tells us 'In the east wall of the porch of Cardigan church is a stone inscribed

"JASON LEWIS, ABEL GRIFFITHS –
Church Wardens 1639".'

Meyrick tells us 'The castle and the ground contained within its outer walls (called the Castle-green) which now belongs to John Bowen, Esq. who is erecting a house on the site of the keep, the dungeons now serving as his cellars'. Carlisle adds, 'the wall between the two towers [is] being lowered, and the green sloped down so as to form a hanging garden'.

The *Carmarthen Journal* states that 'on 31st May 1827, Arthur Jones of Cardigan Town and High Sheriff of Cardiganshire, gave a meal at the Angel Inn in the town for the forty artists and mechanics employed by him in building his new Castle Green home'.

Lewis tells us 'The site of the keep is at present occupied by a handsome modern villa, the cellars of which are formed out of the dungeons of that ancient tower, of which the walls in some parts are from nine to ten feet thick; and the outer ward has been converted into a verdant lawn, tastefully disposed in pastures, the whole effectived by John Bowen Esq. The property now belongs to David Davies Esq. High Sheriff of the county [in 1841] by purchase in 1836'. The builder was David Evans, architect and master builder of Eglwyswrw. Such purchases did not endear the Davieses to the local squireachy who did not consider them as one of their own, as they were in trade.

David Griffith Davies, who founded the Cardigan Mercantile Company, was the son of Thomas Davies of Bridge House, Cardigan, High Sheriff of Cardiganshire in 1826. On his death, his wealth was calculated at £36,251. He married twice, firstly to Anna Letitia Griffiths, who died in 1851, daughter of the Rev. David Griffiths of Berllan, Eglwyswrw parish, vicar of Nevern. The marriage was subject to a pre-nuptial settlement in 1833. He married secondly, Elizabeth Holcombe, daughter of a prominent clergyman from Fishguard.

David Griffith Davies was High Sheriff in 1841 and bought Gellifor in Nevern in 1860. He and his wife, Anna, had a son, David Griffith Davies, JP, d. 1906, later of Castle Green, who married Arabella Anne, the daughter of the Rev. Rees William Morgan Davies – Berrington, rector of Nolton and vicar of Roch, Pembrokeshire. A marriage settlement was made in 1871. David Davies presented the residents of Cardigan with the famous 'whisky clock' on the Guild Hall.

In 1873 the estate was of 193 acres, yielding £85 p.a., but parts of the estate were sold in 1889. *Contemporary Biographies* states 'The mansion is held for her lifetime by Mrs. Davies, widow of David Griffith Davies, JP, after which it passes to her son, David Berrington Griffith Davies'. He is described as of Plâs Llangoedmor, which he bought from H. M. Vaughan in 1924. When he moved to Llangoedmor, David Berrington Davies sold Castle Green to John Evans, an auctioneer, who lived there until the property was sold to Mrs. Barbara Woods in 1940. In January 1998, she was living in a caravan in the Castle grounds.

There are two photographs of the house in *Contemporary Biographies* and an engraving of the exterior in Nicholas's *County Families*.

Grid Ref: SN 1777 4587

Refs: BLG, 1898, i, 381. Blome List, 1673; *Contemporary Biographies,* 1907, 156 – 7; Carlisle; Lewis, *TDW,* 1811; *Carmarthen Journal,* 1827; Burke, *LG,* 1952; Landowners Return, 1873; Nicholas, *County Families;* Meyrick, *Cardiganshire.*

CASTLE HILL, Llanilar

Built of local stone in 1777 and shown on *Colby's Map of 1831*, situated half a mile south of the village of Llanilar and bordering on the east of the A487 to Lledrod. Meyrick tells us 'Purchased in 1777 by John Williams, High Sheriff son of Nat. Williams of the Abbey of Strata Florida in 1801 for his son, John, a minor in 1777. He erected the present mansion and planted the forest trees and firs to a very large amount'. He was the grandson of William Williams (1698-1773) of Pant Seiri near Tregaron, known as 'King of the Mountains or Job of the West' as he was the owner of vast flocks of sheep. The family bore the arms: *azure* a chevron between three stags heads erased.

The Castle Hill family is represented in Llanilar church by two brasses to John Williams. He married Mary, the daughter of Bowen Jones of Trewythen, Montgomeryshire and their son, John Nathaniel Williams succeeded to the property whilst still a minor when his father died in 1806. G. E. Evans tells us in his book *Cardiganshire* 'on the principle, possibly, that one good turn deserves another, the parish testified its gratitude to Mr. John Nathaniel Williams of Castle Hill for hunting the foxes, by consenting that he should erect a pew in the parish church'. Consent was given at a vestry meeting on 17 February 1815 the year John Nathaniel Williams was High Sheriff. He married Sarah Elizabeth, second child of J. Loxdale of Kingsland, Shrewsbury, by his third wife, Jane Phillips, widow. Sarah died without issue in 1862.

By the middle of the 19th century the house had passed to the Loxdale family who had their own estate in Shropshire in the 15th century and who signed their pedigree for Dwnn. Joseph Loxdale, Mayor of Shrewsbury in 1797, High Steward and Deputy Recorder of the Borough of Shrewsbury, married Anna Maria Wood of Bayston, Salop. in 1790. They had two sons, James and John Loxdale; James, and John the younger son (1799-1885), of Kingsland, Shrewsbury, married three times: firstly his cousin, Anne Loxdale (dsp 1848) and secondly Anna Rice, daughter of the Rev. John Watson, DD, of Northants. They had a son, Reginald James Rice Loxdale. John Loxdale's third wife was a widow, Jane Phillips. They had a daughter Sarah Elizabeth, who married the aforesaid John Nathaniel Williams of Castle Hill.

James Loxdale, (1797-1890), third son of Joseph and Anna Loxdale, inherited Castle Hill at the death of his sister Sarah Elizabeth Williams, who died in 1862.

He was Barrister-at-Law, a JP, a Deputy-Lieutenant and High Sheriff of Cardigan in 1867. In 1873 the estate was of 778 acres yielding £286 p.a. James Loxdale died without issue in 1890 and he was succeeded by his nephew, Reginald James Rice Loxdale, born 1859. He was a solicitor and a JP. He married twice. His first wife, Edith Aurelia, daughter of B. Spurgin of Northants and widow of Henry Murray Loxdale, who died in childbirth in 1892. In 1894 he married Florence Mary Pryse, daughter of Sir Pryse Pryse of Gogerddan. Their daughter Myfanwy Louisa Regina married her kinsman, Major J. J. H. Loxdale, son of Joseph Loxdale by Caroline Barbara McLean in 1922. Myfanwy Loxdale married her cousin, J. J. H. Loxdale in 1921. Their son, Dr. Alasdair Loxdale, inherited the estate on the death of his mother, and his eldest son, Peter, now lives there.

The arms of the Loxdales are: *ermine* of a chief *sable* 3 lions rampant *or.* crest: a bull's head couped *proper.* A photograph of the house exists in *Contemporary Biographies of South Wales and Monmouth.*

Grid Ref: SN 6252 7465

Refs: Colby Map, 1831; Meyrick, *Cardiganshire,* 286 (edn. 1907), p. 286; *Contemporary Biographies of South Wales & Monmouth,* 1907, 159; Landowners Return, 1873; G. E. Evans, *Cardiganshire,* 1903, 110; Horsfall-Turner, *Wanderings,* 95.

CASTELL HYWEL, Llandysul Uwch Cerdin

An ancient fortified mansion, sometimes called Humphrey's Castle and shown on the *14th century Rees Map* and *Llandysul Tithe Map of 1841* situated to the east of the B459, between Pontsian and Talgarreg.

The original property of the old family of Lloyd of Alltyrodin. Meyrick tells us, 'Gwilym Llwyd of Castell Hywel, Esq. who was the sixth in descent from Cadivor ap Dinawal, was probably the founder of the first mansion on

the Castle estate . . . the present mansion at Castle Howel is not on the site of that built by Gwilym Llwyd, but close to it'.

An ode to Dafydd ap Llewelyn ap Gwilym Lloyd of Castell Hywel eulogises the noble house and its hospitality; 'the house was well-built and on a large scale and stored with choice wines and provisions.' Another ode says that he is said to have inherited the estate from both his father and grandfather and mentions his late wife, Lleucu. The Lloyds signed for Dwnn.

In 1760, Castell Hywel was owned by David Llwyd of Berllandywyll, Carmarthenshire, but leased to a Thomas Lewis. The next occupant was the Rev. Dafyddd Dafis of Castell Hywel, who was born at Goetre-isaf, Llangybi, and who married Anne Evans of Foelallt, Ciliau Aeron in 1775. They had nine sons and four daughters. The family went to live at Castell Hywel in 1783. The Rev. Dafis opened his famous school in what is now the garden. A number of well-known pupils received a classical education at the school. Dafydd Dafis was also a fine poet. He wrote *englynion to Peterwell,* the home of the notorious Herbert Lloyd, and his collected works were published in *Telyn Dewi* in 1824. He was buried in Llanwenog churchyard in 1827, aged 83 having left Castell Hywel many years before. A photograph of Castell Hywel is shown in *Telyn Dewi* in 1824.

Meyrick wrote 'Dafydd's descendants enjoyed it till it was sold by Mr. Lloyd, who resided at Berllandywyll in Carmarthenshire, to David Lloyd, Esq. of Alltyrodin, the present possessor "who leased the capital messuage and land called Castle Hywel in 1807" late in the occupancy of the Rev. David David, minister of the Gospel', to John Evans of Llandysul, who was a yeoman and resided at Castell Hywel for 21 years.

The house was described in *Telyn Dewi* as a 'spacious farmhouse in the valley of Cletwr Fach. The house remains like it was in David Davis's day: some of the windows have been closed: the *lwfer* is no longer open, but still there'.

By 1841 the estate had passed to John Lloyd Davies Esq. of Alltyrodin, but was still tenanted by a descendant of John Evans, of the same name. The *NLW, Morgan Richardson Deeds* state that a Thomas Parry Horsman, Sheriff of Cardigan in 1879 was living at Castell Howell.

The Castell Howell Estate was offered for sale on 15 June 1882. A Sale Catalogue in *CRO* gives details of: 'The Castle Howell Estate, W. Cardiganshire 1,130 acres to be sold, all in the parish of Llandysul. LOT 1, Castle Howell. Farmhouse, outbuildings, gardens, yard and six cottages and smith's shop. 374a. 3r. 22p. held by James Davis on 21 year lease from 29 September 1875 at £300 p.a. Quarry on farm, bounded by Glandwr farm on N. by Coed-llanau on E. by Esgerddedwydd and on S. and on W. by river Cletwr Fach. LOT 2, Glandwr otherwise Glendyr farm 206 acres17 p. £120. LOT 3, Nantygwiddau 133 acres 6p. £50. LOT 4, Maen y gwinion bach otherwise Rhos y myrson and Blaensychddau 243 acres 26p. and cottage called Ffos-bounded on W. by Maeny-gwinion Mawr farm. LOT 5, Castle Howell Mill, corn grist, with 2 fields belonging, dwelling house and outbuilding 2a. 2r. 36p. LOT 6, Glanrhydydre farm otherwise Glanrhydre 170 acres 26p. and cottage and garden'.

In 1952 Ellis's *Crwydro Ceredigion* has a photograph showing Castell Hywel now a farmhouse.

Where to Stay in Wales 1976 lists 'Castell Howell' as 'now a farm without any traces of its former character and is adapted and organised for holidaymakers'. It includes an illustration.

Grid Ref: SN 4425 4831

Refs: Dwnn, i, 227-8; ibid, ii, 33-4; WWHR, i, 50-1. & iii, 85; Blome List, 1673; Meyrick, *Cardiganshire,* 1810, 194; Lewis, *TDW,* 1840; NLW, Morgan Richardson Deeds, ii, 528 & fo. 2226; Ellis, *Crwydro Ceredigion,* 1952; *Where to Stay in Wales,* 1976, p. 214, illust.; Llandysul Tithe Map, 1841; Rees Map, 14th

Century; Griffith Owen Deeds, No. 4642; NLW, Roy Evans Deeds, 206; CRO, GGMS (Tywal Gloff), fo.19; Davies, *Hanes Plwyf Llandysul,* pp. 102-8; CRO Sc 680 .

CASTELL NADOLIG, Penbryn

Marked on *Colby's Map of 1831* as a farm south of the main road near Temple Bar, between Tan-y-groes and Sarnau. The remains of the old castell lie nearby across the A 487 (T).

Meredydd (descended from Owen and Gruffydd) of Castell Nadolig married Angharad, a descendant of David ap Howell to Cil Gadfarch, Pembrokeshire. Dates are unknown.

The messuages of Castell Nadolig and Tir Bwlch y Clawdd, in the parish of Penbryn were part of the Lewes of Abernantbychan estate in 1650, when James Jenkins was tenant.

In 1760 the house was owned by John Evans.

Grid Ref: SN 2986 5012

Refs: Colby Map, 1831; WWHR, iii, 80; *Dwnn,* i, 103.

CASTELL ODWYN, Llanbadarn Odwyn

West of Tregaron, between Tregaron and Llangeitho, adjacent to Sarn Helen (B4578) modern OS maps show an old fort, Pen y Gaer, near Deri Odwyn.

'Treygfa ne Tai penna Gwaithvoed ychoed, oedd Castell odwyn wrth Llanbadarn Odwyn o fforth y ffynon o vewn Arglwyddiaeth pennarth o vewn Sir Abertivi, a Gwaethfod uchod y fy fawr yn y flwyddyn o oedran harglwydd (1038) ag y gladdwyd ymorth y ffynnon ychod fel y tystia llythrenne ar y faen, y gaed ar ei fedd ef.'

Home of the Moethy family, descended from Ifor ap Cadafor ap Gwaethfoed and Griffith, Lord of Castell Odwyn. The Moethy pedigree is recorded in the *Edwinsford Pedigree Book* as is their history to The Plantagenets, in the reign of King John 1199-1216. Edwinsford states 'Griffith Voel ap Ivor of Castell Odwyn-David ap Griffith Voel-David Fychan or Vongam-Rees Moythy-Howell Moythy followed by Madoc'.

CRO GGMS gives 'Ifor ap Cadifor ap Gwaethfoed-Griffith, Lord of Castle Odwyn-then David Moythe was of Castell Odwyn to Rees Moythe to Rees Moythe to Howell Moythe to Madoc Moythe to John Moythe, who married Catherine, daughter of Meredudd ap Robert-John Moythe's natural son was Twm Shon Catti Thomas, later of Fountain's Gate, son of John and Catherine (c. 1530-1609)'.

The *Harleian Manuscripts* give 'The Posteritie of Kydivor ap Gwaithvoel were Deprived of the Lordsh[ip] in kinge John his time, And Although the Authoritie was evicted from them by conquest, yet they kept a great p[ar]te of their inheritance in possession; as Glynayron, Pennarth, and all those p[ar]ties. Castle Odwyn in Llanbadarn odwyn, and ffowntain gate in the p'ishe of Caron, wch hathe been their principall mansion place, After they hadd lost their Castles and holdes by the sea side, ffowntain gate was Destroid by the normans, viz by one Geffrey Clement and others in Kinge H. the third his time. But castell Odwin was allways mainteyned untill Howell Moythe esquires removed his Dwelling from thence nearer the vale of Ayron. Howell Moythe and Rethergh ap Ievan lloid his coosin Divided their Landes by Gavaelkyd alias gavaelkind, between breethern, wch weakned their posterities. I doe finde in a Chronicle mention on the noblenes of that Sr Gwyn ap Gwaithvoed, being an ancient knight, howe a ffrenche knight possessed his castle by conquest. And he made suite to William Rufus then Kinge of Inglande, that throughe his Licence he mought fought the Combate by sworde with the ffrench man, in a close Chamber, wch being granted him, he slewe the ffrench man, and was restored to his former possession. He afterwards became blinde'.

Grid Ref: SN 6350 6098

Refs: Edwinsford Ped. Book; CRO, GGMS, III (Gwaethfoed); BM, Harleian MSS., 3538. 17th Century, ff. 15, 15a, ffos. 47-8 ex. info. Emrys Williams.

CAWRENCE (TYDDYN CAWRWENS), Llandygwydd

Marked on *Colby's Map of 1831* and modern OS maps and located on a hill overlooking Nant Arberth a mile north of Llechrhyd.

William Griffiths, the son of Gruffydd and Dyddgu, daughter and co-heiress of Rhys ap Nicholas of Cardigan who married Elen, daughter and co-heiress of John Mortimer ap Rhys ap Rhydderch of Towyn, Ferwig. William Griffiths of Tyddyn Cawrens signed his pedigree for Dwnn. He had two sisters, Elsbeth and Ann. William Dyleway, gent., of Haverfordwest owned Cawrens in 1760.

Once the largest farm in the area, Cawrence was sold by the Coedmor estate in the early 1960's to a Mrs. Bevan, who in the late 70's sold much of the land to David George of Dyffryn, Llangoedmor. The farmhouse, the outbuildings and some land were bought by Mr. and Mrs. Malcolm Wilson in 1993. Having renovated the farmhouse they are now restoring the outbuildings. According to Canon James Cunnane, the leading authority on medieval Cardigan, the Welshry held a court at Cauros under the jurisdiction of the Mortimers, Lords of Coedmor, and he believes that the location was on the site of the present buildings.

Grid Ref: SN 2232 4544

Refs: Colby Map, 1831; WWHR, III, 78; *Dwnn*, i, 39. M. Wilson.

CEFN BRECHFA, Llanbadarn Odwyn

There is also a Brechfa in Llangeitho parish, west of Llanbadarn Odwyn. Modern OS maps show Brechfa and Brechfa-fach on high ground west of Llangeitho.

Home of the Gwynn family (descended from Gwaethfoed) in 1610. The family signed for Dwnn and their arms were quarterly coat, Gwaethfoed 1st quarter. Ievan Gwynn married Jenet, daughter of Morgan David Lloyd of Golenydd and they had a son and heir, David Gwyn, Esq., of Cefen Brecha, who married Margaret, daughter of John Stedman of Strata Florida and a daughter Jane, who married John ap Ievan of Park Rhydderch.

Grid Ref: SN 6023 6053

Refs: Colby Map, 1831; *Dwnn,* i, 18; CRO, GGMS, III (Gwaethfoed).

CEFN-COED, Llanbadarn Fawr

On the east bank of the Melindwr, north-east of Capel Bangor, and marked on *Colby's Map of 1831* and as Cyncoed on modern OS maps.

On 6 August 1752, the *Castle Hill Deeds* show '1. Griffith Lloyd of Cencoed otherwise Keven Coed, in parish Llanbadarn Vawr, gt. 2. John Lloyd of same parish, gent.. Surrender of a messuage called Cencoed otherwise Keven Coed, a water mill called Melin Coed, 2 cottages, and a messuage and land called Tyddin Wm Sion, Tyr y Ceven called, Bwlch y Tir Coch, and Tir blaen nant y Bwla in former times but now called Llyest Nant Bwla, in parish Llanbadarn fawr. On 7th and 8th Aug 1752. said John Lloyd leased and released the said lands to Stephen Edwards, and Matthew Evans of Aberystwyth gt. in order to create a tenant to the precipe'.

In 1760 Griffith Lloyd, gt. of Cwmbrwyno and his son John Lloyd of Keven y Coed, both owned Keven y Coed. John Lloyd (d. 1797), married and had a daughter, Elizabeth, his only child. Elizabeth married John Bond, gent. of The Grange, Dorset, High Sheriff in 1814. Her pre-nuptial settlement, dated 16 August 1798, settled Cefn-coed and fifteen other properties in Cardiganshire to 'uses of the marriage'.

Grid Ref: SN 6731 8088

Refs: Colby Map, 1831; NLW, Crosswood Deeds, fo. 290, 293; WWHR, iii, 102; NLW, Castle Hill Docs., 1031-21, 1069.

CEFN GARTH FREFY, Llanddewibrefi

Hwnt-y-garth, Godre'r-garth, Cefn-y-Garth and Garth were farms just west of Llanddewibrefi church marked on *Colby's Map of 1831* and as Garth and Ochergarth on modern OS maps on the eastern bank of the river Teifi.

CRO GGMS tells us that 'Ieuan ddu of Cefen Garth Frefi' was 'sayed to be descended from Gwilym ap Rhys Whith, of Cefn Garth yr enni, county Cardiganshire, Esquire of the body of King Edward the first'.

His son Llewelyn, alive in 1495, bore the arms: *argent* 3 bulls heads couped *sable* attired *or.* He had a son Rees and a grandson David, who married Jane, a daughter of Herbert of Hafod. Their son, Thomas Davids became the Rector of Eglwyscymin.

By 1760 the house was owned by Daniel Evan of Garth.

Grid Ref: SN 6561 5550

Refs: CRO, GGMS (Gwyddno); WWHR, ii 47; ibid, iii, 100; Colby Map, 1831.

CEFN GWALLTER, Llandysul
Shown on *Colby's Map of 1831* as south-west of Castell Howell and on modern OS maps as on the east bank of Cletwr fawr, north-west of Pontsian.

The *Aberglasney Deeds* tell us that John Davies, gent. owned Cefn Gwallter in 1760. His will was dated 24 March 1782. He had a brother, David, and a sister Anne. David Davies lived at Troedrhiwpenyd and was described as 'lately deceased' in 1782.

Anne Davies married Ellis Jones and had a son, Samuel. John Davies had two daughters, and co-heiresses: Gwen, who married a Williams and Mary, who married a Lewis.

By 1848 Evan Davies, farmer, owned Cefn Gwallter.

Grid Ref: SN 4238 4752

Refs: Colby Map, 1831; CRO, Aberglasney Deeds, p. 117; WWHR, iii, 85.

CEFN-GWYN, Llanfihangel Genau'r-glyn
Situated on the east bank of afon Leri, north of Bont-goch and Elerch church.

In his book *Sheriffs of Cardiganshire* Phillips gives Richard Lewis, JP, of 'Cefn Gwyn or Alltfadog' as High Sheriff in 1701. The *PRO List* shows that his name was to be left out of Commission of Peace in 1714-15. He had a son, Lewis Lewis, who was High Sheriff in 1727.

Later notes tell us that Lewis John son and heir of Lewis Lewis of Cefn-gwyn had a daughter who married John Jones, son of George Jones, third brother of Col. John Jones of Nanteos, by Mary Fychan, daughter and heiress of Rhoscellan. They had a son, George Jones, who married Alice Prys. Recently the home of Mr. D. Parry.

Grid Ref: SN 6804 8695

Refs: WWHR, i, 27; Phillips, *Sheriffs of Cardiganshire;* PRO List ex info Emrys Williams.

CEFNMABWS, Llanrhystud
A farm to the east of and near the mansion of Mabws, to the south of the Wyre Fach and shown on *Colby's Map of 1831*.

Ievan Rees Fychan of Cefen Mabros married Elen Fychan, daughter and co-heiress of Meredydd ddu of Uwch Aeron, by Janet, daughter of Llewelyn Griffith Fychan ap David Vaughan ap Meuric Goch (to Edwin). Dates are lacking.

Grid Ref: SN 5715 6835

Refs: Colby Map, 1831; CRO, GGMS, III (Edwin ap Tegl), fo. 8.

CEFNMELGOED, Llanychaearn
A farmstead of great antiquity situated east of the A487(T), south of the village of Blaenplwyf, and marked on *Colby's Map of 1831*. The earliest recorded at Cefnmelgoed was Ievan ap Ievan Fychan who married Tanglwyst, daughter of Llewelyn Howel Meredudd of Pen-y-berth early in the 14th century.

J. Davies tells us in his *Display of Heraldry* that in 1352/3 (26 Edward III) 'Robert ap Meredith of Caerms. (to Owain Gwynedd) was near four score years old before he married; and then in his dotage, fancied and married Angharad, daughter of David ap Llewelyn ap David of Ceven Mulgoed in Cardiganshire, whose wife was the daughter of Rhydderch ap Evan Lloyd of Gogerthan and had issue'. The son and heir of this union, Ievan ap Robert, was the grandfather of John Wynn of the celebrated Gwydir family. Marged, daughter of John Lloyd ap David ap Llewelyn, brother of the aforesaid Angharad, married Rhydderch ap Rhys and Lord of Towyn near Ferwig. Their son, Sir John Gwyn, married Nest, daughter of Ievan ap Tryhaiarn (Trehaearn), of Llanilar and their third son, David, adopted the surname Lloyd and signed for Dwnn in 1596. The eldest son, Morris, is described as 'grythor penkerdd ag aeth ar gerdd dent'.

The *Harleian Papers* in the British Museum state that in 1558, Cefnmelgoed was the home of Rhydderch ap Ievan Lloyd who was outlawed and his lands sold to John Doddington. The *Aberglasney Deeds* tell us that by May 1651, Edward Pryse, gent., was living at 'Keven Melgoed'. He was the third son of Thomas Pryse of 'Glanfroed', and Bridget, daughter and co-heiress of John Griffith, described as of Cil Cemaes, Merionethshire. He married Mary, daughter of John Vaughan of Caethle and in turn, their daughter and co-heiress married Richard Morris of Llanilar, who traced to Edwin. The *NLW Cwrtmawr Deeds,* on 11

December 1703, give details of an 'Agreement between: 1. Elizabeth Jones of Talysarn, parish of Trefilan, widow and executrix of Richard Jones, late of Cwm newidion, gent., and 2. Sir Thomas Powell of Dyffryn Park, Knight – Release of all suits, actions etc. and also release of two messuages called Tyddyn Kefen Melgoed and Tyddyn Glan y Gors-rydd in the parishes of Llanychaearn and Llandeiniol with all conditions of redemptions'.

After World War II Cefnmelgoed was occupied by the Pugh family who left in the late 60's.

Grid Ref: SN 5777 7431

Refs: Colby Map, 1831; John Davies, *Display of Heraldry,* 1709, p. 9; CRO, Aberglasney Deeds, 105; BLG, 1850, II, p. 1650; NLW, Cwrtmawr Deeds, No. 49; WWHR, i, 26-7; PRO, Dale Castle MS., p. 20; BM Harleian Papers, 608, fo. 24; *Dwnn,* i, 53-4; CRO, GGMS, III (Edwinsford), fo. 8.

CILBRONNAU, Llangoedmor

East of Llangoedmor church and south of the B4507, the old highway from Cardigan to Newcastle Emlyn and marked on *Colby's Map of 1831* as Kil-bronne.

The birthplace of the poet Ifor Ceri (John Jenkins) died 1829, and home to others of a distinguished family which include Sir Lawrence Jenkins, Chief Justice of the High Court of Calcutta. The Jenkins were descended from Elystan Glodrudd.

The *Noyadd Trefawr Deeds* tell us that on 10 Jan 1581/2, 'Howell Griffith Lloid and Griffith Lloid ap Rees David Llewellyn, both of Trederoir parish, yeoman, granted two messuages called Kiel y bronnay and Lloyn Adda' in the parishes of Llangoedmor and Llechryd, to John Mortimer, Esq. On the same date they gave him a 'bond in £100 for peaceful possession and further assurance'.

In 1600-1 the *Noyadd Trefawr Deeds* tell us that 'Dyddgu Meredith granted a tenement Keri y bronnay and two pieces called Teir y cleyn poeth and Knowk yr eithin, in Llangoedmore parish, to her son Richard Griffith of the said parish, yeoman, who, on 20 January 1600-1, granted them to Griffith David ap Rudderch, yeoman, of the same parish'.

In 1738 Jenkin Griffith of Blaen-porth, gent, married Maud Griffiths and their daughter, Elinor, married Griffith Jenkins of Cilbronne. Their son, Jonathan Jenkins, heir to his mother, had lands settled on him: the capital messuage of Cilbronnau, 3 parcels called Tyr y Gwern Hiscock, Tir Pen y Bryn and Tir Bronglewyn adjoining Cilbronnau, another messuage in the parish of Llangoedmor, a messuage and land in Verwick parish called Trekeven, a stang called Llain Kefan y Bettel; a messuage and land called Tyr y Garnwen alias Tyr Pen yr Allt and a piece called Tyr Meredith in the parish of Aber-porth.

Jonathan Jenkins married Elizabeth Lewes, youngest daughter of John Lewes of Tredefaid, Pembrokeshire. The marriage was subject to a pre-nuptial settlement on 13 December 1738. Jonathan Jenkins died in 1770 and his only son, Griffith Jenkins, succeeded to his estates. He married Mary, family unknown, and they had four sons.

Griffith died on 13 October 1781 and his will was dated the previous day, and was proved in January 1783.

His elegy, written by Ioan Seincyn mentions that 'his paternal grandmother was of the same blood as Mr. Lloyd of Mabws; his mother related to Lewis of Pantyrodin; his mother and his sister live in Cardigan; his cousins live at Tredefaid; his cousin Mr. Davies of Penyrallt, his uncle John of Palle, his relations of Fachendre, Mr. Morris and relations of Mrs. Jenkins of Cilybronnau, mentions Mrs. Jenkins of Trefwinsor, his cousins from Glanyrynys to Llanllunan and that he leaves a widow and five sons – John the heir, Jonathan, Thomas, Jeremiah, and Griffith, the youngest'.

Griffith and Mary had five sons. The eldest, John, became the Rev. John Jenkins, vicar and clerk of Whippingham, Isle of Wight and he married Elizabeth Jones of Crosswood, Guildsfield, Montgomeryshire. Little is known of Jonathan, Thomas and Jeremiah. G. E. Evans tells us that 'Griffith (the younger) was steward of the manor of Lampeter (under Richard Hart Davis, Lord) and held the leets regularly until 1844 when he was succeeded by Richard David Jenkins who held the office till the last leet in 1883'.

In 1872, the aforesaid Rev. John Jenkins's son, John Heyward Jenkins, of Crosswood Esq. known in 1860 as John Heyward Heyward, barrister, sold Cilbronnau and other lands to his cousin Richard David Jenkins.

Richard David Jenkins, Esq. (1844-1883), was of the Priory in 1861 and for many years agent to the Ffynonne estate of the Colbys. He passed Cilbronnau to his son and heir, Lawrence Hugh Jenkins Esq., born in 1857, called to the Bar in 1883, and who married Catherine Minna Kennedy in 1892. He was knighted in 1901 and became Chief Justice of Bengal in 1899 and Chief Justice of the High Court of Calcutta from 1909-15. He was appointed to the Privy Council in 1915. Cilbronnau was rebuilt c. 1900. His heir was Glodrydd Lawrence Richard Jenkins.

In 1926, there was a sale of furniture at Cilbronnau mansion and on 22 August 1931, the Cilbronnau estate consisting of the mansion, farm and three cottages, and 103 acres was advertised for sale, with a good ground plan. It was described as the home of Sir Lawrence Jenkins and his ancestors for many generations, and 'was completely modernised and remodelled at great expense within the last twenty years . . . the architectural effect of the house is most pleasing; the many gables, the mullioned windows, are suggestive of Worcestershire or Shropshire'.

The house comprised, on the ground floor, 'entrance on south side very artistic porch, entrance hall with oak panelled walls and oak ceiling beams, drawing room of great artistic merit decorated in an Oriental manner, the walls and ceilings hand-painted, one wall completely filled by a painting by Shaeffler depicting *The Worship of the Golden Calf*, another drawing room, with large window recess and marble mantelpiece, inner lounge hall with oak staircase and panelling, con-servatory or winter garden, library with large Early English open hearth and Toddy hole; the vendors (Captain Grismond Picton Philipps and C. L. E. Morgan-Richardson) reserved the right to remove the window with armorial bearings and to replace with plain glass: on the east side is the main entrance with open porch, leading into a hall with flagged floor, cloakroom, basin and w.c.: this hall also communicates with the entrance hall, etc, and leads into the dining room with carved and gilded mantelpiece and overmantel: on the first landing is the billiard room, oak panelled, open hearth, lavatory, w.c.: the other floors contain 12 bedrooms, 3 dressing rooms, 4 bathrooms: the domestic offices include kitchen, servants hall, scullery, housemaids' cupboards, larder, butlers' pantry, wine cellar, servants lavatory, etc: there are outbuildings, gardens, sundial, summer house, fountain; in all 12 acres'. The catalogue continues 'The house itself is really a perfect house and many of the rooms are of quite unique charm and character'.

Cilbronnau became a part of the estate of Cwmgwili in Carmarthenshire through the marriage of Edith Evans to Grismond Philipps in 1897. Edith was the niece of Sir Lawrence Jenkins. Most of the house was demolished in the 1950's only a service wing remains. In 1978 the property was sold by Griffith Philipps.

Grid Ref: SN 2050 4537

Refs: Colby Map, 1831; Meyrick, *Cardiganshire,* 182; Blodau, *Dyfed;* NLW, Noyadd Trefawr Collection, Noyadd Trefawr Deeds, No. 126; WWHR, iii, 78; G. E. Evans, *Lampeter;* NLW, Cwmgwili Deeds.

CILCENNIN, Plas Cilcennin

A short mile north-east of the hamlet of Cilcennin, marked on *Colby's Map of 1831* as Plas Cilcennan and on the *14th century Rees Map* as Cilcennyn. Home of families of Stedman and Vaughan, a cadet branch of Crosswood.

In his *County Families*, Nicholas tells us that 'the village of Cilcennan, whose great house, Plâs Cilcennan, was in the 17th century of considerable note, the property and residence of Harry Vaughan, Sheriff for the county in the time of Cromwell. Near at hand are the barrows called Tri chrug Aeron'.

The story of Plâs Cilcennin was published in the *Welsh Gazette* on 25 March 1948. 'Rowland Stedman, third son of John Stedman of Strata Florida (died 1607), founded Plâs Cilcennin c. 1590 after his marriage in 1587 to Jane, daughter of Hugh Llewelyn Lloyd of Llanllyr (d. 1577) and widow of Jenkin John Howel of Llanybydder. Property in Llanfihangel Genau'r Glyn, Aberystwyth and Llanfihangel y Creuddyn (val. £20 p.a.) was settled on him, and a lease for years of the Grange of Dovarchen (val. £19.10 p.a. above Crown rent of £7), and to have either "a mansion house" or £240 to build one. On his death in 1613, Jane came with households goods and her £300 in lieu of dower'.

John Stedman c. 1590-1623, married his third cousin Anne on 2 March 1611-12. She was the daughter of Sir Thomas Johnes, Kt., of Abermarlais (d. 1604), sister of Sir Henry Soames created baronet in 1643, widow of James Mortimer of Coedmor, born 1586 and educated at St. Mary Hall, Oxford. Anne was married for the third time, in 1624, to Edward Vaughan of Trawsgoed. John Stedman's second daughter and co-heiress, Mary Stedman, who died in 1677, married her own step-brother and brother-in-law, Henry Vaughan (1605-65), second son of Trawsgoed. They inherited an undivided moiety of demesne of Plâs Cilcennin and went to live there and in 1636 took a 99-year-lease of the other moiety from John and Jane Vaughan.

'Henry Vaughan was High Sheriff in 1642 and 1654, and a JP. Plâs Cilcennin was assessed at 9 hearths in 1672. He owned 170 cattle and 547 sheep at the time of his sudden death, before he could sign his will, in 1665, when the Great Plague raged in London. He left three daughters of whom Jane was one. His widow was assessed at 9 hearths in 1672. In his draft will of 1666, Henry Vaughan made bequests to "my grandson Vaughan Price (second son of Sir Matthew Price of Newtown Mont. Bart; my grandson Henry Herbert (2nd son of Morgan Herbert of Havod); my grandson Henry Lloyd (2nd son of Thomas Lloyd of Llanllawddog, Carms.); my wife Mary; my brother John Vaughan of Trawscoed, Esq. and my nephew Edward Vaughan of Trawscoed".'

The *Welsh Gazette* continued 'Jane Vaughan inherited the demesne and one third of the Cilcennin estate. In 1657 she married Sir Matthew Price (d. 1674), of Newtown, Co. Mont.. Their part of the estate passed to their eldest son and heir, Sir John Price, 3rd Baronet (1661-99) dsp and the property passed to his next brother Sir Vaughan Price.

Sir Vaughan Price, 4th Baronet, married Anne Powell of Laugharne, and before his accession in 1699, lived at Plâs Cilcennin and was High Sheriff in 1696. Sir Vaughan Price retained as his agent William Hughes, Attorney, of Tyglyn (will proved in 1712), who had served Henry Vaughan. Hughes was installed at Plâs Cilcennin as tenant. His own nephew, also called William Hughes, (d. 1730) left a widow Mary, who afterwards married John Jones of Tyglyn (1696-1756). John and Mary Jones lived at Plâs Cilcennin for many years. Sir John Price succeeded in 1720 and sold Plâs Cilcennin for £3,364 to James Philipps of Pentypark, Pembs. (b. 1730) with whom Richard Philipps of Coedgain, Carms. was joint purchaser.

The *Crosswood Deeds* state that 'Wilmot, 3rd Viscount Lisburne brought a bill against James Philipps in Chancery in 1758 for recovery of the undivided moiety leased in 1636.' The case was heard in 1761, and in 1765 the *Coleman Deeds* show that 'on Oct. 24th 1765 a certificate of an award was issued, pursuant to a decree of 12th Nov. 1761, setting forth the metes and bounds of Kilkennan Demesne and Lluestwen, belonging to the Vaughans'.

In 1765 the *Welsh Gazette* tells us that the Commissioners responded that Plâs Cilcennin 'now consists of an old decayed mansion which is fallen down and in ruins, a little messuage or farm house built or converted out of some or one of the offices belonging to the said mansion house . . .'. The case was settled in 1767, when James Philipps conveyed his moiety (of the demesne only), and sold the rest of the property in lots in 1765 to Lord Lisburne in exchange for Bronwenau, Lluestwen and £490.

The Lords Lisburne owned Plâs Cilcennin from 1767 until 1888, when, on his father's death, the 6th Earl sold it to the tenant, William Williams, the grandfather of the present tenant (1958).

There had been many tenants. In his diary of 1819, Captain Jenkin Jones wrote 'Walked to Place Kilkenin which is inhabited by a farmer of the name of Evan James, whose father had the house about 20 years ago, it is a house new since my grandfather's time . . .'.

Grid Ref: SN 5313 6041

Refs: Colby Map, 1831; Meyrick, *Cardiganshire,* 259; Rees Map, 14th Century; WWHR, I, 118; Nicholas, *County Families;* i, 133; NLW, Crosswoods Deeds; Captain Jenkin Jones Diary 1819; Story of Plas Cilcennin, *Welsh Gazette,* 25 March 1948; NLW, Coleman Deeds, p. 363.

CILIAU AERON, Cilau Aeron

Probably near Ciliau Aeron church. The farms of Ciliau Uchaf and Penlan Ciliau are marked on *Colby's Map of 1831* and Ciliau Uchaf is south of Ciliau Aeron on modern OS maps.

The pedigree of its Elizabethan owners Lloyd, and then Lewis ap Hugh, viv. 1615-25) are given in *Dwnn* and are traced to Cadifor ap Dinawal.

Refs: Dwnn, i, 16; Colby Map, 1831.

CILCERT, Henfynyw

To the west of Henfynyw church to the north-west of Ffosyffin and near the coast and shown on *Colby's Map of 1831* and modern OS maps.

A house which links the old families of Gwyn and Parry. Thomas Gwyn, a descendant of Griffith married Mary, daughter of James Parry, younger son of John Parry (to Gwyddno), of Llanarth and Ann, daughter of William Jenkins of Cilgerran. They had two sons; James Gwyn, who married Joan, daughter of John Walter, and David Gwyn of whom little is known. The family tree is undated. Their uncle, Thomas Gwyn was of Mynachty.

Refs: Colby Map, 1831; CRO, GGMS, I (EG).

CILFACHAU, Llanddeiniol

East of the A 487 (T) between Llanfarian and Llanrhystud and south of Llanddeiniol church; overlooks the afon Wyre. Marked on *Colby's Map of 1831* also known as Gilfachau, Kilfochay and Kilvache.

Home of the Lloyds descended from Tydwal Gloff. Rhys David Lloyd had a son Thomas, who married Mary, daughter of David Lloyd of Crynfryn. They had three sons and three daughters:

1. John, who succeeded. 2. David Lloyd, was as of London. 3. Sir Richard Lloyd of Huntingdon, Knight. 4. Bridget, who married Jenkin Ieuan. 5. Anne, who married Jenkin David of Gilvachavel. 6. Elizabeth, married William Parry of Pen-y-cwm (to Gwyddno).

John Lloyd married Margaret Parry, daughter of Stephen Parry. They had one son, Stephen, and two daughters, Elizabeth, who married Thomas Price and Anne, who married David Richard of Rhod-mad. Stephen married Elizabeth, daughter of Edward William David of Geneu'r glyn.

In 1672, Elizabeth Lloyd paid tax on 5 hearths. Their two daughters were co-heiresses to Cilfachau. The elder daughter, Margaret married Mathew James of Pengwern in Cenarth, Carmarthenshire, the son of the Rev. David James MA (1615-1682). Mathew James owned Pontycnycau in 1685, and resided at Cilfachau. The younger daughter, Anne, married Edward Price of Rhandir (a younger branch of Gogerddan).

The *Tyglyn Documents* state 'On May 2 1685, Mathew James of Kilvache, gt., granted permission to Henry Jones of Tyglyn, gt., to erect a new weir over the Aeron, and for turning the course of the river to serve a new mill on Henry Jones's lands near Pont Dolvour . . .'.

Mathew James's son, David built Tyglyn Ucha, where he was living in 1730 and was High Sheriff of Cardiganshire in 1734. Later, the house passed to James Lewes, younger son of John Lewes of Llysnewydd.

Grid Ref: SN 5614 7137

Refs: Colby Map, 1831; CRO, GGMS; ibid, I (Tydwal Gloff); ibid, III (Gwaethfoed), 25 ibid, III (Owen ap Bradwen); NLW, Tyglyn Docs, 124.

CIL-FFORCH, Henfynyw

Situated near the sea and north of Henfynyw church, south of Aberaeron and shown on *Colby's Map of 1831* and on modern OS maps.

The home of the Gwynnes in the 17th century and then the Lloyds. Lewis ab Griffith (to Grono Goch of Llangathen, to Elystan) had a son Griffith of Cilfforch, who married Mabli, daughter of Jenkin ab Ieuan Jenkin ap Rhys Lloyd. They had two sons; the elder was Lewis Gwyn Griffith and the younger, Jenkin Fychan whose arms were: *azure* 3 stags heads couped *or*. Crest – nag's head couped ger bridled *or*, a gauntlet *proper* holding ye bridle.

In 1570-80 Lewis Gwyn of Cilfforch, the eldest son of Griffith and Mabli, was Lord of the Manor of Aberaeron alias Llyswen. The *Griffith Owen List* gives Lewis Gwyn Griffith as married to a daughter of Ieuan Lloyd ap Lewis, but Dwnn calls her Gwenllian, daughter of Thomas ap John.

Their son Morgan Gwyn of Cilfforch married a daughter of Rhys Gwyn of Mynachty and they resided there. They had a son and heir Griffith Gwyn, who married Florence, daughter of Ieuan Thomas of Tremoilet. In 1672, Griffith Gwyn was assessed at 4 hearths. After his death Florence married Charles Lloyd, son and heir of Thomas Lloyd of Llanllyr. Charles Lloyd was living at Cil-fforch in 1706. Florence and Griffith Gwyn had a son, Lewis Gwyn of Mynachdy, who married Mary, daughter of John Prys of Rhandir, Cardiganshire, gent. The *Mynachty Deeds* describe a post-nuptial settlement, made on 9 July 1706 between Lewis Gwyn and Mary. Among lands settled were 'a messuage called Ffynnon Ddewi Vach in Henfynyw parish, the capital messuage called Kilforch in Henfynyw (which was at that time the home of Charles Lloyd and his wife Florence), the capital messuage called Mynachtie Mawr, and a messuage called Kriggie bychan (both in Llanbadarn Trefeglwys parish)'.

In 1785, Lewis Gwyn of Mynachty gave a lease of Cil-fforch to John David of Henfynyw, yeoman and Mary, his wife.

By 1807, the Gwyn family had died out and the estate was devised by will to Tyglyn, which was associated by Lewis Gwynn's son Charles by marriage to Bridget, daughter of John Jones of Tyglyn.

G. E. Evans records in his book *Cardiganshire* that it was noted in the Cilcennin parish register on 24 September 1852, 'John Evans of Carne was buried, aged 16, having been drowned at Aberaeron with seven others, returning from a new vessel which had just gone out to sea. All the parties were young people. There were three from the same house called Cilforch'.

Grid Ref: SN 4466 6159

Refs: Colby Map, 1831; NLW, Griffith Owen List (iv); *Dwnn* (i, 58); WWHR, i, 46; PRO, Dale Castle MS., p. 28 (109); Protheroe, C, D, E; Mynachty Deeds, No. 8, No. 247; G. E. Evans, *Cardiganshire,* 1903, 173.

CILGWYN, Llandyfriog

There are two houses of this name. The original seat of the Lloyd family was at the house now known as Old Cilgwyn on a wooded slope about 250 ft. above sea level, and about 1,200 yards north of the Teifi, shown on the *14th century Rees Map,* the *Kitchin Map of 1754* and *Colby's Map of 1831.* In 1509, Dyddgu, daughter of Thomas ap Griffith ap Nicholas, descended from Griffydd ap Nicholas of Dynefur, married Griffydd of Cilgwyn. Their son, David Llwyd married Jonet, daughter of Sir Thomas Phillipps (died c. 1519/20), of Picton by a daughter of Henry Dwnn. The son of David and Jonet, John Llwyd was of Cilgwyn and married Anne, daughter of Sir John Vaughan of Whitland, who was High Sheriff of Cardiganshire 1560, and who died 1567.

Thomas Lloyd, the second son of Jenkin Lloyd and Elizabeth his wife who bought Gilfachwen from his elder brother, was a successful attorney-at-law, often described in genealogies as 'a Ludlow clerk', showing that he practised in the courts of the Council of Wales and the Marches. He was the first of his family to live at Cilgwyn. This came about through his marriage, between 1611 and 1616, probably nearer the latter date, to Mary Lloyd co-heiress of the Cilgwyn estate. Her father Rhys Lloyd was son of John Lloyd (High Sheriff in 1583) whose forebears had been seated at Cilgwyn for many generations and, like the family of Gilfachwen, he traced his pedigree of Elystan Glodrudd. By his wife Elen daughter of Lewis David Meredith of Aber-nantbychan, Rhys had two daughters, Mary who married the said attorney Thomas Lloyd, and Joan who married John Parry of Blaen-pant (died in office as High Sheriff in 1620). Cilgwyn formed part of Mary's portion.

Thomas Lloyd had moved to his wife's home by 1616, for the Letters Patent dated 13 December of that year, appointing him Eschaetor of Cardiganshire, describe him as 'of Cilgwyn, gentleman'.

Having acquired Gilfachwen by purchase, and Cilgwyn by marriage, he added to his possessions by several other purchases both of leaseholds and freeholds. On 27 March 1611 Henry Don Lee of Abercyfor near Carmarthen, esquire, assigned to him a Crown lease of Dol y Gwyddfa in the grange of Manorvorion, formerly part of the possessions of the monastery of Whitland. Later, on 7 September 1621, he obtained a lease for 21 years of the same property from the Earl of Essex (who had acquired the Crown lease), for a down payment of £8, a yearly rent of 13s. 4d., with an obligation to keep the premises in repair. He had second thoughts about this transaction, as shown by an endorsement on the deed which runs, 'This gentleman, Mr. Lloyde within menconed did thinke be payed over muche, and therefore desired that this might not be a precedent to future ages'. Nevertheless, he held on to the property, for having assigned it to Thomas James of Cenarth on 20 September 1631. it was again regranted to Thomas Lloyd by nominees of the Earl of Essex on 1 November following.

He made some minor purchases from Sir Henry Jones of Abermarlais, Carmarthenshire, a parcel of land called Ddol bicka vach in Llandyfriog parish in 1624, and a messuage and garden in Newcastle Emlyn in 1627.

Thomas managed to procure a share of the Cilgwyn estate that had belonged to one of the other co-heiresses, for on 20 July 1631, Charles Lloyd and Sage his wife, of Llanedy, parish, Carmarthenshire, conveyed to him their one-fourth part of over 30 properties including the capital messuage of Cilgwyn. The date of Thomas Lloyd's death is not known. He was alive in November 1649, and no further reference to him has been found. He had two children, 1. John, see later. 2. Elenor who married firstly Griffith Lloyd of Gwernmaccwy (whose uncle Charles Lloyd had been hanged for murdering Mr. Lloyd of Gilfachwen issa) by whom she had five children, and secondly

Morgan Lloyd of Greengrove (brother of William Lloyd of Llanllyr) who died in 1688, his will being proved in 1692.

Soon after the Restoration in 1660, the Lloyds had bought materials lying about the castle of Newcastle Emlyn, when Emlyn castle was dismantled by Cromwell's men, and took what they needed to enlarge the medieval mansion known as Old Cilgwyn.

The only son, John Lloyd, succeeded to Cilgwyn and Gilfachwen. Before his father's death he lived for some time at Gilfachwen Ucha and is described as of that place in a deed dated 20 July 1652, when John Thomas David Lloyd of Llandysul, released his claim in Llayne Carne deg y bore in accordance with an arbitration award.

John Lloyd made a particularly good marriage. His wife, Dorothy, was the daughter of Walter Vaughan of Llanelly, son of Walter Vaughan of Golden Grove, by Mary Rice of Dynevor, daughter of Griffith Rice, whose parents were Rhys ap Griffith and Katherine Howard, daughter of the Duke of Norfolk. Walter Vaughan of Llanelly's eldest brother, Sir John Vaughan was Comptroller of the Household of the Prince of Wales (Charles I), and was elevated to the peerage as Baron Emlyn and later as Earl of Carbery. This august ancestry was further gilded by the fact that Dorothy's father was extremely rich. The post-nuptial settlement was dated 10 June 1639.

It is generally believed that he is the John Lloyd described in a manuscript written about 1661, and printed in the *Cambrian Register* for 1795 – 'John Lloyd, a royalist of an even temper, quitted all offices in 1643, compounded for his delinquency, liveth a retired hospitable life, neither ambitious, nor a contemner of those publique employments that his fortune and capacity do deserve'.

John continued his father's acquisitive policy and was able to obtain a further share of the Cilgwyn estate amongst other properties. On 28 February 1679-80, he made provision for his unmarried daughters and a further jointure on his wife. By this deed he conveyed over 17 properties. John Lloyd of Cilgwyn may have been the man of that name who served as High Sheriff of Cardiganshire in 1683. He was certainly alive in 1680, and died before 1685. His wife survived him and in 1688 joined with her daughters Margaret and Cecil and their husbands in mortgaging lands in Llandyfriog to Nathan Griffiths of Pantcilgane, Carms., in £200. They had the following children:

1. Thomas Lloyd – see later.

2. William Lloyd, married Mary daughter and co-heir of David Jenkins of Dolwlff Llanwenog, by whom he had two sons, David and Walter; the elder son, David Lloyd, married Jenkin Evan of Llygadenwyn's daughter, and their only child, David Lloyd, lost his life at Dolwlff in July 1751 when taking the charge out of a gun.

3. Mary, married John Lloyd of Lloyd Jack, Ystrad parish, and had issue.

4. Anne, married Evan Lloyd of Alltyrodyn and had issue.

5. Elizabeth, married firstly William Lloyd of Pantcilgan (will proved 1684); secondly Nathan Griffiths of Mountain Hall, Llangeler parish, High Sheriff of Carmarthenshire in 1695 and of Cardiganshire in 1706.

6. Margaret married on 30 September 1682, John Bowen of Morfa Bychan in Llanychaiarn parish, and had issue; on the day before her wedding she conveyed her interest under the settlement of 1679/80, to her unmarried sister, Cicil.

7. Cicil, on 10 October 1685 conveyed her interest, under the settlement of 1670/80, to her widowed mother; she married, before October 1688, Thomas Philippe of Lampeter Velfrey, Pembrokeshire (will proved 10 June 1696), and afterwards married Reynald Lewis, younger son of Lewis John of Lan in the same parish; she had no issue.

8. Sage, married before October 1688, David Lloyd of Ffosybleiddiad in Lledrod parish (will proved 28 January 1714-15), and had issue, from whom descend the family of Lloyd-Philipps of Dale Castle.

9. Elinor, married after 1696, Philip Jones of Llether Neuadd, later of Llanina, and had issue.

Thomas Lloyd, the eldest son, took up a military career, and became a captain in the army. He married Jane, widow of Thomas Lewes of Llysnewydd (who had died in February 1672) daughter of Colonel James Lewes of Coedmore, who had been High Sheriff of Cardiganshire in 1664 and of Pembrokeshire in 1641 and 1668. His mother, Mary, was daughter of John Wogan of Wiston, one of Pembrokeshire's oldest families. Coedmore now enters into the chronicle of the Lloyds. It had formed part of the estates of the Mortimers from the Middle Ages, and continued in that family until 20 March 1614-15 when Rowland Mortimer sold it to Sir John Lewes of Abernantbychan, from whom it descended to his great-grandson John Lewes who married Elizabeth Lewis of Llangors, Breconshire. John Lewes became financially embarrassed and on 28 September 1689 mortgaged the Coedmore estate in £400, and later was obliged to convey the property to his first-cousin Walter Lloyd (see below) whose mother Jane was sister to James Lewes of Coedmore, father of the said John. Thomas Lloyd never succeeded to the paternal estate for he died in his father's lifetime, his will being proved at Carmarthen in 1679.

As Thomas and Jane Lloyd had married after February 1672, their three children were minors at the time of their father's death. They were: John Lloyd, see later; Walter Lloyd who lived firstly at Cardigan (1707) being described as of The Priory in 1712–14, and later at Coedmor. On 1 October 1714 he mortgaged part of the demesne of Coedmor, several other messuages, Llechryd water corn mill, Coedmor weir on the river Tivy, and all fishing rights in that river that belonged to the manors of Iscoed Isherwin and Iscoed Mortimer, for £1,200, to Nathaniel Wade of Bristol. On 29 April 1718, Anne Wade of Bristol, widow, and her daughter Anne, released to Walter Lloyd of the town of Cardigan, gentleman, the capital house or burgage 'with a red herring house and garden' adjoining, and certain rent charges, all in the said town. On 8 April 1720, Mrs. Wade assigned the mortgage of 1714 to John Lloyd of Cilgwyn, so that the Coedmore property remained in the Lloyd family. Walter Lloyd was High Sheriff of Cardiganshire in 1722. He married Mary daughter of Dr. Bevan of Carmarthen, and died without issue on 24 October 1722, aged 46. By his will, dated 5 October 1722, and proved in PCC on 23 January 1722-3, he desired to be buried in Llangoedmore churchyard 'as near my seate in the Chancell there and the Bones of my Ancestors and Family as may be convenient without any damage to the said Chancell wall'. He bequeathed barley to the poor of Llangoedmor and Cardigan; to his nephew, Thomas Lloyd (second son of testator's brother John Lloyd late of Cilgwyn) he bequeathed the lordships or manors of Iskoed Mortimer and Iskoed Ishirewern with fisheries and other perquisites thereto belonging, for ever subject to payment of £80 yearly to testator's wife; he charged all his lands and mill in the hamlet of Llechryd with £500 to be paid to testator's nephew John Lloyd of Cilgwyn to enable him to discharge portions, payable under his later father's will, to the brothers and sister of the said John and Thomas Lloyd, and since corroborated by deeds of purchase of one-fourth of the Cilgwyn estate by which a further £100 was charged on the estate and made payable to James Lloyd, brother of the said John Lloyd the younger, 'which James was born after his father's death'; in addition he left to the said nephew John, testator's title to one-third of Hellingwen in Llandyfriog parish; and appointed his nephew Thomas Lloyd to be sole executor. His wife's will was proved in 1729. The third son was James Lloyd of The Priory, Cardigan, entered the service of King William III, and died unmarried, his will being proved in 1717.

John Lloyd (eldest son of Thomas and Jane) succeeded his grandfather to Cilgwyn. The earliest notice found to him is in a deed dated 7 September 1699, when Charles Powell of Llanllwni, gentleman, released to him a fourth part of a messuage called Gwernan in Tredroyre, Tyr llwyn yos and a tucking mill in Pembryn parish. He married Elinor daughter of John Lloyd of Bwuchllaethwen, now called Llangennech Park, Carmarthenshire, descended from the Lloyds of Pryscedwyn (Pontardulais), by Elizabeth daughter of Howel Gwyn of Glanbran.

On 13 November 1701, George Lloyd of Berkeley Castle, Gloucestershire, executor and devisee of the will of William Powell of the Exchequer Office of Pleas in Lincoln's Inn, entered into agreement with John Lloyd, for mortgaging one-fourth of the Cilgwyn estate, but John Lloyd died shortly afterwards, his will being dated 18 March 1701-2. On 17 April 1702, Mrs. Elinor Lloyd purchased George Lloyd's share in Cilgwyn, and on that date charged the estate with £200 to the use of her sons Thomas and William, and with £300 payable to her daughter Jane, with remainder in fee to her eldest son John. Elinor lost no time in seeking another partner, and in December 1702 married Thomas Lewes, of Llysnewydd. He died in 1712, and Elinor then took as her third husband, before 1721, Walter Morley of Capel Tydist, Llangadog, Carmarthenshire. She continued to enjoy an annuity of £50 charged on her first husband's estate, and was still alive in 1748.

John and Elinor Lloyd had the following children: John Lloyd of Cilgwyn, see later. David Lloyd. William Lloyd, who lived at Cilgwyn; his eldest brother granted him an annuity of two guineas on 15 February 1729-30, and he was portreeve of Adpar in 1733. The fourth son was Thomas Lloyd of Coedmore, see later. Their daughter Jane, married John Howells at Penybailey, the pre-nuptial settlement dated 28 May 1725, and had issue. The youngest son, James Lloyd, born posthumously on 8 October 1702, died in the Mediterranean in 1722 or 1723.

John Lloyd, the eldest son of John and Elinor Lloyd succeeded to Cilgwyn. He served as High Sheriff of Cardiganshire in 1731, and appointed his younger brother Thomas Lloyd of Coedmore to be Under-Sheriff. He married firstly in 1722 to Anne, daughter of the Revd. Thomas Davids, rector of St. Thomas, Haverfordwest (then deceased), by Hester his wife. Their pre-nuptial settlement is dated 16 and 17 October 1722, the trustees being Thomas

Phillipps of Cringae, Carmarthen, John Stephens of Haverfordwest, gentleman, Samuel Hughes of Llwynybrain, Carmarthenshire, and Hugh Fowler of Haverfordwest, esquire. She died without issue. He married, secondly, on 7 February 1741, Elizabeth Davies of St. Stephen's parish, Bristol, daughter of John Davies of Bristol, by whom he had three children; a note in *Mr. G. B. Brigstocke's Manuscripts* describes her father as John David of Newcastle Emlyn, corviser.

On 2 August 1721, John Lloyd, his mother Elinor Morley, and her husband Walter Morley of Capel Tydist, Llangadock, gentleman, mortgaged the Cilgwyn estate for £237 to James Johnson of the county borough of Carmarthen, merchant, and on the same date they assigned the Cilgwyn estate to trustees, to secure £50 per annum for Elinor, and John Lloyd further agreed to pay the £237 to the Morleys. The final concords in the transaction, describe the Carmarthenshire part of the property as comprising 5 messuages, 4 cottages, a water grist mill, 9 gardens, and 733 acres in the parishes of Llanfihangel Yeroth and Llangeler, and the Cardiganshire part of the property as 25 messuages, 25 gardens, and 2,200 acres in Llandyfriog and Llandysul, and the moiety of 20 messuages, 10 cottages, a water grist mill, a fulling mill, 25 gardens, and 2,910 acres in Llandyfriog, Trodyroyre, Penbryn, and Brongwyn. Thus by this time, the Cilgwyn estate had grown into a very substantial one. On 29 September 1722 a partition of the estate was made between Stephen Parry of Noyadd Trefawr, Cardiganshire, and John Lloyd.

On 19 September 1724 John Lloyd (described as grandson and heir-at-law of John Lloyd of Cilgwyn, deceased) cleared a mortgage of £400 created in 1665, and paid the money to William Howell of Morvil parish, Pembrokeshire, and Edward Emanuell of Kilgerran parish, and Margaret his wife. The first time, that members of the family are described in legal documents as 'esquire' occurs in 1727, and indicates their rise in the social and economic scale.

Judging from bonds he gave to different people John Lloyd seems to have been pressed for ready cash towards the end of his life. In 1746 he gave a bond for the repayment of £21 to John Owen of Glôg in Clydey parish, Pembrokeshire; in 1747, to Thomas Parry of Carmarthen (£250), Revd. William Propert of Trevaccoon, Pembrokeshire, (£100), Grace Jones of Llether Noyadd, Carmarthenshire, spinster (£30), John Philipps af Cringae, Carmarthenshire (£41). From a note made in May 1747, it appears that a judgement had been entered against him by William Lloyd for £500 plus 56s. 8d. costs, for failing to discharge a penal bond in £250, but on 21 December of that year he was able to discharge a bond for £250 to Thomas David of Troedrhiwffenid in Llandysul parish.

John Lloyd was soon to rest from his worries, for he died on 5 July 1748, and his will, dated 17 May, and proved in London on 6 February following, mentions his sons Thomas and John, both minors, and his daughter Elizabeth; and to his mother, wife of Walter Morley of Capel Tydist, to his mother-in-law Heather Davies widow, and to his wife Elizabeth, he left annuities of £40, £25, and £60 respectively. His wife survived him, and on 15 February 1748-9, the Revd. Edward Yardley, Archdeacon of Cardigan and rector of Llandyfriog, granted a lease for 21 years of that rectory, to Elizabeth widow and relict of John Lloyd of Cilgwyn 'lately deceased'. She afterwards married Thomas Parry, collector of excise at Carmarthen since 20 June 1732. The marriage took place before 29 August 1751, for Parry is described as of Cilgwyn on that date; their only child, Elizabeth Lloyd Parry, died before 15 October 1763 when administration of her estate was granted to Sir Thomas Stepney, Bt., guardian of Thomas Lloyd of Cilgwyn, a minor and 'brother by the mother's side to the said Elizabeth'.

John and Elizabeth Lloyd left three children, all of whom died without issue, namely: Thomas Lloyd of Cilgwyn – see later. John Lloyd who married Anne Price; a deed of 1795 describes him as of Cilgwyn, younger son of John Lloyd deceased; on 9 February 1802, John Lloyd of Cilgwyn, esquire, and Anne his wife, gave a release to Richard Brathwaite of Crinege, Kent, and Thomas Lloyd of Coedmore, esquires, for a legacy under the will of John

Lloyd of Cilgwyn, esquire, deceased; John died about 1803. The daughter named as Elizabeth died about 1754 whilst still a child.

Thomas Lloyd, the eldest son, succeeded to the estate and although he had no children, left a testamentory bombshell, the rumblings of which have not entirely ceased to this day.

He entered the Royal Navy and rose to the rank of captain. He eventually retired, returned to Cilgwyn, and took particular interest in estate management and farming, participated in public life, sat on the bench of magistrates, and in 1800 served as High Sheriff.

He made some alienations as well as additions to his estate, and seems to have been occasionally pressed for money. Gilvachwwn Ucha (also called Tir y Dre) had been mortgaged, and in 1782 James Lewess of Cwmbyar in Llandysul parish assigned the mortgage to Thomas Lloyd.

Thomas Lloyd will be mainly remembered as one of the leading 'improving landlords' of the late 18th century. At one time he had about 3,000 acres under his immediate management, carried out ambitious schemes to enrich the soil, improve livestock, experimented with the growing of grasses and corn, and constructed reservoirs and water courses to ensure that all fields were adequately supplied with that commodity. He was one of the supporters of the Carmarthenshire Agricultural Society, and with his friends the Rev. Lewis Turnor, 'squarson' of Wervilbrook, and Edward Warren Jones of Llanina, was responsible for a general improvement of husbandry in south Cardiganshire. A humane, philanthropic, kindly man, he was extremely popular with all classes, particularly with his tenants, all of whom shared a deep affection for him. A strong believer in granting leases for lives, he said: 'Security for life gives energy to action; and as few men live so long as they wish or expect, improvements are carried on to the last. Hope comforts the tenants, uncertainty the landlords.' Thomas Lloyd compiled a valuable report on agriculture in the southern half of Cardiganshire, for the Government, and was published in 1794. He wrote numerous letters on farming, military and naval matters, on domestic and foreign policy, which reveal him to have been a man of 'advanced' views. He was strongly opposed to slavery, having seen it at first hand in Jamaica where he lived for a short while, and wrote a long letter on the subject to Wilberforce in 1789.

Thomas Lloyd died unmarried on 12 April 1801. By his will dated 29 October 1790, he bequeathed:

All my lands (except Pencellyfawr) to my friends Richard Henry Alexander Bennet of Beckenham, Kent, and Thomas Lewis of Gellydowill, esquires on trust to the use of my friends William Lewes of Llysnewydd and William Owen Brigstocke of Blaen-pant, on trust, as follows: One-third of my estate, to the use of my relation Thomas Lloyd of Coedmore, esquire, for his life, then to his sons and daughters in tail, for ever, and in default of issue, to the use of my friend Richard Braithwaite, esquire, Rear Admiral of the White in the Royal Navy, and Ulrica Eleanora his wife, in survivorship, and then to their two unmarried daughters Jane Maria and Georgina, for lives as tenants in common, and to the heirs of their body, male and female, in tail, and in default, to my right heirs. The other two-thirds part, to the use of the said Richard and Ulrica Braithwaite for ever, with remainder to their said daughters and the heirs of their body in tail male and female. Pencelly otherwise Pencelly fawr, to the said Richard and Ulrica Eleanora Braithwaite for lives – with remainder to their two said daughters. To my brother John Lloyd, an annuity of £400, the use of all plate and personalty and furniture at Cilgwyn, for life: the farm stock, implements, etc, at Cilgwyn were to be sold, and the money devoted to the use of the said brother John: to Mrs Martha Nares wife of John Nares, esquire, barrister at law, annuity of £50: to William Lewis of Cardigan, attorney-at-law, annuity of £40 for life, and after his decease to his wife Margaret for her life; and annuity of £20 as well as the sum of £100 to their daughter Elizabeth Lewis; to Mrs. Gertrude Barber, widow of Mr. Barber, Captain in the army, annuity of £40; he gave annuities to servants, and left the residue to be shared equally between his said brother John Lloyd, and his friend Richard Braithwaite.

The will aroused tumultuous feelings in the breasts of testator's kinsmen at Coedmore, feelings which were hardly allayed by seeing two-thirds of the Cilgwyn estate passing to strangers in blood. Lloyd and Braithwaite had served together in the Navy, the latter rising to become an Admiral, and there seems to be no reason other than friendship to explain why Lloyd disposed of the property in the manner he did. All sorts of rumours and tittle-tattle flew around, and for many years formed the staple conversation piece in Tivyside drawing rooms when old ladies (of both sexes) delighted in probing other people's private lives as relentlessly as a surgeon hunting after gall-stones. Amongst the less noxious of these fictions is that chronicled by the Rev. W. J. Davies in *Hanes Llandyssul* (1896) and repeated by Horsfall-Turner in his *Walks and Wanderings through Cardiganshire.* We are told, 'About 1760, two old sea captains, Lloyd of Cilgwyn and Captain Braithwaite, who were comrades and had fought side by side, had had the misfortune to lose their ships. In a spot of despondency, they agreed to toss to decide whose estate should be sold to buy new ships for both, and Captain Lloyd won. The new vessels were obtained, Lloyd was unlucky again and lost his ship through fire. He died a single man in 1801, and left by will the greater part of his estate to his old friend now Admiral Braithwaite. The Admiral resided here for a short time but did not long survive his friend. The Fitzwilliams are descended from the Admiral'.

Meyrick tells us that, 'The house then passed into the ownership of Benjamin Hall, High Sheriff in 1830 and E. C. H. Hall and then to the Fitzwilliams family. *Contemporary Biographies of South Wales and Monmouthshire* tell us: 'In this parish was Emlyn Cottage where Anne Brigstocke, née Williams, resided during her widowhood with her daughters and her husband's cousin, Miss Mary Brigstocke of Robert's Rest, Carmarthenshire. Mr. Fitzwilliams afterwards purchased this property and built a new house on it, which is now named Cilgwyn.' It became the main residence of the Fitzwilliams family. C. H. Lloyd Fitzwilliams was High Sheriff in 1884. The Rev. Griffydd Evans, vicar of N.C.E. wrote 'Mr. C. H. L. Fitzwilliams informed me that when Mr. Fitzwilliams pulled down the Old Mansion during the erection of the present Cilgwyn he found that the house of the Restoration Period incorporated a wing of the older house; that in one part of this there was a wall 8ft thick, containing a zig-zag passage, the ends of which had been built up, leaving a thick oak door inside. The doorway was pointed, and there were other fifteenth century notes of time. The best of the timber in Old Cilgwyn was used in the construction of the new residence, and thus some of the oak is preserved in the present Cilgwyn. Emlyn B. Williams observed that by 1860 'The old mansion of Cilgwyn has no longer a gentleman within its walls'.

By 1932 a sale of portions of Cilgwyn estate took place. *Carmarthenshire RO* states that there were 157 lots, all minor items, cottages, fields, building sites, houses and small holdings. Lot 128 was the exception, being Gilfachwen-Uchaf, close to Llandysul – a farmhouse and buildings with 114 acres.

There exists in an official pamphlet, a photograph of Cilgwyn mansion in 1949, by then a Baptist Missionary Society Conference Centre. Francis Jones notes that the old house was demolished, and from its materials the large barn (still there) was built.

Refs: Blome List, 1673. Meyrick, *Cardiganshire,* 187, & 1810 (edn. 1907, p. 187); *Hanes, Casnewydd Emlyn,* B. Williams, 1860; WWHR, i. 16; WWHR, iii, 82; *Y Cymm,* 1922; Rev. Griffydd Evans, *Contemporary Biographies of South Wales and Monmouthshire,* 1907; NLW, Cilgwyn Dcts, No. 208-9; *Journal of Ceredigion Antiquarian Society,* 1976; NLW, *Penarth,* 140; NLW, MS., Pen. 156; SC 509, Carmarthen RO; NLW, Cilgwyn Collection Map; Francis Jones 'Lloyd of Gilfachwen, Cilgwyn and Coedmor' (abridged), *Ceredigion,* 1976.

CILPYLL, Nancwnlle

To the north of the river Aeron, on the eastern bank of Nant Gwenffrwd, east of Parc Rhydderch and north of the B4342, a long mile east of Llangeitho. Marked on *Colby's Map of 1831,* but not named on modern OS maps.

Earliest known occupant was Thomas ap Owen, fifth son of Rhydderch ap Ievan Llywd of Glynaeron by Maud Clement, who had three natural children by Jane, daughter of Ievan

Lloyd hen. Dwnn gives the pedigree of earlier owners. The pedigree of the eldest son of the liaison, David Lloyd is given in Powys Fadog; David Lloyd of Cilpyll ap Thomas ap Owain ap Philip ap Rhydderch ap Ievan Lloyd of Glyn Aeron ap Ievan ap Gruffydd Foel ap Ifor ap Cadifor ap Gwaethfoed, Lord of Cardigan, arms given as; *or* a lion rampant regardant *sable*.

David Lloyd's daughter, Gwerfyl Gwyn married firstly Maurice ap Rhys, vivens 1563, of Llanywared in Llangurig in Arwystle. His son, Rees, had two sons, Richard ap Rees Gwyn and William Gwyn, who was Gentleman to the Duchess of Lennox in 1627. Richard ap Rees Gwyn, the eldest son, had a son, Rees, who married Lucy, daughter of Rees of Nanty-chendy in Llangyryd (Llangurig). Their son, Richard Gwyn, vivens 1642, married Jane, daughter of Thomas Rhydderch Jenkin David Park of Glyn Aeron.

On 8 May 1642 Richard Gwyn, of Kilypyll, Nancwnlle, gent., mortgaged Melin Kilypyll water corn mill, in £30. J. Davies's *Display of Heraldry* has a Gwyn living at 'Cilypyll' until at least 1716. Richard was succeeded by Rees Gwyn who resided at Glynaeron.

By the middle of the 18th century, John Morgan, gent., owned Cilpyll. In 1769 he married Margaretta Eleanora, daughter of the late John Parry of Cwm Cynon, Llangrannog parish.

The *NLW Morgan Richardson Deeds* tell us of 'a pre-nuptial settlement of John Morgan of Cilpill, gent., and Margaretta Eleanora only living daughter of John Parry of Cwmeynon, of Llangrannog parish and Hester, his wife, a messuage called Kilpyll in parish Nantcwnlle and Morva Howell in parish. Penbryn'. Margaretta's portion was £500. In 1786, John Morgan of Cilpyll was one of the trustees of a pre-nuptial settlement of John Daniel of Cwrt Mawr and Anne Rogers.

Margaretta Eleanora, daughter of John and Margaretta Morgan, married Sylvanus Howell of Ffynnonfelen, Carmarthenshire in 1795. The marriage was subject to a pre-nuptial settlement. The Roy Evans deeds state: 'On June 11 1795. 1. Sylvanus Howell of Ffynnonfelen, Llanwinio parish, Carms., Esq. 2. Margaretta Elinora Morgan, spinster, 3rd daughter of John Morgan of Kilpill, parish. Nantcwnlle. 3. Said John Morgan. 4. John Howell of Tegfynydd, Llanfallteg parish, Esq. and William Jones of Ystrad Walter, gent., both of Carms. 5. Benjamin Griffiths of Penhendrue, Llanwinio Parish, gent., and Rev. Rice Williams, clerk, vicar of Nantcwnlle, release, to settle a jointure on M. E. Morgan, intended wife of said Sylvanus Howell, of messuages and lands called Ffynnon-felen, parish Llanwinio, and Morva Howell, parish Penbryn, Cards'.

Eleanora and Sylvanus were married at Nancwnlle church on 12 June 1795. Sylvanus Howell was described as of Morfa, parish of Penllwyn, bachelor. Margaretta had two older sisters; Esther, who married the Rev. Hugh Lloyd of Penwern, Cilcennin, clerk, and Anne who married John Mortimer of Trehowell, Llanwnda, Pembrokeshire at Nancwnlle in 1797.

By 1866 ownership had passed to Thomas Jones, gent., aged 66, who was succeeded by his son, John Jones in 1889.

Grid Ref: SN 5978 5893

Refs: Colby Map, 1831; *Dwnn,* i, 41, 87; *Powys Fadog,* ii, 265; CRO, GGMS; WWHR, II, 150; Morgan Richardson, i, 182; BM, Add. MS., 9865, vol. II; *Arch. Cam.,* 1867, p. 269; Griffith Owen Deeds, No. 6733; CRO, GGMS, I; NLW, Protheroe, I, fo. 67; CRO, GGMS III (Gwaethfoed); J. Davies, *Display of Heraldry,* 1716, p. 60; NLW, Bronwydd Deeds, No. 3344; NLW, Roy Evans DD, No. 205; CRO, Archibald Williams Deeds.

CIL-RHUG, Llanbadarn Odwyn

Home of the Lloyd family. Not found on the *Colby Map of 1831* but on the modern OS map there is a Maesrhug just south of Blaenpennal, on the eastern bank of the Aeron, south of the B4577 a mile from its junction with the A485.

Cilrhug, also known as Cilyrug uwch Aeron, Cilrhug, Cilrhyg and Kilrhug. The herald Dwnn recorded the pedigree of the early owners.

Thomas of Cilryg was descended from Griffith Foel (to Cadifor ap Dinawal), and passed Cilrug through six generations to John David Lloyd, who was the owner at the beginning of the 17th century. In 1609 John

David Lloyd, gent., of Cil-rhug married Jane, daughter of Ieuan ap Lewis ap Howel ap y Bedo of Llangeitho. They had two children, Morgan, vivens 1609, and Eissac (Isaac).

By 1672, John Lloyd, gent, married to Judith, daughter of John Pryse of Rhandir, was assessed at 3 hearths. His will, dated 28 July 1695, showed that he owned lands in Llansantffraid parish. They had three sons and a daughter: John, who succeeded whilst still a minor, Morgan, Magdalen and Rees, the youngest son.

In 1758 the Cil-rhug estate consisted of Park y llan, Stafell wen, Llain wen, Pensone, Lluest y gors, a water corn grist mill called Melin Cilypull, Tal y Uriv [sic], all in Llanbadarn Odwyn. Tyddyn y lletty du, Lletty du ucha, Cefn y wern, all in Llandewi brefi, Troedyrhiw Hir, in Nantcwnlle' as well as Cilrhug, the family home.

John Lloyd, married Catherine and had three sons and two daughters. This was a tragic time for the Lloyds. In a letter written to Francis Jones by Tudor Barnes, of Aberystwyth, dated 9 June 1977, he quotes the affidavit of Thomas Lewis of Kilrugh, in the parish of Llanbadarn Odwyn, Cardiganshire, farmer, given on 6 November 1812.

'Thomas Lewis says that he is about 79 years old and has lived with his father at a farm called Cappengwynfyl and as a servant at a farm called Glynacha, both about 2 miles from Felinissa farm, p. Llanbadarn Odwyn, from his childhood until he was 25 years old; that he then removed to a farm called Wenallt nearly 2 miles from Felinissa, where he lived for about 16 years, then he went to reside at a farm called Cwmmelen, close to Felinissa and lived there as a tenant for 36 years, from whence he removed about 21 years ago to Kilrhue. He says that Felenissa, from the time of his first recollection has always been reputed and considered to be part of the Kilrhug Estate. The deponent continues by saying that he was well acquainted with John Lloyd, gent., who was in possession of the Kilrhug estate about 1758; that John Lloyd had three sons only, i.e. Thomas, who died a great number of years before his father, unmarried (the deponent being then about 9 years old), John Lloyd and David Lloyd and two daughters only, i.e. Elizabeth, the wife of Thomas Lewis of Trecoll parish Llanbadarn Odyn, who together with her only child died several years before her father in childbirth, and Mary Lloyd, spinster.

'The deponent believes that John Lloyd, the son, died about 7 years after his father, being then about 32 years old; that David Lloyd, who at the time of his death, was about 25 years old, survived his brother, only 4 years or thereabouts; that John Lloyd, the son, and David Lloyd always resided at Kilrhug and that they were both bachelors at the time of their death. On the death of David Lloyd, his sister Mary Lloyd took possession of the Kilrhug estate and continued in possession until her decease, which happened about 1792, she being then a spinster. The deponent concludes that to his knowledge neither John Lloyd, the son, David Lloyd nor Mary Lloyd left wills.'

There is a copy of the will made by John Lloyd, the father, included by Tudor Barnes in his letter.

Copy Will (made on 15 May 1758) of John Lloyd, gent., 15 February 1814, of Keelrhug, p. Llanbadarn Odun:

'To be buried in the churchyard of Llanbadarn Odun. To his brother, Daniel Lloyd, one teal of pilcorn and his best clothes. To his sister, Mary Herbert, one teal of pilcorn. To his sister, Jane Jones, half a teal of pilcorn. To his daughter, Mary Lloyd – £120 and 'furniture of bedchamber'. To his son, John Lloyd, all those lands in p. Llanbadarn Odun called Park yr llan, Stafel wen and Llainwen and pennsone *[the document is torn here]* and Lluest u Gors, a water corn grist mill called Melin Cilupull and his mansion house called Kulrhug and Tale a uri. To Catherine, his wife, £15 yearly out of the property above mentioned for life, then to his son, John Lloyd and his heirs.

His son, John Lloyd is to pay six score and £10 to testator's other son, David who is also to have £6 yearly out of Park u lan. To his son, David and his heirs, all his lands and tenements in p. Llandewi Brevy, co. Cards., called Tuddun u

Lletty du and Cefen a wern and Lletty du ucha, and Tenements and lands in p. Nantcwnlle, Co. Cards, called Troedurhiw hir. The rest of his goods to his son David, whom he appoints sole executor and trustee of his [testator's] grand daughter Anne Lewis until 21 years old.'

What Thomas Lewis, farmer, failed to say in his affidavit, or did not know, was that Mary Lloyd, sister of John Lloyd, the son, was murdered. *Ceredigion* tells us that 'the murder was planned by her manservant David Evans, who had two accomplices, John Benjamin (aged 18) of Llangeitho, labourer, and John Samuel of Llandewibrefi, shoemaker. When Cilrhug was deserted except for the victim, David Evans, and accomplice Benjamin entered the house and strangled her with his hands on 16 March 1792. The motive was robbery. The three were apprehended; Benjamin pleaded guilty to killing her and was brought before the Great Sessions.

On 4 December 1812 an affidavit was signed by David Lloyd of Broncapel, Tregaron, gent, referring to the estate of Mary Lloyd, late of Cilrug, his first cousin.

The long association of the Lloyds with Cilrhug then ceased, for in 1873, the *Landowners Return, 1873* gives 'Eleanor Thomas of Cilrhyg' as owner of 81 acres yielding £64 p.a.

Grid Ref: SN 6093 5912

Refs: Dwnn, i, 28, 241; Protheroe MS. (Long Book), fo. 67; CRO, GGMS, I (Tydwal Gloff); III (Gwaethfoed); NLW, Deri Ormond Deeds, No. 196; Coleman Deeds, No. 164; *Ceredigion,* v, 1966, p. 267; WWHR, iii, 100; Landowners Return, 1873.

CILYGWYDDYL, Llanllwchaearn

There is a Cefn Gwyddel in Llanllwchaearn, half a mile north of Cross Inn on the A486 to New Quay.

Ieuan's son, David of Cilygwyddyl had a son, David du, whose son David had a daughter Janet. She married David Gwyn of Mynachdy in Llanbadarn Trefeglwys.

Their pedigree was recorded by Dwnn as descending from Gruffydd of Mynachty. Dates are lacking.

Grid Ref: SN 3887 5768

Ref: Dwnn, i, 31.

COEDLANNAU-FAWR, Llanwenog

Now a farmhouse in the north-west part of the parish near the lands of Castell Hywel, west of Cwrtnewydd and shown on *Colby's Map of 1831* as Coed lana Fawr and -Fach. On modern OS maps the place-name Coedlannau is printed between two large farms.

The home of the ancient family of Lloyd of Coedlannau. Richard Lloyd married Hester and had two sons, David and John, but he died whilst they were still minors.

His will, dated 1729, proved in 1730 tells us: 'my wife Hester, my eldest son David Lloyd, second son John Lloyd, my brother-in-law Thomas Richard and his daughters Lettice and Mary Richard, my godson Richard Davies son of my cousin William Davies of Maesmoy, my brother-in-law Jenkin Jones'.

Richard Lloyd had two sons; David Lloyd became the Presbyterian minister of Llwynrhydowen, and was known as a poet. He married twice: firstly Jane, daughter of Jenkin Jones, who was his cousin, on 5 August 1752 and had a daughter, Jane, who married Thomas Thomas of Llanfair. He married secondly Letitia, who on her mother's side came from Lloyd of Ffosybleiddiad and on her father's side from Castell Hywel. John Lloyd, the younger son, succeeded to Coedlannau, but never married.

Letitia died in January 1812. The son, Richard, was the heir. He became a Unitarian minister of Heol Awst, Carmarthenshire and succeeded to Coedlannau upon his uncle's death. Richard died on 27 September 1727. In his will, dated 2 June 1727, he left a horse to his mother, half of Coedlannau to his brother, John, and the other half (charged with £100 for his sister, Margaret), to his brother, Charles, who also had the Coedlannau farmhouse. The second son John, was a schoolmaster who married Ann, daughter of the Rev. D. Davies, vicar of Bangor (he died in 1842). Their son, the Rev. David Lloyd MA, LLD, was a prominent Unitarian. Charles Lloyd (1766-1829), the third son, was also a Unitarian minister and a notable scholar. His biography, *Particulars of the Life of a Dissenting Minister* was published in 1813. He lived at Coedlannau from 1800-1.

G. Eyre Evans tells us in *Cardiganshire*: 'On the inner walls of Llanwenog church is painted a large coat of arms, with scroll, of the ancient family of Lloyd of Coedlannau; the name of one "Charles Lloyd, gent." with that of Bowen being likewise now visible. They were church-wardens when the mural painting was executed: a marble tablet to the Rev. Charles Lloyd, LLD, of Coedallannau Fawr, a remarkable man, first minister of the Unitarian chapel, Capel y Groes; he was third son of the Rev. David Lloyd, Presbyterian minister of Brynllevrith where he was born on 18 December 1766. Charles became a Presbyterian minister and was buried at Lampeter. He was married twice, firstly to Ann Knight of Pulborough, Sussex (died 23 May 1829), and had 8 children, and secondly to Sara Maria Smith by whom he had a son, Francis Vaughan Lloyd (born 1811).

[Francis Jones noted here that the Charles Lloyd entry in *DNB* has inaccuracies .]

Charles Lloyd, gent., third son of the Rev. D. Lloyd, succeeded to Coedlannau. In 1861, Elias Jones owned Coedlannau. He died on 25 May 1861, aged 49, and was the first to be buried at the church of St Joan, built 1853-5 on Pontysgawen land at Dyffryn Cletwr-fach.

Grid Ref: SN 4671 4810

Refs: G. Eyre Evans, *Cardiganshire,* 1903, 54-5; G. Eyre Evans, *Lloyd Letters*, 1754-1786, pr. 1908; Lloyd Family Records, p. 59 also pedigrees pp. 13-14; WWHR, iii, 87; Colby Map, 1831; Davies, *Hanes Plwyf Llandysul,* pp. 180, 185-8.

COED-LLYS, Llanilar

Lying two miles south of Llanilar village and marked on *Colby's Map of 1831* and modern OS maps. Cadwgan Llwyd 'o Goed y Llys yn Llan Ilar' signed for Dwnn.

In 1760 the Rev. Albany Wallis of the Inner Temple owned Coedllys. He was a London solicitor who later bought Peterwell. He died on 3 September 1800, aged 86.

Grid Ref: SN 6220 7369

Refs: Dwnn, i, 22; Colby Map, 1831; WWHR, iii, 95.

COED-MAWR, site unknown

Samuel Hughes of Penhill, Carmarthenshire, JP, in 1705, married Elizabeth, daughter and co-heiress of Thomas Lewis of Coedmawr, Cardiganshire.

C. Vaughan Pryse-Rice, in 1900 tells us: 'It is necessary to realise that the Lewis's of Coedmawr were a separate family and owned a separate house called Coedmawr, to the Lloyds of Coedmore, as we learn a certain Captain Thomas Lloyd of Coedmore living in 1693 married Jane, daughter of John Lewis of Coedmawr.'

The pedigree of Coed-mawr is given in the *Bodleian Manuscripts.*

Refs: BL, Bodleian MSS., Add c. 177-9; PRO List.

COEDMOR[E] Llangoedmor

Home of the Mortimers, Lewes's and the Lloyds. Marked as 'lord's demesne' on the 14th century *Rees Map.* 'Coedmore, the seat of Thomas Lloyd, Esq, is a noble mansion, situated on a lofty eminence overlooking the River Teivy, commanding a fine view of Kilgerran Castle . . . contiguous to the seat formerly stood Castel Cevel, the ancient mansion of the lords of Coedmore. The old mansion was down where the garden is, on lower ground than the present house.' *South Wales Squires* gives 'the present house is of comparatively modern erection, for the old mansion stood nearly a mile to the westward; however the fine walled gardens remain on their original site. They contain a picturesque gazebo with a steep roof, which bears the date 1694'. Meyrick writes: 'Coedmore – first owned by the Clermont family – then by the Langleys – then the Mortimers. The Mortimers lived first at the old house called Castell Cevel in Coedmaur. Leland alludes to it as "Coit Mawr Castel, nune Coitmore by Tyve, betwyxt Giltearran and Cardigan, nune vestigia tantum extant. It is yet in the name of a barony to one Mortymer of Cardiganshire".'

Francis Jones wrote in his essays on the Mortimers of Coedmor: There can be little doubt that the name Coedmor is a compliance of Coed Mawr (the great forest), for it is known that this area comprised a large woodland (part of which still remains), stretching from

Cardigan so far as Llechryd and possibly beyond.

The first known holders of Coedmor were the Mortimers. Roger de Mortimer, described in records as 'of West Wales', received part of Genau'r glyn in north Cardiganshire after the Welsh War of 1276-77, and he may well have held Coedmor at the same time. In 1280-1 Bogs [sic] de Knovil delivered 50 librates of land in the king's washes in the commote of Genau'r Glyn to Roger de Mortimer and on 27 December 1284 the King granted the said lands to Roger de Mortimer. Roger also held a moiety of the commote of Iscoed. During the war of 1282, Roger de Mortimer and Geoffrey Clermont were centenars of infantry raised in west Wales for service against Llywelyn ap Gruffydd. In January 1283 Roger, who commanded 20 horse and 20 foot, was appointed constable of Llanbadarn Castle. In 1287 Roger and Hugh de Mortimer were among Tibetot's officers serving in the war against Rhys ap Meredydd, and in that year Roger was appointed constable of Newcastle Emlyn. However, in November 1287 Rhys captured the castle, held Mortimer a prisoner and slaughtered his garrison. The date of Roger's death is unknown, but it was probably before 1294. His widow, Nest, was alive in 1300 and receiving dower from her late husband's lands. The ancestry of this Roger de Mortimer is unknown. He is sometimes given by later genealogists as a younger son of Roger de Mortimer of Chirk, and brother of Joan de Mortimer who sold Chirk to Richard Fitzalan, but this is incompatible with the dates and cannot be accepted. He may have been a kinsman of the Chirk family but there is no evidence to establish the relationship.

Coedmore then became the property of Llewelyn Mortimer who married Angharad, daughter of Meredydd ab Rhys, Prince of Cardigan. Their son Roger inherited and he married Gwenllian, daughter of Einon Vaur of the Wood. Their son Edmund married Eva, daughter to Rhys David ap Rhys ap Llewelyn ap Cadwgan of Carag and they had a son Owen Mortimer who married Angharad, daughter of Rhys David Thomas of Gwernan and they in turn had a son, Richard Mortimer who married Elizabeth, daughter of Owen ap Rhys ap Llewelyn ap Owen. Their son John married Rydderch ap Rhys, Lord of Tywin, and their son John who was married to Eva, daughter of Lewis David Meredydd of Abernantbychan. This John Mortimer, Baron of Coedmawr, lived at Castell Cevil in Coedmawr and his daughter whose name is unknown, had a natural daughter named Jane by Sir Rhys ab Thomas, and a natural son by Griffith Vaughan of Corsygedol when Governor of Cilgerran Castle. This son was named Tydyr, and from him is descended Dr. Theodore Price, formerly Principal of Hart Hall, Oxford. John Mortimer had a son, Richard who married Catherine, daughter of Rowland Meyrick, Bishop of Bangor. Their son Rowland married a daughter of James Lewes of Abernantbycan on 20 March 1617 and granted Coedmor to his brother-in-law, Sir John Lewis of Abernantbychan in exchange for the grantee's Carmarthenshire estate of Castle Lloyd, near Laugharne, and a sum of £200. The Lewis family held Coedmore for a further three generations until 25 March 1700. Sir John Lewes (1580-1656), was High Sheriff and married Bridget, daughter of Sir Richard Pryse of Gogerddan, and had a son, James. Colonel James Lewis was High Sheriff of Cardiganshire in 1664, and married Mary Wogan. They had a daughter, Jane, and a son, James Lewes. Jane Lewes married firstly Thomas Lewes of Llysnewydd who died in 1672, and secondly Captain Thomas Lloyd of Gilfachwen, will proved 1679. They had a son and heir John Lloyd of Cilgwyn, will proved 1702 at Carmarthen, whose eldest son, John was of Cilgwyn and the second son Thomas Lloyd was of Coedmor. He had inherited it from Jane's and Thomas's second son, Walter

Lloyd who had bought Coedmor back from the Wade family of Bristol.

In March 1700 John Lewes, who was in financial difficulties, sold Coedmor to Nicholas [or Nathaniel] Wade of Bristol. Eventually, in 1714, Walter Lloyd, son of Jane and Thomas Lloyd and therefore first cousin to John Lewes, acquired Coedmore, part of which he then mortgaged back to the Wades. Walter married Mary daughter of Dr. Bevan of Carmarthen. He was High Sheriff in 1722 and died without issue on 24 October 1722.

The Lloyds established a tin works at Llechryd called Coedmor Forge. Thomas Lloyd, born about 1696, younger son of John Lloyd of Cilgwyn succeeded to Coedmor. Not a great deal is known about him. He was party to the marriage settlement of his sister Jane in 1725, and in 1727 gave a release to his elder brother John of Cilgwyn, for a legacy of £100. He married, pre-nuptial settlement dated 14 May 1725, Mary daughter of Morgan Howell of Gwernmaccwy, and co-heiress of her brother Oliver Howell of Mountain Hall, Llangeler.

Thomas Lloyd died on 12 April 1737, and his will dated 8 January 1736-7 was proved on 30 May 1737. His widow remarried, before 1741, to John Lloyd of Cardigan, gentleman, a younger brother of Thomas Lloyd of Bronwydd. He had five children, all minors in 1741: Walter Lloyd, aged 14 in 1741, see later. John Lloyd, to whom his father bequeathed £100. He lived in Cardigan town, and was there in 1760 when he gave his elder brother a receipt for legacies due under their father's will. James Lloyd, to whom his father bequeathed £100, died under 16 years of age. William Lloyd, to whom his father bequeathed £100 on, died shortly after becoming 16 years of age. Their daughter, Jane, to whom her father bequeathed £300; she was under 18 in 1737, never married, and was living in Cardigan town in 1780, when her brother Walter settled an annuity of £30 on her for life, charged on Blaenwnnen farm in Llangoedmore parish.

Walter Lloyd married, in Dublin, Anna Posthuma younger daughter and co-heiress of a Carmarthenshire landowner, William Thomas of Pentowin (he died in 1740) in Mydrim parish, and his wife Anne daughter of Rice Thomas of Castell Gorfod, barrister-at-law. She was born in 1740 after her father's death, hence one of her Christian names. The elder daughter and co-heiress, Hesther (or Easter) Thomas, married in 1758, George Bowen of Llwyngwair and had issue. Anne, mother of these girls, married again, to John Morgan of Cardigan. The sisters were fortunate, for their maternal uncle, William Thomas of Castell Gorfod, left his valuable estate between them.

No clue has been found to explain why the marriage took place in Dublin. The circumstances suggest an elopement. In order to put the matter beyond all doubt, the bridegroom procured affidavits, afterwards carefully preserved with the family muniments. Thus, one sworn on 2 June 1760 before John Tew, Lord Mayor of the city of Dublin, by William Beeby of St. Mark's parish, Dublin, Thomas Lloyd 'late of Cardigan town, but now and for some months, past, of the parish of St. Andrews, Dublin, gentleman', and John Morris servant to Walter Lloyd of Cardigan town, esquire, affirmed jointly, that they were together in a room in St. Peter's parish, Dublin, between 4 and 5 p.m. on 29 October 1759, where they saw Walter Lloyd being married to Anna Posthuma Thomas late of Cardigan town, spinster, according to the form and ceremonies of the Church of England, by the Rev. Chaworth Chambre, curate of St. Andrew's church, Dublin, and that the enclosed paper was written by him. The enclosure read – 'Dublin May 31st 1760. I hereby certify that on Monday October 29th 1759 Walter Lloyd and Anna Posthuma Thomas were joined together in the holy state of matrimony according to the Laws and Statutes of this Kingdom, by me, Chaworth Chambre.' Three post-nuptial settlements were executed – on 19 August 1760, 13 March 1762, and 27 November 1766. In the first, Walter, described as of the town of Cardigan, settled the Coedmor estate to the uses of the marriage, and any children; his wife's portion was £1,600; her dower in case of widowhood to be £150 a year; with power to raise £1,200 for younger children.

Walter Lloyd was a Justice of the Peace, and served as High Sheriff of Cardiganshire in 1761. His will and codicil were dated 3 December 1783 and 18 December 1785, and he died about 1786-88. His widow remarried in 1789, to one

Joseph Mills, and was again a widow by 1805. She died on 22 July 1814, having made her will on 9 October 1810.

Walter and Anna Posthuma Lloyd had the following four children: Thomas Lloyd, baptised at St. Mary's Cardigan on 16 September 1760 – see later. Anna Maria, baptised at St. Mary's Cardigan on 27 December 1762; she was living, unmarried, at Fishguard in 1815. Elizabeth, baptised at St. Mary's Cardigan, on 27 December 1762 (probably a twin with her sister); she married the Rev. John Williams, Wesleyan Methodist minister, described in the pre-nuptial settlement, dated 12 January 1811, as late of Denbigh but now of Tirllwyd in Llangoedmor parish. He was living at Holyhead in 1816, and at Spring Gardens, Carmarthen in 1832. Lastly, Easter Lloyd, unmarried and living in 1783.

Thomas Lloyd of Coedmor was a magistrate, and in 1798 High Sheriff of Cardiganshire. It was he who inherited one-third of the Cilgwyn estate from his kinsman Captain Thomas Lloyd. On 30 April 1790 he bought the farm of Forest near Cilgerran, from John Symmons of Slebech, for £3,000. He died on 21 September 1810, aged 51. His will, dated 15 February 1804 was proved in PCC on 19 June 1811.

His wife was an Englishwoman, and this was the first time that any member of the family had married a person of non-Welsh antecedents. She was Elizabeth, fourth daughter of Edmund Probyn of Newland in Gloucestershire, by Sophia daughter of Richard Dalton of Knaith in Lincolnshire. The marriage took place in 1791, the pre-nuptial settlement being dated 13 August of that year. After her husband's death, she lived at various places – at Plâs Bridell in 1824, Cardigan in 1839, and at Richmond where she died in her 83rd year in November 1852, having been a widow for some 42 years. She was buried at Petersham. They had the following six children:

Thomas Lloyd of Coedmor, born 1 November 1793 – see later. Oliver Lloyd born 16 July 1801, married in 1828 Anna Maria daughter and sole heiress of Captain James Richard Lewes Lloyd of Dolhaidd in Carmarthenshire. She died in 1830. Oliver Lloyd who lived at Dolhaidd, died in London in 1840, leaving two daughters: 1. Maria who married on 28 October 1851 Lieut. Thomas Elliott of the 77th Foot, who settled at Dolhaidd, and had issue; and 2. Emmeline, born 7 January 1830, who married William Owen Brigstocke of Gellydywyll and Blaen-pant, and had issue.

The third son was Walter Lloyd, a Lieutenant in the Royal Navy; on 28 August 1820, Walter and a companion sailed from Aberystwyth in an open boat for Cardigan, and about eight of the clock in the evening, when off Aberystwyth, a tremendous squall of wind arose, the boat sank and both men were drowned. The fourth son, Francis Edmund Lloyd, born 18 February 1807; he went to sea, and died of fever aboard *HMS Blood.* Their two daughters were; Sophia, born 2 May 1792, lived at Bridell, executrix of her mother; her own will was dated 4 April 1860, and Anna, born 19 February 1797, married on 28 November 1822, John Probyn of the Manor House, Longhope, Gloucestershire, and had issue. Her marriage portion consisted of £1,000 under the parents' marriage settlement, and £300 under her grandmother's will.

The eldest son, Thomas Lloyd succeeded to Coedmor. In his younger days he was a noted athlete, and one of his exploits was long remembered in the district, for more than one reason. In the summer of 1825, he challenged Mr. Lucas, a solicitor practising in Cardigan, and considered to be one of the best runners in Wales, to a foot-race from Cardigan across the Prescelli hills to Haverfordwest, for a wager of £50. The distance to be covered was about 30 miles, and Mr. Lloyd was to have one mile start, each runner to be accompanied by a mounted servant of the other to see that the rules were observed. The race started at 7 o'clock in the morning, and Mr. Lloyd won handsomely, reaching Haverfordwest an hour before his rival. As soon as the news reached the Cardigan district, where Lloyd was particularly popular, the people went wild with joy – bonfires, deep potations, and bell-ringing to celebrate Coedmor's victory. So energetically did the men of Cilgerran set to work, that the church bells were smashed beyond repair. Afterwards a move was made to bring the muscular campanologists before the Court of Arches, but this was dropped, and finally Anthony Abel Gower of Glandovan sent the bells to Bristol where they were recast and rendered fit for further service in less exuberant hands.

Thomas Lloyd became a prominent public figure; a Justice of the Peace and Deputy Lieutenant, and in 1816, when only twenty-three years of age, served as High Sheriff, and in 1854 was appointed Lord Lieutenant and Custos Rotulorum of Cardiganshire. His Lieutenancy was of short duration for he died at Coedmor on 12 July 1807 in his 64th year. His will, dated 14 May 1850 was proved in PCC on 24 October 1857, the personalty sworn under £20,000. Thomas Lloyd's wife, Charlotte Longcroft was heiress of a moiety of the Llanina estate. She was born in Haverfordwest in 1799, and on 23 March 1819 married Thomas Lloyd at St. Mary's church in that town. She died on 5 May 1866. By their pre-nuptial settlement, made on the day of the wedding, the Coedmore estate was settled to the uses of the marriage, and included manors and lordships of Iscoed Isherwen, and Coedmor otherwise Iscoed Coedmor otherwise Iscoed Mortimer, the capital messuage and demesne of Coedmor, and 33 properties, all in Llangoedmor parish, the fishing weir, called Coedmor Weir, and the right of fishing in the Teifi belonging to the manor of Iscoed Isherwen.

Thomas Lloyd and Charlotte (Longcroft) his wife had four sons: The heir, Thomas Edward Lloyd, born 12 April 1820, educated at Rugby, admitted 19 January 1839 to the Middle Temple was 'called' on 8 November 1844, and practised at the Chancery bar. He sat as Member of Parliament for Cardiganshire for the years 1874-80, and was a Justice of the Peace. Among his friends was the statesman, Disraeli. He died on 23 September 1909, and was buried at Llangoedmor. His will dated 6 February 1909, was proved on 14 December, the gross value of his estate amounting to £179,836 2s. 5d. He married twice; firstly on 27 April 1850 at St. Clement Danes church, Clemena Frances Phillott second daughter of the Rev. David Daniel of Jesus College, Oxford, chaplain at Hampton Court, son of John Daniel of Cwrt Mawr, Cardiganshire, and she died in March 1882; and secondly, on 27 August 1885 at St. Thomas church, Portland Square, Eliza Mary daughter of the Rev. George Bennett, rector of Bede, Suffolk, sister of Sir Ernest Bennett, MP, She survived her husband and died on 30 December 1947, at the advanced age of 90. Thomas Lloyd left an only child (by his first wife), Edith, born on 10 April 1856, who married her father's groom one Albert Camillus Coghlan. Albert died in March 1898, and his wife on 23 February 1908 aged 52, without issue.

The second son, Edmund Lloyd, born 29 January 1822, became a solicitor. On 5 April 1864 he was appointed Treasurer of the county of Cardigan, being then living at Aberaeron. By his wife Fanny (daughter of William Andrus), he had eleven children, namely: Thomas the heir, Charlotte Sophia, Edmund George Rowley, he had three children, William Thomas, Robert, and Emmeline, Charles Edward, Walter Henry, Gertrude, Emmeline, Alice Maria, William Oliver, Camilla Grace ('Milly'), Jessie Kate, twin with 'Milly'.

The third son was Walter Lloyd, born 7 December 1822. The youngest son, Charles Oliver Lloyd, born 9 June 1825, entered the Royal Navy as a Volunteer (First Class), and in 1840 when serving on board *HMS Daphne* fell from aloft and was killed; he was buried at Smyrna where a tombstone commemorates him.

Walter Lloyd, third son of Thomas and Charlotte Lloyd of Coedmor, born at Coedmor on 7 December 1823, entered on a military career, and became a captain in the 11th Regiment, Madras NI, Indian Army. He eventually returned to Wales, was appointed a Justice of the Peace, and lived for a time at Glyntaf, in Carmarthenshire. About 1858-9 he emigrated and settled at Deepdene, Richmond, in the South African province of Natal. He sat as a member in the Cape parliament, and died on 17 September 1879, at Carlton House, Berla, Durban. His will was made on 16 March 1871 as of Alexandra Road, St. John's Wood, when on a visit to England, and a codicil added on 15 September 1878. He married on 18 June 1856 at St. Paul's church, Durban, Marion Fanny Grice of Durban. He had eleven children, namely: Walter Lloyd, the heir – see later. Edward Charles Oliver Lloyd of Natal. Lewis Howard Lloyd – see later. Llewellin who left two children. Louisa Florence, Agnes Marion, Mabel who married Judge Robinson of Salisbury, Southern Rhodesia, by whom she had a son, Sir Victor Robinson, attorney-general of Southern Rhodesia, and chairman of the Rhodesian Constitutional Council. Helen who died unmarried before 1871. Catherine, Alice Gertrude and the eleventh child Amy Georgina.

Walter Lloyd (eldest son of Walter and Marion Lloyd) of Natal married Louise Thompson, by whom he had a son Walter John ('Jack') Lloyd of Natal. W. J. Lloyd married Euphemia Craig (who married secondly C. S. Richards), by whom he had a son Ian Stewart Lloyd.

Ian Stewart Lloyd, born on 30 May 1921, was educated at Michaeltower, the University of Witwatersrand, and King's College, Cambridge, and Administrative Staff College, Henley. He became President of the Cambridge Union, and leader of the Cambridge tour of the USA in 1947. He graduated BA, proceeded MA, in 1951, and MSc in 1952. He was Economics Adviser to the Central Mining and Investment Corporation in 1949-52, Member of the South African Board of Trade and Industries 1952-55, Director of Acton Society Trust in 1956, Chairman of the United Kingdom Committee. He has been Economic Adviser to British and Commonwealth Shipping since 1956, and Director of Research from 1956 to 1964. In 1964, and again in 1970, he was elected Member of Parliament (Conservative) for the Langstone Division of Portsmouth, and in 1974 for the Havant and Waterloo Division. In 1951 Ian Stewart Lloyd married Frances Dorward Addison daughter of the Hon. W. Addison, CMG, OBE, MC, DCM, by whom he had three sons: 1. Jonathan Stewart Lloyd, Grenadier Guards; 2. Mark William Lloyd; 3. Peregrine Murray Addison Lloyd.

We now turn to Lewis Howard Lloyd, younger son of Walter and Marion Lloyd. He lived at Durban, Natal, and married Charlotte Winifred Gladys Treffry-Goatley of Goatley Lees, Isle of Thanet. He was a Justice of the Peace and a Deputy Lieutenant.

He died at Durban on 7 January 1930 and his will (dated 28 February 1927) was proved on 30 July of that year. His estate was valued at £31,177 12s. 0d. L. H. Lloyd left five children:

1. Edward Howard Lloyd born at Durban on 13 February 1913, in due course inherited the Coedmor estate, and came to live at the mansion on the death of Mrs. T. E. Lloyd in 1947. Educated at Cheltenham College, he served in the Pembrokeshire Yeomanry, and became captain during the Second World War. He was for some time a member of Cardiganshire County Council, and Master of the Tivyside Foxhounds. He married Ella Marjorie Ninon, daughter of J. H. Phillips of Newport, Monmouthshire. Captain Lloyd died on 4 December 1966, and was buried with his ancestors at Llangoedmor. He left two children: 1. Edward David Mortimer Lloyd, born 15 May 1940, educated at Cheltenham College, and of Coedmor; 2. Pamela Mary, born 6 January 1936, married Mr. Smith of the USA, and has issue.

2. Dudley Walter Lloyd of Hafodwen, Llechryd, born in Durban, educated at Hilton College, South Africa and the University of London (BA), a writer, died unmarried in December 1971.

3. Thomas Howard Lewis Lloyd, born at Coedmor, and later of St. Dogmaels.

4. Helen Gladys, born in Durban, assistant matron in a hospital at Pretoria, South Africa. She married, firstly, Mr. Da Silva of Portugal (div) by whom she had two daughters, and secondly Mr. Brown, by whom she had a son.

5. Gloria Clare, born at Aberystwyth, married Anthony Eldridge by whom she had three daughters, Rowena, Sandra, and Mary.

In the foregoing pages we have followed the trail of an ancient family from the banks of the Severn and the Wye to the fertile land that flank the waters of the Teifi, passing through some eight hundred and fifty years of time. The family of Lloyd illustrate the remarkable power of endurance of the *uchelwyr,* their resilience and tenacity, and their ability not only, in many instances to retain the lands patiently acquired by their forebears, but their capacity as leaders of the community in which they lived. The history of the Lloyds is the history of the survival of the old Welsh tradition.

The Tivyside Photographic Souvenir, Pen y Lan has a photograph of Coedmor, 1871, which shows a large L-shaped 2 storeyed building. In 1873 the *Landowners Return* gives the estate to be very substantial, at 1,519 acres and £1,046 p.a.

In 1983 the house was still owned by a Lloyd, one David Lloyd, a descendent of Thomas and Jane Lloyd of Coedmor.

Refs: NLW, Griffith Owen List (iv); Blome List, 1673; *Dwnn,* i. 34-5; Burke, *LG,* 1850; Lewis, *TDW,* 1840; CRO, Plas Llanstephan Ord., p. 82, Deeds Nos. 262-3; H. M. Vaughan, *South Wales Squires,* 1926, p. 100; *Pembs.* IV, 495, fo. 18; CRO, GGMS, III (Edwinsford), fo. 4-5; Meyrick, *Cardiganshire,* 1810, p. 182; Landowners Return, 1873; Francis Jones 'Lloyd of Gilfachwen, Cilgwyn and Coedmore' (abridged), *Ceredigion* (1976).

COEDMOR, Henfynyw

Near Ffos-y-ffin, south of Henfynyw church but is not marked on *Colby's Map of 1831* or on modern OS maps. The home of Philip Pugh and his wife, Ann, daughter of Dafydd Jones of Coedmor and half-sister to Peregrine Musgrave, a prominent Quaker from Haverfordwest. They were the parents of the Rev. Philip Pugh (1679-1760) who built Llwynpiod chapel at his own expense.

Ref: Francis Jones Archives.

COEDMOR, Llanddewibrefi

Coedmor Uchaf and Isaf, marked on *Colby's Map of 1831* as west of Betws Leucu and near the border with Llanddewibrefi parish. Shown on modern OS maps as half a mile east of B4578 (Sarn Helen).

Jenkin Jones, son of John ap John Llewellyn of Caron and his wife Angharad, daughter of Ieuan Thomas and Maud, daughter of David Bowen David Powell of Olmarch (to Gwaethfoed) descended from the Clements, Lords of Caron, married Margaret, daughter of David ap Rees ap Lewis of Glyn Aeron. In 1679-80 the *NLW Bronwydd Deeds* give the entry '1. Feb 4th. Jenkin Jones of Coed Mawr, gt. and Llewelyn Pughe, clerk of Henfynyw. Thomas Lloyd of Bronwydd, Esq. Bond in £5,000 to perform covenants in indenture of even date'.

Jenkin and Margaret had three sons, John, David and Walter. John Jones was '*subpromus* Dni Regum Caroli, 2nd, Jacobi 2o and William III'.

Grid Ref: SN 6310 5785

Refs: CRO, GGMS, III (Gwaethfoed); Colby Map, 1831; NLW, Bronwydd Deeds, No. 666.

COED-Y-FOEL, Llandysul

A farmhouse named Coedfoel Uchaf on modern OS maps on high ground 1¾ miles north-north-east of Llandysul, half a mile south-east of Prengwyn, and marked on *Colby's Map of 1831*.

According to the *Golden Grove Manuscripts* Thomas Lloyd of Coed-y-foel, second son of Ievan ap David Foel of Gelliladron, Llanllwni (Carmarthenshire) descended from Tewdwr Mawr. 'Thomas Lloyd had a daughter Eleri, who married William ap Ievan ap Thomas ap Saer y Cwm of Gwain y Meirch in Llangeler (Carmarthenshire) and their daughter Lleucu married Richard Llwyd of Penlan in Llangeler.'

Other owners were Ievan ap Henry, Ievan ab Ieuvan alias Coch yr Aur, who married Jane, daughter of David Thomas of Gellifaharen and David Henry who married Gwenllian daughter of Thomas Lloyd of Ffosesgob of the Alltyrodyn family.

In 1841, David Charles was the owner and occupier of Coedfoel, farming 87 acres 1 rood 9 perches, but by 1873 the *Landowners Return, 1873,* gives Coed-y-foel owned by the same or another David Charles with 130 acres paying £81 p.a.

Some fragmentary pedigrees are given for this house but are undated.

Grid Ref: SN 4297 4355

Refs: Colby Map, 1831; PRO, Dale Castle MSS., p. 30 (113) & p. 29; WWHR, i, 50, 51-2, & 1, 18; CRO, GGMS, I (Gwynfardd); Landowners Return, 1873; CRO, Golden Grove MSS., II Adv. Cardiganshire.

COED-Y-PARC, Betws Bledrws
There is a Coed-y-Parc in the parish of Betws Bledrws, south-west of the church and south of the main road to Lampeter marked on *Colby's Map of 1831*. The house is located but not named on modern OS maps.

In his will dated 31 August 1667 and proved in Carmarthen in 1669, Sir Francis Lloyd of Maesyfelin left to his wife, Lady Mary Lloyd (daughter of the Earl of Carbery) the capital mansion called Coed y Parke, and other property for her life.

Blome's List 1673 gives Lodowick Lewis of Code y Park, gt., although the dates are missing. In the 18th century the house was also owned at some time by the Jones family; David Jones and his daughter, Anne, who married Edward Lloyd, son of John Lloyd of Brynog by his wife, Anne Pugh.

Grid Ref: SN 5937 5170

Refs: WWHR, i, 10, n. 3; Colby Map, 1831; CRO, GGMS, III (Gwaethfoed), p. 30; Blome List, 1673.

COEDYPERTHI, Betws Ifan
Situated south-east of Betws Ifan church and shown on *Colby's Map of 1831* as Coed Perthe, and to the east of the road from Brongest to Betws Ifan on modern OS maps.

The house formed part of the Abernant-bychan estate in 1650, and was tenanted by Lleuen Thomas and Thomas David. It was among the properties mortgaged by John Lewis of Coedmore, Esq. on 12 July 1682 (taxed at 3 hearths) to John Matthew of Lodington, Southampton, Esq. The mortgage remained for many years and was assigned several times to different persons. Finally on 27 June 1734, the messuage and land called Penybanc, otherwise called Coed Perthy Issa in Troed-yr-aur parish, was released to John Morgan of Cardigan Esq. In 1702, the farm was in the tenure of Thomas Harry at rent of £3 p.a. John Morgan later released it to Abel Griffith. In 1755, Abel Griffith made his will as of Coedyperthy, but later he was of Llwyn-y-brain (Carmarthenshire). His kinsman, James Griffith, gent., lived at Coedyperthi in 1759.

Grid Ref: SN 3107 4725

Refs: CRO, Aberglasney Deeds, p. 50; Colby Map, 1831.

CREUDDYN, Llanfihangel-y-Creuddyn
Creuddyn was an ancient commote of North Cardiganshire.

Rees Llewelyn, descended from Rhys ap Robert (to Gwynfardd Dyfed) married Efa (or Margaret) daughter of Rhys ap Adda Fychan of Creuddyn in Cardganshire. Adda Fychan was the progenitor of the Vaughans of Crosswood (Trawsgoed), who moved there early in the 14th century following his marriage to Tudo, heiress of Crosswood.

Astonishingly, according to *CRO, GGMS (Gwynfardd),* their son Jenkin paid Hearth Tax on 140 hearths of his mother's estate in Creuddyn. He married a daughter of Rees Goch of Creuddyn and their son David married a daughter of David Lloyd David Prytherch (to Gwaethfoed). The family flourished but little is known of whether they remained at Creuddyn or whether Creuddyn was ever a residence or merely the name of the commote and parish. It is not identified on OS maps.

Refs: CRO, GGMS (Gwynfardd).

CROSSWOOD, see TRAWSGOED

CRUGBYCHAN, Ferwig
The house stands overlooking the sea and is an old farmhouse to the north of Ferwig, four miles from Cardigan; marked on *Colby's Map of 1831* as Crug and on modern OS maps as Crug Farm. Francis Jones noted that it was much modernised when he visited it in 1965.

The medieval family was descended from Rhys of Crugbychan, Lord of Caerwedros. He was succeeded by his son, Ievan and then Rhys and Phillip. Phillip's daughter and heiress, Elen, married Philip ap Thomas, a grandson of Rhys ap Meredudd, Lord of Tywyn (to Gwynfardd). Owain ap Rhys Phillip signed for Dwnn on 24 January 1588. He married Elen, daughter of David Lloyd Griffith ap Rhys ap Gwernan (to Elystan). Elen's mother was Janet, daughter of Sir Thomas Philipps of Picton. Their son Nicholas took the name Bowen and, according to the *Griffith Owen Deeds* he married Elizabeth, the daughter and heiress of Owen ap Rees of Kilrhyiwe (Cilrhiwe), Pembrokeshire, but Dwnn states that he married Elizabeth, daughter and heiress of Owen ap Phillip of Llanfihangel Penbedw.

Nicholas Bowen had a son and heir, George and three daughters. George married Elizabeth, the daughter of George Philipps of Cardigan. One of the daughters, Elinor, married Edward Lloyd of Frood (Ffrwd) of Carmarthenshire. The names of the other daughters are not given. George and Elizabeth were living at Crugbychan in 1620.

By 1643, George Bowen's son, John, had succeeded and was married twice. Firstly to Fortuna Prynallt (ap Rheinallt), daughter and heiress of Hugh Prynallt of Morfa Bychan of Llanychaearn parish, and secondly, to the daughter of Thomas Pryse of Glanfrêd, Llanfihangel Geneau'r-glyn. John Bowen had one brother and five sisters. His brother, Hugh remained a bachelor, his sister Elen married Owen Bowen of Ferwig; Lettice married Nicholas Owen, vicar of Aber-porth and Mary married Thomas Morgan of Ferwig. Anne was married twice; firstly to John Williams of Ffoslas, Carmarthenshire, and secondly to Richard Lewys of Trefynys.

It would appear that the Bowens then lived at Morfa Bychan as *Griffith Owen Deeds* state that 'on 6 Feb 1653, John Bowen of Morva Bychan, gt., mortgaged to Robert Lloyd of Cardigan, gt., the capital messuage called Krigbuchan and a close or park adjoining called Park yr hendy in the parish of Verwig in £250'.

John and Fortuna had four sons and two daughters. George, who succeeded, Hugh, who was 'with the Duke of Abermarle', Nicholas, Charles, Mary, and Fortuna who married Owen Jones, son of Thomas John ap Edward of Nanteos. George Bowen married Elizabeth, daughter of Hugh Lloyd of Lloyd Jack. After his death she married John Lloyd of Nantgowry.

Deeds dated 1680 show '1. Elinor Lloyd, widow (of John Bowen and John Lloyd) relict and administratrix of Robert Lloyd, late of Cardigan, gt., deceased, and 2. Hywel Davies of Laugharne, Carms., and Elizabeth uxor, only daughter and heiress of said Robert and Elinor Lloyd. Quit claim of the capital messuage and land called Krigbuchan and messuages called Kriglas, Park yr Hendy, all in the parish of Verwig and formerly mortgaged by John Bowen, gt., to said Robert Lloyd.' In 1682 John Bowen of Morfa Bychan married Margaret Lloyd, daughter of John Lloyd of Cilgwyn. The service was conducted by the Rev. Charles Bowen [probably his uncle]. The Bowens had ceased to live at Crugbychan by the early 18th century.

The *Griffith Owen List* tells us that, 'in 1757 Anne Tindall of Carmarthen, widow, gave a lease for lives to Roger Rees of the parish of Verwick, yeoman, of a messuage and land called Crig, otherwise Crigbuchan in the parish of Verwig'. At this time, Meyrick states, 'This is now simply a farmhouse; and such is its condition today with no features surviving to indicate its former status.' A figure and plan of the house can be seen in *Carmarthen Studies 1974*.

Grid Ref: SN 1789 1513

Refs: Colby Map, 1831; NLW, Griffith Owen List, iv, Griffith Owen colln; *Dwnn,* i, 62; WWHR, i, 32-3, 56; ibid, iii; PRO, Dale Castle MS., p. 25 (98), 31; *Carmarthen Studies,* 1974, pp. 67, 92; NLW, Morgan Richardson Deeds, i, 153; CRO, GGMS I (Gwynfardd); ibid, II (Ideo), fo. 8; Protheroe MS., ii, fo. 90.

CRUGMOR, Llangoedmor

Located two miles north-east of Cardigan town, south of the A487 (T) below a hill mentioned in the Mabinogion and where in the 18th century tradition tells of Siôn Philip who was unjustly hanged after being falsely accused of stealing a black ram, the property of the notorious Herbert Lloyd of Peterwell who coveted his land. Marked on *Colby's Map of 1831* as Crugmawr . . . also known as Krigmore.

The home of the family of Owain ap Rhys Lloyd (to Rhys Chwith, thence to Ceredig, Lord of Ceredigion), who signed for Dwnn in 1591. Owain ap Rhys Lloyd married Lleucu, daughter of Owen ap Rhys ap y Bedo. They had seven children, John, Morgan, Rhys, Thomas, William, Nicholas and Catherine. John ap Owen, eldest son, married Alice, daughter of John Garnons of Herefordshire, and they had a son Thomas.

The *Guide to Cardigan and District* states: 'the farm below the hill on its south side, called Crugmawr Farm, formerly the residence of a distinguished family named Turnor.'

The *Noyadd Drefawr Deeds* in 1535-6 give: '1. Hangharott verch Meredyth glyn of Cardigan.

2. John Mortimer. Quit claim of two messuages in town of Cardigan and five acres called Cregevawr' Further, the *NLW, Cwrtmawr Deeds* state 'On 21st June 1671, between: Thomas Knolles of Crugmore, gt. and 2. Thomas Powell of Llechwedd dyris Esq. and Walter Pryse of Tynoheer, Montgomeryshire, gt. Articles of agreement re a marriage to be solemnised between the said Thomas Knolles, and Alice Lloyd of Ynysheer, Cards.; and also a marriage between John Knolles son and heir apparent of said Thomas Knolles., and Dorothy Lloyd, one of the daughters of Thomas Lloyd deceased and the said Alice. The property to be settled includes the capital messuage called Crigmore, and messuage called Tir y Court, and cottage, several parcels adjoining called Tir y barthen, and a close called Tir y barthen, in ph. Llangoedmore; a capital messuage called Killerkin, a messuage called Tythyn Troed yr Rhiw and parcels called Killvach Eynon and Parke y Keven in ph. Manerdyvy, Pembs., and 3 messuages including one called Trekoone in ph. St. Dogmells, Pembs.'

Thomas Knolles of Crugmore married Alice Lloyd, widow of Thomas Lloyd of Ynyshir. Thomas was assessed at 2 hearths in 1672. Their son John, described as of Ynys-hir, married the daughter of Thomas and Alice Lloyd in 1680. Thus, Thomas Knolles was step-father and father-in-law of the bride, and Alice was step-mother and mother-in-law of the bridegroom and the bride and groom were step-brother and step-sister.

Before 1690, Thomas Lewes of Crygmore had married Bridget Lewes, daughter of Col. James Lewes of Coedmor. Thomas Lewes's will was proved on 12 February 1690 by his widow, and all his estates in Cardiganshire were divided between his two daughters, one of whom died unmarried in 1721 and the other, Mary, married Samuel Hughes of Penhill, Carmarthenshire, gent. Samuel Hughes, by now of Crugmore, was a JP in 1705 but his name was ordered to be removed from the Commission of Peace in 1714-15, 'he being dead'.

In 1760, John Turnor, gent., of Crugmor, also owned one third of Trevorgan. According to Meyrick he was, 'probably the father of Capt. John Turnor, RN who was born at Crugmor in about 1760 and died in 1801'.

Grid Ref: SN 2071 4741

Refs: Dwnn, i, 85; Blome List, 1673; WWHR, iii, 78; PRO List; NLW, Cwrtmawr Deeds, No. 1449; NLW, Noyadd Trefawr Deeds, No. 69, EE & W, 4335; *Guide to Cardigan and District,* W. E. James, Cardigan, 1899, p. 51.

CRYNFRYN, Nancwnlle

Marked on *Colby's Map of 1831* as in the north of the parish and located on modern OS maps by the B4576 two miles north of Bwlchllan. A property of great antiquity.

Hanes Llangeitho tells us, "To the north-west of Llangeitho is Crynfryn which was an old dwelling house: the first occupant was Meurig Goch and the next was Dafydd Llwyd Fongam'.

Francis Jones writes, 'On 25 April 1978 my wife and I and Lloyd-Johnes called to see Crynfryn. The old mansion is now ruined and roofless, part of it made into the outhouse. It stood on the side of the farmyard, with a fine prospect from it, very old outhouses and a good deal of timber. A modern commodious farmhouse has been built in the late 19th century about 100 yards away from the old mansion on a knoll. Proprietors are Mr. and Mrs. Murton, farmers. Crynfryn is on top of a hill overlooking the countryside between Pencwch to the north and Bwlchllan to the south, a very remote spot'.

David Lloyd traced to Selyf, King of Dyfed, and Meurig Goch of Cil-y-cwn. He was the first Lloyd of Crynfryn. His father, also David, was Under Sheriff in 1554. The Lloyds of Bronwydd are lineally descended from this family. David Lloyd, descended from Howel ap Rees (to Tydwal Gloff), was married twice; firstly to Margaret, daughter of John Price of Newton, Montgomeryshire and secondly to Margaret, daughter of Hugh Lloyd. David Lloyd was the second of five children. His elder brother, Morgan Lloyd was vicar of Llanboidy, and his younger brother Thomas was rector of Llangynllo. It is from Thomas that the Bronwydd family was descended. David Lloyd's youngest brother was Richard, and his only sister Joan, who was married firstly to Rees David of Glan-y-wern and secondly to John James, 'to ye Cantors'.

David Lloyd and his first wife, Margaret Price had four children – John Lloyd who succeeded and was High Sheriff in 1638, Edward Lloyd of Carmarthenshire who married a daughter of Rowland Williams, vicar of Pen-carreg, Mary who married Thomas Lloyd of Gilfachavel and Margaret who married John Griffith Bevan Trahaearn.

John Lloyd of Crynfryn, was High Sheriff in 1638 and a Royalist. He was, according to the *Cambrian Register,* compounded for £140. 'A Royalist of an even temper, quitted all offices in 1643, compounded for his delinquency, liveth a retired hospitalle life, neither ambitious, nor a contemner of these publique employments that his fortune and capacity do deserve'. In his *Annals and Pedigrees of Lloyds and Edwardes of Crynfryn* John Davies tells us that 'On 6th Oct. 1645 John Lloyd of Crynfryn adhered to the King, but when Parliamentarian forces appeared in Wales he submitted as shown by a Certificate given by Maj. Gen. Laugharne on 10 Nov. 1645. He took the National Covenant and negative oath and declared his submission to Parliament at Cardigan on 6th Oct., 1645. He is seized of a few freehold tenements in Llan-santffraid, a house and garden in Capel Gwynfil and in parishes Llanddewibrefi, and Llangeitho, of yearly value of £18.16.8. He is tenant for life of Crynfryn of yearly value of £10, also of Dôle and a water grist mill in Galltryalangy of £15, also of other small tenets worth £27.14.0. His personal estate is valued at £50. He pays an allowance of £4.6.8 Chief Rent issuing out of the property. This is a true and Just particular of his Estate, which he humbly submits to be fined by this Honourable Commission, having seven Motherless Children and far indebted, which he prays may be taken into consideration at the imposing of his fine'.

Only three of John Lloyd's children are known – David, Catherine, and Isold who married Thomas Jones of Llwyngaru in Caron, son of John Jones and Katherine Stedman and their daughter and heiress, Elizabeth, married Edward Vaughan of Trawsgoed. John Lloyd's son, David Lloyd, High Sheriff in 1662, married Grace Lloyd, the daughter and co-heiress of Capt. Evan Lloyd of Plâs y dyon (Plasduon) in Llanwnnog Montgomeryshire (to Einion ap Seisyllt). When David Lloyd's will was proved in 1660, the Inventory of Goods showed – '4 horses £6. 1 grey horse £5. 11 young horses £10. 1 bull £2.10.0. 5 young bulls £2.10.0. 20 kine £43.13.0. 9 two year old [cattle] £6.15.0. 8 three year old cattle £12. 8 yearlings £3.4.0. 6 calves 12/-. 205 sheep on 6 various farms £30. 37 platters £15. Plate, silver, and furniture £141.0.6. Total £266.6.6'.

In 1672 David Lloyd paid tax on 5 hearths. David and Grace Lloyd had three sons and four daughters:

1. David who succeeded.

2. Walter of Olmarch who married Anne, daughter and co-heiress of John Lloyd of Ystrad Corrwg, Llanawddog and they had two sons and one daughter.

3. Morris, an apothecary in Salop.

4. Elizabeth who married Richard Lloyd of Mabws.

5. Bridgit who married firstly Morgan Lloyd of Rhiwarthen and secondly George Devereux.

6. Anne who married Thomas Johnes of Llanfair Clydogau and Dolaucothi.

7. Mary who married firstly James Lewis of Glasrug and secondly William Lloyd of Rhiw-arthen.

The *Crosswood Deeds* state that 'In 1677, second son Walter Lloyd took out a lease for 30 years from Edward Vaughan of Trawscoed Esq. a corn mill in the parish of Caron, called Full-brook Mill, at £6 p.a., a fat hog at Candlemas and 6 chickens at Michaelmas'.

David Lloyd, who succeeded, was High Sheriff of Cardiganshire in 1694. He was married twice; firstly to Margaret Lloyd, eldest daughter of Samuel Lloyd of Nantymeicked [sic], Montgomeryshire and secondly to Margaret, the daughter of Lewis Owen of Peniarth, Merionydd, relict of Thomas Pryse of Glanfrêd.

The *Annals of Crynfryn* say that from his first marriage, David and Margaret Lloyd had a daughter, Grace, about whom a curious legend was told in the district. 'When Mrs Lloyd was *enciente* of Grace, an astrologer was called in to give information as to the stars under which the child would be born. When the critical time came, he begged the birth should be postponed as the stars were in an alarming conjunction.

Every effort was made to comply, and at last a child forced its way into the world, and given the name Grace. The astrologer said that the situation of the planets was slightly improved, but that Venus was still perilously in the ascendant. He urged that the child from the age of ten should be made a kind of Vestal Virgin, till old enough to be given away in marriage. Every care was taken to isolate her from men-folk. But the heavenly bodies defeated the parents' vigilance, and when about 17 years old she gave birth to a child, named Edward. The family thereupon smothered Grace between two feather beds. Edward was given to the wife of a swineherd who lived at Lluest y Moch to be brought up as their own child.'

When he grew up, Edward contested some of the Lloyd property, especially the wild horses and cattle kept at Rhos-y-cwm some 2 to 3 miles in the direction of the sea, against Mr. Jones an attorney who had bought the Crynfryn property in about 1746, and now lived there. Edward and his son John, aged about 17, having made a raid on the horses, were pursued, and were caught up by Mr. Jones' party as they mounted Rhiw Lluestwen. Shots were exchanged. Edward was killed, but the boy escaped.

From David Lloyd's second marriage there were two sons and a daughter. Little is known of John and Richard Lloyd, but Margaret Lloyd married Thomas Edwardes of Cae Madog and their son John Edwardes was known as Shoni bach, poet of Bryncethin.

Grace Lloyd was married three times: firstly to Thomas Lloyd of Berllandywyll, Carmarthenshire, and had a son, David Lloyd, who died April 1726, secondly, to Bennet Dyer, barrister, of Aberglasney, Carmarthenshire, High Sheriff in 1735, and thirdly, to the Rev. John Williams, vicar of Catherington, Hampshire. They were married before March 1740. Grace died on 10 November 1743 and was buried at Catherington.

John Jones, born on 25 March 1725, bought Crynfryn in 1746 and a new house was built. The *Annals of Crynfryn* state 'The old house came down and another was built by contract. Iantor Moelfryn and Gotto Lluestmoch carried all the stones on a handbarrow from Colbeugroes Quarry'. John Jones was a solicitor of Aberystwyth, the second son of John Jones, the elder of Tyglyn and Plâs Cilcennau and Bridget, daughter of David Parry of Noyadd Trefawr. John Jones the elder lived with his son, John the younger, for a time at Crynfryn before his death in 1756. In the 1760 election John Jones, the younger, acted as agent for John Pugh Pryse, the Whig candidate. Lewis Morris called John Jones, the younger, 'an avaricious, driving attorney'. He married Mary, youngest daughter of Thomas Lewis of Llwyngrawys. They had two sons, John and William, both of whom died unmarried, and five daughters. The family left Crynfryn for Ystrad near Carmarthen but Anna Maria was born at Crynfryn in 1748. She married Thomas Jones and their son John Jones of Ystrad became an MP for Carmarthenshire. Magdalen Jones married John Bateman, Clerk of the Peace of Haverfordwest. Elizabeth was married twice; firstly to Evan Bonville and secondly to D. J. Edwardes of Rhyd-y-gors. Bridget Jones died unmarried and Francis married the Rev. J. Jenkins, vicar of Meidrym, but died without issue.

Grid Ref: SN 5830 6136

Refs: Colby Map, 1831; *Dwnn,* i, 41; WWHR, i, 21-3; Griffith Owen List (iv); Blome List, 1673; Meyrick, Cardiganshire, 256; John Davies, 'Annuls & Pedigrees of the Lloyds and Edwardes of Crynfryn, and other families in the parish of Nantcwnlle'; *Cambrian News,* 1931; NLW, Crosswood Deeds, p. 117; Cambrian Register, I, p. 167; PRO, Dale Castle MS., p. 22 (88); CRO, GGMS, I (Tydwal Gloff), III, David Morgan Collwyn ap Tangno, p. 11; PRO List; *Hanes Llangeitho*, 1859, p. 11.

CRYNGOED, Llanarth

Marked on *Colby's Map of 1831* as just over two miles east of Llanarth village and one mile to the east of Neuadd mansion, on a slope south of the upper reaches of Afon Dryw between Cwm Mawr and Nantyrefail.

The *Protheroe Deeds* tell us that 'Hugh ap Thomas ap Watkin ap Rees Vichan ap Davidh Bevan Bool aur. This David Bevan Bool aur was so named from a golden boul that he got by an exployt in London, for as the report goes there was some noble man that gave the report that he [who] threw the boul furthest should have it, and he was the man; this David Bevan Bool aur lived at a place called of Cryngoed where there is an old castle to be seen to this day'. The above Hugh's male descendent lived at Noyadd Llanarth. According to William Lewes, Llwynderw, Ieuan Bwl aur was 8th in male descent from Madoc Danwr of North Wales.

Grid Ref: SN 4570 5756

Refs: CA, Protheroe MS., c, vi; Colby Map, 1831.

CWMBWA, Llanbadarn Fawr

Home of a family of Lloyd, descended from Gwaethfoed, situated south of Penrhyncoch, near Melin Cwmbwa. Marked on *Colby's Map of 1831.*

Meredydd ap Rhys ap David Llwyd of Cwmbwa (to Gwaethfoed) married Elinor, a daughter of David Llwyd. Their son David married Catherine, the daughter of Richard Powell, who was Sergeant at Arms to Henry VIII. David Llwyd was High Sheriff of Cardiganshire in 1577. His son Meredith, married Mary, daughter of John Watkin of Pen-y-berth. Their son and heir, David married Magdalen, daughter of Watkin Lloyd of Abertrinant, parish of Llanfihangel-y-Creuddyn and had one son, Meredith and three daughters, Catherine, Dorothy and Gwen. Meredith married Elizabeth, daughter of Edward William of Allt Fadog; Catherine married Moog Herbert of Rhiwbren, Llanarth; Dorothy married John Edward of Allt Fadog; and Gwen married David ap Hugh of Dolfor (to Edwin), son of Hugh ap Richard of Abermagwr.

Meredith Lloyd, of Cwmbwa, c. 1656, succeeded his father and had a son David, and a daughter, Magdalen, who married John Hugh of Ty yn Llwyn in Llangwyryfon parish. David Lloyd married Sulen, daughter of Watkin Morgan of Cwmnewidion. They had a son and heir, Meredith. In 1672 Margaret Morgan, widow, was shown as of Cwmbwa and assessed for 4 hearths. Meredith Lloyd, born in 1675, gent., succeeded his father and attended Brasenose College, Oxford. He matriculated in 1695 at the age of 19. He had one sister, Hannah, baptized 22 August 1678 at Llanbadarn Fawr, and one brother, John, baptized 21 February 1679/80 at Llanbadarn Fawr. Meredith Lloyd's daughter, Susannah, married Hugh Griffith (died 1731) of Penbombren, by whom she had 3 sons of whom nothing is known.

The element, Bwa, in the place name Cwm bwa, may refer to Y Bwa Bach (Little Hunchback), whose wife, Morfudd, of fair hair and dark eyebrows, sometimes given the epithet Llwyd, is referred to in thirty *cywyddau* by Dafydd ap Gwilym, the most distinguished Welsh medieval poet, reputedly born at Brogynin, Penrhyncoch, who wooed her even when she became a wife and mother. Ebowa baghan (Bwa Bach) is named in a list of witnesses at Aberystwyth in the Assizes Rolls for 1344. There are several place-names in the vicinity called Madog.

Grid Ref: SN 6505 8375

Refs: Burke, *LG,* 1850; NLW, Cwrtmawr Deeds; Colby Map, 1831; CRO, GGMS, I (Adv. Dem.); CRO, GGMS, III (Gwaethfoed) (Edwin); Letter from David Jenkins CBE, JP, Aberystwyth and *Bro Dafydd ap Gwilym*, 1992..

CWMBERWYN, Tregaron

In the valley of Nant Berwyn, Tregaron, east of Tregaron on the mountain road to Soar-y-Mynydd, sheltered by the mountain of Craig y Fintan and Craig Pantseiri and marked but not named on *Colby's Map of 1831*.

The Rev. D. C. Rees writes in *Tregaron*: 'Home of the Herberts, about 3/4 mile from Tregaron. Now a large sheep farm, on an old site. Under a bedroom window is a stone inscribed C.H. 1690, i.e. Charles Herbert who also farmed Pantysheriff. In Tregaron churchyard there was a tombstone inscribed "Here lieth James Herbert of Pantysheriff who died . . . 1684".'

The house had been modernised and changed by 1900.

Grid Ref: SN 7190 5831

Refs: Colby Map, 1831; The Rev. D. C. Rees, *Tregaron,* 1936, p. 57.

CWMCYNFELYN, Llangorwen

Located in woodland near the hairpin bend on the B4572 between Waun-fawr and Clarach and overlooking Cardigan Bay. Formerly called Cwmcynfy or Abercwm Cynfil, a farm house named Hen Gwm stood near the existing property. The first recorded occupier of Cwm was Mathew Evans, twice Mayor of Aberystwyth (1734 and 1760) and described by Lewis Morris as a solicitor of 'the lowest kind, inebriate and haughty who sold parts of his estate to meet his insatiable need for intoxicating liquor'. When he died Mathew left his estate to his nephew, Mathew Davies of Wileirog-uchaf, a farm between Clarach and Borth. He was High Sheriff of Cardiganshire in 1790. Mathew Davies married Jane Richards, daughter of Roderick Richards and his wife Anne, daughter of Jenkin Lloyd of Clochfaen, Montgomery and Abaty Cwm-hir, Radnor, of the neighbouring Plâs Penglais. According to a descendant, George Checkland Williams, Mathew Davies, through a woman friend, bought land from the Pryses of Gogerddan and others and his estates included Wileirog, Wallog and Rhoscellan, all adjoining properties. They had two daughters, and co-heiresses; Jane, the eldest married Isaac Lloyd Williams (1771-1846), who was educated at Trinity College, Oxford, and Chancery barrister of the Inner Temple of Lincoln's Inn, the son of David Williams of Ty'n-y-wern and Ystrad Teilo, Llanrhystud parish, who descended from Gwilym ap Sion of Ynys-wen in Llanegwad, parish north Carmarthenshire. The younger daughter, married General Lewis Davies, a member of the Davies family of Perthygwenyn near Llannon and later of Crugiau, Rhydyfelin and Tan-y-bwlch and father of Mathew Vaughan Davies, later Lord Ystwyth. The present house dates from about 1770 and was built by Dixon, the architect, from stones quarried near Wallog.

The eldest son of Isaac Lloyd Williams and Jane, his wife, was Mathew Davies Williams, born in London in 1800 who lived at Cwm following the death of his father in 1846 and who spent two years living at Bodfrigan (Lodge Park) where two of his children were born, while a new roof was put on Cwm, where a further seven children were born. Mathew Davies Williams died in 1860 and following litigation between members of the family which cost a great deal of money, Mathew Davies Williams sold parts of the estate to Pryse Pryse of Gogerddan, who when a toddler, took his first steps at Cwm. The eldest son, Colonel George Williams, lived successively at Rhoscellan, Wallog (where his sister lived later) and Ffynnon Caradog where he died and was succeeded by his son, George Checkland Williams.

Cwmcynfelyn was occupied by a Captain Cosens, a retired Army officer and his family in 1881, and in 1888 Henry Bonsall, one of the Fronfraith family was of Cwmcynfelyn when he was defeated by William Morgan, a Bow Street coal merchant and grandfather of Lord Elystan Morgan, in the first County Council elections. David Howell JP migrated from Llanbrynmair to marry a daughter of Thomas Jones of Great Darkgate Street, Aberystwyth, and his drapery store, built on the site of the old Talbot Inn, remained a leading store in Aberystwyth for many years. David also lived at Cwmcynfelyn in the early years of the 20th century.

The most prominent member of the Williams family of Cwm was Isaac Williams (1802-1865) second son of Isaac Lloyd Williams. Educated at Harrow and Fellow of Trinity College, Oxford, he was a leading poet, hymn-writer, theologian and friend of Keble, Hurrell Fronde and later Newman's curate at St. Mary's, Oxford. Isaac Williams was mainly responsible for building Llangorwen church on land given by his father (who also gave an endowment of £1,000). It was built of the hard blue stone of the country from around Wallog. The interior is of Bath stone and based on the east end of Newman's church at Littlemore near Oxford. The consecration in December 1841 was in Welsh, the first that had been known. The eagle lectern was presented by John Keble, and the stained glass window in the west wall was later donated by John Francis JP of Wallog, in memory of his daughter, Kate, who died in 1888. The altar was of stone, the first since the reformation. Isaac Williams died in 1865.

In 1988, Mrs. Rosa Price, a native of Llandysul, bought the mansion and grounds from

Mrs. Beryl Thomas, daughter of Haydn Thomas, of Aberystwyth. Mrs. Price has restored both house and grounds and Cwm is now a residential and nursing home housing 44 residents.

Grid Ref: SN 6038 8348

Refs: Meyrick, *Cardiganshire, 310,* 311, 375, (1810) edn. 1907, 311. Mynachty Deeds, No. 41; Colby Map, 1831; Dwnn, *Heraldic Visitations* (1846); WWHR, iii, 102. Lewis, WJ. *Born on a Perilous Rock,* 1980: *Y Bywgraffiadur.*

CWM CYNON, Llandysiliogogo

Located a quarter of a mile south of Llwyndafydd and marked on *Colby's Map of 1831* and described as being in a valley some distance from the hamlet of Ciliau Uchaf in Llandisiliogogo parish. Lewis tells us 'Here is an ancient mansion called Cym Cynin, the property of the family of Parry, now converted into a farmhouse'. Meyrick states, 'anciently a place of more grandeur than present'. George Parry of Cwm Cynon (grandson of Harry of Cwmtudu, traced to David ap Ieuan, Llwyndafydd to Tydwal Gloff), married Margaret, daughter of John Price, vicar of Llanllwchaeron. In his will, dated 28 December 1647, George devised properties called Tythin Cwm Kynon and others in that parish.

His brother, David William Parry, paid the Lay Subsidy for Cwm Cynon in 1577 and 1601 and was succeeded by his son, George, who married Anne, daughter of Thomas Price, who was the elder brother of Owen Price of Myddfai, Carms. George was succeeded by his eldest son, Thomas, who married Margaret, daughter and co-heiress of John Lewes of Gernos. The marriage settlement, dated 20 December 1714, included, 'the capital messuage and lands called Cwmcynon. Their eldest son, John Parry, married Heather Howells of Penybank, Llanfihangel-ar-Arth, niece and heir-at-law of Llewelin Lloyd, late of Saffron Mead, Esq. deceased. John died in 1747 when the administration of his estate was granted to Hesther, his widow. According to *CRO, GGMS,* John was succeeded by his son, Llewelin Parry, High Sheriff of Cardiganshire in 1772 who appointed Thomas Hawker of Aberystwyth, gent, to be his Under-Sheriff. Carlisle, *TDW*, 1811 states, 'Cwm Cynon or Cynon's Vale (which is four miles distant from Capel Cynon) was the seat of the Parrys of Gernose. King Henry VII with the army that joined him under Sir Rhys ap Thomas, encamped for the night on a small eminence opposite Cwm Cynon on their march to Bosworth. The country people relate a story of the golden goblet left behind him and claimed afterwards, by the King's Orders, by the Vaughan of Golden Grove in the county of Carmarthen, where they say it is kept to this day'. Meyrick states, 'it (Cwm Cynon) still belongs to the descendants of the Parrys of Gernos (1810). No traces of the mansion remain.

Refs: NLW, Morgan Richardson Deeds, i, 159, 165, 170, 177, 179, 180, 184; Lewis, *TDW,* 1840; Meyrick, *Cardiganshire,* 1810, edn. 1907, p. 233; Colby Map, 1831; D. J. Davies, Llanarth, 65; NLW, Griffith Owen Colln; CRO, GGMS, I (Tydwal Gloff) 44-5; Carlisle, *TDW,* 1831; WWHR, i, 21.

CWM EINON, Capel Dewi

Situated north-east of Capel Dewi off the B4459, marked on modern OS map and *Colby Map of 1831.*

William Davies is the first known owner of Cwm Einon. He was born in 1780 and was the grandson of Thomas and Elizabeth David, formerly of Crugwheel (Crug-y-chwil), who settled at Bro Gwenog, and was the son and heir of John Davies of Bwlch-mawr and Mary, daughter of John David Jenkin of Llanfihangel-ar-Arth, Carmarthenshire, who had 12 children in all.

William Davies married Mary, of Lluest Cornicyll, in Llangybi parish, who was born in 1782. Mary died on 26 May 1857 aged 75 and William on 8 April 1870 aged 90. He was buried at Capel Dewi.

William and Mary Davies had nine children, of whom little is known, except for one daughter Elizabeth (1813-1873), who married a John Lloyd and they had three children, a son, Thomas Lloyd, who married, but of whom little is known and two daughters – Margaret and Mary. Margaret Lloyd, born in 1853, married William Jones of Pantyrychen, Goodwick, Pembrokeshire, who died in 1922, and

Mary Lloyd, born in 1855, who married Charles Sadler on 28 February 1901 at Highgate St. Michael, Middlesex.

Margaret and William Jones had five children; William John Jones, born in 1876, of Harbour Village, Goodwick, Pembrokeshire, who married Margaret, surname unknown. Two daughters, Elizabeth, born in 1880 and Mary Anne, born in 1882. David, born 24 December 1884, also of Harbour Village and Walter, born in 1890, and who served with the Rifle Brigade and was killed in the first Battle of the Somme on 16 July 1916.

Grid Ref: SN 4598 4305

Refs: NLW, MS. 8732 E, fos. 26-43.

CWMBARRY (CWM BERN), Penbryn

This house could well be Cwm Bern which is located a mile south-east of Tre-saith on the bank of an un-named stream which runs into the Saith. David Thomas, alias Dai Mawr, of Cwmbarry in Penbryn, married Gwenllian, youngest daughter of Thomas Bowen of Bwlchbychan. They had a daughter, Mary, who was in the service of James Lewes of Penralltybie in 1690. Also shown is Owen John David Trahaearn of Cwmbarry, whose daughter, Catherine, married John Davies ap David ap Rhys Moethe. No dates are given.

Grid Ref: SN 2880 5087

Refs: CRO, GGMS, I (Tydwal Gloff); ibid, III (Gwaethfoed).

CWM HAWEN, Llangrannog

Home of the Lewes family, descended from Ednowain of Bradwen. Marked as Cwm Owen on *Colby*'s *Map of 1831,* standing on a slope above the valley of Nant Hawen brook, east of Llangrannog village, about a mile south of Pontgarreg, but more correctly named Cwm Hawen. Also known as Cwmawen. Evelyn Hope calls the home 'Cwmhawen Fawr in parish of Llangrannog. There are traces of a considerable plâs at Cwm Hawen Fawr'.

John Lewes was the first of his family to live at Cwm Hawen early in the 17th century. On his marriage to Elen Jenkin, daughter and heiress of Thomas Jenkin ab Evan Lloyd of Cwm Hawen, Descended from Ieuan Lloyd of Cwm Hawen and Rhys Griffith (as of Lloyd of Crynfryn).

John Lewes, younger son of Lewes David Meredydd of Abernantbychan, and Elen had a son, James, who lived at Cwmawen c. 1612. James married twice; firstly Mary, daughter and heiress of Edward Morgan David Lloyd of Glascrug and secondly Elizabeth, daughter of Henry Don Lee of Pibwr. From the first marriage there was a notable son and heir, John Lewes of Glascrug and Cwmawen, the fierce Puritan and author of *Contemplations of these Times*. From his second marriage, a son Thomas Lewes described as 'sometime of Cwm Owen' was assessed at £5 and paid 40/- Lay Subsidy. He married Bridget, daughter of James Lewes of Coedmor.

James's son, John Lewes was High Sheriff of Cardiganshire in 1635. He married Magdalen, daughter and heiress of Rees, 3rd son of Morgan David Lloyd of Glascrug. They had one son, John, and two daughters, Mary and Elizabeth. Mary married John Phillips of Dolhaidd Isa, Penboyr, Carmarthenshire, and Elizabeth married Evan Gwyn of Cwntyda Issa, (Cwmtudu-isaf).

John Lewes, the younger, married Lowri, daughter of Hugh Tydyr of Llanegrn. John, the younger, pre-deceased his father by nearly ten years (will proved 1664, his father's in 1674 and his mother's in 1685). In 1672 John Lewes, the elder, and Mrs. Magdalen Lewes, widow, were assessed for 5 hearths.

John and Lowri's son, James, married Mary, daughter of David Lloyd of Crynfryn. James died without issue and *CRO GGMS* tells us that 'the whole estate descended to ye issue of Mary and Elizabeth aforesaid', his aunts.

Meyrick says 'Cwm Owen, formerly a seat of the Lewes's, James Lewes, Esq., having no issue, the estate of Cwmowen descended to the daughter of John Lewes, viz. Elizabeth wife of Ieuan Gwynn of Cwmtydy and her heirs. It is now the property of the Saunderses', but according to the family tree from the *Golden Grove Manuscripts* it descended to Mary and John Phillipp's daughter Mary, who married David Lloyd of Wern Newydd, who died at sea without issue. The estate then reverted to the descendants of the younger sister and John

Phillips of Dol-haidd and Cwm Hawen, whose daughter married John Phillips, gent., of Moel Ifor, Llanrhystud parish. In Llangrannog church was an ornamental pew belonging to Moel Ifor, Llanrhystud and Cwm Hawen, dated 1718.

Grid Ref: SN 3383 5363

Refs: Colby Map, 1831; Blome List, 1673; WWHR, i, 25, 34; Meyrick, *Cardiganshire,* 232; NLW, Crosswood Deeds, p. 77; CRO, GGMS, III (Owen ap Bradwen); E. Hope *Llangrannog and the Pigeonsford Family,* 1931; G. E. Evans, *Cardiganshire,* 1903, 78.

CWM HYAR, Llandysul

Situated in the north of the parish and shown on *Colby's Map of 1831*, near Melin Gefail, and on modern OS map east of A486 between Croeslan and Ffostrast just under one mile west of Dyffryn Llynod. Also known as Cwm Yar and Cwmhyar and found on the *Tithe Map, Llandysul, 1841.* An ancient homestead, formerly the house of William ap John Lloyd who traced to Gwynfardd. *CRO GGMS* states that his son was Walter and his grandson William Lloyd Walter, the first to be described as 'of Cwmhuar'.

The *Carmarthenshire Deeds* in Pembrokeshire RO refers to a Deed dated 2 March 1687/8:

'1. David Evan of Llandysul and William David of Cwmgwedmerth, Penbryn, Cards., Gent. 2. John Lewis of Llandysul, gt. 3. Lewis David of Penbryn, gt. Deed to lead uses of a Recovery of a messuage and land called Cwm Hyar and several pieces of land in Llandysul'.

By 1738 the property was owned by John Lewis, gent. and formed part of the pre-nuptial settlement between his daughter, Mary, and James Lewis, the younger, second son of James Lewis of Llanllawddog, Carmarthenshire, gent. The settlement included the messuage and land called Cwmhyar, several pieces of land, and a messuage and tucking mill called Tir Tucker Teg also in Llandysul parish.

The *NLW Morgan Richardson Deeds* tells us that 'the estate was added to, in 1752, by John Bowen of Llanfihangel Ystrad parish and his wife Margaret, when they gave to James Lewis of Cwm Yar messuages called Gwern Tyr Shead alias Tyr Pant Y Castell, Tyr Twy Bach and Tyr y velyn ban, in the parish of Llandisilio gogo'.

During 1758-9 tax was levied at 4d. in the £1. Cwm Hyar was assessed at £7 and paid 2/4d. in tax. James Lewis's will was dated 17 June 1783 and was proved on 8 July 1789.

On 25 November 1819, at the end of George III's reign, James Lewis was granted a faculty to erect a pew in Llandysul church. The *Carmarthenshire Deeds* in Pembrokeshire RO state that 'On 4-5 Aug. 1820 1. James Lewis of Cymhyar, gent. Priscilla his wife, and their eldest son John Lewis of Narberth, gent. 2. Mary Bowen of Narberth, spinster. 3. John Willy of Haverfordwest, gent. 4/- Thomas Jones of Carmarthen, gent. 5. Williams Evans of Haverfordwest and Lewis Evans of Cardigan, gent. 6. William Bowen of Haverfordwest and William Williams of Gumfreston. Esq.', were witnesses to the pre-nuptial settlement of John Lewis and Mary Bowen – properties called Cwmhyar, with cottages and pieces of land, a messuage and corn grist mill called Tir Tucker Teg, all in Llandysul (described in the Exemplification as 5 messuages, 10 cottages, 10 gardens, 5 water corn grist mills, 10 barns, 10 stables, 10 cowhouses, 10 beasthouses, 10 curtilages, 500 acres land, 100 acres pasture, 50 acre meadow, 50 acre wood and underwood, 20 acres moor, 100 acres furze and heath, in Llandysul parish)'.

James Lewis, the son of John and Mary, married Jane Martha Davies of Penybailey, spinster. This marriage was also subject to a pre-nuptial settlement, on 30 November 1837 between '1. John Davies of Penybailey, Llangunllo, Esq. 2. James Lewis of Cymhyar, gent. 3. Jane Martha Davies of Penybailey, spinster. 4. John Howell Davies of Penybailey, Esq. and the Rev. William Davies of Llwyngorras, Pembs. Pre-nuptial settlement of James Lewis and Jane Martha Davies – messuage and land called Corrws and Blaentrossel in Llandyfriog ph'.

James Lewis subscribed to Dwnn's *Heraldic Visitations* (1846), and his daughter and heiress, Priscilla Willy Lewis, married Lloyd Price, son of W. D. Price of Castell Pigyn in 1856. Their son, Meredydd Lewis Willy Lloyd Price, born 11 May 1857, qualified as a solicitor in 1882. He died at the age of 81 in 1938.

Francis Jones noted in 1975 that Cym Hyar

was still an interesting house and was inhabited by a farmer, Mr. Thomas.

Refs: Tithe Map, Llandysul 1841; Carmarthenshire Deeds in Pembrokeshire RO; Colby Map, 1831; Mr. Thomas 1975.

CWM MEUDWY, Llandysul

There is no Cwm Meudwy on *Colby's Map of 1831*, but there is a Cwm-idiau one mile north-west of Llandysul, and this identical place is marked on modern OS maps as Cwm-Meudwy and located south of the A486 Llandysul to Horeb road. Also known as Cwm Fydw and Cwm Moydw.

Thomas ap David Lloyd Griffith of Cwmoydw in Llandysul, descended from Lloyd of Faerdref, traced to Tewdr Mawr. Thomas, was the second son of David Llwyd of Faerdref in Llandysul parish, married Catherine, daughter of Philip Howell ap John Lloyd (descended from Gwynfardd). Thomas and Catherine had a son, John, and a daughter who married Henry Thomas of Llandysul. John Thomas and his wife, Elizabeth, tragically buried three of their sons, James, Titus and Daniel on 14 October 1796, cause of death unknown.

The *Llandysul Tithe Map of 1841* gives the Rev. Thomas Lloyd as owner of Cwm Meudwy with David Thomas as its tenant.

Grid Ref: SN 4030 4150

Refs: WWHR, i, 52-3; PRO, Dale Castle MS., p. 30; Lloyd Family Records (Peds. p. 21); Llandysul Tithe Map, 1841; CRO, GGMS (Tewdwr), I, p. 40.

CWMNEWIDION,
Llanfihangel-y-Creuddyn

Marked on *Colby's Map of 1831* as three farmsteads – Cwmnewidion-isaf, -ganol and -uchaf, but only Cwmnewidion-isaf is named on modern OS maps. The farm lies on the north bank of the Newidion, north-east of Abermagn, off the B4340 near the experimental farm of Trawsgoed. The Cwmnewidion referred to here is the original settlement sited at Cwmnewidion-isaf, formerly named Place Cwmnewidion, and in earlier times the nucleus of an estate of some substance. The earliest reference can be traced to the early 16th century when Ievan ap Morris (traced to Cadifor ap Dinawal), is referred to as of Cwmnewidion. He was succeeded by his son, Hugh David Fychan and his grandson, David Fychan, who married Jane, eldest daughter of Morris ap Richard of Trawsgoed, ancestor of the Vaughans, later Earls of Lisburne. Jane died c. 1587. David Fychan was succeeded by his son, Hugh David Fychan, whose heiress, Elizabeth, married as her second husband, Edward Stradling, who was living at Cwmnewidion in 1652 when he gave a receipt to Edward Vaughan of Maenarthur for £33.16.0 being the first three years' rent of the capital messuage and lease of Cwmnewidion 'now in the tenure of said Edward Stradling under a 21 year lease'. The *Crosswood Deeds* refer to a grant dated 1 April 1615, from John Lloyd of Ystrad parish, gent., and Bridget, daughter and heiress of Richard ap Hugh, gent., deceased, his wife, to Edward Vaughan of Trawsgoed, Esq., of a moiety of a capital messuage called 'Cwmnewidion (in the tenure of David Lloyd ap Rhydderch, and Ellen, late wife of Hugh ap Richard) and other properties all in the township of Maenarthur in Llanfihangel-y-Creuddyn parish and lately the property of the said Hugh ap Richard, deceased'. In 1659/60 Edward Vaughan of Cwmnewidion made his will which was proved in London on 9 August 1660. It states, 'To my nephew Edward Vaughan, all the tenements conveyed to my servant, Thomas Robert, to my use during life of Elizabeth Stradling (daughter and heiress of Hugh David Vaughan of Cwmnewidion, gent., dec.), on trust to pay my sister Margaret Lloyd £10 p.a. for life; to my nephew John Herbert a bay mare and £10; to my brother James Vaughan £10 p.a. for life; residue to my nephew and executor Edward Vaughan of Trawsgoed'. Edward Vaughan was a brother of the famous Sir John Vaughan (1603-74), Chief Justice of the Common Pleas. In 1672 Margaret Morgan of Cwmnewidion was assessed for 4 hearths in the Hearth Tax and the *NLW, Cwrtmawr Deeds* record '1687/8 Jan 17 agreement between: 1. Benjamin Morgans of Cwm Newidion, gt., and Margaret Morgans of Cwm Bwa [Llanbadarn Fawr parish] widow, and 2. William Powell, gent., bond for observance of covenant in deed of even date'. Susan, daughter of Watkin

Morgan of Cwmnewidion married David Lloyd of Cwm Bwa. On 12 January 1691/2 the *Crosswood Deeds* state: 'Lease for 7 years from John Vaughan of Trawsgoed, gent., to William Pugh of Llanfihangel-y-Creuddyn, gent., of a tenament called Cwmnewidion in said parish, £8 p.a. a hen and 20 eggs at Shrovetide or 6d and a heriot of the second best beast.'

Cwmnewidion-ganol was probably built at this time and later in 1760, Lewis Pugh of Rhos-y-rhiw owned the property. Further, a Deed dated 1698/9, names Richard Johnes of 'Cwmnewidion, gent.' By the end of the 17th century various names and surnames are associated with what was by then two or even three settlements. In 1692 Charles Herbert is named as owner of Cwmnewidion. He was a descendant of Elizabeth, daughter of Hugh David Fychan, whose first husband was Charles Herbert of Pengelli, Brecs. His daughter, Elizabeth, married a Lloyd of Aberllolwyn and to her will, dated 19 October 1744, is added a codicil on 6 April 1768. Elizabeth lived to a grand old age. It was through the marriage of Elizabeth that the estate passed to Cornelius Griffiths and his wife, Anne, who lived at Cwmnewidion in 1760. Later, through the profligacy of Cornelius, the family was forced to alienate the estate and at his death at the end of the 18th century, it was sold to Wilmot Vaughan of Trawsgoed. Cwmnewidion remained the property of the Vaughans until the Trawsgoed estate was sold after World War II. The three farms of Cwmnewidion are now owned by former tenants.

Grid Ref: SN 6805 7450

Refs: Colby Map, 1831; NLW, Cwrtmawr Deeds, 1039, 239, 133; CRO, GGMS, III (Gwaethfoed); NLW, Mynachty Deeds, 7 AE, 12356, E, p. 87; NLW, Crosswood Deeds, pp. 37, 55, 78, 79, 86, 130, 184; JF(Ll) Deeds: alvo 1655-6; NLW, Crosswood Deeds, p. 77; WWHR, iii 96.

CWMTUDU (CWM TYDU), Llandsiliogogo
Marked as Place Cwm Tydu on *Evan Bowen's Map of 1754* but the precise location is uncertain. *Colby's Map of 1831* notes the settlement on the coast and it is likely that the original plâs of Cwm Tydu has long since disappeared, and it is also possible that the farmstead of Cwm Tydu became two farms in the uchaf and isaf principle. The settlement of Cwm Tydu is situated on the Cardigan Bay coast equidistant between Llangrannog to the south and New Quay to the north where the afon Ffynnon Ddewi runs into the sea. The family associated with the house is ancient. Llywelyn Foel is the first recorded connection in the 13th century. He was followed in turn by his son, Dafydd, and his grandson, Griffith, who was living at Caerwedros in 1316. In 1357 the family is represented by Dafydd of Llwyndafydd, whose second wife, Gwenllian, was the daughter of Adda Fychan of Llanddwy, Llanfihangel-y-creuddyn parish. Their son, Rees Dafydd (1399-1443), married Agnes, daughter of Rees ap Adda Fychan, again of Llanddwy. The family can be traced to Blegwyryd ap Dinawal and the first to be located at Cwm Tydu is Harry ap Thomas ap Philip ap Rees Dafydd, who was living there between 1541 and 1575. Harry married Elen, daughter of Adam Ievan ap Jenkin Llwyd of Cemaes. Their son, David, was the first to adopt the surname Parry and he was followed by his second son, David William Parry, who is described as 'of Cwm Tydu' between 1591-5 and was alive in 1632. Anne, an heiress of Cwm Tydu and the widow of Jenkin Lloyd, married the Rev. John Lewes of Llysnewydd, who was born in 1616/7. Jenkin Lloyd settled Cwm Tydu and other lands in Llandisiliogogo to the uses of his daughter's marriage – lands he had purchased from John Lloyd, gent., and Margaret, his wife, who was descended from David Parry of Cwm Tydu through his daughter who married Thomas Nicholas Lloyd who traced to Jenkin Lloyd of Cemaes. It is at this time that we come across references to a second homestead, when Elizabeth, daughter of John Lewis of Cwm Hawen, Llangrannog parish, married Evan Gwyn of Cwm Tydu-isaf. He paid tax for three hearths and Joyce Lewis for four in the Hearth Tax in 1672.

Descended from the Gwyns were the Phillipses of Moelifor in Llanrhystud parish and the Saunders Davieses of Pentre, Maenordeifi. After 1796, when there is a reference to a David Jenkins 'of Cwmtydu, farmer', the records are silent. In Lewis, *TDW* (1840) it is stated, fancifully perhaps, 'In Cwm Tydwr are the foundations of some ancient buildings, which, according to tradition, are the remains of the ancient castellated mansion of the Tudors'. More accurate is the description of Evan Rees in his *South Wales Coast*: 'The remains of this town (the farm) are not now to be seen. It stood half a mile from Traeth Cwm Tydyr, up the Cwm.' The site may possibly be identified with the area of Pen-y-parc which is located on modern OS maps. In the same volume, 'Non' (Miss Gwladys Evans), says, 'It (Llandisiliogogo parish) is one of the few remaining parishes in Wales uncorrupted by the English customs and speech'. She quotes the late Stephen Evans JP, who stated that 'if Welsh should ever come to die, it would last be heard in one of the dingles of Llandisiliogogo when some poor old woman would ejaculate with her dying gasp, "Ych a fi".'

Grid Ref: 3550 5674

Refs: Bowen Map of South Wales, 1754; Colby Map, 1831; Lewis, *TDW*, 1840; *Dwnn,* i, p. 84; NLW, Morgan Richardson Deeds; NLW, Great Sessions Papers CRO; NLW, Griffith Owen Deeds, No. 1255; CRO, GGMS, I (Gwynfardd); ibid, III (Owen ap Bradwen); WWHR, ii, p. 21; BM, Additional MSS., 39749 (Woods MS.) fo. 167.

CWM UL (CWM YL), Llandysul

Marked on *Colby's Map of 1831* as Cwm-ul and located half a mile north-west of Troedrhiwffenyd, on the bank of a small stream and about one and three quarter miles north-west of Llandysul village. Not marked on modern OS maps.

John Lewes of Cwm ul in Llandysul was the son of James Lewes of Cilfache and the grandson of John Lewes of Llysnewydd and his wife, Jenet. John Lewes was married twice; firstly to Mary, daughter of Jenkin Thomas, vivens 1674, of Dyffryn Llynod and his wife, Elen Lewes of Gernos, and secondly to a daughter of John Walter. They had a son, John Lewes, and a daughter.

In 1841 the *Llandysul Tithe Map* gives: 'Cwmul. David Evans, Thomas Saunders, and Martha Jones, owners. William Davies tenant. The holding was of 212 acres .'

Grid Ref: SN 4020 4308

Refs: Colby Map, 1831; CRO, GGMS, III (Owen ap Bradwen), fo. 8; Llandysul Tithe Map, 1841.

CWRRWS, Llandyfriog

Also Corrws. Cwrrws Fawr and Fach and Felin Cwrrws, situated half a mile east of Llandyfriog church, near Aber-banc and shown on *Colby's Map of 1831*, but not named on modern OS maps.

David ab Owen ap Meredudd (to Tydwal Gloff) of Corrws in Iskoed, gent. married a daughter of Griffith Llewellin Perkin of Tre-rickert, Nevern. Their daughter and heiress, Dyddgu, married Mathias ap Owen of Rickerton. Pembs, second son of Owen ab Owen of Pentre Ifan, and brother to Sir James ab Owen. Mathias died in November 1540.

The chronology of the families of Corrws is unclear, but David ap Howel of Corrws had two sons, Llewelyn ddu, and Rees, who married Elliw, daughter of Llewelyn Howel Gwyn Benarw (to Tewdwr). Llewelyn ddu's son, Ieuan of Corrws, had two co-heiresses. One (name unknown), married David ap Llewelyn of Cil-y-blaidd, Pencarreg, Carmarthenshire (to Rhydderch ap Tewdwr), and Gwenllian, who married firstly Meredydd Phillip (to Cadifor Fawr) of Cilsant. After his death she married for the second time, this time to Meredith ap Ieuan of Dolfawr 'a man of Great Possessions,' and from this marriage they had a daughter, Jenet, who married Rees Llewelyn ap Llewelyn Rhys ddu Sgwier digri.

Grid Ref: SN 3475 4180

Refs: Dwnn, i, 239; Colby Map, 1831; PRO, Dale Castle MS., 81; CRO, GGMS, I (Tydwal Gloff), fo. 33, 37; NLW, Griffith Owen Deeds, 2nd Bk., p. 272.

CWRT MAWR, Llangeitho

Formerly the home of distinguished theologians, academics and men of letters. Located on *Colby's Map of 1831* and on modern OS maps, two miles north of Llangeitho and a quarter-mile south of the B4577. The place-name suggests a homestead of some antiquity though records are not found until the middle of the 18th century. In 1760 John Pugh, second son of the Rev. Philip Pugh, Blaenpennal, and brother of Philip Pugh of Tyglyn Aeron, owned the property and lived at Cwrt Mawr. A monumental inscription to a John Daniel is found in Llangeitho churchyard which states that he owned and lived at Cwrt Mawr in 1786.

Meyrick tells us: 'It is a reputable farmhouse and the property of Mr. John Daniels.' A suggestion of Cwrt Mawr's antiquity is given by Lewis who states, 'The old mansion of Cwrt Mawr . . . at present in the occupation of a farmer'. Cwrt Mawr today is primarily identified as the home of the distinguished Davies family and their descendants, several of whom were notable preachers, bankers, academics, writers and prominent promoters of the Welsh language and culture. The earliest reference to the Davieses is to one David Davies (1745-1804), described as of Machynlleth and a prominent Quaker. He married Jonnet (1747-1822), daughter of Robert Jones, Y Plâs, Aberllefenni, Montgomeryshire. His youngest son, Robert (1790-1841), settled in Aberystwyth and married Eliza, daughter of the famous hymn-writer and Methodist minister, David Charles of Carmarthen, by his second wife Sarah (1798-1876), daughter of Samuel Levi Phillips, a Jewish banker and converted Christian of Haverfordwest and Mary Jones of Prendergast, his wife.

Robert established a Sunday School at Trefechan, Aberystwyth and it was at his house in Great Darkgate Street that the Confession of Faith of the Calvinistic Methodists was prepared. Robert's youngest son, Robert Joseph Davies (1839-92), a freeholder of Llanbadarn Fawr, married Frances Humphreys of Nant-y-llan, Llandyfaelog, great-niece of the Rev. Peter Williams, Methodist clergyman and author, best known for his edition of the Bible, published in 1770. Robert Joseph was appointed JP for Cardiganshire and following his marriage in 1863, spent the remainder of his days with his wife at Cwrt Mawr, which his younger brother and his mother, Eliza, had purchased some years earlier. Robert died in 1892 and is buried at Llangeitho. Robert and Frances had four children: Sarah married the Rev. J. M. Saunders.The heir, David Charles Davies became the Director of the Field Veterinary Museum of Chicago. Anne Jane married as her first husband Thomas Edward Ellis (1855-1899), Liberal MP for Meir. and Chief Whip from 1894, whose premature death deprived Victorian Wales of its natural leader. Their son, Thomas Iorwerth Ellis, became a lecturer, headmaster and was a prolific author. For many years he was the secretary of Undeb Cymru Fydd. His six volumes in *Cyfres Crwydro Cymru* series (1953-9), are well-written travel books published from 1952. In *Crwydro Ceredigion,* T. I. Ellis provides an evocative account of the Sunday School conducted for many years by his grandmother in the large kitchen at Cwrtmawr. The youngest son, John Humphreys Davies (1876-1926), author, Registrar and later Principal of UCW, Aberystwyth from 1919 until his early death. His interest in Welsh culture was extensive; his books and manuscripts were later presented to the NLW Aberystwyth and are known as the *Cwrtmawr MSS.*

Robert Joseph Davies extended the original Georgian house at Cwrt Mawr in the 1860's. A description of the house is given in a biography of John Humphreys Davies written by his nephew, T. I. Ellis: 'The ground floor had a hall with a large room on either side (2 parlours) with oak floors: the stairs and balusters also of oak rose from the other end of the hall. There was another room near the foot of the stairs on the right and behind that was a dairy. On the other side of the stairs a door opened to the large kitchen beyond which was a small kitchen. On the first floor there were five bedrooms and on the second floor seven bedrooms. The farmhouse was about 200 yards from the mansion.'

A photograph of Cwrt Mawr and a Welsh poem written in praise of the house and the Davies family by Iolo Caernarfon, appears in *Cymru Vol. VI* in 1893. A further photograph is included in *John Humphreys Davies* by T. I. Ellis, published in 1963 and also in the September 1971 issue of *Country Quest.* The front elevation shows a range of three windows with three storeys and a pillared front entrance.

Owned in the 1960's by Prof. Jawetz of the UCW, Aberystwyth and then by the Evans family whose ancestor founded the Evans Evans travel company and was Mayor of Camden in the 1930's. The house has six acres of land-scaped gardens and woodland designed by a Mr. Gold of Carmarthen at the end of the 19th century. David Davies Conservative Assembly Member for Monmouthshire is a descendant of the Davies family of Cwrt Mawr.

Grid Ref: SN 6210 6210

Refs: Colby Map, 1831; Lewis, *TDW;* Meyrick, *Cardiganshire,* 255; WWHR, iii, 101; *Cymru,* vol. vi, 1893; *John Humphrey Davies*, T. I. Ellis, 1963; *County Quest,* Sept. 1971, p. 43; NLW, Cwrtmawr MSS.

CWRTNEWYDD, Llanwenog

The hamlet of Cwrtnewydd is located on the B4338 between Dre-fach and Gors-goch. The house referred to here is located less than a mile from the present hamlet and is marked on *Colby's Map of 1831*.

Davies in *Hanes Plwyf Llanwenog* states: 'The first mansion in Llanwenog was at Rhuddlan Teifi, called Yr hen gwrt, but hardly any remains there now. Later the second mansion, Cwrt Newydd was built on the banks of the Cledlyn stream; it was called Llys Newydd in Cromwell's time: the field below the house is called Cae Ffwrndy. Family of Saer y Cwm.'

According to the *Dale Castle Manuscript,* in c. 1600, John Webb or Webley came out of England to Cardiganshire. He had a son, Philip John Webb. Meyrick tells us in *Cardiganshire* 'Somewhere near Llanvaughan was the dingle in which lived the son of John Webley of Court Newydd, who followed the occupation of carpenter in it, where his family were termed *Tylwyth Saer y Cwm;* the family of the Carpenter in the vale . . . Cwrt Newydd is now the property of Mr. Thomas of Allt goch'.

Philip John Webb had a brother, David, who was known as David, *Saer y Cwm.* His family tree descends through seven generations: David to Thomas (who lived there in 1760 and owned part of Ffosyffald in Llanwenog parish), to Ieuan to Thomas of Cwrt Newydd to John to Lewis to John ap Lewis to Mary, who married David ap Richard of Llandovery. Their son was the famous Rhys Prichard (1579-1644), the vicar of Llandovery and author of *Canwyll y Cymru*, a volume of stanzas on Christian life published in 1681.

By the middle of the 19th century, John Evans lived at Cwrt Farm. He married Anne (d. 1845), the daughter of David Beynon and Mary née Evans. Anne's brother was Jenkin Beynon of Llaethlliw (1778-1849). John and Anne Evans had one daughter and two sons: Mary, the ultimate heiress (1815-56), who married Thomas Thomas of Llanfair (d. 1860), the son and heir, David Beynon Evans (1817-55), and the Rev. Evan Evans, clerk (1820-63). Both sons died without issue. On 25 June 1863 the Rev. Evans mortgaged the Llaethlliw estate in £25,000. He died 27 December 1863.

Mary Thomas had issue, but the house passed from the family at this time as Anne Thomas, daughter of Mary, married Evan Jones, gent., of Tyssul Castle, Llandysul, in 1877. Her brother, David Thomas (1846-1882) of Llanfair succeeded to Llaethliw and Dol-llan. John Thomas, b. 1852 is shown as of Llanfair, and Mary Thomas, the youngest daughter, died in 1868, whilst still a minor.

The Court (Cwrt) Estate was auctioned on 19 December 1879. A document in Carmarthen RO says 'The Court Estate in the parishes of Llanwenog, Llanwen, Penbryn, Llanfihangel Ystrad (Cards.), and Llanllwni (Carms). The total acreage was 843 acres and annual rental £508.10.0. The properties to be sold were Court, otherwise Court Newydd. Llanwenog parish, 208.1.7 acres, yielding £117.7.6 p.a. with David Jones as tenant. Alltgoch, in Llanwenog parish being 265.1.1 acres, tenant David Jones paying rent of £124 and Morfa Uchaf in the parish of Penbryn. 161.1.3 acres near Llangrannog village being a farm of 161 acres with a rental of £120'.

Grid Ref: SN 4957 4830

Refs: Colby Map, 1831; WWHR, i, 46-7; ibid, iii, 87; Meyrick, *Cardiganshire,* 215, 217; PRO, Dale Castle MS., p. 28; Davies, *Hanes Plwyf Llanwenog,* 1939, pp. 73-4; SC7, CRO; NLW, Morgan Richardson Deeds, vol. 1.

CYFOETH Y BRENIN,
Llanfihangel Genau'r-glyn
Site location unknown
Not named on modern OS maps but located on *Rees Map of South Wales* in the 14th century. The place-name suggests great antiquity and the name brenin (Lord) refers to the English penetration early in the 12th century. In 1136 Owain and Cadwaladr ap Gruffudd, from Gwynedd, razed Castell Gwallter to the ground. The castle was given to Gilbert de Clare by Henry I and was built by Walter Bec. The castle was sited adjacent to the village of Llandre, north of Bow Street, west of the B4353 to Borth. The Lordship or Manor of Cyfoeth y Brenin was located in Llanfihangel Genau'r Glyn and the neighbouring parish of Talybont. The Cyfoeth y Brenin School Board established in 1871 consisted of Cyfoeth y Brenin, Cynnull Mawr, Tirymynach with Henllys and Broncastellau, all located in the vicinity. Whether Cyfoeth y Brenin was ever a farmstead or as noted is a name given to a particular area is not clear. However, the notes tell us that in 1754, Anne, daughter of James Daniel of Cyfoeth y Brenin married Richard James of Llety Evan (Llety Ifan Hen), near Bont-goch. The arms of James Daniel are given as: *Argent* a (pale) and lozengy *sable*. Thereafter the records are silent.

Refs: Rees, South Wales in the 14th century (map); *Ceredigion,* III, 3 (1958), 207-30; ibid, VIII, 100-140 (1976), pp. 100-140.

CYMERAU, Eglwys-fach
Located on modern OS map west of the A487 (T) between Furnace and Glandyfi in north Cardiganshire and on *Colby's Map of 1831*. Formerly the home of Major-General Lewis Pugh, CB, CBE, DSO, who left Cymerau in 1978 to live in Montgomeryshire and who died there in 1981 aged 73. Lewis Pugh was the son of Major Herbert Owain Pugh DSO, who was born at Aber-mad, Llanilar parish, on 9 July 1874. Herbert Owain, was in turn the son of Lewis Pugh MP. For portraits at Cymerau see Steegman, II, *South Wales.*

A memorial stone dedicated to Major-General Pugh of Cymerau was erected by the Burma Star Association on the side of a hill below Cymerau and unveiled in 1984. Cymerau is now the home of Mr. and Mrs. H. Bredow, who bought the house and grounds in the 1980's.

Grid Ref: SN 6955 9629

Refs: Colby Map, 1831; Mod. OS Map; Steegman, II, *South Wales,* p. 22.

CYNNULL-MAWR,
Llanfihangel Genau'r-glyn
Located directly south of Talybont and west of the A487 (T) road north of Rhydypennau. Marked on *Colby's Map of 1831* as Cynyll Mawr and in 1657 was part of the Gogerddan estate. The first recorded resident, Evan Watkin, was the son of Evan Watkin, probably a kinsman from Moelcerni, a substantial holding overlooking Cardigan Bay in the parish of Llanfihangel Genau'r-glyn. Evan Watkin, senior, who owned the property in 1760, was Mayor of Aberystwyth on six occasions between 1735 and 1757, probably the nominee of the Pryses of Gogerddan who with other gentry dominated the life of the town. His elder daughter married one of the Hugheses of Castell Du, in Llanwenog parish, and his younger daughter married, in 1749, William Jones of Gwynfryn, Llangynfelyn parish near Cors Fochno whose son, Basil Jones, educated at Shrewsbury School, was Bishop of St. David's from 1874-1897. A third generation Evan Watkin became a schoolteacher in England. Llanfihangel Genau'r Glyn, an educational charity named The Edward and Watkins's Charity was established in the parish. Hugh Edward of Cynnull Mawr gave £5 in 1758 and Evan Watkins of the same place another £20 in 1760 for the education of the poor children of the parish. Lately the home of Mr. H. Williams.

Grid Ref: SN 6540 8724

Refs: Colby Map, 1831; WWHR, iii, 104, 116; NLW, Coleman Deeds, No. 120; Nicholas, *County Families*, i (Jones of Gwynfryn); *Ceredigion,* IV, i, 58 (1960).

ANYFFOREST (Tanyfforest), Llangybi

Francis Jones places this property in Llangybi parish and it is located both on *Colby's Map of 1831* and modern OS maps half a mile south of the village off the A485. Thomas Lloyd of Danyfforest was the third son of Sir Walter Lloyd of Llanfair Clydogau, High Sheriff of Cardiganshire both in 1643 and 1644. He married Jane, daughter of Sir Marmaduke Lloyd of Maesyfelin and their only daughter married Thomas Johnes, heir to Dolau Cothi. In 1760, Griffith Jones was the owner and occupier of Danyfforest and by 1775, his son, David Jones, gent., had succeeded to the property.

Grid Ref: SN 6075 5225

Ref: Colby Map, 1831; Phillips, *Sheriffs of Cardiganshire;* WWHR, iii, 90; NLW, Will of David Jones, Deri Ormond, 1775.

DERI ORMOND, Betws Bledrws

Unwanted by the family, the third house on the site was demolished in 1953. The Lodge, a miniature of the main house and Deri Ormond Tower built between 1821-1824 have survived. Marked on *Kitchin's Map of 1754* as Derry Wormwood and on *Colby's Map of 1831* as Derry Ormond, the house was situated in fine parkland a mile north-east of Betws Bledrws. Formerly the home of the Lloyd, Jones and Inglis-Jones families. The first recorded occupier, Thomas Lloyd, younger son of David Lloyd of Crynfryn, married Margaret, daughter of Thomas ab Owain of Bronwydd. Their second son was the Rev. Thomas Lloyd, later Rector of Llangynllo, his will was proved in 1629. He married a daughter of Bryne of Pant Dafydd, and left Deri Ormond to his second son, Rhys Lloyd, who was married to a daughter of John Parry of Blaen-pant. Their son, Thomas, married Magdalen Robinson of Gwersyllt, Denbighshire, whose will was dated 6 April 1680. Their son, Thomas Lloyd, High Sheriff in 1680, owned Deri Ormond in 1684 and married Bridget, daughter of James Jones of Dolaucothi. Thomas Lloyd died in 1692 but his widow was still living at Deri Ormond in 1709. She married secondly, John Williams of Talley, who had died before 1708.

The *Edwinsford Deeds* state that: 'In 1708-9 March 9. 1. Bridget Williams of Derry Wormwood, Cards. Widow and relict of John Williams, late of Talley, Esq. dec. 2. Thomas Williams of Talley, gt, son and heir of the deceased John Williams. Grant of Lands of the said John Williams in the parishes of Talley, Cayo, Llanycrwys, Killycombe, Llanfynydd, Llandilofawr and Llansadwrn, Co. Carm. and Llandewifrefy, Co. Cards.' Thomas and Bridget Lloyd had a son, also Thomas, who married Ann, daughter of Lewis Wogan of Wiston and Cilrhiwe, parish of Llanfihangel Penbedw, Pembrokeshire. Bridget was the grand-daughter of James Lloyd of Cilrhiwe who died in 1707.

By 1733, Thomas and Ann's eldest son, James, owned the property although his father's will was not proved until 1737. The *Deri Ormond Deeds* state: 'On 10th May 1733. Morgan Lloyd of the parish of Bettws Bledrws and his eldest son John Lloyd, corvisers, sold houses called Tuy Sienkyn Phillip near a parcel [of land] formerly enclosed by Morgan Lloyd and near the lands of James Lloyd, Esq. called Y ddery wrman in parish Bettws Bledrws formerly part of Tyrpen y Coed Isan.'

In 1741 David Jones, cattle dealer and drover, settled at Deri Ormond. David and Sarah, his wife, were tenants of James Lloyd at Nanthenfoelfawr and paying rent of £30 in 1741, had contracted to buy Deri Ormond from James Lloyd of Bronwydd in 1758 for £700 and by 1760 David Jones was the owner. His brother, Theophilus Jones, farmed nearby at Blaen-plwyf. Both were earnest Methodists. David's wife, Sarah, was the second daughter of Jenkin Jones of Glyn, Llangeitho and granddaughter of John Jones of Llwyn-rhys, the first nonconformist minister in Cardiganshire. Deri Ormond became the centre of Methodism; meetings were held in the house and in the big barn that David Jones built there in 1770. William Williams, Pantycelyn, often preached in the barn on Saturday evenings on his way to Sunday communion at Llangeitho during the great Methodist revival. The old farmhouse has long since vanished.

David Jones became High Sheriff of Cardiganshire in 1773 and died in 1775 heavily in debt with a mortgage of £2,000 on Deri Ormond. By his will he bequeathed to: 'Mary Bowen, spinster, daughter of William Beynon of Kilyposte, Carms, £40. To Elizabeth Beynon and Judith Beynon, two other daughters of William Beynon, £20 each. To David Jones, son of Griffith Jones of Danyfforest, gent., £20. To my nephew Theophilus Jones of Blaenplwyf, £20. To my niece, Amelia Jones, eldest daughter of my late brother Theophilus, £6. To my nieces Sarah, Elizabeth and Gwenllian Jones, spinsters, three other daughters of my late brother Theophilus £6. To my nephews and nieces, Timothy, Thomas, Mary and Anne Davies, sons and daughters of my sister Anne, wife of David Davies, late of Brithdir, £20 each. My other nephew, Stephen Jones, of my late brother, Theophilus Jones, to have Deri Ormond after my widow.'

Although David Jones left Deri Ormond to his wife for her life and then to his nephew, Stephen, his creditors brought a case against the executors in the Court of Great Sessions in 1781, and an order was made for the sale of Deri Ormond, otherwise known as Ormond's Oaks, which was bought on 12 January 1782 by a John Lewis on behalf of John Jones, surgeon and apothecary of Gracechurch St., London, for £1,575. This John Jones, son of Richard Jones was, at the age of 20, apprenticed for seven years to James Jones, apothecary of Grafton Street, Soho. Ultimately James Jones left a half share in his property to his apprentice. John Jones was 37 when he bought Deri Ormond and lived with his English wife in Brunswick Square. He bought further freeholds in Cardiganshire and was High Sheriff in 1789. In due course he demolished the old house and built a new dwelling further along the hillside described as a square little eight roomed house. His son, Thomas John Jones (1745-1817), succeeded his father and established Banc y Llong at Aberystwyth with two others in 1806. The partnership was dissolved in 1814. Thomas J. Jones died at Brunswick Square in June 1817, aged 72. His son, John Jones jnr, commissioned C. R. Cockerell to design a new house for him at Deri Ormond and demolished his father's house. A 200 foot tower was built on a hilltop. Work on the house began in 1824 and was completed three years later at a cost of £6,211. The *Deri Ormond Deeds* of 31 March 1824 state: 'An agreement with John Foster of Pembroke St, Portland Square, Bristol, carpenter and builder to build a mansion house at Derry Ormond.'

In 1828, John Jones married Charlotte Jesson of Hill Park, Kent. A son, John Inglis, was born the following year at Portland Place, London, and was followed by three daughters, and for the next six years the family commuted between Deri Ormond and London. In 1834-5, an addition in the Italian style was proposed, but tragedy struck the family before the additional work was completed with the death of John Jones early in 1835. For the next 16 years the great house stood empty. Lewis in *TDW* states: 'Deri Ormond, the seat of John Jones, Esq. an elegant modern mansion, erected in 1827 and beautifully situated under the shelter of a lofty hill covered with luxuriant plantations: the grounds, which are tastefully laid out, are ornamented with a small sheet of water, formed by the expansion of a rivulet by which they are intersected, and over which there is a bridge of handsome design. Though not upon a very large scale, this is one of the best houses in the county, and forms an interesting feature in the scenery of the place.' Meyrick writes: 'The Jones family, successful in the drover's trade, acquired the property in the second half of the 18th century. The seat of John Jones, Esq. and late of David Jones, has been lately rebuilt.'

In 1850 John Inglis Jones came to live at Deri Ormond and was High Sheriff of Cardiganshire two years later. He was responsible for building the local school, the station on the Milford and Manchester railway and the saw-mills. The *Landowners Return of 1873* states that Deri Ormond was an estate of 4,278 acres yielding an annual rental of £2,570. By 1895 it was over 11,000 acres and at the end of the First World War, 16,000 acres. John Inglis Jones had died in 1879 and was succeeded by his son, Wilmot. He married the formidable Winifred, a daughter of Alfred Montalto, and they had four children – three boys, and a girl, Elizabeth, later a notable writer and biographer. The family changed its name to Inglis-Jones by Deed Poll in 1898. The golden age of the landed estate was in decline. When Wilmot Inglis-Jones died in 1949, only 462 acres of a once great estate remained and the mansion was sold in 1950 for £3,000. The new proprietor had no intention of living there and in 1953 the building was demolished. The old clock was pulled down by a tractor and the lead and brass sold; the lead for £800 a ton. A piece of the wall-panelling can be seen at the Castle Hotel in Lampeter. *The Anglo-Welsh Review* published an article with photographs of the mansion entitled 'Derry Ormond Tower: A Welsh Landscape Artefact' by Austen Wilks. Nicholas printed an engraving of the house in *County Families* while Steegman listed portraits previously in the house.

Grid Ref: SN 6075 5225

Refs: Kitchin Map, 1854; Colby Map, 1831; Meyrick, *Cardiganshire;* Lewis, *TDW* (1840); Nicholas, *County Families* (1872 & 75); *Ceredigion,* Vol. II, pp. 27-37 (1954); ibid, Vol. X, 3 (1986), pp. 287-99; WWHR, iii, p. 88; Edwinsford Deeds 2646; Steegman II, *South Wales;* NLW, Deri Ormond Deeds, 24, 71-2, 238; Landowners Return, 1873; NLW, Vol. XXII, 2 (1981), pp. 214-225; *Anglo-Welsh Review,* Spring (1975), pp. 89-113;

DINAS CERDIN, Llandysul

Marked on *Colby's Map of 1831* on the bank of the river Cerdin south of the ancient Iron Age hill-fort which is sited on a spur in the vale of Cerdin. There is a Blaen (source) Cerdin further north and there are many Cerdin names in the vicinity. On modern OS maps, Dinas Cerdin is marked to the east and north of the A486 from Croes-lan and less than a mile south-east of the village of Ffostrasol. In the Llanfrene quarter of Llandysul parish in 1758 was a farm called Dinas Cerdin y Llethr. Further south towards Llandysul were Abercerdin (at the confluence of the Teifi and Cerdin), and Glyn Cerdin. The ancient hill-fort Dinas Cerdin is situated on the land of Dinas Cerdin farm. Meyrick states: 'Dinas Cerdin and Blaen Cerdin – these estates belonged to the Lewis family, descended from Morydd, King of Ceredigion; it is still in the possession of a descendant of David Lewis.'

The first of this ancient family to settle at Dinas Cerdin was Jenkin, son of Meredydd ap Ieuan of Capel Cynon. Jenkin married the daughter and heiress of Rhys Dafydd Ieuan of Llwyndafydd. Their son, Meredydd, married Jane, daughter of Thomas ap John Lloyd who was descended from the Castell Hywel family who traced to Cadifor ap Dinawal. The first of the family to take the surname Lewis was David Lewis, who married Catherine, daughter of John Phillip Howell Lloyd of Dolhaidd. Their eldest son, John Lewis, whose elegy and pedigree was noted by Griffith Rhys in 1706, married Elizabeth, daughter and heiress of Rhys Dafydd of Glyn Adda in Llanllawddog parish, whose wife was Lleucu, daughter of Griffith Rhys Llewelyn Watkin of Pant-swllt. A copy of the elegy to John Lewis was found at Pen-y-banc Isaf, Abergwili, and presented to the NLW by J. Lloyd Edwards Esq. A further copy was presented to Francis Jones by Miss Nesta Jenkin Lloyd and is deposited in his file of the Lloyds of Pen-y-banc, Carmarthenshire.

Another prominent member of the Dinas Cerdin family, James Lewis, was ordained Minister of Pencader Congregational Chapel in 1706. He also had charge of the chapel at Pantycreuddyn. W. J. Davies in his *Hanes Plwyf Llandysul*, states that James Lewis came from a superior family who traced their lineage to Morydd, King of Ceredigion in the 9th century. John Lewis (1707-1766), who married Catherine, daughter of John Davies, was born at Blaen Cerdin. He assisted his father at Pencader and Pantycreuddyn and was ordained in 1743 and took charge of both his father's chapels as well as Rhyd-y-bont. He died aged 59 in January 1766. James Lewis, whose elegy has survived, was succeeded by his son, David, who was twice-married; firstly to Sarah, daughter of the Rev. David Evans, Rector of Bangor Teifi, and secondly to Mary, daughter of Edward Evans of Llwynffynnon, by whom he had two sons, John, the heir, and David, who died unmarried in 1771. John married Catherine, daughter of John Davies, by whom he had a son, John, and a daughter, Elizabeth, ultimately heiress of Dinas Cerdin. John and Catherine died within days of each other in the autumn of 1788. Their only son, John, had pre-deceased his parents in 1787 and it was John's son, James, who inherited his grandfather's estate. James Lewis married Rachel Thomas of Derwyn but there were no children of the marriage. Although he had a sister, Catherine, it was his aunt, Elizabeth, sister of John Lewis, who inherited the estate. Elizabeth Lewis, who died aged 78 on 27 January 1842, had married Thomas Evans and he, upon his wife's death, inherited Dinas Cerdin. Thomas Evans died on 8 April 1845 aged 84. There is a tablet to John and Catherine Lewis and their daughter and son-in-law on the south-side of the chancel in Llandysul parish church. David Lewis Evans, son of Elizabeth and Thomas, married Mary Thomas of Llawr-cwrt, Talgarreg. David died on 20 December 1868, aged 76. His memorial stone at Sant Ffraid church, Tre-groes, shows their arms: three lions.

David and Mary Lewis's son, Lewis Lewis Evans, inherited Dinas Cerdin and married Mary, daughter of Jenkin Thomas of Cwm-hyar. They had four children, David, Elizabeth, who died in 1878, Mary Eliza and John Thomas Lewis. Benjamin Williams (Gwynionydd), in his prize-winning essay, *Hanes Castell-newydd-yn-Emlyn,* published in 1860, states: 'From the Lewis family of Dinas Cerdin, descend the late Rev. James Lewis, Pencader, the Rev. Christmas Evans, The Rev. David Lewis Jones and the present Dr. J. H. Jones.' To these names may be added cadet branches of Dinas Cerdin at Carrog, Llanddeiniol parish and Tre-faes, in the parish of Llanilar. The former was the home of Lewis Lewis, a young Methodist clergyman, who died at the age of 27 in 1764 whilst still in deacon's orders, and the Rev. John Lewis of Rhiw-goch, who played a leading role in raising funds to re-build his parish church of Llanrhystud in 1854, and was also a member of the Lewis family of Tre-faes. Other notables among the Lewis's with Dinas Cerdin connections were, Evan Lewis (1818-1901), Dean of Bangor, and his brother, David, sometime head teacher of Twickenham Grammar School. His nephew, also David (1814-1895), was a keen rower and became Vice-Principal of Jesus College, Oxford and a curate to John Henry Newman at St Mary's. David embraced the Roman Catholic Church with his mentor in 1846. David's younger brother, Evan Lewis, was educated at his uncle's school in Twickenham and followed his brother to Jesus College. He took Holy Orders in 1842 and was an enthusiastic promoter of the Oxford Movement in the Diocese of Bangor.

Grid Ref: SN 3860 4685

Refs: Colby Map, 1831; C/A Box 36/XV/fo. 3 W6; WWHR, i, p. 37; Meyrick, *Cardiganshire;* PRO, PRO, Dale Castle MS., p. 26 (101); W. J. Davies, *Hanes Plwyf Llandysul* (1896), pp. 177, 216-22; Benjamin Williams (Gwynionydd), *Hanes Castell-Newydd-yn-Emlyn* (1860), p. 55; Protheroe, C, VI; TM (1840), *Llandysul; Ceredigion,* Vol. VII, No. 3/4 (1974-5) pp. 332-349.

DÔL(E), Llandygwydd

Formerly situated on meadow land near the confluence of the Teifi and Cuch and bordering the main road between Cenarth and Llechryd, marked on *Colby's Map of 1831*. The *Beckinsale Collection* at the CRO has a plan of Dôle surveyed in 1844 by W. Evans for P. Griffiths Esq. the owner. The plan shows five fields totalling 47 acres with the 'old mansion house' marked in the centre of the property. A lane leads north to the main Cenarth to Cardigan road. Stradmore Mansion overlooks Dôl and the fields may now be located immediately north-east of Newbridge saw-mills on the flood plain between the main road and the Teifi.

The *Llwyndyrus Deeds* state: 'On 28th Sept. 1783, James Symmons of Slebech and Rev. Charles Symmons, rector of Narberth and Robeston Wathen, released the messuages called Ddole and Berllan in Llandygwydd parish to Sylvanus Nugent of Penygored, Cilgerran parish in Pembrokeshire.' In 1784-5 Sylvanus Nugent mortgaged the properties called Dole, Stradmore and Pwll Llacka. In 1787 Sylvanus

Nugent released Dôle to John Forester of the Foreign, Walsall, co. Staffs. and William Davies of Clun Meredydd, parish of Whitchurch, Pembrokeshire. In 1789 John Forester, now of Dole, mortgaged the property to Thomas Tucker of Sealyham, and c. 1789 Forester mortgaged Dôle to James Nathaniel Taylor of Stradmore Vale, Cards. On 18 March 1801 J. N. Taylor mortgaged the capital mansion house with its demesne lands called Stradmore and Pwll Llacka, the messuage and its demesne lands called Ddol or Dole, and the messuage called Galltybwla and Dôl Gelli Gwmfur, with furniture and effects of Stradmore house, to Metcalf Graham Steele of Sion Hill, parish of Kirk-by-Wisk, Yorks, and in the same year Metcalf Graham Steele mortgaged it to James Nathaniel Taylor, late of same.'

In 1807 Metcalf Graham Steele owned Thornville, formerly called Ddol. On 26 August 1842, a declaration was made by Lewis Evans of Cardigan, solicitor, that a house was built on the estate called Dôle, and that the proprietor, a Mr. Steele, changed the name to Thornville, and that the old name was restored by Sir Henry Strachey, Bart., of Sutton Court, Somerset.

Grid Ref: SN 2458 4125

Refs: Colby Map, 1831; Lewis, *TDW* (1840); WWHR, iii, p. 79; NLW, Llwyndyrus Deeds; CRO, Beckinsale Deeds.

DOLAU Y, Llanwenog, see HIGHMEAD

DOLAU GWARTHEG, Henfynyw

Situated near the border with Llanddewi Aberarth parish and marked on *Colby's Map of 1831* and on modern OS maps in the Aeron valley a mile south-east of Aberaeron on the main A472 road towards Ystrad Aeron. Horsfall-Turner states '. . . Dolau Gwartheg, the home of the Anglesey missionary Alban Griffiths . . .'. Alban was the third and youngest son of Thomas Griffith, all of whom took Holy Orders – John, born in Parcneuadd, Aberaeron in 1820, and rector of Neath and Llantwit from 1855, and Arthur, later Rector of Llanelly, Breconshire. Their grandfather, Thomas, was the son of Arthur Griffiths of Llangolman, Pembrokeshire, who married his cousin, Janet, daughter of George Lloyd of Cwmgloyn. Alban Griffiths was educated at Abergavenny and was appointed curate at Ebbw Vale by the Bishop of Llandaf. Due to ill-health, he moved to north Wales and was appointed vicar of Llanallgo on Anglesey. He established secular and Sunday schools and was much loved by both church and chapelgoers. He died at the Royal Hotel, Caernarfon, on his way home to Ceredigion less than a year after his arrival in north Wales. His death in 1862 at the early age of 33 years was a severe blow to the people of Anglesey.

Grid Ref: SN 6140 4630

Refs: Colby Map, 1831; Nicholas, *County Families,* ii, p. 629 (2nd edn., 1875); Horsfall-Turner, *Wanderings*, p. 110; Benjamin Williams, *Enwogion Ceredigion,* pp. 86-7.

DOLAUGWYRDDION,
Llanbedr Pont Steffan

Marked as Dôle Gwrddion on *Kitchin's Map of 1754,* as Dôle Gwyrddon on *Emanuel Bowen's Map of South Wales* and Dôle Gwyrddion on the *Colby Map of 1831.* On modern OS maps two farms are marked Dolaugwyrddion-isaf and -uchaf, located south of the A475 main road between Pentre-bach and Llanwnnen on meadowland on the northern bank of the Teifi three miles south-west of Lampeter. The first recorded reference to Dolaugwyrddion is the marriage of Dyddgu, a daughter of Morgan Dafydd Goch of Dôle Gwyrddion who married Ieuan, the son of Ieuan Goch, who traced to the Castell Hywel family and Cadifor ap Dinawal, and his wife, a sister of Dafydd ap Ieuan of Cilie. Dyddgu and Ieuan ap Ieuan Goch had a son, David, who adopted Evans as his surname. David Evans, later of Llechwedd Deri and described as 'an inpecunious free-holder', became High Sheriff of Cardiganshire in 1641, built Peterwell on the site of an ancient well and founded the dynasty which, in due course, was to produce the notorious Sir Herbert Lloyd. David's daughter Sarah, married Daniel Lloyd of Lacques, Llansteffan parish and Dolau Gwyrddion became the property of the Lloyds and let to tenants.

It is likely that Dôle Gwyrddion became two farmsteads -isaf and -uchaf at about this time. In 1672, Hugh and John Davies were taxed at 5 hearths each at Dôle Gwyrddion.

Lettice, the daughter of Thomas Davies of Dolau, married Hugh Philipps, second son of Thomas and Elizabeth Philipps of Cilsant, Llanwinio parish. Their daughter became the heiress. A traditional tale of this time concerning Dolau Gwyrddion is related by Dafydd Nunn, one-time steward and tree planter at Peterwell, who heard the tale from his father. The young son of Pentre Sion went to London to endeavour to make his fortune, failed and joined Cromwell's army. He did well, was promoted and was made an official for wood measuring at the Deptford shipyards. He became known as William Jones. Pentre Sion at that time included, in addition to the present farmhouse, the farms of Hendryd, Pentre-bach and Dôl Drement. For his service to Cromwell, William Jones received Dolau Gwyrddion and in due course, settled there. He married a Miss Hughes, a daughter of the old wealthy family of Llysfaen. They had a son who died in infancy and a daughter. The daughter married the son and heir of Dafydd ap Sion of Ffynnon Fair and became *iure uxoris* of Dolau Gwyrddion. Their son was Morgan Jones who fell in love with Elen, one of the daughters of Sir Watkin Wynn, Dyffryn Llynod in Llandysul parish. Her family opposed the union as he was not of a sufficiently good family and because he had fought against King Charles in the Civil War. For ten years the young couple met secretly. On three occasions Elen was sent to France to stop her clandestine meetings with Morgan. On her return following the third visit, she developed *y frech wen* (smallpox). When Morgan heard of her plight he visited Dyffryn Llynod secretly at midnight to see and console his lover. Alas he contracted the dreaded disease and they both perished within a day or two to each other. They were both aged 40. Elen was buried in Llandysul but Morgan's wish to be buried with her was ignored and he was laid to rest at Lampeter, where his tombstone could be seen until destroyed at a subsequent restoration of the church.

A ballad written by Thomas Dafydd, a 19th century poet and published by Sion Rhydderch at Shrewsbury, was reprinted in 1820. Its title was *'Can serch yn rhoddi hanes carwriaeth Morgan Jones o Dolegwyrddion a gariad Mary Watkins o'r Dyffryn Llynod a fuont feirw o serch un at y llall, ac a gladdwyd yn yr un beddrod yn mynwent Llanbedr, yn cynnwys rhybudd i rieni fo yn erbyn ieuo eu plan lle godasantt eu serch'.* The ballad was written to warn parents against interference when their offspring placed their affections. It consists of 33 four-line stanzas describing the tragic love-affair of Morgan Jones of Dolau Gwyrddion and Elen Watkins of Dyffryn Llynod, who were buried together at Lampeter.

The *Edwinsford Deeds* state that, 'on 14 March 1722/3 William Jones of Talley, gent, and Mary, his wife, transferred to Jane Davies, a widow of Dolau Gwyrddion in the parish of Lampeter, a mortgage to secure £50 on properties in Caio parish'. Jane, the daughter of John Davies of Dolau, married three times. Her first husband, by whom she had a son, William, alive in 1726, was a Price of whom nothing is known. Her second husband, John Davies, by whom she had a daughter, Jane. Jane married as his second wife, David Lloyd of Clun-y-march, Llansawel, a descendant of the Lloyds of Alltyrodin, Llandysul. She then married William Lloyd of Laques. A *Cardiff Central Library Deed* states that on 25 March, 1733, 'articles of agreement were drawn between William Lloyd of Laques, Jane Lloyd of Dolau Gwyrddion, widow, and William Williams of Rhydarwen, Carms. and Morgan Davies of Coomb', before the intended marriage between William Lloyd and Jane and that Jane would receive £50 per annum for life if widowed and to raise £1,000 for the younger children. The *Griffith Owen Deeds* state that Elinor Davies, a widow, had lived at Dolau until 1739, but that she had died before July 1746. By 1760, Daniel Lloyd of Laques had succeeded to Dolau Gwyrddion. He was appointed JP in 1762 and married Sarah Evans, daughter of John Lloyd of Trefenty, son of David Evans of Llechwedd Deri, who was the son of Ifan Goch of Dolau Gwyrddion. In 1792, Daniel, the son and heir of Daniel and Sarah Lloyd, married Marie Eleanora Colburne of Carmarthen. A pre-nuptial settlement was agreed between Daniel Lloyd the elder of Laques and his eldest son, William Lloyd of the same, and Marie Elinora Colburne. The lands settled on the marriage were, Dolau Gwyrddion Uchaf and Isaf, and Danyrallt-fach (let at £118 pa), Bolahaul, Pantsgawen (£10.16.0 pa), and

Dôl Drement , let at 6 guineas all in the parish of Lampeter Pont Steffan, for the use of Daniel and Maria and then to the use of William Lloyd, William Colburne and William Morgan. In 1825, William Lloyd the elder of Laques sold Dolau Gwyrddion, then a property of 333 acres and yielding £240 a year in rent for £7,250.

By 1841, William Price, late of Felindre in the parish of Llanfihangel Ystrad and Portreeve of Lampeter in 1844, was living at Dolau Gwyrddion-uchaf, while the *Landowners Return of 1873* states that a William Price was still the owner of a property now of 133 acres and yielding £122 per annum in rent.

Grid Ref: SN 5556 4670

Refs: Emanuel Bowen Map of South Wales; Colby Map, 1831; *Arch. Camb.,*1861, p. 24; WWHR, i, p. 41; ibid, iii, p. 89; PRO, PRO, Dale Castle MS., p. 27; NLW, Edwinsford Deeds, No. 2592; CRO, GGMS II, Cadifor Fawr; Landowners Return, 1873; Cardiff Central Library Deeds; Bethan Phillips, *Peterwell, The History of a Mansion and its Infamous Squire* (Llandysul), 1983, pp. 14-15.

DOLCLETWR, Llangynfelyn

Described by Evan Isaac as one of the most peaceable homes in Wales (*un o gartrefi tangnefeddus Cymru*). A small estate on the edge of Cors Fochno near the river Cletwr situated east of the parish church and marked on the *Colby Map of 1831.*

From 1611-30 Hugh Lloyd was the owner of Dolcletwr. He was the son of Hugh Lloyd ap John Lloyd of Dolcletwr, ap Hugh John Lloyd of Brysgaga, ap John Lloyd ap Thomas ap Griffith ap Ieuan ap Meredydd. By 1731, Lewis Lewis was the owner of Dolcletwr and High Sheriff of Cardiganshire in 1727 and appointed JP in 1740. The *Noyadd Trefawr Deeds* state: '1727 Aug. 28. 1. Lewis Lewis of Dôl Cletwr, Cards., Esq. present High Sheriff. 2. John Jones of Cardigan, gent. Revocation of appointment of 2 to be under-Sheriff.' The same deeds note that: 'In 1727 Dec. 7. Lewis Lewis of Dôl Cletwr Esq. and Jane, his wife, Richard Lloyd of Mabws Esq., Edward Jones of Llanina, Esq. and Margaret, his wife, lease of possession to Thomas Pugh of Machynlleth, gent, of

messuages called Brysgaga, Broncastellan and lands in the parish of Llanbadarn-fawr and Llanfihangel Genau'r-glyn.'

William Jones was the owner of Dolcletwr in 1736. He died in October of the same year aged 36. His son, also William Jones, gent., was a JP, and is named as the freeholder of the property in 1760. He was High Sheriff in 1766 and died on 5 April 1779, aged 48 years. William and his wife had two daughters, Jane, the heiress, and Margaret Evans, who was natural. Jane married John Watkins of Bryn-gwyn, Rhydypennau, and she died at Brysgaga aged 72 in 1845. Their son, W. J. Watkins, sold Brysgaga to Sir Pryse Pryse of Gogerddan. Jane Watkins, daughter of Jane and John, married David Humphreys of Nant-llan, Llandyfaelog, Carmarthenshire. They had a daughter Frances, who married R. J. Davies of Cwrt Mawr, Llangeitho. Their son, John Humphreys Davies, was Principal of UCW Aberystwyth from 1919 until his death in 1926. Meyrick states: 'Dol Cletwr or Cletwr Mead, is now the property of Major Gilbertson, who received it from his maternal uncle, William Jones.' William Jones of Brysgaga and formerly of Dolcletwr died in 1772. His sister Mary, was Major Gilbertson's wife. Their son, William Cobb Gilbertson, a lawyer, was born in London in 1768. He settled at Brysgaga in 1780 and two years later moved to Aberystwyth. Before the end of the decade, Gilbertson was residing at Dolcletwr and two of his children by his first wife, Mary, daughter of Thomas Pelham Hopley, from Aberystwyth, and who lived for a time at Dolcletwr, were baptised at Llangynfelyn parish church. Gilbertson's second wife is unknown, but his third wife was Elizabeth, the younger daughter of the Rev. Isaac

Williams, vicar of Llanrhystud, whom he married at Llansanffraid in 1811. Eight children were born to William and Elizabeth. Bishop Basil Jones of Gwynfryn bought Dolcletwr from Mr. Gilbertson when the latter moved to Cefn Gwyn, Bontgoch. Elizabeth died in 1846 when William was 77 years old. One of their younger sons, Lewis Gilbertson, born in 1815, attended Jesus College, Oxford and enjoyed a distinguished academic career. He became a Fellow and later Vice-Principal of his old college. He was ordained in 1838 and from 1841 to 1852, was the incumbent of Llangorwen church, north of Aberystwyth. There the influence of the Oxford Movement, inspired by one cousin, Isaac Williams (1802-1865), and built with the money of another, Mathew Davies Williams of Cwmcynfelin, became apparent in the stone altar, the first erected in Wales since the Reformation. To fulfil his father's wish, Lewis Gilbertson also built a church at Elerch and became the first vicar of the new parish in 1869. James Griffiths, tenant, was a retired Merchant Navy master-mariner and grandfather of the present occupier, Mrs. Gwen Davies, who bought Dolcletwr from the Gwynfryn estate in 1977. Having spent a lifetime at sea and wishing to extend his farming activities, Capt. Griffiths moved to Dolcletwr with his wife and four children, from y Gelli in Llangynfelyn. The estate extended from Lodge Park in the north, across Cors Fochno, and included the villages of Tre'r-ddol (formerly Tre Dolcletwr) and Taliesin (formerly named Comins y Dafarn Fach), as far as Ynys Capel. According to Mrs Davies, Dolcletwr was once a public-house called The Wildfowler (Tafarn Dolcletwr), brewing its own beer from hops which still flourish in the hedge-rows of Dolcletwr. The house includes the only example of pre-glazed glass in Cardiganshire and was originally built of cruck construction in c. 1200. This was exposed and preserved during renovations at the house.

Grid Ref: SN 6564 9230

Refs: PRO Lists; Colby Map, 1831; AC (1917), p. 149; Meyrick, *Cardiganshire;* NLW, Bronwydd Deeds, No. 7242; ibid Noyadd Trefawr Deeds, Nos. 429 & 587; Horsfall-Turner, *Wanderings* p. 221; J. R. Phillips, *Sheriffs of Cardiganshire;* Mrs G. Davies, Dolcletwr; *Ceredigion,* vol. vii, pp. 337-8; ibid, vol. viii, p. 251.

DOL-FAWR (Dolfor), Ciliau Aeron

This property is located on *Colby's Map of 1831* and on modern OS maps. The present house called Dolfor, is located on the southern bank of the Aeron west of the minor road which runs north from Ciliau Aeron towards Pennant. It is not to be confused with Dôl Fawr located near Ystradmeurig which was farmed by the monks of Ystrad Fflur (Strata Florida). Early records show Ieuan of Dolfawr, whose son, Griffith ap Ieuan of Dolfawr Aeron married Nest, daughter of Griffith ap Llewelyn of Morfa Bychan, Llanychaearn parish. Their son, Gruffydd Chwith of Dolfawr had a daughter who married Henry ap Phillip descended from Gwaethfoed Fawr, King of Ceredigion in the 11th century. From their son, Gruffydd ap Henry, is descended the family of Lloyd of Llanllyr. Griffith ap Henry in turn was descended from Phillip ap Rhydderch who gave his name to Parc Rhydderch, Llanbadarn Odwyn parish. Another kinsman Dafydd Llwyd ap Dafydd ap Rhydderch was the progenitor of the Pryses of Gogerddan. Formerly the family were notable Royalists and Ieuan ap Gruffydd Foel swore allegiance to the Black Prince in 1343. They were also patrons of the great medieval poets including Dafydd ap Gwilym, Iolo Goch and Gruffydd Llwyd. Gruffydd ap Henry's daughter and heiress, Joan, married Hugh Llewelyn Lloyd who made his home at Llanllyr and raised a distinguished family. The *Golden Grove Manuscripts* state that 'Meredydd ap Ieuan of Dolfawr, by Aberaeron a man of great possessions', married Gwenllian Wen, daughter of Ieauan Llewelyn David of Corws (Cwrrws), relict of Meredudd Phillip of Cilsant, Llanwinio parish, Carmarthenshire. They had a daughter, Jenet, who married Rhys ap Llewelyn ap Rhys Ddu *y Sgweiar Digri* (the mirthful squire). Jenet and Rhys had three sons, one of whom, Ieuan of Pen-y-wern, was the progenitor of the Lloyds of Maenordeifi in Pembrokeshire. Llewelyn ap Phillip, who married Agnes, daughter of Meredydd, heir of Porth Hofin in Aberporth parish. Their son was Lewis of Llaethdir and Llanuwchaeron although Protheroe states, 'Lewis of Llangrannog and Llaethdir'. Rhys Ddu otherwise Rhys ap Gruffydd ap Llywelyn, Sheriff of the whole county in 1394-5, was a lessee of royal lands at

Silian, Trefilan and Talsarn. He later became Owain Glyn Dwr's lieutenant until the surrender in 1408. Rhys was captured in Shropshire, taken to London and executed at Tyburn. His body was drawn and quartered and his head set on London Bridge.

Grid Ref: SN 4987 5965

Refs: Colby Map, 1831; CRO, GGMS (Tydwal Gloff), fos. 33 & 37; Protheroe, C, D & E; *Ceredigion,* VII, No.1 (1972), pp. 14-39; ibid, V, No. 2 (1965), pp.154-7. J.D. Emrys Jones.

DOL-GOCH, Tregaron

Located on the west bank of the upper Tywi adjacent to the Cardiganshire-Breconshire border and marked on *Colby's Map of 1831*, *Kitchin's Map of Breconshire,* east of Llanddewibrefi and Tregaron and on modern OS maps amongst the huge forestry plantation of the Tywi forest. Modern motoring maps denote a youth hostel at Dol-goch which is located south of the mountain road from Tregaron to Abergwesyn. This farmhouse will forever be remembered as the birthplace of the remarkable William Williams (1698-1773), who received the sobriquet *Brenin y Mynydd* (King of the Mountain) and 'Job of the west' in deference to his astute business acumen as a sheep and horse-dealer. William's father, David Williams of Dol-goch was High Sheriff of Cardiganshire in 1725 and his two sons William and Nathaniel, (later of Mynachlog-fawr and Castle Hill, Llanilar), undertook the duties in 1751 and 1776 respectively. The first of the family associated with Dol-goch was John Williams, born in Llanddewibrefi parish who moved to the isolated farmstead following his marriage to Johan Price, sister of Walter Price of Llanfair Clydogau in 1661. The marriage settlement appears in the *Castle Hill Documents* which also includes, on 8 May 1711, a record of an agreement between the burgesses and other inhabitants of Tregaron and William Williams of Dol-goch to divert the river Brenig. In the *Crosswood Deeds* for January 1721/2 is recorded: 'Lease (counterpart) for 21 years, from the Right Hon. John Edward, Lord Viscount Lisburne, to William Williams, of the parish of Caron, gent. of tenements called Dolgoch, Gaiach, Cwmduy, Hirnant, Nant-y-bont, in the said parish of Caron. Yearly rent 10 guineas and a heriot of 5 guineas. Consideration 5 guineas.'

Grid Ref: SN 7920 5875

Refs: Colby Map, 1831; Kitchin's Map of Breconshire; NLW, Crosswood Deeds; ibid, Castle Hill Documents, No. 702; D. C. Rees, *Tregaron: Historical and Antiquarian*, 1936.

DOL-GOCH, Troed-yr-aur (Trefdreyr)

Situated south-east of Troed-yr-aur church near the river Ceri and shown on *Colby's Map of 1831*. On modern OS maps it is located on the western bank of the Ceri half a mile south-west of Brongest. G. E. Evans in his *Cardiganshire*, published in 1903 states: 'Here, Llewelyn ap Gwilym Fychan, Lord of Cardigan, resided, and held that great Eisteddfod about the year 1360.'

Benjamin Williams (Gwynionydd) in his *Hanes Castell-newydd-yn-Emlyn*, states that Dafydd ap Gwilym, the great medieval poet lived there. *'Mae y Ddolgoch ar lan Ceri yn Nhroedyraur o fewn tair milltir i Emlyn.'* Llewelyn ap Gwilym Fychan owned both Dol-goch and Cryngae in the parish of Llangeler and was the uncle of Dafydd ap Gwilym. The *CRO GGMS* state that Gwilym Chwith ap Llywelyn of Cryngae in Emlyn, was descended from Ednyfed Fychan. Horsfall-Turner writes: 'In the vale of Troedyraur, in the nook below the parish church, where the modern farmhouse of Dolgoch retains the name and inherits the woodland environment of an ancient homeland. The mansion of Dolgoch carries us backward in recorded events to the days of the Plantagenet Kings, when this palace and that of Cryngae across the Tivy vale were in the possession of a descendant of Ednyfed Fychan of Penmynydd, Ynys Mon, Llewelyn ap Gwilym Fychan, Constable of Castle Emlyn, at his residence of Dolgoch. Llewelyn, in his days of peace held an Eisteddfod . . . In earlier days, Dolgoch was the home of Dr. Morgan, a physician of some repute, with whom served the literary John Morgan MD, a native of Trefilan in the Aeron vale, author of *An Advertisory Sketch of Pethagovas.* By 1760, the Rev. Samuel Jones, clerk, owned Dol-goch. Thereafter the records are silent.

Grid Ref: SN 3175 4436

Refs: Colby Map, 1831; Benjamin Williams (Gwynionydd), *Hanes Castell-newydd-yn-Emlyn;* G. E. Evans, *Cardiganshire* (1903), p. 271; Horsfall-Turner, *Wanderings.*

DOL-WEN, Llanwenog

Located both on *Colby's Map of 1831* and on modern OS maps due south of Dre-fach on meadowland on the eastern bank of the river Cledlyn. There is a Dolwen-fach nearby.

The *Glassbrook Collection* tells us of an agreement dated 28 February 1738 between: '1. Nathan Griffiths of Dolwen in Llanwenog parish, gent. and Elizabeth his wife, Thomas Griffiths, Rector of Penegoes, Mon., their son and heir, Catherine Griffiths and Mary Griffiths, spinsters, eldest and second daughters of the said Nathan and Catherine, and 2. Anna Pughe of Mathafarn, Mont., spinster , mortgage in £400 of the capital messuage called Dolwen, Tir Kors Gledlyn, Tir y ddolwen and cottages called Tir y ddol in Llanwenog, 3 messuages called Tir Eskeir Anglis, Tir y Kelyn and Tir y Skybor, lands called Llain ymyl y rhyd galed and Y Gors Goch in Llanon parish, Cards.' The same Collection notes that in 1747, William Lloyd of Brynbrane, Cynwyl Gaeo parish, gent., bought the capital messuage of Dol-wen from the Rev.Thomas Griffiths, son and heir of Nathan Griffiths late of Dolwen, gent. deceased, for £1,077.11.4. No further details are included.

Grid Ref: SN 5033 4542

Refs: CRO, Glassbrook Collection, No. 13 (Additional 2).

DOL-WLFF, Llanwenog

Also known as Dolwolf and marked on *Kitchin's Map of 1754* as Dole Wolf and on *Colby's Map of 1831* as Dol Wolf. The property is located on modern OS maps south of Alltyblaca on the bank of the meandering Teifi near the B4337 half a mile north of Llanybydder. Nearby is the old encampment of Castell Dolwlff. The first recorded reference to the name is when Philip ap Ieuan Llwyd, of Dol-wlff, married Lleucu, daughter of Dafydd Llwyd Howel of Maesycrugiau, Llanllwni, Carmarthenshire. Philip was a descendant of Gwilym Lloyd who traced to Maesyfelin, seat of the Lloyd family formerly of Llanllyr, Talsarn. Gwilym was succeeded in turn by his son, Dafydd Lloyd, and his grandson, Jenkin Lloyd, who married a daughter of Ieuan Llwyd of Llanfair Clydogau. His son, Llewelyn, married a daughter of Hywel Fawr, a descendant of Grono Goch, Constable of Castell Dryslwyn in 1280-1.

Philip ap Ieuan Llwyd and Lleucu, his wife, were succeeded by their son, John, who was living at Dol-wlff in 1617. John married Maud, daughter of Gwion Llewelyn Lloyd of Llanfechan, Llanwenog parish. The Lloyds of Llanfechan were High Sheriffs of Cardiganshire on four occasions between 1599 and 1710. Jenkin, the son of John Phillip and Maud, married Mary, daughter of Walter Williams of Pencarreg, a stone's throw across the Teifi in Carmarthenshire. Mary Jenkin was a widow by 1680 for on 8 April of that year the *Noyadd Trefawr Deeds* relate: 'An agreement between: 1. Mary Jenkins of Dol Wolfe, parish of Llanwenog, widow, and her daughter, Jane Jenkins, exor. James Williams of Trevigod, parish of Llanbeder Pont Stephen, gent. surrendered two messuages called Tir Dol Gwm and Tir pen y lan in the parish of Pencarreg, Carms. Consideration £160.'

David and Mary Jenkins had three daughters and co-heiresses. The eldest daughter, also named Mary, married William Lloyd, second son of John Lloyd of Cilgwyn in 1681. The second daughter, Lettice, married Roger Pryse of Llangamarch, Breconshire, and the third, Jane, married Rhys Lloyd of Cil-y-blaidd, third son of David Lloyd of Alltyrodyn, Llandysul. Rhys was a JP for Carmarthenshire from 1685-88 during the reign of James II. William and Mary Lloyd had a son, David, who married Sage, daughter of Jenkin Evan of Llygadenwyn. The *Crosswood Deeds* state that on 30 March 1716: 'A lease for a year and release from David Lloyd of Dolwoolfe, gent. Sage, his wife and Walter Lloyd, his brother, of a messuage in Llanwenog parish to Rees Davies of Bangor Tivy parish, Esq.' Records in the CRO state that in 1737/8, the Dol-wlff estate consisted of 6 messuages, 6 cottages and 1,640 acres in Llanwenog parish. David and Sage's son, David, tragically lost his life at Dol-wlff in July 1751 when removing the charge from a gun and by 1753, Dol-wlff was in the tenure and occupation of Walter Lloyd, William Evans and Margaret, widow of David Wogan. Walter Lloyd, David Lloyd the elder's brother, was uncle and heir-at-law of the young David who died intestate.

Sometime between the years 1759 and 1767, Walter died, also without making a will. Walter Lloyd had married Catherine Jones and a pre nuptial settlement was drawn up on 10 April 1753. Catherine's portion was £30. Following Walter's death, Catherine married Dafydd Jones, gent. of Pen-y-bont (1725-1797). Dafydd was a notable scholar and school-master who ran a school at Dol-wlff between 1755 and 1780 and later taught at Llanybydder. He translated the *Eucharista of Hugo Grotius,* which was published in Carmarthen in 1765. With the support of local gentry and a gift of £15 from Jesus College, Oxford, he visited Palestine and wrote a detailed journal of his visit. Among Dafydd's pupils at Dol-wlff was the acclaimed scholar and bard, Dafydd Davies (Dafis Castell Hywel 1745-1827), and Lewis Lloyd of Cwmtofach, Llanwrda, who became a wealthy London banker. Lewis Lloyd's son, became Lord Overstone, MP for Hythe, who developed modern banking and died a millionaire. Dafydd Jones died on 14 December 1797 and was buried in Llanwenog churchyard. By 1783, John, the son of Walter and Catherine, had succeeded to Dol-wlff. Meyrick writes: 'The last owner of the place was John Lloyd (now living), who sold it to Herbert Lloyd (died 1814), attorney of Carmarthen, for an annuity of £30 and other considerations. Dol-wlff was let then to tenants.

Grid Ref: SN 5225 4487

Refs: Kitchin Map, 1754; Colby Map, 1831; WWHR, i, pp. 40-1, 51; ibid, III, p. 87; Meyrick, *Cardiganshire,* p. 216; CRO, GGMS (Tydwal Gloff), p. 20; NLW, Crosswood Deeds, No.136; PRO, Dale Castle MS., p. 27; NLW, Griffith Owen Deeds, No. 6271; ibid, Noyadd Trefawr Deeds, No. 383; Evans, *Lampeter,* p. 40; Davies, *Hanes Plwyf Llanwenog* (1939), p. 60; CRO, Wilson Deeds; D. H. James, *A Guide to Llanybydder* (1908), p. 18.

DOLYCHENNOG (DOLCHENNOG), Ysbyty Ystwyth

Francis Jones places this farm in the parish of Gwnnws. This parish is divided into Uchaf and Isaf which are separated by Ysradmeurig and Ysbyty Ystwyth parishes. On the *Colby Map of 1831,* Doluwchganog is marked on the southern bank of the Ystwyth adjacent to that river's confluence with the Milwyn. On modern OS maps, Dol-chenog is located at the same location as the Doluwchganog on *Colby's Map* and Coed Dol-chenog is nearby. This places Dolychennog in the parish of Ysbyty Ystwyth. John Parry of Dolychennog, gent, died before October 1760. The *Coleman Deeds* mention a deed of partition between the three daughters and co-heiresses of the Dolychennog estate comprising, at that time, of 18 properties in Gwnnws parish. In 1760, Elizabeth, the eldest daughter, married David Jones of Penbont-bren-fawr, Gwnnws parish. Jane, the second daughter, married Thomas Jenkins of Erw-barfau in the parish of Llanbadarn Fawr, who is described as the owner-occupier of the property, and Anne, the youngest daughter married Evan Griffiths of Bryn-llys, Gwnnws.

Grid Ref: SN 7877 7382

Refs: Colby Map, 1831; NLW, Coleman Deeds, No. 147; WWHR, iii, p. 97; W.T. James, Llanilar.

DOL-Y-GORS, Eglwys Newydd (Hafod)

Marked on *Colby's Map of 1831* as Dol-y-Gors north west of Hafod Uchdryd mansion north of Pont-rhyd-y-groes and Ysbyty Ystwyth. On modern OS maps the farm is located on the road leading from Devil's Bridge to Pont-rhyd-y-groes on marsh land near Nant Cell. Lewys Dwnn gives the pedigree for the Herberts of Dol-y-gors in 'Kwm Ystwyth' for which the family signed in 1593. Cwm Ystwyth, at that time, was the haunt of cattle rustlers, living beyond the law and the Herberts, who were connected with the Welsh Herberts headed by Lord Pembroke, migrated the short distance to this isolated and dangerous community in the 16th century from Montgomeryshire in search of mineral wealth. They bought up expired 99 year farm leases granted to the last tenants of the abbey of Ystrad Fflur at the Dissolution. These farms, which included Dolybeudy and

Dol-y-gors, formed the nucleus of the estate of the Herberts, later of Hafod Uchdryd.

William Herbert married Margaret Vaughan of Trawsgoed (Crosswood), a sister of John Vaughan. In 1632, Charles I summoned all freeholders with an income of £40 or more in land or rent to attend his coronation to be knighted. It was not a summons wholeheartedly welcomed by the gentry for it involved payment of £50 in fees and £20 on each subsidy levied. As many of the gentry defaulted, a commission was appointed and those who would not pay were summoned to appear before it. 'William Herbert of Dol-y-Gors gent. appeared not. Morgan Herbert his son alledged in the behalf of his father that he was at the tyme of the Coronation was ffower score yeres owld and cannot travell and he the said William Herbert hath not been to any great Sessions or quarter sessions houlden within the county for the space of these ffowerteene yeres now last past.'

Also in 1632, Sir John Lewes of Abernant-bychan in Penbryn parish, arbitrated between John Vaughan of Trawsgoed and Morgan Herbert of Hafod Uchdryd regarding disputed lands in Cwm Ystwyth which Lewes awarded to the Herberts for £300 and £22 chief rent due to the Crown. It was Morgan Herbert, who in 1620, received permission from the church authorities to build a new church for the parish of Llanfihangel-y-Creuddyn, which is still known as Eglwys Newydd. In his will, proved in 1649, Morgan Herbert of Cwm Ystwyth named John Vaughan of Trawsgoed as a creditor for £250. It appears that the £300 due to the squire of Trawsgoed for Hafod land had not been paid. The *Cwrtmawr Documents* mention a John Herbert of Dol-y-gors, gent, both in 1671 and 1676. By the beginning of the 18th century the estate passed to Thomas Johnes of Llanfair Clydogau, who married Jane, heiress to William Herbert who died in 1704.

Grid Ref: SN 7450 7410

Refs: Colby Map, 1831; NLW, Crosswood Deeds, p. 46; *Ceredigion,* VI, No. 2 (1969), p. 154; ibid, III, No. 1 (1956), pp. 91-3; Cwrtmawr MS., Nos. 1480 and 210.

DYFFRYN, Aberporth

The village of Aberporth is divided in two by a stream that flows through the valley to the sea. The land on the eastern shore belonged to Dyffryn and is still called Banc y Dyffryn. That on the west was owned by Plâs Aberporth and is referred to as Banc-y-plas. Marked on *Colby's Map of 1831* and on modern OS maps as being a little to the south of the village of Aberporth to the east of Nant Howni. Francis Jones notes that Griffith, the second son of Jenkyn ap Thomas of Panterlis in Llandygwydd parish (now called Pant-y-llys), a descendant of Elystan Glodrudd, settled at Dyffryn which he purchased in 1649. He also owned Penrallt, also in Aberporth. His son, Jenkin ap Griffith, lived at Dyffryn in 1675 and had a son, Griffith Jenkin, who married Elen, daughter and heiress of Jenkin ap Griffith ap Dafydd of Cilbronne. Their son was the first of the Jenkins' to settle there. A map-book of the Trewern estate near Whitland, drawn in 1826 by Alfred Thomas, surveyor and agent, shows that Dyffryn was a farm of 200 acres, which formed part of the estate of John Thomas Beynon of Trewern.

Grid Ref: SN 2610 5075

Ref: Colby Map, 1831; Nicholas, *County Families*, i, 196-7; NLW, 21983C, Map-book of the Trewern Estate of J. T. Beynon

DYFFRYN BERN, Penbryn

Situated a mile from Cardigan Bay south east of the coastal village of Tre-saith and named on *Colby's Map of 1831* as Dyffryn Beron, a mile south of Penbryn church. In his *Guide to Cardigan and District*, W. E. James states, 'The farm of Dyffrynbern, on the lands of which stands a monumental stone, generally known as the "Dyffrynbern Stone": it is 4th or 5th century and is inscribed CORBALENCI IACET ORDOVS' (The body of Corbalengus lies here, an Ordivician).

Nicholas Morgan of Eglwys-wen in Cemaes, married Ann, daughter of David Lloyd of Llanborth, parish of Penbryn. Their son, Thomas, who lived at Llanborth, married Priscilla Edwards of Haverfordwest in 1705. They had two sons and a daughter: Nicholas, who married Mary Reynolds of Blaiddbwll, Llanfyrnoch parish, Pembrokeshire, and David, who married Anne, daughter of Griffith Thomas of Dyffryn Bern. Mary married twice, firstly to Ieuan, whose surname is not known, and then to David Howel of Cilrhedyn, Carmarthenshire. On 9 July 1771, David Davies, otherwise David ap Ioan ap Dafydd ap Griffith ap Dafydd ap Morris, who owned property and land in Troed-yr-aur and neighbouring parishes, married Anne, eldest child of Griffith and Katherine Jenkins of Dyffryn Bern. Their son, David, baptised in 1788, studied medicine and had an illustrious Army career before his retirement in 1838. He married his first cousin, Margaret Coakley, daughter of the Rev. Henry Jenkins, Rector of St James, Montego Bay, Jamaica, in the old Royal Palace in 1810. Griffith and Katherine had 11 children, six sons and five daughters. Jenkin, the eldest, 'died in his chair at noon on Saturday, 13 January 1821', aged 76 years. Jenkin was followed by his bachelor brother, John, who in turn, was succeeded by the third son, the Rev. David Jenkins, later collated to the rectory of Llanllwchaearn in 1779, a benefice which lasted for 57 years. He was followed by his son, Henry, Rector of Stanway and later Dean of Divinity at Magdalen College, Oxford. He died in 1874 aged 87 years and was followed by his first cousin once removed, the Rev. David Henry Davies, incumbent of Llannon, whose widow, Anne, and daughter, Margaret, decided that the property should be sold. Dyffryn Bern passed out of the family at an auction held at the Emlyn Arms, Newcastle Emlyn, on 20 August 1910.

Grid Ref: SN 2878 5119

Refs: WWHR, i, p. 49; ibid, ii, p. 80; PRO, Dale Castle MS., p. 29; W. E. James, *Guide to Cardigan and District* (1899), p. 31; Colby Map, 1831; Tithe Map and Schedule, Penbryn parish; *Ceredigion,* Vol. VI, No. 2, 1969.

DYFFRYN CLETWR, Llandysul

This property, probably later known as Glan Cletwr, was situated on the banks of the Cletwr which flows south from near Post-bach and meets the Teifi at Abercletwr, east of Llandysul. Francis Jones records only that John Tew of Llansawel, Carmarthenshire, had a son, Howel, who, in turn, had a daughter, Gwen, who married David Lloyd of Castell Hywel, parish of Llandysul, MP for Cardiganshire from 1536 to 1547. Gwen was given Dyffryn Cletwr as her portion. Their son lived at Castell Hywel.

Ref: Lloyd Family Records (Pedigrees, p. 8).

DYFFRYN HOFFNANT (Dyffryn Hownant), Penbryn

Dyffryn Hoffnant is located on modern OS maps half a mile north of Sarnau a little to the north of the minor road which runs to Penmorfa and Penbryn. Dyffryn Hownant, of which no trace remains, was located north of the present farmhouse. This Dyffryn Hownant, in turn, was a replacement for an even earlier residence of the same name which stood on the site of a car park in front of the Victorian farmhouse of Llanborth, overlooking the deeply-sided valley of the Hoffnant or Hownant. J. Geraint Jenkins in his article on Penrhyn Beach in *Ceredigion*, notes that the old mansion was the home of nobles and the influential Fychan or Vaughan family, kinsmen of the Lord of Tywyn, Rhys ap Rhydderch, patron of the poets and the owner of extensive lands in Penbryn parish and south Ceredigion, who traced to Gwrwared. Morgan Johnes of Dyffryn Hownant, a member of the Towyn family, signed for Lewys Dwnn on 15 January 1588. The old mansion at Llanborth was abandoned in the 17th century and the family set up home at another residence, Dyffryn Hoffnant, a mile up the valley from the coast. Described as a 'house of great charm', the Vaughan family lived there until the middle of the 18th century when the stones from the dilapidated house were used in the construction of farm buildings and walls. Nothing remains of either residence today and the present Dyffryn Hoffnant is a little south of the old house.

The earliest reference to the property is in 1539 when a bond for £26.6.8 was arranged between 'Rees ap David ap David ap Ievan Duy of the commote of Mabwynion, gent., and Lewis ap David ap Meredydd, for peaceful possession of lands in Dyffryn Hoddnant'. Richard Vaughan married Letitia, daughter of John Scourfield of Moat, Pembrokeshire. He was the son of Morgan ap John of Dyffryn Hoffnant by Margaret, daughter of Jenkyn ap Ieuan Lloyd. The pre-nuptial settlement of John Vaughan, son and heir-apparent of Richard Vaughan and Lettice Bowen of Upton, Pembrokeshire, widow of John Lewes of Abernantbychan, drawn up in October 1634, included the capital messuage called Plâs Dyffryn Hofnant in Penbryn parish. Richard Vaughan sold his patrimony to his brother, Thomas, attorney-at-law, who settled in London. He was succeeded by his sons, Richard, who lived at Dyffryn Hoffnant, and Thomas Vaughan, a barrister-at-law. Richard Vaughan was assessed at 5 hearths in 1670 and he was the last of the Vaughans of Dyffryn Hownant. He lost the entire estate at a London gambling table and in due course, Albany Wallis, a London attorney with a practice in Norfolk Street off the Strand, who represented the notorious Herbert Lloyd of Peterwell, became the main beneficiary. Meyrick states: '. . . (Dyffryn Hownant) once belonged to the Vaughan family but afterwards became the property of Albany Wallis Esq., and is now in the possession of Colonel Bailey Wallis. He was the son of a Lady Bailey, the main beneficiary of Albany Wallis's wealth following his death in 1801.' The Dyffryn Hoffnant estate quickly passed to the Harford family who also owned Llan-borth and who re-modelled Falcondale, near Lampeter. The great house of Dyffryn Hownant fell into disrepair and was later demolished.

Grid Ref: SN 2960 5213

Refs: Dwnn, i, pp. 55, 59, 61, 176; Meyrick, *Cardiganshire,* p. 212; NLW, Cilgwyn MSS, No.158; Colby Map, 1831; Griffith Owen List, iv; WWHR, i, pp. 25-7; NLW, Alcwyn Evans, 12356E, p. 224; PRO List; *Ceredigion,* Vol. IX, No. 4 (1983), pp. 351-2; Bethan Phillips, *Peterwell,* pp. 222-3.

DYFFRYN LLYNOD, Llandysul

Situated in woodland north of Tre-groes in Dyffryn Cerdin, north of Gorrig and shown on *Kitchin's Map of 1754, Colby's Map of 1831* and on modern OS maps. The medieval chapel of Llanffraid stood on the land of Dyffryn Llynod in a field now called Cae'r Capel. On *Speed's Map of 1610,* it is called Llanfra and on *Kitchin's Map* it is named Llanfrai. John ap David ap Llewelyn ap Gwilym Lloyd, descended from Gwilym Griffith Goch Rhys Rhydderch, who traced to Cadifor ap Dinawal, had two sons and two daughters. Anne married Harry Philip and Lleucu married Ieuan Llwyd. Griffith Lloyd had a son, John, who, according to Francis Jones, 'bought Griffith Lewis' wife, being Maud Philipps' and descended from Cadifor Fawr, and a daughter, Dyddgu, who married Morris ap Morris of Llanrheithan, Pembrokeshire. Thomas John, the eldest son and heir, married twice. His first wife was Gwenhwyfar, daughter and heiress of Jenkin Rees Griffith ap Ieuan of Llwyndafydd. Upon her death, he married Catherine, daughter of David Llwyd Griffith of Cilgwyn. By his first marriage, Thomas had a son, Jenkin Thomas of Dyffryn Llynod who signed for Dwnn on 18 January 1588/9. Jenkin married Mary, daughter and co-heiress of David Llwyd ap David Morgan of Glancletwr. From his second marriage Thomas John had a son and two daughters. David, the eldest child, later of Gellifraith, married Mary, daughter of Lewis David Meredydd of Abernantbychan. Gwenllian married Lewis Gwyn Griffith of Aberaeron and Elen married David Lloyd of Gilfach-wen. Jenkin Thomas had a son, Thomas Jenkin, living in 1609, who married Lucy, daughter of Rowland Stedman, originally from Ysrad-Fflur, but then of Cil-cennin, by Jane Lloyd, daughter of Hugh Llewelyn Lloyd of Llanllyr. Stedman died in 1613. Thomas and Lucy had a son, Jenkin, who married Elen, daughter of Thomas Lewes of Gernos. They, in turn, had four sons and a daughter; Thomas Jenkin succeeded to Dyffryn Llynod, John became a mercer in Carmarthen, Harry, of whom nothing is known, and Jenkin Jenkins, of 'ye Life Guard to King Charles II'. The only daughter, Mary, married John Lewes of Cwm-ul, Llandysul, son of James Lewes of Llysnewydd. Thomas Jenkins paid tax on six hearths in 1672 and four hearths for an 'unfinished' house. Thomas married Anne, daughter of George Brown of Winterbourne, Gloucestershire, relict of Jenkin Lloyd of Faerdref whose will was proved in 1660. Thomas and Anne had a son, Thomas and three daughters. Thomas died without issue and the daughters, Anne, Elizabeth and Mary, became co-heiresses when their father died in 1696.

Francis Jones states that 'the last of the family in the male line, Thomas Jenkins of Dyffryn Llynod Esq. in 1680 died unmarried in the 18th century and the estate passed to his three sisters who had married Bristolians, namely Anne, wife of a Mr Tomlinson, Mary, wife of William Birt. A suitor for the hand of one of the daughters was told that he would have to supply: *Deunaw gwr a deunaw cledde, Dennaw gwas yn gwisgo lifre, Dennaw march o liw'r sguthanod, Cyn Codi'r ferch o Ddytffryn Llynod.* [Eighteen men and eighteen swords, Eighteen servants in livery clad, Eighteen charged the colour of wood pigeons before leading a daughter from Dyffryn Llynod.]

Mary, wife of Peter Davies inherited Dyffryn Llynod and their son, John Edwardes Rogers, was later of Abermeurig. Meyrick states: 'Dyffryn is now part of the Abermeurig estate and the property of Mrs Edwardes of that place.' The original estate book of Dyffryn Llynod for 1691-1748 was copied by George Eyre Evans at Abermeurig in 1909. Christmas Evans, the distinguished preacher and hymn-writer was born at Esgair-wen on Dyffryn Llynod land in 1776. Close to the house is a tree planted in his memory in 1930. Francis Jones and his wife, Ethel, visited Dyffryn Llynod in 1980. It was then owned by D. A. Green and his wife, who had bought it in 1965. It was a two-storeyed residence with a range of three windows. Above the central window was a date-stone inscribed 'JE 1785'. The rooms were large and commodious with fine old oak beams and had been restored and modernised by Mr. and Mrs. Green. The outbuildings had early features with splendid roof timbers. There was a small garden and a pleasant orchard with a stream running through the lawns and under a bridge producing a most pleasing feature. The main buildings were located on a slope beyond the stream. Francis Jones was informed that in the 1930's, Dyffryn Llynod was owned by Mr. Rogers Lewis of Abermeurig who sold it to Philip Jones, a farmer who specialised in growing seed potatoes on the 200-acre holding. An essay written by John Davies, who worked at the NLW and who died in 1939, outlines the pedigree of Elen Wyn of Dyffryn Llynod and the Wyns of Llandysul.

Grid Ref: SN 4055 4550

Refs: Kitchin Map, 1754; Colby Map, 1831; *Dwnn,* i, 58; WWHR, i, 21; CRO, GGMS (Tydwal Gloff), fo. 26; ibid, III (Owen ap Bradwen); Blome List, 1673; Meyrick, *Cardiganshire,* 199 (& pedigrees); W. J. Davies, *Hanes Plwyf Llandysul,* 1896, pp. 100, 228-9; *TCAS.* Vol. XXIII, 1932, p. 95; Llandysul Tithe Map, 1841; NLW, MS., 8710.

DYFFRYN PAITH,
Llanfihangel-y-Creuddyn

The property, like Llechwedd Dyrys in the same area, no longer exists, but is marked on *Colby's Map of 1831.* The Paith rises near Pen-uwch farm and flows west to join the Ystwyth at Rhydyfelin, south of Aberystwyth. The earliest reference to Dyffryn Paith is in the 16th century when Richard Morris Jenkins of Dyffryn Paith, whose mother was Catherine Herle of Breconshire, married Jane, widow of David Morris Fychan of Cwmnewidion and daughter of Morris ap Richard of Trawsgoed. Francis Jones also mentions a marriage between Jenkin ap Ievan Goch of Dyffryn Paith and Catherine, daughter of Sir John Vaughan. Sir Thomas Powell of Llechwedd Dyrys is described in the *NLW, Cwrtmawr Deeds* as of Dyffryn Paith which he occupied in 1691 following the marriage of his son, William, to Avarina Le Brun of Nanteos. Sir Thomas remained there until 1704. In 1760 the Rev. John Richards is described as a freeholder of Dyffryn Paith. In 1798 John Parry, a member of the Ty Ucha family of Llanilar and a solicitor in Aberystwyth married Elizabeth, daughter of John Lewis of Aberystwyth and widow of Thomas Hughes of Hendrefelen. Their eldest son, John Thomas Herbert Parry married Mary Davies in 1839 and they resided at Glanpaith. Their marriage settlement agreed on 4 September settled on them the capital messuage of Glanpaith and 12 other properties in Llanbadarn Fawr and Llanrhystud parishes as well as houses in Aberystwyth. In 1873 letters of administration of the estate of Mary, late wife of John Parry of Glanpaith were granted to her husband and a year later Squire Parry of Glanpaith was reminded by the Gosen Chapel Committee that rent of 14/- pew rent was due from the late

'Lady Parry'. Their son, John, lived at Dyffryn Paith in 1918.

Refs: Colby Map, 1831; NLW, Cwrtmawr Deeds, Nos. 49, 92, 462, 1102; WWHR, iii, 98; CRO, GGMS (Tydwal Gloff).

DYFFRYN SAITH, Penbryn

Situated one mile south-west of Penbryn church in the valley of the Saith and marked on *Colby's Map of 1831* on the east bank of the river near Tre-saith. Dyffryn Saith was the home of the Williams family descended by illegitimacy from the Lords of Tywyn. William ap Thomas had a son, David William of Dyffryn Saith whose son, Thomas, married Mary, daughter of John Jones of Morfa-isaf between Penbryn and Llangrannog. Their son, Michael Williams, was a founder member of Penmorfa Chapel during the upsurge of Methodism in the 18th century. In due course following a tragic love affair, Michael emigrated to the West Indies where he died a very rich man. His brother, William, married Elizabeth, daughter of David Evans of Bwlch-y-crwys and his sister Elen married Griffith Morgan of Ty-hen, south-west of Penbryn church. In 1760 Ellis David held the lease of Dyffryn Saith.

Grid Ref: SN 2825 5123

Refs: Colby Map, 1831; NLW, AE 12356 E, p. 226; WWHR, iii, 80.

Welsh girl in the costume of Cardiganshire, from a watercolour circa 1830

EMLYN COTTAGE, Llandyfriog

Built c. 1802 and marked on *Colby's Map of 1831* as on the site of the present mansion, which is located just north of the A475 in Adpar, Newcastle Emlyn. Built from a plan by Nash as a 'bijou rustic villa' for the Hall, later Fitzwilliams family.

Anne Brigstocke lived at Emlyn Cottage during her widowhood with her daughters and Mary Brigstocke, her husband's cousin. Emlyn Cottage was partially pulled down in the 1860's by Charles Home Lloyd Fitzwilliams and the present Cilgwyn mansion was built around it.

Grid Ref: SN 3142 4090

Refs: Colby Map, 1831; *Ceredigion,* VIII, No. I (1976), p. 91; Leslie Baker-Jones, *Princelings, Privilege and Power* (Llandysul), 1999, p. 143.

ESGAIR-GRAIG,
Troed-yr-aur (Tredroyr)

Marked Esgair y Graig on *Colby's Map of 1831* and Esgairgraig on modern OS maps and located a short mile north-east of Beulah. David Parry, who was alive in 1769, married Rachel Lewis, the daughter of John Lewis of Blaencerdin, a kinsman of the Lewis family of Dinas Cerdin. Rachel was a sister to James Lewis of Cwmduar who traced to Morydd, Prince of Ceredigion. Anne, David Parry's sister, married James John. D. Emrys Williams states that 'David Parry . . . married Miss Bevin, and his grandson Mr. D. Parry-Jones, now of Esgergraig, owns part of his ancestral estate of Dinas Cerdin'.

The *Mynachty Deeds* mention a David Parry 'of Esgirygraig in the parish of Tredyroir, gt.' who lived there in 1783. David and Rachel had a daughter, Mary, who married Morgan Jones, a minister of the Gospel at Tre-lech, Carmarthenshire. Their son, David Parry Jones married and had two sons, David and Theophilus Parry Jones.

Grid Ref: SN 3012 4671

Refs: Colby Map, 1831; WWHR, iii, 82, ex info D. Emrys Williams; Mynachty Deeds, No. 29; NLW; Morgan Richardson MSS., No. 2697.

ESGAIR TANGLWST,
Troed-yr-aur

Marked on *Colby's Map of 1831* and on modern OS maps as Tanglwst, just north-east of Rhydlewis. In 1760 John Bowen owned and occupied Tanglwst. In the east wall of Troed-yr-aur church is a tablet with a shield quarterly a lion rampart in each quarter, to Owen Bowen, gent, who died in 1802, and the Rev. Edward Bowen, vicar of Llanthony and curate of Maenordeifi, Pembrokeshire, who died in 1806, aged 37.

Grid Ref: SN 3510 4811

Refs: Colby Map, 1831; Horsfall-Turner, *Wanderings,* p. 156; WWHR, iii, 82.

ESGAIR-WEN, Llandysul

Christmas Evans (1766-1838), Baptist minister, and one of the foremost Welsh preachers, the son of Samuel Evans, bootmaker, and Joanna, his wife, was born at Esgair-Wen on Christmas Day 1766. His biographer traced his descent from Morydd, Prince of Ceredigion c. 830. He was employed by a local farmer and it was while he was working at Castell Hywel that he learnt to read and write. Esgair-wen no longer stands and the only indication of its location is a tree planted in a field on Dyffryn Llynod farm in memory of the great preacher.

Grid Ref: SN 4055 4550

Refs: Turner, Cardiganshire, 215; Crwydro, *Ceredigion,* p. 94; Y Bywgraffiadur.

ESGAIR-WEN, Llannarth

Francis Jones notes only that Esgair-wen was a mansion built in the Tudor period between Llwyndafydd and Llangybi. Marked on *Colby's Map of 1831* and on modern OS maps as Esgair-wen and Esgair-wen-Fach, one and a half miles south of Mydroilyn, north-east of Talgarreg. Near it is Blaen Cletwr. No further details are given.

Grid Ref: SN 4523 5997

Refs: Colby Map, 1831; W. J. Lewis, *Ceredigion,* 1955; *Atlas* Hanesyddol, map opp. p. 23.

FADFA Y (FADFAY), Llandysul

Found on *Colby's Map of 1831* and on modern OS maps a mile and a half south-south-east of Talgarreg, near Capel Bwlch-y-fadfa and about a mile north-west of Castell Hywel on the banks of the Cletwr Fawr. Also shown on *Emanuel Bowen's Map of 1754.*

In 1676 John Rees of Bwlch y Fadfa, Llandysul parish, gent, gave a grant 'in consideration of £50, of Tir Blaen Cletwr alias Tir Blaen Cletwr Fawr in Llanarth parish, to Lewis ap Evan of Llanarth parish, yeoman'. The *Bronwydd Deeds* record on 26 August 1676: 'Opinion of (Sir) John Powell on a deed and settlement of Vadva estate made by John Rees upon David Jones and Maud, his wife; with copy of same'. The pre-nuptial settlement of John David and Maud Thomas, spinster, eldest daughter of said Thomas David, dated 1 September 1676 mentions, 'messuages and land called Bwlch y Vadva, Tythin y Gors and Tir y Pan Gwndwa in parish Llandisilio and Tir Nant Cribwr in parish Llandysul.' On 27 January 1716/17, the *Bronwydd Deeds* gives the legal opinion of Henry Lloyd regarding the title of John Davies to the Fadfa estate. John Davies of Fadfa died on 29 May 1713 and probate was granted on 8 August 1727. On 2 April 1728, David Thomas of Llandysul parish, gent, and Mary, his wife, the eldest daughter of John Davies late of Fadfa, gent. deceased, witnessed an agreement made between Deborah Jones of Llangoedmor parish, widow, second daughter of said John Davies, Thomas Jones of Cenarth parish, gent. and Hester, his wife, third daughter of said John Davies, and Lettice Davies of Fadfa, youngest daughter of said John Davies, and Edward Lloyd of Wern-llaeth, Cardiganshire, Esq., John Morgan of Cardigan Esq., David Lloyd of Lloyd Jack Esq., and James Lewis of Gellidywyll Esq., of a lease for one year of the capital messuage and land of Fadfa, otherwise Bwlchyfadfa, Tir y Gors and Pant y Gwyndwn in the parish of Llandisiliogogo, a messuage and land called Gelli Angharad, parish of Llanarth and messuages and land called 'Tyr Nant y Cribwr and Tyr Glan Ythan, Llandysul parish and messuages and land called Tyr Dyffryn Velin,

Llyne Tyr Griffith ap Evan Du, Ty Du and Llwyn yr Hwch, in Silian parish, and a water corn grist mill in said parish of Silian, Co. Cardiganshire. On 25 April 1728, the *Bronwydd Deeds* records a Partition deed of the estate between the said children of John Davies. By 1760 David Thomas of Fadfa, owned 'Camnant (Fadfa)' in the parish of Llandysul.

Grid Ref: SN 4291 4938

Ref: WWHR, iii, 85; Bronwydd Deeds, Nos. 2595, 2595a, 2596, 2822, 2884, 2889; Colby Map, 1831; Emanuel Bowen, *Map of South Wales*, c. 1760; J. F. Deeds, 779.

FAENOG, Y, see FEINOG

FAERDRE-FACH, Llandysul
(also known as PARC MAWR)

The *Carmarthen Antiquary* states: 'This was the Grange of Maerdref Gwynionydd, which in 1331 Meredydd ab Owen confirmed the grant which the Lord Rhys had made of it to Talley Abbey in 1197.' Marked on *Colby's Map of 1831* and on modern OS maps to the east of the B4476 between Llandysul and Pren-gwyn. The main residence was called Parc mawr (later Faerdre-fach), and there were special quarters for VIP's at Ystafell. When Talley was dissolved in 1536, the Grange of Maerdref was kept in hand by the Crown until 1596 when Queen Elizabeth I granted it to David Williams, Sergeant-at-Law and Attorney General of south-west Wales. He broke it up and leased Parc Mawr and Gellifaharen, then in possession of Lleucu Llaw Goch, to David ab Ieuan, gent., and William David, both of Llanfihangel-ar-arth, for 31 years at a rental of £7.13.1 a year.

In the 17th century, Parc Mawr became the freehold property of the family of Fforest, Cilgerran, Pembrokeshire. Towards the end of the 17th century, David Thomas divided the estate between his two daughters, Gwen receiving Parc Mawr, and the other daughter the portion which later became known as Faerdre-fawr. She married a Lewis of Llannerchaeron. Gwen married Thomas Jones of Danyrallt, Llangoedmor. His mother was the daughter of David Lloyd of Brynele, Nancwnlle, whose cousin of Crynfryn, in the same parish, married a Johnes of Llanfair Clydogau.

Thomas Jones also owned Llanio, but was living at Faerdre-fawr (Parc Mawr) when High Sheriff in 1760.

Thomas and Gwen had several sons: Daniel, who died in his teens, David, a bachelor, who squandered the estate before he died, Richard, who through the influence of his youngest brother, Walter, became the vicar of Kingsbridge, Devon, and his grandson became rector of Exeter College, Oxford. John married a daughter of Fron-wen, Llanarth, and their grandson was John Jordan Jones, Capt. RN (great-grandfather of Miss Jordan Jones, a teacher at Llandysul Grammar School at the beginning of the 20th century). Walter married Letitia Jones of Nantremenyn, Pont-siân, the sister of Sylvanus Jones, in 1746. This Walter lived under the patronage of Sarah, the old Duchess of Marlborough, and was in her household at the time of her death and she left him an annuity of £30 p.a. payable quarterly by the Spencer branch of that family and which he lived to enjoy for forty years or more.

Walter had two sons, the elder, who married Margaret Rogers of Brynele, inherited Llanio and Faerdre-fach, and the younger became the rector of Ruckinge, Kent. The elder son died in 1808 leaving his two estates to his son, Dr. Walter Jones, who had married Elinor Davies of Gorwydd, Llanddewibrefi, sister of Sir David Davies who was Queen Adelaide's doctor. Dr. Walter Jones had two brothers, three spinster sisters, and another sister who was widowed when her husband, Dr. Rogers of Abermeurig, was drowned fording a river in flood when returning from a call. Dr. Walter Jones mortgaged Faerdre to David Davies of Blaen-y-wern in Llanfair Clydogau for £800 and three years later sold the property to the mortgagee for £4,800. David Davies placed James Davies (1779-1859), a son of Davies of Gelliffraith,

Tre-groes, who had recently married Margaret Lewis of Llawr-cwrt, as his tenant at Faerdre. They lived there till 1830, when, on the death of the owner, the trustees sold Faerdre to David Jones of Gellifaharen. James Davies, the tenant, then moved to Bryngrannod but in 1857, at the age of 78, he returned to Faerdre to spend the last two years of his life there. At the sale on 19 June 1857, Faerdre was bought by Thomas Davies (son of said James Davies) for £4,600.

Grid Ref: SN 4208 4237

Refs: Carmarthen Antiquary, Vol. III, 196; Colby Map, 1831; W. J. Davies, *Hanes Plwyf Llandysul,* 1896, p. 345; CRO, GGMS, I (Tewdwr), fo. 40; ibid, III; *Gwaethfoed,* fo. 34.

FAERDREF-FAWR, Y, Llandysul

Faerdre-fawr farm, in the Teifi Valley, is located north-east of Llandysul near the ancient site of Castell Gwynionydd village and marked on *Colby's Map of 1831* as Fairdre-fawr and -fach, and on the 14th century *Rees Map of South Wales* as a grange belonging to the monks of Talley. Meyrick states: 'Now a farmhouse, was formerly a place of some consequence, and distinguished by the additional title Vawr.' Faerdre was the home of the Lloyds who were descended from Rhydderch ap Tewdwr. Howell ap Rees ap Howel ap David ap Philip ap Einon of Pencarreg, who traced to Tewdwr Mawr, had a son, Griffith ap Howel of Faerdref, Llandysul Uwch Cerdin, who married Joan, daughter of Ieuan John Griffith alias Lloyd, descended from Gwynfardd Dyfed. They had many children. The eldest son, Ieuan, married Elen, daughter of David Lewis of Gernos, and daughters, Mary, who married Griffith Ieuan David Philip and Gwenllian, who married David Lewis Gwynn. Another daughter, Elizabeth, married twice; firstly to David Lewis of Gilfach-chwith and secondly to Lodwick Lewes of Brynhenlle. John Lloyd was the eldest son of Ieuan and Elen Lloyd. He married Jane, daughter of Morgan Herbert of Hafod Uchdryd whose will was proved in 1649. Another son, William, was apparently, 'murther'd basely by 2 gentlemen in ye anarchy of Oliver Cromwell.' Meyrick is mistaken when he states: 'This John Lloyd died without issue, but his father's sister having married into the Lewis family of Llanerchaeron, carried this estate to them having become heiress to it; and it has been in the family ever since, Colonel Lewis of that place enjoying it.' It was John's son, Ieuan, who married Jane, the daughter of Sir Henry Vaughan of Derwydd, whose will was proved in 1702, who died without issue. Ieuan's brother, Jenkin alias Ieuan David Lloyd, married Elen, daughter of David Lewis of Gernos. Jenkin Lloyd was educated at Jesus College, Oxford, and became chaplain to Oliver Crom well as well as being MP from 1654-6. His will, dated 20 February 1659/60, was proved by Griffith John on 22 September 1660. Jenkin became an itinerant preacher and in 1658 published *Christ's Valediction* – a treatise of 220 pages.

He married Anne, daughter of Hugh Browne of Bristol. Anne married secondly Thomas Jenkins of Dyffryn Llynod. Ieuan Lloyd had another brother, John and eight sisters: Elinor, who married her first cousin, John Parry of Llanerchaeron, Jane, died a spinster, Mary married Thomas David of Vaidre Vach. The fourth sister Anne married William Lloyd of Pantgilgan, Catherine died a spinster, Bridget married twice, firstly Lodowick Lewes and secondly Walter Price of 'Llanfairclydoey' (Llanfair Clydogau). Margaret died a spinster and the youngest sister, Cissil, married twice, firstly David Jones, vicar of Llangeler and secondly William Lewes of Llwynderw. Jenkin's son, John, who married Mary daughter of Morgan Herbert of Hafod, died without issue. The estate passed to the Llanerchaeron family and Faerdre remained in their possession, occupied by tenants, until sold in 1918.

Grid Ref: SN 4275 4286

Refs: Dwnn, i, 149: WWHR, i, 19; Meyrick, *Cardiganshire,* 198; *Hanes Plwyf Llandysul,* pp. 189-190; W. J. Davies; PRO, Dale Castle MS., p. 21; NLW, Cwrtmawr Deeds, No. 254; NLW, BRA (1955); Llandysul Tithe Map, 1841.

FALCONDALE, Llanbedr Pont Steffan

Shown on *Colby's Map of 1831* and on modern OS maps in woodland bordering the A482 road towards Aberaeron a mile north-west of Lampeter. According to the *Deri Ormond Deeds* a house called Falcondale was built by Daniel

Evans, a Lampeter banker, formerly of Llechwedd Deri and Peterwell. It was empty in 1820 and soon after was rented by the vicar of Lampeter, John Williams, who ran a boarding school for boys there. At the Easter Court Leet of 1831, David Evans of Falcondale, banker, was admitted burgess of Lampeter, the last to be so admitted before the Reform Bill of 1832. He was still living there in 1834.

The house has long been associated with the Harford family of Blaise Castle, Gloucestershire, who came to Cardiganshire early in the 19th century. The family, descended from a wealthy Bristol family of bankers, had acquired the Peterwell estate when J. S. Harford married the daughter of Richard Hart Davies, MP for Colchester and a native of Bristol, who had arrived in Lampeter in 1812. The Harfords chose not to renovate Peterwell and erected a new residence at Falcondale.

The first Harford, John Scandrett, author and art collector, never lived in Wales and took little interest in the new house. He did, however, express to Bishop Thomas Burgess of St David's, his wish to build a college to prepare local boys for the church. In 1859, his nephew, John Battersby Harford, who provided Lampeter with a pure water supply, decided to add extensively to the small house at Falcondale which after his marriage to Miss de Bunsen, became their home. The new Falcondale was described as a house 'in a vaguely similar style to Hafod'. J. B. Harford was High Sheriff in 1855. The Falcondale estate of 5,782 acres had a rent roll of £4,256 a year in 1873. J. B. Harford and his wife had two sons, Frederick Dundas, born in 1862, a career-diplomat, who was High Sheriff in 1920, and John C. Harford, High Sheriff in 1886, a Major in the Pembrokeshire Yeomanry and a distinguished public servant. He became a Cardiganshire County Councillor and is described by Kenneth Morgan as the 'most politically active landowner' between 1880 and 1914. J. C. Harford had married into the powerful family of Raikes and he contested the Cardiganshire seat in 1895 and 1900. His wife, whom he married in 1893, was the second daughter of the Rt. Hon. H. C. Raikes. J. C. Harford died in 1934.

Falcondale was sold to the County Council in 1951 who converted it into an old people's home. It was sold in 1957 for £35,250 to H. L. Smith of Llwyngwril, Meirionydd. It is now a country hotel. Steegman, ii, *South Wales* (1962), gives details of the portraits formerly in the house.

Grid Ref: SN 5650 4912

Refs: Colby Map, 1831; NLW, Deri Ormond Deeds, 268a and b; *Ceredigion,* vol. ii, No. 3, 1954; G. E. Evans, *Lampeter,* p. 44; Steegman, ii, *South Wales* (1962); Landowners Return, 1873; *Ceredigion,* V, No. 4 (1967); ibid, VII, Nos. 3/4 (1974/75), pp. 224, 317-8.

FEINOG (VEINOG), Dihewyd

Faenog, Felin Faenog and Faenog-uchaf are marked on *Colby's Map of 1831* between Mydroilyon and Dihewyd. The reference given is for Feinog-isaf, mentioned as the capital messuage in various deeds. They are also marked on modern OS maps as Feinog-ganol. The home of the Hughes family from the early 18th century to the early 19th century. Hugh David of Feinog, married Honor, daughter of Thomas, second son of Thomas Lewes of Gernos and had a son, David, and a daughter Margaret, who married Lewis Pugh descended from Saer y Cwm of Cwrtnewydd. They had a son, Lewis Pugh.

David Hughes, alive in 1705 succeeded his father and bought Harmeston Hall, Steynton, Pembrokeshire. David married and had two sons and two daughters; Charles, the heir, and John, who married Susan Barron of Lambston in 1743. The elder daughter Elizabeth, married William Parry of Haverfordwest, a brazier, and Catherine the youngest.

Charles Hughes of Feinog, gent., married Elizabeth, the youngest daughter of Evan Thomas of Gilfach, Llangeler, Carmarthenshire, by a daughter of Griffith David of Moylon. The pre-nuptial settlement was agreed on 4 December 1744 which settled the capital messuage called 'Vaynog otherwise Veinog vawr or Veinog Issa'. Charles is described as a freeholder of Feinog in 1760. They had a son, David Hughes of Vaynog, gent., who was the eldest son and heir. In 1789 he married Sarah, daughter of John Lewis and Elizabeth his wife, of Llannerchaeron.

John Hughes of Llanychaeron, Esq., had a natural daughter Mary, by Rebecca Thomas, described as a 'single woman'. Mary married Rees Bowen of Vainog, gent. The post-nuptial settlement signed on 9/10 November 1815 settled Llety coch, Stavell-wen, Penybont and Penygraig, in the parish of Dihewyd to their uses. Evan Jones of Penrhiw was trustee.

The old mansion was pulled down late in the 19th or early in the 20th century and a new farmhouse erected there. Now commonly called Faenog.

Grid Ref: SN 4688 5610

Refs: Colby Map, 1831; WWHR, iii, 89; Protheroe MS., G. VI; NLW, Griffith Owen Deeds, No. 6782-3.

FERWIG, Y Ferwig

A parish and hamlet immediately north of Cardigan town. Its land extends to the coast on the east, and south to the Teifi estuary and includes Gwbert and the ancient residence of the Lords of Tywyn. The location of this residence is unknown. The *Noyadd Trefawr Deeds* give details of a bond in £100 for performance of covenants on 22 January 1577/8 between Owen ap David and Rhys ap Bowen, 'both of the parish of Verwike, Cards., yeomen, and John Mortimer Esq., following the marriage of Griffith ap Rhys, son and heir of the said Rhys, and Catheryn, ferch Thomas'.

Rhys Philip of Ferwig had a son, Owen ap Rhys Philip, who married Katherine, the natural daughter of David Lloyd Griffith Prys. They had two daughters and three sons. Elen married John Prys ap John of Ferwig, Elizabeth (died c. 1614), married John ap Owen Fychan (died 1605), of Argoed, Pembrokeshire. The eldest son, Nicholas ap Owen, married Elizabeth, daughter of Owen Phillips of Llanfihangel Penbedw, Pembrokeshire, Morgan, who died in his youth, and Mathias ap Owen who married Mary, daughter of David Phillips of Cilsant, Llanwinio, Carmarthenshire. Dates are lacking.

Grid Ref: SN 1825 4950

Refs: NLW, Noyadd Trefawr Deeds, No. 322; Egerton MS., 2586, fo. 302; Francis Jones, *Historic Houses of Pembrokeshire and their Families,* p. 2, 1996,

FOELALLT Y, Llanddewibrefi

A house of great antiquity, located on *Colby's Map of 1831* and on modern OS maps half a mile south-east of Llanddewibrefi, on the north bank of the river Brenig. The early home of Herbert Lloyd, later of Peterwell. In his *Tours of Wales* in 1804 Fenton writes: 'At the opening of a retired vale environed with high barren hills, about a quarter of a mile or less above the church is Foelallt, a mansion of some note in former days, but shewing nothing of its pristine consequence.' Meyrick states: 'this seat, which stands to the east of the church belonged formerly to a family of the name of Williams. The Williamses traced to Sir Rhys ap Griffith, Lord of Llansadwn, and so to Ednyfed Fychan.'

John Williams who lived at Foelallt in 1685 was descended from Thomas ap Rhys Cantwr of Llanddewibrefi, ap Ieuan ap Griffith ap Thomas ap Sir Rhys Hen of Llansadwrn and Abermarlais, a distant cousin of Henry Tudor and a second cousin to Sir Rhys ap Thomas. The Rev. David John Williams, the son and heir of the said John Williams, sold the estate to Walter Lloyd, the son of Jonathan Lloyd of Llanfair Clydogau who settled at Foelallt. Walter was appointed Attorney-General for Carmarthenshire, Cardiganshire and Pembrokeshire in 1715 and was MP for the County of Cardiganshire from 1734 to 1741. He married Elizabeth, daughter and heiress of Daniel Evans of Peterwell (Ffynnon Bedr) Lampeter, by Mary Herbert of Hafod. They had four children amongst whom were John, who eventually succeeded to Peterwell, and Alice, who was baptised on 27 February 1724 and who married Jeremiah Lloyd. Her marriage portion was £1,000. Alice and Jeremiah Lloyd moved to Maesyfelin (Millfield) where Jeremiah acted as steward to the estate. He was appointed JP in 1763 and a Clerk of the Peace and Coroner for Cardiganshire in 1770. He died at Carmarthen on 12 June 1780 and was buried at St. Peters, Carmarthen.

John Lloyd, barrister, the eldest son of Walter and Elizabeth Lloyd, succeeded his father to Peterwell. He was MP for Cardiganshire from 1747 until his death in 1755. In 1750 he married Elizabeth, daughter of Sir Issac Le Hemp MP of Gunthorpe Manor, Norfolk. Elizabeth brought with her a portion of £80,000. She was a lady-in-waiting to the Queen and George II gave the young couple a pair of gold wine coolers as a wedding present. John Lloyd also succeeded to the estate of his brother-in-law, Sir Lucius Lloyd at Maesyfelin in 1750. He died prematurely on 29 June 1755 and is buried at Lampeter. Walter and Elizabeth's second son, Herbert, who had succeeded his brother John to Foelallt in 1749, inherited Peterwell and in 1755, Maesyfelin. His turbulent life has been recorded elsewhere. Herbert committed suicide on 19 August 1769 and died without legal issue. In his article 'The Lesser County Houses of Cardiganshire' H. Lloyd-Johnes writes: 'The second son Herbert Lloyd (later Bart) lived at Voelallt. In 1740 Herbert Lloyd gave £2.2.0. towards rebuilding the church tower of Cardigan. Sir Herbert's first wife was a Miss Bragge of whom little is known. [This Elizabeth Bragge was an heiress from Essex who brought with her a dowry of £15,000. Elizabeth died five days following the birth of their first-born, also named Elizabeth, in March 1743.] Herbert's second wife was Anne, daughter of William Powell, Nanteos, and the widow of Richard Stedman of Strata Florida. She was 18 years older than her husband when they married in 1745. Domestic unhappiness drove her from Peterwell and she returned to Voelallt, probably about 1760, and was well known for her philanthropy to poor neighbours.'

Edward Richard of Ystrad Meurig wrote: 'Daw Anna i dywynnu, Cyn nenmawr cân imi, Di weli blwy' Dewi' n blodeuo.' Horsfall-Turner writes: 'Not far from the village of Llanddewibrefi was the venerable mansion of Voelallt, under the shadow of the rocky mountains. Here resided Lady Lloyd the second wife, unhappy in wedlock, of Sir Herbert of Peterwell. She survived him and was buried at Strata Florida.' Herbert Lloyd's sister, Elizabeth, married John Adams of Whitland and it was their son, John, who eventually inherited Peterwell, Maesyfelin and Foelallt, together with encumbrances totalling £54,000. The *Deri Ormond Deeds* record that in May 1776, John Adams of Peterwell, Esq., sold the Foelallt estate in the parishes of Llanddewibrefi and Llanfair Clydogau, subject to the life inheritance of Dame Anne Lloyd, to Thomas Johnes of Croft Castle, Herefordshire, Esq., for £3,500. Thomas Johnes, the younger, then sold it to Thomas Smith, son of George Smith of Nottingham, who lived at Cwrt Henry, Carmarthenshire.

Herbert Lloyd-Johnes in Ceredigion, states: 'The writer has been told that the house had as many windows as days in a year, while a more modest account made it weeks instead of days! In actual fact Voelallt was a typical small house dating from the seventeenth century.' Thomas Smith married Mary . . . and they had three sons and two daughters, Thomas the younger, George, who died in 1843, Robert, Mary, and Frances, who married John Richards of Co. Worcester and Southwark, Esq. John Jones of Deri Ormond bought the interest in Foelallt of Robert, Frances and George in 1823, 1846 and 1857 respectively. Foelallt was advertised for sale by direction of the executors of the late George Smith on 23 October 1856. The Sale Catalogue states: 'Foel Allt House, which stands on the banks of the River Brefy or Brennig at the entrance to a ravine of considerable beauty and interest, surrounded by a Park and Plantation of about 80 acres . . . though in itself a residence of no pretensions. Approached by a carriage drive with Lodge entrance. Ground Floor – Dining room, housekeepers' room, large kitchen, wash-house, bake-house, store closets, larder etc. Upper Floor – Drawing room, 3 bedrooms, a dressing room, and 2 large attics in the roof. In the rear – a courtyard, dairy with cheese room over, Turf house, outbuildings, station yard with coach house, 3 stall stable, cow byre, dog kennels etc. Lawn, garden and shrubbery extend to river Brefy.'

The house was occupied by Robert Sibbold, as yearly tenant at the moderate rent of £45 per annum. In his *Historical Notes*, J. Rowlands writes: 'Foelallt, now almost in ruins was owned by J. Inglis Jones. A miracle was said to have happened at the building of Llanddewibrefi church. On that occasion the two oxen employed were overladen and one died from the effort of dragging the load up the hill. The other, at the loss of his companion, bellowed nine times and suddenly the hill opened and a way was made for him to draw the load.' The miracle is commemorated in these lines:

Llanddewibrefi fraith
Lle brefodd yr ych naw gwaith
Nes holltodd Craig y Foelallt.

H. Lloyd Jones writes: 'Foelallt was pulled down by the then owner, the late Mr Wilmot Inglis Jones, within living memory. By today [1953] it is difficult even to discover the site.' Francis Jones notes that the house has totally disappeared except for the garden, but the site is still visible.

Grid Ref: SN 5485 6690

Refs: Colby Map, 1831; PRO, Dale Castle MS., pp. 26, 101, 102; WWHR, i, pp. 37-8; C/A Box 36 copy by WL from DE. s.n. 'the Cantors'; *Cymru,* July 1902, p. 15; Turner, *Wanderings,* p. 253; J. Rowlands, *Historical Notes,* 1866, p. 83; Fenton, *Tours in Wales in 1804,* p. 7; Meyrick, *Cardiganshire,* p. 253; H. Lloyd-Jones, *'The Lesser Country Houses of Cardiganshire', Ceredigion,* vol. II, No. 2. 1953; PRO List; *Welsh Gazette,* 27 Dec. 1923; *Arch Cam.,* 1861, pp. 158, 161; NLW, Deri Ormond Deeds, Nos. 63-4, 111; Bethan Phillips, *Peterwell, The History of a Mansion and its Infamous Squire.*

FOUNTAIN GATE (PORTHYFFYNNON), Tregaron

The home of Thomas Jones, antiquary and bard, better known, perhaps fancifully, to generations of schoolchildren as Twm Sion Cati, the Welsh Robin Hood, but in truth, 'the most accomplished heraldic bard of his day'.

Meyrick describes the property: 'on a hill, south-east of the town, are shewn the ruins of Fountain Gate, called by the people, Plâs Twm Sion Catty.' It is maintained that Porthyffynnon was one of Gwaethfoed's (died 1038), properties situated near the Flaenog, half a mile east of Tregaron. The Rev. D. C. Rees tells us: 'Hardly a vestige remains. Some forty years ago (1894) when stones removed from the ruinous walls were being carted away, two square stone blocks were found; one with a lion rampant within a border engrailed, the other with a lion rampant within a plain border. The stones are carefully preserved by Mr. H. P. Evans at Werna.' The stones and carvings are characteristic of the 16th century. The arms are those of Rhys ap Tewdwr. One stone also showed a faint outline of I.P.L., I.P. Sketches of the heraldic stones appeared in the *Western Mail* on 2 March 1926. 'At the Lampeter meeting of the Cambrians in 1931, were exhibited two stones with carved heraldic shields on them, taken from Porth-ffynnon; the first showed a lion rampant within a plain border; and below the shield the initials J.D.; the second, a lion rampant within an indented border, with indistinct initials below the shield: the style of the shields and letters suggested the period c. 1550-1600'.

It is said that Porth-y-ffynnon was built on the ruins of an old hafod which belonged to the Gwaethfoed family. They were deprived of the Lordship in King John's time, 'yet they Reape a great parte of their inheritaunce in possession, as Glynayron, Penarth and all those parts, Castle Odwyn in Llanbadarne Edwyn and Fountayn Gate in the parish of Caron, which hath been theire principall mansion place after they had loste their castles and houlds bye the seaside'.

Thomas Jones was the natural son of John, son of David ap Madog ap Howel Moethau and Catherine, the natural daughter of Meredydd ap Ieuan. Thomas signed his pedigree for the herald Dwnn on 30 December 1588. His work and place in Welsh heraldic and genealogical performance is outlined in Frances Jones's essay *An Approach to Welsh Genealogy.* Professor Glanmor Williams in *Wales and the Reign of Queen Mary I* suggests that Thomas Jones was one of the Marion 'martyrs'. Two years later (1557), a small group of exiles, all of whom had connections with west Wales, joined John Knox's congregation at Geneva. They included Thomas Jones of Fountain Gate who arrived in May 1557. Francis Jones states 'He was a cousin of Dr. John Dee (1527-1608), mathematician and astrologer and Fellow of Trinity College, Cambridge'.

In Extracts from *The Private Diary of John Dee* it records that on 29 November 1579 John had received a letter from Mr. Thomas Jones. On 28 November 1590 he records, 'My cousin, Mr. Thomas Jones came in the end of the term, about St. Andrew's even. A week later he writes, 'Mr. Thomas Griffith my cousin from Llanbedr came to see me and stay all night with me, and allso Mr. Thomas Jones, and in Monday morning went by water to London and so the said day homeward. On 10 August 1596 Dr. Dee records, 'Mr. Thomas Jones of Tregarron came to see me to Manchester and rode toward Wales, bak agayn the 13th day to meet the catall coming'. Three days later, 'Mr. Jones rode towards Wales'.

Thomas was probably married twice. His first wife was Anne, daughter of Hugh Lewis ap David who traced to Tewdwr. He married secondly Johan, the widow of Thomas Rhys Williams of Ystrad-ffin, a rich landowner and High Sheriff of Cardiganshire in 1579 and 1596. Johan was the daughter of Sir John Price of the Priory, Brecon. In his will dated 17 May 1608 Thomas Jones bequeathed nine head of cattle to his base son, John Moethe and the residue of his property to his beloved Johan. The inventory of his goods amounted to £139. Among debts due to him was from Griffith David, 'my son-in-law'. The will was proved at Carmarthen in 1608. According to the Fenton Manuscripts, Thomas had three children, Rees, John and Margaret, who married William Morgan of Llanfihangel Crucorney. The *Golden Grove Manuscripts* state that Margaret was the wife of Rees Moythe, Thomas's son.

By 1657 Thomas Lloyd was of Porthyffynnon and on 2 November 1682, Katherine Lloyd, widow, sold a messuage in Ystrad parish to Christopher Philips of Builth, gent. The capital messuage called Fountain Gate alias Porthyffynnon was mentioned in the marriage settlement of William Powell of Llechwedd Dyrus and Avarina Le Brun of Nanteos, dated 1 April 1690. In 1691 William Powell of Nanteos, Esq. mortgaged Fountain Gate and other lands in the parish of Caron but Porthyffynnon was still part of the estate of Powell of Nanteos in 1718.

Grid Ref: SN 6820 5950

Refs: Archaeologia Cambrensis, 1931, 386, photograph; J. G. Wood, *Principal Rivers of Wales,* 1813, 147. *Chanc. Proc.,* c. 8 Mitford 325/56, 1657; NLW Llanllyr Deeds, Nos. 70-71; Lewis, *TDW,* 1840; *Llyfr Baglan,* p. 123; Meyrick, *Cardiganshire,* 1808; Fenton, *Tours in Wales;* Dafydd H. Evans, Twm Sion Cati *in Coleg Dewi a'r Fro,* 1984, pp. 8-22, with photograph of site of Fountain Gate, p. 14; *Dwnn* i, 7, 45, 46; *TCAS,* vol. IX, 1913, p. 16; NLW, Cwrtmawr Deeds No. 200, 324, 1648-9; Francis Jones *'An Approach to Welsh Genealogy',* 1948, pp. 383-385; CRO, GGMS III, *Gwaethfoed* (Cardiganshire); Extracts from *The Private Diary of John Dee,* ed. J. D. Halliwell, Camden Society (XIX), London, 1842; Prof. Glanmor Williams, *'Wales and the Reign of Queen Mary',* in *Welsh History Review,* vol. 10, No. 3, 1981, p. 353.

FRONFRAITH, Llanbadarn fawr

Also known as Vronvraith and located on *Colby's Map of 1831* and on modern OS maps as due east of Aberystwyth, south of the minor road between Cwmpadarn and Capel Dewi, adjacent to the main railway line. Nicholas described it in County Families as 'a plain substantial mansion in the vale of Rheidol'.

Meyrick states, 'Vronvraith formerly belonged to Mr Lloyd of Tan y Castell, from whom it was purchased by John Morgan (to Gwaethfoed). He left it to his eldest son, Thomas, who, about the year 1784 sold it to Sir Thomas Bonsall, knight, whose family now possess it'.

Thomas Bonsall (1730-1808), was the son of George and Mary Bonsall of Ecton, Staffordshire, and mined the famous Ecton vein. He came to the Ysbyty Ystwyth area and worked the Cwmystwyth Mines originally as a manager and later as a lessee. Thomas is reputed to have made a fortune of over £40,000 mining in north Cardiganshire. In a letter dated 24 January 1789 from Thomas Bonsall, Fronfraith, to his brother Richard he writes: 'About 1786 went to live where I purchased, on the

North of the river Rhydol, within three miles of Aberystwyth. Here was a comfortable house when I purchased and which by additions, I have made a very good house. God has been very good unto me in bountifully bestowing a sufficiency of blessings of life. I have purchased estates in Cardiganshire to the amount of about £300 p.a. clear, have some thousands out at interest secured by mortgages, and several thousand employed in different businesses . . . the same Providence has given me ten fine children – 6 sons and 4 daughters – all healthy, and sound, and fair to look upon. The eldest daughter near 18; the youngest, a boy, of 18 months old. Thanks to God we have had no funerals yet. The sons were together with us all the late Holy Days. The two eldest sons, John and Thomas, are at School at Shrewsbury, from which place they returned yesterday; both in the Greek Testament. One daughter, Sarah, is mostly with her aunt Owens at Aberystwyth, and three sons go daily to Llanbadarn School.'

Thomas Bonsall married Winifred, daughter of Isaac Williams of Fronfraith who was related to the Williams of Ty' nwern, Llanrhystud. He was High Sheriff of Cardiganshire in 1795 and knighted the following year. He died in 1808, aged 78.

Little is known of Sir Thomas's daughters except that Mary the youngest, married James Hughes, the first Mayor of the reformed Corporation of Aberystwyth who lived at Glan Rheidol. Sir Thomas's sons were: John, Thomas, who died an infant in January 1797, George who built Glan Rheidol, and William a surgeon who founded the local dispensary at Aberystwyth in 1821, which became the Infirmary in 1838. Joseph who died young and Issac Bonsall, later the rector of Llanwrin and chairman of the Machynlleth Bench.

His grandson, Henry Bonsall, who lived at Cwm, Clarach, was defeated in the first County Council election by William Morgan, a Bow Street coal merchant and grandfather of Elystan Morgan. Henry was the author of Records of the House of Bonsall, which was privately printed in 1903.

Sir Thomas's eldest son, John George William Bonsall, succeeded to Fronfraith and was High Sheriff of Cardiganshire in 1866. The *Landowners Return of 1873* lists the estate of Fronfraith as 1,658 acres, yielding an annual rental of £818. In 1904 John Joseph Bonsall of Fronfraith and Galltlan, Montgomeryshire, who married Emily Hughes of Glanrheidol, was High Sheriff. The family motto was *Goreu Ach y Goruchaf.*

Grid Ref: SN 6180 8190

Refs: Colby Map, 1831; Meyrick, *Cardiganshire*, 311; *Burke,* 19, 1952;. Malkin, 1804, *South Wales* (reprint 1970), p. 371; Nicholas, *County Families,* i, 190, 1872; Add Morris Letters II, p. 918; Henry Bonsall, *Records of the House of Bonsall,* pr. 1903; *The Cambrian Travellers' Guide,* 1813, p. 42; Deri Ormond Deeds, 387; Landowners Return, 1873; J. Davies, 'Llansilin, Display of Heraldry', *Ceredigion,* VI, No. 1, 1968, p. 22; ibid, VIII, No. 4, 1979, p. 419; *Cardiganshire County History*, vol. 3, p. 431.

FRONWEN, Llanarth

Marked on *Colby's Map of 1831* and modern OS maps a quarter of a mile south-east of Llanarth. Rhys ap Gruffydd of Fronwen married a daughter of Ieuan ab John of Blaencletwr and Nantremenyn, Pont-sian, but dates are unclear. In 1760 Daniel Lewis owned and lived at Fronwen and in 1781 the property was assessed for tax at £9. Daniel's daughter married the Rev. John Jones, vicar of Edern, Caernarfon and their son John Jordan Jones was a Captain in the Navy and a JP and lived at Fronwen. The Jones family were still living at Fronwen in 1913 and a Miss Jordan Jones was a teacher at Llandysul Grammar School.

Grid Ref: SN 4287 5724

Refs: Colby Map, 1831; D. J. Davies, *Llanarth,* 34-37 and pedigree.

FFOSESGOB, Llandysul

Shown on *Colby's Map of 1831* and on modern OS maps, north of Llandysul and south of the minor road leading from Prengwyn to Tregroes north of Llandysul village. The *Lloyd Family Records* state that: 'By Letters Patent dated 37 Elizabeth, in consideration of £30, a lease was granted to David Williams for 31 years at 7/- per annum, of a messuage and land called Ffoshesgob Ffoshesgob in the parish of Llandysul, now or late in tenure of Rhys ap Ieuan David Teg.' In the following year, David Williams, Sergeant-at-Law, assigned the lease of Ffosesgob to Ieuan ap Ieuan ap Howel of parish Llandysul, yeoman. Administration of the last will and testament of Ieuan ap Ieuan ap Howell of the parish of Llandysul was granted to David ap Rees and his wife, Mary, ferch Ieuan, actual and lawful daughter of deceased, on 5 October 1613. The inventory of his goods detailed 3 horses and 2 mares of the value of £4, 42 beasts – £27.6.8, 210 sheep – £21. The household utensils and implements for the house – £5.2.2. Poultry – 2/-, Corn – £23.6.8. Ploughs – 6/8d, 6 harrows with iron pins – 13/4d, 24 hurdles – 6/-, 4 swine –13/4d. A messuage called 'Ffoshesgog alias Ffoshosgold was held by lease, being parcel of the Grange of Maerdreff alias Vaerdriff, in parish Llandysul, valued at £24. Debts due to deceased by specialties and without specialties £50. Total £156.16.0.'

Ieuan ap Howel of Ffosesgob had a son, Ieuan ap Ieuan ap Howel, who had a daughter, Mary, living in 1624. She married David Rees David Llewelyn Lloyd of Castell Hywel. They settled at Ffosesgob and had four sons and one daughter: Ieuan Lloyd of Alltyrodin, Thomas David Lloyd of Ffosesgob, living in 1665, David of Caerau, Rhys David, of Llwynrhydowen and Gwenllian, who married David Ieuan of Pant, Cenarth parish. Thomas David Lloyd, who lived at Ffosesgob between 1642 and 1665, succeeded his father to Ffosesgob. He married Catherine, daughter of Morris Griffith of Glan-dwr. They had three sons and three daughters. David Lloyd Thomas David, who succeeded to the property, Rhys, of Llanfair, who married Angharad, second daughter of Evan ap Evan alias *Coch yr aur* of Pantysgawen. The third son, Ieuan Thomas David, living in 1709, married Gwenllian, daughter of David Morris of Coedymynach in Llangeler parish. The eldest daughter, Gwenllian, married David Henry of Coed-y-foel, Mary married Ieuan Thomas Beynon, gent., of Abercefel, and Margaret married John David John Griffith of Glan-dwr. David Lloyd Thomas David, living in 1665, the eldest son, succeeded his father at Ffosesgob and married Elen, daughter of Thomas David Aaron of Pantyrorlech. Their marriage settlement was agreed in 1663. They had two sons, Thomas and Rees David.

Thomas married his cousin, Margaret, daughter and co-heiress of Rees Thomas David. The union was subject to a pre-nuptial settlement made on 20 November 1688. Thomas David's will was dated 1 April 1731 and proved in the same year. Thomas and Margaret David had several children. David Thomas succeeded to Ffosesgob and married Mary. His will was proved in 1758 and he died without issue. In 1760, the family sold the property to John Williams, gent. of Pythin, Carmarthenshire. Meyrick records that Ffosesgob, 'belongs to a respectable freeholder descended from the Lloyds of Castell Hywel family'. The *Tithe Schedule of 1841* for Llandysul lists Thomas Thomas, Esq., as the owner with Mary Thomas as tenant.

Francis Jones writes: 'I visited Ffosesgob on St. George's Day 1980, and met there William Davies whose family have been there for four generations. Recently he sold it to his nephew who will live there. He told me that the original plas was in the valley below the present house which is a very old and interesting building of two storeys, the upper storey having a range of four windows. A stream runs through part of the farmyard, and alongside (outside) the wall of the court before the house, and serves a ty bach (lavatory), in the corner of the dwelling house. It stands on high ground, below the crest, overlooking a deep dingle, both sides heavily wooded. The drive is long, and has a beautiful avenue of well-grown trees. Mr. Davies told me that his younger brother had died earlier in the year, and he only had to live a little longer and he would have drawn his old age pension. He went to the local C of E church as it was handy, but the family is buried at . . . (a Non-conformist chapel whose name escapes me).'

Grid Ref: SN 4168 4413

Refs: Colby Map, 1831; Llandysul Tithe Map, 1841; Meyrick, *Cardiganshire,* 195; Lloyd Family Records, Appx., pp. xvi - xix & Peds. pp. 19-20; PRO, Dale Castle MS., pp. 29, 30; WWHR, i, 51-2; CRO, GGMS I (Tydwal Gloff), fo. 21.

FFOSHELYG, Llandysul

A farm adjacent to Dyffryn Llynod, half a mile north of Tre-groes and shown but not named on *Colby's Map of 1831* and modern OS maps. Gwenllian Rhys, the daughter of Jenkin ap Rhys ap Griffith of Penrallt Gwerchyr, descended from Llewelyn Foel who traced to Blegywryd, married Rhys Lloyd of Ffoshelig, who was descended from Gwilym Lloyd of Castell Hywel. They had many children: Jenkin, who succeeded to Ffoshelyg, John Fychan ap Rees David ap Llewelyn described in 1552 as a yeoman, Jane, co-heiress, who married David Prydderch of Pantstreimon and Maud, co-heiress, who married Lewes Bevan Lewes of Aber-mad. Another daughter married Griffith Jenkin, and Tanglwst married Richard Morris of Trawsgoed. Anne, was married to Thomas David Rees Gwyn Gwilym Llewelyn of Cil-y-cwm and the youngest son was Rhydderch ap Rees David ap Llewelyn.

Jenkin Lloyd, who succeeded his father at Ffoshelyg, had a daughter, Mary, who was his heiress. She married Phillip Bryne of Llangynllo and later of Llanfair Trelygen and the property passed to him in 1552. Mary had a son by Francis Read in *vita conjugis*, called David Read (Ryd). The *Bronwydd Deeds* record that on 14 July 1562, 'Phillip Brwyn of Fos helyke, gent.,' bought Bronwydd. Philip was leasing and releasing land in 1589 and on 8 July 1611, the *Bronwydd Deeds* state: 'A release of a messuage of land to Thomas Lloyd, where said Thomas Lloyd dwells, called Bronwydd.'

It is not clear whether Mary Bryne actually married Francis Read, but their son, David, succeeded to the estate. The Read family had signed for Dwnn and were a branch of the Castell-mael, Llangain, Carmarthenshire family. David Read had a son, Thomas, described as of Ffoshelyg, who married Gwenllian, daughter of Thomas Lloyd of Castell Hywel. Their daughter and heiress, Elizabeth, married Francis Lloyd, the fourth son of Hugh Lloyd, son of Llewelyn Lloyd of Llanllyr. They had a son, Hugh Lloyd, who inherited Ffoshelyg from his mother. Hugh married Anne, daughter of George Lloyd of Castell Hywel. Hugh Lloyd's will was dated 23 March 1635/6 and proved on 5 April 1636. An inventory of his goods and chattels amounted to £103. Meyrick writes: 'It is still in the possession of a descendant of the Lloyds.'

Hugh Lloyd was succeeded by his eldest son, Morgan. The other sons were Francis and John and a sister, Barbara. Morgan Lloyd of Ffoshelyg was High Sheriff in 1687 and married Elizabeth, daughter of Edward Jones of Nanteos. Morgan's will was dated 1687 and an inventory was taken in 1688. Their son, Hugh Lloyd, succeeded to the estate. He was High Sheriff in 1701 and married Bridget, the heiress of Sampson Llwyd of Dolaullannerch, Clydau, Pembrokeshire. The marriage was subject to a post-nuptial settlement in 1695. Hugh Lloyd's will, dated 13 April 1700, was proved on 4 August 1703. Bridget's will was dated 1713; an inventory was taken in 1737 and the will was proved on 19 June 1738. They had nine children all of whom were left £100 each by their father except for Elizabeth, who received £150. The children were: Morgan, who succeeded his father, Thomas, later of Dolaullannerch and John Lloyd whose will dated 30 March 1720. Elizabeth married Charles Gwynne and Elinor married Walter Jones of Llandysul, gent. while Mary remained unmarried. Anne married Henry Jones of Arberth, formerly of Lampeter Velfrey. Bridget, whose will was dated 14 March 1732/3 and Margaret, the youngest, married Benjamin Davies of Clydau, a tanner.

Morgan Lloyd, who succeeded to Ffoshelyg, married his cousin Sarah Davies, daughter of Margaret and Benjamin Davies. They were childless. By 25 November 1791, Thomas Gough late of Haverfordwest, is described as, of Ffoshelyg, and in 1798 a Martha Gough is referred to as a widow living at the property. The *Tithe Map of 1841* names Rees Thomas as the owner-occupier of Ffoshelyg, a holding of 232 acres.

Grid Ref: SN 4091 4588

Refs: Modern OS Maps; Llandysul Tithe Map, 184; *Dwnn,* i, p. 91; WWHR i, p. 20; Blome List, 1673; Meyrick, *Cardiganshire,* p. 195; PRO, Dale Castle MS., pp. 21-22; NLW, Bronwydd Deeds, Nos. 679, 695, 2042, 2115, 2203, 2310, 2312, 2330, 2868, 2870; ibid, NLW, Cwrtmawr Deeds, 823; ibid, BRA 898, Nos. 25, 107, 181, 205, 274; ibid, 11807 D ff. 64-66; CRO, GGMS I (Tywal Gloff), p. 25.

FFOSRHYDYGALED, Llanychaearn

Nicholas writes in his *County Families*: 'The mansion of Ffosrhydgaled . . . is a substanstial building in the domestic style of architecture, of recent erection, and standing on a slope commanding a view of the beautiful Vale of Ystwyth. Mr Davies is erecting (1871) in the near neighbourhood an elegant residence in the mixed Gothic style, which has command of still more charming scenery.' Ffosrhydygaled is marked on *Colby's Map of 1831,* and on modern OS maps as an hotel west of the A487(T) between Chancery and Blaen-plwyf, south of Aberystwyth. The *Ffosrhydgaled Deeds* relate that on 30 September 1753, James Lloyd of Mabws, gent., 'released Ffos Rhyd Galed, Ty yr y Rhos and Cwrt y Cwm otherwise Spite Chancery, in Llanychaearn to John Davies of town of Cardigan, gent.' On 23 December 1754, the same John Davies released the above properties to John Morgan of Ffynnon-wen, of the parish of Llanafan, gent.

The Davies family, who built the present residence, hailed from Montgomeryshire. Joseph David of Machynlleth (1711-1792) and his wife, Mary (née Owen) (1712-1792), had a son, James, and a daughter, Elizabeth, who married Hugh Davies of Machynlleth, a banker (1748-1815). The Davies family bore the arms: *or* a chevron between 3 boars heads with the motto, *Y cyfiawn a flodeuant.* (The just shall flourish.) James and Mary had two sons, David, living in 1772, and Morris. Hugh and Elizabeth had two daughters, Mary and Jane. Jane married Thomas Lewis and their daughter Elizabeth, married R. D. Jenkins of Cilbronnau, Llangoedmor parish. Their son was Sir Lawrence Jenkins (1858-1928). Morris Davies, later of Ffosrhydygaled, married his cousin, Mary. The marriage was subject of a prenuptial settlement agreed on 14 October 1814.

Morris Davies was High Sheriff in 1829. He ran profitable businesses in Trefechan, Aberystwyth. He owned several limekilns and sold lime to local farmers and was also a corn merchant, buying barley in Llanrhystud and Llannon and transporting it to north Wales to be sold. When he died in 1835, his nephew, James Davies came from Machynlleth to succeed his uncle. He was High Sheriff in 1846, a JP and a Deputy-Lieutenant of Cardiganshire and lived at The Green, Trefechan. James married Elizabeth, daughter of Edward Evans, son of Pierce Evans JP of Upton Castle, Pembrokeshire. They had five daughters and a son, Morris Davies, of Ffosrhydygaled, born in 1843. He was called to the Bar at the Inner Temple in 1867. The *Landowners Return* lists James as owning 749 acres yielding a rental of £716 per annum. He married twice. In 1876, he married Mary Anne Elizabeth, eldest daughter of George William Parry of Llidiardau, Llanilar. The marriage was subject to a pre-nuptial settlement on 25 April 1876. Mary died in 1888 and in 1890, Morris married Mary Laura Philipps, eldest daughter of Thomas Bonsall of Glanrheidol, the widow of Col. John Allen Lloyd Philipps of Mabws, Llanrhystud and Dale Castle.

James George Morris Davies, born 1879, was the son of his first marriage. He became the land agent of the Hafod estate and married a daughter of the Summers family of Rosemoor, Haverfordwest, who was a ladies' maid at Hafod. The Davies's were followed at Ffosrhydygaled by members of the Smiths Crisps family, the last of whom – two elderly spinsters – died during the 1950's. By 1981 the house had become an hotel.

Grid Ref: SN 5779 7646

Refs: Colby Map, 1831 Nicholas, *County Families,* i, 191, 1875; Landowners Return, 1873; NLW, Ffos-rhydgaled Deeds, 15-18; W. J. Lewis, *Born on a Perilous Rock,* Aberystwyth (1980), p. 104; Francis Jones, *Historic Houses of Pembrokeshire and their Families,* p. 189, 1996,.

FFOSYBLEIDDIAID, Lledrod

Formerly the home of a most distinguished and ancient family, latterly Lloyds, who through Cadwgan Grach of Carrog, Llanddeiniol parish, descended from Owain Gwynedd. Marked on *Colby's Map of 1831* and named Ffos on modern OS maps, one mile south-west of Ystradmeurig, half a mile north-west of Swyddffynnon, on a lower hill-slope, adjacent to a tributary of the Teifi. H. Lloyd Johnes in his series of articles, *The Lesser Country Houses of Cardiganshire*, gives the following description: 'The present farmhouse is small and mean-looking, and retains no features of interest and only the ruins of what at one time must have been substantial out-buildings confirm that this was once the home of one of the oldest families in Cardiganshire.' Mr Osborne Jones of Ystrad-meurig wrote to Lloyd Johnes in 1951, that when he visited Ffosybleiddiaid in 1893, 'the ground floor was occupied by a huge kitchen slanting towards the fireplace and paved with cobble stone. At the west end opposite to the fire there was a small narrow room, and an outer kitchen on the south side of the house. There was no upper floor, except a few boards placed upon rafters where the Ystradmeurig students who lodged there slept. Their study was the tiny room at the west end'. The picture drawn by Mr Osborne Jones depicts a residence both rude and medieval in appearance. 'Alas, in the early years of this century the cobbled floor was pulled up and the huge kitchen divided by cheap wooden partitions.'

Meyrick visited Ffosybleiddiaid, c. 1809, when it was a farmhouse, but it had been recently the residence and was still the property of James Lloyd who had moved to his wife's more commodious home at Mabws. The Lloyds are said to have been Jacobites. David Lloyd, a naval captain and an old sea comrade of James II, is mentioned in Macauley's *History of England*. After James II's death he retired to private life, and is said to have died in 1722, aged 79. His younger brother, Oliver Lloyd was page to James II. Another member of the family was John Lloyd of Pound, born at Ffosybleiddiaid in 1726, who became Clerk of the Check at Plymouth Dockyard and a JP in Devon. Reynolds painted his portrait. His younger brother, Vaughan Lloyd, was born at Ffosybleiddiaid in 1736, entered the Royal Artillery and was present at the Battle of Minden, the siege of Gibraltar and served in the West Indies. He became Commandant of the Garrison at Woolwich and was promoted full General in 1814. He died in 1817. The last of the family at Ffosybleiddiaid was James Lloyd (1721-1800), who farmed there and managed the estate. He married Anna Maria, only child and heiress of Richard Lloyd of Mabws, Llanrhystud parish, MP for Cardigan. James Lloyd acted for some time as Secondary to the Court of Great Sessions for the Carmarthen circuit and became a JP.

The earliest reference to the property is when Morgan ap Meredydd, descended from Rhys Ddu, married Margaret, the daughter of Ieuan ap Gruffydd ap Rhys of Caeo, Carmarthenshire, by Gwenllian, daughter of Morgan ap Llewelyn ap Gwilym Llwyd. They had a son, David Llwyd of Ffosybleiddiaid who lived there in 1550. The family signed for Lewys Dwnn in 1588 and its arms were: a lion and *sable,* ducally gorged and chained *or.* The crest was as in arms, and the motto *Ducit amor patriae (Ar Dduw i gyd).* David Llwyd married Mary, daughter of Rhys ap David Llwyd ap David ap Rhydderch of Gogerddan. Their son was Oliver Lloyd, alive in 1593, who married Gwenllian, daughter of Rhydderch ap David ap Llewelyn ap Cadwgan by Margaret, daughter of David Llwyd ap Ieuan ap Lewis of Aber-mad, Llanychaearn parish. They had a son, David Llwyd of Ffosybleiddiaid (1582-1636), who married Gwladys, daughter of Richard Herbert of Pengelli, Llanfeugan, Brecon. Their son, Oliver Lloyd (1610-1668), married Jane, daughter of John Lloyd, brother to Thomas Lloyd of Llanllyr, High Sheriff in 1647. On 2 October 1648, the *Crosswood Deeds* record that a grant was given by John Vaughan of Trawsgoed Esq., to Oliver Lloyd of Ffosybleiddiaid, gent., of 'Fose y blined and Llwyn y parke', (in the tenure of David Lloyd Oliver, gent., at £3.15.0 p.a.) and 12 other properties in the granges of Blaen Aeron and Mefennydd, reserving to grantor a perpetual yearly rent of £9.8.8. Oliver and Jane Lloyd had two sons, John, who succeeded his father to the estate, and David. Captain David Lloyd of the *Philobasilicos*, the second son, was the sea comrade, agent and a favourite of James II. He was the Captain of a Man-of-War, of a troop of the Royal Regiment of Horse and Groom of the Bedchamber to the King. He attended James II during most of the King's troubles following his Abdication. The *Golden Grove Manuscripts* give the following anecdote in the hand of Theophilus Jones: 'David Lloyd was Captain of a Man-of-War and followed his master James II to France; when one night complaining of the ingratitude of his daughters; 'Mary must be excused (says he), her heart and mind and thoughts are entirely her husband's and governed by his w[hims], but Anne should not have forsaken me; she however fell into bad company and therefore a good deal may be said for her likewise. Not a word for her either' says Lloyd as he was leaving the room, 'Both Bitches, by G—!' from U.S. member of the House of Balcarras penes Col. James Lloyd, Mabws.

David Lloyd died on 4 January 1722/3. John Lloyd, the elder son, succeeded to Ffosybleiddiaid. He was a barrister and was admitted to Gray's Inn on 20 February 1656. He married Elizabeth, daughter and co-heiress of Thomas Lloyd of Wernfellig and Llanllyr. In 1670 John Lloyd paid tax on 4 hearths. Papers at the Pembrokeshire Record Office record: 'The Ffosybleiddiad estate owned in 1689 by John Lloyd Esq., of Cwmelin, Cardiganshire, and Elizabeth his wife consists of the capital messuage of Tythyn Ffoes y bleidded, and 14 properties in the parishes of Lledrod, Llanbadarn Odwyn, Gwnws, Llanilar, Caron and Llangeitho, houses in the town of Caron, and lands, unspecified, at Morfa'r Esgob, and the profits of an annual fair held on the Tir y dre called Ffair dydd Gwyl Ifan; which were settled on themselves and their son David Lloyd of Ffoes y Bleiddied, gent., on 13th Dec. 1689 (a post-nuptial settlement of John Lloyd and Elizabeth)'. They had two sons, David and John Lloyd. John, the younger son was a Captain under William III and David, the elder son, succeeded to Ffosybleiddiaid. He was a JP in 1705 and married Sage, the daughter of John Lloyd of Cilgwyn. An inventory of goods was taken when David Lloyd died in 1714, mentions the following rooms in the house: 3 upper garrets, 5 beds and furniture, the Porch chamber (bedroom), Middle Chamber, Little Chamber, New Chamber, the room above and over the parlour, The Parlour, The Hall, room over the kitchen and kitchen.

David Lloyd's will, proved on 28 January 1714, mentions messuages callen Gwernfeilig in Llanfihangel Ystrad parish and Cil-y-bwn in Trefilan. David and Sage's son, John Lloyd, was Mayor of Carmarthen in 1739 and was the patron of his son's friend, Edward Richard, founder of the Grammar School at Ystrad Meurig. In his book *Edward Richards of Ystrad Meurig* D. G. Osborne-Jones, referring to the Lloyds writes, 'the family as a whole were distinguished for their loyalty to their friends'. John Lloyd married Mary, only daughter of James Philipps of Pentypark, Pembrokeshire, who traced to Cadifor Fawr. They had four sons and one daughter: James Philipps Lloyd, John Lloyd, Thomas Lloyd, Vaughan Lloyd and Briana, who died unmarried in 1814. D. G. Osborne-Jones continues: 'James Lloyd, the eldest son, an old Harrovian was Edward Richard of Ystrad Meurig's lifelong friend; John Lloyd of Plymouth, second son of Ffos y bleiddied, was a pupil at Edward Richard's school at Ystrad Meurig in 1735 and later lived at Danyrallt'. Vaughan Lloyd (1736-1817), married Sarah Fluker, the widow of Major Fluker and second daughter of Main Swete Walrond of Antigua. He died on 16 June 1817 leaving a son, James Lloyd, who died unmarried. James Philipps Lloyd succeeded his father, John Lloyd. Born on 22 October 1721, he was educated at Harrow, trained as a lawyer, and was the friend and patron of the aforementioned Edward Richard. On 4 June 1750, he married Anna Maria, only child and heiress of Richard Lloyd of Mabws and Ystrad Teilo by

Lettice Games of Tregaer, Breconshire. They had four sons and one daughter. John Lloyd, born 1753, the eldest son described as of Ffosybleiddiaid, Mabws and Ystrad Teilo, was High Sheriff of Pembrokeshire in 1785 and of Cardiganshire in 1806. Richard, the second son, born in 1755 died aged 22 in 1777, James Philipps Lloyd-Philipps, the third son, took the additional surname of Philipps when he inherited the Pentypark estate. Vaughan, the fourth son, died in 1772. Letitia Mary, the only daughter, born in 1751, married Admiral Thomas of Llanfechan. John Lloyd, the eldest son, married Eleanor Allen, daughter of John Allen of Dale Castle on 8 July 1776 and became the Allen-Lloyds and later, the Allen Lloyd-Philipps. Although the family prospered, it no longer lived at Ffosybleiddiaid. The house was occupied by tenants such as David Richards, who farmed there with his wife, Letitia, in 1757. He was followed by his son, also David. By 1843, the property was owned by Major Lloyd-Phillips of Mabws and tenanted by David Meredith who leased 389 acres, with the house, outbuildings, yard, garden, roads and water. In 1888, Ffosybleiddiaid was sold to Lord Lisburne and became part of the Trawsgoed estate.

Grid Ref: SN 6875 6705

Refs: Colby Map, 1831; *Dwnn,* i, 17, 36; WWHR i, 30; *Burke,* 1850; PRO, Dale Castle MS., p. 24; Blome List, 1673; NLW, Crosswood Deeds, pp. 23, 74, 142; Meyrick, *Cardiganshire,* 278; H. Lloyd Johnes, *'The Lesser Country Houses of Cardiganshire', Ceredigion,* ii, 4, pp. 241-3, 1955; NLW Coleman Deeds, Nos. 142, 165; Lloyd Pedigrees, p. 58; NLW, Cwrtmawr Deeds, Nos. 211, 295, 398; P RO, D/LP, No. 5/62. *Historical Notes,* J. Rowlands, 1866. p. 90; Theakstone & Davies Pedigrees, 1913, s.n. *Lloyd of Ffos y Bleiddied;* D. G. Osborne-Jones, *Edward Richard of Ystradmeurig,* 1934; CRO, GGMS (Tywal Gloff), 1; Francis Jones, *Historic Houses of Pembrokeshire and their Families,* 1996,.

FFOSYBONTPREN, Llanilar

Marked on *Colby's Map of 1831* as one mile south-west of Llanilar village. Also known as Ffosbonpren and occupied throughout this period by tenant farmers.

John Lewes of Llysnewydd in Llangeler parish, Carmarthenshire, the son of David Llewelyn of Gernos, married Janet, the daughter of William David Lloyd and co-heiress of Glandyweli, Carmarthenshire. They had two sons, Thomas and David. David, the second son was of Pant-y-fen and married Anne, daughter of John Parry of Tredefaid, Pembrokeshire. Thomas Lewes, elder son was described as of Ffosybontpren and Tredefaid. He married Eleanor, daughter of James Vaughan of Gelligati, Cenarth, who was the second son of Thomas Vaughan of Clunfyrddin, (Farthingshook), Pembrokeshire. Their son was John Lewes of Ffosybontbren and Tredefaid. He married Elizabeth, daughter of Watkin Lloyd of Wern Newydd, Llanarth. They had two sons, Thomas Lewes, coroner, who married a daughter of John Thomas of Cilciffeth, Pembrokeshire and the Rev. Watkin Lewes of Penybenglog, Pembrokeshire who, in turn, married Anne Williams of Ambleston, Pembrokeshire and became the father of Sir Watkin Lewis, alderman of the City of London.

Grid Ref: SN 6137 7377

Refs: Colby Map, 1831; NLW 12356E, 501; CRO, GGMS III (Owen ap Bradwen); Francis Jones, *Historic Houses of Pembrokeshire and their Families,* 1996, and *Historic Carmarthenshire Homes and their Families,* (Brawdy Books), 1997.

FFWRNEITHIN, Llanarth

Marked on *Colby's Map of 1831* and on modern OS maps as north-east of Mydroilyn and west of Dihewyd. John Lewis Williams, the poet, is named as of Ffwrneithin late in the 17th century, although precise dates are not given. He was a descendant of Ieuan Thomas ab David, Saer y Cwm, Cwrt Newydd, and son of Lewis Williams, a younger son of Williams ab Ieuan. His nephew was Thomas Williams, physician of Trehale, near Mathry, Pembrokeshire, who emigrated to America in 1725.

Lewis Pugh was also of Ffwrneithin. His son, Rev Hugh Pugh, vicar of Llangrannog married Mary, daughter of Lewis Gwynn, of Mynachdy, who was living in 1721. By 1760 Thomas Pugh, gent., owned and occupied Ffwrneithin. His seal to a deed in 1772 was a stags head and neck couped. In 1797 David Daniel, gent., lived at Ffwrneithin.

Grid Ref: SN 4628 5609

Refs: Colby Map, 1831; WWHR, i, 46, 54; PRO, Dale Castle MS., p. 30 (115); NLW, Griffith Owen Deeds; NLW, No. 6283; CRO, Beckinsale Collection.

FFYNNON BEDR
see PETERWELL

FFYNNON GWERFYL
see WERVILBROOK

FFYNNON LLEFRITH, Llangrannog
Marked on *Colby's Map of 1831* and on modern OS maps a long mile north of Plwmp.

Harry of Cwmtudu, from the family of David ab Ievan of Llwyndafydd who traced to Tydwal Gloff, had two sons, David Parry and William ap Harry of Cwm Cynon. David had two sons George, of Llangrannog, who had a son, Parry of Rhydyglomen, and Philip Parry, who had a natural son, Harry Philip who lived at Ffynnon Llefrith. He married Catherine Beynon, daughter of David Jenkin Beynon of Llangrannog and they had a son, David Parry. William ap Harry of Cwm Cynon had a son, David William Parry, who had a daughter Anne, who married David Thomas of Ffynnon Llefrith. Dates are sadly lacking.

Grid Ref: SN 3638 5425

Refs: CRO, GGMS, I (Tydwal Gloff), 44-5; Colby Map, 1831.

GARTHFREFI, Llanddewibrefi
Now the farm called Garth, to the west of Llanddewibrefi village and near the banks of the river Teifi. There are three farms named Garth within one and a quarter miles of Llanddewibrefi marked on *Colby's Map of 1831* and on modern OS maps; the history of each is somewhat confused. We know that Evan Dhu was of Garth vrevi and Garth Ystrad and that his great-grandson was the Rev. Thomas Davids, clerk, who married Grace, daughter of John Hall by Jane Laugharne. Their eldest son James married Frances, daughter of Thomas Mores of Hollwell, Oxfordshire by Hester, daughter of William Johnson of Wydford, Oxon. Dates are lacking.

Francis Jones notes that Daniel Evans, Quaker, of Garth, son of Anne died c. 1783. His descendant, Daniel John Evans of Gorwydd, and later of Garth, married Margaret Milne. Their children tragically died young – a son in childhood and a daughter, who married Dr. John Rowland of Pontrhydfendigaid and died in 1890, aged only twenty-three, having given birth to three sons and a daughter. Daniel, inherited the Garth estate died in 1901. Rowland John, who was of Argoed died a year before his elder brother in 1900. The third son, Robert, who lived at Garth and served as a Cardiganshire County Councillor died in 1928 aged sixty, his wife having pre-deceased him by six months aged fifty-five.

Grid Ref: SN 6475 5534

Refs: Colby Map, 1831; Llansteffan MS., fo. 43; D. Ben Rees, *Hanes Plwyf Llandewibrefi,* 1984, p. 66.

GELLI, Trefilan
Gelli is shown on *Colby's Map of 1831* and on modern OS maps north-west of Trefilan church. A sale catalogue of 1980 states that 'The front part of the house seems to be late 18th early 19th century. To the rear is a wing which is possibly 17th century. It is said to be by Nash but there is no evidence of this. The house contains entrance porch, front hall, drawing room, dining room, living room, back hall, kitchen, larder and cellar. On the first floor: Boxroom, four bedrooms and bathroom. On the second floor: Bedroom, sitting room and bathroom. There is a walled garden, outbuildings and grounds'.

Lewis Rogers of Gelli, son of Thomas and his wife, Anne Hughes, formerly of Llanychaearn, was appointed JP in 1748 and High

Sheriff in 1753. He was a lawyer and agent to Sir Robert Smythe, the winner by 500 votes over Thomas Johnes, the younger, in the Cardigan Borough Election of 1774. The result was overturned on petition to the House of Commons. Lewis Rogers had been involved in other elections and had been an agent at Ilchester, Somerset, where an election was declared void and a new writ issued. Rogers was accused of perjury and committed to Newgate prison. Only his deteriorating health secured his release. He is described as 'a very shady character'. Lewis and his wife, Anne, daughter of John Edwardes, Abermeurig, were tenants at Llanllyr when their son, John was born. John was educated at Ystrad Meurig at the school run by the Rev. John Williams, who was married to his aunt. He studied medicine at Guy's Hospital, London, and in Edinburgh, before returning to Gelli and caring for patients 'both rich and poor without fear or favour'. In 1846, whilst returning home from a call late at night with his servant that his coach overturned in the Aeron at Talsarn which was in flood and Dr. Rogers drowned. He was 61 years old. He and his wife, Anne, daughter of Thomas Jones of Llanio, had five children including Letitia (1825-1882), from whom the Rev. John Lewis, vicar of Llanrhystud, and the Rogers-Lewis of Abermeurig descend. A younger son, Henry, a clergyman in Essex was High Sheriff of Cardiganshire in 1820.

Grid Ref: SN 5463 5737

Refs: Colby Map, 1831; NLW, Mynachty Deeds; *Ceredigion,* vi, No. 4 (1971), p. 347; *Caerfyrddin,* 1869, pp. 213-4; ibid, vii, (1972), p. 55: Benjamin Williams, *Enwogion Ceredigion*; WWHR, iii, pp. 95, 149-160.

GELLI FAHAREN, Llandysul

Marked on *Colby's Map of 1831* as Gelly Fyharen and on modern OS maps a mile and a half north of Llandysul off the B4476 road to Pren-gwyn. The earliest reference to this property states that David Thomas of Gellifaharen married Elen, daughter of David Lloyd Griffith of Faerdref and his wife Jane, daughter and coheiress of Rhydderch David Prydderch of Pantstreimon. In 1760 David Davies of Gellifaren also owned Gellifaren-Fach in the same parish. By 1830 David Jones owned the farm and he also bought Faerdre-fach . His son, John, followed him at Gellifaharen and The *Llandysul Tithe Map of 1841* shows the property as being of 154 acres and 9 p. The *Landowners Return of 1873* lists John Jones as owning 172 acres worth £102 per annum and Mrs. Jones, also of Gellifaharen, owned 377 acres rated at £131. In *Hanes Plwyf Landyssul,* W. J. Davies tells us *'Arwyddair teulu y diweddar Mr. John Jones [Gellifaharen] yw "Gwirionedd a Gwladgarwch".'* (Truth and Patriotism.)

According to Daniel Jones in his *Hanes Plwyfi Llangeler a Phenboyr,* one Samuel Oliver of Nantgarreg, farmer, who was alive in 1899, is said to have once lived at Gellifaharen.

John Jones (1834-1884), the son of David and Jane Jones, whose mother was a granddaughter of Dafydd Dafis, Castell Hywel, married Mary Moses of Ton, Cwm Nedd. He was a prominent lawyer who became Registrar of the County Court in Swansea. He was also a pioneer farmer at Gellifaharen who built substantial outbuildings for his animals. When the Unitarian congregation of Llwynrhydowen were forced to leave their chapel, John Jones was instrumental in securing Capel y Graig, Llandysul for them. He died in tragic circumstances whilst returning with his family from Capel y Graig in July 1884. John Jones and the children's governess were killed on Wesley Hill, Llandysul, when thrown from the carriage and his wife and four children were injured.

Grid Ref: SN 4195 4317

Refs: Colby Map, 1831; PRO, Dale Castle MS., p. 29, iii, 30 (114); W. J. Davies, *Hanes Plwyf Llandyssul,* 1896, p. 228; WWHR, iii, 85; Jones, *Llangeler and Penbryn,* p. 125; Llandysul Tithe Map, 1841; Landowners Return, 1873; Daniel E. Jones, *Hanes Plwyfi Llangeler a Phenboyr* (Llandysul), 1899.

GELLIFRAITH, Llandysul

The house is shown on *Colby's Map of 1831* and on modern OS maps as lying half a mile west of Dyffryn Llynod bordering the minor road which follows the Cerdin river towards Bwlch-y-gros. Meyrick, in *Cardiganshire* says 'Anciently a seat of the Lloyds and afterwards of the Phillips's, is a curious ancient building; the roof and pointed arches of the doors and window giving it a claim to such a title'. The last of the line was Thomas Phillips who died without issue. Their pedigree traced back to the Lloyds of Blaenythan, the home of a second son of Llwyndafydd. 'The estate is now the property of David Lloyd of Alltyrodin, Esq.'

In 1629 Rhys Lloyd gent. was living at Gellifraith. He and Sir John Lewis, Kt., of Abernantbychan, were trustees to the pre-nuptial settlement of Thomas Lewes of Gellidywyll, Carmarthenshire, gent., and Mary, daughter of David Llwyd of Pantstreimon in the parish of Llandysul, dated 20 January 1618/9. David Lloyd Thomas John of Gellifraith had a daughter and heiress, Jane, who married Phillip ap James ap Phillip, a descendant of the Lloyds of Llwyndafydd. Their son, John, who took the patronymic Phillip as his surname, married Anne, daughter of Hugh Bowen of Upton Castle, Pembrokeshire. Their son, Thomas ap Phillip, married Gwenllian, daughter of Phillip Thomas Phillip of Tre-main. There were no children of this marriage. Thomas Phillips gave the whole of the estate, other than the Gellifraith tenement, to Thomas Phillips of Cryngae, his godson, the son of John Phillips of Dol-haidd. The estate of Rhyd-y-bont, Llanybydder parish, and the tenement of Gellifraith, Llandysul, passed to the daughter of David Lloyd, living in 1761. Major Jones gives sundry fragments of pedigrees, all undated. Gellifraith was rated for the parish rate at £12 for tax at 4d. in the pound in 1758/9. By 1841, Delme Seymour Davies, Esq., was the owner, with James Davies as tenant.

Grid Ref: SN 3997 4532

Refs: Colby Map, 1831; WWHR, i, pp 17 & 34-50; Meyrick, *Cardiganshire,* 1810, edn., 1907, p. 200; PRO, Dale Castle MS., pp. 25-26; W. J. Davies, *Hanes Plwyf Llandysul,* pp189 & 296; CRO, GGMS I, fo. 26; NLW, Noyadd Trefawr Deeds, No. 307.

GERNOS (GYRN), Llangynllo

This house, now derelict, is situated a mile north east of Bronwydd, and is marked on *Colby's Map of 1831* and on modern OS maps east of the B4334 road from Aber-banc to Penrhiw-pal at Coed-y-bryn. *Bowen's Map of South Wales in 1760* indicates 'a fish pond nearby'. In modern times it became known as Mount Gernos. The house formerly belonged to John ap Rosser, descended from Meurig, grandson of Rhys Fychan ap Rhys Mechyll ap Rhys Grug, who married Cissil, daughter of Gwilym Thomas Hir. The property passed to the Lewis's by marriage with a daughter of Rhys ap John who was of the same descent as Llwyd of Cilgwyn. David Lewes of Gernos (will proved 1611), married Gwenllian, daughter of Thomas Parry of Noyadd Trefawr and had five sons; Thomas, who married Lettice, daughter of Thomas Lloyd, third son of Llanllyr, George, Clerk, Treasurer of St David's, later of Clydau parish, John of Llysnewydd, Richard of Pantyrodyn and Lodwick, who became Coroner for Cardiganshire and married a daughter of David Lloyd of Faerdref, Llandysul.

Thomas Lewes, the eldest son, and Lettice had two sons and two daughters, David, the heir, Thomas, who became a mercer in Carmarthen. Thomas, son of David and Gwenllian Lewis, murdered his own mother, daughter of Thomas Parry of Neuadd, for which deed he was hanged.

Elen, who married Jenkin Thomas and Gwenllian who married John Rees Jenkin. David Lewes, who succeeded to Gernos, married Mary, a daughter of Sir John Lewes of Abernantbychan and had three sons and two daughters. His eldest son, John, married Sarah Wilkes of Somerset. He served as High Sheriff in 1672 and in the same year Gernos was assessed as having 7 hearths. He was known as John the elder and latterly lived at Troed-y-rhiw, encouraging local writers such as Moses Williams. His son, John the younger, inherited and lived at Gernos. He married Margaret, daughter of Walter Jones of Llwynyffortiwn. His youngest brother, Erasmus Lewis, entered Jesus College, Oxford on 22 February 1683/4, aged twenty, graduated BA in 1688 and was ordained by the Bishop of Winchester on 21

September 1690. He was collated vicar of Lampeter and rector of Betws Bledrws on 17 December 1695. He resigned both livings in 1743 and died in 1744 in his eighty second year. He was a scholar and a poet and assisted John Rhydderch to compile his *English and Welsh Dictionary* published at Shrewsbury in 1725. Some of his englynion were contained in a manuscript volume, *Briwsion o'r Brydyddiaeth Gymreig*.

John Lewes was appointed JP in 1705 and High Sheriff of Cardiganshire in 1711. David, the second son of John and Margaret, succeeded and married Lucy, the daughter of Edward Jones of Llanina. The marriage was subject to a pre-nuptial settlement. Among lands settled were 'the capital messuage known as Tyr y Gernos Issa, Tyr y Gernos Ycha, Tyr Dole Goch, Tyr bach y Crydd, Tyr bach y Rhew and Tyr Eithin Duon'. David Lewes was High Sheriff in 1726 and died a year later. Having had no issue, his four sisters, Mary, Elizabeth. Margaret and Sarah became co-heiresses. Margaret married Thomas Parry of Cwm Cynon who later bought the shares of the co-heiresses. They had a son, John Parry, who married Hester, daughter of John Howells of Penybeili, her portion being £200. John died in 1747. Hester was the heiress of her uncle, Llewelyn Llwyd, of Dolgrogws. She married secondly, Watkin Watkin of Gwnnws, who died in 1776. The Parrys remained at Cwm Cynon and Gernos was occupied by Lewis Llwyd, second husband of Elizabeth Lloyd, who was living at Gernos in 1737. He was High Sheriff of the county in 1756. Lewis Lloyd was followed by Llewelyn Parry, High Sheriff of Cardiganshire in 1772. His will was dated 12 January 1824 and was proved on 31 May 1824. His natural son, Thomas Parry, became the heir of Gernos. On inheriting the property he took the name Thomas Llewelyn Parry. He helped to establish the independent chapel of Bwlch-y-groes in the parish of Llandysul in 1833 and a new mansion was built at Gernos. He died on 12 November 1836 and his will was proved on 31 December 1836. He had a natural daughter, Judith Parry, born in 1827, who lived with Mrs. Judith Jones of Newcastle Emlyn. Judith Parry married Gwinnett Tyler, a lieutenant on HMS *Leander* and brother of Lt.-Col. George Henry Tyler of Cottrell, Gloucestershire. The marriage was subject to a pre-nuptial settlement in March 1852. They had three daughters and a son, Gwinnett George Tyler, who married Constance Webley who lived at Glanhelyg, Llechryd, after his death in 1906. The *Landowners Return of 1873* shows the estate consisted of 2,051 acres returning a rental of £778 per annum. In 1884 there were mortgages of £20,000 on the estate. In 1882 Gwinnett Tyler established a woollen mill at Maesllyn.

Part of the Mount Gernos estate was advertised for sale in 1907. The entire estate was sold in 1926 in 70 lots amounting to 1462 acres including the main residence with 63 acres and the home farm of 94 acres. A Sale Catalogue of 1926 describes the residence as having, with demesne of 63 acres, dining room, drawing and morning rooms, library, smoking room, eighteen bed and dressing rooms, bathrooms, lavatories, kitchens, pantries, a new wing of out-offices and outbuildings; and a home farm of 94 acres. The old mansion, spoilt by the addition of two wings by Middleton of Cheltenham in 1870, had 18 bedrooms, florid stonework, a Gothic wooden staircase and a stained glass screen between the inner and outer hall. Thereafter it housed pigs and remained derelict.

Grid Ref: SN 3640 4515

Refs: Colby Map, 1831; NLW, Griffith Owen List (iv); Emanuel Bowen Map of South Wales, c. 1760; NLW, Morgan Richardson, i, 169, 176, 209; PRO List; Meyrick, *Cardiganshire,* 202; CRO, GGMS III (Owen ap Bradwen); G. E. Evans, Lampeter, 64-67, & refs there; 1905; NLW, BRA, 898, Nos. 69 & 70; Landowners Return, 1873; W. J. Davies, *Hanes Plwyf Llandysul,* pp. 51-2; S.A. 668. & Evan Davies, *Hanes Plwyf Llangynllo;* Thomas Lloyd, *The Lost Houses of Wales,* 1986 p. 50.

GILFACHAFAEL, Llanddeiniol

Situated a long mile north-east of Llanrhystud on a southern slope, east of the river Wyre and marked on *Colby's Map of 1831* and on modern OS maps. The *Golden Grove Manuscripts* state that the house was owned by Jenkin David who married Anne, the daughter of Thomas Lloyd of Cilfache in Llanddeiniol by Mary, daughter of David Lloyd of Crynfryn. They had a son who married Gaenor, daughter of Jenkin Jones of Coedmor in Pencarreg, the widow of Llewelyn Pugh of Llannerchaeron. Dates are lacking. However we do know that one George Parry of Gilfachafael was a JP in 1772.

Grid Ref: SN 5585 7037

Refs: CRO, GGMS I; ibid, II (Adv. Cards.); ibid, III (Tydwal Gloff); Colby Map, 1831.

GILFACH BERTHOG, site unknown

This location is unknown. According to The *Golden Grove Manuscripts* a Jones of Gilfach Berthog had a daughter, Judith, who married John ap Zaccheus, son of Zaccheus ap John and Rebecca daughter of Ievan of Llechwedd Deri, descended from Tydwal. Zaccheus ap John was the son of John, natural son of Ieuan of Parc Rhydderch. Dates unknown.

Refs: CRO, GGMS, III (Gwaethfoed), fo. 34.

GILFACH-CHWITH, Llandysul

Located on *Colby's Map of 1831* and modern OS maps north of the A475 main road between Penrhiwllan and Horeb. David Lewis of Gilfach-chwith was the grandson of Philip Howel of Blaenythan and Elen, daughter of Lewis David Meredydd Owen, who traced to Bradwen. David Lewis married Elizabeth, daughter of David Lloyd Griffith Howel of Faerdre, Llandysul, and secondly Lodwick Lewes of Brynhinlle who also traced to Bradwen. David and Elizabeth had a son, John Lewis, who succeeded to the property and married Anne, daughter of George Lloyd of Castell Hywel. Their daughter and heiress, Cisill, married Thomas Howells of Penybeili, the son of John Howell Morgan. No dates are given.

Grid Ref: SN 3870 4275

Refs: Colby Map, 1831; CRO, GGMS (Gwynfardd and Tydwal Gloff).

GILFACHREDA, Llanina

Gilfachreda, now the name given to the hamlet on the main road between Llanarth and New Quay. Marked on *Colby's Map of 1831* as Gilfachrheda, the house is situated on the road half a mile south of Llanina. This house formerly belonged to the Wern Newydd estate, Llanarth. In his *Wanderings*, Turner mentions the property in name only. In 1837 the house was owned by Thomas Lloyd and Charles Longcroft. The latter lived at Llanina Mansion.

Grid Ref: SN 4509 5880

Refs: Colby Map, 1831; Horsfall-Turner, *Wanderings.*

GILFACH-WEN ISAF, Llandysul

The lands of Gilfach-wen lie to the west and within a mile of Llandysul, on a long slope stretching down to the banks of the Teifi. At some time in the Middle Ages the property became divided Gilfach-wen Isaf and Gilfach-wen Uchaf. Both homes have a good southerly aspect and are protected from the north winds by land that rises to 500 feet. Marked on *Colby's Map of 1831* as Gilfach-wen and Gilfach-wen -isaf.

In his *Topographical Dictionary of Wales* Lewis described Gilfach-wen Isaf thus: 'A small but elegant mansion, forming one of the most pleasing objects on the banks of the river Teifi. It is beautifully situated in the midst of thick groves and backed by luxuriant and extensive woods; but from the judicious disposition of the trees, the house with the river winding beneath it, forms a conspicuous and beautiful feature in the landscape.'

Meyrick tells us that 'the earliest known family there was Llwyd, descended from the same root as those of Dyffryn Llynod, a branch of the Llwyds of Castell Hywel not to be confused with the Lloyds of Gilfachwen Uchaf. The property retains some of the characteristics of a gentleman's residence and consists of a small attractive mansion, together with a farmhouse and the usual outbuildings'.

Thomas ap Jenkin ap Thomas ap Hywel Fawr of Gilfach-wen -Isaf, who descended from Elystan Glodrydd, married Angharad, daughter of David ap Rhydderch of Pantstreimon. Their son, David married Gwenllian, the daughter of

John Gwion Llewelyn Lloyd, who traced to Tydwal Gloff. Their son, also David, who married Anne, daughter of Morris David ap David, sold Gilfachwen-Isaf to Howel Phillips, gent. David Lloyd's son, the third David, was thereafter described as of Waungilwen in Penboyr parish. He died on 10 February 1695. Meyrick writes 'the last of the family to live there was Mary, daughter of Thomas Philipps of Cringa, who left her share of the estate from her own nephew to the present possessor, the Rev. John Lloyd, who was related to her only as being derived from the same stock'. In the latter half of the eighteenth century, through marriage, it became the property of the county family of Waunifor, who built the residence that has substantially survived until the present day. John Lloyd owned Gilfach-wen Isaf in 1760. Writing in 1840, Lewis describes the house as 'Gilfachwen, the seat of the Rev. Thomas Lloyd, is a small but elegant mansion'. A year later The *Llandysul Tithe Schedule of 1841* tells us that the Rev. Thomas Lloyd was the owner-occupier of the property of 204 acres. Thomas Lloyd of Gilfachwen wrote to W. O. Price in April 1864: 'I am afraid poor Harry has got into a bad set at Oxford. Probably he is easily led; if so, he may fall into great embarrassments. Let him beware of Oxford Tradesmen, for of all Creditors, the world cannot produce a more unconscionable set. They offer young men every facility to run into debt; and I have known these debts remain as an incubus upon many for years after they have left the University, seriously interfering with their after progress in life. He must be put under an allowance. At the rate he is now going on £500 a year would be little enough for him. £150 would be ample, with an occasional bonus, if he be obliged to have a private tutor, which he will very probably require . . . With kind regards to your circle.' Thomas Lloyd wrote to Miss Davies of Hill House College, Haverfordwest in September 1865: 'Enclose cheque of £50 "to square our account" my daughters Jane and Fanny at school. My eldest son practices his profession at Llandysul and boards here. My son Tom is home on his vacation. Anna and Maria are the only girls with us. Mary is at St. David's and Jane at Cardigan.' By 27 July 1868 Thomas

Lloyd had died. Fanny his daughter married Meredydd Lloyd Price of Bryn Cothin, Nantgaredig, Carmarthenshire.

The *Landowners Return of 1873* tells us that John Lloyd of Gilfach-wen, a solicitor who died in 1889, is listed as owning 638 acres returning £474 p.a. and Mrs. Lloyd held 97 acres at £86 p.a.

Francis Jones visited Gilfach-wen Isaf on 21 May 1974 and describes it as '. . . a cube, of c. 1800 which is in excellent preservation and lived in until a few months ago. The farmhouse and outbuildings are just behind it and nearer the road. It is now owned by J. Oswyn Evans, Danycoed farm, who has recently cut down the fine timber in the grounds mainly on the east side of the house'.

Grid Ref: SN 4037 4074

Refs: Colby Map, 1831; Meyrick, *Cardiganshire,* 1810 edn. 1907, p. 197; Landowners Return, 1873; Lewis, *TDW;* CRO, GGMS (Elystan Glodrudd), fo. 33; Llandysul Tithe Map, 1841; Davies, *Hanes Plwyf Llandysul.*

GILFACHWEN UCHAF, Llandysul

This property is closer to Llandysul than Gilfachwen Isaf and is marked on *Colby's Map of 1831* as Gilfachwen. This was the original home of the Lloyds, descendents of Elystan Glod-drudd, who later settled at Cilgwyn and Coedmor. Nothing remains to indicate its former status, but the original mansion is said to have been located in a hayfield below the house where the ridges and foundation lines can still be seen.

The *Golden Grove Manuscripts* tell us that Jenkin ap Rees ap David ap Howel Vychan ap Rhys Foel ap Rhys ap Rhydderch ap Cadifor ap Dinawal 'built ye house at Gilfachwen'. David, younger son of Thomas ap David ap Gruffydd ap Gronw Goch was followed by his son, Rhys, who settled here as a result of his marriage to Angharad, the daughter and heiress of the above Jenkin ap Rees. The pedigree recorded by Lewys Dwnn states that Rhys ap David and Angharad had two sons, Howel Fychan who succeeded to Gilfachwen Uchaf and Gruffydd, who married a daughter of Thomas ap Gruffydd ap Nicholas, and received Cilgwyn in Llandyfriog parish. A great-great-grandchild of this marriage brought Cilgwyn to a son of Gilfach Uchaf. According to Dwnn, Howel married Angharad, daughter of Jenkin ap David ap Rhydderch of Parc Rhydderch, by whom he had the following children:

David ap Howel Fychan, the heir; Rhys ap Howel Fychan of Penrallt Fochno who married and had issue; Eva who married Gruffydd ap Evan Howel ab Einion ab Ieuan ap Gruffydd ap Rhys ap Llywelin and Lleucu, who married John Lloyd ap Gruffydd Gwyn.

David ap Howel Fychan, the heir, married Angharad, daughter and heiress of David ap Ieuan Lloyd ap Gruffydd ap Cadogan of Gelliladron in Llanllwni. They had nine children: David, Howel, Gruffydd, John, Dyddgu, Elen, Margaret, who married Jenkin ap Thomas ap Howel Fawr of Gilfachwen Isaf, Elen, the younger, and Jane. The eldest, David ap David, sometimes called David Llwyd ap David, succeeded and married Gwenllian, daughter of Thomas ap Howel Fawr of Gilfachwen-isaf.

David added considerably to his property between 1538 and 1561. Like all the gentry of the period he was a practical farmer. The rents were used to provide liquid assets to buy more land or to lay out in mortgage. He died in 1568, his will dated 12 April and proved on 7 December of the same year. To his wife, 'Mawd ferch David,' by way of dower, he left one third of his personal and real estate. The inventory of his goods, attached to his will, indicate his farming activities. He owned 4 oxen (valued at £4), 8 kine (£5.6.8), 9 young bullocks (£3), 5 heifers (£1.5.0), 4 labouring nags (£3.6.8), 4 mares (£1.6.8), 140 sheep (£14), 32 lambs (£1.12.0), swine (4s), corn (£8) and household stuff (£6).

David ap David and Gwenllian had ten children, as recorded by *Dwnn:* Jenkin, the eldest son, who succeeded to the estate and Griffith, a natural son, married Elizabeth, daughter of Ieuan ap Howel ap Gwalter. Their marriage settlement dated 22 November 1555, settled the lands of Dol y llan and Alltfedw to their use. His father also bequeathed to him Tir Dol-y-Llan in Llanfihangel-ar-arth parish, Carmarthenshire and the house adjoining, by 'the gret stone' called *y maen llwyd*, to hold until his brother Jenkin paid £26.13.4 to him. The third son was Ieuan to whom his father bequeathed 'Tyddyn y Nant Fedw and Tir y ty hen ynghwm Gwythel' in Llanfihangel-ar-arth parish to hold until his brother Jenkin paid him £26.13. The fourth son, Morris, inherited 'Tir Pen Ffynnon y Fwyalch and Tir y Bercor' in Bangor Teifi parish, to be held again until his brother Jenkin paid him the sums of £20 and £13.6.8. Again, the youngest son, was Rhys, his father bequeathed Tir yr Allt Fedw in Llanfihangel-ar-arth to hold until his brother Jenkin paid him £26.13.4. The daughters of Howel and Angharad were: Margaret, Dyddgu, to whom her father left a cow. She married Thomas ab Ieuan ap Henry. Elen was also left a cow and married Thomas ap David ap Griffith. Gwenllian, married Ieuan ab Ieaun ap Howel and Lleucu who was devised 13s. 4d in her father's will.

Jenkin, the eldest son, described in contemporary documents as Jenkin Lloyd ap David ap David, gent., succeeded to Gilfachwen Ucha and his children adopted the name Lloyd as their permanent patronymic. He married Elizabeth, daughter of David ab Ieuan Lloyd Fychan of Llanfair Clydogau who traced his lineage to Cadifor ap Gwaethfoed. On 15 April 1582 he made his will which was proved on the 24th of that month. He desired to be buried in Llandysul church; gave 7 shillings to David Evans, clerk, 'my ghostly father', 4 pence to the cathedral church of St. David's and 20 shillings towards the repair of the bridge of Llandysul.

His widow, Elizabeth, survived him for many years and her will, dated 8 August 1609 was proved on 19 July 1610. They had four sons and three daughters. David Lloyd succeeded and the next eldest brother, John was, by his father's will, to be one of the tutors of his younger brothers and sisters.

On 10 January 1588 David and John paid 3s. 4d to the deputy-herald Lewys Dwnn for recording their coat of arms and pedigree. Their arms were described as a shield of six quarters- the arms of 1. Gronw Goch; 2. of Elystan Glodrudd; 3. of Cadifor ap Dinawal and three others that came into the family 'through marriages', not specified by Dwnn. David Lloyd married Elen, daughter of Thomas ap John ap David ap Llywelin of Gellifraith. The marriage was the subject of a post-nuptial settlement agreed on 10 April 1573.

In 1602 David was in need of ready cash and on 2 June of that year, he mortgaged Tir Pant-y-moch for £13.6.8. to Thomas Llewelyn Lloyd of Llandysul, gent. He was in greater trouble in the following year, for on 26 May 1603, the Bishop of St. Davids issued a letter recording the excommunication of David Lloyd Jenkin at the instance of Thomas David Llewelyn Lloyd and Phillip ap Howell, gentlemen. Sadly, the nature of the offence is not stated. David died before 1609. His eldest son, usually called David David Lloyd succeeded to the estate. He seems to have had some difficulty in keeping solvent. On 30 October he granted capital messuages and parcels of land to his brother, Thomas. This was the beginning of a downhill ride which resulted in the release of most of his lands including 1,320 acres of land in Llandysul parish to Thomas and much of the rest to a yeoman John ap Ieuan Thomas. He died before 19 June 1617 and his widow released the capital messuage called 'Plas y Gilvagh Wenn ywcha' to his brother-in-law Thomas Lloyd then living at Cilgwyn. Jane was his second wife, his first having died without issue.

Thomas Lloyd, second son, who bought Gilfachwen Uchaf from his elder brother, was a successful attorney-at-law, often described as a 'Ludlow clerk', and was qualified to practise in the courts of the councils of Wales and the Marches. He was the first of his family to live at Cilgwyn through his marriage between 1611 and 1618 to Mary Lloyd, co-heiress of the Cilgwyn estate. Later he was able to buy a further share in Cilgwyn when Charles Lloyd and Sage, his wife, conveyed their one-fourth part to him. Thomas and Mary's only son, John Lloyd, succeeded to Cilgwyn and Gilfachwen. Before his father's death he lived for some time at Gilfachwen Ucha (also called Tir y dre) and is described as of that place in a deed dated 20 July 1652.

Gilfachwen Ucha then ceased to be the main family home and was mortgaged and then sold by the Lloyd's before the end of the 18th century. In 1760 it was held on lease by Thomas John, yeoman, where he remained until his death. His will was dated 13 April 1790 and proved on 1 May 1790. In 1841 the *Tithe Schedule* shows that Gilfachwen Ucha, a tenanted holding of 101 acres, occupied by David Thomas, was owned by Benjamin Edward Hall, Esq., whose father-in-law, Admiral Richard Braithwaite inherited two-thirds of the Cilgwyn estate following the death of Thomas Lloyd, a bachelor, in 1801.

Francis Jones visited the property on 21 May 1974. He writes, 'The present farmhouse has been completely modernised and the outbuildings changed into holiday houses. The stable, close to the farmhouse was rebuilt in 1928 and inset in the wall is a stone bearing the date 1928 and the crest of a demi-lion rampant holding a sword, point upwards, in the fore-paws, on a torse, and above the crest a label bearing the words *vive ut vivas*. Immediately below it is a stone bearing the following inscription, I.E. 1733, which had been in the wall of the old stable. Another stone in the wall of the barn attached to the stable has a tablet engraved T. L. E. 1800. The old mansion stood in the meadow just below and to the left of the present farmhouse'. It was then owned by Mr. K. M. Thomas of Am Nawr, Llandysul who visited the property with Francis Jones.

In 1913 the house was bought by Mr. and Mrs. D. L. Jones. The whole property is now in private use.

Grid Ref: SN 4089 4063

Refs: Colby Map, 1831; *Dwnn,* i, 57-8; ibid, ii, 30; WWHR, i, 16-18; Meyrick, *Cardiganshire,* 196; Llandysul Tithe Map, 1841; CRO, GGMS I (Tydwal Gloff), 37; Abridged from Francis Jones, *'The Lloyds of Gilfachwen, Cilgwyn and Coedmore'*, *Ceredigion,* 1978; NLW, Cwrtmawr Deeds, No. 1157.

GLANARBERTH, Llangoedmor

Formerly a large house on high ground with a commanding view of the Teifi, located on modern OS maps above Llechryd. A photograph taken between 1860-1870 was published in *The Tivyside Photographic Souvenir.* Amateur theatricals were provided by Mrs. Lort Phillips for the gentry at Glanarberth in the last quarter of the 19th century. Among the actors performing 'Orange Blossoms' by J. P. Woolmer, were the Count de Palatine, the Misses Jones of

Pen-y-lan, Capt. Jones-Parry, Ty-llwyd, Miss Howells of Glas-pant and Master Lort Phillips. Following the entertainment the guests, 'fifty of the elite of the county families of Tivy-side', took supper. Formerly the home of the Lort Phillipses, it was destroyed by fire in the 1970's and the stone used for other building projects.

Grid Ref: SN 2203 4380

Refs: Modern OS Maps; *The Tivyside Photographic Souvenir,* C. Allen, Tenby, 1871; NLW, Morgan Richardson Deeds, i, 137; *Cardiganshire & Tivyside Advertiser,* 23 January 1987; *Ceredigion,* vol. viii, No. 2 (1977), p. 174.

GLANCLETWR, Llandysul

This homestead is marked on *Colby's Map of 1831* and on modern OS maps a little north of Pont-sian on the banks of the Cletwr Fach.

Morgan Llwyd of Glan Cletwr, was the fifth son of David Llewlyn Llwyd of Castell Hywel, married Jenet, daughter of Rhydderch Thomas of Pantstreimon. Morgan's son, David Morgan Llwyd succeeded and married Gwenllian, daughter of David William Fychan of Llangathen. His son, David Llwyd, succeeded and married a daughter of David Llewelyn Llwyd of Castell Hywel. They had two daughters, Maud and Mary, co-heiresses to the estate. Maud, married William Llwyd of Glandyweli, also a descendant of Castell Hywel and they had four daughters, Gwenllian, Catherine, Jenet and Elen. Gwenllian married firstly David Lloyd of Maesycrigie and secondly, Griffith Lloyd Walter. Elen married Richard Lewes of Pantyrodyn. Mary married Jenkin Thomas of Dyffryn Llynod ap Thomas ap John ap David Llewelyn. This marriage was the subject of a pre-nuptial settlement agreed on 17 May 1550. The famous Baptist preacher, Christmas Evans, worked as a farm labourer at Glancletwr in his youth.

The *Llandysul Tithe Map* tells us that John Lloyd Davies of Alltyrodyn was the owner in 1841 and the tenant was James Jones. the property at this time was 188 acres.

Grid Ref: SN 4396 4671

Refs: PRO, Dale Castle MS., p. 22 (88), 23 (93); WWHR, i, 21, 27-28; CRO, GGMS, I (Tewdwr); Llandysul Tithe Map, 1841; Colby Map, 1831.

GLANDENIS (Glandenys), Silian

Marked but not named on *Colby's Map of 1831* and named on modern OS maps south-east of Silian near the bridge of the same name. The home, in 1860, of William Jones, High Sheriff of Cardiganshire in the same year. He was the son of John Jones of Blaen-nos, Carmarthenshire, by Mary, daughter of William Jones of Ystradwalter and Plâs Llanfair, near Lampeter. In 1873 William Jones's estate totalled a substantial 2,744 acres with a rental of £1,424 p.a. His wife, Anne Isabella, was a daughter of James Fenton of Dutton Manor, Lancashire. William and Anne were married in 1876. William died in 1897.

Glendenis with 39 acres were offered for sale in May 1930. The ground floor comprised: the lobby, entrance hall, dining room, plus bay, morning room, drawing room, library. Through the side entrance – w.c. still room, kitchen, laundry, scullery, servants' hall, boot room, butlers' pantry, back passage, paved yard and underground cellar. On the first floor were 8 principal bedrooms and dressing rooms, 3 maids' bedrooms. bathroom, housemaids' pantry and sink. airing cupboard, linen closet, w.c. outbuildings, walled kitchen garden and hothouse (peach house, vinery and greenhouse).

The property was bought by Professor John Cayo Evans of Derw, Lampeter. In 1975 it was owned by the late Julian Cayo Evans, horse-breeder and sometime member of the Free Wales Army jailed for being a member of a quasi-military organisation.

Grid Ref: SN 5810 5092

Refs: Colby Map, 1831; Nicholas, *County Families,* 1875, p. 198; Landowners Return, 1873.

GLANDULAS, Betws Ifan

Situated half a mile east of Betws Ifan and marked on *Colby's Map of 1831* and on modern OS maps on the banks of the Dulas. In 1650 Coedy-perthie, Glandulas and Pantybara in the parishes of Betws and Troed -yr-aur (Trefdreyr), were occupied by Lleucu Thomas and Thomas David, paying £17 rental. These properties formed part of the estate of Lewes of Abernantbychan . Glandulas became the home of the Davies family during the 18th and 19th centuries. *NLW Morgan Richardson Deeds* tells us that a Mr. Davies of Glandulas married Elizabeth . . . , and their son, David Davies later owned Glandulas. David's marriage to Elizabeth Hughes was the subject of a post-nuptial settlement agreed on 13 November 1784.

Grid Ref: SN 3125 4765

Refs: CRO, Aberglasney Collection; Colby Map, 1831; NLW, Morgan Richardson Deeds, Nos. 1997-8.

GLANDYFI, Eglwys-fach

Situated in a superb location south of Dyfi Junction station and north of Eglwys-fach off the A487 (T) to Machynlleth and is marked on *Colby's Map of 1831* and on modern OS maps as Glandyfi Castle. It was built c. 1810 by George Jeffreys, High Sheriff of Cardiganshire in 1819. He appointed John Hughes of Allt-lwyd, gent, to be his deputy. The *Glan Paith Deeds* show us that George Jeffreys of Glandyfi Castle was a party to the lease for fourteen years of a capital messuage called Aberllolwyn and parcels of land called Cae-gwyn and Caecefnsgubor, all in the parish of Llanychaearn. Meyrick states that Glandyfi Castle became the home of Major John Spurrell, a retired Cavalry officer, born in 1855, of a Norfolk family. He married Mary Maud Fagan in 1893.

Grid Ref: SN 6925 9675

Refs: Colby Map, 1831; NLW, Glan Paith Deeds, 124 & 221; *Cardiganshire County History,* vol. III, pp. 247, 282.

GLANEIRW, Blaen-porth

The mansion is located between Blaenporth and the Aberporth crossroads, on the A487 (T) seven miles north of Cardigan and a mile east of Blaenporth. Marked in *Colby's Map of 1831* and on modern OS maps the present house stands on the site of Eirw Castle. The *Landowners Return of 1873* tells us that it was the home of

T. Harman Brenchley with 110 acres of the value of £68 per annum. A Sale Catalogue for the year 1929 describes the mansion as follows: Ground floor – a front entrance protected by a porch, hall, drawing room, wide staircase, kitchen, butlers' pantry, servants' hall, pantries, scullery, store room, underground dairy and cellars, behind the library with access from the outside is the coachman's room. The main staircase leads to the first floor only; the staircase from the back entrance hall leads to both first and second floors. On the first floor, a bedroom over the library with dressing room, 2 w.c.'s, bedroom over dining room, dressing room over entrance hall, long dressing room (used as lumber room), nursery, smoking room, w.c., and back stairs. On the second floor – one very large bedroom, four moderate sized bedrooms, box-room. The outbuildings included a laundry, coachhouse, stable, carpenters' shop, fruit and potato rooms, also farm buildings, a walled garden, tennis and croquet lawns. Attached to the property at this time were 55 acres. Harman Brenchley was succeeded at Glaneirw by his son, Herbert Walter Harman Brenchley, born at Pigeonsford, Llangrannog in 1861. He was educated at Winchester and Jesus College, Cambridge. Until his retirement he was a Lt. Colonel in the Middlesex Regiment. In recent years, Glaneirw has been occupied by a Community employed in pottery and the visual arts.

Grid Ref: SN 3125 4765

Refs: Colby Map, 1831; Landowners Return, 1873.

GLANFRÊD, Llanfihangel Geneu'r glyn

Glanfrêd stands south of the river Leri, north-east of Llandre off the road to Borth and is marked on *Colby's Map of 1831* as Glan Fred. Meyrick tells us 'Glanvread, an old mansion, formerly situated on the left bank of this river and the site is now occupied by a good farmhouse'.

Sion ap Gruffydd ab Ieuan ap Siencyn of Glanfrêd signed his pedigree for the herald Dwnn on 30 December 1588. His will was proved in 1613. His only daughter and sole heiress, Bridget, married Thomas, the younger brother of Sir Richard Price MP of Gogerddan in 1597. Thomas Pryse was admitted to the Inner Temple in 1588 and served as MP for Cardigan 1597-1601 and High Sheriff for Cardiganshire in 1609. His will was dated 12 September 1623 and following his death, Bridget married John Pugh of Ynysgreigiog and both were living at Glanfrêd in 1629. Bridget had ten children all of whom made good marriages, including Lettice, who married four times. Sion Cain wrote an elegy to Thomas and in 1625 wrote a *cywydd* to Bridget and their son, Thomas, the younger, born in 1598 who succeeded to the estates of Glanfraed and Ynysgreigiog that yielded £500 a year in 1650. He married Elizabeth, daughter of John Parry of Noyadd Trefawr, in the parish of Llandygwydd. They had ten children including Bridget Pryse, whose liaison with Edward Lloyd of Llanforda, Oswestry, a distant relation, produced Edward Llwyd the eminent scientist and philologist born c. 1660 who became a Fellow of the Royal Society and Keeper of the Ashmolean Museum in 1691.

Thomas Pryse was High Sheriff in 1626 and died in 1681. He had a son, another Thomas, who in 1650 when he was 17 years old, married his cousin, Susan, daughter and heiress of Richard Pugh of Dolyfonddu, Montgomeryshire, a cadet branch of Mathafarn. Her estate was worth £300 a year and her portion was £900. His second wife, Jane, whom Thomas married in 1683, was the daughter of Edward Meriden of Shropshire. He was High Sheriff in 1688 and died on 28 May 1688 at Edge in Shropshire. Thomas, the eldest son of Thomas Pryse and Susan Pugh of Dolyfonddu, was living at Glanfrêd in 1676 and died before 1688 in his father's lifetime. In 1676 he married Margaret, daughter of Lewis Owen of Peniarth, Meirionnydd, a prominent Royalist during the Civil War. Following her husband's death, Margaret married David Lloyd of Crynfryn, Nantcwnlle. Lewis Pryse, born in 1683, inherited Gogerddan in 1694 following the death of his kinsman, Sir Carbery Pryse. Lewis Pryse was a Jacobite and became MP for Cardigan Borough, until expelled for non-attendance in 1716. He married Anne, daughter of John Lloyd of Aberllefenni, Meirionnydd. He died on 11 August 1720 and his son, Thomas Pryse of Gogerddan died in 1745. Lewis's three daughters Mary, Margaret and Jane became his co-heiresses. They each inherited £3,500. Mary, the eldest daughter, inherited Glanfrêd and the Aberllefenni estate. Margaret married a Corbett of Ynysmaengwyn and Jane married James Philipps of Pentypark, Walton East parish, Pembrokeshire.

Mary, Lewis's eldest daughter, brought Glanfrêd to her husband John Campbell of Stackpole Court, Pembrokeshire, from whom it descended to the first Lord Cawdor who advertised it for sale in 1802. Glanfrêd was described: 'Part of Glanfraed Farm, 131 acres, a genteel dwelling house, offices and excellent out-buildings. The house is very substantial and well fitted up, part lately rebuilt, and the whole thoroughly repaired fit for the residence of a

Gentleman at a very considerable expence' and further 'Part of Glanfraed Farm, 160 acres, in the possession of Richard Owen tenant-at-will'.

On 2 April 1802, Lord Cawdor gave a lease for eighteen years at an annual rental of £160 to John Gevers of Glanfraed, 'of the capital messuage called Glanfraed, the iron forge belonging, and other messuages and fields, all in Llanfihangel Geneu'r-glyn'. The *Deri Ormond Deeds* show that on 23 May 1803 Glanfraed was sold by Lord Cawdor to John Jones of Gracechurch Street. London, Esq., later of Deri Ormond, subject to the leases of John Gevers and Humphrey Jones, for £7,050. The *Deri Ormond Deeds* include a plan of the Glanfraed estate c. 1803. In 1852, Jonathan Bunce, son of David Morgan and Anne James, was born at Pwll-glas, Llandre, one of the largest holdings of the Gogerddan estate. He married Jane, daughter of David Rees of Pantygwyfol. Llanilar, and lived at Glanfrêd. Their son, James Latimer Morgan, born at Glanfrêd in 1887, became Secretary to the Welsh Agricultural Council in Aberystwyth having previously served in London in charge of the secretariat of the Agricultural Commissioners for Wales. He was educated at King's College, London and married Gwen Elizabeth Thomas in 1915. They lived at Isfryn, Llandre. The last Morgan at Glanfrêd was Ieuan Morgan and his wife, Sarah Alice, who farmed there until their retirement. Recently the house was sold and the farmland bought by neighbours.

Grid Ref: SN 6333 8775

Refs: Colby Map, 1831; *Arch. Cam.,* 1917, 139ff; *Dwnn,* i, 44, 46; PRO, Dale Castle MS.; WWHR., i, 7-8; CRO, GGMS III (Gwaethfoed); Blome List, 1673; NLW, Griffith Owen List (iv);. Meyrick, *Cardiganshire,* 323, 329;. Sale Catalogue (printed); Cawdor Muniments; NLW, Noyadd Trefawr Deeds, No. 381; Deri Ormond Deeds, 67,141, 145, 148-9, 150; CRO, Cawdor (Addl.) Collection; Lewis, *TDW,* 1811; *Ceredigion,* vol. I, (1950), p. 79; *Who's Who in Wales,* 1920; Francis Jones, *Historic Houses of Pembrokeshire and their Families,* pp. 164, 196, 1996.

GLANHELYG (Glanhelig), Llechryd

The Tivyside Photographic Souvenir c. 1871, shows a modern house of two storeys. It is marked on modern OS maps east of the A484 in the village of Llechryd opposite Nantcrymanau farm. Maria Webley-Parry, of Noyadd Trefawr, married, as his second wife, William Owen Brigstocke of Blaen-pant. She induced him to build Glanhelyg on Tyrhos fields as a residence for her two maiden sisters, Elen and Eliza. 'One of these sisters, having weak watery eyes, fell in love with William Buck at Stradmore, and as he did not respond, she pretended to fall ill and went to bed. He took no notice of her health, so she sent for him to give him a dying message. He came to see her and she took a tender farewell and fished out from under her pillow an old silver turnip-watch which she desired him to accept in memory of her. He departed with the watch, but paid no further attention to her health. After a time she realised that her love could not be reciprocated and she got up from her bed, said she was better and wrote to Mr. Buck and asked for the return of her old silver watch as it had only been given in expectation of death'. Miss Elen Webley-Parry of Glanhelyg in 1873 owned 63 acres with a rental of £45.

With the deaths of Elen and Eliza in 1892 and 1894, Glanhelyg became the property of Mrs. Constance Gabler, formerly Tyler, of Gernos. In turn Glanhelig passed to Katherine Maria Antoinette, the wife of Admiral Herbert Willes Webley Hope, who had spent much of her childhood at Blaen-pant. The Admiral's mother was Elen Jordan of Rhydycolomennod (Pigeonsford), Llangrannog. The Hopes had three children, Elen, Adrian and Jacqueline. In 1929 Elen married David Heneker, son of General Sir William Heneker, an Irish-Canadian, whose wife was a Jones of Felindre, Llandovery. David Heneker, a distinguished musician composed the music for *Half A Sixpence* and other shows. David and Elen's son, Peter, inherited Glanhelyg in 1971. A former executive for London Weekend Television, he became the first National Organiser for CAFOD Wales and was honoured with the Knights of St. Gregory Medal by Pope Paul II. He married Josephine Ann, daughter of James William and Kathleen Lewis-Bowen of Clynfyw and have five sons. The Henekers built a residence on the Glanhelyg estate and have sold the mansion to Mr. R Holtam, a painter, and his wife, a homeopathic practitioner.

Grid Ref: SN 2138 4455

Refs: G. R. Brigstocke's Family MSS.; Landowners Return, 1873; Francis Jones, *Historic Houses of Pembrokeshire and their Families,* pp. 37, 38, (Brawdy Books), 1996; Mr. & Mrs. P. Heneker.

GLANLERI, Llanfihangel Geneu'r Glyn

As the name suggests this house is located on the banks of the Leri on the outskirts of Borth near to where the B4353 road runs under the main railway line. Glanleri is a house of great antiquity. The first recorded owner was Rhydderch ap Rhys, mentioned in the poems of Dafydd Nanmor in the 16th century, whose father Rhys ap Meredudd was Lord of Towyn and the owner of vast estates in south Ceredigion. Upon the death of his elder brother, Thomas ap Rhys, Rhydderch took up residence at Towyn and was Esquire to the Body of Henry VII and held various government posts in west Wales. Rhydderch made three important marriages. His first wife was Margaret, daughter of John Llwyd ap Dafydd ap Llewelyn ap Dafydd of Cefnmelgoed, Llanychaearn parish. His second wife was again Margaret, this time a daughter of Sir John Lingen, county Hereford. Rhydderch married finally, Janet, daughter of Thomas ap Gruffydd ap Nicholas, a member of the powerful house of Dinefwr. He was succeeded at Glanleri by his second son, John, who became known as John Fychan (Vaughan) which became the patronymic of the family. John married Maud, daughter of Thomas Rhys Lewis of Llwyn Iorwerth near Penllwyn in the parish of Llanbadarn Fawr. They had eight children. The sixth son, Morris Fychan of Glanleri, High Sheriff in 1612, died without issue and was succeeded by his brother Morgan, whose son Dafydd married a sister of Rhys Lewis of Rhiwarthen. Their son, Francis Fychan, High Sheriff in 1694, was married to an unknown Mary, and their daughter and heiress, Mary, married Richard Ingram of Glanhafren, Montgomeryshire. They had two children, Francis and Mary. Francis, High Sheriff in 1737, died unmarried in 1741 and was succeeded by his sister who married the Rev. John Gwyn, vicar of Llanfihangel Genau'r-glyn. In the list of *Cardiganshire Freeholders of 1760,* Edward Jones, gent., of Rhoscellan-fach, Llangorwen, is listed as the occupier of Glanleri. Edward was a younger son of Nanteos. Francis Jones noted that the next occupier of Glanleri was Henry Lewis Edwarde-Gwynne, a captain of the 62nd Regiment on half-pay. He was a member of the Rhyd-y-gors family which included David Edwards, Deputy-Herald, who compiled a vast collection of pedigrees and coats of arms. Henry may have taken the additional surname Gwynne when he succeeded to Glanleri following the death of the Rev. John Gwyn. Henry, who died in 1866, served in the Napoleonic wars and in India, and is mainly remembered for enriching our cuisine when he brought from India a recipe for a sauce which became known as Worcestershire Sauce.

The next occupiers of Glanleri were connected to the Griffiths family of Ty-nant, Tal-y-bont, formerly of Cwm Rhaeadr, near Derwen-las, Montgomeryshire. One of the family, Griffith Griffiths (1799-1845), son of Griffith and Elizabeth Griffiths of Ty-nant, became a Church of England missionary in Jamaica, Another, Susan Griffiths, married Mathew Davies Williams of Cwmcynfelyn, Clarach. Also related to the Griffiths family was Frank Richards, whose wife, Polly, was from Pentre, Cwm Ystwyth. Mr Richards farmed at Glanleri for many years. Their son, James, established a caravan park on part of the farm, and was a generous benefactor of Aberystwyth Town F.C. He married Dora, elder daughter of Mr. and Mrs. J. Phillips of Nantybenglog, Capel Seion. Their son, Rheinallt, is now of Glanleri.

Grid Ref: SN 6175 8858

Refs: Colby Map, 1831; NLW, Griffith Owen List (iv); *Dwnn,* i, 43-4; WWHR, i, 32; *Arch. Cam.,* 1917, 150; Burke, *LG,* 1850, i, 520; Nicholas, *County Families,* i, 179; PRO, Dale Castle MS., p. 26 (92); CRO, GGMS I (Gwynfardd); CRO, GGMS III (Edwin) fo. 4-5; NLW, Cwrtmawr Deeds No. 142; Mrs. D. Richards.

GLAN MEDENI, Betws Ifan

Located on modern OS maps a long mile south of Betws Ifan and to the west of the road to Brongest. Abel Walters of Perthcereint started building a small residence near the banks of the river Medeni in Betws Ifan parish. The house became known as Medeni Villa, then Lodge, then Blaen Medeni and finally Glan Medeni. Francis Jones, in his article *Walters of Perthcereint* states that Abel moved into the finished house in 1836 with his daughters, Frances and Jane. Their brother, John, inherited Aberglasney in 1841 and became Walters-Philipps. In September 1843 Rebecca rioters invaded the house and shouted abuse at the Walters sisters. For their own safety, Frances and Jane moved to a house in Newcastle Emlyn in 1844. An elegy in Welsh to Frances Walters by Benjamin Williams (Gwynionydd) was published in Cardigan when Frances died in 1851. Jane returned to Glan Medeni where she remained until her death in 1881. An inventory taken of goods at Blaenmedeni on 21 July 1851 valued the furniture and other effects at £412 and mentions the following; kitchen, outer kitchen, dairy, dining parlour, drawing room and two bedrooms. The *Landowners Return of 1873* gives Jane Walters as owner of 258 acres with a rental of £159 per annum.

Francis Jones visited the house in the 1960's and found it to be in good condition. It was then occupied and owned by Captain Peter Browning and his wife.

Grid Ref: SN 2995 4705

Refs: Francis Jones, 'Walters of Perthcereint,' *Ceredigion,* 1969, 168-200; Landowners Return, 1873.

GLAN NANT-Y-COU (Glan Nantycoy), Cellan

Marked on *Colby's Map of 1831* but not named on modern OS maps. Located on the banks of the Cou, a tributary of the Teifi off the B4343 between Cwmann and Cellan. The *Carmarthenshire Deeds* tell us that in 1800 this house was occupied by John Evans, senior, gent., his wife, Diana, and their son, John Evans, junior. John, senior's will was dated 11 October 1810 and administration of his will was granted to his widow, Diana, on 21 December 1813. Thereafter the records are silent.

Grid Ref: SN 60254 8160

Refs: PRO, Carmarthenshire Deeds; Colby Map, 1831.

GLANPAITH, Llanbadarn Fawr

Not named on *Colby's Map of 1831* but located on modern OS maps north of the B4340 from Penparcau to New Cross on the lane leading to Nanteos. The pre-nuptial agreement of John Thomas Herbert Parry of Glanpaith and Mary Davies, made on 4 September 1839, includes the capital messuage of Glanpaith. The *Glanpaith Deeds* contain a copy of a ground plan of John Parry's house drawn on 21 March 1866. John Parry was living at Glanpaith in 1872 when the *Landowners Return, 1873,* listed his acreage as 440 acres, attracting a rental of £361. Letters of Administration of the will of Mary Parry made in 1842 were granted on 26 May 1873. John Parry succeeded and was described as of Glanpaith in 1918. An interesting letter in the Glanpaith papers relates a request from the Gosen MC Chapel Committee "desiring payment" of fourteen shillings pew rent due from the late Lady Parry. The house has descended through the female line to the present day.

Grid Ref: SN 6048 7891

Refs: Colby Map, 1831; Glan Paith Deeds, 110, 162, 236, 242, 348; Landowners Return, 1873.

GLANRHEIDOL, Llanbadarn Fawr

Marked on *Colby's Map of 1831* and on modern OS maps south of Capel Bangor off the minor road which runs parallel to the Rheidol towards Devil's Bridge. Samuel Lewis wrote in 1840, 'Glanrheidol, the residence of James Hughes, Esq.', who was chiefly instrumental in having the road made from Llangurig through Goginan to Aberystwyth. He built and endowed the church at Capel Bangor and helped to make the Aberystwyth harbour serviceable. He was the first mayor of the reformed Corporation of Aberystwyth and was a successful advocate.

James Hughes, one of the founders of the Roberts and Evans firm of solicitors in Aberystwyth, was Clerk to the Magistrates and also Borough Treasurer. As solicitor for the impoverished Nanteos estate, he once offered a bottle of wine to one of his friends for every gate he could find on a certain farm. His brother, John, a surveyor, lived at Lluest Gwilym and was Clerk of the Markets at Aberystwyth. James married Mary, youngest daughter of Sir Thomas Bonsall of Fronfraith. Henry Bonsall, commonly known as HB, was born at Glanrheidol in 1862 and in 1903 he wrote the *Records of the House of Bonsall*, a 48-page published work, now held at the National Library of Wales. The *Landowners Return of 1873* names three men as living at Glanrheidol; James Hughes, owning 1,298 acres at a rental of £794, Thomas Bonsall as having 1,800 acres at £1,269 and J.G. Bonsall 30 acres with a rental of £14. *Ceredigion Record Office* has a copy of the Glanrheidol and Penbryn estates sale catalogue of 1903.

Grid Ref: SN 6630 7938

Refs: Colby Map, 1831; Ceredigion RO, ADX/119/48-9; Henry Bonsall, *Records of the House of Bonsall; Aberystwyth,* Evans, 1903; S. Lewis, *Topographical Dictionary of Wales 1840;* Landowners Return, 1840; E. G. Bowen, *History of Llanbadarn Fawr*, 1979, p.124 *Ceredigion,* Vol. II, No. 2 (1953), p. 118; ibid, Vol. IX, No. 1 (1980), pp. 64-8; ibid, Vol. X, No. 4 (1987), pp. 357-67.

GLANRHOCA, Llanddewibrefi

Situated to the south-west of Llanddewibrefi adjacent to the Teifi by a minor road which leads to Llangybi and marked on *Colby's Map of 1831.* Earliest known records state that Jenkin Davies, of Glanrhoca who traced to Cadifor ap Dinawal, made a will on 19 May 1750, just before his death, and it was proved in June of the same year. Joshua Davies is given as of Glanrhoca in 1760. Details of a deed written in 1791 in the *Deri Ormond Deeds* state that Evan Phillip sold Ffos-yr-ych in the parish of Betws Bledrws to David Davies of Glanrhoca, for £55. In 1796 David Davies, and Jenkin Davies of Maesycrugiau, Llanllwni, took a lease for 21 years of lands in the parish of Llanddewibrefi from Owen Llwyd of Abertrinant. David Davies, High Sheriff of Cardiganshire in 1802, made his will on 18 July 1792, making a settlement on his son and heir Jenkin, by Mary, his wife, leaving him Glanrhoca and seventeen other properties in various parishes. On his monument in Llanddewibrefi church are the lines: *'Praises on Tombs are Trifles vainly spent, A man's good name is his best Monument.'*

Jenkin married Sarah, daughter of John Bowen of Waunifor, Llandysul and his wife, Margaret. Sarah was the heiress to her brother Thomas Bowen of Maesycrugiau, who died in 1789 The pre-nuptial settlement of 21 July 1792 mentions over 50 properties which were part of the Maesycrugiau estate. Sarah died in 1827 and Jenkin in 1836. Their four children all died without issue, the last in 1858.

Meyrick states that Glanrhoca was 'a seat belonging to Jenkin Davies of Maesycrygie'. Confusion can arise within this family as explained by Phillips in his book *Sheriffs of Cardiganshire* who tells us 'The Glanrhoca estate has descended from father to son, the name being constantly either Jenkin or David, for upwards of three hundred years. The principal seat of this family is at Maesycrugiau, Carmarthenshire'. In the 1851 census, Glanroca is listed as a farm of 127 acres.

Grid Ref: SN 6320 5355.

Refs: Colby Map, 1831; NLW, Morgan Richardson Deeds, ii, 476; Meyrick, *Cardiganshire,* p. 54; Phillips, *Sheriffs of Cardiganshire;* NLW Deri Ormond Deeds, No. 86-87, 90-1; CRO, Carmarthenshire Deeds; Horsfall-Turner, *Wanderings,* 250; D. Benjamin Rees, *Hanes Plwyf Llanddewibrefi,* 1984 p. 152.

GLANYRAFON, Llanfihangel-y-Creuddyn

This farm is found south of the Rheidol, south-east of the village of Llanbadarn Fawr near the halt on the Vale of Rheidol Railway to Devil's Bridge and the industrial estate and is marked on *Colby's Map of 1831.* Aldborough Lloyd-Williams of the Gwernan family was of Glanyrafon, Penwenallt and Tre-wen, all in Cardiganshire. He married Florence Mary Graham, daughter of John Stevenson of

Cheltenham, who died in 1900. When his father died in 1890, their son, Aldborough Rupert Caulfield Lloyd-Williams, succeeded to the property. He was educated at Marlborough College and Trinity College, Cambridge, gaining his BA in 1902. He became known as the Lord of the Manor of Glan-yr-afon. In 1906 he married Isabella Rosina, daughter of Walter John Trapnell of Clifton. Their son, Ian Aldborough Caulfield Lloyd-Williams, was born in 1909.

Grid Ref: SN 6155 8044

Refs: Colby Map, 1831.

GLAN-Y-WERN, Llanfair Clydogau

Francis Jones notes that there is no Glan y Wern on *Colby's Map of 1831* but there is a Blaen y Wern, a Wern-fawr and a Wern-y-glyn all located on modern OS maps east of Llangybi between the A485 and the Teifi. The *NLW, Cwrtmawr Deeds* mentions a deed in trust by the Rev. Thomas Lloyd of Llangynllo, clerk of Bronwydd estate, dated 14 March 1613/14. Among the properties named is a messuage called 'Tythin Griffith Person, alias Tir Glan-y-wern' in Llanfair Clydogau parish. Thomas Lloyd, who died c. 1630, was the brother of David Lloyd of Crynfryn, Nantcwnlle and Joan Lloyd who was married twice; firstly to Rees David of Glan-y-Wern and secondly to John Jones who traced to the Cantors.

Walter Pryse was the son of Hugh Pryse of Blaen-y-wern by Anne, widow of Hugh Lloyd of Ffoshelyg, daughter of David Lloyd of Castell Hywel. Walter was twice married. His first wife was Bridget, widow of Lodwick Lewes, daughter and co-heiress of John Lloyd, Faedre, Llandysul, who died childless. Walter Pryse, gent., was certainly of Glan-y-Wern in 1661 when he married Mary, the sister of Thomas Powell of Llechwedd Dyrus, Esq. The marriage was the subject of a pre-nuptial settlement agreed on 18 October 1661 between Walter Pryse, his mother Anne, widow, Thomas Powell and Morgan Lloyd of Ffoshelyg, gent. Included were the messuage called 'Glanywern, messuages called Llwyn Meilir in Llangybi, Tir y Wern Fach and Tir y Kilgwyn, a messuage part of the demesne land of Kilgwyn and a parcel heretofore part of the said demesne land, all in Llangybie, messuages called Tir y Maes and Felin in Llethr Phillipp in Betws Bledrws, a messuage called Tir Gorwydd y Kwm in the same parishes, a water mill called Melin Llangybi and the Lordship or manor of Llangybi and Betws'. Walter Pryse died c. 1690 and Thomas Powell inherited Glan-y-wern. Later, Sir Thomas sold it to Thomas Lloyd of Bronwydd for £700.

Grid Ref: SN 6205 5330

Refs: CRO, Chanc. Proc. 1695; NLW, Cwrtmawr Deeds, Nos. 59, 275, 429, 437, 558, 1032, 1607, 1637 & 1676; CRO, GGMS, I (Tydwal Gloff); Colby Map, 1831.

GLENNYDD, Llanfihangel-y-Creuddyn

Situated south of New Cross on the north bank of the Ystwyth opposite Llanilar and marked on *Colby's Map of 1831* and on modern OS maps. Formerly a small estate later enveloped by larger and more powerful neighbours. The *Crosswood Deeds* refer to Rees David ap Jenkin, Esq. of 'Golenyth', who in 1571 was the arbitrator in a dispute between Morgan Herbert of Llanwnws, Morris Thomas ap Morris, gent. of Llanilar and David Thomas Esq. of the parish of Llanfihangel-y-Creuddyn. On 5 March 1604/5, according to the *NLW Cwrtmawr Deeds* 'Rees Gwynn ap Richard of Golennydd mortgaged a messuage called Tyddyn Keginan in Llanfihangel y Creuddyn to Rees Goch Griffith of the same parish'.

Lewys Dwnn lists Griffith ap Ieuan ap Jenkin, descended from Gwaethfoed as living at Golennith. His will was proved in 1613. In 1625 Richard Gwyn of Glennydd, gent., mortgaged the capital messuage of Glennydd and other lands in Llanfihangel-y-Creuddyn to Edward Vaughan of Trawsgoed, and two years later the same Richard Gwyn surrendered all his interest in the capital messuage called Glennydd and other properties to the same Edward Vaughan.

Rhys Gwyn ap Richard had previously mortgaged Tyddyn Ceginan to Rhys Goch ap Gruffydd. A Dafydd ap Harry of Glennydd, who died in 1643, son of Harri Morris Goch by Jane, daughter of Richard Morris Fychan, descended from Adda Fychan, married Mary Morris. They had eight children from which the Parry families of Rhod-mad, Ty'n berllan, Gilfachafael and Llidiardau descend. David ap Harri had a brother, Richard, who died in 1633. His son, Phillip Richard ap Harri, married Bridget David of Llwynhywel. Another son of Dafydd ap Harri, George, who died in 1681, had a natural son, Samuel George Parry, who married the daughter of Owen Jones, a younger son of Nanteos by Fortuna Bowen of Crug-bychan. Glennydd remained a part of the Trawsgoed estate occupied by tenant-farmers.

Grid Ref: SN 6305 7585

Refs: Colby Map, 1831; NLW, Crosswood Deeds, pp. 14, 46, 47; NLW, Cwrtmawr Deeds, No. 146; PRO, Dale Castle Deeds, p. 27 (106); CRO, GGMS, I (Tydwal Gloff) & II (Gwaethfoed); *Dwnn,* i, 46.

GLYNAERON (GLYN UCHAF),
Llangeitho

Meyrick tells us 'Though now an insignificant farmhouse, this property was formerly the residence of people of consequence in this county. Ieuan ab Griffith was the first of Glyn Aeron. His son Ieuan Lloyd succeeded to it after his death and bequeathed it to his son, Rhydderch, the poet, who married Maud, daughter of Sir William Clement, Lord of Caron'.

This homestead is situated north-east of Llangeitho called Glyn Uchaf on *Colby's Map of 1831* and mistakenly, Yr Glyn, on modern OS maps and located near the river Aeron. According to David Morgan in his *Hanes Llangeitho*, the original Glyn Aeron stood near Castell Odwyn. It is stated that the first occupant of Glyn Aeron was Ieuan, son of Gruffydd Foel of Castell Odwyn. He was succeeded by his son, Rhydderch, who owned *Llyfr Gwyn Rhydderch*, a manuscript of medieval Welsh prose, including the *Mabinogion* romances. Poets, including Dafydd ap Gwilym enjoyed the patronage of this family and they held offices under the Crown. Rhydderch ab Ieuan Llwyd was an authority on the Welsh Laws. Horsfall-Turner in his *Wanderings,* states, 'The farmhouse of Glyn, once a residence of the "Llwydiaid o Blas Rhydderch" was later [that] of David Lewis, MO, who was born in Nantmedd below Llanio. Educated at Llangeitho, Ystrad Meurig and in London . . . he entered the Navy. After 13 years as a Navy Surgeon he returned to his native country bringing with him an African prince who he had named "John Cardigan". From Glyn, Daniel Rowland took his wife. The present home bears a corner stone dated with 'Peter Davies, yr 1818'.

This Peter Davies was of Caerllygest, grandson of David Edwards of Abermeurig, and he married Magdalen, one of three heiresses who inherited the estate from their father, Jenkin Jones, the dissenting minister who died in 1725. Another sister married David Jones of Deri Ormond, High Sheriff in 1773. In turn, Jenkin's brother, David, one of the twelve children of John Jones of Llwyn-rhys, the first dissenting minister in Ceredigion who died aged 82 in 1722, was a captain in the King's Guards who is said to have saved King William's life at the Battle of the Boyne. David was also a prolific author and among his achievements is *A Complete History of Europe from 1600 to 1716*, which runs to 18 volumes. He wrote also: *The Secret History of Whitehall* in 1697, *History of the Turks* in 1701, *Life of King James II*, 1702, *History of the House of Brunswick* in 1715, *A Translation of Pezron's Antiquities, 1702*, amongst other titles.

Descendants of the same family still owned Glyn Uchaf in 1913.

Grid Ref: SN 6275 6031

Refs: Meyrick, *Cardiganshire,* 255; CRO, GGMS III (Gwaethfoed); CRO, Davies, *Hanes Llangeitho;* David Morgan, *Aberporth,* 1859, p. 11.

GLYNMEHERIN, Llanwenog

Marked on *Colby's Map of 1831* as Clun Maherin, north of Cors goch and on modern OS maps as between Cwrtnewydd and Gors goch. In 1760 the Rev. Mr. Thomas of Olmarch owned Glynmeherin. In the late 19th century it was the home of the Jenkins family including David Jenkins, otherwise Dafydd Siencyn, who kept a diary widely quoted in *Hanes Plwyf Llanwenog* by D. R. and Z. S. Cledyn Davies. His son, William Jenkins born in 1825 married a daughter of John Davies of Llanbydder, became a shopkeeper and auctioneer and died in Ffos-y-ffald in 1878. At that time Glynmeherin was a holding of over 200 acres. Francis Jones noted that there were some old carvings in the farmhouse 'now owned by Mr. Jenkins'.

Grid Ref: SN 4865 4975

Refs: Colby Map, 1831; Modern OS Maps; WWHR, iii, 87; D. R. & Z. S. Cledyn Davies, *Hanes Plwyf Llanwenog* (Aberystwyth), 1939, pp. 106-117.

GOGERDDAN PLÂS, Llanbadarn Fawr

Until 1949 this was the home of the Pryse ap Rhys family, an ancient and powerful family of distinguished politicians, lawyers and patrons of bards. Now the site of IGER, formerly the Welsh Plant Breeding Station, the plâs is located south of Bow Street on the road to Penrhyn-coch. Gogerddan was built originally in the latter half of the 15th century, but most of the present building is of much more recent date. During reconstruction work in 1949, workmen uncovered a massive oak beam dating from the early 16th century.

David Jenkins tells us that 'the Pryses of Gogerddan traced their lineage back to Gwaethfod, Lord of Cardigan (c. 1057). Their arms are: *or* a lion rampant regardent *sable*, and the family crest – a lion rampant regardant *sable,* holding between the paws a fleur-de-lis *or*, and their motto *Duw a'n bendithio* (May God bless us). The earliest known deed showing the Pryses at Gogerddan is 20 October 1334 which includes the place name and refers to lands in the neighbourhood that may possibly have formed the nucleus of the estate. One of the most important of the antecedents of the Pryse family was Rhydderch ab Ieuan Llwyd of Parc Rhydderch in the parish of Llangeitho. He was a man of some affluence and influence during the latter half of the 14th century'.

The family were proud of their lineage and were generous patrons of the Welsh poets. Some thirty-five *cywyddau* and *englynion* were written to various members of the Gogerddan family *'I blas Gogerddan heb dy dad'* including Dafydd ap Gwilym's elegy to Rhydderch Evan Llwyd.

Dafydd Llwyd, son of Dafydd ap Rhydderch lived at Gogerddan, although there are some doubts about who was the first of the lineage to settle at the property. Dafydd Llwyd married Gwenllian, the daughter of Maredudd ap Llewelyn. Odes to Dafydd were written by

Dafydd Nanmor and by Gutun Goch Brydydd. Their son, Rhys undertook a pilgrimage to Rome and married Catherine, daughter of Rhys ap David Llwyd. Lewys Mon and Lewis Trefnant both wrote *cywyddau* to Rhys. Their son, Rhisiart, married Elliw, the daughter of William ap Siancyn and Rhisiart had a number of *cywyddau* dedicated to him by Huw Arwystl, Matthew Brwmffild and Sion Ceri, as well as an elegy by William Llyn.

Sion Prys, the son of Rhisiart, married Elizabeth, daughter of Thomas Perrott. Sion Pryse, became the first to use the patronymic and was the first member of the Gogerddan family to become a Member of Parliament. He also served as High Sheriff of the county in 1580. Thomas Jones (Twm Sion Cati) of Porthyffynnon, drew the Pryse pedigree in 1590 and at Gogerddan at this time was a large dining-table shaped from a single tree. Richard, eldest son and heir of John Pryse, married Gwenllian, daughter and heiress of Thomas ap Rhys ap Morris ap Owen of Aberbechan, near Newtown, Montgomeryshire. He was High Sheriff in 1586 and 1604 and the Member of Parliament for Cardiganshire 1584-5, 1588-9, 1593, 1601, 1614 and 1621-2. He was appointed a Member of the Council of the Marches on 7 July 1602 and was knighted in July 1603. David Jenkins tells us 'On 17 April following, the House of Commons ordered Richard Pryse to be sent for by the Serjeant-at-Arms to answer certain charges concerning his conduct as sheriff of the county at the parliamentary election of 1604, when a double return was made for the Boroughs'. Sir Richard died in February 1622/3. He was succeeded by his son, Sir John Pryse, referred to as of Aberbechan, Montgomeryshire, called to the Inner Temple in 1608. He married Mary, daughter of Sir Henry Bromley of Shawardine, Shropshire.

His son, Richard, succeeded to the property and estates and bought himself a baronetcy on 9 August 1641. He was High Sheriff of Cardiganshire in 1639 and 1655 and as MP from 1646-8. His eldest son, Sir Richard Pryse, second baronet, was an ardent supporter of Cromwell and held many offices during his administration, but was regarded by many as something of a loose canon. *The Parliamentary History of Wales* states 'He ran through several publique offices under all Governments that have been from 1652 to this time, but more by the direction of his father-in-law Mr. (later Sir), Bulshode Whitlock, father of Elizabeth, his first wife, than by his own desires'. He married as his second wife, Mary, widow of Anthony Van Dyck, the artist, whose portraits hung at Gogerddan for many years. In 1672 Gogerddan was assessed at sixteen hearths, an indication of its size and importance. A schedule of furniture at Gogerddan in 1675 names the following rooms: the Cockloft, Green Chamber, Red Chamber, Painted Chamber, Crasse Chamber, John Lewis's Chamber, my Lady's Chamber, Mr. Middleton's Chamber, Smithfield, and over Smithfield.

Sir Richard Pryse died without issue and was succeeded by his brother, Sir Thomas Pryse, the third baronet, who died unmarried also without issue in 1682. Sir Carbery Pryse, a nephew, then succeeded to Gogerddan and became Member of Parliament for Cardigan from 1690-4. His election, however, was the subject of much wrangling in the county and subject of a petition to the House of Commons which eventually declared him the victor with a majority of one. When Sir Carbery died unmarried in 1694 the baronetcy expired and the estate devolved to his cousin, Thomas Pryse of Dole, son of John Pryse of Glanmeryn, MP for Cardigan Borough from 1741-5. He married Mary, daughter of David Lewes Esq. of Dolhaidd Uchaf. Thomas, who by one account was 'zealous in supporting the plunder of a shipwreck' died at Gogerddan in May 1745 when he was 30 years old. He was Mary's third husband and first cousin to her first husband, John Pryse of Glanmeryn. In 1690, lead was discovered at Bwlch yr Esygair Hir, (Esgair-hir), on part of the Gogerddan estate. The area became known as the 'Welsh Potosi' and following the Act of Parliament empowering all subjects to work their own mines, the news was conveyed to Gogerddan within 48 hours and great fires were lit on the surrounding hills.

Thomas's son, Richard, died unmarried in 1742 and the estate passed to Lewis Pryse, Thomas's kinsman of Glanfred, who later sold the mining rights to Humphrey Mackworth for £16,000. Lewis became MP for Cardiganshire in 1701, when still only eighteen years old. He was a Jacobite sympathiser and was eventually expelled from the House of Commons for non-attendance due to being 'laid up with a severe attack of gout'. He married Anne, daughter of John Lloyd of Aberllefenni.

Evelyn Lewis tells us that 'the older part of Gogerddan was the same in 1745 as is seen today. To judge from estate plans, a terraced front and ornamental grounds were added about the year 1750, whilst in the early part of the last century an old portion of the house was pulled down, which may possibly have included some of the original 15th century buildings'.

Lewis and Anne died childless and it was therefore another Thomas who succeeded his cousin and half-brother, Richard, who died in his youth at Gogerddan. Thomas married Maria, daughter of Rowland Pugh of Mathafarn, Montgomeryshire, but their son John Pugh Pryse died unmarried in 1774 and the estate passed to Lewis Pryse who sold the Priory estate in Cardigan to Thomas Johnes of Woodstock and Abernantbychan, Penbryn parish, and married Margaret, heiress of Edward Ryves of New Woodstock, Oxfordshire. They had two children, Margaret who married Edward Loveden Loveden of Buscot Park, Berkshire in 1773, and Lewis, who pre-deceased his father and died unmarried on 25 September 1776. He was buried at Llanbadarn Fawr, as was his father some two years later. Edward Townsend had taken the name and arms of Loveden on 27 June 1772. He was the son of Thomas Townsend of Cirencester and was MP for Abingdon, Berkshire. He and Margaret had three sons and three daughters Pryse, who inherited Gogerddan, Edward, Walter, Jane, Margaret and Jane Elizabeth.

Pryse Loveden (1774-1849) was of Gogerddan and Buscot. He took the surname Pryse by Royal Licence in 1798. He was married twice; firstly in 1798 to The Hon. Mrs. Agar, the second daughter of Lord Ashbrooke, who died on 14 January 1813 and secondly, in 1815 to Jane, daughter of Peter Cavallier of Stepney and Guisborough, Yorkshire, who died on 23 March 1846. Pryse was MP for Cardigan Borough from 1818-20, 1820-35, 1837-45 and 1845-49, a political career which spanned thirty one years. He and his second wife, Jane, had three sons: Pryse Pryse who succeeded to Gogerddan, Colonel Edward Pryse of Peithyll, who was MP for Cardiganshire from 1857-68, Lord-Lieutenant of Cardiganshire and Lt.-Colonel and Commandant of the Royal Cardiganshire Militia. He died unmarried on 29 May 1888, aged 71. The third son, John Pugh Pryse, born 10 September 1818, assumed the name Vaughan in 1866. He served as a JP and Deputy-Lieutenant for Cardiganshire. He was of Bwlchbychan and had issue.

Pryse Pryse succeeded his father and on 18 July 1849 he further complicated his family tree by reverting to the surname and arms of Loveden. He married Margaretta Jane Rice of Llwynybrain, the daughter of Major Walter Rice. Pryse Pryse Loveden was MP for Cardigan Borough from 1849-55. He died on 1 February 1855 aged 40. Margaretta subsequently married a second time, on 19 May 1859, Henry Charles Fryer of Lytchett Ho, Dorset.

The family name became even further complicated when Pryse Pryse's son, Pryse, succeeded him. He took the surname Loveden by Royal Licence on 14 May 1855, then took the surname and arms of Pryse on 28 July 1863. In *South Wales Squires*, H. M. Vaughan tells us 'Sir Pryse was the builder of the present mansion, insisting on the older portion of the house being retained in the now long edifice. On the other hand, the trustees of the estate wisely wished entirely to rebuild the house on the wooded slope facing south above the splendid level lawns that form the chief feature of Gogerddan'.

Sir Pryse Pryse, born on 15 January 1838 was a JP and Deputy-Lieutenant of the county. He became the 1st baronet of the second creation on 28 July 1866, was a Cornet in the Royal Horse Guards and a Colonel of the Royal Cardiganshire Militia and a subscriber to Dwnn's *Heraldic Visitations* in 1861. He died in 1906, within a week of being bitten by a fox at the age of sixty-eight. He had five sons and two daughters. The eldest son was Pryse Pryse, born 11 December 1859, who married Louisa, third daughter of Colonel William Parker Howell of Pen'rheol, Carmarthen, on 2 June 1881. He died without issue in January 1900 and is remembered for being much derided by his school-mates at Eton for appearing in a homespun suit made by a local tailor and by offering the boys of Uppingham school, evacuated to Borth, a cricket pitch at Gogerddan in the

Old Gogerddan

1870's. The second son, Sir Edward John Webley-Parry-Pryse, became 2nd baronet on the death of Pryse Pryse in 1900. He was appointed a JP and was a Deputy-Lieutenant and served as High Sheriff of the county in 1908. On 3 November 1892 he took the additional surname and arms of Webley-Parry by Royal Licence when he married Nina Catherine Angharad, only daughter of David Kedgwin William Henry Webley-Parry of Noyadd Trefawr. Sir Edward also died without issue on 20 October 1918. As Master of the Tivyside Hunt he became infamous for hunting hounds on the day of the funeral of Queen Victoria in January 1901. He and a select group of friends enjoyed a day's hunting when every other pack in the Kingdom refrained.

On his death, the third son, Sir Lewes Thomas Loveden Pryse, 3rd Baronet, succeeded his brother Edward. Lewes was born on

5 February 1864 and lived for a time at Aberllolwyn, Llanfarian, and was married twice, firstly in 1894 to Florence Madeline, daughter of Colonel F. R. Howell of Trewellwell, St David's parish by whom he had a son, John Pryse Howell Loveden (d. 1934), and then in 1938 to Gwendoline Marjorie, adopted daughter of David Howell of Cwmcynfelyn, Clarach. Sir Lewes died on 23 May 1946. Lady Marjorie later lived at Ffynnon Caradog, became Master of Foxhounds after Lewes' death. She was still keeping the Gogerddan Foxhounds and hunting hounds herself in the 1980's on foot.

The fourth son, Richard Humphrey Edmund Pryse who died at Ty-mawr in 1929 was 'eccentric, unstable and alcoholic' and took to the road as a vagrant. George Rice Pryse Saunders, succeeded Sir Lewes and became 4th baronet of Glanrhydw and Gogerddan, and took the additional name and arms of Saunders in 1932. He married Geraldine Mabel, daughter of C. M. Abadam of Middleton Hall in 1895.

The fifth son, Herbert William Pryse, who lived at Ystrad, Nantgaredig was declared a bankrupt in 1898 and worked at the Daimler factory at Coventry and died at Cwmsymlog in 1946.

The eldest daughter, Margaret Louisa, married Captain Edward Athelstone Lewis Powell, JP, DL, of Nanteos, and the youngest, Florence Mary, married Reginald James Rice Loxdale of Castle Hill, Llanilar, in 1894.

Sir George and Lady Geraldine had a son, Pryse, and a daughter, Margaret. Sir Pryse Loveden Pryse-Saunders-Pryse of Glanrhydw who took the additional Pryse in 1949 became the 5th and last baronet He married Emily Georgiana Compton Cavendish and died without issue in 1962. Margaret married Godfrey S. Briggs in 1930 and lived at Ty-Mawr, Cilcennin.

Having lived at Gogerddan for 600 years, the Pryse family relinquished the Plâs and the estate, which once consisted of 30,000 acres in Cardiganshire alone, was dispersed. The Lodge Park estate amounting to over 7,000 acres was sold in 1930 to the Forestry Commission and the remainder, some 3,700 acres was sold in 1948. Portraits that were formerly hung in the house can be seen in Steegman's *South Wales II*. An engraving of the house can be found in Nicholas's *County Families*.

Grid Ref: SN 6295 8363

Refs: TCAS, vol. I, p. 26, Evelyn Lewis; Rev. D. Davies *Telyn Dewi*, , 1927, pp. 111-112; Nicholas, *County Families,* 1872 & 1875, p. 126; *South Wales News,* 10 July 1934; H. M. Vaughan, *South Wales Squires,* 1926, p. 53; NLW, Griffith Owen List (iv); *Dwnn,* i, 44-45, 284, ii, 23; WWHR, i, 5-6; PRO Chanc. Rl., Mitford, 179/214; *NLW Journal,* 1953-4, pp. 81, 176, 353; David Jenkins, *The Pryse Family of Gogerddan,* NLW, VIII, i pp. 81-96; ibid, VIII, ii pp. 176-198; Steegman, *South Wales II* (1962); Jennifer Edkins, *Gogerddan Mansion and Estates* (Aberystwyth), 1989; *Cardiganshire County History,* Vol. 3, p. 54.

GREENGROVE (GELLI GWYRDDION), Llanfihangel Ystrad

Described by George Eyre Evans as 'one of those delightfully roomy passage houses, which gladden the hearts of all true novelists. It carries its cool refreshing name from its well-wooded situation'.

Located near the road from Aberaeron to Temple Bar, adjacent to the Theatre Felin-fach complex, lying at right angles to the slope and marked on *Colby's Map of 1831*. The house is now incorporated into the offices of a dairy company. Francis Jones noted 'It is still a pleasant house, being well-maintained. Meyrick describes it as 'standing pleasantly in the charming Vale of Aeron it was once the property of Thomas Lloyd of Wernvylig who gave it to his third brother Morgan Lloyd. The Lloyds are long extinct and the last of that name sold it to the father of John Vaughan of Tyllwyd, Esq'.

The *Blome List of 1673* names Morgan Lloyd of Greengrove as being descended from Morgan Lloyd of Llanllyr, a brother of William, also of Llanllyr and Thomas Lloyd of Wernfeilig. Morgan Lloyd married Elinor, daughter of Thomas Lloyd of Cilgwyn in 1669. He was High Sheriff of Cardiganshire in 1677 and died in 1688. Their daughter and heiress, Jane, married Sir Charles Lloyd of Maesyfelin, natural son of Sir Francis Lloyd by Bridget Leigh of Carmarthen. Following Jane's death on 20 July 1689, Sir Charles married as his second wife Frances, daughter of Sir Francis Cornwallis of

Abermarlais. She died on 20 January 1751 having had two sons and four daughters. One of the daughters, also Jane, married twice, firstly a disastrous marriage to her father's servant James Tanner. The *Lloyd Family Pedigrees* refer to an action brought before the Great Sessions in 1732. Morgan Lloyd of Greengrove owned an estate worth £200 a year and settled the same on his daughter and heiress, Jane, when she married Charles Lloyd of Maesyfelin in 1684. Morgan Lloyd had been so irritated at the inequality of the match with James Tanner that he had procured the said James Tanner to be 'pressed a soldier and sent into ye late wars in Flanders, and during the absence of the said James Tanner and while he was abroad in the service of his nation, and without his consent or privy, the said Sir Charles Lloyd and Jane Lloyd suffered a commons recovery, in which the said James Tanner did not join, in order to bar and defeat the other'.

H. Lloyd-Johnes tells us in *The Lesser County Houses of Cardiganshire* that the couple were divorced, but Jane does not appear to have enjoyed the Greengrove estate for long after her father's death, as by 1732 a Herbert descendant of Morgan Lloyd's elder brother, Thomas Lloyd of Llanllyr was contesting the estate in the court of Great Sessions. It was probably this Herbert who sold Greengrove to Dorothy, Lady Lisburne and her son Edward Vaughan in 1754.

Dorothy had an eventful life. Her husband, John Vaughan, the 2nd Viscount, was a drunken womaniser and gambler. His first wife, Anne Bennet, had died childless in 1723. On 10 January 1725, in bizarre circumstances, John, in a drunken haze, married Dorothy, second daughter of Capt. Richard, an Irish army officer of Henblas, Llanwnog, Montgomeryshire in a ceremony performed by John Gilsley, vicar of Llandinarn.

Dorothy's sister, Cordelia, was married to David Lloyd of Breinog, agent to the Trawsgoed estate. The 2nd Viscount, an MP, spent much of his time in London but a daughter was born in 1727. The marriage, such as it was, quickly deteriorated and Dorothy left Trawsgoed in 1729 never to return and lived with her father at Henblas. In 1733 she gave birth to a son, Edward, in Cheshire. The 2nd Viscount died in 1741 and was succeeded by his brother, Wilmot Vaughan. Dorothy's son, Edward, and Wilmot became involved in legal actions which came to a head in 1754 when Edward, then aged 21 years, relinquished his claim to the Trawsgoed estate and title in return for a £200 lump sum and an annual pension of £200 to be increased to £300 on the death of his mother, Dorothy, the Dowager Lady Lisburne. The Dowager secured an annuity of £88 from the Trawsgoed estate and later lived with Edward at Greengrove, which, according to some, they purchased, while others speculate as to the involvement of David Lloyd of Breinog, the Trawsgoed agent and the Dowager's brother-in-law.

Dorothy remained at Greengrove where she drove around the grounds in a small carriage drawn by a pair of mastiffs. She died in 1791 aged 81 years and was buried at Llanfihangel Ystrad where her memorial reads, 'Her Ladyship was remarkable for her Humanity and ever employed in work of Beneficence and Charity'. Edward Vaughan had, according to a descendant, H. M. Vaughan of Llangoedmor, 'a rather feeble intellect' and married Anne Williams in 1759 and had three children: Edward, David and John. Edward married a Mrs. Taylor and inherited his father's real estate. The second son, David, died aged 16 and did not live to inherit Breinog under the terms of the will of David Lloyd, his great-uncle, which passed to his brother, John, who was to assume the surname Lloyd on the succession, but significantly did not pass it on to his heirs. John Vaughan Lloyd born in 1764, married Jane, eldest daughter of Herbert Evans of Dolau (Highmead) in 1788.

G. E. Evans describes Greengrove in *Cardiganshire* 'Edward Vaughan either rebuilt or re-roofed the house – I incline to this latter, for two beams in the airy attics are inscribed – E.V. 1765 and E.V 1771. The earlier of these dates may mark the year of his marriage . . . and the latter perhaps is that of the time, when to oblige his wife, who naturally objected to a leaky roof, he restored it'.

John Vaughan Lloyd was High Sheriff in 1775. During his shrievalty a prisoner was sentenced to death at Cardigan Assizes, but the

High Sheriff spirited him away to Greengrove where he was employed as a labourer on the estate. However, 'when awkward enquiries began to be made,' the unfortunate man was strung up on a tree in the grounds.

Francis Jones notes that John was the only surviving son and his descendants remained at Breinog and later at Plâs Llangoedmor, and Greengrove was let and occupied by tenants.

Grid Ref: SN 5180 5750

Refs: Colby Map, 1831; G. E. Evans, *Cardiganshire,* 1903, 49; Meyrick, *Cardiganshire,* 238; Blome List, 1673. NLW, Griffith Owen Collection; PRO, Dale Castle MSS., No, 76; WWHR, i, 6-7; NLW, Edwinsford Deeds, 28, 32; Lloyds Family Pedigrees, XV; H. Lloyd-Johnes, 'The Lesser County Houses of Cardiganshire,' *Ceredigion,* vol. II, No. 2, (1953) pp 85-88. Morgan G., *A Welsh House and its Family. The Vaughans of Trawsgoed,* 1997, pp. 77-102.

GROGWYNION (PENGROGWYNION), Llanafan

The reference given is for the site of the former Grogwynion lead mine on the north bank of the Ystwyth between Llanafan and Pont-rhyd-y-groes. There is a Pengrogwynion nearby. John Ball, gent., is listed in 1760 as a freeholder of a property in Aberystwyth living at Grogwynion. Also listed is a William Ball of Rhos-y-rhiw, Llanfihangel-y-Creuddyn. We do not know the definition of gent. in the 18th century, but in the modern sense, John Ball was no gentleman. In 1763 when employed as mining agent to the Company of Mine Adventurers he ran a 'truck' shop, and out of a sum of over £30 paid to a group of miners as wages, only 3/0d. was paid in cash. The remainder had to be taken in goods from his shop at extortionate prices. Ball was dismissed for corruption and robbing the miners by Lewis Morris, the Crown Agent. John Ball, a native of Devon, arrived in north Cardiganshire a poor man, yet by 'toadying to the gentry, cheating the miners and blackmailing shipowners' he became a shipowner and proprietor of much estate in Aberystwyth, especially at Trefechan. He leased a property to John Lloyd of Aberdyfi, Collector of Taxes, which became the Customs House. At the instigation of Herbert Lloyd of Peterwell, John Ball was appointed JP in 1762 and together with Johnes of Aber-mad and Lloyd himself, turned north Cardiganshire into a lawless region in the middle of the 17th century. John Paynter of Hafod wrote of Ball to Lord Powis, 'Convicted for the third time for imprudently keeping an ale-house – no magistrate can stop the career of that lawless fellow.' A Thomas Ball was mine captain at the Lisburne mine in 1869. Local tradition in Llanafan has it that Grogwynion was the only property in the parish of Llanafan not owned by the Vaughans of Trawsgoed. The story goes that a Pryse of Gogerddan and the owner of Trawsgoed were spending the evening at a London house. The latter staked Grogwynion in a race involving two common flies. He lost and the property passed to the Pryses of Gogerddan.

Grid Ref: SN 7230 7245

Refs: NLW, Cwrtmawr Deeds, No. 727; WWHR, iii; *Ceredigion*, Vol. XIII, No. 1 (1997), p. 30; ibid, Vol, II, p. 91; ibid, Vol. III, p. 286, 290; Bethan Phillips, *Peterwell* (Aberystwyth), 1997, p. 145.

GWARCOED EINON, Llandysul

Located north east of Capel Dewi, on the banks of the Einon which flows to the Cletwr. Nearby are Cwmeinon and Esgaireinon. The earliest reference is to Rees ap David Llewelyn Lloyd of Gwarcoed Einion whose daughter, Mary, married Jenkin John Phillip of Dol-wlff who was alive in 1617. Their son, David Jenkins of Dol-wlff married Mary, daughter of Walter William of Pen-carreg. They had three daughters, Mary, Lettice and Jane, all co-heiresses. The next family to live at Gwarcoed Einion was that of John Evans, whose daughter Gwenllian married Rhys Thomas of Llanfair-perthy-cynddyn. Their son, Thomas Thomas was living at Llanfair in 1778.

Grid Ref: SN 4675 4410

Refs: Colby Map, 1831; PRO, Dale Castle MSS., p. 27; CRO, GGMS, I (Tydwal Gloff).

GWASTOD, Betws Leucu

Located on the banks of the Aeron north of Abermeurig and a home of great antiquity. The 17th century house which has been added to and restored, is of cruck construction with the quarters called the *neuadd* and a gable end, the *penuchaf*.

The home of a family of Lloyd, there in 1613, descended from Gruffydd Foel of Glyn Aeron. Their pedigree was written by the herald Lewys Dwnn.

Earliest records indicate that Gwastad Gwrda was the home of Morgan ap Sion ap Thomas who traced to Rhydderch.The earliest resident was David Lloyd Morgan, who was living in 1613. He married Ann, the daughter of Thomas ap Owen of Rolleston, Pembrokeshire. Their son, David Lloyd married Rachel, daughter of Samuel Hughes of Allt-goch. David died without issue. His sister, Joan, married Daniel Jones of Llanio and another sister, Bridget, married Daniel Rowland of Caron, son of Rowland Rees David Walter and Margaret, daughter of John David David Rees David Lloyd of Cilrhug. Thomas, the second son, became vicar of Nantcwnlle, whose wife came from Herefordshire and their son, David Lloyd, married Margaret, second daughter of William Lloyd of Pantgilgan, Carmarthenshire. David Edward of Cae Madock in the parish of Nantcwnlle, an ancestor of Edwardes of Abermeurig, died in 1670 and his will, proved in the same year mentions the furniture in Cae Madock and 'ye old cupboard from Gwastod'.

In 1672 Walter and David Lloyd, gent, are listed paying tax on 4 and 3 hearths, respectively. On 1 August 1751, the *Castle Hill Deeds* show that 'Thomas Lloyd of Gwastad Gwrda gt. and Thomas Jones of Cwm y glaw and Richard Allin of Trebane, both in Carmarthenshire, gents. made articles of agreement for the conveyance of messuages called Bonyurne, Esker Vach and Wayne Wenn in the parishes of Llanddewibrefi, Caron and Llanilar, Cardiganshire'. In the list of Cardiganshire freeholders of 1760 Thomas Lloyd, son of David who died in 1731, owned and lived at Gwastod. Thomas Jones, lawyer of Cwm-y-glaw and Richard Allen are listed as freeholders of Gwastod. Thomas Lloyd had two daughters, one of whom, Joan, married Daniel Jones of Llanio as his second wife. She died childless.

In 1800 the estate was at its peak and consisted of 2,000 acres with properties in Betws Leucu, Nancwnlle, Llanddewibrefi and Cil-y-cwm and Cynmyl Gaeo in Carmarthenshire. A map of Gwastod was drawn by Richard Jones in 1801. During the first half of the 19th century Price Lewes, third son of William Lewes and Joan, the daughter of Thomas Lloyd of Bronwydd was given Gwastod and the land 'up to Llwyn-y-groes and up to Blaenrhiwallen and Hafod-y-gors'. Price, born in 1796 and educated at Brazenose College and Lincoln's Inn, was the younger brother of John Lewes of Llanllyr. He was High Sheriff of Cardiganshire in 1863 and died unmarried in London in 1878, aged 83. Apart from Felindre, which he bequeathed to his brother, John, he left his estate partly to his nephews, Price Lewes, later of Tyglyn Aeron and William Lewes of Llysnewydd. Francis Jones visited Gwastod in 1975 when it was owned and farmed by Benjamin Jones.

Grid Ref: SN 5670 5687

Refs: Iorwerth Peate, *The Welsh House,* p. 70; *Journal of the Welsh Bibliographical Society*, VI (1943), p. 14; *Dwnn,* i, 245; Meyrick, *Cardiganshire,* p. 253; NLW, Llysnewydd DD, Bundle 76; WWHR, i, pp. 33-4; ibid, vol. ii, pp. 152-3; ibid, vol. iii, pp. 77-11; *Cardiganshire Freeholder,* 1760; CRO, GGMS, I (Tydwal Gloff); ibid, III (Gwaethfoed), fo. 34; PRO, Dale Castle MSS., p. 25 (98); *Ceredigion,* VI, No. 4 (1971), pp. 347-8.

GWERNAN(T), Troed-yr-aur (Tredroyr)

Located in woodland north-east of Troed-yr-aur and marked on *Colby's Map of 1831.* According to G. E. Evans in *Cardiganshire* 'Gwernant is a well-known mansion . . . formerly stood in the hollow, but the present house on the summit of the hill was built by John Lloyd Williams early in the 19th century. He was a descendant of Einion ap Dafydd Llwyd of Wern Newydd, and in no way connected with the earlier family who owned Gwernant, they deriving from Goronwy Goch, Lord of Llangathen'.

Lewis Glyn Cothi dedicated an Ode of Praise to Hywell ap Dafydd ap Goronwy, *O*

Wernan yn Nhredreyr, descended from Elystan Glodrudd, and mentions the noble mansion he had built 'where wealth and every comfort was to be had' – and describes the house as *Ugain 'ty ag un toad, ac yn ty gwin bad.* Lewis also wrote an elegy to Hywel, whose wife was Anne Perrot, daughter of Sir Thomas Perrot. Descendants of Gronwy Goch (fl. 1300) settled at Gilfach-wen, Emlyn, Cilgwyn, Cefn-y-coed in Llanegwad and at Crugbychan when Owen ap Rhys married Elen, daughter of Dafydd Llwyd Griffydd ap Rhys of Gwernan, whose son was Nicholas Bowen (ap Owen). Francis Jones states that Elizabeth Bowes-Lyon (later Queen Elizabeth, the Queen Mother), claims descent from Gwernan through the Hughes (ap Huw) family of Uxbridge, one of whom, Grissold married firstly, Edward Neville, Lord Abergavenny, who died at Uxbridge on 10 February 1588/9 and secondly Francis, Earl of Cumberland at the end of the 16th century. In 1564 John ap David Lloyd of Cilgwyn Esq., made a gift of 'the manor or tenement of Gwernon Place and land called Tir Llewelyn ap Ieuan gall, in Troed-yr-aur parish, to Lewis David ap Merededd, Esq. Rees Lloyd, son of said John, married Elen, daughter of said Lewis, and Gwernan, part of Cilgwyn estate was settled on this marriage'. They had two daughters; Mary, who married Thomas Lloyd, a 'Ludlow clerk', formerly of Golfach-wen, who settled at Cilgwyn, and Joan, who married John Parry of Blaen-pant. Thomas later purchased the shares of the other co-heiresses to Gwernan, held by Charles and Sage Lloyd of Llanedi and Charles Powell of Llanllwni, and thus Gwernan became part of the Cilgwyn estate. Francis Jones notes that a partition of the Cilgwyn estate, comprising 6,000 acres, was made between Stephen Parry of Noyadd Trefawr and John Lloyd in 1722. Stephen's sister, Mary, married Charles Evans of Capel Gwnda and Llwyndyrus in 1720. Charles died at Gwernan in 1736 and one of the seven children, Cesar, lived at Gwernan and died without issue, and Rhys of Llanarth, described in 1769 as executor of his father's estate, married a Miss Jones and their son was John Evans of Gelli, Llanarth. In 1791, Frances Gwyn of Noyadd Trefawr, who married a spendthrift, sold Gwernan and other properties in Troed-yr-aur and Penbryn to James Bowen of Cardigan. In 1795, he sold the properties to John Lloyd Williams who assumed the additional name of Lloyd following his marriage to Mary Lloyd, heiress of Llwynrheol, Llanarth.

John Lloyd-Williams, a surgeon in India during his working life, descended from Einion ap Dafydd Llwyd of Wern Newydd, Llanarth, built the Georgian mansion and decorated the park with trees representing the battle positions of troops during an Indian campaign. He was High Sheriff of Cardiganshire in 1805. He married Martha Louisa, daughter of Morley Saunders of County Wicklow, by Martha, daughter of the Earl of Aldborough. Her large dowry contributed towards the lavishness of the new house at Gwernan. The estate grew through purchase and mortgage and the family developed a model home-farm of 440 acres which boasted six different breeds of cattle. John Lloyd-Williams also had shares in a vessel trading between Bristol, south Wales and Liverpool from which he expected a return of £240 a year. He died in 1835 and was succeeded by his son, Edward, born in 1796, who was a barrister in Edgbaston, a JP and Deputy-Lieutenant of Cardiganshire. In 1820 he married Dorothea de Pipe, the daughter of James Bell, of Uttoxeter, Staffordshire. Edward Lloyd-Williams spent much of his time away from Gwernan. In her will written in 1859, his wife complained that her husband was 'forever abroad'. The family held trading links in India and the Far East for over a century. Edward was intensely disliked by the locals at Troed-yr-aur, a hatred which was manifested during the Rebecca riots. Edward was succeeded by his son, Caulfield Tyne Lloyd-Williams, born in 1818 and High Sheriff of Cardiganshire in 1869. Caulfield had interests in the Pembrokeshire coalfield and the Moreton mine in Saundersfoot brought him royalties of 1/- a ton for coal and 6d. for culm. Caulfield was succeeded in 1898 by Gilbert Henry Lloyd-Williams, born in 1871, whose father was Caulfield's first cousin. Gilbert was a tea-planter in India when he inherited Gwernan. A bachelor, he lived in a lodge on the estate and sold the mansion to the eccentric Thomas Ford(e) Hughes of Nantgwylan and Aberceri who imported an elaborate organ from Paris and assembled it at Gwernan. Gilbert Lloyd-Williams imported a Scandinavian bungalow in 1903 and erected it in a superb location south of the mansion. In 1913 Gilbert sold the greater part of the estate, re-purchased the mansion from Forde Hughes and lived at Gwernan until his death during the Second World War. Gwernan is now a ruin and the home farm is occupied by the Nicholls family. The Scandinavian bungalow is now called Calderbrook with 12 acres of land. In *My People* by Caradoc Evans is a photograph of Nanty, a group of eight cottages built by the Lloyd-Williams family for estate workers, now also demolished.

Grid Ref: SN 3338 4605

Ref: Colby Map, 1831; *Dwnn,* i, 37, 77; NLW, Noyadd Trefawr Deeds, p. 85, No. 48; ED Jones Lewis Glyn Cothi, I, 214, 218, 470; NLW, Griffith Owen Deeds, No. 2375; NLW, Bronwydd MS. (Peds.), c. 1700, fo. 94b; G. E. Evans, *Cardiganshire,* 1903, 271; NLW, Cwrtmawr Deeds, 207, 628; CRO, GGMS (Gwynfardd), p. 30; CRO, GGMS (to Elystan Glodrudd); Francis Jones, *God Bless the Prince of Wales,* 1969, 70-73; Burke, *LG*, 1850, ii. 1599; ibid, 1898, ii, 1604; Meyrick, *Cardiganshire,* 204; Carlisle, *Topographical Dictionary of Wales,* 1811; Leslie Baker-Jones, *Princelings, Privilege and Power* (Llandysul), 1999.

GWERN-Y-MEDD, Llangoedmor

Marked on *Colby's Map of 1831* and on modern OS maps as Gwern Medd to the east of Cilbronnau and just north-east of Noyadd Wilym. Formerly owned by Sir John Lewes of Abernantbychan who in 1611 quit his claim on the capital messuage called Gwern y medd and other lands in the parish of Penbryn to David James, a tenant of George Owen, the antiquary, at Coedwynog, Pembrokeshire. In the survey of the Lordship of Is-coed (Uwch Hirwern) in 1651, Thomas Lloyd paid *Gwestfa* or Chief Rent of 1/3d. for Tir Gwern y Medd. During the early years of the 18th century, Gwern-y-medd became part of the Llwyngrawys estate of Thomas Lewis. In 1760 it was held by his eldest son, David, who married Mary Greswood and lived at Malvern Hall, Worcestershire. Gwern-y-medd remained the property of the Lewis family, who moved from Llwyngrawys to Clynfyw, Maenordeifi in the 1750's, until sold in 1912. In 1886, Gwern-y-medd was occupied by Daniel Owen, a tenant, who paid an annual rental of £56.

Grid Ref: SN 2132 4531

Ref: Colby Map, 1831; NLW, Morgan Richardson, 671; WWHR, iii, 78; Francis Jones, *Historic Houses of Pembrokeshire and their Families,* pp. 40-41, (Brawdy Books), 1996; *Ceredigion,* Vol. VI, No. 4 (1963), pp. 374-387.

GWNDWN, Llangrannog

Situated near Capel Gwndwn, south-east of Wervilbrook (Nant Gwerfyl), and marked on *Colby's Map of 1831* and modern OS maps. Watkin Watkin gent., is listed as the freeholder of Gwndwn and Capel Cynon in 1760. Watkin married twice; firstly to Elizabeth, an only child of Rhys and Jane Jenkins of Cyd blwyf, Llanllwchaearn and Llanina. They had five children: Jane, who married Thomas Rees, Elizabeth who married David Moses, John, David and Mary. In accordance with the terms of Watkin's will John and David were left 'my physics books and the bookcase'. Watkin's second wife whom he married in 1758 was Hester, daughter of John Howells of Penybeili and niece and heiress of Llewelyn Llwyd of Saffron Mead. Hester had been married previously to John Parry of Cwn Cynon, gent., of Llandisiliogogo parish. Their marriage settlement was dated 26 June 1739 and letters of administration were granted Hester on 8 July 1747 following John's death. Their eldest son, and his mother's heir, Llewelyn, was living at Gernos in 1782, and his will was proved on 12 January 1824. He had a natural son, Thomas Parry of Hammersmith, gent. in 1799 and of Gernos in 1824. Watkin and Hester's marriage was also the subject of a pre-nuptial agreement signed on 19 December 1758. Watkin and Hester had two children; Thomas, his father's heir, inherited Gwndwn, and Hester, described as a spinster of Llanllyr in 1790, married John Thomas of Aberduar, Llanydder, a surgeon and apothecary. This marriage settlement is dated 31 May 1790, and Hester's portion was £300. John Thomas and Hester had four children, the eldest son, Watkin William Thomas became a vicar of Dinas, Pembrokeshire, John Howell, Esq. lived in Lampeter in 1847, and the youngest son, Thomas Parry, a surgeon, later lived at Aberceri. The only daughter, Hester Eleanora, married the Rev. Thomas Rees, clerk of Pritchard-fach in the parish of St. Mary's, Cardigan. Watkin Watkins, the freeholder of 1760, was an early convert to Methodism and became Steward of the Societies at Blaen-hownant, Twr-gwyn and Llwyndafydd. At a Society meeting at Dolberthog, Llandrindod, in May 1743 it was resolved, 'that Bror Watkin Waykins should qualify himself to be a Scribe or Emanuensis to Bror Daniel Rowland and Bror [Howell] Davies'. A letter written by Watkin Watkins of Gwndwn is published in *Welsh Piety* in February 1758 and Morgan Rhys published one of his hymns in *Golwg ar y Ddinas Noddfa* in 1770. Watkin entertained Howell Harries at Gwndwn in 1742.

Grid Ref: SN 3630 5175

Refs: Colby Map, 1831; NLW, Morgan Richardson Deeds, i, 189, 196, 784; WWHR, iii, 84; *Ceredigion,* Vol. V, No. 1, pp. 5-7.

GWYNFRYN, Llangynfelyn

South of Llancynfelyn church off the minor road from Taliesin to Ynys-las. Formerly known as Gweddynys, a name recently resurrected in a modern house built at Neuadd-yr-ynys adjacent to Gwynfryn. The home of William Basil Tickell Jones, Bishop of St. David's from 1874 until his death in 1897. The Jones family had close links with Pen-bontbren and Cynnull-mawr, Tal-y-bont and Brysgaga, Bow Street. A daughter of Thomas Griffith of Penbontbren married William Jones of Brysgaga c. 1720. Their son, William, married firstly, Jane, daughter and co-heiress of Evan Watkin of Cynnull-mawr in 1749 and then in 1772, Anne, widow of Lewis Morris,

and heiress of Penbryn, Goginan. She died in 1785. Their son, William, described as of Troed-y-rhiw, Llanbadarn Fawr, married Mary Tilsley of Llandinam, Montgomeryshire in 1780. Twenty properties in Elerch and Llancynfelyn were settled to the uses of the marriage. Their son, William Tilsley Jones, High Sheriff in 1838, was living at Gwynfryn, built in 1814 'on a low eminence called Ynys Cynfelyn,' in 1821, when he married Jane Tickell of Cheltenham, Gloucestershire. The Cardiganshire estate, but not Gwynfryn itself, was settled on the newly-weds. They lived in Cheltenham where William Basil Tickell Jones was born in 1822. Educated at Shrewsbury School and Trinity College, Oxford, he became a Fellow of Queen's College. William was ordained deacon in 1848 and priest in 1853 and followed his friend Archbishop William Thomson to the Diocese of York in 1865. He married Frances Charlotte, daughter of the Rev. Samuel Holworthy of Croxall, Derbyshire, in 1856. From 1867-74 he was Archdeacon of York until installed Bishop of St David's in 1874.

Frances died without children in 1881 and William married Anne, daughter of George Henry Loxdale of Aigburth, Liverpool in 1886. There were three children – William Basil Loxdale, born in 1890 and his sisters, Gwladys Mary Loxdale and Audrey Dorothea Loxdale. The Bishop died in 1897 and his wife, Anne, in

The Coach House

1905. In 1850 William had conveyed to the minister and churchwardens of Llancynfelyn, a parcel of ground, part of the Dolcletwr estate, for erecting a school for the education of the poorer classes of the parish. In 1873 the Crynfryn estate was nearly 1,500 acres with an annual rental of £713. In 1884, he granted to Peter Furguson of Glasgow and James McIlquaham of Bridge Street House, Aberystwyth, a lease to prospect for lead, copper and other minerals, under Dolcletwr, Tafarn Fach and Fuches-goch in Llangynfelyn with liberty to use the buildings erected for working the Pwll Roman mine and to divert water from the Cletwr. William, born in 1890 was an officer in the Royal Flying Corps and was killed in action during World War I. His sister, Audrey, appointed JP in 1926, married an Evans of Pengelli, Newcastle Emlyn (brother of Wil Ifan, poet and writer). Gladys, daughter of Bishop Basil Jones, married the Rev. J. A. Griffin. They had three daughters. Their eldest daughter, Anne, married Major J. A. Lloyd-Williams, M.C. On retiring from the Army they lived at Birchgrove. Their eldest son, Simon, now lives at Moelgolomen, Bontgoch, which he farms. Gwynfryn was sold in the late 1940's along with Tanllan, two cottages and about 20 acres of land. It passed through several hands until bought by Huw Phillips, a native of New Quay, who has adapted the elegant mansion as a home for the elderly. The coat of arms of the Jones's is stunningly depicted in the stained glass in the entrance hall of Gwynfryn.

Grid Ref: SN 6465 9175

Refs: Colby Map, 1831; Nicholas, *County Families;* Lewis, *TDW;* Landowners Return, 1873.

HAFOD, Eglwys Newydd

Haford was the grandest house ever built in Cardiganshire and was situated in the beautiful upper reaches of the Ystwyth near Pont-rhyd-y-groes and marked on *Colby's Map of 1831.* 'Three men stand out in Hafod's history; Thomas Johns (1780-1816) who created it, the Duke of Newcastle who lived there between 1832-1846 who revived it . . . and John Waddingham who resuscitated the estate'. There have also been three houses at Hafod, that of the Herberts, pulled down in about 1783 by Thomas Johnes, and rebuilt by him in 1783, from a design by Baldwin of Bath. The house burnt down in 1807 and was again rebuilt by Thomas Johnes.

In medieval times, all, or most of the land, belonged to the Abbey of Ysrad Fflur. In 1547 Richard Devereux held a lease of Hafod and other Abbey lands. According to Nicholas in *County Families* the earliest stock there was that of Fychan, descended from Cadifor ap Dinawal. A daughter of William ap Rhys Fychan married, as his second wife, Sir Richard Herbert of Powys, after which the Herberts removed to Hafod. Lewis *TDW* and other sources tell us that Morgan Herbert had a house built at Hafod 'having embarked in the mining adventures of the neighbourhood which from the nature of the ground and the badness of the roads, being inaccessible except during the summer, obtained the appellation of Havod, signifying a summer residence'. Morgan's descendants married into some of the best Cardiganshire families. The land was heavily planted with 'Oaks and other forest trees' in the 16th century

Thomas Johnes

due, in the most part, to serve as a defence against the prevailing lawlessness of the area. William Herbert had a chapel built on Hafod land in an attempt to teach the locals the 'rudiments of religion'. This was the church at Eglwys Newydd built in 1620. Morgan was a prominent supporter of the Solemn League and Covenant in 1635 and his daughters married respectively Daniel Evans of Peterwell and John Lloyd of Ystrad Teilo, Llanrhystud.

The Herberts named their elder sons Morgan and Richard alternately through several generations. A Morgan Herbert married Mary Vaughan (Fychan) daughter of Henry Fychan of Cilcennin. This Morgan was High Sheriff of Cardiganshire from 1657-1660. He paid tax on 8 hearths, a reflection of the size of Hafod in 1670. His will was proved in 1688 and his son, William, succeeded to Hafod. He married Rebecca, a daughter of Thomas Hill of Shrewsbury. William was High Sheriff of Cardiganshire in 1689. He died on 13 June 1704 aged 47 years and was buried in the chapel built by his ancestor. His will was dated 1704. His daughter, and heiress, Jane, married Thomas Johnes of Llanfair Clydogau, High Sheriff in 1705, the owner of considerable lands in west Wales. Hafod was then let to tenants. Jane died soon after her marriage and when Thomas died without issue, Hafod became the property of his cousin, also Thomas Johnes, of Pen-y-bont, Tregaron who was a cousin of John and Herbert Lloyd of Peterwell. Thomas, his wife and family of two sons and two daughters left Pen-y-bont and moved to Llanfair Clydogau. The elder son, also Thomas, 'led a riotous and frivolous life in London. His excesses necessitated his marriage to a wealthy bride, namely Elizabeth, the daughter and heiress of Richard Knight of Croft Castle, Herefordshire, whose portion was £70,000.' The couple chose to live at Croft Castle, with Elizabeth's parents, but Thomas visted Cardiganshire fairly frequently, was High Sheriff of the county in 1705 and was appointed Custos Rotulorum of Cardiganshire.

In 1763 the tenant at Hafod was John Paynter, who had been in the mining business before becoming Lord Powis's agent. He was High Sheriff in 1763. He is described as 'clever, ruthless and full of vanity – a social climber, who reneged on his promise to make all necessary repairs to Hafod, but did rid it of its poltergeist', or so he boasted. However, 'the mischievous imp or poltergeist that haunted the older mansion threw everything into disarray both within and without the house' and before building the new house, Thomas Johnes had the spirit exorcised, it was 'captured' and allowed to go 'provided he took himself to Devil's Bridge and with an ounce hammer and tin-tack cut off a fathom of rock. This accomplished he would be released. The tapping of his little hammer can still be heard at Devil's Bridge'.

When Thomas Johnes, the Custos, died in May 1783 his son, Colonel Thomas Johnes suceeded and visited his more remote Cardiganshire properties for the first time. He discovered in himself a love of the wild scenery and a determination to improve the land and living conditions of the peasants and had new plantations established around Hafod. His young wife, Mary, daughter and heiress of the late Rev. Henry Burgh of Monmouthshire, died on 1 April 1782.

In 1783/4 Thomas married his cousin Jane Johnes, and the blissfully happy couple lived at Hafod where their daughter Marie Anne

(Mariamne) was born in 1784. In June 1786 the foundations for a new house at Hafod were laid, designed by Thomas Baldwin of Bath. The house was 'an elegant Gothic fantasy, all pointed windows and pinnacles', according to J. Summerson, Nash 'made alterations and enlargements in the period 1793-96, and the octagon library, added in 1793, was almost certainly his work' (although Johnes himself is also attributed as its designer). He also added a dome and cupola and a costly marbled interior.

In 1796 the *Journeys of Sir R. C. Hoare* described Hafod as 'the seat of Mr. Johnes, . . . the house is of singular, and not an elegant, species of Gothic architecture . . . one room [is] fitted up with a very fine Gobelin tapestry. The library [is] circular in its form with a gallery supported by marble columns of the ancient doric order without bases; the proportions are much too heavy. The conservatory of the above is a hundred feet in length [and] joins the library. There is a good picture of Vandyke . . . the house is certainly not very advantageously placed, facing a barren mountain . . . the largest trees are sycamore, which I have always thought the hardiest of trees'.

Charles Wilkins tells us in *Tales and Sketches of Wales* that, 'to the south, near the river was a big ice house'. Although pressing debt forced Col. Johnes to economise, he planted 2,065,000 trees on his lands at Hafod. His duties as Lord-Lieutenant and MP gave him the opportunity to improve the welfare of the local people, including public transport, postal services and tourism. A general view of the mansion and its setting was painted by J. M. W. Turner in 1798.

Mariamne Johnes, the only child, developed a spinal deformity in her teens which caused her many years of pain and probably contributed to her early death. She led a reclusive life on account of this, and became a notable botanist and artist. Eminent men such as Sir Joseph Banks and Dr. James Edward Smith, President of the Linnaean Society, corresponded with her and distinguished men of the Arts visited, played and debated at Hafod. She had a royal academician as her drawing master and an Italian opera singer, Giuseppe Vigaoni as her singing master. Her father built her a special 'pensile' garden in the grounds in which she

Mariamne about 9 years old

worked and painted. On her death the garden was abandoned as the memory of its owner haunted it for her distraught parents. Hafod drew society to its door across the mountains, and from it came the translations of Froissart and the Chronicles of de Joinville and de la Brocquière from the pen of Thomas Johnes. Financial troubles were always with him, and yet he still spent money on a generous scale. To promote the publishing of his books he started the Hafod Press which ran for seven years. However, his duties in London called him, and it was early in the morning of Friday 13 March 1807 when Col. Johnes was away in London on Parliamentary business that fire broke out in the attics at Hafod. By the time the family, friends and servants were evacuated, the house and its precious library of irreplaceable manuscripts, books and essays was beyond saving.

Thomas and his family rented Castle Hill near Aberystwyth and set about rebuilding Hafod. Johnes wrote to George Cumberland, 'all Nash's buildings are gone; and you will say, perhaps, no loss. But Baldwin's stand firm. I shall employ him again, for he is an able, and, I believe, an honest man' In a letter dated 2 September 1807 to her brother, John Johnes, of Dolecothi, Eliza Johnes then living at Castle Hill, Llanilar wrote 'Your letter of the 29th reached me yesterday at the Devil's Bridge [Inn], where we had all gone to celebrate the commencement of the rebuilding of Hafod – and likewise that of Mr. Johnes birthday. God grant him and my sister health to see it completed, and long to enjoy it. The contractors have bound themselves under a heavy penalty to get it under cover by Christmas – the walls standing is a saving I am told, of ten thousand pounds. Mariamne could not summon courage to go to see it in its present desolate state . . .'

Baldwin of Bath re-designed the new mansion and Thomas part-furnished it with some of the auctioned contents of Fonthill in Wiltshire. Although the new house had taken longer to finish than was at first envisaged, Thomas Johnes was delighted with the result. The mansion was 'a wonderful improvement on the other'. When Thomas and Jane's daughter, Mariamne, died on 4 July 1811, Thomas was a broken man neither he nor his wife recovered from the blow. Mariamne was buried in the Gothic church at Hafod, where a marble monument to her memory was erected designed by Sir Francis Chantrey. The church itself was destroyed by fire in 1932. Elisabeth Inglis-Jones tells us 'As for his finances, they were going from bad to worse . . . no longer able to stay their headlong descent towards ruin' Thomas was forced to start selling his assets, from timber to books.

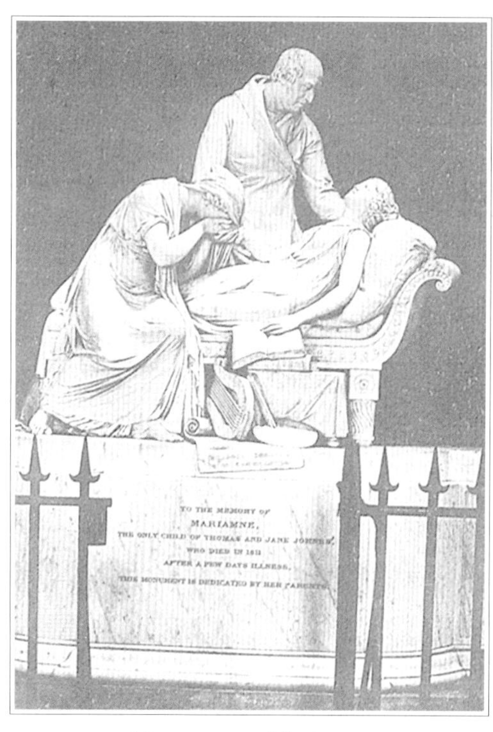

Monument to Mariamne

In 1813, the reversion of Hafod was offered for sale and purchased by a Mr. Claughton with a large down payment and the remainder on Thomas' death, thereby rescuing the Johnes from their pecuniary difficulties. A little after the sale, Thomas's mother died; a circumstance that could have rendered the sale of Hafod unnecessary had it happened sooner. Due to Thomas's failing health, Thomas and Jane spent their winters at Langton, near Dawlish, Devon, and only the summers at Hafod. Thomas died on 20 April 1816 at Langton. Jane took his body back to Hafod, and buried him with their child and went back to Devon, never to return to Cardiganshire again. She died in 1833 in Exeter, Devon.

Hafod was left empty for the seventeen years of Jane's widowhood. Claughton had 'got out of his purchase'. The place had been 'thrown into Chancery' and was rapidly deteriorating. Hafod and its contents were sold under an Order of Chancery to the 4th Duke of Newcastle for £70,000 in 1832 and he took possession of it shortly before Jane's death in 1833. For the next twelve years it was his principal residence. The Duke was an elderly and unpopular widower much hated throughout the country. However, he farmed on a massive scale and instituted many improvements and reclaimed much waste land. He was credited with 'bringing the Durham bull' into Wales which much improved the Welsh stock. When he returned to Clumber he stripped Hafod of anything of value and sold the estate to Sir Henry de Hoghton, High Sheriff 1849, who pulled down much of the house and employed Nash's former pupil, Anthony Salvin, to embellish the mansion. Salvin added a tall tower of the companile type at the south-west corner of the house. The work was never completed. Hafod was once again put up for sale and bought by a Llanelli speculator who lived there for a time but died a bankrupt.

From 1872 to 1940 Hafod was owned by the Waddinghams, a Lincolnshire family of farming stock. John Waddingham had made his fortune as a merchant and cloth manufacturer in Leeds. He became a wealthy man by shrewd investment in the railway industry both in Britain and abroad. He was married to Margaret Wilkinson and they had three children, John, Janet and Margaret. When he died in 1890 he left a personal fortune of £253,000 (or ten million pounds at present day values). John Waddingham retired from business in 1846 and bought the Guiting Grange estate near Cheltenham for £35,000 and in 1872 he bought the Hafod estate from the bankrupt William Chambers. John set about improving the estate and the house which Sir Henry de Hoghton had left greatly unfinished. By 1927 the Hafod estate comprised over 15,000 acres with a rent roll of £2,165. It is estimated that when John Waddingham died at Guiting Grange his annual income was £15,000 p.a. – more than that of the Lisburnes of Crosswood or the Pryses of Gogerddan. In his will John set up a trust fund to ensure income to maintain the estate. His son John was left the Guiting estate and James, the eldest son, was given the Hafod estate where he had lived since 1872. Educated at Cheltenham College and Oriel College, Oxford, James became a fluent Welsh speaker and student of Welsh poetry and literature. In 1883 he married Sarah, daughter of James Davies of Ffosrhydygaled. James was 43 years old and Sarah, 51. Sarah restored the church at Eglwys Newydd and built a church and vicarage at Devil's Bridge. She died in 1910. Despite the building of the Vale of Rheidol Light Railway and the sale of timber for pit props, the Hafod estate and the Waddinghams simply ran out of money. In 1932, with three faithful retainers, he removed to North Parade, Aberystwyth, where he died in 1938 aged 98. His funeral at Eglwys Newydd was attended by twelve clergymen, and the hundreds of mourners paid generous tribute to the man and his achievements at Hafod where he is still fondly remembered today.

The Hafod estate was sold in 1940 to W. G. Tarrant, a builder from Surrey and he lived there until his death two years later. Tarrant was born in Hampshire in 1875 and married Henrietta Foy in 1896. They had five children. W. G. Tarrant established his own building business and became a reputable builder who built the St. George's Hill Estate near Weybridge and the Wentworth Estate, both with their own golf courses. During the depression Tarrant got into financial difficulties but recovered and built Wellington bombers at Byfleet during the War. How he came to know about Hafod is a mystery. He paid £46,000 for the estate of 13,000 acres. He employed upwards of 150 men on timber working in Cwm Ystwyth. He also converted the existing water driven sawmill to hydro-electric power which also lit the mansion. A tall man, standing over six foot, and of stout build, his death from a heart attack in March 1942 was totally unexpected. His widow sold the estate to T. E. Davies of Worcester for £23,000; he sold it on to a timber merchant, J. J. Rennie of Wrexham for £17,750. In August 1946 Hafod mansion was declared vacant for rate purposes and following the sale of most of the estate to the Forestry Com-mission in the 1950's and the stripping of the interior, the mansion degenerated into a derelict state and in August 1958 it was blown up with dynamite.

Grid Ref: SN 7625 7350

Refs: TCAS, Vol. 1, 1910, pp. 20-23, 51-54; Jones, *Wales Illust.,* 1830; Nicholas, *County Families,* pp. 177-8; Warner (1797), p. 67, *Destruction of the Country House*, A. Salvin, Photo No. 162; *Tales and Sketches of Wales,* Charles Wilkins, (Cardiff); *The Cambrian Tourist,* 1823 edn., pp. 157-165; *Peacocks in Paradise,* E. Inglis-Jones, pp. 19, 20, 23, 48, 215, 240; Meyrick, *Cardiganshire,* 1810 edn., p. 256; D. E. Bonner, *'Hanes Hafod Uchfryd', Cymru,* xxxix (1910), 157; Cumberland, *Attempt to describe Hafod*, 1796; J. Davies, *'The Herberts of Hafod', Old Wales,* 1906, pp. 147-151; *Giraldus* (J. Rowland), *'Hafod', Haul,* 1862, p. 115; E. B. Morris, *'Hafod Ychtryd', Cymru,* xxxii, 1907, p. 272; J. E. Smith, *Fifteen Views of Hafod,* 1810; *Hafod Brython,* iv, p. 227; NLW, Dolecothy Letters; *'Architectural Development of Hafod* 1786-1807' John A. Thomas, *Ceredigion,* Vol. VII, Nos. 1973, 174/5; Colby Map, 1831; *Journeys of Sir R. C. Hoare,* 1793-1810, ed.; Thompson, p. 63; Lewis, *TDW,* 1834; Edwinsford, No. 2751; Landowners Return, 1873; WWHR, i, 18-19; Blome List, 1673; Henry Hoghton, 1849; *Thomas James Waddingham,* 1892;

Barber, *Tour,* 1803, pp. 120-1; Malkin, *South Wales,* 1904, p. 349; Horsfall-Turner, *Wanderings,* pp. 43-47; NLW, MS. 6878, fo. 120, *Tour in 1805*; J. Summerson, *John Nash,* p. 59; *Welsh Life in the 18th Century,* Twiston-Davies and Edwards, pp. 201-204; *Arch. Cam.* Painting by Stothard, 12847, p. 352; ibid 1879, p. 164; *Country Life,* 11 Nov. 1954, p. 1673; *Lost Masterpieces*, Chantrey; *Buildings and Prospects,* John Piper Architectural Press, 1948, pp. 35-48; *Old Wales*, 1906, pp. 147-51, 218, *'Huberts of Hafod'*, J. Davies; *Wales*, 6, No. 2, 1946, p. 45-54, *'Hafod and Thomas Johnes'*, E. Inglis-Jones; *'Thos. Johnes of Hafod'*, 1784-1816, Dafydd Jenkins, 1948; *Y Cymmr,* xxxv, 1925; *Some Letters of Thomas Johnes of Hafod* 1749-1907, H. M. Vaughan with photos of Hafod; *Red Dragon,* 10, 1886, p. 132, *Col. Johnes*, by W. R. Williams; *Cambrian News,* 22 August 1958; *'End of Hafod Mansion'*, Anon; *Country Life,* 1958, pp. 252-3, fo. 888; ibid, 2 October 1958 p. 725; *'Last Look at Hafod'*, *An Attempt to describe Hafod,* Geo. Cumberland, 1796; *Ceredigion,* Vol. XI, No. 1, (1988-9), pp. 59-71; ibid, Vol. XI No. 4 (1992), pp. 385-401.

HAFODAU, Llanbadarn Fawr

Located in the hills to the south of Goginan and marked on *Colby's Map of 1831.* Nicholas in *County Families* states 'The Jones family have been resident at Hafodau since early in the 16th century and William Johnes [Jones] was the owner-occupier in 1760. William Jones had a son, also William Jones of Llwyn-y-groes, near Lampeter who was born at Hafodau in 1828. He married Margaret Jones Hughes, daughter of Thomas Hughes, DL of Neuadd fawr, Lampeter. William Jones, the younger, was still alive in 1875.

Grid Ref: SN 6955 8038

Refs: Colby Map, 1831; Nicholas, *County Families*, i, 198; WWHR iii, 102.

HENBANT FAWR, Llandygwydd

Marked on *Colby's Map of 1831* as just over half a mile north of Blaen-pant but not named on modern OS maps. Reynold Jenkins of Blaen-pant owned Henbant Fawr, worth £8 p.a. and let it to John William Jenkins. Gabriel Lewis, a near relative of Reynold Jenkins, lived with him at Blaen-pant 'in the nature of a steward and had been very serviceable to him for many years'. Gabriel fell in love with Eleanor Talbot, for many years a servant with Reynold, and they married in about 1668.

Reynold Jenkins granted to them for lives, in survivorship, Henbant Fawr at a peppercorn rent. In 1678 Gabriel died and in 1683 Eleanor married Thomas Herbert who died in 1725.

The heir to Henbant Fawr was Elizabeth Brigstocke (nee Jenkins), the grand-daughter of Reynold Jenkins, and wife of William Brigstocke of Blaen-pant. In 1728, Eleanor Herbert the widow, Caesar Evans of Gwernan, gent, and Anne Parry of Noyadd, widow, tried to hold a title to Henbant Fawr to frustrate Mrs. Elizabeth Brigstocke of Blaen-pant, the rightful owner.

A schedule of *Brigstocke of Blaen-pant Deeds* includes Henbant alias Pistill Blaen-dwrdu occupied by Eleanor Herbert, widow, dated 2 April 1732. By 1746 a John Lloyd was living at Henbant Fawr.

Grid Ref: SN 2568 4485

Ref: Colby Map, 1831; Chanc. Pro. 1728.

HENBANT-FAWR, Llandysul

A 'pleasant small mansion of two storeys, with central entrance porch rising the whole height of the house with pediment in roof'. Located on *Colby's Map of 1831* as south of Alltyrodin near the west bank of the Cletwr are Henbant Uchaf and Henbant Isaf farms. Now named Henbant Fawr and Bancyrhenbant they are situated on the lower slope west of the river Cletwr and opposite Capel Dewi shown on modern OS maps and on the *Llandysul Tithe Map of 1841.* Meyrick tells us, 'This is now only a farmhouse and originally belonged to a branch of the Allt yr Odin family'.

The house was put up for sale in 1975 and described thus 'Henbant Hall, a Georgian house reputed to be built by Nash, and once the home of the Countess of Ellesmere, stands in an elevated position overlooking the Valley and the surrounding countryside, faces south and is a dwelling of great charm and character. The dwelling is built of stone, part rendered with a Caernarvon slated roof, and the accommodation comprises: Main entrance hall, drawing-room, dining-room, lounge, kitchen, inner hall, cloakroom, larder, half-landing with Nash window, master bedroom, 3 double bedrooms, master bedroom and secondary bathroom. Externally there is an old stable block. A level driveway joins the house to the parish road and pasture land surrounds the house. There is a ¼ mile of salmon and trout fishing on the River Clettwr. In front of the dwelling there are two duck flight ponds and trout ponds'.

The first known occupier was David Rhys David Llewelyn Lloyd who traced to Castell Hywel. He had a son, David of Caerau who married a daughter of Roger Prys of Caerau in the parish of Llandysul. Their son was Rhys David of Henbant. He had two sons, David Rhys of Henbant, living in1709, who married Mary David, the daughter and co-heiress of Rhys Thomas David of Llanfair berthy Cynnddyn, and Evan Rhys of Llandysul, joiner, who married a daughter of William fab Evan bach o Gwenllian Siars David.

David and Mary Rhys had a son, Rees David, who married Anne Evan, the daughter of Henry Evan of Court in Llangeler. David Rees owned Henbant in 1760.

Llandysul church has a monumental inscription to a Samuel Davies of Henbant who died in 1822 aged 72. The *Llandysul Tithe Map of 1841* records David Davies as the owner-occupier, holding 62 acres. At this time, Henbant isaf was owned by the Rev. David Davies, with John Davies as tenant of a holding of 42 acres, and at Henbant Ucha, James Jones was the owner-occupier of a small farm of some 50 acres.

Grid Ref: SN 4490 4290

Ref: Colby Map, 1831; Mod. OS Map; Meyrick, *Cardiganshire,* 1810 (ed. 1907, p. 199); CRO, GGMS, I (Tydwal Gloff), fo. 13; Turner, *Wanderings,* 212; WWHR, iii, 85; PRO, Dale Castle MS., p. 30; Llandysul Tithe Map, 1841; John Francis, Thomas Jones & Sons, Estate Agent details.

HENBLAS, Ystradmeurig

Although Francis Jones does not give a location this property was probably situated on the edge of Tregarron Bog at Ystradmeurig. It was a school producing priests and academics. It was founded by Edward Richard in 1734 and he was followed as headmaster by John Williams and his son, another John.

It was later the home of John Allen Lloyd of Dale Castle descended from the Lloyds of Ffosybleiddiaid, and Philipps of Pentypark, Pembrokeshire. In 1801 he married Elizabeth Bishop of Stormington, Sussex. He died in 1805, two years after his second son, Harry James Lloyd (1803-1879), was born. Harry Lloyd married Martha Llewellin of Pembrokeshire, and they had a son Richard Lloyd

(1842-1887), who was of Henblas. In 1871 he married Martha Elizabeth Barrow and had a son Richard Llewellin Lloyd (1872-1938), who inherited Pentypark. He was High Sheriff of Pembrokeshire in 1912. He married Beatrice, daughter of William Williams, solicitor of Aberystwyth. They had three daughters, one of whom married a Warren Davies and had a daughter and heiress Grace, who married Peter Trevelyn Jones of Llwyndafydd. She died in 1986.

Grid Ref: SN703 6762

Refs: Francis Jones Archives; *Ceredigion,* II, 1950, pp. 38-42

HENBLAS ABER-MAD, see ABER-MAD

HENDRE- FELIN, Spytty Ystradmeurig
Marked on *Colby's Map of 1831* as between Ystradmeurig and Ysbyty Ystwyth and on modern OS Maps on a minor road adjacent to the old Cruig-yr-hendre lead mine. The *Hendre Velen Deeds* of the Hafod Vilitra family state that 'in 1620 Morgan Hubert of Dol-y-gors, gt, settled Hendre Velen, in the occupation of Richard ap Ieuan, on Thomas Morgan Herbert of Spitty Rhwystwyth, gt, and his wife Mary ferch Richard.' We are also told that 'In 1666 Hendre Velen was mortgaged by Thomas Morgan Herbert of Spyty Ystwyth, gt, to Sir Francis Lloyd of Maesyfelin. In 1676 Richard Herbert of Hendre Felen, gt, Mary his wife, their son and heir apparent Thomas Herbert of Hendre-felen, gt., and Mary Richard of Hendre Velen, widow of Thomas Herbert the elder, gt, deceased, mortgaged Maes y Brandy'.

In 1691 Charles Lloyd of Maesyfelin, Esq. transferred the mortgage of Hendre-felen to William Hughes of Tyglyn, gent., then aged 56. His son, Thomas Hughes, the elder, of Hendre Felen Esq. was High Sheriff in 1716. He was one of the early patrons of Edward Richard, founder of the Grammar School at Ystradmeurig. He married Elizabeth; they had two sons, John and Thomas, the younger. John married Eleanor, daughter of Athelstan Morris of Maesmawr, Montgomeryshire. John Hughes's will was dated 20 February 1736.

They had two sons, Thomas who succeeded his father, and John, and a daughter, Susannah. John Hughes, the second son, was born in 1726 and lived at Morfa Bychan. Thomas Hughes was appointed JP in 1748 and High Sheriff in 1760. He married Elizabeth, second and youngest daughter of John Lewis of Aberystwyth. The marriage was subject to a pre-nuptial settlement, agreed on 31 October 1788. Thomas Hughes died on 8 May 1790 in his 67th year. His daughter Elizabeth married Capt. Francis Thomas Gibb JP of Bath, who was of Hendrefelen in the 1840s. He became High Sheriff of Cardiganshire in 1843. This marriage was also the subject of a pre-nuptial settlement on 1 July 1823. Elizabeth died at Greenford Lodge on 23 May 1856 also in her 67th year. Her husband died on 30 October 1881 in his 90th year. There is a memorial stone to him at Ysbyty Ystwyth. Their son, Francis Griffith Gibb, JP was of Greenford Lodge, near Southall, Middlesex.

Grid Ref: SN 7225 6990

Ref: Colby Map, 1831; Cambrian Register, vol. 3; NLW, Hendre Velen Deeds; Phillips, *Sheriffs of Cardiganshire.*

HENDRE PHYLIP, Llanddewibrefi
Francis Jones has not identified the location of this house.

John Davies of Hendre Phylip came from a wealthy family. He married Jane . . . and they had a son, the Rev. John Davies, born in December 1795 and entered Queen's College, Cambridge, where he graduated in 1820, BD 1831, DD 1844. Thereafter he held English livings. He was honorary Canon of Durham Castle and a prolific author. He retired in 1860 and died on 21 October 1861 at Ilkeley Wells, Yorkshire. He married Mary Hopkinson and they had at least four children, two of whom, John Llewelyn Davies and Sarah Emily Davies became prominent educationists.

Sarah was born on 22 April 1830 and died on 13 July 1921. She was an early advocate of higher education for women, an author, and was a founder of what later became Girton College, Cambridge. She died on 13 July 1921. Her brother, the Rev. John Llewelyn Davies (1826-1916), was educated at Repton School and Trinity College, Cambridge. He married Mary, the eldest daughter of Judge Sir Charles John Crompton (1797-1865). John Davies was Hulsean Lecturer, Cambridge, and Lady Margaret Preacher at Oxford and chaplain ordinary to Queen Victoria from 1881. He, also, was an advocate of higher education for women and was the joint author (with D. J. Vaughan) of a translation of *The Republic of Plato*. He was a keen mountaineer. He died at Hampstead, leaving 'two sons of great promise' and three sons who were Fellows of Trinity College, Cambridge, and two further sons of whom no comment was made.

Refs: Francis Jones Archives; DNB Clergy List.

HIGHMEAD (DOLAU), Llanwenog

In *A Guide to Llanybyther* D. H. James describes Highmead thus: '. . . the river Teifi hems the uneven borders of the three Dolau's – the mansion and the two farms of that name are in full view . . . the stately mansion of Dolaubach, or as it is now more commonly called Highmead, the residence of the popular Lord Lieutenant of Cardiganshire.' Located on *Colby's Map of 1831* and marked as a school on modern OS maps, the mansion lies on the north bank of the Teifi south-west of Llanbydder. The house was built in 1777 on a site previously occupied by Dolau-bach (Low Mead).

The *Transactions of Cardiganshire Antiquary Society* states 'The present mansion, with a commanding view of the Vale of Teivy, was first built in 1777. Though this house is modern, the spot has been celebrated in ancient times for its palaces. Before this mansion was built, there stood quite close to this spot, an older seat known as Dolau Bach or Lowmead. There are many people who call Highmead Dolau Bach, but it is in fact, Dolau Mawr. To the east of the mansion are two farms still called Dolau Canol and Dolau Uchaf. According to tradition, the palace of Pryderi, son of Pwyll was at Rhuddlan Teifi in Ceredigion, and it is believed to have been within Highmead park, somewhere on the river side. Nearby, to the west, at the confluence of the Cledlyn and the Teifi is a place still called Rhuddlan, and to the north-east of that spot are the three farms of Cefn- rhuddlan -isaf, -ganol and -uchaf'.

The family is descended from the Lords of Castell Hywel to Dafydd Llwyd Gwyon of Llanfechan, High Sheriff of Cardiganshire in 1599. In his will dated 20 May 1611, he mentions sums of money ranging from forty shillings to forty pounds and refers to three sons and four natural daughters. To his heir Siencyn Llwyd Gwyon he left the mansion at Llanfechan and lands in eight parishes in the Teifi valley. Siencyn's son David, in his will, dated 4 May 1666, mentions 'my lands called Dolefawr'. David's son, Edmund, of Rhydybont married Ann, daughter of Ifan of Llylgad Enwyn and had a daughter, Elizabeth, who married John Evans of Carmarthen (d. 1757 aged 39).

Their son, Herbert Evans of Lowmead, built the present mansion on his mother's estate. Nicholas wrote 'The mansion at Highmead was built in the year 1777 by Herbert Evans, Esq. great-grandfather of the present proprietor, near the house of Lowmead (used by his father John Evans as a hunting lodge) on part of the Llanfechan estate, which belonged to his mother . . .'. Herbert Evans died on 21 April 1787, aged 44.

Hanes Plwyf Llanwenog records *'Bu'r Milwriad H. Davies-Evans am 60 mlynedd yn organydd yr Eglwys, a'i rodd ef ydyw'r organ fawr a hadd y eglwys Llanwenog'.* At the church there is a tablet to Herbert Evans of Y Dolau Bach and his wife 'Ann Goch' in 1807, and also a tablet to their daughter Anna, wife of Sir George Williams, Bt., of Llwynywermwd.

In 1804 during his tour of Cardiganshire Fenton wrote 'I called at Highmead on Mrs. Evans (a sister of Sir Watkin Lewes), drank a glass of wine and ate a biscuit there. Then on through her beautiful plantation to Lampeter'.

In 1810 Meyrick recorded that Highmead is 'now the property of Major Evans, son of Herbert Evans, Esq. Major Evans' paternal ancestors were of Glantowy, Carmarthenshire. There is a very extensive farm belonging to this estate, and it is said of the late Mrs. Evans, the Major's mother, that though a lady, her agricultural knowledge and practice far exceeds that of any man in the country'.

Major Evans married Elizabeth, the daughter of Lord Robert Seymour of Taliaris, and widow of William Davies of Penlan, Llanfynydd. In a letter that he wrote to G. Eyre Evans he described Lowmead as 'the same as Hendy, the Highmead farm. The old house formerly had a second storey with dormer windows, but it was at best but a small place'. He inherited his mother's interest in horticulture for in 1815 he won the Silver Medal for planting the largest number of trees in Cardiganshire.

Major Evans advertised Highmead to let in *The Cambrian* on 12 December 1807 and described the house thus: on ground floor, breakfast parlour, dining room, drawing room; on first floor, 4 best bedrooms; attic storey, 4 good bedrooms, 2 small bedrooms : there were domestic offices, stabling for 12 horses, coach house; the whole in good repair, having been newly roofed and painted within these two years; land from 1 to 600 acres is to be let with the house'. Major Evans died in 1848 and his family placed a commemorative tablet in Llanwenog church.

Colonel Herbert Davies-Evans succeeded his father and was High Sheriff in 1870 and Lord-Lieutenant of Cardiganshire from 1889 to 1924. He married Mary Eleanor Geraldine Jones, daughter of David Jones of Pantglas. They had four children: Herbert, Viola, Delme and Alan. Herbert died in 1930. The *Landowners Return for 1873* records that the estate was of 2,808 acres bringing a rental of £1863.

In 1956 Highmead became a school for the disabled. Francis Jones visited it in 1962, it was still a school in 1975 but closed some years ago.

Grid Ref: SN 5020 4313

Refs: Colby Map, 1831; *Trans. Cards. Antiq. Soc.* Vol. 1. No. 3 (1913), p. 5; Lloyd Family Records, p. 42; Cledyn Davies, *Hanes Plwyf Llanwenog,* 1939, pp. 71-2, 1939, p. 71; D. H. James *A Guide to Llanybyther, Bailibedw, Maesycrugiau,* 1908, p. 13; Meyrick, *Cardiganshire,* 1810, ed. 1907, p. 216; *The Cambrian,* 12 Dec. 1807; Fenton, *Tours in Wales* (1804), 13, p. 10; Nicholas, *County Families* (1875 edn.), 194, illus. on p. 137; Landowners Return, 1873; *Lampeter* (1905), Col. H. Davies-Evans to G. Eyre Evans pr. on p. 41.

LAN-LAS, Llanddewi Aber-arth

Lan-las is on the north bank of the Aeron, two miles south-east of Aberaeron village, opposite Llanerchaeron Mansion and north-east of Llannerch Aeron church, and is marked on *Colby's Map of 1831* and on modern OS maps. Formerly the home of Lewis, descended from Cadwgan Grach of Carrog.

Horsfall-Turner tells us that 'Lan-las was formerly the home of the Parry family and the Venerable Archdeacon John Parry, rector of Troed yr Aur, who died in 1727, was born here. The family descent has been traced back through the centuries to Llewelyn Fawr, and Llanaeron mansion was built to replace the old Lan-las by Col. Lewis nearly a century and a half ago'. Lewis ap Hugh, descended from Sgweier Digri married Janes, the daughter of Rees James of Tyglyn. Their son, the Rev. Hugh Lewis, vicar of Llangrannog, married Anne, daughter of John Parry who traced to Gwyddno. They had four sons, John the eldest, married Elizabeth Griffiths of Erryd, Carmarthenshire, they also had a son, John. William, the second son, married Eleanor, daughter of Evan Price of Rhydybenne, Carmarthenshire, relict of William Lewis of Llwynderw. The other sons, Hugh and Charles, both died unmarried.

William Lewis of Lan-las was appointed a JP in 1748 and was High Sheriff in 1747. He had been given Lan-las by his aunt, Anne Parry who was the daughter and co-heiress of Stephen Parry. She died in 1721. When William Lewis died childless in 1789 he left Lan-las to his nephew John Lewis, who was married to Elizabeth, daughter of Thomas Johnes of Dolaucothi and Pen-y-bont. They had two sons and five daughters; William who succeeded to Lan-las and later to Llwynderw, John who succeeded to the Llanerchaeron estate and lived at Plâs Llaethliw, Mary Anne who married John Lloyd of Welsh St. Donats; Magdalen, who married Charles Morgan of Carmarthen, Sarah married David Hughes, Jane and Elizabeth Wilhelmina.

William Lewis married Corbetta Williama Powell, daughter of Dr. Powell of Nanteos.

Lan-las remained part of the Llannerch estate until at least 1924. In the *Tithe Schedule of 1844* Lan-las was owned by John William Lewis who farmed 41 acres with the remainder of the 124 acres farmed by John Phillips, son of John and Jane Phillips of Cefn-gwyn, Llanbadarn Trefeglwys.

Grid Ref: 4814 6075

Refs: Horsfall-Turner *Wanderings in Cardiganshire* 109-10. (publ. after 1902); Colby Map, 1831; NLW, Griffith Owen Deeds, Nos. 6794-5; CRO, GGMS, I (Tydwal Gloff), p. 34. Bryngwyn Papers.

LAWN, THE, see TREFECHAN

LODGE PARK (BODFRIGAN),
Llangynfelin. Also known as BODVAGE

Lodge Park, standing magnificently above the Dyfi estuary', is forever associated with the Pryse family of Gogerddan who used it originally as a hunting lodge. The house is also known as Bodfrigan. The *Bronwydd Deeds and Documents* mention that the house was once leased by Magdalen Lloyd, a widow, formerly of Bronwydd. The hunting lodge was built by the Pryses at the end of the 16th century as the centre of an enclosed deer park of 150 acres containing 60 deer. Such hunting lodges are rare in Wales.

Sir Hugh Myddleton of Denbigh came to north Cardiganshire in 1617 with the stated intention of developing the coal industry. He did not find coal, but discovered a great deal of lead and silver. He was on very good terms with the Pryses and his daughter married Sir Richard Pryse. Myddleton lived at Bodfrigan until his death in 1631. Five years later, Thomas Bushell bought the rights to the mines from Lady Myddleton and eventually established a mint at the castle in Aberystwyth and lent a huge sum of money to Charles I. Bushell also resided at Lodge Park. In the trees a little to the north of the Lodge is a well, known as *Ffynnon Bushell.* Bushell is reputed to have murdered his wife and placed her body in the well whose waters still run winter and summer. When Sir Carbery Pryse hit a pure vein of silver near the surface at Esgair-hir, he mined 200 tons of the precious metal and, due to government regulations which secured all silver for the Crown, he hid his valuable asset at Lodge Park. Later in Parliament, he and others challenged the right of the Crown to the silver and sponsored an Act of Parliament which enpowered all subjects to enjoy and work their own mines. What became of the silver is not known. Lodge Park was used as a dower house of Gogerddan and was often let to other gentry.

In 1774 John Lewis, estate and election agent of Lewis Pryse, gave notice to William Jones, the squire of Brysgaga, Bow Street and, 'of the holding of Bodfrigan', for voting against the Gogerddan interest in the election of 1774. In 1793, 36,000 oaks, 7,000 ash and 2,500 Scots pine were planted around the Lodge and in the 1830's, Mathew Davies Williams of Cwm-cynfelyn lived at Lodge Park for two years while a new roof was put on the family residence at Clarach. The present house is Georgian or early Victorian. During the 1870's and 80's it was the home of Henry Fryer and his wife, Margaret (née Pryse), who were attended by eight retainers. Fryer, a solicitor in Aberystwyth, became the first Clerk of the new Cardiganshire County Council and he was also registration agent for the local Liberal Association. Pryse Pryse died at Lodge Park following a fox-bite in 1906, but little is known of the house in the first half of the 20th century. Mrs. Briggs (née Pryse), later of Plasymynydd, lived there during World War II and it was also utilised as a country club, and the home of J. W. Musty, professional at Borth Golf Club and a Colonel Halford. Mrs. Briggs had a reputation for eccentricity. The Pryse connection with Lodge Park was broken in the early 1950's when it was sold. Ponsford Engineering bought the estate in the late 60's with the intention of building a development of 150 chalets in woodland around the house. Fortunately their planning application was turned down. A modern bungalow replaced the old summer-house and Lodge Park was allowed to deteriorate. In 1996 Mr. M. Hayes, a sound engineer, bought the property and 7 acres of the surrounding land. He lives at Lodge Park with his wife and family. He has a deep appreciation of the historical importance of the house and grounds and is committed to a complete restoration of both.

Grid Ref: SN 6535 9365

Refs: Ceredigion, Vol. I, No. 2 (1951), pp. 183-9; NLW, Bronwydd Deeds, No. 2477; Evan Isaac, *Coelion Cymru,* 1938 pp. 100-1. M. Hayes.

LOVESGROVE (GELLI ANGHARAD), Llanbadarn Fawr

The first recorded owner was Rhys Lloyd who married Sibyl, daughter of Richard Pryse of Rhandir, Llangwyryfon. Her brother, John, was a coroner and was alive in 1691. The *Cwrtmawr Manuscripts* record an agreement between Richard Herbert of Cwmyddalfa, Montgomeryshire and Rees Lloyd of Lovesgrove, dated 6 October 1675, 'Release of a messuage called Tyddyn Dol y Knew and a parcel called Gweirglodd y Maen ar Pythyll, situated between Ffynnon Ddewi on the south and a tenement called Pwllcrwm on the north, all in the parish of Llanbadarnfawr'. The will of Walter Jenkins of Llanwnnen, gent., proved in March 1718/9 states: 'to my nephew Walter Jenkins, property called Lovesgrove, alias Brynglas in Llanbadarnfawr parish which I hold in my mortgage.' The *Hearth Tax of 1672* lists Evan Edward as of Lovesgrove. He also owned Nant Ceiro.

At the end of the 18th century, Lovesgrove was owned by Sir Robert Vaughan of Hengwrt, Meirionnydd. In 1811 it was acquired by the heavily indebted William Edward Powell, the young squire of Nanteos. Lovesgrove was immediately mortgaged for £4,000 and shared out between the Aberystwyth creditors of the estate. In 1843, Lovesgrove was bought for £7,500 by John Evans, a prosperous lime merchant and trader who kept a shop in Commerce House, Bridge Street, Aberystwyth. His great-grandfather, Ifan ap Siencyn, from Trecastell, Llanwnog, Montgomeryshire, married Catherine, daughter of Lewis Owen of Waun-fach, Llanegryn, one of the notable families of Merionnydd. John Evans was the son of Gruffydd Evans of Tir-main, Tywyn and his wife Anne, daughter of John Jones of Tafolwern, Llanbrynmair. John Evans married Elizabeth, daughter of Lewis Pugh of Abermad. It is said that her dowry was made up of golden sovereigns equivalent to her weight. Fortunately for her father, Elizabeth was a slim, small lady. John Evans added his wife's surname to his own and the family became Pugh Evans. John and Elizabeth had three sons. The second, Lewis Pugh Evans (1837-1908) inherited Abermad following the death of his bachelor uncle, Lewis Pugh, on condition that he took the name and arms of Pugh. He became Lewis Pugh Pugh and had a distinguished career in India as a barrister and Attorney-General in the Indian Government. He built Aber-mad Man-sion and Cymerau, Eglwys-fach and was Liberal MP for Cardiganshire from 1880-5. He married Veronica Harriet, daughter of James Hill, Bengal, and died in India in 1908. The third son of John and Elizabeth was Gruffydd Humphrey Pugh Evans (1840-1902), educated at Lincoln College, Oxford, and called to the Bar in 1867. He followed his elder brother and became a barrister and was a member of the Viceroy's Council for twenty years. He was knighted in 1892. In 1873 he married his sister-in-law, Emelia Savi, another daughter of James Hill and had seven children. He built the present mansion in 1883. Sir Gruffydd was followed at Lovesgrove by his second son, Lewis Pugh Evans, born in 1881. Following his education at Llandovery College and the Royal Staff College, Lewis entered the Black Watch in 1899 and fought in the Boer War and was regularly promoted. In the Great War, whilst commanding a battery of the Lincolnshire Regiment, Lieut.-Colonel Evans was awarded the Victoria Cross 'for the most conspicuous bravery and leadership'. In 1918, he married Dorothea Margaret Seagrave, eldest daughter of John Carbery Pugh Vaughan Pryse-Rice and Margaret, his wife, of Llwyn-y-brain, Llandovery. Lewis left the Army with the rank of Brigadier-General and became active in local affairs and was a progressive and successful farmer. Their only son, Gruffydd Eric Carbery Vaughan Evans of Aberglasney died in 1950 during his father's lifetime. He and his wife, Barbara Noel Rogers of London had married in 1943 and had two sons, Christopher Lewis Vaughan Pryse Evans, born in 1945 and Roger David Loveden Evans born in 1947. Christopher succeeded his grandfather when he died in his 90's. In 1982, Lovesgrove, along with 22 acres was advertised for sale.

Lovesgrove has been converted into two residences. Mr. Tim Farn of Bangor Garage, Capel Bangor, has recently renovated and extended Lovesgrove Lodge.

Grid Ref: SN 6286 8163

Refs: Colby Map, 1831; Burke, *LG,* 1952; Nicholas, *County Families,* edn. 1875, i 195; WWHR, iii, 103; NLW, Cwrtmawr Deeds, No. 17; CRO, GGMS III (Gwaethfoed); Landowners Return, 1873. E. G. Bowen *The History of Llanbadarn Fawr,* 1979, pp 103-6; *Ceredigion,* IX I pp. 62, 66; *Who's Who in Wales,* 1st edn. 1921; W.J. Lewis, *Born on a Perilous Rock,* 1980, p 110.

LLAETHLLIW, Henfynyw

Marked on *Colby's Map of 1831* as two miles south-east of Aberaeron, south of the main road and south of Llanerchaeron church and Llanerchaeron mansion, and adjacent to Neuadd Llwyd chapel.

The first recorded family to reside at Llaethlliw were descended from Rhys ddu Sgweier Digri to Cadifor ap Dinawal. Lewis Dafydd and Jane, his wife, the daughter of Sir James ab Owen of Pentre Ifan, had a son Hugh Lewis, whose great-grandson, the Rev. Hugh Lewis, vicar of Llangrannog and Llandisiliogogo, and Archdeacon of Cardigan, was the owner of Plâs Ciliau Aeron. His wife Anne was the younger sister of Stephen Parry of Llanerchaeron and granddaughter of John Parry. John, the son of Hugh and Anne Lewis lived at Llaethlliw when his father died in 1732. The marriage settlement in 1716 of John Lewis and Magdalen Jenkins, his first wife, included Plâs Llaethlliw and a dozen other properties in Dyffryn Aeron. Elizabeth Lewis, John's second wife was the first to live at Llanerchaeron. Llaethlliw appears to have been sold, for Francis Jones notes that in 1760 the property was owned and occupied by Thomas Beynon. Llaethlliw does not appear in the Llanerchaeron rent roll of 1786. The Beynons lived at the property for a further hundred years. Following Thomas came David then his son Jenkin Beynon, whose will, proved in 1849 mentions his nephew, the Rev. David Beynon Evans (1817-55) and his niece Mary, wife of Thomas Thomas of Llanfair, Llandysul. Their daughters inherited £1,000 each and Llaethlliw was left to the Rev. Evan Evans (1820-63) of Llanwenog who mortgaged the estate for £25,000 shortly before his death. The entire estate was sold to tenants at the beginning of this century.

Grid Ref: SN4750 5963

Refs: Colby Map, 1831; WWHR i, 40, iii 95; NLW, Morgan Richardson Deeds, i 271-2; NLW, Glansevin Coll., No 1935, p. 257; NLW, 12356 E, 503.

LLANBORTH, Penbryn

Situated in a valley at the foot of a steep slope, known locally as Cwm Lladron (smugglers' valley), immediately east of Penbryn church, near the estuary of the river Hoffnant. It is marked on *Colby's Map of 1831* and on modern OS maps. The seat of Rhys ap Rhydderch, Lord of Tywyn, and his descendants the Lloyds and Morgans, also descended from Gwynfardd Dyfed. Henry VII is said to have stayed at Llanborth (and a dozen other places), for the night, on his way to Bosworth.

Lewis in *TDW* states 'Llanborth is by some thought to be that celebrated by Llywarch Hen as the field where Geraint ab Erbin, a King of Devon was slain with a vast number of followers, and who is supposed to have been interred on a farm in this parish still called Porth Geraint . . . was formerly an ancient mansion belonging to the family of Rhys ap Rhydderch of Tywyn and in default of heirs it fell to the Lord of the Manor'. Meyrick writes 'Llanborth . . . still bears marks of antiquity. Its polished doorway, antiquated windows and ivy-mantled roof bespeak the many centuries it has witnessed'. Lewis, in *TDW* adds 'This estate . . . in default of an heir it was escheated to the Lord of the manor, Sir Herbert Lloyd of Peterwell, about fifty years ago and is now in the possession of Colonel Bailey Wallis who sold it to R. Hart-Davis'.

Rhys Fychan ap Rhydderch of Tywyn in the parish of Ferwig had children by both his wives and three natural sons, one of whom was John who married Anne, daughter of David Lewes of Gernos. They had three sons, David Lloyd of Llanborth, Thomas Lloyd was a solicitor who married in London, and William ap John married Elen Lloyd, the daughter of Evan David Lloyd of Faedre, Llandysul.

David Lloyd of Llanborth married the daughter of David Llwyd Gethin, alias Kyffin, and they had two sons and one daughter. George Lloyd, who succeeded to Llanborth, Howel Lloyd who died without issue and Anne Lloyd who married Nicholas Morgan of Tygwyn Eglwys-wen, Cemaes, the natural son of Morgan John, Lord of Towyn by Lleucu, daughter of David Lloyd ap Griffith ap Philip. Nicholas Morgan paid tax on three hearths in 1670. They had three sons, James, Thomas and Griffith Morgan. George Lloyd of Llanborth married Joan Griffith of Llanarth. A memorial inscription in the church states that George Lloyd died on 2 May 1678, aged forty-seven-and-a-half. His wife Joan died on 18 January 1699, aged 77. They had one son, David Lloyd of Llanborth, who was without issue in 1695, and who died after 1705.

The *Griffith Owen Collection* tells us that 'in 1650 David Lloyd of Pantbetws granted three messuages and land called Llanborth and Tir Tre Dafydd in the parish of Penbryn, two cottages called Tir y Brag and Tir Trevo, and the water corn-mill called Melin Llanborth to Rev. John Lewes of Cwmtudu and Evan David Phillip of Penbryn, and Pantybetws in Betws Ifan parish to secure the payment of the grantors debt'.

The Llanborth estate went to David's cousin Thomas Morgan who married Priscilla Edwardes of Haverfordwest, Pembrokeshire on 15 November 1715. They had two sons and one daughter, Nicholas Morgan of Ty-gwyn, alive in 1723, who married Mary Reynold, daughter of Thomas Reynolds of Blaiddbwll, in the parish of Clydau, Pembrokeshire, David, who succeeded to Llanborth, and Mary, who married twice, firstly to Ieuan (surname unknown), and secondly to David Howell of Cilrhedyn. David Morgan of Llanborth was also of Tyhen. He married Anne Thomas, daughter of Griffith Thomas of Dyffryn Bern, their child pre-deceased him, and Griffith died on 19 May 1770, aged 73. There is a memorial inscription to him in Penbryn church and poignantly also 'here lies the body of D.D. of Llanborth who died 29th May 1769, aged six'.

In her book *Llangranog and the Pigeonsford Family,* Evelyn Hope relates that Dorothy, daughter of James Bowen of Llwyngwair, Pembrokeshire, who married George Price of Rhydycolomennod, High Sheriff in 1759, was a Methodist who frequented Penmorfa chapel every Sunday and that 'before the Chapel was built the services were held in a large room in the old farmhouse at Llanborth, which has since been pulled down. The room had a gallery and was evidently part of an old Mansion. Madam Price used to sit in the gallery'.

In a Sale Catalogue of the Peterwell Estate, dated August 1807, it states; 'Llanborth, 147 acres, let to David John at £52.10.0. p.a. and Llanborth Mill and land let to Evan David at £11.11.0. a year is included'. Llanborth quickly passed to R. Hart-Davis and the Harfords of Falcondale. On 22 December 1821 the Peterwell Estate Papers show that 'Benjamin Jones of Ffynnonfadog, Penbryn parish, farmer, and Anne his wife, only child and heir of David Davies of Aberporth, gent, and William Davies of Llanborth in Penbryn, farmer, released a dwelling house and appurtenences in the town of Lampeter, to John Jones of Deri Ormond'. The present farmhouse of Llanborth is a Victorian building.

Grid Ref: SN 2950 5213

Refs: CRO, GGMS (Gwynfardd), p. 31; CRO, GGMS [Urien], fo. 14-15; Croyden Deeds; NLW, Griffith Owen Deeds; ibid, Griffith Owen Collection; Colby Map, 1831; D. Roy Evans Deeds. 1; Meyrick, *Cardiganshire,* 210-211; PRO, Dale Castle MS., p. 29, No. 83; NLW, Peterwell Estate Papers; NLW, Bronwydd Deeds, 7114-5; WWHR, i, 15, 48-49; Evelyn Hope, *Llangrannog and the Pigeonsford Family,* 1931., p. 13; *Guide to Cardigan and District;* W. E. James, *Cardigan,* 1899, p. 32; S. Lewis, *TDW,* 1840.

LLANCYNFELIN, Llangynfelyn

Situated on the northeast edge of Cors Fochno east of Ynys las near the parish church and marked on modern OS maps. Gruffydd ap Meredith descended from Brochwel Yscethrog had a son Roland, who married Jane, daughter of Ieuan ap David ap Robin Lloyd of Peny-buarth, Carmarthenshire. Their son Gruffydd ap Roland married Catherine, daughter of Richard ap John Fychan ap Rhydderch ap Rhys ap Meredydd, Lord of Towyn. They had a son Rhys ap Gruffydd who signed for Dwnn as

Rees Griffith in 1613. He married Jane, the daughter of John ap Hugh ap Sion Lloyd a descendant of Howel Goch. They had two sons, Roland and John who were both alive in 1613.

Grid Ref: SN 6435 9175

Refs: Meyrick, *Cardiganshire,* 330; *Dwnn,* i, 242.

LLANDDWY, Llanfihangel-y-Creuddyn

Marked on *Colby's Map of 1831* and on modern OS maps south of the main road, south-west of Llanfyhangel-y-Creuddyn church, on the banks of the Ystwyth between Abermagwr and Glan Ystwyth. The mansion of Llidiardau is a short distance to the south west. Earliest recorded owner of this house is Adda Fychan of Llanddwy in Creuddyn who claimed descent from Collwyn ap Tangno from Meirionnydd. Adda's father, Llywelyn Fychan was reeve of Creuddyn in 1301-2 and Adda, in turn was beadle of the same commote from 1326-28, escheator for Carmarthenshire and Cardiganshire in 1344 and later attorney for the Constable of Cardigan Castle. Early in the 14th century he married Tudo, daughter and heiress of Ieuan Goch of Trawsgoed (Crosswood) and became progenitor of the Vaughans. Adda had a son, Rhys ap Adda Fychan who succeeded to Llanddwy and a daughter, Gwenllian, who was the second wife of David ap Ieuan descended from Blegwydd ap Dinawal of Carrog. His first wife was Nest, daughter of Llewelyn of Llanfair by whom he had a son Rhys David. He married his step-cousin, Agnes, daughter of Rhys ap Adda Fychan and they had a son, Philip ap Rhys, from whom descended the Jenkins of Carrog.

On September 29 1687 the *NLW Cwrtmawr Deeds* record a release from David Morgan and Thomas Morgan, both of Llanilar, gents., to Sir Thomas Powell, Sergeant-at-Law, a Baron of the Court of Exchequer of Nanteos, of the capital messuage called 'Tythyn Llanddwy in the parish of Llanfyhangel y Croythin'.

Grid Ref: SN 6482 7468

Refs: Colby Map, 1831; NLW, Cwrtmawr Deeds, 552; PRO, Dale Castle MS. 83; WWHR. ii, 15; Ralph A. Griffiths, *The Principality of South Wales in the Later Middle Ages,* I.

LLANDYSUL, Llandysul

Location unknown. John ap David ap Llewelyn Lloyd, descended from the Castell Hywel family, had a natural son John Lloyd of Llandysul, described as 'fidler'. He had two sons, John Lloyd Pwt y galon, fidler, and Jenkin Lloyd. John Lloyd also had a son David John Lloyd, 'fidler', who was alive in 1726.

Refs: CRO, GGMS I (Tydwal Gloff), fo. 27.

LLANDYSUL, Llandysul. Location unknown

Ieuan Griffith Lloyd of Forest Brechfa, Carmarthenshire, had a son Griffith Lloyd of Forest who married a daughter of Gwilym Prys Philip David of Llwynhywel. He had a son David Lloyd, and a grandson, Griffith Lloyd, who had three sons. The eldest, David Lloyd of Forest, married Barbara Rice of Dynefwr, while Francis Lloyd the second son married Margaret Llwyd, daughter of Griffith John Llewelyn Llwyd of Gwernmacwydd. Their son, Lodwick Lloyd, later of Llandysul, married a daughter of Thomas Lloyd of Llanllyr. Thomas Lloyd, third son, was of Yspyty Ifan in Llanegwad, in Carmarthenshire. Dates are unclear.

Refs: Francis Jones Archives.

LLANERCHAERON, Ciliau Aeron

For over 350 years the home of ten generations of the Lewes family. The mansion, built by John Nash in 1794-5 for Major William Lewis to replace an earlier *Plâs,* was bequeathed to the National Trust in 1989 and recently fully restored. Named Llan Ayron on *Colby's Map of 1831,* and Llanaeron on modern OS maps, it is located two miles south-west of Aberaeron north of the A482 to Ystrad Aeron. Nicholas states 'In old times called Uwch Aeron, Llan-Uwch Aeron and corrupted to Llanerchaeron'.

In his *Wanderings,* Horsfall-Turner states, 'Llanaeron called Llanerchaeron or Llanuchaeron. Here the grey of Llanaeron mansion built to replace the old Llanlas by Colonel Lewes nearly a century-and-a-half ago . . . '.

The first member of the family to live at Llanerchaeron was Llewelyn Parry second son of Thomas Parry of Pentre, Maenordeifi, Pembrokeshire, who bought the 500 acre estate from the Gwynne family of Mynachty in 1634 for £140. The Parry family, originally from St. Dogmaels, Pembrokeshire, were descended from Rhys Chwith, Esquire to the Body of Edward I. Llewelyn's uncle, Llewelyn Thomas Parry, also of Pentre had purchased Tyglyn Aeron and erected a new home there early in the 17th century. Both Llewelyn and his son, John who succeeded him at Llanerchaeron married daughters of the Lloyds of Faerdre, Llandysul. John's wife, Eleanor, later inherited part of the Faerdre estate. Llanerchaeron was a substantial property in 1672.

John Parry, who died in 1690 was followed by his eldest son, Stephen, who married Anne, daughter of Morgan Lloyd of Ffoshelyg. Stephen consolidated and extended the estate. He and his wife had two daughters, Mary and Anne

but lacked a male heir, and when Stephen died in 1718, he was succeeded by his nephew, Lewis Parry, being both the son of his brother John Parry of Pantyrodin, and his daughter Mary's husband. Lewis and Mary had a son John Parry, who was a barrister and married Anne, daughter of Walter Lloyd of Peterwell. After John Parry's death, the estate was inherited by his uncle, John Lewis of Llaethlliw.

Meyrick tells us 'Llanychaeron House, now the seat of Colonel Lewis, has an elegant effect, standing in a handsome park, plentifully adorned with noble trees. It was anciently called Ychaeron, and the first mention made of it is when it was the residence of the Parry family, the first of whom that lived at it was Llewellyn Parry, second son of John Thomas Parry of Noyadd Trevawr'. The house was of substantial size; John Parry paid tax on six hearths in 1672. Lewis describes the house as 'formerly the residence of the family of Parry, and now the seat of Major Lewis, is an elegant modern mansion, delightfully situated in the vale of Aeron, commanding a fine view of that river, and embossed in well-wooded grounds, skirted by a small park'.

John Lewis of Llaethlliw had a son, also John, who married Elizabeth Johnes, daughter of Thomas Johnes of Penybont (later Dolau-cothi), on 31 March 1749. Their son was Colonel William Lewis of Llanerchaeron, and their daughter, Magdalen, who married Charles Morgan of Quay St., Carmarthen, solicitor and Clerk of the Peace, who died on 25 November 1833, aged 76. They had a daughter, Mary Elizabeth Morgan, 1797-1881, who, in 1823, married Sackville Henry Frederick John Gwynne of Glan-bran.

Colonel Lewis married Corbetta Williama, a daughter of Dr. Powell of Nanteos. Colonel Lewis was High Sheriff in 1792 and was a great benefactor to the church. Carlisle tells us 'the church was erected jointly at the expense of the parishioners, and Colonel William Lewis, but most from the liberality of the latter; which worthy gentleman has also caused a handsome edifice to be erected for the minister, in a delightful, picturesque situation, not a quarter of a mile from his own elegant mansion, at Llan ych Aeron'.

Colonel Lewis and his wife Corbetta had a son, John, who succeeded, and a daughter, Eliza Williama Anne, who married William Lewes of Llysnewydd on 11 Feb, 1812. The marriage took place at Bath. John William Lewes, only son was of Llanerchaeron; he was a JP, DL, and High Sheriff in 1840. He married a daughter of the Rev. George Mettam of Barwell, Leicestershire but they had no issue.

Grid Ref: SN 4335 4091

Refs: Meyrick, *Cardiganshire,* 1810, edn. 1907, p. 259, 260; Lewis. *TDW,* 1814; Phillips, *Tour,* 1805, 53; NLW, Coleman Deeds, Nos. 134 & 141; J. G. Wood, *Principal Rivers of Wales,* 1813, pl. 1, 163; Carlisle, *TDW,* 1811, AE 12356E; Horsfall-Turner, *Wanderings,* pp. 109-110.

LLANFAIR, Llandysul

In his notes Francis Jones includes both Llanfair and Llanfairperthycyndym. For Llanfair he wrote 'see Llanfairperthycyndym – one assumes that it is one and the same house'. Now a stone-built residence situated in a loop of the Teifi, between the confluence of the Teifi and the Cletwr and marked on *Colby's Map of 1831.* In 1752 the house was owned by Rhys Thomas, gent. Thomas Thomas succeeded and was married twice; firstly to Jane, daughter of the Rev. David Lloyd of Llwynrhydowen by whom he had a son and heir David, and secondly to Anne David. David Thomas married Mary . . . they had three sons and a daughter. Thomas Thomas succeeded to the estate and Rees, who was living at Dolau died in 1865 without issue. David became curate of Carmarthen and was alive in 1875.

Thomas Thomas married Mary Evans, the daughter of John Evans of Cwrt farm, Llanwenog by Anne Beynon, sister of Jenkin Beynon of Llaethliw, *vivens* 1815-56. The *NLW Morgan Richardson Deeds* relate 'in the mid-19th century. testimonies were recorded concerning Mrs. Howell Davies (formerly Miss Thomas) while an under-servant to Mr. Thomas Thomas: mentioning her duties, the set-up of the servants, her ill-treatment by her brother, her schooling, her courtship, and that, 'During the twelvemonths . . . never heard her speak one word of English'. Thomas Thomas had two sons and three daughters. Captain David Thomas of Llanfair 1846-82, the elder son, also succeeded to Llaethlliw and was High Sheriff in 1874. He was buried on 1 March 1882. The house was let by the trustees of the late David Thomas for nine years to Captain Arthur Connop Newland of Mustbury, Axminster, Devon, at a rental of £70. The estate was sold on 16 September 1884.

There was a further sale on 28 May 1908 when the house and estate were advertised for sale and were described as: Residential Estate called Llanfair, with farm and lands adjoining, known as Bank Llanfair, a small holding called Cyfing, otherwise Lodge Llanfair, all in the parish of Llandysul in all amounting to 170 acres to be sold. Mansion House: Ground Floor – Entrance hall, Drawing and dining rooms, Library or Smoking rooms, Gun room, Kitchens, Servants Hall, Laundry, Dairy, Larder, Store room, Boiling house, Wine and beer cellars in basement. Upper Floor – 7 bedrooms, 4 dressing rooms, 2 bathrooms, Lav, W.C. good outbuildings and farm buildings. Bank Llanfair farm (let to Evan Evans – 50 acres £60 p.a.).

Llanfair Lodge was advertised for sale again

in 1955 ; it was by then a demesne of 18 acres, and had a timbered porch, the dining room was 24ft by 14 ft and was formerly two rooms, with timbered ceilings, a fire-place at either end, the oak panelling which divided the rooms was 'still available if required', and in the lounge the oak-beamed ceiling had carved corbels.

Until 1974 it was the home of Mrs. Gladys Fraser, later Douglas, a noted breeder of Jersey cattle. It is now the residence of Captain John Kidd and his wife, Gwenllian, younger daughter of the late J. Hext Lewis of Llanllyr.

Grid Ref: SN 4335 4091.

Refs: Colby Map, 1831; NLW, BRA 898, No. 10; NLW, Morgan Richardson Deeds, i, 271, 289;

LLANFAIR CLYDOGAU, Llanfair Clydogau

Formerly the home of the Lloyds and Johnes. Nothing of the Plâs remains.

The earliest reference to this house is in 1550, when David ap Evan Lloyd Fychan, who was descended from Gwaethfoed was living at Llanfair Clydogau. He was High Sheriff in 1550, 1557 and 1570-1, when he was 79 years old. His son, Jenkin ap David, was High Sheriff in 1578 and 1590-1, married Margaret, daughter of John Stedman of Ystrad fflur (Strata Florida). He died on 17 November 1591 and his will was proved on 5 February 1592. It was recorded that he held the following lands in fee: 'Manor of Kellan

(worth 26/8. 91 messuages in Llandewibrefi, 14 messuages in Nantcwnlle, a tenement in same parish, 6 messuages in the chapelry of Betws in Llanddewibrefi, 2 in Llangyby, 4 in Ystrad, 3 in Bettws Bledrws and 7 messuages in Llanfair-clydogau. Several messuages in Lampeter, certain lands and tenements in Llandisilio, a tenement called Castle Moithen in the hundred of Moithen, Llanarth. 12 messuages in Llanio and Gwynfil in Llanddewibrefi, 7 messuages in Caron 15, messuages in Llanbadarn Odyn, 4 messuages in Llangeitho and 19 messuages in Caron, a total of 177 messuages in Cardiganshire as well as messuages in Carmarthenshire, in the parishes of Meidrim, Llansawel and Llanysmail'.

John Lloyd, son and heir of Jenkin and Margaret Lloyd, married Jane, the daughter of Sir Walter Rice of Newtown. He was born in 1573 and became High Sheriff in 1603. He died in 1603 at the early age of 29, and his young son Walter Lloyd succeeded. Walter married twice: firstly Elizabeth Pryse of Glanfrêd, by whom he had issue, and secondly to Bridget Pryse who had no children. Walter became MP for Cardiganshire, was an ardent Royalist and was a Member during the Long Parliament. He was knighted by Charles I. Sir Walter and his wife Elizabeth had six sons: Thomas who succeeded, and married twice; firstly to Jane, the daughter of Sir Marmaduke Lloyd and then to Alice, daughter of Robert Corbet, Ynysymaengwyn. They had three daughters: Elizabeth, the co-heiress, who married Thomas Johnes of Dolau Cothi, Anne who married her cousin, Walter Lloyd and Corbetta, a spinster. Jonathan, the second son of Sir Walter and Lady Elizabeth married Margaret, daughter of Edward Vaughan of Trawsgoed. Their son was Walter Lloyd of Foelallt, who married Anne, daughter and co-heiress of Thomas Lloyd. They had a son also called Walter, a barrister, who was Attorney-General on the Carmarthenshire circuit, MP for Cardiganshire from 1734 to 1741, and was buried at Lampeter on 22 February 1747. In 1713 he married Elizabeth, the daughter and co-heiress of Daniel Evans of Ffynnon Bedr. They had nine children: Daniel and Walter died young. John Lloyd married Elizabeth Le Heupe, the daughter of the wealthy Sir Isaac Le Heupe. Her dowry was £80,000. John Lloyd became MP for Cardiganshire from 1747 to 1755, and was buried at Lampeter on 29 June 1755. They had no children. The fourth son was the notorious Sir Herbert Lloyd of Peterwell who was created a Baronet on the accession of George III. Walter Lloyd's daughters were: Mary who died in infancy, Anne, 1719-46, who married Sir Lucius Lloyd of Maesyfelin, Elizabeth who married John Adams of Whitland and Alice who married Jeremy Lloyd of Mabws. Sir Herbert succeeded his brother John and was created a Baronet on 26 January 1763. He married a Miss Bragge who, tragically, was buried a few days after her infant daughter on 30 March 1743. Herbert married as his second wife, Anne Stedman, daughter of William and Avarina Powell of Nanteos, the widow of Richard Stedman of Strata Florida.

It was Thomas Johnes and Elizabeth (née Lloyd) who succeeded to Llanfair Clydogau. Thomas Johnes was the son and heir of James Johnes of Dolaucothi and was living at Llanfair Clydogau in 1674 when he was High Sheriff. The house was of magnificent proportions and was assessed in 1670 at 11 hearths. They had a son, also Thomas Johnes who married Anne, daughter of David Lloyd of Crynfryn, Nantcwnlle. E. Inglis-Jones writes in her article 'Deri Ormond' in *Ceredigion* that 'In the 1740's Thomas Johnes lived there with wife and family. There is a tradition that Thomas Johnes had a son who 'cut a dash' in the London fashionable world, and once had a house party for friends at Llanfair, among them Sir Charles Hanbury Williams, Henry Holland, a Lord of the Treasury, Richard Rigby, a favourite of the Prince of Wales, and John Lloyd of Peterwell. They played for high stakes night after night, and young Thomas Johnes and John Lloyd lost very heavily. A year or two later Thomas Johnes married the heiress of Croft Castle near Ludlow, and went to live there for the rest of his life. When his father died early in the 1750's, Llanfair was dismantled and left empty. It stood decaying and crumbling for years before it fell down and the stones were carted away'.

Meyrick tells us, 'Plâs Llanvair Clydogan, now in ruins, was formerly a magnificent residence and during the time of Thomas Johnes, Esq., father of Colonel Jones of Havod Ychdryd, was frequently honoured by the company of Lord Thurlow . . . It is now the property of J. Beadnel, Esq., who bought it from Colonel Johnes'. Lewis in *TDW* writes 'This mansion latterly belonged to the family of Johnes, and was the residence of the father of the Lord-Lieutenant of the county till his marriage, after which time it was suffered to fall into a state of decay. It was a building of very great antiquity. The walls in some parts were five-yards in thickness and in several parts of the building there was the date 1080. It is now a ruin having fallen down within the last few years'. J. G. Wood adds: 'The mansion of Llanfair Clydogau was suffered to fall into decay when the family became possessed of Hafod. Perhaps the proximity of the mines had something to do with its desertion'.

Herbert Lloyd-Johnes in his article in *Ceredigion* tells us 'Llanfair Clydogau – a few hundred yards west of the present church is a paved pathway from the house to the church which can still be seen in places. The house was demolished to provide materials for the new house at Hafod, but it had ceased to be their home after Col. Johnes's father, also a Thomas, moved to his wife's house at Croft Castle at Ludlow. The opening of a lead mine in the vicinity no doubt hastened their departure'.

Francis Jones writes, 'No remains of the place are there today, but near the entrance to the lawn there is still a great oak tree, but now withering, which doubtless belonged to the days of the Plâs.'

Grid Ref: SN 6240 5125

Refs: Dwnn, I, 38, 63-4, 84; WWHR i, 11-12; WWHR iii, NLW, Griffith Owen List (iv); J. G. Wood, *Principal Rivers of Wales,* 1813, 149; *Arch. Cam.* 1861, 158, n; Meyrick, *Cardiganshire,* 1810, edn 1907. p. 229; H. Lloyd-Johnes (1800-1876); *Ceredigion,* vol. III. No. 1, 1956; Lewis, *TDW;* E. Inglis-Jones, 'Deri Ormond', *Ceredigion,* vol. II, No. 3, 1954; CRO, Dale Castle MS., p. 22 (88); *Cymru.* July 1906, p. 22; Lloyd Peds. & Records, p. 16; Horsfall-Turner *Wanderings;* Fenton *Tours in Wales,* 1804-1813, p. 7; CRO, GGMS III (Gwaethfoed).

LLANFAIRPERTHYCYNDYN, Llandysul

There is also a Cefn Llanfair, Lodge Llanfair and Allt Llanfair near the banks of the Teifi south-east of Faedre fawr. The ancient chapel of Llanfair stood in the meadow below Plâs Llanfair, but sadly no traces remain. In his notes Francis Jones wrote, 'For Llanfair see Llanfairperthycynddyn – one assumes that it is one and the same house'.

Thomas ap David of Llanfairperthycyndyn, younger son of David ap Rhys David Llewelyn Lloyd of Castell Hywel had a son, Rhys of Llanfair, alive in 1709, who married Angharad, daughter of Ieuan ap Ieuan of Pantysgawen. They had three daughters who became co-heiresses to the estate. Margaret married her first cousin Thomas David of Ffosesgob descended from Castell Hywel, son of David Thomas, and brother of Rhys. Thomas David's will was proved in 1731. Mary married David Rees of Henbant descended from Castell Hywel. They had a son, Rhys David of Henbant who married Anne Evan, the daughter of Harry Evan of Court Manorforion and Catherine married Evan David Rees.

Thomas and Margaret David's elder son, David Thomas, succeeded to Ffosesgob but he died without issue and his will was proved in 1758. In the same year Llanfairperthycyndyn was rated in the parish tax at £8.

Rhys Thomas, the second son succeeded to Llanfairperthycyndyn and married Gwenllian, daughter of John Evans of Gwarcoed Einon, Llandysul. They had two sons, Thomas Thomas of Llanfairperthycyndyn and John Thomas of Ffosesgob. Thomas Thomas married Jane, the daughter of the Rev. David Lloyd of Coedlannau, Brynllefrith and Castell Hywel. Their elder son, David Thomas married

Mary, the daughter of John and Susannah Edwards of Wernmacwydd. The younger son the Rev. Thomas Thomas born in 1789 was a Unitarian Minister of some note who died of consumption in August 1818, aged 29 and was buried beneath the communion table of Pantydefaid chapel. David Thomas died on 1 August 1845, aged 61, and Mary, after a long widowhood, on 19 September, 1876 aged 89. They had a son, Thomas and a daughter, Margaret, who married the Rev. Thomas Davies, the Rector of Llangynllo. Their daughter Susannah Gwenllian married R. T. P. Williams, a solicitor of Haverfordwest. One of their sons, George Edgar Robert Williams, also a solicitor of Haverfordwest, had a son Howell Williams, of Haverfordwest, alive in 1978.

Thomas Thomas had a son David. The *Landowners Return of 1873* showed that David Thomas of Llanfair was listed as having an estate of 2,560 acres, with a rental of £1,204 p.a. A coat of arms was assigned to David and John Thomas in 1874. This was: *azure* a lion rampant holding between its paws a spear head *or* between 2 flamiches *or* each charged with a scaling ladder *sable.* The crest was on a wreath issuant from a wreath of oak *or* a wolf head erased *sable,* in its mouth a spearhead *or.* The Motto was, *Clemens et Verax.*

Grid Ref: SN 4347 4095

Refs: Colby Map, 1831; PRO, Dale Castle MS., p. 30 (113, 114); WWHR, i, 52; W. J. Davies, *Hanes Plwyf Llandysul,* 1896, pp. 204-5, 228; Llandysul Parish Tax 1758-9; Landowners Return, 1873; CRO, GGMS I (Tydwal Gloff), p. 21; Lloyd Family Records (ped. pp. 19-20).

LLANFAIR TRELYGEN,
Troed-yr-aur (Trefdreyr)

Marked on *Bowen's Map of 1754* as Treligon and on *Colby's Map of 1831* as Llanfair Treflygen. It was once a small parish, some three and a half miles north-east of Newcastle Emlyn, near Llangynllo church south-east of Cred-y-bryn, but its church was in ruins before 1840 when its population numbered 124. The remains of Eglwys Llanfair can still be seen and there is a Ffynnon Fair nearby.

The home of the Bryne (also spelt Brein or Bruyn) family. Henry Bryne, gent., was assessed at 4/- as his chief rent payable to the Lord of the Manor in 1651. William Bryne Esq. had a son Thomas, later of Llanfynnon-wen, who married Gwenllian Lloyd. They had a son Philip, who married Gwenllian, the daughter of Ieuan ap y Bedo Du of Lampeter. They had a son and heir, George. George's eldest son John, gent. married Katherine, the daughter of Owen ap Rhys Lloyd of Llangoedmor in 1613. They had four sons, David, who died an infant, David, Harry and Edward, and two daughters, Sage and Ann. The family pedigree was recorded by the herald Dwnn and bore the arms: *or* a double headed eagle *sable.*

Grid Ref: SN 3432 4415

Refs: Dwnn, i, 19; Colby Map, 1831; Emanuel Bowen Map, 1754; Melville Richards, 'Gwynionydd Is Cerdin in 1651,' *Ceredigion,* iv, No. 4, pp. 388-99.

LLANFECHAN (LLANVAUGHAN),
Llanwenog

Formerly a chapelry belonging to Llanwenog, and the home of the Lloyd and Thomas families. It is situated on the north-west bank of the Teifi west of Alltyblaca and is marked on *Colby's Map of 1831* as Lan Vaughan and on modern OS maps as Llanfechan. *Hanes Llanwenog* records 'Plasty Llanfechan, a Plâs from 1300 to 1800. It is said that the estate owner could see, *gynifer a chwe ugain [120] o dyddynod o'i eiddo yn nyffryn Teifi.* (as many as 120 of his cottages from the windows of Llanfechan). It became a ruin after the death of Admiral Thomas in 1810'.

Gwion Lloyd, who was living at Llanfechan, from 1566-76, the son of Llewelyn Llwyd ap Dafydd, who traced to Castell Hywel, married Gwenllian, the daughter of Howel Jenkin Rees David Thomas descended from Tewdwr of Blaentren. They had eight sons and the eldest son, David Lloyd Gwion, succeeded to the estate and married Elen, the daughter of James ap Sir John Williams of Panthowell, Carmarthenshire. David Lloyd Gwion was High Sheriff of Cardiganshire in 1609. His will was dated 20 May 1611 and proved on 30 October 1611. As there were no legitimate heirs he left the Llanfechan estate to his natural son Jenkin.

Jenkin Lloyd was High Sheriff in 1613 and married Elen, the daughter of Morgan Thomas of Llansawel. In his will dated 7 March 1647 and proved on 29 January 1648 he gives details of '2 messuages mortgaged to me by Evan Gwyen, Esq. in £200, in the parish of Llanwenog, one called Keven Rhyddlan alias Kaer Dyron, and the other Tir karn Dafydd Lloyd gefen Rhyddlan. My messuages and land in the parish of Llansawel, Carmarthenshire, which I bought from Francis Howell, now deceased, gent., 2 messuages and land in the parish of Llanwnnon called Tir y vronvelen and Tir krygkwok alias Tir y Lletty talgrwn'. His will then listed all his other lands in other parishes.

Jenkin Lloyd's son David succeeded to the property. He married Anne Owen, the natural daughter of George Owen of Henllys, Pembrokeshire. David Lloyd's will was dated 4 May 1666, shortly before his death. In his will he listed his property, which included Blaen Tren and his lands called Dole Mawr (Highmead).

Jenkin Lloyd succeeded his father. He was the eldest of five sons; his brothers were Edmund, David, Griffith and Rawleigh. In 1672 Jenkin Lloyd of Llanfechan, gent, and his mother, paid tax on 1 and 7 hearths respectively. Jenkin married Catherine, daughter of Oliver Lloyd of Ffosybleiddiaid, and they had three sons and three daughters: David Lloyd who succeeded to the estate, John Lloyd of Castell Hywel who married Mary, the daughter of Sir Francis Cornwallis, relict of Thomas Lloyd, Thomas, who had a natural daughter, Mary, by Rachel Williams of Dolgwm and a natural son John, an apothecary, by Mary Llewelyn. Another daughter Elizabeth married Nathan Griffith of Dolwen and Mary married Richard Morgan of Llysfaln, and another daughter who married Mr. Philipps of Wythfawr. In *A Guide to Llanbydder* D. H. James tells us 'Jenkin Lloyd was interested in church music. His name and date was inscribed on one of the church bells of Llanwenog- now, alas, recast'.

David Lloyd succeeded his father and was a JP and High Sheriff in 1710 He drowned in 1714 and the PRO Lists relates that 'David Lloyd of Llanvaughan, JP, was removed from Commissioners of Peace, "being dead". His will dated 30 July 1711 was proved on 25 October 1716. His brother, John Lloyd of Castell Hywel inherited Llanfechan and the estate then passed

to his son Charles Lloyd. He married Margaret, daughter of David Lloyd of Ffosybleiddiaid. They had at least three sons and one daughter. Evan Lloyd succeeded to Llanfechan, David lived at Gilfach-wen, John in Cringae (Cryngae), and Sage, who married the Rev. John Thomas, vicar of Llandysul in 1744 and later vicar of Llanllwni.

In 1857 *The Cambrian Journal* related this story 'There was a tradition that one of the Lloyds of Llanvechan lost a valuable gold watch on Mynydd Llanbyther, whilst out hunting, about the middle of the last century. From that mountain the neighbouring people procure their peat. Some twenty years ago there was an old man of the name Dafydd William Pantycraph upon whom Providence had recently frowned, his two sons having disappeared. One morning however, when in the act of adding fuel to his fire, this long-lost watch made its appearance, and enabled the old man to recoup his losses'.

John and Sage Thomas had five sons: James Thomas, a surgeon on the Isle of Man married Anne . . . and their daughter Maria, the coheiress of Llanfechan married Lieutenant R. Macdonald who served with the 80th Foot. Charles Lloyd who was born on 28 April 1747 married and had a daughter, Elizabeth who married John Davies Esq., of Llanfechan in 1773. Admiral John Thomas married Letitia Maria, the eldest daughter of James Lloyd of Mabws, while Richard (1754-1821) had a natural daughter, Judith, who married David Edwards of Blaencae Noyadd, Llanllwni.

Evan Lloyd (1720-1773) who succeeded to Llanfechan, was the father of John Lloyd, the antiquary and musician. Another of the family on the mother's side was the bard David Thomas (Dewi Hefin) 1828-1909. His son, David Thomas OBE, was President of the Cambrian Association; other descendants were the Rev. D. Gwynog Rees (1865-1934) of Gellionnen, and Miss Mary Thomas of Parc y Clochydd, antiquary.

In *County Families* Nicholas writes 'Llanvaughan or Llanvychan, that is, little church, was formerly a chapel belonging to Llanwenog. At present an elegant mansion stands on the site of this chapel, and is now the residence of Admiral Thomas who married Letitia Maria, sister to John Lloyd, Esq, of Mabws . . . After the chapel was pulled down, a house was built in its stead, which became the property of Gwynon Lloyd, third son of Llewelyn Lloyd of Castell Howell, whose descendants continued in possession of it till the year 1759, when it was sold to John Davies Esq. of Llwydsiac, and afterwards bought by Admiral Thomas in the year 1786, who pulled down the old house, and erected the present elegant mansion . . . A colonnade leads to the saloon, on one side of which is the drawing-room and on the other the dining-room, and in which is a handsome double flight of stairs leading to the bedrooms. The offices have all judiciously been placed behind the house, so that though it is spacious it has a very neat and compact appearance. In the kitchen garden, by the side of the gate, is an ancient inscribed stone about nine feet three inches in breadth. The inscription may be read as follows *'Trenactus hic iacit filius Maglogni'* who was buried in all probability, in the chapel called Capel Whyl, as this stone was found in the eastern wall of the ruins of that building, a few feet below the surface of the earth'.

John Davies from Llwydsiac (Lloyd Jack), Ystrad Aeron, bought Llanfechan in 1759 and lived there for 25 years until Admiral John Thomas, the third son of John and Sage, bought Llanfechan in 1786. He was born at Cefncoed, Llanllwni on 26 October 1751. He was baptized privately on 3 November 1751. He became a troublesome boy and a delinquent teenager. His behaviour was such that he was sent away to sea where he displayed such bravery and daring that he quickly came to the attention of his superiors. The prize-money secured from the French made him a rich man and enabled him to buy the ancestral home. He was appointed Admiral of the Red in 1799 and later Admiral of the White. He served in the Royal Navy for 39 years and was severely wounded in several engagements. He was DL and JP for Cardiganshire and Carmarthenshire.

The *Arch. Cam.* records state that 'during the repairs to Llanfechan House, and the alterations of the adjacent grounds, the owner of the mansion has taken special precautions to provide for the safety of the Trenacatus Stone'. Admiral Thomas died at Llanfechan on 26 May 1810, in his 59th year and was buried in the family vault at Llanllwni, Carmarthenshire. After his death the mansion was sold to Captain Delme Seymour Evans, who was the father of Colonel Davies Evans of Highmead. In an advertisement that appeared in *The Cambrian* on 12 September 1812, the house was 'to be let, ready furnished. Llanvaughan House, consists of a large dining-parlour, drawing room, a small breakfast-room or study; a large kitchen, servants' hall, cellars, butler's pantry, house-keeper's room, brewing kitchen etc. 7 bed-chambers, 2 dressing rooms, and garrets; 2 four-stalled stables, saddle-room and coach-house for three carriages; large garden, stocked with fruit trees, shrubberies'.

By 1837 the house was much dilapidated and on 8 June 1841 Miss Louisa Thomas, co-heiress conveyed three-quarters of Gwarallt and Llanfechan to Captain D. S. Davies, and ten years later, Miss A. C. Macdonald, daughter of Maria and Lieutenant MacDonald, conveyed the remainder to him.

An engraving of the house appears in Nicholas's *County Families* in 1872. Francis Jones visited Llanfechan house in the 1960's accompanied by the Misses Jenkins-Lloyd of Parcyronnen, Carmarthenshire. It was by then a complete ruin, only some walls were left standing.

Grid Ref: SN 5163 4547

Refs: Colby Map, 1831; *Dwnn,* i, 40-1; WWHR, i, 29; Blome List, 1673; Meyrick, *Cardiganshire,* 191, 215; Lewis, *TDW;* Nicholas, *County Families* (1872. vol I, p. 137) also 1873. 204; *The Cambrian Journal,* 1857, p. 66; ibid 12th Sept. 1812, advert; *Arch. Cam.* 1866, 196; ibid, 1861, pp. 42-3; ibid, 1878, p. 343; J. G.

Wood, *Principal Rivers of Wales,* 1813, pl. 1, p. 151; NLW, Morgan Richardson Deeds, i, p. 185; Carlisle, *TDW,* 1811; Lloyd Family Records. p. 37, 42. (Peds. p. 29) & Appx. pp. i - iv, ix-xii, & Peds. pp. 15-18; CRO, GGMS I (Tydwal Gloff), fo. 24; Davies, *Hanes Plwyf Llandysul* pp. 198-200, & 226-7 and *Llanwenog* 1939, pp. 65-7, pp. 72-3; PRO List 1714 & 1715; Theakstone and Davies, Lloyd ped., p. 15, Llanfechan; D. H. Haines, *A Guide to Llanybydder*, 1908, p. 21.

LLANFFYNNON-WEN Llangynllo

There is a Ffynnon-wen, a farm east of Bronwydd, south-west Cardiganshire, north-east of Llanyfriog church marked on *Colby's Map of 1831* and on modern OS maps.

Thomas Bryne (Brein), Esq. of Llanffynonwen had a son Philip Bryne who owned Bronwydd. His son George Bryne married Mary, daughter of Lewis David Meredydd of Abernant-bychan. Their daughter Sage, married Thomas ap David of Crynfyrn, MA, vicar of Penbryn and Llangunllo. They had four sons and four daughters, all alive in 1613.

There was also a Hugh Bryne of Llanffynnonwen who had a son, William Bryne who had a son Thomas who married Anne, daughter of Gwilym ap Gwilym of Carmarthen. They had a daughter Jonet who married Rhys Lloyd of Coedtren, Llanbydder, who traced to Rhydderch ap Tewdwr.

Grid Ref: SN 3625 4325

Refs: Colby Map, 1831; *Dwnn*, i, 16, 19, 41; Ld. I, 17.

LLANGOEDMOR(E), Plâs Llangoedmor

Standing at the gateway of the Teifi valley, off the old B4570 Cardigan to Newcastle Emlyn; the home of gentry families for over four centuries.

In 1550 the Plâs was the seat of Rhys Lloyd, whose grand-daughter, Catherine married John Bryune later of Bronwydd, and it was owned by his descendants until Jacobean times when it passed to the possession of the Lloyds of Mabws and Ystrad Teilo.

In 1728, the property, consisting of Tir y Place and other farms and two mills in Llangoedmore parish, was mortgaged to Catherine Mansell, widow, and in 1738 Richard Lloyd of Mabws directed that they be assigned to Sir

Edward Mansell, Bt., of Trimsaran, for the use of Catherine Mansell's devisees. In 1757 the mortgage was assigned to Richard Knight of Ludlow, Esq. and on 10 October 1758 the properties specified in the mortgage were sold for £2,500 to John Lloyd. He was of Ffosybleiddiaid, younger son of John Lloyd (1690-1748) by Mary Philipps of Pentyparc (1701-1781). John held the post of Clerk of the Check at HM Dockyard, Plymouth, Devon.

At the time of the sale Richard Lloyd of London wrote a letter to Thomas Johnes Esq. (Dolaucothi) 'As to the Llangoedmore Estate I leave it to you to close with the present offers or not . . . the capital tenement goes but for £21 per annum, yet its worth was £30 and there is withal a good house fit for any gent. of middling fortune to live in, with many conveniences and most excellent outhouses. The subsisting lease may be an objection, but there but one life now in being which may, I suppose be bought in . . . Mr. Owen of Rhiwsaeson tenanted Llangoedmor yet seldom at it'.

During the years 1758-60 John Lloyd greatly improved and enlarged the old Elizabethan house, retaining one of its original wings. An interesting feature of the interior decorations was the panelling placed in the dining-room and a carved mantelpiece said to have been brought on horseback from London. Both were removed towards the middle of the present century. On 20 February 1786 John Lloyd sold 'Tir Place with adjoining fields, Tir Phillip Coedmore and a meadow called Park Issa Tyr Lloyd dan yr eglwys, all of which are now called Plâs Llangoedmor' for £1,600 to 'David Edward Lewis Lloyd, squire of Dolhaidd near Newcastle Emlyn', who lived there for some years. John Lloyd, JP died at Pound near Tavistock, Devon in 1806, aged 90.

David Lloyd later mortgaged the property to Mary Eliza Lawrence of Cardigan for £1000, which he redeemed in 1796. Shortly afterwards it changed hands again. On 3 June 1801 David sold Plâs Llangoedmor to the Rev. Benjamin Millingchamp for £3,500 and the furniture for a further £200. Up to this time the Plâs had always been held by families surnamed Lloyd. David Lloyd had a receipt from the Rev. Millingchamp, on the same day, for £200 'for all goods and furniture in the mansion and outhouses of Llangoedmore Place (excepting goods locked up in a garret in the new part of the said mansion house and all books and a bookcase)'.

Born in Cardigan, the Rev. Mr. Benjamin Millingchamp was a distinguished scholar. He was the son of Joseph Millingchamp, collector and Customs Officer of Cardigan and Anne Gambold. Educated at Oxford, Benjamin Millingchamp took Holy Orders and became a naval chaplain. He married Sarah Rawlinson of Grantham (she died in 1869, aged 95) and from 1779 he served on Admiral Hughes's flagship *The Superb* in Indian seas and took part in several actions. In 1782 he was appointed chaplain of Fort St. George, Madras, where he served and made his fortune under the East India Company until his return to Britain in 1797. He was Rural Dean of Cemaes, Prebendary of St. David's Cathedral, became a Doctor of Divinity of Oxford in 1821 and was appointed Archdeacon of Carmarthen in 1825. He was a Persian scholar and brought to Plâs Llangoedmor a valuable collection of Persian manuscripts later presented to the National Library of Wales by H. M. Vaughan. He made his will on 17 August 1828, died on 6 January 1829 and his will was proved on 30 December 1830. He was buried at Llangoedmor.

The property passed to his daughter and heiress, Sarah Millingchamp, who married Colonel Herbert Vaughan of Brynog, formerly of the Perthshire Light Infantry and grandson of Edward Vaughan who was the son of Dorothy, Viscountess Lisburne and David Lloyd, the agent of Trawsgoed estate.

Herbert and Sarah Vaughan had four children. The eldest son, Herbert, died of wounds received in the Crimea in 1855. Emily Sarah married Thomas Harman Benchley of Glaneirw, had three children and died in 1926 in her 99th year. Edward Percival died of cholera in Bombay in 1864 and John Vaughan (1830-1881), who married Julia Ann, daughter of Thomas Charles Morris of Bryn Myrddin and Cwm, Llansteffan and who remained at Llangoedmor. John and Julia Ann, in turn, had five children. Herbert Millingchamp (1870-1948), John Percival, who died in India in 1906, Captain Edward Vaughan of Westward Ho! who died in 1943, Julian, who lived at Maesgwyn, near Llanboidy, and finally, Charles. Herbert Millingchamp Vaughan, the last of the Vaughans to live at Plâs Llangoedmor. He was educated at Clifton College and Keble, Oxford, which he loathed and as a young man spent his winters in Italy and produced biographies, books on art, science fiction and novels.

During the years 1830-36 great improvements were made to the mansion. An old wing was demolished and a fine façade with pillared entrance was added to the western end.

H. M. Vaughan, who was High Sheriff of Cardiganshire in 1916, and the author of *South Wales Squires* has left a vivid and informative account of life in the mansion in Victorian times. '. . . The present house has a good façade, built early in 1830, in the reign of William IV; whilst the portion behind dates chiefly from the middle of the eighteenth century. From the secluded rose garden on the south side you can easily tell by the quoining where the older and newer portions join. There was formerly standing a much older wing of the house, low and gabled, jutting out from the main building to the west, which appears in old views of Llangoedmor. This was demolished by my grandfather some ninety years ago [c. 1836] when he added the present western front. It now has three reception rooms, the main feature being the drawing-room furnished by W. Owen of Haverfordwest in the reign of William IV. The dining-room was long and panelled with a fine mantelpiece reputed to have been brought by horseback in the mid-eighteenth century. '

A catalogue at the Carmarthenshire Record Office details a three day 'Antique Furniture Sale' to be held on instructions of H. M. Vaughan on 18-20 March 1924. For sale was furniture, china, glassware, silver and plated ware, old paintings and paintings on silk, and many books. Herbert Millingchamp Vaughan settled at Tenby. The house had been purchased by David Berrington Griffiths Davies, JP of Castle Green, Cardigan and later of Parc-y-gors. It was sold after the Second World War to two brothers named Birt. The Birts then sold to Mrs. Cuff who was herself selling it when Frances Jones visited Plâs Llangoedmor on 31 August 1979. He writes, 'The house was in first-class condition and was well-maintained. The old fireplace, that had been placed in the dining room in the eighteenth century, had been removed about thirty years ago and replaced by a horrid kind of brickwork, wholly out of keeping. I was told that the old fireplace is now in the National Museum of Wales in Cardiff, which I will see when I go there next month. I was told that Berrington Davies had sold it, sometime after World War I to two brothers called Birt and it is they who removed the fireplace. The cellars are large and go under all the house. They are arched and excellently preserved and wholly free from damp. The present facade with porch and a pediment at roof height was made in the 1830's. There are eight chimneys'.

In July 1979 the property was described as an impressive house standing in mature, well-established grounds of eight acres or thereabouts. The house had three fine reception rooms, drawing room, dining room, study, small sitting room, cloakroom, two kitchens, sculleries, utility room, nine bedrooms, four bathrooms and five second floor bedrooms.

In 1980 the Plâs and 8 acres of grounds were bought by Neville George and his wife, Jane (née Trinder), from Mrs. Cuff who ran a famous pony stud in Llangoedmor. The Georges, who are from a prominent Pembrokeshire family, have two children – James, an accountant and Justin, a conservationist. Neville, who is the kinsman of David George of Dyffryn Farm, Llangoedmor, farms 300 acres at Denant near Haverfordwest. On their first night at Llangoedmor, with renovations as yet incomplete, the Georges were disturbed by an apparition of an elderly lady, dressed in an elegant, sweeping gown, who provided some entertainment by dancing around the bedroom. She made a repeat appearance some time later. The house has been restored and enjoys glorious views of the Teifi and the Pembrokeshire hills beyond.

Grid Ref: SN 1970 4594

Refs: Colby Map, 1831; Lewis, *TDW; Family History* by H. M. Vaughan in WWHR, vi, pp. 109-111; H. M. Vaughan, *South Wales Squires,* 1926, pp. 7-19, illust. of house; H. Lloyd-Johnes, The Lesser Country Houses of Cardiganshire, *Ceredigion,* 1955, pp. 241-3; NLW, Dolau Cothi Letters; Burke, *L.G.* 1952; *Dwnn,* i, 19; NLW, Morgan Richardson Deeds, ii, 302, 304; CRO, sc. 514; John Francis Estate Agents particulars; Francis Jones, *Lloyds of Plas Llangoedmor;* Ex. Info. J. George.

LLANGYBI, Bettus Bledrws

Also known as Llangybi y Ty Dan y Forest. It was probably a large old house in the village, the property of the Lloyd family who owned Dany-forest in the same parish. There is a possibility that this is the same house. Griffith Lloyd's pedigree (traced to Gwaethfoed) was recorded by the herald Dwnn in 1613. David of Llangybi ap Llewelyn ap David Fychan had a son, David Llwyd of Llangybi who had a son Griffith. Griffith's son, Mathew Griffith moved across the border to Pembrokeshire and the other son David Griffith married Lleucu, daughter of Owen William. Their son was the Rev. Griffith David, clerk, who married the daughter of Jenkin William Bowen of Pencarreg. They had a daughter Elizabeth, their heiress, and she married David Jones of Betws, ap John David of Penwernhir by Strata Florida. By 1636 Thomas Griffith was living at Llangybi. Meyrick notes that the property was later owned by Captain Powell of Nanteos.

Grid Ref: SN 6087 5318

Refs: Colby Map, 1831; *Dwnn,* i, 25, 27; CRO, GGMS III (Gwaethfoed), fo. 36; NLW, Cwrtmawr Deeds No. 95, 1185,147, 1336. No. 8.

LLANGWYRYDDON, see RHANDIR

LLANINA, Llanina

Situated close to the shore a mile north of New Quay, near the small chapel of St. Ina which belongs to the mother church of Llanarth. Formerly the home of the Musgrave, Gwyn, Jones, Longcroft and Lloyd families. The church at St. Ina was the last in Wales to fall to the Reformation. H. Lloyd-Jones tells us in his article *The Lesser County Houses of Cardiganshire*: 'An excellent example of the smaller Welsh country house. Almost untouched, it has been the home of the smaller squirearchy since its construction in the latter half of the 17th century. It is L-shaped, and very small, with a long panelled dining room. A small square parlour leads out of this, and a large kitchen makes up the ground floor. The kitchen contains in situ a clock spit which appears in working order. The upper floors contain a panelled bedroom over the parlour and contains some interesting closets and cupboards which appear in unexpected places. The staircase is broad and handsome, and in period. There is also a charming olde world walled garden'.

In the one acre walled garden is a magnificent mulberry tree, vine grafted, estimated to be over 1,000 years old and 200 lb. of fruit is harvested from it annually. It is believed that Llanina was the site of a monastic foundation and traces of medieval cells can be found in the grounds. The leaves of the mulberry were fed to silkworms for the production of vestments for the community. The small chapel close to the house, used as a studio by Augustus John during the 1930's, was a Mass Centre for pilgrims on their way to St. David's.

H. M. Vaughan in *The South Wales Squires* elaborates on the house 'One of the few examples of the old untouched Welsh Squires's home that I know of, and that is still inhabited is Llanina . . . The house is very small, and its main feature consists of a long low panelled dining-room which runs the whole length of the house . . . The only other reception room at Llanina is a small square parlour, opening from the dining room . . . Yet, although so meagre according to our modern standard, there is a good deal of space in this quaint old mansion of the Longcrofts, who succeeded an older family of Jones of Llanina. Over the parlour is the chief guest room, which has a curious ghost story attached to it where at certain times a lady's white hand, severed and bleeding at the wrist, is said to hover over the bed to the discomfiture of its occupant'.

Ernestus Musgrave, an early owner of Llanina, from a Yorkshire Catholic family, married Deborah Gwyn of Moel Ifor, Llanrhystud, and their eldest son Peregrine, was born at Llanina in 1644. Meyrick tells us that 'Llanina once formed part of the Moelifor family possessions, but Daniel Gwyn left it by will from his own brother John Gwyn, to his half-brother Edward Jones of Llanina, by which the Jones's became possessors of the Llanina estate. Some suspicions having arisen as to the manner the will was obtained, and possibly the right of this bequest, the question was tried in the reign of Charles II and the Gwyns of Moel Ivor lost the cause by the supposed treachery of their own attorney'. Lloyd-Johnes continues 'When Daniel Gwyn was dying, without issue, he left Llanina estate to his half-brother Edward Jones, descended from Cadwgan Grach of Carrog. Daniel's will was contested by the Gwyn family, but Edward Jones remained in possession and became High Sheriff in 1679'. He was the son of Richard Jones and the grandson of Edward Jones of Nanteos and his wife Margaret. He had a son, also Edward Jones, JP in 1705 and High Sheriff in 1729, who married a Margaret . . . and they had four children: Phillip Jones who succeeded to the estate, Edward Jones, who died before 1776, Grace, who was the executrix of her mother, who married David Lloyd Newnam 'her present husband' and Mary, who pre-deceased her mother. The *Coedmore Deeds* tell us that Margaret Jones's will dated 22 October 1776 specified: 'To my daughter-in-law Catherine Jones of Trewern, Pembrokeshire, widow, and my son Phillip Jones, and my three grandchildren, £200 to be shared between them, charged on the estate of my late husband Edward Jones by virtue of deed made on 26 May 1725 between said Edward Jones and Henry Price of county borough of Carmarthen, gent., To my dear grandson Edward Warren

Jones £500. To my daughter-in-law Catherine Jones and her three children, Edward, Jane and Catherine, 20 guineas between them. To my daughter Grace Newnam, my share of the personal estate of my late daughter Mary Jones. To the poor of the parish of Llanina, Llanarth and Llanllwchaiarn, £10 between them. To the said Grace Newnam all my other personal estate for her alone without her present husband David Lloyd Newnam notwithstanding her coverture, and I nominate her sole executrix: my good friends James Lloyd of Mabus and John Davies, esquires, to help her'. Grace Newnam was also the executrix of her husband's will, dated 18 October 1777; he had bequeathed all to her. The will was proved on 3 June 1777 by the executrix.

Phillip Jones of Llanina married Catherine Warren, heiress to Trewern, Pembrokeshire. Her will was proved in 1793 and they had three children: Edward Warren Jones, Jane and Catherine, all alive in 1776. Edward Warren Jones succeeded to his father's estates and was High Sheriff in 1796. From his father who descended from the Joneses of Nanteos, he had inherited the estate of Llanina, and from his mother Catherine Warren, co-heiress of the Warrens of Trewern and Longridge he inherited further valuable properties in Pembrokeshire. He was also a kinsman of the Lloyds, for his great-grandmother was Elinor daughter of John Lloyd of Cilgwyn by Dorothy Vaughan his wife. He died in 1807 and his heiress, Elizabeth, married Captain Edward Longcroft RN. Tradition has it that Captain Longcroft was the excise officer for these parts, and met his wife during his anti-smuggling duties.

The Longcrofts were an interesting family, seated at Willford in Wiltshire since the days of Elizabeth. One of them, the Revd. Robert Longcroft, vicar of St. Mary Portsea, was chaplain in ordinary to King William III. His grandson, Robert Longcroft married the wealthy Elizabeth Bearcroft of Carshalton, Surrey, and their eldest son Edward entered the Royal Navy. Edward Longcroft was First-Lieutenant of the *Formidable* in the action of 12 April 1782, served as Flag-Lieutenant to Admiral Rodney, and attained the rank of post captain. He married Elizabeth Baylis at Kingston, Jamaica,

in 1782, and had five children by her.

How and why Captain Longcroft of Havant Hall in Hampshire, came to Llanina is not known, but he was living there before 1807, with his wife Elizabeth and their three children, Edward Henry, Charles Richard, and Charlotte, and was on terms of close friendship with Mr. Jones. Captain Longcroft died on 16 August 1812, aged 62, and his wife on 23 February 1819, aged 49, and both were buried at Llanina.

The *Coedmore Deeds* tell us that the terms of Edward Warren Jones's will, dated 19 Aug. 1807 specified, 'To Edward Longcroft, son of Edward Longcroft of Llanina, Esq, and John Brooks of Noyadd, Esq. all my realty in parish Llanarth, Llanina, Llanllwchaiarn, Cidplwyth, in Co. Cards; Llechryd on Cards; Llanfihangel Yaroth (ar Arth), Llanllwyny, Llanbyther, Trelech ar Bettws, in Co. Carmarthenshire; Nevern, Cil-gwyn, Llawhaden, and Bletherston, in Co. Pembrokeshire: on trust to raise and pay £200 p.a. to my sister Jane Margaret Jones, spr., £200 p.a. to my sister Catherine Mathias; £200 p.a. to Elizabeth wife of Edward Longcroft of Llanina, £20 p.a. to my natural daughter Mary Jones alias James. A moiety of the realty to my god-daughter Charlotte Longcroft, daughter of the said Edward and Elizabeth Longcroft, with remainder to the use of Thomas Williams of Haverfordwest Esq. and Samuel Harries of Cryglas, Esq. during the life of the said Charlotte, in trust to preserve the contingent uses, then to Charlotte's issue in tail male and female, and in default to the uses of my god-son Charles Richard Longcroft, son of said Edward and Elizabeth Longcroft, and his heirs with remainders over. The other moiety to my said god-son Charles Richard Longcroft, with remainder. My personalty to be given equally between Charlotte and Charles Richard Longcroft. Edward Longcroft and David Hughes to be joint executors'. A codicil dated 29 November 1823 adds 'To Hannah Evan, otherwise Beynon, in Llanina parish, single woman, £200, and to her natural daughter Hannah Evan otherwise Jones £400 when she becomes 18, the interest thereof towards her maintenance till she becomes 18'. A further codicil dated 24 August 1824 confirms the previous codicil and the '£400 to Hannah Jones my natural or reputed daughter; also confirms the like sum of £400 to my natural daughter Jane Jones otherwise Evan (daughter of Hannah Evan otherwise Beynon) when 18'. Hannah Jones, the natural daughter of Edward Warren Jones was married on 26 March 1839 at St. Mary's church, Cardigan, to John Rowlands of Cardigan.

Shipwrights in New Quay lived in tied cottages owned by the Longcrofts at Cei Bach and Llanina. When threatened with eviction if they did not vote Tory at the 1832 election, they built themselves some cottages at Hengell known as the Arba.

Edward Warren Jones's godson Charles Richard Longcroft succeeded to Llanina and was High Sheriff in 1834. He presented a silver cup and paten to Llanina church in June 1875 to which a flagon was added in 1884. In 1873 his son C. K. Longcroft lived at Llanina. The *Landowners Return* of that year tells us that Llanina was a substantial estate of 2,709 acres, with a rental of £1,158 p.a.

Llanina was sold between the Wars and an auction was held at New Quay in 1925 when the household effects of Air Commodore Longcroft were sold. In 1939, Baron Howard de Walden bought Llanina from Col. Whittaker and lived there with his family for the duration of the war. A guest in the loft above the coach-house in the summer of 1945 was Dylan Thomas, whose escapades in New Quay are not always fondly remembered. Baron Howard de Walden sold Llanina to Col. J. J. Davies and his wife Betty in 1951. In 1967 the property was sold to Holimarine. Llanina deteriorated and a demolition order was served by the Council. All seemed hopeless until Mr. James Maurice, a London banker, persuaded the authorities to place a compulsory purchase on the property and to sell Llanina to him. Fortunately his offer was accepted and Mr. Maurice, and his family moved to Llanina. Mr. Maurice has rebuilt the ruins. Francis Jones visited the property in 1968.

Grid Ref: SN 4050 5978

Refs: 'The Musgraves of Llanina', WWHR iv, 1914, 193-200; Meyrick, *Cardiganshire*, 1810 edn., 1907, p. 236; D. J. Davies, 'Llanina', 38-40. TCAS; H. Lloyd Johnes 'The Lesser Country Houses of Cardiganshire', *Ceredigion,* 1955 & 3, 1956-9, pp. 89-90; H. M. Vaughan, *South Wales Squires,* 1926, 65-7; *Arch. Cam.,* 1959, p. 339; ibid, 1863, p. 264; ibid, 1880 p. 216; CRO, GGMS I (Elystan Glodwydd), fo. 30; PRO List; G. S. Cards. 31 Charles II, calumptus pedigrees; CRO, GGMS II (Adv. Cardiganshire), fo. 189, Landowners Return, 1873; Francis Green MS., vol. 23, p. 125; Haverfordwest Public Library; CRO, Coedmor Deeds (Box 3); *Ceredigion,* vii, No. 3/4. (1974/75) pp. 284-5; Francis Jones, *Historic Houses of Pembrokeshire and their Families,* p. 35, 1996 (Brawdy Books); Mr. Maurice, Llanina.

LLANIO-FAWR, Llanddewibreifi

Marked on *Colby's Map of 1831* and on modern OS maps as near Pont Llanio in the north-west corner of the parish and east of Sarn Helen, the old Roman road.

The earliest reference to this property is to Griffith Coch, the natural son of Ieuan (who traced to Gwyddno), brother to John of Parc Rhydderch, and Griffith Lloyd of Cellau. Griffith's son, John Griffith, married Margaret Lloyd, daughter of David Lloyd of Crynfryn. They had two sons: Daniel Jones of Llanio Fawr, and Richard Jones of Lletherod (Lledrod) who married Gwenllian, daughter of Morgan ap Rees ap Oliver of Ffosybleiddiaid. Daniel Jones succeeded to Llaniofawr, and was alive and married by 1703. He was married twice.

His first wife was Elenor Lloyd, daughter of David Lloyd (to Tydwal) of Brynele by Elenor daughter of Griffith Lloyd of Gwernmacwydd. His second wife Joan, was the daughter of Thomas ap David Lloyd ap Morgan of Gwastod Gwrda. By his first marriage he had three sons; Thomas Jones, JP, of Llanio, alive in 1698, who succeeded to the home, John Jones, alive in 1703, and David Jones who married a daughter of Henry Jones of Abermangoed.

Thomas Jones married Gwenllian Davies, daughter of Thomas Davies of Faedre-fach, by Mary Lloyd, daughter and co-heiress of John Lloyd of Faerdre, Llandysul, by Margaret Herbert, daughter of Morgan Herbert of Hafod Uchdryd. Thomas Jones was High Sheriff in 1739-40 and died whilst in office. He had two sons, David and Walter Jones, gent, owner and occupier of Llanio Fawr in 1760. Walter married Lettice, daughter of Walter Jones of Nantremenyn, who was born in 1715 and who died in 1798, aged 83. They had two sons. The elder, Thomas Jones died on 5 December 1805 in his 57th year. He had married Anne Margaretta Rogers of the parish of Nancwnlle who died 17 October 1828 in her 67th year. The younger son was Daniel Jones, clerk, Rector of Ruckinge, Kent who died on 26 July 1822, aged 72.

Thomas and Anne Jones had two sons, Walter Jones, elder son of Llanio-fawr, and Daniel Jones younger son who died 8 April 1829, aged 30. Walter Jones, a surgeon, succeeded to the estate and married Elinor . . . They both died at a relatively early age, Elinor on 24 April 1843, aged 43 and Walter on Christmas Eve 1850, aged 49. A memorial inscription on a slate tablet was erected in the chancel of Llanddewibrefi church.

The estate then descended in unbroken line until the death of Samuel Evans Jones aged 70 in 1907. The *Landowners Return of 1873* lists Llanio-fawr as an estate of 728 acres, with a rental of £ 110 p.a. A brass tablet in the chancel of Llanddewibrefi reads, 'In Affectionate Rememberance of Samuel Evans Jones, the Last of the Jones's of Llanio, Cardiganshire, who died March 8 1907 aged 70 years. He lived in peace and died in hope'. He was succeeded by his nephew Mr. D. D. Evans, a founder member of the Cardiganshire Antiquarian Society, who died in 1966 aged 89 years. Until the early 1950's Mr. Evans was the King's Royal Keeper, whose duty it was to report illegal encroachments in the area. One of his privileges was the right to shoot in the area covered by the Crown's rights without having to buy a licence.

In 1978 Francis Jones wrote 'Mr. D. D. Evans of Caer Llanio, owner of Llanio Fawr, has a son who now lives at the old home. He tells me that there is a stone in the wall of the house inscribed 1663, and that apart from two bow windows, the old house is unchanged'.

Grid Ref: SN 6438 5718.

Refs: WWHR, i, 19; Francis Jones Archives; WWHR, iii, 114; Colby Map, 1831; CRO, GGMS III (Gwaethfoed), & CRO, GGMS I (Tedwr) ex. inf. E. D. Jones (NLW); H. Moll, *Description of Wales,* 1740, p. 264; Landowners Return, 1873; *Ceredigion*, iii (1958) p. 243.

LLANLLYR, Llanfihangel Ystrad

Located south of Talsarn and the Aeron adjacent to the B4337 road towards Temple Bar. Leland tells us, in his *Itinerary*, that 'Llanllyr was a nunnery of White Nunnes in Cardiganshire apon the brook of Aeron. It was a celle of Stratflere, and stood from Stratflere X miles in the by-way to Cairdigan. The village hard by it is caullid Talesarne Greene'. Irish sources relate that nuns came to Llanllyr as novices from Ireland. In *Llanllyr, 1180-1980,* by J. Hext Lewes, published in *Ceredigion,* an account is given of its history. 'About 1180 a priory of Cistercian nuns was founded at Llanllyr by the Lord Rhys and at the Dissolution it passed to the Crown, who leased it, in 1537, to Gruffydd ap Henry ap Ieuan ap Philip ap Rhydderch of Glyn Aeron, for 21 years. The lessee's tenant at Llanllyr was Griffith ap Henry ap Phillip ap Rhydderch of Lloyd Jack ap Ieuan Lloyd of Glynaeron (Llangeitho). A new lease was granted in 1553 to William Sackville one of the Servers of the Queen's Board, and John Dudley, both of Dorking'.

Gruffydd's daughter and co-heiress, Siwan, married Hugh Llewelyn Lloyd, High Sheriff in 1567, 3rd son of Llewelyn Lloyd of Castell Hywel. He died in 1577 and his IPM taken on

24 December 1577 says that he died 'seized of the site of the late monastery of Llanllyr'.

Morgan Lloyd of Llanllyr (1544-1604), married Elizabeth, daughter and heiress of Lewis ap Henry ap Gwilym ap John ap Llewelyn Lloyd, descended from Gwyddno Garanhir. He was High Sheriff in 1576, 1585, 1594 and 1599 and a brother to Griffith Lloyd, second Principal of Jesus College, Oxford (1572-86), and Regnus Professor of Civil Law at Oxford. Lewys Dwnn recorded his pedigree. Morgan died on 6 October 1604 and in his will dated 4 April 1604 he left an annuity of £6.13.4 to each of his sons Griffith, John and Francis for their lives. The IPM of Morgan Lloyd taken at Talysarn on 25 September 1605 states 'that he was seized of in demesne as of fee: Site of the late monastery of Llanllyr; also 1 messuage, 1 mill, 100a. arable, 10a. meadow, and 40a. pasture in Llanllyr, worth £3.6.8. p.a., 1 messuage, 30a. arable, 10a. meadow, 10a. pasture, in Ciliau Aeron, worth 3/4d. 11 messuages, 340a. arable, 70a. meadow, 100a. pasture in Ystrad, worth 30/-. 4 messuages, 40a. arable, 30a. meadow, 20a. pasture, in Dehewid, worth 10/-. 1 messuage, 10a. arable, 5a. meadow, 5a. pasture in Llanwnen, worth 2/-. 17 messuages, 620a. arable, 40a. meadow, 110a. pasture in Trefilan, worth 24/-. 3 messuages, 60a. arable, 40a. meadow in Llanbadarn Trefeglwys, worth 10/-. An island called 'the Ilande of Cardigan,' containing 40a. arable, worth 6/8. 1 messuage, 20 a. arable 10a. meadow, 20a. pasture, in Llanarth 16d. 1 messuage, 20a. arable, 10a. meadow, 20a. pasture in Nantgwnlle, 2/-. 2 messuages, 40a. arable, 10a. meadow, 10a. pasture in Cilcennin, 2/-. 1 messuage, 1a. arable, 3a. meadow, 3a. pasture in Llanbeder, 3/4d. 1 water corn mill in Llanbeder, 10/-, a total of 1,927 acres.'

In 1604 the Llanllyr estate rental value was £8.11.4 per annum. In 1613 Elizabeth Lloyd was still living at Llanllyr and in 1615 was holding one-third of her husband's estate in dower, in addition to holding two-thirds of the family estate. She also held for life 10 messuages in the parishes of Abergwili, Llanegwad and Llangathen, Carmarthenshire worth 20/-. Their son, Thomas Lloyd, held two thirds of the estate on his mother's death and considerable acreage elsewhere (some 960 acres). Thomas Lloyd was married twice; firstly to Jane of Llanarth and secondly to Lettice Pryse, the daughter of Sir John Pryse of Gogerddan. They had a son and heir, John,(1607-13) who died on 21 August 1613. Thomas's daughter, Bridget, became his sole heiress at the age of 14 years 9 months. She married the 2nd Earl of Carbery who became owner, *iure uxoris* when Bridget died childless. The Earl exchanged Llanllyr with David Parry of St. Dogmael's for lands in Llangeler and Penbryn and a sum of money. Parry died in debt, about 1642. His will was proved by PCC in the same year, while his heirs maintained that he died intestate but that, 'rude notes were set on foot' by Sir John Lewes and executors after his death 'purporting to be notes for making his will'. In 1648 his trustees sold the capital messuage called Llanllyr and other lands to Thomas Lloyd of Wernfeilig who was also the tenant of Llanllyr, on his accepting the debts of £2,600. Thomas Lloyd married Lettice Pryse, daughter of John Pryse of Glanfrêd and they had three daughters; Bridget who married Thomas Lloyd of Berllandywyll, Elizabeth who married John Lloyd of Ffosybleiddiaid, and Lettice, who married Edward Carew of Rochester. Thomas's will, dated 25 June 1649, left Llanllyr to his brother William, with legacies to his three daughters To his widow, Lettice, he left six named rooms in the house and two fields during widowhood. She married again to a Bowen of Crugbychan, and took her daughters to live there.

When William Lloyd succeeded to the estate of Llanllyr it caused great trouble in the family as his younger brother, Morgan Lloyd of Greengrove, challenged William's claim to Llanllyr alleging that William had, 'got into his hands all the deeds, evidences and writings of Thomas Lloyd after his death, his daughters being then very young', and that William, when his brother Thomas bought Llanllyr for £2,800 'could not have been a joint purchaser of Llanllyr because at that time he had no visible estate whereby he could possibly purchase so great a property'. William Lloyd had, in fact, become heavily involved financially, as the *Llanllyr Deeds* records a transaction on 4 July 1648 between: 'Sir John Parry of Abernant-bychan, John Parry of Dolyfonddu, Mont., gt., and Thomas Parry of

St. Dogmaels, gt., release to Thomas Lloyd, Esq. and William Lloyd, gt., both of Llanllyr, the capital messuage called Llanlire, and Melin Llanllire and messuages in the parishes of Ystrad, Dihewyd, and Trevilan, and the tolls of the fair of Tallyesarne, and two messuages in Llanbadan Trefeglwys, being the estate of the late David Parry of Noyadd, Esq. dec.'

In 1656 William Lloyd mortgaged the Llanllyr estate for £800 to William Sumner of Great Pelicott, Buckinghamshire, gent., High Sheriff in 1669. However, less than one month later issued a defeasance of the above land. In 1660-1, William Lloyd of Llanllyr, brother and heir to Thomas Lloyd of same, Esq., dec., mortgaged lands, but *not* the capital messuage of Llanllyr, to said William Sumner. He mortgaged other lands to James Lewis of Coedmor then on 17 September 1662, the said William Lloyd mortgaged the same lands to Henry Sumner and Thomas Harborne, gent., of Buckinghamshire. William and his son, Henry, were taxed for 6 hearths in 1672.

When William Lloyd died in 1688, Sumner foreclosed and put his son, Henry Sumner, and a bailiff at Llanllyr. Bridget Lloyd, the daughter of Sir Walter Lloyd of Llanfair, Clydogau (claiming dowry as William Lloyd's widow), came back at the head of a crowd of friends, before the case was heard in Chancery. The Lloyds stormed the house, impounded Sumner's cattle, beat his servants, carried away his hay and 'started to pull the house down and did not desist until Henry Sumner fled in terror'.

In 1696 Llanllyr was described as a decayed house in the hands of a tenant, but remained in the ownership of Sumner and his heirs. On 10 June 1720 it was sold by Henry Sumner to John Lewes, (1680-1742), who was married to Hester Beynon of Castell Gorfod. John was a merchant, Mayor of Carmarthen in 1724 and of Cardigan in 1731 and 1736, and High Sheriff of Cardiganshire in 1730. He found the old house let for £13 p.a. to Evan Lewis, a pious, nonconformist minister who had come there from Cilgwyn, Llangybi. John was the eldest son of David Lewes, second son of the Rev. John Lewes of Llysnewydd (1616-63).

John Lewes (1711-83) of Llanllyr, and of Llysnewydd after his cousin's death, was High Sheriff of Cardiganshire in 1752, and Mayor of Cardigan in 1768. He married Rebecca Price of Dyffryn (1719-82). William Lewes, his cousin of Llysnewydd, married Joan Lloyd of Bronwydd and died in 1828 without issue. John Lewes, (1793-1860), the third son of John, and a Captain in the 23rd Light Dragoons, fought at Waterloo. He married Mary Anne Lloyd (1802-42), daughter of John Vaughan Lloyd of Brynog and was given Llanllyr as his marriage portion and went to live there.

He was followed by his son, another John, (1829-1900) was Lt.-Col. of The Buffs, which he formed in 1847. He fought in the Crimea and planted the British flag on the Redan Tower during the Crimean War and was henceforth known as 'Redan Lewes'. He married Mary Jane Griffiths of Llwyndyrys in 1858 and with her money bought his father out of Llanllyr. In 1873, the estate was 749 acres, with an annual rental of £457.

It was a year later that Llanllyr was enlarged to accommodate the nine children of John and Mary. The original house was pulled down in 1859. The stones of the old house were used to build the new one and the bricks for the top storey at the front of the new house were actually baked in the meadows alongside the claypit.

J. Hext Lewes tell us that the new house was 'on the other side of the farmyard . . . its foundations and cobbled yard can still be seen'. The top storey at the back of the house was added in 1874. One small building of the old house remained in 'use as a carpenter's shop' till about 1880. During the earlier demolition of the old Llanllyr, which was the site of chapel older than the medieval nunnery, part of a squared pillar-stone with incised crosses and an inscription in Latin was discovered. It reads:

TESQUITUS DITOC/QUA
DOMNUACO/LLO FILIUS ASA/ITGEN
DEDI (T),

'The sacred place of Ditoc, Domnuacollon, son of Asaitgen or Ollon, son of Asaitgen gave to Domnuac . . .'.

The stone records the donation of land to the church. It stands in the garden south-west of the house. In a letter, written in 1896, Colonel Lewes wrote: 'I remember part of the old house at Llanllyr and I have always understood that the stone in question was found in the old building, with the other part of it, which unfortunately was broken up. This main building was used to build the present house.'

Col. John Lewes and Mary were followed at Llanllyr by his son, another John (1860-1931) who married Louisa Hext from Cornwall in 1890. The Hext family were originally from Somerset. In 1900 the Llanllyr estate, extended by purchases and legacies, had grown to 1,300 acres, half of which was sold to meet death duties and the redemption of a mortgage. When Col. John Lewes died in 1931, his widow, Louisa lived at Llanllyr until 1947 when she handed the estate over to her son, Capt. John Hext Lewes, OBE, RN, FRAgS, Lord-Lieutenant of Cardiganshire (1956-74) and Dyfed (1974-8). He consolidated the estate and converted 200 acres of marsh bog into pasture. He married Nesta Cecil, daughter of Capt. Fitzroy Talbot and had a son, John, now of Llansawel, and two daughters, Loveday (a Cornish name), and Gwenllian, now of Llanfair.

Loveday Elizabeth Talbot Hext Lewes, now at Llanllyr, married Robert Gee, a London lawyer and businessman. Together they have restored and modernised the house at Llanllyr. They have three children; Matthew, Patrick and Emma, who is married to Nicholas Barran. Matthew, the eldest son, graduated in Agriculture from the University of Reading and is married to Carolyn Angela (née Edwards) of Talsarn. They have two sons, George Cooper Alun John Lewes and Joshua Llyr Robert Price Lewes. Matthew runs the farm and 100 of the 400 acres are given over to growing organic vegetables.

Grid Ref: SN 5435 5596

Refs: Meyrick, *Cardiganshire*, 1810, p. 238; NLW, Griffith Owen List (iv); *Dwnn*, ii, 25; Llwyd, *Parochalia,* III, 80; 'Llanllyr, 1180-1980,' J. Hext Lewis, *Ceredigion,* 1971, pp. 341-9; Landowners Return, 1873; NLW Llanllyr Deeds, Nos. 3, 4 & 5; *Arch. Cam.* 1896, p. 123; Lloyd Family Records, pp. 24 & 26; John Leland, *The Itinerary in Wales,* (1906), p. 51. Ex. Info. The Gee family, Llanllyr.

LLANWENOG, Llanwenog

Location of this mansion is unknown. In an Ode to Dafydd ap Thomas Fychan of Llanwenog in Gwynionydd, descended from Cadifor ap Dinawal and Gwaethfoed he is described as 'Dafydd gadben Llanwenog'.

Refs: LGC II, 290

LLECHWEDD DERI, Llanwnnen

Marked on *Colby's Map of 1831* and on modern OS maps as two farms -uchaf and -isaf, about half a mile north-west of Llanwnnen village, south-west of Cribyn, on the side of a hill, on the banks of a small stream running to the Granell. Llechwedd Deri Isaf is on the site of the old mansion. The first known occupier was David Evans, descended from David ap Ieuan who was descended from Cadifor ap Dinawal. Ieuan Coch married the heiress of Rhys ap Griffith of Llechwedd Deri Uchaf. His son, also Ieuan of Dolaugwyrddion married Margaret Lloyd, daughter of John Lloyd Jenkins, the second son of Jenkin Lloyd David of Gilfachwen. The *Crosswood Deeds* detail a grant from John Vaughan of Trawscoed, Esq. to David Evans of 'Llechwedd y dery, gent, of lands in the grange of Havodwen, Cardiganshire'; and on 11 September 1637 another grant from John Vaughan to David Evans.

David Evans was High Sheriff in 1641, bought the Peterwell (Ffynnon Bedr) estate and built the first house of Peterwell and resided there. He had four sons and two daughters. His eldest son Thomas Evans was described as of Ffynon Bedr, his second son John Evans of Trefenty was High Sheriff in 1688, and his third son, Rees, married Anne, daughter of Francis Lloyd of Llanstephan and they had three daughters. Erasmus Evans, MA, the youngest son, was vicar of Lampeter and later of Buxton. Eleanor Evans married Lewis Lloyd of Llangennech who was High Sheriff of Carmarthenshire in 1654, and Sarah Evans married Daniel, third son of Rees Lloyd of Laques. Thomas Evans, the eldest son was High Sheriff in 1654. During the Civil War he was first an ardent Royalist and then joined the Roundheads. He grew rich exploiting his authority, confiscating lands and plundering churches for silver plate and treasures considered 'idolatrous trappings' by

Cromwell's men. The misfortune of the Peterwell family later is put down to the sacrilegious conduct of Thomas Evans. In 1722 Llechwedd Derry Issa and Ycha, formed part of the Evans of Peterwell estate, and later of the Lloyds and in that year the estate was partitioned between the co-heiresses, and the two farms given to Walter Lloyd and Elizabeth, his wife. The farms were let to tenants until sold to William Williams, Pantseiri, Tregaron, following the demise of the Peterwell estate late in the 18th century.

Grid Ref: SN5063 5050

Refs: Colby Map, 1831; PRO, Dale Castle MS., p. 27, sn. Llechwedd deri; CRO, GGMS III (Gwaeth-foed) fo. 34, & AE 12356E, fo. 495; Protheroe MS., c. xx (E. Pryse), C/A XII (WL); *Arch. Cam.* 1861, p. 24 ff, also CRO, GGMS I (Tydwal Gloff); NLW, Crosswood Deeds, pp. 59 & 64.

LLECHWEDD DYRYS,
Llanfihangel-y-Creuddyn

Not marked on *Colby's Map of 1831* but was located south of the B4340 Penparcau to New Cross road, south-west of Nanteos. Ieuan, the natural son of Griffith ap Llewelyn Lloyd, descended from Llewelyn Caplan of Dyffryn Aeron, owned Llechwedd Dyrys. His son, Howell, married Elen, daughter and heiress of Lewis David Meredydd of Llangwyryfon and they had a son Phillip ap Howel. Phillip married Elliw, the daughter and co-heiress of David Lloyd of Creuddyn. They had two sons, David Philip Howel of Llechwedd Dyrys, and Thomas Powell who married the daughter of Nicholas Bowen of Crugbychan.

David Philip Howel of Llechwedd Dyrys married the daughter of John ap Edward of Nanteos, who acquired the mansion when he married Sian ferch Morris. They had one son, John Powell who succeeded to the estate, and four daughters. The eldest daughter married John Morys Rees Goch of Creuddyn. The second daughter was married firstly to John Prynallt and secondly to David Lloyd of Aberbrwynen, and they had a daughter, Elizabeth who married her cousin Sir Thomas Powell. The third daughter of David Philip Powell married Morgan John Lewis of Nantybenglog, Pembrokeshire and the youngest daughter married Hugh Prichard of Abermagwr.

John Powell (ap Howell) of Llechwedd Dyrys married Jane Pryse, the daughter of Thomas Pryse of Glanfrêd. The *NLW Cwrtmawr Deeds* show that the marriage was subject to a pre-nuptial settlement made on 23 October 1629 between '1. David Phillip Powell of Llanbadarn vawr, gent., and John Powell of same, his son and heir apparent; 2. Thomas Prise of Ynysgreigog, Cardiganshire, Esq.; 3. Walter Lloyd of Llanfairclydogau, Esq. Edward Prise of Ynysgreigog, gent., Hugh Prichard of Llanfihangel Creuthyn, and Morgan John Lewis of Llanbadarn vawr, gent. Lands settled were the messuages called Llechwedd Dyrys, 21 other messuages, a water corn grist mill called Melin Ycheldre, a close, and two houses and gardens, all in Llanbadarn Fawr and Llanfihangel-y-Creuddyn'. John and Jane Powell had a son, Thomas Powell, who was Sergeant-at-Law in 1684, and in 1687 was 'one of ye judges of Westminster', and appointed a Baron of the Exchequer, and later knighted. He owned Llechwedd Dyrys from 1662 to 1684. Sir Thomas married his cousin, Elizabeth, and they had two sons and one daughter. The *Crosswood Deeds* show that on 9 January 1662/3 a release was made from Thomas Powell to John Vaughan of all his interest in a tenement in Llanfihangel y Creuddyn. Sir Thomas's children were: William Powell who succeeded him, Richard, who died unmarried and Mary Powell, who married Thomas Owens of Llynllo, Montgomeryshire. William Powell married Avarina le Brun, daughter and co-heiress of Cornelius le Brun of Cologne described as a Hugenot engineer, who had married Ann, daughter and heiress of John Jones of Nanteos. The marriage was subject to a pre-nuptial settlement on 1 April 1690. They had three sons and two daughters; Thomas Powell, who married the daughter of Sir John Frederick of Kent, but who died suddenly at Russell Court, London, John Powell who died unmarried, and William Powell, who was the rector of Geneu'r Glyn, and who succeeded to Nanteos. Llechwedd Dyrys became unoccupied and was later abandoned and became ruinous.

Grid Ref: SN 61550 7825

Refs: PRO, Dale Castle MS., p. 28; NLW, Cwrtmawr Deeds, Nos. 218, 953, 1323 & 1626, 324;

NLW, Crosswood Deeds, p. 89; Blome List, 1673; Meyrick, *Cardiganshire* 1810 (ed. 1907), 218; NLW, Bronwydd Deeds, No. 2861; CRO, GGMS III (Edwin ap Tegl), also (Gwaethfoed) fo. 24; WWHR, i, 45.

LLECHWEDD-Y-CWM, Llanwenog

Now called Llechwedd and located a mile south of Llanwenog in woodland east of the minor road towards Maesycrugiau. The home of a family who traced to Castell Hywel, and took the surname Phillips. Philip ap Ieuan, descended from Cadifor ap Dinawal had two sons, David ap Philip of Llechwedd y Cwm, who married Catherine Fu, the daughter of Eynon Fu of Glandyweli and Griffith Philip, who was vicar of Llangeler. David ap Philip had a son, Ieuan ap David. Dates are lacking. David Phillips of Llechwedd y Cwm married Eleanor Scourfield, daughter of William Scourfield of Moat, Pembrokeshire. They had two daughters who were co-heiresses, Jane, who married John Rogers of Laugharne, a coroner, and Mary, who married William Phillips of Cwm Nantddu. In 1722 when the Peterwell estate was partitioned among the co-heiresses, Miss Letitia Evans was assigned 'the capital messuage and lands called Llechwedd y Cwm', in the parish of Llanwenog.

Grid Ref: SN 4913 4450

Refs: NLW, J. Alcwyn Evans, 12356 E, C/A Protheroe, B.1.

LLET(T)Y MEURIG,
(also known as Clapsini), Tregaron

Marked on *Colby's Map of 1831* and on modern OS maps as a short mile east of Tregaron on the mountain road leading to Cwm Berwyn formerly called Clapsini. In 1668 the *Crosswood Deeds* give details of a Walter Vaughan of Moor Cottage, Herefordshire, gent., and his son and heir apparent, Edward Vaughan described as of Lletty Veiricke in 1671/2. There is a gravestone in the churchyard at Tregaron to David Rees, Clapsini, who died in 1817. A large stone on the stable wall bears the lettering 'TR 1739.'

Grid Ref: SN 6920 5930

Refs: Colby Map, 1831; NLW, Crosswood Deeds, pp. 95, 105; The Rev. D. C. Rees, *Tregaron,* 1936, p. 57; NLW, Cwrtmawr Deeds, No. 1480.1110.

LLIDIARDAU, Llanilar

The mansion and home farm (124 acres) of the Llidiardau estate was purchased by David Parry in 1739 from Elizabeth Thomas of Cwmnewidion for £132. Earlier owners were Phillip David (1611-35) and his son, John Phillip David and Gwenllian, his wife, owners from 1672-1692. Marked on *Colby's Map of 1831* and on modern OS maps a mile east of Llanilar, south of the B4575 to Trawscoed. The Parry family are descendants of Adda Fychan of Llanddwy, David ap Harry of Glennydd and the Parrys of Tyddyn y Berllan (Ty'n berllan), a farm east of Llidiardau. This family, according to Meyrick, 'have been in possession of this, and many other estates near it, ever since the time of Queen Elizabeth'.

An early reference mentions a Morgan David Parry, Esq. of Tython y Berllan, who died in 1674. He was followed by his son, David and grandson Morgan, who died unmarried in 1759. He in turn, was succeeded by his nephew David, the first of Llidiardau, who married Mary Parry, widow of John Jones, vicar of Cardigan. David's uncle John, brother of Morgan (1675-1759) donated communion cups to St. Ilar church in 1751. Meyrick states, 'No parish in the Diocese of St. David's has a more unique and intrinsically valuable cup than that which is the chief gem of St Hilary's Chest. It is a silver cup of simple funnel-shape, gilt-lined, four and a half inches high, and studded all round with golden Swedish coins, of early 18th century date, and one coin as large as our crown piece in the bottom'. The inscription reads, 'the Gift of John Parry, Messenger in Ordinary to their Majesty's King George ye 1st and 2nd, to the Parish Church of Llan Hilary, in the County of Cardigan, 1751.' John Parry brought the chalice from Stockholm, where he lived for many years, in 1720. The use of the cup was reserved for the great festivals of Easter and Christmas.

Thomas Parry (1746-1819) succeeded his father, David, in 1763. He married Elizabeth, daughter of Nathaniel Williams, of the Old Abbey, Ystrad Fflur. Thomas was a deputy-lieutenant and magistrate for the county. 'He has made a very pretty place of this, which, besides being a good farm, has a fine plantation of firs and other timber'. The family arms are *argent* a chevron *azure* between three fleur de lis of the second in a chief *azure* a mullet pierced *argent,* crest a lion rampant'.

The original will of Viscount Lisburne of Trawsgoed of 1741 mentions 'a friend and kinsman' Thomas Parry of Aberystwyth and Llidiardau attorney-at-law to whom he bequeathed his law books, his best gold watch and £50.

Following the death of Thomas Parry, his widow, Sarah, lived in Walworth, and his only son, George Williams Parry (1785-1838), High Sheriff of Cardiganshire in 1823 succeeded to Llidiardau. Thomas had attempted to dissuade George in 1809 from marrying Anne Hughes, a daughter of a breech-maker from Machynlleth.

In 1873 the Llidiardau estate of George William Parry (1811-74) who was married to Elizabeth Hughes of Glanrheidol, by then of great age, is recorded as 3,561 acres with an annual rental of £1,947. He died the following year having secured his request for 'eight sittings in the nave and four sittings for his servants' which he claimed was his by a 'prescriptive right' to the bench he had occupied since 1832, prior to the restoration of Llanilar church in 1874.

He was succeeded by the third George William Parry (1852-1927), High Sheriff of Cardiganshire in 1885 and a deputy-lieutenant and JP. He married Emma Charlotte, descended from the Richardes of Plâs Pen-glais, the daughter of the Rev. Charles Marriott, Rector of Charlton Musgrave, Somerset. Their children were George William Randolph Marriott Parry (1885-1974), Thomas Rufus (1885-1974) and Ena Elizabeth Penelope (1894-1983).

Francis Jones relates a tale of one of the Parry's of Llidiardau, who was a well-known miser. Among his methods of avoiding spending money was to place straw in his boots instead of having new soles.

George Williams Randolph Marriott Parry, married Edith St Ives, (1882-1977), daughter of Captain Walter Croker St. Ives Partridge of Hampshire, in 1932. Both he and his brother, Rufus served in World War I, when his father

was unwilling to recruit local youths for the Poppy Fields of Flanders. His mother, Emma, lived in Aberystwyth in a home which she named 'Gates'. His sister, Ena, the first female car driver and cigarette smoker in the Llanilar area, lived at Llanfarian and died un-married in 1983. The estate was sold in 1956 and the small acreage remaining farmed by locals. In recent years the Pugh family lived at Llidiardau.

Llidiardau, altered and extended by the architect, Richard Kyrke Penson, in the 1850's, is now the family home of Mr. and Mrs. Gary Stalbow. They have renovated the house, a wing of which was demolished many years ago, and restored the garden to its former glory. The Rattray family live in the former home farm and the land is let to neighbours.

Grid Ref: SN 6378 7467

Refs: Colby Map, 1831; Meyrick, *Cardiganshire,* 285-6, 1811; Nicholas, *County Families,* 1875; Landowners Return, 1873; NLW, Glan Paith Deeds, 110, 114, 162, 236, 242; H. M. Vaughan, *South Wales Squires,* p. 205. Ex info H. J. Llewelyn Jones.

LLOYD JACK (LLWYD SIAC),
Llanfihangel Ystrad

Situated in Dyffryn Aeron one mile west of Llanllyr between the A482 and the dismantled railway and the Aeron and marked on *Emanuel Bowen's Map of South Wales,* c. 1760, *Colby's Map of 1831* and on modern OS maps. Llwyd Jack and Lloyd Jack are said to be corruptions of the earlier Clwyd Jack. The family signed their pedigree for the herald Dwnn. David Lloid ap Hugh o'r Clwyd Jack bore the arms: 1. Gwaethvoed; 2. Kidrych ap Gwaethfoed; 3. Ynyr; 4. *or* a griffin segreant *vert;* 5. Urien; 6. Bledri; 7. Tewdr; 8. Jestin ap Gwrgant.

An early reference reveals that David Lloyd ap Hugh of Clwydsiack married Angharad, daughter of John ap Howell John. David was descended from the Pryses of Goggerddan, and was High Sheriff of Cardiganshire in 1597. He had a son, Morgan Lloyd, who married Elen, daughter of James Lewis of Abernantbychan, Penbryn parish. They had a son, Hugh of Lloyd Jack, High Sheriff in 1648 and 1673, who married Anne, daughter of John Parry of Blaen-pant, Llangoedmor. His will was proved in 1679. John and Anne had two sons, John who succeeded to the estate, and Morgan, who was alive in 1668, was of Bryngelyn in the parish of Llanfihangel Ystrad. He married Lettice, daughter of John Price ap Walter Price of Blaen-pant.

John Lloyd married Mary, daughter of John Lloyd of Cilgwyn and they had four sons; the eldest, Hugh, Thomas of Gwernfilyg who had a son, John Lloyd; Griffith and John Lloyd of Breinog (Brynog) who married Anne, daughter of Hugh Pugh.

John and Anne had four sons and four daughters: David, his will proved in 1769, John, Charles, Edward, who married Anne, daughter of David Jones of Coed y Parc, Mary who married Thomas Jones of Brynely, Anne, who married Decimus Price, Margaret and Jane.

Hugh Lloyd, High Sheriff in 1697, married Mary, daughter of David Lloyd of Alltyrodin and they had two sons and three daughters. Edward Lhwyd in *Parochalia* writes: 'Hugh Lloyd of Lloyd Sach Esq. and present High Sheriff of the county in 1697-8 bore the arms: *black* lyon rampart regardant armed 2 langued gules in a field *or,* in the name and tenure of heirs male for severall generations past'. On 25 August 1698 administration of his estate was granted to Hugh Lloyd's chief creditor, John Bowen of Morfa Bychan. Hugh's eldest son David succeeded. The second son, Walter Lloyd married Mary Lewes, daughter of Griffith Lloyd of Porthyneuadd and had a son, Hugh Lloyd. The eldest son David Lloyd, High Sheriff in 1718, was married twice; firstly to Dorothy, daughter of David Lloyd of Ffosybleiddiaid, and secondly to Catherine, daughter of Evan Pryce of Rhydybenne, relict of Rees David Morris of Bangor. They had a son Hugh, who pre-deceased his father, dying unmarried in February 1742. David Lloyd died in May 1743 and Lloyd Jack fell to David's nephew Hugh Lloyd, son of his brother Walter, whilst he was still a minor on 28 May 1746. The *Edwinsford Deeds* record that on 28 May 1746 a document was agreed between '1. Thomas Williams, Edwinsford, Esq.; 2. Hugh Lloyd of Llwyd Jack, Cardiganshire, gent., aged 18, nephew and heir of David Lloyd of Llwyd Jack, Esq., deceased, and David Lloyd, Gwernveilig, Cards, gent., guardian of said Hugh; 3. Lewis Rogers of Gelly, parish Trevilan, gent., Assignment of a mortgage to secure £1,583.13.3. of a capital messuage and demesne lands called Tyr Griffith Powell, otherwise Tyr Llwyd Jack, and messuages and land therewith held, messuages and land called Tyr Pant Vrew, otherwise Tyr y Vroe, Llain y wisg Codd goon, and many others (named) in the parishes of Llanfihangel Ystrad and Dihewid'.

Hugh Lloyd married Mary, but died intestate in 1756 and his wife married David Davies and in 1760 he was said to be enjoying her dower out of Lloyd Jack. Mary survived both her husbands. Meyrick tells us that, 'the last male, Hugh Lloyd died leaving three daughters and co-heiresses, one of whom, Anne, married John Davies of Maes, Esq. the estate thus became the property of said John Davies'. On 25 July 1799 the Church in Wales Records tell us that 'The Subchanter and Vicars choral of the Catholic church of St. Davids gave lease for 21 years of Llansantffraid parsonage, to Herbert Lloyd Davies of Lloyd Jack, Cardiganshire'.

Anne and John had a son, David Davies. A poignant obituary in *The Cambrian* on 4 October 1806 informed its readers that: 'Lately, in the prime of life, at Llandrindod Wells, where he went for the recovery of a long and painful illness, which he bore with Christian fortitude and resignation, David Davies, Esq., of Lloyd Jack House, Cardiganshire, JP. John Davies, Esq., of the same place, his father, left four sons, who all died within five years, the eldest, married and did not survive three months, and his widow also died within two years. The other three brothers died bachelors and in the bloom of life. Therefore now remaining of that most ancient family only their disconsolate mother and sister.' On the 14 June 1806 *The Cambrian* published the obituary of Thomas Davies: 'Died at Lloyd Jack House, in the 29th year of his life, Thomas Davies, Esq., youngest son of the late John Davies, Esq., buried at Pencarreg on 4th March 1796 of the same place. He was a gentleman of great work, and is most deservedly lamented by all who knew him, especially the poor, to whom he was a generous benefactor.' His mother lived for many years after his death; she died on 21 June 1823 aged 76.

The sale notice of the Lloyd Jack Estate in *The Cambrian,* 1 September 1804, describes the estate: 'In the beautiful and fertile Vale of Ayron, consisting of the capital demesne, farm and lands called Lloyd Jack, and 18 other farms, in the whole about 1,400 acres of good arable, meadow and pasture, let at low yearly rents, amounting to all the clear yearly rent of £675. Part of the estate consists of an elegant modern built dwelling house at Ystrad, adjoining the demesne lands aforesaid, and which contains on the ground floor, 2 parlours, a dining room, kitchen, outward kitchen, servants hall, laundry, dairy, pantry and cellar. On first floor: five good bedchambers with dressing rooms: and on the attic storey bedroom which will hold 8 beds for servants, lately erected for the residence of the Proprietor of the estate, with suitable offices, a good garden in a pleasant and sporting county. There are a great number of very respectable gent's seats in the neighbourhood. The turnpike from Lampeter to Aberaeron runs through the centre of the property, and has a post which passes the door of the mansion house five times a week. The mansion is about six miles from the sea and seaport of Aberaeron, and is about the same distance from the market town of Lampeter.'

The accounts and rentals of the Lloyd Jack Estate for 1811-14 are shown in the *Griffith Owen Deeds* and a document in 1812 mentions Anne Davies, late of Lloyd Jack, but now of Aberystwyth, widow and executrix of David Davies late of Lloyd Jack, Esq., who was the administrator of Herbert Lloyd Davies of Lloyd Jack, Esq., dec. (whose wife had pre-deceased him in 1805). The rental of the Llwyd Jack estate was taken in 1814 by Mrs. Anne Davies, widow. In 1813 *The Cambrian Traveller's Guide* tells us that, 'Llwyd siac was formerly the residence of the Lloyds, but is now almost in ruins. The estate now belongs to Counsellor Touchett.' Meyrick adds that 'the estate is now settled on Counsellor Touchett's son'. In 1819, the *Deri Ormond Deeds* shows an entry for Mary Rees of Lloyd Jack, widow. An elegy *'er cof am Dafydd Jenkin Rees o Lloydjack'* by David Davies of Castell Hywel, was published in *Telyn Dewi* in 1824.

Grid Ref: SN 5286 5636

Refs: Colby Map, 1831; Emanuel Bowen Map of South Wales, c. 1760; *Dwnn,* i, 15, 80-81; WWHR, i, 23-4; Blome List, 1673; Meyrick *Cardiganshire,* edn. 1907, p. 237; Edward Lhwyd, *Parochalia,* III, 80; *The Cambrian*, 1 Sept. 1804 & 4th Oct. 1806; PRO, Dale Castle MS., p. 20; Church in Wales Records; NLW, Griffith Owen Deeds, Nos. 8539 & 1163-4; Edwinsford Deeds, 664, 708, 2611; *Historical Notes,* J. Rowlands, 1866; NLW, Deri Ormond Deeds, 214; David Davies, *Telyn Dewi* (1824); G. E. Evans, *Cardiganshire,* 1903, 148; *The Cambrian Traveller's Guide,* 2nd edn. 1813, p. 11.

LLWYNCADFOR, Llandyfriog
(formerly Llanfair Trelygen)

Marked on *Colby's Map of 1831* and on modern OS maps as about one and a quarter miles north-north-east of Llandyfriog church. Formerly the home of Rhys, descended from Elystan Glodrudd, and the Davids, descended from Tydwal Gloff.

The earliest reference mentions Meredydd of Llwyn Cadfor, who traced to Tydwal ap Rhodri Mawr, had a son Owain, and a grandson David, all of Llwyn Cadfor. David's daughter Efa, married Rhys ab Hywel Fawr of Gilfach-wen Isaf descended from Elystan. Their son was Rhys whose son, Richard married Lleucu, daughter of Morris ap Owen ap Howel of Pengelli in Cenarth. They had a son, Rhys, who married Lleucu, daughter of Rhydderch David Evan Du of Blaen-y-nant in Llandyfriog. Their son John married Jane, daughter of Thomas Davies, vicar of Llandysul, called *y Ficer Coch,* and they too had a son, Rhys, who married Joan, daughter of Rhys Thomas Prydderch Evan Du of Pentre du in Llandyfriog and Gerddi-bach. They had two sons, David and Harry, a corviser.

David married Angharad, daughter of Morgan Thomas Prydderch.

In *Hanes Castell-Newydd-yn-Emlyn* the author states that the former owners lost their wealth and sold Llwyncadifor. Methusalem Davies was then owner. He had a brother, Richard and three sisters. Richard was the vicar of Cenarth and married Margaret, the daughter of Thomas Rees of Emlyn, a drover. Methusalem Davies's sisters were Elizabeth, Mary, who married James Williams, son of William James of Cilycwm and another sister who married Ifan Gruffydd of Twrgwyn, Troed-yr aur 'ye Welsh poet'. Methusalem Davies was the vicar of Pencarreg from 1727-32. He died without issue and bequeathed his estate to his nephew, also Methusalem, the son of his brother Richard. The Rev. Methusalem Davies, vicar of Llanfair Trelygen, clerk, married Grace, the eldest daughter of James Williams of Waun, Henllan, Cardiganshire, gent. The marriage was subject to a pre-nuptial settlement made on 25 May 1732 which settled the messuages of Llwyncadfor and Tir-y-bryn in the parishes of Llanfair Trelygen and Llandyfriog on the newly-weds. Their son, James Davies, also became a clergyman. Meyrick tells us that David Davies, Esq., descended from Tydwal Gloff, was also a later owner. By 1848 Mary Howell, late of Allt-y-gog, Abergwili parish, widow, was described as of Llwyncadfor.

Grid Ref: SN 3390 4275

Refs: Colby Map, 1831. Meyrick, *Cardiganshire,* 188; B. Williams, *Hanes Castell-Newydd-yn-Emlyn*, 1860, p. 53; WWHR, iii, 83; ibid, i, 47-8; PRO, Dale Castle MS., p. 29; CRO, GGMS I (Elystan), fo. 33; NLW, Cwrtmawr Deeds, No. 126; NLW, Cilgwyn Docs., No 120.

LLWYN-COED, Aberporth

Located on *Colby's Map of 1831* and on modern OS maps as south of Aberporth and north-east of the airfields at Blaenannerch. Francis Jones recorded memorial inscriptions at the churchyard which reads:

1. Yma y gorwedd cyrph 5 o blant Dafydd Evan, Llwyncoed. Evan a fn farw Meliefin 24, 1791, oed 6 dydd. Esther a fu farw Rhagfyr 18 1793 yn 13 mlwydd oed. Jane a fu farw Rhagfyr 29 1793 yn 6 mlwydd oed. Ann a fu farw Rhygfyr 30 1793 yn 9 mlwydd oed.

2. Dafydd Evan o Lluncoed yn y plwyf hwn, a Sarah ei wraig, a John ei fab. Dafydd a fu farw Mawrth 22, 1828 oedran 77. Sarah a fu farw 15 Mawrth 1811, oedran 56. John a fu farw 13 Awst 1811, 34.

3. Mary gwraig Thomas Davies o Llwyn y Coed, farw Medi 21, 1837, 44. John mab hynaf y Thomas a Mary Davies uchod, fu farw 2 Gorff 1845, 20.

Grid Ref: SN 2585 5000

Refs: Colby Map, 1831; Francis Jones Archives.

LLWYNDAFYDD, Llandysiliogogo

Llwyndafydd will forever be associated with Dafydd ab Ieuan, who tradition holds entertained Henry Tudor, Earl of Richmond on his historic journey to Bosworth Field in August 1485. Marked on *Colby's Map of 1831* and on modern OS maps as a village, in the valley of Ffynnon Ddewi which enters the sea at Cwmtudu. The remains of Castell Caerwedros is nearby.

Dafydd ab Ieuan of Llwyndafydd who was descended from Blegwryd ap Dinawal, married as his first wife, Nest, daughter of Adda Fychan of Llanddwy on the banks of the Ystwyth in the parish of Llanfihangel y Creuddyn. It was Dafydd who extended the hospitality and, in some tales, even his daughter, to Henry, Earl of Richmond who is said to have repaid his host with the gift of the Hirlas Horn, which was later held by the Lords of Cawdor of Gelli-aur and Stackpole. The son of the purported assignation, Harry, was by some accounts, the progenitor of the Parrys in Cwm Cynon, Gernos and other locations. It is believed that many Parrys are the descendants of this night of passion.

From Dafydd ab Ieuan descended Rhys, and then Harry of Cwmtudu to David Parry, who married the daughter of Lewis Llewelyn Llwyd. Their son, William Parry of Cwm Cynon, married Elizabeth, the daughter of James ap Rhys ap Morgan of Aberarthen. Deio ab Ieuan Du (fl. 1460-80), a medieval poet from north Cardiganshire addressed an ode to Thomas Andras of Newport, Pembrokeshire, requesting two swans as a gift for Ieuan ap Siencyn Llwyd of Llwyndafydd. He states that there is a deep pool *(llyn dwfn)* for the swans there. Deio ab Ieuan Du was the poet who gave the Welsh nation *Y Ddraig Goch ddyry cychwyn* (set forth the Red Dragon), in a poem thanking Sion ap Rhys of Glyn-nedd for the gift of a bull and a heifer. Richard ap Dafydd ab Ieuan's daughter and heiress Elen, married Ieuan ap Siencyn Llwyd, the second son of Jenkin Llwyd and his wife, Efa, of Blaiddbwll, Clydau. They had a son, Adda of Llwyndafydd, and a daughter Lleucu, who married Dafydd ap Llewelyn ap Gwilym, the second son of Castell Hywel. The poet Lewis Glyncothi wrote an elegy to Lleucu and an ode to her husband. Adda ap Ieuan had three sons Thomas, John and Rhys, and it was Hugh, son of Thomas ap Adda ap Ieuan, who succeeded to Llwyndafydd.

Grid Ref: SN 3713 5550

Refs: Colby Map, 1831; Meyrick, *Cardiganshire,* p. 233; Horsfall-Turner *Wanderings,* 132-3. *Dwnn,* i, 40, 58, 80, 82-3; WWHR, i, 10, 34; Lewis, *TDW,* 1840; PRO, Dale Castle MS., *Works,* pp. 258-61; C/A Protheroe MS., iv.

LLWYNDYRYS, Llandygwydd

This property formed part of the estate of the Bishops of St. David's and was the home of the Birts, Wogans, Symmons and Griffiths. Located on *Colby's Map of 1831* and on modern OS maps a long mile east of Llechryd north of the A484 to Cenarth and overlooking the Teifi. The first reference to this house is when Gwen Anwyl, daughter and heiress of Gruffydd William Madog of Llwyndyrys, married Rhys Fychan (Vaughan) of Corsygedol (Meirionydd), the son of William Fychan who settled at Cilgerran late in the 15th century and was Constable of Cardigan in 1507. Later in the 16th century Llwyndyrys was occupied by a John Welley, the son of James Welley of Knighton, Radnorshire, a mercer, and his wife Penelope, the third daughter of William Jenkins of Carrog, Llanddeiniol parish, and his wife, Elizabeth, daughter of Morgan Llwyd of Lloyd Jack, Llanfihangel Ystrad. John Welley was followed at Llwyndyrys by Robert Birt, son of Robert Birt of Shropshire and his wife, Elizabeth, daughter of Sir Richard Strangeways, and grandson of Robert Birt, whose father was of Birt Hall in Essex.

Robert Birt, the first of the Birts to live at

Llwyndyrys married Jane, daughter of Sir Thomas Trenchard. Their second son, also named Robert Birt, was the senior bailiff of Carmarthen in 1556 and Mayor in 1564. He married Elizabeth [or Eva] Read, daughter of Edward Read of Carmarthen. They had two sons and two daughters. John, the eldest, succeeded to Llwyndyrys, and Robert, who was the senior bailiff of Carmarthen in 1587 and Mayor in 1593. He married Jane, daughter of Griffith Lloyd and they had three daughters. Elizabeth Birt married twice; firstly to Einon Philipps and secondly to Sir John Wogan of Boulston. Bridget, the second daughter was also married twice; firstly to James Prydderch of Nantyrhebog and secondly to Michael Ferrier, the Town Clerk of Carmarthen.

John Birt of Llwyndyrys married Anne, daughter of Lewis Davies of Carmarthen. John Birt was senior bailiff of Carmarthen in 1583, Mayor in 1591 and High Sheriff of Cardiganshire in 1598. He signed for Dwnn on 26 July 1591. John and Anne had three sons and two daughters. His son, Thomas Birt, succeeded and married Maud, daughter of William Walter of Roch Castle, Pembrokeshire. The second son was John Birt, Jr., alive in 1619. The youngest son, Robert married Frances Hayward of Fletherhill, Pembrokeshire. His will was proved on 14 January 1648/9 and mentions 'my wife Frances, my son Robert Birt, my nephew James Hayward son of Thomas Hayward of Rudbaxton, Pembs., gent., dec.' Of the three daughters Elizabeth Birt married Hugh Parry of Cwmtudur and Lucy married John Revel. Thomas Birt's will was proved on 3 February 1647/8, and Maud died in July 1671. Her will was proved at Carmarthen later that year. Their only son Robert married Winifred or Gwenffrwd, daughter of Thomas Jones of Dolaucothi and widow of David Lloyd of Porthrhyd and Castell Hywel. Winifred died in August 1675 at Vaenor, Manordeifi, Pembrokeshire. Robert Birt had two daughters and co-heiresses, Mary, and Winifred. Mary married M. Salmer, a French doctor of St. Clement Danes, and Winifred, will dated 16 October 1721 and proved in 1723, married William Brigstocke of Llechdwnny, Llandyfaelog. Llwyndyrys was certainly of commodious proportions for in 1672, Mary and Winifred Birt were assessed at 7 hearths and Richard Birt at 3.

Mary sold the estate to Sir William Wogan of Llanstinian, Pembrokeshire, who died without issue in 1710 and Llwyndyrys passed to his nephew Thomas Symmons of Martel, also Pembrokeshire. The house was tenanted for some years. In 1721, Stephen Parry of Noyadd Trefawr made a bequest to his brother-in-law Charles Evans 'of Llwyndyrys', who had married his sister, Mary. Charles later lived at Gwernan where he died. Thomas Symmons's will dated 28 July 1730 describes him as being of Llwyndyrys. His son, John took possession of the family estate and in 1749 he gave a 'lease of Llwyndyrys in the parish of Llandygwydd, a house and garden thereto belonging in the village and chapelry of Llechryd and house commonly called the Counting House in the same village'. Amongst the properties that formed the estate at this time were Stradmore, Dol, Penlan and Berllan, the Manor of Llandygwydd and messuages called Llwyndyrus, Scotland and Henbant, all in the parish of Llandygwydd. John Symmons sold part of the heavily mortgaged estate to the mortgagee, Peter Holford, in 1782.

In 1800, under an Act of Parliament, for the redemption of Land Tax, The Bishop of St. David's sold the Manor and Lordship of Llwyndyrys to the Rev. Thomas Griffiths, Prebendary of Llandygwydd. Meyrick writes 'The present mansion was erected a few years ago by the Rev. Thomas Griffiths, and stands upon an elevated spot, overlooking the Teifi . . . In the grounds is the site of the original edifice, which was moated; and the second residence now forming part of the offices to the new building. Under the new house, on the left hand, close to the turnpike road leading to Cardigan, is a large mount or tumulus, in height about eight yards'. Lewis in *TDW* adds that the Bishop sold both the manor and Lordship of Llandygwydd and the estate of Llwyndyrus, and that the new mansion was near the site of the old episcopal palace. Horsfall-Turner states 'that the restored mansion replaced the old castellated home'. A photograph of Llwyndyrys taken in 1871 by Charles Allen of Tenby and published in *The Tivyside Photographic Souvenir* shows a square block of two storeys, pillared entrance, and a long domestic wing on one side. The main block has a range of three windows and is early 19th century. The wing of two storeys, lower than the main block, is probably earlier. At the side of the pillared entrance is a mounting block of three steps.

The Rev. Griffiths, who died in 1813, had a son, also Thomas, who married Mary Anne, daughter of John Iggulden, Esq. of Deal, at the Queen's Square Chapel, Bath, in May 1808. They had a son Thomas Iggulden Griffiths, described in 1831 as' late of Bath but now of Deal, Kent'. In 1825, three Griffiths were described as of Llwyndyrys; George Woolgar Griffiths, the Rev. Charles Griffiths and Mehetabel Griffiths. In 1832 John Griffiths married Elizabeth Anne, eldest daughter of the late James Brown Esq. of Purbrook, Hampshire, on 22 June 1826.

On 10 June 1874 the *Llwyndyrus Collection* states that there was a request by Charles Marshal Griffiths of the Inner Temple, barrister and owner of Llwyndyrus estate, and Sarah Anna Griffiths to Messrs John Griffiths of Treforgan, Llangoedmor, and James Kingsford of The Strand, London, and Rev. Henry Manning Ingram of Littledean's Yard, Westminster, clerk, trustees of their marriage settlement, to secure £3,000 on mortgage to the said C. M. Griffiths. In 1920 Llwyndyrys was owned by Major John Hugh Sandham Griffiths, second son of the late Charles Marshal Griffiths Q.C. In 1890, he married Emily, daughter of the late Rev. E. J. Selwyn of Pluckley Rectory, Kent. Educated at Highgate and Sandhurst, Major Griffiths served in India and Burma. Sir John Lynn Thomas, the son of Evan Thomas of Cwmgefeileis, Llandysul, formerly of Strad-more (Ystrad Mawr) and a distinguished surgeon bought Llwyndyrys in 1924. Sir John, knighted in 1919, was the first Consultant Surgeon to practise in Cardiff. He was also an inventor of surgical instruments. Sir John was responsible for the establishment of the Prince of Wales Hospital for Limbless Soldiers and Sailors at Rhydlafar, Cardiff. In his retirement he took up archaeology. When Sir John Lynn Thomas died in 1939, Llwyndyrys was bought by Louisa Hext Lewes of Llanllyr and was used during World War II as a Red Cross Convalescent Home for wounded soldiers. It is now a Residential Home and has been recently extended.

Grid Ref: SN 2378 4345

Refs: NLW, Griffith Owen List (iv); *Dwnn,* i, 83; WWHR, i, 35-6; ibid, iii, 79; ibid, xiv, p. 232; Symmons of Martell and Llanstinian; Lewis, *TDW,* 1840; Horsfall-Turner, *Wanderings,* 199; NLW, Llwyndyrus Collection; NLW, F. Green Deeds. No. 12; Meyrick, *Cardiganshire,* 1810 edn., 1907, p. 184; Carlisle, *TDW,* 1811; PRO, Dale Castle MS., p. 25 (100), 26.

LLWYNGARU (LLWYN Y GARY), Caron

Marked on *Colby's Map of 1831* as Llwyn-y-gary on the banks of the Berwyn, two miles east of Tregaron in woodland north of the mountain road towards Diffwys.

Formerly the home of the Jones family. The first recorded inhabitant was John Coch, who descended from Collwyn ap Tangno, and had three sons. The eldest, Ieuan Jones who married the daughter of John David Lloyd of Llangybi whose daughter and heiress, Maud, married Morgan Herbert of Hafod. The second son, Thomas Jones married Maud, the daughter of Ieuan o'r Wythied, and their grandson, David, later of Ludlow was Cryer to Judge Turner. John, the youngest son of John Coch lived at Llwyn-garu and married Katherine, daughter of John Stedman of Ystrad Fflur. Their son Thomas, the last in the male line, married Isod, daughter of John Lloyd of Crynfryn by the daughter of Watkin Morgan David Lloyd. Their heiress, Elizabeth, married Edward Vaughan son of Walter Vaughan, a younger son of Trawsgoed. Edward and Elizabeth's daughter, Elizabeth, married Watkin Lloyd, a younger son of Rhiwarthen, Goginan. The pedigree of Jones of Llwyngaru is given, by the Deputy-Herald, David Edwardes of Rhyd-y-gors (c.1630-90), in the *Bodleian Manuscripts.* Walter Lloyd of Llwyngaru died on 29 March 1678 and in his will he left legacies to his brother, Evan Lloyd of Genau'r-glyn, clerk, and to Walter Lloyd, junior of Crynfryn, nephew of the testator, being the son of Grace Lloyd of Crynfryn. The will was proved in PCC. The testator had a sister, Catherine. Among properties named by testator were Fullbrooke Mill and Cefen y Maes-glas in Caron. A reference to a David Hughes of Llwyngaru is given in the Vestry Book of St. Caron's church for October 1801. Hughes was allowed 12/- to send John Jones to Swansea. The parish registers of St. Caron's lists a Walter Davies, farmer of Llwyngaru between 1782 and 1795.

Grid Ref: SN 7050 5891

Refs: Colby Map, 1831; Bodleian MS., Add. C. 177-9, David Edwardes; CRO, GGMS, I (Tydwal Gloff), III (Collwyn ap Tedwr); CRO, GGMS II (Adv. Cardiganshire) GRB notes; J. Francis Deeds (Llanllawddog), Nos. 105, 28. Feb. 1678-9.

LLWYNGRAWYS, Llangoedmor

Located on *Emanuel Bowen's Map of South Wales,* and *Colby's Map of 1831* and on modern OS maps two miles east of Cardigan, north of the old B4570 road to Cwm-cou and Newcastle Emlyn. The first known family at Llwyn y grawys was that of Thomas. Thomas Jenkin had five sons, one of whom was natural, and a daughter. The eldest son, Jenkin Thomas succeeded to the estate. The other sons were David, John, Thomas, and another John, who was a natural son and a daughter, Margaret. Jenkin Thomas of 'the capital messuage called

Llwyn y Graws, gent,' married Margaret . . . family unknown. In his will, dated 30 March 1668, he left the property to his wife and the remainder to the children of his brother, Thomas ap Thomas.

The eldest son, John, succeeded to the estate. John Thomas was brought up in Oxford and educated at the University there. He became a leading non-conformist preacher and ministered at Llechryd for many years. He was a member of a mixed Baptist and Independent congregation who met at, among other places, Rhosygilwen, Cilgerran, the home of Jenkin

Jones, formerly of Brithdir-fawr, north Pembrokeshire, a puritan and a Captain in Cromwell's army, who died in 1698. John Thomas was the first witness to Jenkin Jones' will. John took part in an historic debate with John Jenkins of Rhydwilym, on the merits of infant baptism at Pen-an farm on the slopes of the Frenni-fawr. He later built a chapel at Llechryd and was a man of great influence in south Cardiganshire and was held in high regard. In the *Clynfyw Papers* at the NLW it is recorded, 'On 6th August 1719 Jane Thomas of Penyrallt vach, Llangoedmore parish, widow and relict of John Thomas, late of Llwyn y Grawys, gent., dec. bargained and sold messuages and land in the said parish called Pant y Butler and Park Llwyd, to Thomas Lewis of Llwyn y Grawis, gent.' Thomas Lewis had formerly owned the Blackpool Forge at Canaston, Pembrokeshire. In 1719 he became associated with Coedmor Forge at Llechryd-isaf and bought the tools, plate and implements of the Forge which he controlled for many years. In 1744, Thomas Lloyd of Llechryd, glover, mortgaged two houses and a field in Llechryd to Thomas Lewis for £25. In 1749, he leased Melin Aber-cuch and converted it into an iron forge. A man of considerable business acumen, Thomas Lewis had ready money which enabled him to lend to owners who mortgaged their properties as security and were often unable to redeem them. It was thus in 1719 that Jane, wife of the aforementioned John Thomas of Llwyngrawys released Pantybwtler and Parc-llwyd, both in Llangoedmor parish, to Thomas Lewis as settle-ment for the £88.12.0 mortgage due on the property. In 1714 Thomas had married Mag-dalen (also known as Maud), daughter and heiress of Thomas David Thomas, a cousin of John Thomas, who inherited Llwyngrawys. Thomas and his wife had five children. David, the eldest, JP for Cardiganshire in 1748, married an heiress, Mary Greswood from Malvern, and lived there. Thomas married Ann, heiress of James Harries of Wern-gou, Clydau parish. The eldest daughter, Mary, married John Jones of Llanbadarn Fawr. Elizabeth married as her first husband, John James of Tyglyn Aeron, and secondly, Philip Pugh (1706-80), son of the Rev. Philip Pugh of Llwynpiod. John Lewis, the third son of Thomas and Magdalen, died in 1742. Magdalen Lewis died in 1729 and Thomas married, as his second wife, a widow, Catherine Lewis of Llanbedr Velfrey, Pembrokeshire, in 1735. Their only child, William, who married Margaret Bowen of Pantyderi, Llanfair Nant-gwyn, remained at Llwyngrawys when his father purchased the Clynfyw estate in Maenordeifi parish from Owen Davies, Receiver-General of Westminster Abbey and his wife, in 1753. In 1757, Thomas Lewis married his third wife, Jane Owen, heiress of Clunyrynys, Ferwig. Their daughter, Dorothy, born in 1763 later became the third wife of the Rev. William Williams, a notable Baptist minister of Tre-fach, also in Llanfair Nantgwyn. The descendants of these unions are the Lewis-Bowen family of Clynfyw. Llwyngrawys was let to tenants and later sold. Francis Jones visited the house and wrote; Visited (but not examined) by me on 14 May 1983. House and outbuildings adapted for visitors. Seems well kept. Comparatively small. Long adapted to farming usage (it) lies on a gentle slope'.

Llwyngrawys is now owned by David George who farms the neighbouring Dyffryn farm. Llwyngrawys is let to tenants. David George was the unsuccessful Conservative candidate for the Cardiganshire constituency in the 1970 General Election.

Grid Ref: SN 2185 4600

Refs: Emanuel Bowen Map of South Wales, c. 1760; Colby Map, 1831; *Blodau Dyfed* (1824) p. 217; Clynfyw Deeds, Box 1; Taliaris Deeds, Echedale, p. 5; NLW, Noyadd Trefawr Deeds, No. 672; CRO, GGMS I (Gwynfardd) p. 19; WWHR, ii, p. 155; Meyrick, *Cardiganshire*, p. 122; CRO, Coedmor Deeds, Box 8. Ex info. Mr and Mrs. T Lewis-Bowen.

LLWYNHYWEL, Llanilar (formerly Rhostie)

Marked on *Colby's Map of 1831* and modern OS maps a mile and a half south of Llanilar east of Rhos-y-garth. The first reference to this house is late in the 17th century when Bridget David of Llwynhywel married Philip Richard, son of Richard ap Harry of Cefn-coch, Llanilar, (died in 1633) by Gwenllian, daughter of one Llywelyn. Richard was descended, through his father David ap Harry of Glenydd, from Adda Fychan of Llanddwy in the parish of Llanfihangel-y-Creuddyn, an important Government official in the area in the middle of the 14th century.

In 1777, James Parry, third son of David Parry of Llidiardau and Mary, widow of the Rev. John Jones, vicar of Cardigan, married Elizabeth, daughter of Evan Morgan of Trawsgoed Lodge (1754-1813). James came to prominence a year later in 1778 when he was convicted of the manslaughter of Morgan Morgans on the night of 7 March. Morgan Morgans 'much in liquor' entered the kitchen at Llwynhowel and when James Parry saw him 'did violently assault . . . and did fasten the said linen handerchief about the neck of the said Morgan Morgans . . . of which choaking strangling and suffocating the said Morgan Morgans then and there instantly died'.

The previous year James Parry had mortgaged Llwynhowel to Catherine Jones, a widow of Aberystwyth. James and Elizabeth had a daughter, Mary, who married Samuel Rush Meyrick (1783-1848), antiquary and barrister at the ecclesiastical and admiralty courts. He built Goodrich Court near Ross-on-Wye and was the author of *The History and Antiquities of the County of Cardigan* (1809-10). His most important work was his edition of Lewys Dwnn's *Heraldic Visitations of Wales and part of the Marches* (1846), essential reading for students of Welsh genealogy and heraldry. His son, Llywelyn (1807-37), an equerry to the Duke of Sussex, died unmarried.

Llwynhywel eventually became part of the Castle Hill estate and farmed by tenants. In 1944, David John and Nancy Lloyd Evans settled at Llwynhywel and purchased the holding from the Castle Hill estate in 1955. The farm is now run by Mr. and Mrs. Irwell Evans and family.

Grid Ref: SN 6363 7235

Refs: Colby Map, 1831; Castle Hill Docs., No 839; Ex info. Mrs. N. Evans.

LLWYN-IORWERTH, Llanbadarn Fawr

Marked on *Colby's Map of 1831* and on modern OS maps as Llwyn Ierwerth-uchaf and -isaf four miles east of Aberystwyth and north of Penbryn off the A44 (T) road towards Ponterwyd. The family who settled at Llwyn Iorwerth were of great antiquity, descended from Edwyn ap Owen ap Hywel Dda. The earliest reference in the Notes is to Lewis, the son of Llewelyn Fychan Ieuvan Ieuvan Fychan, and Margaret his wife, who traced to Adda Welw. Lewis was twice married. His first wife was Agnes, heiress of Llewelyn ap David of Aber-mad, from whom descended the Lloyds of Aber-mad. As his second wife, Lewis married Dyddgu, daughter of Meredudd ap Llewelyn of Penybuarth. Their son, Rhys, who married a daughter of David ap Richard ap David Parke, was followed by Thomas ap Rhys of Llwyn Iorwerth. Thomas's daughter, Maud, married as her second husband, John ap Rhydderch of Towyn, from whom descends the early Glanleri family. Thomas was followed at Llwyniorwerth by Watkin Thomas, who signed for Dwnn in 1588 and married Elen, daughter of Richard Pryse of Gogerddan. Watkin and Elen had two children, Elizabeth, who married Morgan David Lloyd of Glascrug, from whom the Lloyds of Rhiwarthen descend, and a son, David Lloyd, who married Mary, daughter of John Stedman of Ystrad Fflur. In 1760 Llwyn Iorwerth-isaf was occupied by John James, who married Catherine, daughter of William Jones, a freeholder of Hafodau, Goginan. Their children were Thomas, born in 1766 and Elizabeth, baptized on 4 February 1768.

Grid Ref: SN 6475 8112

Refs: Colby Map, 1831; NLW, Griffith Owen List (iv); *Dwnn,* i, 48; WWHR, i, 31, 32; CRO, GGMS III (Edwin), fo. 4-5; CRO, GGMS (Gwynfardd) p. 29; O. Pemb. IV, 467, No. 2; C/A Protheroe MS., C, VI.

LLWYNRHYDOWEN, Llandysul

Marked on *Colby's Map of 1831* and on modern OS maps adjacent to the B4459 just south of Rhydowen overlooking the Cetwr. In the same vicinity are Tomen Rhydowen and Rhyd Owen, formerly part of the Grange of Taly-llchau. Alltyrodin is nearby. The home of Rhys, younger son of Alltyrodyn.

The Lloyds of Llwynrhydowen were descended from Rees ap David ap Llewelyn ap Gwilym Llwyd of Castell Hywel who traced to Cadifor ap Dinawal. His son, David of Alltyrodin married Mary, daughter of Ieuan ap Ievan ap Howel of Faerdre. Their second son, Rhys, is the first named at Llwynrhydowen and his son, David ap Rhys succeeded. David's son, Rhys David ap Rhys married Jane, daughter of Thomas Bowen of Bwlchbychan. Their son, another David, who died in 1709, married Jane, daughter of David Lloyd John of Camnant and lived there. Evan, the second son of David ap Rhys, had a daughter Jane, who married the Rev. Jenkin Jones, born in Trefle, Llanwenog, author and minister, who built the Arminian (later Unitarian) chapel of Llwynrhydowen in 1733. Jenkin Jones died in 1742 and it was his son-in-law, David Lloyd of Coedlannan who married Jenkin's daughter, Jane, and published his *Hymnau* in 1768. The congregation of Llwynrhydowen were turned out of their chapel in 1876 when Gwilym Marles was the minister, by the playboy squire of Alltyrodin, who, influenced by his agent, also evicted ten-ants who cast Liberal votes at the 1868 election.

Grid Ref: SN 4454 4500

Refs: Colby Map, 1831; ped. NLW, J. Alcwyn Evans 12356 E; WWHR, ii, 52; CRO, GGMS (Tydwal Gloff).

LLWYN-RHYS, Llanbadarn Odwyn

This property may be the property now known as Cwm-y-glyn. Marked on *Colby's Map of 1831* but not named on modern OS maps, half a mile north-east of Llangeitho. The house is chiefly remembered as the home of John Jones, recognised as one of the first, if not the first, dissenting minister in the county.

The first recorded occupant was John ab Ieuan Llwyd who was descended from the Clement family of Tregaron who married Angharad, daughter of Ieuan ap Thomas who traced to Rhydderch of Glyn Aeron, as recorded in the *Golden Grove Manuscripts.* Their son, the aforementioned John Jones (c. 1640-1722) married, in 1660, Margaret, sister to David Edwards, another notable preacher of Deri Odwyn, who owned Llwyn-rhys. Their second son, Jenkin Jones of Coed Mawr, Llanddewibrefi was buried at Cardigan in 1705. John and Margaret Jones had at least twelve children. The eldest, David Jones (1660-1724) was a Cavalry Officer and wrote:

Tragical History of the Stuart Family, 1697;
The Secret History of Whitehall, 1697;
1717 ditto, brought up to date;
1701 History of the Turks;
1702 Life of King James II;
1702 History of William III;
1715 History of the House of Brunswick;

Translation of Pezron's Antiquities of Nations (French);

Anglo French Wars and Salic Law;

Complete History of Europe from 1600 to 1716 in 16 volumes;

Lives of Sir Stepen Fox, of Dr. South, of Earl of Halifax, and of Dr. Radcliffe;

Detection of the Court and State of England.

Jenkin Jones and his wife, Mary, had several children. Sarah married David Jones, of Deri Ormond, drover, and High Sheriff in 1773 who died a debtor in 1775.

In 1782 Deri Ormond was sold to John Jones. Llwynrhys became the property of Rogers of Abermeurig, purchased from the Jones family. In his book *The Abermeurig Family* J. H. Davies tells us 'The house still remains much as it was in his day [John Jones, dissenter, d. 1722], and one portion called 'Y Groes' is shown which was specially erected for the purpose of a conventicle. It is a very small room, leading out of the kitchen, and could only at best have held a few persons. Still it is probably one of the oldest relicts of the non-conformity of the 17th century, and Mr. Rogers has carefully preserved it from decay'.

Horsfall-Turner tells us that, 'The straw-thatched mansion stands today in much the same condition as when in 1672 Morgan Hywel was licenced to be a congregational teacher at the house of John Jones of Llanbadarn Odwyn. After sundry knocks against the doorways, and the hams and baskets hanging from the roof, we managed to enter the kitchen which appeared to be in almost total darkness for a time. A spacious room it was, with a monster fire-place and a yawning black chimney, its tiny window was deep set in the thick wall, a blackened oak beam stretching many feet into the room supported the loft which was entered by a ladder close to the door. On the left of the door a bedroom six feet high and very small with earthen floor, was called the preacher's room. In this very room Morgan Hywel held forth to his far-gathered congregation . . . John Jones's son was brought up with an excellent knowledge of languages and thus became highly valued by James II into whose service he had entered. As a prolific writer on contemporaneous history he became widely known. After he had been absent for some years, Captain Jones visited his parents. The old people saw him crossing the fields and wondered who the military gentleman could be. The times were dangerous for non-conformist preachers and naturally enough the old man feared apprehension and hid away in a loft. The son, still unrecognized by his mother, entered the house and asked for the master. In perfect fear the old dame fainted away and from the loft came her husband in haste. Hurried explanations followed. The Captain had brought down a special permission for the preacher to conduct public services, and as the house was limited in capacity, a cross was soon erected in the wider expanse without, from which the message could be proclaimed more widely'.

Grid Ref: SN 6318 5985

Refs: Colby Map, 1831; NLW, Griffith Owen Deeds; B. J. J. Teulu, *Llwynrhys in Cymru,* 25, 1903, 221-3; CRO, GGMS; J. H. Davies, *The Abermeurig Family;* WWHR, ii, 154 (1913); Horsfall-Turner, *Cardiganshire,* pp. 263-4, & sketch of the old Llwynrhys house (p. 264).

LLWYN-Y-GROES, Llanwnnen

This property and Castell Du are associated with Neuadd-fawr. It is situated north-west of Llanwnnen, near Capel-y-groes on the west bank of the Grannell and marked on *Colby's Map of 1831.*

In 1760 it was owned by Hugh Bevan. Anne Jenkins of Llwyn-y-groes married Thomas Jones of Neuadd-fawr who was High Sheriff of Cardiganshire in 1764 and who died in 1813 aged 91. In 1862, William Jones of Llwyn-y-groes owned a freehold rent charge on Esgeronnen-fach in Llanybydder parish.

In *TDW* Lewis writes 'In the vale of the Granell, is Llwyn y Groes, the deserted seat of the family of Jones of Neuadd in the adjoining parish. The mansion, which is spacious and handsome, is finely situated in the midst of flourishing plantations, and the grounds comprehend much beautiful scenery'. In 1908 David Robert Jones of Llwyn-y-groes inherited Neuadd-fawr and Castell Du under the terms of the will of Alice Mabel Hughes, widow of Thomas Hugh Rice Hughes of Neuadd-fawr.

Grid Ref: SN 5236 4811

Refs: Colby Map, 1831; WWHR, iii, 90; Lewis *TDW,* 1840.

LLWYN YR HEOL, site unknown

Mary Lloyd of Llwyn yr Heol (of Castell Hywel stock) married Thomas Williams, who took the additional name Lloyd on marriage. Their son was Lloyd-Williams of Gwernant.

LLYSFAEN, Llanwnnen

Marked on *Colby's Map of 1831* and on modern OS maps as Llysfaen -uchaf and -isaf, as a long mile north-west of Llanwnnen village, on the banks of the Grannell. In 1760 Richard Morgan owned and lived at Llysfaen. He was High Sheriff of Cardiganshire in 1767.

Refs: Colby Map, 1831; WWHR, iii, 90.

ABWS, Llanrhystud
Marked on *Colby's Map of 1831* and on modern OS maps one and three quarter miles south-east of Llanrhystud, on the south bank of the Wyre fach in Cwm Mabws. The site of two houses, one built in the early 1600's of greystone and replaced in the middle of the 18th century. Nearby are Penlan Mabws, Cefn Mabws and Mabws-hen, which suggests a location of great antiquity. Plâs Mabws was the seat of an ancient family of the same stock as the Lloyds of Ystrad Teilo.

Rhydderch ap Rhys Goch ap Ieuan ap Rhys Fychan ap Rhys Ddu ap Llewelyn ap Cadogan was descended from Cadifor ap Dinawal. Rhydderch married Elen, daughter of Lewis ap Ieuan ap Lewys of Aber-mad. Their son, Richard ap Rhydderch, who married Lleucu, daughter of William ap Llewelyn, signed for Lewys Dwnn in 1613, who described the property as 'Y Plâs: Mabws Fawr'.

David ap Richard married Elizabeth, daughter of Henry ap Richard ap John ap Rhydderch. His brother, Ieuan, described as of Llanbadarn, married Elen, daughter of John Pryse of Gogerddan. Their eldest son, David Llwyd, rector of Llangoedmor, died unmarried and devised the estate to his brother, Richard, of Mabws and Ystrad Teilo, who married Gwen, daughter of Morgan Herbert of Hafod Uchdryd. Their son, Erasmus, married Elizabeth, daughter of David Lewes of Gernos, and was assessed at three hearths in the return for 1672. Erasmus was succeeded by his son, Richard, High Sheriff in 1671, who married Elizabeth, daughter of David Lloyd of Crynfryn, Nancwnlle, High Sheriff of Cardiganshire in 1662. Her portion was £500. It is probable that it was at this time that the family moved to Mabws from Ystrad Teilo where they had resided for centuries. In the *Trefaes Deeds* is a reference to a deed dated 1-2 October 1723 to which Richard Morris of Carrog and Richard Lloyd of Mabws were party. The deed mentions 'the dwelling house of Richard Lloyd called New Mabws', built of greystone. In 1730, Richard Lloyd of Mabws Esq. subscribed to *Laws of Hywel Dda* (Welsh and Latin) and was MP for Cardigan Borough from 1729-1741. He married Lettice, heiress of Edward Games of Tre-gaer, Brecon. On 4 June 1750 Anna Maria (1728-1786), daughter and heiress of Richard Lloyd of Mabws and Ystrad Teilo married James Lloyd of Ffosybleiddiaid (1721-1800), and it was this James who built the mansion of Mabws soon after his marriage in 1750.

Meyrick tells us, 'Mabws . . . is a very large edifice, situated in a vale. It was erected by James Lloyd Esq. of Ffos y Bleiddied and Ystrad Teilo, father of John who married Elinor, daughter of John Allen of Dale Castle, in Pembrokeshire. As she was an heiress, he, in her right, possessed Dale Castle' (and in his own right inherited Mabws and Ffosybleiddiaid).

In his *Visitation of Seats* Burke describes the house, 'it is an English manor-house built of blue stone and standing upon high ground, of large size and exceedingly commodious. Up the centre of the building runs a spacious staircase lined with handsome carved oak . . . and most of the rooms are floored with the same material'.

John Lloyd (1753-1820) and Elinor Allen were married in 1776. John was High Sheriff of Pembrokeshire in 1785 and Cardiganshire in 1803. It was from this union that the Lloyd-Philipps of Dale Castle, descend. John's brother, James (1762-1837), inherited Pentyparc, Walton East parish, near Clarbeston Road in 1823 from the descendants of Mary Philipps, his great-grandmother, who had married John Lloyd of Ffosybleiddiaid early in the 18th century. James, who added Philipps to his surname, commanded the 86th Regiment during the Egyptian Campaign of 1801, leading it across the desert from Suez to Cairo. He died at Mabws on 11 April 1837, aged 75 years. James and his wife, Winifred (nee Thomas), who lived at Mabws until her death, had two sons, James

Beynon (d. 1865) and Frederick Lewis Lloyd-Philipps, who died without heirs at Pentyparc in 1902.

In the *Tithe Schedule of 1839,* Mabws estate was of 2,682 acres with an annual rental of £1,561. The Rev. Isaac Williams (1734-1811), vicar of Llanrhystud for 40 years, lived at Mabws in 1760 as a tutor for the young James Lloyd.

The 'Particulars of Sale of Freehold Estates of the late John Lloyd of Dale Castle, Pembs, called the Mabws and Foesybleiddiaidd Estates', were advertised to be sold at auction at the Talbot Inn, Lampeter on Monday 5 July 1824. Among the more interesting lots were 4 lime-kilns and an old mill which were situated on the seaside, where any quantity of sand and sea-weed could be procured for manure, and formed part of the flat called 'Llansaintfread Flat', celebrated for the growth of Barley. The turnpike road from the town of Aberystwyth to the town of Cardigan lay near this lot. Also included was a water corn grist mill called Felin-fawr, which adjoined the previous lot on the seaside. The mill was 'in full work, had a constant supply of water and had lately been put in complete repair'. Farms were offered which were held on a lease for three lives; a lot of five messuages and land which were subject to an annuity of £80 during the life of a 'female now aged about 50 years or thereabouts'. Three farms were subject to an annual fee of farm rent to the Earl of Lisburne; also included was 'an unoccupied garden and its appurtenances in Tregaron, the Red Lion Inn, in Llanrhystud with stables, gardens and land and the rights of "Tolls, Pitchings or Dues of Fairs" held at Ystradmeurig'.

In *Out with the Cambrians* published in 1933, Evelyn Lewes of Llanllyr writes 'I specially remember the Frederick Lloyd Philipps of Pentyparc who died in the year 1902. Probably Mr. Lloyd Philipps was one of the very few Pembrokeshire landowners of his time who could converse in Welsh, but it was appropriate that he should be able to do so, for he was born at Mabws, one of the most venerable houses of Cardiganshire, and his forebears were the Lloyds of the still more ancient house of Ffosy-bleiddied, who traced their descent from the illustrious King of all Wales, Rhodri Mawr of Mervyn Frych'.

Mabws, along with about 50 acres, is now occupied by Mrs. Gunton and her two sons. Local tradition maintains that Mabws-hen nearby, was the location of the original *plâs.*

Grid Ref: SN 5650 6855

Refs: Colby Map, 1831; Meyrick, *Cardiganshire,* 1810, edn. 1907, p. 266; WWHR, iii, 93; Landowners Return, 1873; Evelyn Lewes, *Out with the Cambrians,* 1933, p. 33; *Dwnn,* i, 161, 28; Nicholas, *County Families,* 1875, I, 206; *Ceredigion* Vol. VII, Nos. 3/4 (1976), p. 343; Burke, *Visitation of Seats,* iv (1858), 92; NLW, Griffith Owen Deeds, 5001; Llanrhystyd Tithe Apportionment Map, 10 September 1839; NLW, Trefaes Deeds; PRO ADX/16.

MAENOREIFED, Llandygwydd

There are several Eifed place-names in the area. Marked on *Colby's Map of 1831* and on modern OS maps on the banks of the Teifi north of the A484 a mile east of Llechryd. Thomas Pryce, a merchant of Cardigan town, and living in 1766 had a sister, Bridget, who married a Wagner (see Aber-porth Plas). They had a son, John Wagner, who married and had two children, the eldest of whom, Thomas Richard Pryce Wagner lived at Maenoreifed from 1839 until he died in 1878. His will was proved in 1879. He left his realty to his nephew, John Frederick Mitchell who was his sister's son.

A photograph taken c.1870 and published in *The Tivyside Photographic Souvenir,* shows the house to be a small well-proportioned attractive property, probably of the 18th century; comprising of two storeys, a range of three windows and a pillared entrance. Following his marriage to Aline Margaret, elder daughter of John Vaughan Colby of Ffynone, Maenordeifi, Colonel Cecil John Herbert Spence-Jones and his wife lived at Maenoreifed prior to his assuming the name Spence-Colby following the death of his father-in-law in 1919 when the young pair moved to Ffynone. Maenoreifed is now owned by Mr. and Mrs. Tom Craig who have carried out extensive renovations to the property.

Grid Ref: SN 2319 4363

Refs: Colby Map, 1831; *The Tivyside Photographic Souvenir.*

MAESBANGOR, Llanbadarn Fawr

Located just south of Capel Bangor and marked on *Colby's Map of 1831* and on modern OS maps on the banks of the Melindwr. Meyrick tells us that, 'the house here belonged formerly to a family named Lloyd, now extinct'.

The Lord Chief Justice, Sir John Pratt married as his second wife, Elizabeth, the daughter of the Rev. Hugh Wilson rector of Llandinam and Canon of Bangor. Elizabeth died in 1728. Their son Charles (b. 1713) became the 1st Earl Camden.

According to the *Golden Grove Manuscripts* Richard ap Rhys of Gogerddan had three sons, one of whom was William Llwyd of Maesbangor who married Maud, daughter of Harry Thomas of Cwmtudu. They had four sons. The eldest John Prys Llwyd, who married Mary, daughter and heiress of Rhys ap Jenkin ap William, and had two sons; Thomas, who married a daughter of Thomas Lewis Morgan of Rhiwarthen, and Edward Lloyd who married and had issue. The second son of William and Maud was Richard, and the third son was Morris William of Penrallt who married and had issue. The fourth son was Rhys.

In 1760 Bulstrode Lloyd, gent., owned Maesbangor and at some time it was the home of Mr. Scawen Lloyd. The pedigree of the Lloyds of Maesbangor is given in the *Bodleian Manuscripts.*

Grid Ref: SN 6562 7995

Refs: Colby Map, 1831; Bodleian MSS., Add. C. 177-9, D.E.; WWHR, iii, 102; CRO, GGMS, III (Gwaethfoed).

MAESYFELIN,
Llanbedr Pont Steffan (Lampeter)

This property, described as 'a Jacobean edifice', once stood east of Lampeter near the present-day rugby ground and is marked on *Colby's Map of 1831.* Meyrick states 'This house no longer exists as a place of consequence, a farmhouse only now serving instead of the original mansion, to which it was formerly an appendage. It stood on the side of a little river, called Dulas, and not far from the mill which occasioned its name. It was the property of a family of Lloyd, allied to those of Allt yr Odin, and Castle Howel'.

Lewis in *TDW* tells us that 'The ancient Lords of this place are represented to have been men of great wealth: their mansion was delightfully situated on the declivity of an eminence to the west of the town; and there are still some remains of a causeway, which, according to tradition, led from it to the western door of the church.

The castle of Lampeter is stated to have been demolished towards the end of the twelfth century by Owain Gwynedd . . . it is supposed to have stood in a meadow on the right of the road leading to Aberystwyth, the site being marked by a lofty artificial mound surrounded by an entrenchment'. Built on the site of a 14th century building, Maesyfelin was the home of Thomas Griffith, originally of Mynyd-dhywel, Lampeter, who was High Sheriff of Cardiganshire in 1574. He was followed at Maesyfelin by Marmaduke Lloyd, son and heir of Thomas Lloyd, Chancellor of St. David's Cathedral, and a nephew of Marmaduke Middleton, Bishop of St. David's. Marmaduke Lloyd was educated at Oxford and was called to the Bar in 1608. He married Mary, daughter of John Gwyn Stedman of Ystrad Fflur and they had nine children. A fervent Royalist, captured with his son, Francis, at the Battle of St. Fagans, Marmaduke became a General for Wales and the Marches and Chief Justice of Brecon. He was knighted in 1622 and died before November 1651 when his will was proved and the Maesyfelin estate, along with other lands in Shropshire, Somerset, Montgomery, Carmarthenshire and Cardiganshire, passed to John Lloyd, his brother-in-law of Peterwell.

One of Sir Marmaduke Lloyd's best friends was Rhys Prichard (1579-1644), vicar of Llandovery and author of *Canwyll y Cymry,* published in full in 1681. Rhys's son, Samuel, was drowned in the Tywi. According to tradition the vicar held the sons of Sir Marmaduke responsible, as Samuel had dared to aspire to the hand of their sister. Vicar Prichard is said to have laid a curse on Maesyfelin:

> *May God with heavy curses chase*
> *All Maesyfelin's villain race*
> *For they have drowned in Tywi's tide*
> *Llandovery's flower, Cymru's pride.*

Melltith Duw fo ar Maesyfelin
Ar bob carreg a phob gwreiddyn
Am dafly blodau tre Llandyfri
Ar ei ben i Dywi i foddi.

Sir Marmaduke was succeeded at Maesyfelin by his son, Francis, MP for Carmarthenshire 1640-4, Comptroller of the Household of Charles I, and knighted at Oxford in 1643. He married Mary, daughter of John Vaughan, Earl of Carbery and kept a mistress, Bridget Leigh at Maesyfelin. She was the mother of his sons, Lucius and Charles. He died in 1669 and was buried in Lampeter. Maesyfelin was certainly commodious, Lady Mary Lloyd was assessed at 13 hearths in 1672. Lucius predeceased his father and Charles Lloyd (1655-1704), the younger brother succeeded to the estate. Educated at Oxford his first wife was Jane, daughter of Morgan Lloyd of Greengrove and his second, Frances, daughter of Sir Francis Cornwallis of Abermarlais, bore him two sons and four daughters. He was High Sheriff of Cardiganshire in 1690, knighted in 1693 and created a baronet in 1708. He represented Cardigan Borough in Parliament from 1698-1701. He died in 1723 and was succeeded by his son Charles Cornwallis Lloyd, the second baronet who died at the age of 24. Charles was succeeded by his brother Lucius who married Anne, daughter of Walter Lloyd of Peterwell. Lucius died without an heir in 1750 and the Maesyfelin estate went to John Lloyd, his brother-in-law of Peterwell. In his will drawn up in 1745, with a codicil added in 1750, mention is made of over 50 properties, mostly in Cynwyl Gaeo, a cornmill, a 20 year lease of the church of Llanbedr Pont Steffan, and the tithes and obligations of Llanwenog parish and the rectory and church of Llan-y-crwys.

Lady Lloyd (Sir Lucius' mother) lived in her old home for another three years, until she died and then the great days of Millfield ended. The Rev. William Edmunds described it thus: 'the glory of Maesyfelin fell to the dust'. Later, Alice, a married sister of John Lloyd of Peterwell lived there. She had married Jeremiah Lloyd, coroner for Cardiganshire, who resided at Maesyfelin in the 1750s, and their son Herbert Lloyd, attorney of Carmarthenshire was born there. It is said that a great quantity of the materials of the house were carried away to enlarge and adorn the mansion at Peterwell. In 1804 when he was in the Lampeter area described in his *Tours in Wales* Fenton wrote 'I mounted my horse, crossed the River Dulas at Millfield, (Maesyfelin), and ascended the Summit of Mynydd Allt Goch'.

In 1860, the Rev. William Edmunds, Master of Lampeter School wrote 'At present there is nothing to be seen of Maesyfelin. A few neat cottages for workmen are built near the spot where the old mansion stood. Some of the foundations of the house were dug up some 25 years ago by the farmer who occupied the land. A gentleman who visited the place not long afterwards, brought away as a relic a carved stone. He describes it as 'the lowest stone of a door jamb, chamfered on one edge, and finished off below with an oak leaf on the slope where the chamfer ended in the square angle at the bottom'. This stone was conveyed to Dolaucothi (residence of John Johnes, Esq., descended from Maesyfelin) . . . The mansion of Maesyfelin is described as an old place, built in the pointed style'.

Grid Ref: SN 5775 4870

Refs: Colby Map, 1831; E. Inglis Jones, 'Derry Ormond,' *Ceredigion,* vol. II, No. 3, 1954; *Arch. Cam.* 1860, pp. 169-70, 172, 176-8, 272-80, ibid, 1881, pp. 236-7; Maesyfelin in *Welsh Gazette,* 11th Jan. 1906 & Chwedlau Maesyfelin, on 25th July 1946; Old Lampeter Families, Rev. William Edmunds, reprint from *Arch. Cam.* 1860, p. 21-2; *Cymru,* Oct. 1901, 237-241; Blome List, 1673; WWHR, i, 9-11; Meyrick, *Cardiganshire,* edn. 1907, 223-4; *The Cambrian Journal,* 1857, 62; Fenton, *Tours in Wales,* 1804-13, p. 11; Lloyd Family Records, p. 29; George E. Evans, *Pamphlet on Peterwell*, 1900; Lewis, *TDW,* 1840; Bethan Phillips, *Peterwell,* pp. 1-12.

MOELFRYN, Llanbadarn Trefeglwys
Marked on *Colby's Map of 1831* and on modern OS maps as Moelfryn-mawr, with Moelfryn-bach, and Moelfryn-maen as neighbouring properties in the east of the parish, west of Penwych.

Richard Herbert, son and heir of Morgan Morgan Herbert, gent., of Gwnnws parish, descendant of the Hafod family, married Margaret, daughter of Morgan David Jenkins of Moelfryn whose will was dated 11 January

1664/5. The marriage was subject to a pre-nuptial settlement dated 20 December 1630, Margaret's portion being £140. They had a son Morgan Herbert, gent., of Moelfryn who lived there at the end of the 17th century. In 1672 a Richard Herbert, Esq. of Llanafan parish paid tax on eight hearths. Morgan Herbert's will was dated 21 June 1706. He and his wife, Jane, had three sons and one daughter. Richard Herbert, the eldest son succeeded to Moelfryn. The other children who were alive in 1710 were Thomas, John and Mary, who married David Hugh of Cilcennin, the son and heir of Hugh Richard of Penbryn parish, gent. Their marriage was subject to a pre-nuptial settlement in May 1705. Richard Herbert, eldest son and heir is named as of Moelfryn in 1710. He married Magdalen Lloyd, sister of John Lloyd of Cilyrug, (Cil-rhug), gent. This marriage was also subject to a pre-nuptial settlement on 14 November 1698, Magdalen's portion being £100. The Notes also mention a Morgan Herbert, gent., vivens 1755 who married Catherine who was described as 'widow in 1759, her husband being lately deceased'. In 1760, the year following Morgan Herbert's death Edward Evan was the owner-occupier of Moelfryn-mawr.

Grid Ref: SN 5780 6250

Refs: Colby Map, 1831; J. F. Deeds 803,.809, 786, 791; WWHR, ii, 91.

MOEL IFOR, Llanrhystud

Former residence of the Gwyn and Phillips families, located on *Colby's Map of 1831* and on modern OS maps, adjacent to the A487 (T) above the Carrog stream, north east of Llanrhystud. Meyrick tells us 'now only a farmhouse, was formerly the residence of two ancient families . . . situated on the side of a hill. Moel Ivor is supposed by some to be the same as Llanrhystud Castle, mentioned in Powel's *History of Wales*, and it stood formerly opposite the present house on the other side of the valley. It was pulled down in the reign of Queen Elizabeth, about the year 1565, by Jenkin Gwyn, when he served the office of High Sheriff for the county; and a large mansion house erected where the present one stands. The family who afterwards inherited it, principally resided at Dolhaidd and Cringae in Carmarthenshire [and] this venerable old mansion became neglected and so ruinous that about twenty years ago it was pulled down, and the present farmhouse built in its stead'.

The Llanina estate once belonged to the Gwyn family of Moeli Ifor. The family were deprived of it by means of a fatal will, the legality of which was disputed in the reign of Charles II, but the attorney deserted and they lost the case. In his *Historical Notes* J. Rowlands tells us that 'It is stated that he was bribed by the other side. In the time of Cromwell, the same attorney acted as an agent to the Protector in this county. He was evidently an unprincipled man'.

Among the early owners of Moel Ifor was Owen Gwynn who served as High Sheriff of Cardiganshire in 1552. The Gwynns traced to Cadifor ap Dinawal through Llewelyn ap Cadwgan of Carrog and Rhys Ddu y Sgweier digri. Jenkin Gwynn was the next owner of Moel Ifor to serve as High Sheriff in 1564. He was the father of Ieuan Gwynn who had a daughter Deborah, who married Ernestus Musgrave, whose family had fled to Wales from Yorkshire to escape religious persecution. Their son, Peregrine, moved to Pembrokeshire and was a prominent Quaker. Deborah's second husband was David Jones of Coedmor in Pencarreg, ap John ap David ap Owen. Ieuan Gwynn Jenkin, married a female descendant of Rees Lloyd Llewelyn of Ffoshelyg and was High Sheriff of Cardiganshire in 1613 and again in 1623. The line of the Gwynns ended in two co-heiresses who married two brothers; Magdalen married John Phillips of Dolhaidd and Bridget married Richard Phillips. At about this time Elinor Gwynn, widow of Moel Ifor, married a Richard Jones, her portion being £500. The house was possibly tenanted in 1672; according to the *Blome List* Richard Herbert was living at Moel Ifor in that year and paid tax on five hearths.

In 1703 Richard Phillips of Moel Ifor was High Sheriff of the county and was appointed a JP in 1706. Richard and Bridget had three sons and three daughters who all subscribed to *Laws of Hywel Dda* in 1730: Richard, Daniel, John, Magdalen the co-heiress, who died unmarried.

Elizabeth married the Rev. Watkin Lewes of Tredefaid, Pembrokeshire. Jane who was the last grand-daughter of the last of the Gwynns of Moel Ifor, married Erasmus Saunders of Pentre, whose daughter and heiress, Susan, married Dr. David Davies, of Pentre, formerly of Llandovery and the Moel Ifor estate which had already been passed to the Phillips of Dolhaidd passed to Saunders Davies of Pentre. Erasmus Saunders of Moel Ifor was appointed JP in 1748.

In 1751 a post-nuptial settlement was agreed between the co-heiresses and their spouses, which gave a third of the messuages and lands of the late Richard Phillips, including a tucking mill and a corn grist mill, to Elizabeth and her husband, the Rev. Watkin Lewes of Penybenglog, Meline parish, Pembrokeshire.

In *County Families* Nicholas tells us that towards the end of the 18th century Moel Ifor, having become decayed, was taken down and a farmhouse was built on or near the site of the old mansion. The *Llanrhystyd Tithe Apportionment* of 10 September 1839 shows that David Saunders Davies was the owner with John James as tenant of the 180 acres. David Saunders Davies also owned several farms in the area as well as Felindre Moel Ifor (18 acres), Felindre Tucking Mill (3 acres) and Moel Ifor Mill or Felinganol (6 acres). Moel Ifor was occupied by a series of tenants and then sold. The present owner-occupiers are the Evans family.

Grid Ref: SN 5473 7063

Refs: Colby Map, 1831; *Dwnn*, i, 38, WWHR, i, 42-3; PRO, Dale Castle MS.; Blome List, 1673; Meyrick, *Cardiganshire,* 267; Nicholas, *County Families,* i, 176, 177; CRO, GGMS, *Cardiganshire,* 34 Charles II (1682-3); *Historical Notes,* J. Rowlands *Historical Notes,*1866, 103; Llanrhystyd Tithe Apportionment, 10 Sept. 1839; *The Cambrian Travellers Guide.* 2nd edn., 1813, p. 9.

MORFA BYCHAN, Llanychaearn

Formerly a grange belonging to the abbey of Strata Florida (Ystrad Fflur), situated on the coastal plateau west of Chancery, four miles south of Aberystwyth. An old house, now demolished, it had a Gothic doorway, post and panel partitions and an ancient barn which is now part of a holiday park. Marked on the 14th century *Rees Map,* on *Colby's Map of 1831* and on modern OS maps.

The first known occupier Ieuan Llwyd, was descended from Llawdden, the *praepositus* of the Commote of Perfedd in 1351-2. He moved from Morfa Bychan to Genau'r Glyn, and it is with the latter location that he became mostly associated. Dafydd ap Gwilym wrote a *cywydd* to him. Ieuan's son, Gruffydd ap Llewelyn of Morfa Bychan, married Anne Vaughan, daughter of Ieuan Llwyd Ieuan Griffith Foel who traced to Gwaethfoed. Their son Rhys ap Gruffydd (Rhys Ddu) was Governor of Aberystwyth Castle and lived at Morfa Bychan. Rhys Ddu was one of Owain Glyndwr's trusted lieutenants in the county. He had served as Sheriff of Cardiganshire in 1394-95 and leased royal lands at Silian, Trefilan and Talsarn. A man 'of few scruples' he later joined Glyndwr and remained with him until the end when Rhys was put to death and his head set on London Bridge.

Rhys Ddu had two daughters, Elliw, who married Maredydd ap Owen, Lord of Towyn and another daughter who married Meredydd ap Gronw ap Meyler (Meilyr).

In 1544 Thomas John ap Rhydderch of Morfa Bychan was High Sheriff of Cardiganshire. He was married to Elizabeth, daughter of Richard Mortimer of Coedmor. Thomas was succeeded by his son, Morris and his grandson, Rheinallt Morris, who married Maud, daughter of Thomas Morris Fychan. Rheinallt's grand-daughter Fortuna married John Bowen of Crugbychan. In 1610, one Reginald Morris is described as of Morfa Bychan having three messuages as security for a loan to David Lloyd ap Ieuan of Aber-mad.

Francis Lloyd, of the Aber-mad family, and his son and heir, Thomas Lloyd, were 'of Morfa Bychan' in 1669. They agreed to mortgage a messuage called Tir perth Rees ucha and three parcels of land called Tir Thomas y Gof all in the parish of Llanychaearn to James Jones of Dolaucothi. It would appear that the family no longer held the property in 1673 as Francis Lloyd was described as 'late of Morfa Bychan' when party to a deed, and in 1681 again when together with his son and daughter, also described as late of Morfa Bychan, he took out a further mortgage on the aforesaid messuage and lands.

John Bowen was succeeded by his son George Bowen of Crugbychan who married Elizabeth Lloyd, daughter of Hugh Lloyd of Lloyd Jack. They had a son, John Bowen, a minor in 1672, (and still living in 1806), described as of Morfa Bychan who married Margaret Lloyd, daughter of John Lloyd of Cilgwyn on 30 September 1682. Their son, John Bowen, was the last of the Bowens and he sold Morfa Bychan to Thomas Lloyd, second son of David Lloyd of Ffosybleiddiaid. In 1760 John Hughes was of Morfa Bychan. Meyrick writes, 'Morva, formerly called Morfa Bychan, is the residence of Miss Hughes, who inherited Aberllolwyn in this parish'.

A note in the Ceredigion Museum in Aberystwyth where an ancient partition is displayed (1985) states, 'The post-and-panel oak screen was rescued by Mr. John Jervis of Bryneithin when Morfa Bychan was demolished. The screen would have separated the main room or hall of the house from two small rooms behind it'.

The property was demolished by the Agricultural College, Aberystwyth in 1975.

Grid Ref: SN 7712 5655

Refs: Colby Map, 1831; Meyrick, *Cardiganshire,* 283; Tax Eccl.; CRO, GGMS I (Gwaethfoed) p. 30; ibid, III (Edwin); P. Smith, *Houses*, maps 37, 39, Ceredigion Museum, Aberystwyth; Gwaith David ap Gwilym 14; NLW, Cwrtmawr Deeds, Nos. 121, 232, 1225-7, 1315; Hywel Roberts, *Ceredigion,* VIII I, 1972, p. 21. WWHR, i, 55; CRO, GGMS (Gwynfardd), p. 25.

MORFA-MAWR, Llansanffraid

This ancient holding stands one mile south-west of the village of Llanon, near the sea and is marked on the 14th century *Rees Map of South Wales* and *Colby's Map of 1831* and on modern OS maps.

Rhys ap Gruffydd granted lands to the Cistercian monks of the Abbey of Strata Florida and the grange of Morfa-mawr became a sub-station of the Abbey. It extended from the river Arth north along the coast to the Ysig, a rivulet which enters the sea at Morfa-mawr. The grange extended east to Tryal-mawr and across country to Aberarth, a circumference of seven miles. Llywelyn ap Grffudd in his march into South Wales in 1256 spent the first Wednesday in Advent at Morfa-mawr. At the Dissolution the grange was purchased by Richard Devereux whose son became Earl of Essex and the tenants held the land on lease.

Thomas Gwyn ap Morgan Fychan was a JP. He was married twice; firstly to Gwenllian, daughter of Hugh Llewelyn Lloyd of Llanllyr, and secondly to Elen, daughter of Rhydderch ap Rees Fychan. Thomas died in 1622, having had a son, Huw, and two daughters; Margaret, who married Huw Bevan Lloyd ap y Cantor of Ynysfergi, and Dorothy who remained a spinster. Huw Gwyn married Mary Gruffydd, daughter of Morys Gruffydd of Plasnewydd, Anglesey. He signed his pedigree for the herald Dwnn on 24 January 1588. The Gwyn family who settled at Morfa-mawr were descended from Phylip ap Rhydderch ab Ieuan Llwyd of Glyn Aeron. Huw Gwyn, his brother Rhys and his father, Thomas, were all subjects of *cywyddan* of late medieval bards. Huw Gwyn predeceased his father in 1601, and his widow, Mary, married Anthony Stanley, Constable of Harlech Castle.

Huw and Mary had a son, Rowland, and a daughter Jane, who married Edward Owen of Pencrug in Llanbadarn Fawr. Rowland married Jane, daughter of Henry Watkin of Newcastle Emlyn and they had two sons; Thomas Gwyn who went to Holland and Huw Gwyn of Carmarthen, who married Anne Morgan, sister of David Morgan of Abergwili who traced to Elystan.

Hywel Roberts tells us in his valuable article in *Ceredigion* that Gruffudd Hafren wrote a *cywydd* describing the pleasures to be enjoyed at Morfa-mawr. Huw Llwyd Fyr wrote a *cywydd moliant* to Dafydd ab Ieuan ap Phylip ap Rhydderch of Glyn Aeron and that Dafydd Goch Brydydd composed one to Thomas Morgan. Ieuan Tew wrote two *cywyddan* to Thomas and Huw Gwyn and Rhysiant Philip wrote a *cywydd* to Huw Gwyn, and Sion Mawddwg wrote a *cywydd* to Huw and his wife Mary.

Grid Ref: SN 5038 6565

Refs: Rees Map, 14th Century; Colby Map, 1831; *Dwnn,* i, 80, 81-2; NLW, Griffith Owen List (iv); O Pemb., iv, 476; *Annales Camb.* p. 91; Tax Eccles. 1291; NLW, Cwrtmawr Deeds, No. 677; CRO, GGMS III (Gwaethfoed); Powis Castle Deeds, 16227; Hywel Roberts, *Ceredigion VII,* 1972, pp. 31-3.

MYNACHTY, Llanbadarn Trefeglwys

Situated about three miles east of Aberaeron village and south of the river Arth and marked on *Colby's Map of 1831.* Formerly the home of the Gwyn family of great antiquity. Previously known as Crugypebyll and near to the ancient castle of Dineirth built by Richard de la Mare, a follower of Richard de Clare, in 1110. In 1530 Llewelyn Dafydd ap Rhydderch held a 99 year lease of Crugypebyll from the Abbot of Strata Florida. In 1536 the reversion passed to the Crown on the dissolution of the abbey and was later granted to Richard Devereux and his son, the first Earl of Essex. According to Francis Jones' notes, the first of the Gwyns, a family destined to have a long association with Mynachty, was Lewis Dafydd Gwyn, son of Dafydd Gwyn, who was the son of Adda ap Meredydd of Trawscoed by his second wife,Gwerfyl daughter and co-heiress of Llewelyn Goch and traced by Dwnn to Llewelyn Gaplan of Aberaeron and so to Edwin ap Gronwy. Lewis Dafydd married Lleucu, the daughter of David Llwyd David Phillip, (according to Dwnn she was the daughter of Lewis ap David Lloyd) of Plâs Ciliau Aeron. Their son, Huw Gwyn, whose will was proved in 1606, and who predeceased his father, left a son and heir, Morgan Gwyn, who was High Sheriff of the county in 1614 and assessed at £5 in the Land Survey of 1628. He was still alive in 1645. He married the daughter of Morris Gruffydd yr Aer of Carmarthenshire. In 1631 John Vaughan, Morgan's distant kinsman, bought the reversion of the estate from Robert, third Earl of Essex, whose grandfather had bought it from the crown in 1564.

Morgan Gwyn's son and heir, Rhys Gwyn married Gaynor, the daughter and heiress of James Williams, whose will was proved in 1661. She was a widow in 1651 when she bought the reversion and fee farm of Mynachty from John Vaughan. They had a daughter and sole heiress, Elizabeth, who founded the second dynasty of Gwyns to live at Mynachty.

Elizabeth married Morgan Gwynn ap Lewis Gwyn ap Gruffydd of Cilfforch, Henfynwy, who traced to Gono Goch of Llangathen. Morgan paid tax on five hearths in 1672. His will was proved in 1682 and Elizabeth's one year later. They had a son and heir, Griffith Gwynn, who married Florence, daughter of Evan Thomas of Tremoilet, Carmarthenshire. Florence married as her second husband, Charles Lloyd, son of William Lloyd of Llanllyr. Their son, Lewis Gwynne was High Sheriff in 1702 and married Mary, daughter of John Price of Rhandir, Llangwyryfon, which was subject to a pre-nuptial settlement involving 22 properties in 1706.

Charles Gwynne, although only the fourth son of the marriage, inherited Mynachty, his brothers having died without issue. Charles married Bridget, daughter of the first John Jones of Tyglyn Aeron, Ciliau, by Bridget daughter of David Parry of Noyadd Trefawr. They had three sons and two daughters, all of whom died without issue. Charles Gwynne was High Sheriff in 1744 and died in 1749. His son, Lewis Gwynne was High Sheriff in 1771 (with John Jones of Aberystwyth as his Under-Sheriff), and died in 1805, a bachelor and without issue. In his *Visitation of Seats (1852)* Burke tells us that, 'The old house, built about two hundred years ago, was pulled down in the middle of the last century, and a new house built upon its site by Lewis Gwynne. Since then large additions have been made to it by the present owner'. Lewis Gwynne left Mynachty for their lives to his cousins Alban and Susanna Thomas Jones of Tyglyn.

The notice of Lewis Gwynne's death appeared in *The British Press* on Friday 6

The staircase at Mynachty

December 1805. 'He lived very private, though possessed of an extensive estate and accumulated an immense fortune, the bulk of which he has left to the Rev. Alban Thomas Jones of Tyglyn together with his real estate, except a small part of which he bequeathed to Mr. Edwards, youngest son of D. J. Edwards Esq., of Job's Well near Carmarthen. He had in his house when he died such a quantity of gold that a horse could not carry the weight to convey it to Tylgyn about a mile off, and when put on a sledge it was with difficulty he could draw it there. The amount in gold is One Hundred Thousand Pounds, besides Fifty Thousand Pounds in the Stocks. He was generous to the poor, always a friend to the necessitous, and an upright gentleman'. A small simple tablet stands at the side of the parish church of Llanbadarn Trefeglwys which says: 'He was a man, take him for all in all, We ne'er shall look upon his like again' – *Shakespeare*. It was Lewis Gwynne's cousin Susanna who became his heiress. She had married against her parent's wishes, another cousin, a penniless widowed Hampshire curate, aged 45, with five children, named Alban Thomas, whom her parents had described as 'an old mad clergyman . . . the oddest in nature'.

Charles Wilkins tells us in *Tales and Sketches of Wales* that 'Alban Thomas was the son of Alban Thomas of Rhos, Aberporth, vicar of Blaenporth. He was educated in London and became a doctor. His friend, one Moses Williams, a scholar, bookworm, dusty and cobwebbed with old lore, who spent his time in the British Museum, and when on a visit to Sir Hans Sloane's house, he met a young lady with whom he fell violently in love. He asked Alban to see the lady and to propose on his behalf, but she told the ambassador that she had no love for Moses. But Alban had fallen in love with her himself, and in due course proposed. She said 'If you can show me your coat of arms and prove you are entitled to it, I will be your wife. But I couldn't think of marrying anyone who had not the right to bear arms'. Alban wrote to his father who was interested in genealogy and heraldry, and in due course he received a beautiful pedigree illuminated with arms, tracing his descent from the Lords of Towyn. This he took to the lady and within a few months Alban led to the altar one who possessed both grace of person and a long purse. They lived happily in London until Mrs. Thomas took ill and died. Alban Thomas returned to Wales and married Miss Jones of Tyglyn, and he took the name Alban Thomas Jones. When his wife inherited Monachty from her Gwynne relatives, he took the name Alban Thomas Jones Gwynne. The unsuccessful suitor Moses Williams became the rector of Llanwenog where he vegetated very tranquilly, cultivating turnips, and, at his leisure hours, literature'. For variations of this tale see J. Rowlands' *Historical Notes.*

Alban Thomas Jones Gwynne (1751-1819), assumed not only the last name but also the arms of his late cousin, and with his second wife, Susannah Maria, Tyglyn (1754-1830), became the third family of Mynachty Gwynnes and it was they who built Aberaeron village and quay following a private Act of Parliament. Alban's mother was sister to Bridget, wife of the aforesaid Charles Gwynne, and Susannah Maria's grandfather was a brother of the same Bridget. In his book *Cardiganshire* Evans tells us that at the church of Llanbadarn Trefeglwy: 'On the wall over against the Holy Table is an unusual marble slab, probably the largest in the county, whereupon are recorded the names and dates of most of the children of the Rev. Alban Thomas Jones Gwynne of Tyglyn; together with those of their husbands and wives'. Thereafter the Mynachty estate descended to Alban's only son also named Alban Thomas Jones Gwynne, by his first wife, Martha Aston. He was known as Col. Gwynne. In 1808 he married Mary Anne, daughter of John Vevers of

Hereford. His son and heir was Alban Lewis Thomas Jones Gwynne (1809-65). He married Jane Crawshay Bailey of Nantyglo, Monmouthshire in 1847, was High Sheriff of Cardiganshire in 1853 and served as a Captain in the 62nd Regiment. His son, Alban Gwynne (1852-1904) married Mary Edith, daughter of John Battersby Harford, of Falcondale and Blaise Castle, Gloucestershire, who died in 1917. An engraving of the exterior of Mynachty can be found in Nicholas's *County Families* (1872). In 1873 *The Landowners Return* gives 'A. G. Gwynne of Mynachty as owning 422 acres, yielding £139 p.a. A. Lloyd Gwynne with 113 acres worth £49 p.a., and Mrs. Gwynne as 315 acres at £123'.

Their son Alban Lewis Gwynne was born in 1880, and was appointed a Lieut. Commander in the Royal Navy. He married Ruby, daughter of Col. Bond, of the Indian Army in 1912, and had, with other issue, a son Alban Patrick, born in 1913. Alban Lewis Gwynne sold Mynachty to a Captain Briggs. A Sale Catalogue of 1936 describes it as of 'Georgian character with a southerly aspect, comprising on the ground floor: entrance hall with stone paved floor, morning room communicating with a small winter garden drawing room, dining room, smoking room, domestic offices, store room, butler's pantry, servant's hall, kitchen, scullery, fine oak staircase, cellars. On first floor: five bedrooms, housemaid's cupboard, two w.c.s, bathroom, day nursery, night nursery, linen cupboard. On second floor: three large rooms for servants. To the rear of the house, extensive buildings, yard, larders, store-rooms, coach-house, laundry, boot room, stables, etc., walled garden, three greenhouses for peaches and nectarines, and farm buildings'.

Captain Briggs subsequently married Elinor, only daughter of Capt. and Mrs. George Rice Pryse of Ty Mawr, Cilcennin. When Capt. Briggs died Mynachty was sold to Ivor Jones who owned it in 1958. The present occupiers are Mr. and Mrs. Nigel Symmons-Jones.

Grid Ref: SN 5050 6205

Refs: Colby Map, 1831; *Dwnn,* i, 31; WWHR, i, 46; WWHR, iii, 91; Burke, *L.G.* 1852; Burke, *Visitation of Seats,* i (1852), 130; Nicholas, *County Families* (1872 & 1875), p. 132, vol. I; Meyrick, *Cardiganshire,* 1810, edn. 1907, p. 262; Landowners Return, 1873; Charles Wilkins, *Tales and Sketches of Wales,* Cardiff, 1879, pp. 314-318; J. Rowlands, *Historical Notes,* 1866, 145; Howell and Beazley, *Guide to South Wales,* 1977, 67; Evans, *Cardiganshire,* 1903, 184-5, 278; *The Cambrian*, 7th Dec. 1805; CRO, GGMS III (Edwin); NLW, Mynachty Deeds No 247. *Ceredigion,* VIII, 1977, pp. 224-236.

NANTCEIRO, Llanbadarn Fawr

Located a mile east of Llanbadarn north of the A44 (T) road. Not marked on *Colby's Map.* The first recorded occupant is Thomas Morgan who married Catherine . . . who died in 1836. In 1833 their son, John Morgan, married Elizabeth, daughter of John Evans of Prohurst, County Limerick. Elizabeth died in 1868 and John in 1870. They had a son John Thomas Morgan, born in London in 1842 and educated at Shrewsbury and Jesus College, Oxford. He became a JP and D.L and served the office of High Sheriff in 1890. In 1869 John married Frances Hannah, daughter of Robert Goddard Jones of Blackheath, Kent. They had one son and three daughters: John Herbert Morgan who died in 1879 predeceasing his father, and daughters Harriet Beatrice, Gertrude Elizabeth, (who married Major Hugh Edward Bonsall of Galltlan, Cardiganshire in 1896), and Gwendolyn Frances. John T. Morgan, a doctor, was the first representative of Llanbadarn Fawr on the newly-formed Cardiganshire County Council in 1889. Nantceiro was recently the home of the distinguished scholar, R. Geraint Gruffydd, formerly Librarian of the National Library of Wales and Director of the Centre for Advanced Welsh and Celtic Studies.

Grid Ref: SN 6145 8094

Refs: Meyrick, *Cardiganshire*, p. 371.

NANT-DDU, Llangrannog

A stream named Nant Ddu rises near Nanty-mawr and flows past Nanty-fach into the Hawen half a mile from the sea at Llangrannog. Nanty is a recent corruption of Nant-ddu, (the black stream). It is marked on *Colby's Map of 1831.* Meyrick describes it thus 'formerly a place of some consequence when belonging to the Lewes's . . . It is now the property of a family named Saunders. Rhys Lewes is the last of that name mentioned in the *Heraldry Manuscripts.* This estate came to the Lewes family by marriage, George Lewes having married the daughter and heir of [Rhys]-Llwyd, who had previously possessed it'.

Late in the 16th century Rhys Llwyd of Nant-ddu had a daughter and heiress who married George Lewes, son of Rhys Lewes of Penbryn, who was the fourth son of Lewes David Meredydd of Abernantbychan. They had eight children, all of whom were alive in 1609: Rhys Lewes of Nant-ddu who succeeded his father and David, James, Harry, Elizabeth, Gwenllian, Bridget and Jane.

Grid Ref: SN3210 5270

Refs: Meyrick, *Cardiganshire,* 1810, ed. 1907, 230; Colby Map, 1831; PRO, Dale Castle MS., p. 25 (100); WWHR, I. 35; NLW 12356 E, 498.

NANTGWYLAN, Llangynllo

Situated south-east of the hamlet of Penrhiwpal south of the B4334 towards Coedybryn and located on both *Colby's Map of 1831* and modern OS maps. Sometimes named Nantyddwylan. In 1760 it was owned and occupied by John Hughes, gent. A Miss Hughes of Nantgwylan, heiress to the Faenog estate near Mydroilyn, married the Rev. David Davies, vicar of Llanfihangel-y-Creuddyn whose son, Thomas Davies, High Sheriff in 1835 and generally known by the sobriquet 'pec o'r pen', married Elizabeth Lloyd, whose mother also Elizabeth, heiress of Abertrinant, married Col. Owen Lloyd, son of Thomas Lloyd of Bronwydd. Thomas Davies was a self-made man and following his marriage to Elizabeth Lloyd attended public dinners and meetings accompanied by a mentor who would instruct Thomas on points of etiquette. At social gatherings he would be expected to bow acknowledgement and was prompted by his minder with the words 'Now then, Mr. Dafis, pec o'r pen'.

Thomas owned extensive properties in Pembrokeshire and the marriage settlement prior to his marriage to Elizabeth Lloyd mentions Myrtle Hill and other lands in the parish of Steynton including East Harmeston, and holdings in Mydroilyn, Llanarth, and also Faenog and Faenog Mill in Llanerchaeron and Dihewyd. Turner in his *Wanderings*, refers to the tombstone of Thomas Davies of Nantgwylan who died in 1811, aged 37 years, on the vestry floor of the church at Llangynllo. He was the father of 'Pec o'r pen'. By 1846 Thomas Davies was living at Aberceri and in 1866 he was succeeded by his son, the ultra eccentric Thomas, who assumed the name of Ford Hughes.

Grid Ref: SN 3287 4565

Refs: Colby Map, 1831; NLW, Bronwydd Deeds, 2064-5, 2067; Turner, *Wanderings,* 157; H. M. Vaughan, *South Wales Squires,* 1926, pp. 91-2; WWHR, iii, 83; NLW, Griffith Owen Deeds, Nos. 1382 & 4620.

NANTEOS, Llanfihangel-y-Creuddyn

Situated in a superb location in the tranquil vale of the Paith three miles south-east of Aberystwyth, north of the B4340 between Southgate and New Cross and located on both *Colby's Map of 1831* and modern OS maps. Nearby is a hill-fort enclosure named Old Warren Hill. Formerly called Neuadd Llawdden after the descendant of Hywel Dda referred to by medieval poets, who was long associated with the Commotte of Perferdd and Lord of the Manor of Uwch Aeron early in the 14th century.

The residence of the Jones and later of the Powell families, formerly of Llechwedd Dyrys a short distance away across the Paith. The Powells came to Nanteos through the marriage in 1620 of William Powell, son and heir of Sir Thomas Powell, a King's Bench judge and Baron of the Exchequer during the reign of James II, descended from Edwin ap Gronow through Llewelyn Caplan, and Avarina, eldest daughter of Cornelius le Brun and Anne, heiress of Col. John Jones. John ap Edward is the first associated with the property. His son, Edward Jones, married Margaret Lewis of Abernantbychan and had four sons. The second son, John, was a Royalist Colonel in the Civil War who defended Aberystwyth Castle, and was appointed High Sheriff in 1665. He married Mary, daughter of Jasper Cornelius le

Brun, born in Cologne of a Huguenot family, who came to Wales and made his fortune in lead mining which enabled him to purchase estates in the Tregaron area. He paid tax on six hearths in 1672. The marriage settlement of his daughter, Avarina and William Powell of Llechwedd Dyrus dated 1 April 1690 mentions, 'the capital messuage called Nanteos alias Neuadd Lawdden, a house and garden thereto belonging formerly a tucking mill called Velin Vach alias Melin Lowdden . . . and a parcel called Lleine Llawdden,' all in the parish of Llanbadarn-fawr. Also mentioned are Tyddyn Nanty benglog and Fountaingate alias Porthyffynnon on the parish of Caron and many other properties. The tenants of William and Anne Powell deposited their hard-earned rents into a copper vessel which was made in Tregaron in 1674. William and Anne had three sons, Thomas, who succeeded to the estate, John, who died in Africa and the Rev. William Powell (1705-80) who married Elizabeth, daughter of Athleston Owen of Montgomeryshire. The ghost of Elizabeth Owen is said to haunt one room. Her husband presented her with valuable jewellery. As she was childless she had no one to whom she wished to leave the jewellery on her death, and was afraid that it might pass to her sister-in-law whom she hated. So she hid the jewels in a secret place in the house. For centuries the treasure has been sought.

Thomas Powell was MP for Cardigan Borough from 1725-27 and for Cardiganshire from 1742-27. He married Mary, granddaughter of Sir John Frederick, Lord Mayor of London in 1662. Mary brought her consider-able dowry to Nanteos in a great iron chest, fitted with seven locks, and with her husband, supervised the building of the Georgian mansion in 1739, described by Burke as a 'massive, imposing edifice of Doric Order,' to replace the earlier residence on the 11th century site. The great oak staircase was made from local timber. The new mansion was completed in 1757. The later additions were constructed in 1838-9.

Thomas Powell died suddenly of an apoplectic fit in a London street in 1752 and the estate devolved to his surviving brother, the studious Dr. William Powell LWD (1705-80), Oxford educated and ordained in Lincoln, William and his late brother took an active part in running the lead and silver mines on the estate and became involved in expensive litigation with the Crown regarding the rights to ownership of the waste land. It was through the marriage of their sister, Anna, to Richard Stedman that the extensive lands of the Ystrad Fflur estate came to the Powells. Relics from the abbey of Ystrad Fflur included the famous *Cwpan Nanteos* (the Holy Phial of Strata Florida), reputed to possess curative properties. The Cup, variously described as a portion of the Cross of Calvery or the Cup used during the Last Supper, was extensively loaned out (in return for collateral) over a wide area. Such was the belief in its healing properties that its rim was extensively chewed and became worn away. It is now deposited in a bank-vault. With the addition of the Ystrad Fflur estate, the Powells owned 30,000 acres from Devil's Bridge and Ponterwyd to Aberystwyth and included the extensive sheep walks of the upland wilderness above Llanddewibrefi. William Powell was succeeded by his son, Thomas (1745-97), High Sheriff in 1785 who married Eleanor Corbett of Ynysymaengwyn, Meirioneth. Thomas founded what became the Welsh Girls' School at Ashford. Eleanor and Thomas had four children; William, who succeeded to the estate, his brother Richard and two sisters. William Edward Powell (1788-1854) was High Sheriff in 1810, MP for Cardiganshire from 1816-54 and Lord Lieutenant of the County. Following schooling at Westminster and college at Oxford, William bought an army commission and left the running of Nanteos to agents. The estate, due partially to a series of family settlements, was heavily in debt. Malkin wrote in 1804;

'Nanteos is a family mansion belonging to the Powells, but rented during the just expiring minority by a Mr. Pocock . . . want of taste in the placing of their houses is very generally imputed to the Welsh gentry . . . At Nanteos, in the true sporting style, the dog kennel is the principle object from the front of the house; but it is disguised like something of a temple. The gardens are remarkably good. There was a celebrated harper at Nanteos about a century ago, who played there sixty-nine years. His portrait is preserved'.

When William came of age in 1809 the debt burden was over £20,000. Despite the difficulties of the estate, William and his mother Eleanor continued to lead the profligate lives to which they had become accustomed. He with his string of race-horses and she living in style in London, Bath and Dublin. Eleanor, with debts of over £5,000, even fled to France to escape her creditors. William Edward Powell also had four children by Mary Selina Genet who lived in London, the result of a long-standing liaison. Each child received £50 under the terms of his will.

It fell to William T. R. Powell (1815-78) MP for Cardiganshire from 1859-65, to attempt to revive the fortunes of the estate. Land and property to the value of £80,000 was sold between 1868 and 1873 when the estate was reduced to 21,000 acres with a rental of £9,054. The succeeding life-tenant at Nanteos was the eccentric George Powell (1842-84), poet, scholar and friend of Byron, Swinburne, Longfellow and Wagner, who described Nanteos as 'my beautiful but unhappy home'. He preferred the atmosphere of the inns and taverns of Aberystwyth. He published volumes of poetry and donated 900 books to the Aberystwyth Literary Institute. George famously shot the prize bull of the estate when handed a gun by his father and told to shoot the first animal he saw in the parkland. He died aged 40 the year following his marriage to Dinah Harries of Goodwick, Pembrokeshire, who upon her remarriage to an American, Ulysses T. Whildin of Illinois in 1883 saw her annuity, which was charged on the Nanteos estate, reduced to £250. George was succeeded by a cousin, William Beauclerk Powell (1834-1911), and it was William and his son Edward Athleston Lewis Powell (1870-1930) who carried out extensive sales of land and property which saw the estate dwindle to 4,000 acres. Some of the proceeds were utilized on much needed repairs and rebuilding of tenant homes and farms. Edward Powell married Margaret Louisa Joan, elder daughter of Sir Pryse Pryse of Gogerddan thereby uniting two great houses of North Cardiganshire, albeit in decline. Their only son, William Edward George Pryse Wynne Powell, born in 1899, was killed in action in France five days before the Armistice. Various claims of male relations to the estate were rejected and when Edward Powell died in 1930, the male line of the Powells of Nanteos came to an end.

Margaret Powell was a close friend of Lord Ystwyth of Tan-y-bwlch. She arranged assignations by raising a sheet on the flag-pole on the roof of Nanteos which could be seen by his Lordship at his home across the Ystwyth.

Margaret, who in later years carried a brass ear-trumpet and was a lady of great dignity and determination, died in 1952. A great niece of Mrs. Powell, Elizabeth Mirylees and her husband James, a retired major, succeeded to Nanteos, but the upkeep of the 60 roomed mansion was such that most of the 2,250 acres and the house were sold in 1967. The new owners, Geoffrey and Rose Bliss restored the property and lived at Nanteos until 1980 when the mansion was again sold. It is now an hotel and conference centre.

Grid Ref: SN 6205 7863

Refs: CRO, GGMS (Gwynfardd), p. 30; NLW, GS Cards., 1676-77, 1682-3; NLW, Cwrtmawr Deeds 203, 324, 1620; Landowners Return, 1873; *Ceredigion*, IX, No. 1 (1980), pp. 58-77; Blome List, 1673; Burke, *Visitation of Seats,* i (1852), p. 244; *Country Quest,* May 1976; D. J. Evans, *Hanes Capel Seion* (1935).

NANTREMENYN, Llandysul

Marked on *Colby's Map of 1831* and modern OS maps north-west of Pont-sian, on a steep slope above the Cletur-fawr.

The earliest known inhabitant of Nantremenyn is Ieuan Thomas, son of Dafydd ap John 'Saer y Cwm', whose younger son, John was of Nantremenyn. John had five sons and two daughters. Ieuan John who inherited Blaen Cletwr, Thomas John who succeeded to Nantremenyn, David John, Morris John and Hugh John. The eldest daughter, Elizabeth, married Morris David, and Mary married Francis Rhys Pritchard. Thomas John who succeeded his father, John, to Nantremenyn married and had five sons and three daughters. His son, also Thomas, married Gwenllian, daughter of Henry Henry of Coed-y-foel. They had two daughters, Anne married Walter Eynon, and Margaret, who married Samuel Williams, vicar of Llandyfriog. Their son, Moses Williams MA Oxford, FRS (1685-1742) was born at Glaslwyn, Llandysul, and was a parson, scholar and antiquary of some repute.

William Jones of Nantremenyn bore the arms of Tewdwr Mawr. His son, Sylvanus Jones (1742-1810), was an antiquary and genealogist. William's daughter, Lettice, married Walter Jones of Llanio, who bore the arms of Gwaethfoed, in 1746.

Hanes Plwyf Llandysul states that Sylvanus Jones compiled a manuscript of pedigrees of Cardiganshire and Carmarthenshire families from the manuscripts of William Lewes of Llwynderw, which he completed on 8 December 1760. Meyrick used the pedigrees in his *History of Cardiganshire.* Sylvanus Jones owned Nantremenyn, Cwmdyllest and other properties. He was buried at Llandysul on 7 June 1810, aged 86. His grandson was John Sylvanus Jones, innkeeper of the King's Head in Llandysul.

By 1827 the estate was owned by Rees Jones, gent. In 1841 the *Llandysul Tithe Map* gives the Misses Jane and Mary Jones as the owners with Eleanor Evans as tenant of 152 acres. Thirty-two years later the *Landowners Return, 1873,* shows that Jane Jones owned 162 acres yielding a rental of £90.

Grid Ref: SN 4286 4710

Refs: Colby Map, 1831; Modern OS maps; PRO, Dale Castle MS., p. 29, iii, 30-1 (115); Landowners Return, 1873; WWHR, i, 50, 54; The Rev. W. J. Davies, *Hanes Plwyf Llandysul,* 1896, pp 172-3; Llandysul Tithe Map, 1841.

NANTYBENGLOG (ISAF),
Llanbadarn-y-Creuddyn

Located south of the A4120 Aberystwyth to Devil's Bridge road a mile east of Capel Seion on a south-facing slope overlooking the Paith. Formerly a small estate, Nantybenglog-ucha is the neighbouring property. The earliest reference to the property is the reference to the marriage of Morgan John Lewis of Nantybenglog to a daughter of Sir Thomas Powell, King's Bench judge, early in the 17th century. In 1675, John Jones, son of Rees Jones of Nantybenglog, gent, married Joan, daughter of Philip Swancott and sister of Richard Swancott of Machynlleth. The pre-nuptial settlement dated 20 March 1675/6 refers to land in Llanilar and Llanbadarn Fawr parishes. By 1697/8 Richard Jones was of Nantybenglog. He was the grandson of Mary Jones, widow of Abermangoed, Carmarthenshire. By 1709 John Jones was living at Julianstowne Bridge in the county of East Meath in Ireland when he sold Nantybenglog alias Nantybenglog Isaf and parcels called 'Llain y maen Gwyn, Llain pen y Cryg, Llaine y Delyn and the cottage thereon, Llainhir, Llain Kefen Llech and Llain y gors, a messuage called Tir or Tyddyn y bryn whith, Nant yr Hydd and Tyddyn y Genfron', all in the parish of Llanbadarn to William Powell of Nanteos.

Nantybenglog was let to tenants who included John Morgan (1777-85), and Morgan Morgan, born at Troedrhiwlasgrug and grandfather of D. R. Morgan of North Parade, Aberystwyth (1803). In 1873 the tenant was William Goose, whose son, educated at Ardwyn County School, became a doctor. Before the end of the 19th century, David and Margretta James came to Nantybenglog and their daughter, Elizabeth Jane, married James Phillips, son of Evan and Margaret Phillips of Bryn-gwyn, Llanilar. James, who was a pioneer in agricultural practice, installed one of the first milking parlours in the country at Nantybenglog. Ifan, the younger son, succeeded to the tenancy and when the Nanteos estate was put up for sale in 1967, he purchased the 150 acre farm. He later sold the farmhouse and 60 acres to Mr. A Axford, a consultant at Bronglais hospital. The large farmhouse on the hill was built in 1906 to replace the older residence adjoining the farm buildings.

Grid Ref: SN 6425 7838

Refs: NLW, Cwrtmawr Deeds, Nos. 203, 400, 821, 1004; CRO, GGMS III (Edwin); Mrs. L. Morris, Tre-main.

NANT-Y-LLAN, Tre-main

This is the farm south-west of Tre-main parish church and marked on *Colby's Map of 1831* and on modern OS maps. The *GGMS* tell us that Thomas Phillips of Nant-y-llan was an attorney in the Great Sessions and that he married Elizabeth Pryse, daughter and co-heiress of Edward Pryse of Cefnmelgoed, the younger brother of Thomas Pryse of Glanfrêd by Mary, daughter of John Vaughan of Caethle, Merionethshire.

Grid Ref: SN 2407 4838

Refs: Colby Map, 1831; CRO, GGMS, III (Gwaethfoed), p. 24.

NAVY HALL, Lledrod

Situated half a mile north of Bronnant, west of the B4578 towards Lledrod and marked on *Colby's Map of 1831* and on modern OS maps. Rice Edwards of Navy Hall was appointed JP in 1760. His younger brother, John Edwards of Clynybuarth, Llangeitho, had four sons: Richard, Samuel, John and Daniel. Rice Edwards of Navy Hall, was alive in 1748, was a Captain in the Royal Navy. In 1760 he was of Navy Hall but in his will dated 24 September 1778, he was described as of Aberystwyth. The will was proved in PCC '48 Warburton'. He left his clothes to John Dudlike. His eldest son and heir, Richard Edwards, married Frances Vaughan, daughter of John Vaughan of Dolgwm, Carmarthenshire. The marriage was the subject of a pre-nuptial settlement drawn up on 14 January 1766. Rice Edwards, son of Richard, became heir of Navy Hall in 1778 whilst still a minor.

It would appear that the family ceased to hold the property as we know that the house belonged to Herbert Lloyd of Carmarthen, attorney, at the time of his death in 1814, and that by 1843, Jane James was the owner with William Jones occupier of the 146 acres consisting of the fields, Henberllan, Cae Morris, Cae Llowyddu, Cae dan Byttyr, Fron Black Hall, Bron hevel fryn, Cae Hwel mawr and bach. Cae dan Man hiwel.

Navy Hall, now a holding of 100 acres, is farmed by Trevor Jones and his mother who moved to Lledrod in the 1930's from south Wales.

Grid Ref: SN 6387 6812

Refs: Colby Map, 1831; WWHR, iii, 96; Lledrod parish Tithe Apportionment, 12 June 1843.

NEUADD-FAWR, Llanwnnen

A double-pile house in the hamlet of Tref-y-coed in Llanwnnen parish which Samuel Lewis described as 'the neat residence of Thomas Jones, Esq., standing on a well-wooded eminence, north of the turn-pike road, forms a conspicuous and pleasing object in the approach to Lampeter'. Marked on *Colby's Map of 1831* and modern OS maps within a mile of Llanwnnen to the north-east across the river Grannell.

Thomas Jones of Neuadd-fawr was a self-taught surgeon who married Anne Jenkins of Llwyn-y-groes, which was on the western bank of the Grannell. He served as High Sheriff of Cardiganshire in 1764 and died in 1813 at the age of 91. He had one son, Thomas Hugh Jones, (1778-1847), and three daughters. Anne, the eldest, married David Jones of Beilibedw in Llanllwni parish, and the second daughter, Margaret, married Thomas Hughes of Castell-du, in Llanwnnen. The youngest daughter, Mary, died unmarried aged 28.

Thomas Hugh Jones succeeded to the property worth £1,000 a year, and was by profession a doctor who became a well-known bone-setter. He was also intimately acquainted with the genealogies of the families of Cardiganshire and subscribed to Dwnn's *Heraldic Visitations* (1846). He died unmarried in 1847 and was buried in a vault of his own design in a field on the estate. He was succeeded by his nephew, Thomas Hughes of Castell-du.

Thomas's son, Thomas Hugh Rice Hughes, JP, DL, of Neuadd-fawr, married in 1899, Alice Mabel, daughter of Alfred Sterry of Dan-y-coed, Glamorganshire by Alice Rosine Crawshay, whose first husband was William Crawshay Dennis of Bradford House, Devon, who died in 1898. Thomas Hughes died in 1902 and Alice in 1919. In her draft will, drawn up in 1908, Alice Mabel Hughes of Neuadd-fawr, mentions the following relatives: 'My late husband, Thomas Hugh Rice Hughes, my sister Eva Gwendoline Toller, my niece, Priscilla Toller, daughter of the said Eva, my brothers Henry Crawshay Sterry and Alfred Crawshay Sterry'. She left Neuadd-Fawr and the Castell-du estates, and other bequests, to David Robert Jones of Llwyn-y-groes, Llanwnnen.

The break-up of the estate came on 17 June 1931 when the Neuadd-fawr estate, comprising the house and 1,690 acres and the smallholdings Waungron and Hendy Cottages, plus Castell-du, was offered for sale in 79 lots. On the ground floor was an entrance hall, dining and drawing room, library, lavatory, kitchen, pantry, scullery, farm kitchen, dairy . On the first floor were three principal bedrooms and dressing rooms, three maids' bedrooms, bathroom, w.c. and two lumber rooms. In the courtyard were 9 blocks of outbuildings. Castell-du was described as a 'dwelling house with two front rooms, two bedrooms, back-kitchen, dairy, six bedrooms, outbuildings along with two cottages called Tancastell and Tydwgi'.

In 1977 Mr. William Jones was living at Neuadd-fawr.

Grid Ref: SN 5363 4796

Refs: Colby Map, 1831; J. Islan Jones, *Ymofynydd*, 1955, 84-7; D. Cledlyn Davies, *Welsh Gazette,* 23 March 1950; Lewis, *TDW,* 1840; *Arch. Cam.* 1860 (The Rev. William Edmunds); Dwnn, *Heraldic Visitations* (1846); CRO, Sc 535.

NEUADD LLAN(N)ARTH, Llanarth

Located two miles east of Llanarth north of the road towards Derwen-gam. Marked on *Kitchin's Map of 1754, Emanuel Bowen's Map of South Wales* c. 1760 and as Noyadd on *Colby's Map of 1831*. Neuadd Farm is nearby.

The early family associated with Neuadd is that of Hugh ap Thomas ap Watkin ap Rhys Fychan ap David Bevan Bwl Aur whose son was David ap Hugh. David had a son, Hugh ap David, who married a daughter of Pant-streimon. They had two daughters, one of whom married Thomas Lloyd of Llanllyr and the other married Edward Morgan of Glasgrug.

James Griffiths, described as owner-occupier of Neuadd in 1760, married Gwenllian Lloyd, daughter of Watkin Lloyd of Wern Newydd. Their daughter, Frances married the Rev. James Brooks, MA, a deacon in 1726, vicar of Llanarth in 1727, a JP and alive in 1741. David Griffiths, son of James, married Jane, daughter of John Lloyd of Pantygilgan, Carmarthenshire.

The Oxford Book of Welsh Verse contains what Francis Jones describes as 'this splenetic districh' written by Evan Thomas, the local cobbler, (c. 1710-1770) 'To the Lady of Neuadd Llanarth for imprisoning the author's goat for two days for grazing too close to the Hall.

Y Rhawnddu, fwngddu, hagar,
Beth wnest ti i'th chwaer, yr afar?
'Run gyrn a'th dad, 'run farf a'th fam,
Pam rhoist hi ar gam yng ngharchar?

You black-haired, black-mared witch
What did you to your sister the goat?
Same horns as your Dad,
same beard as your Mum,
Why did you falsely imprison me?

Meyrick tells us that 'Noyadd Llanarth is the seat of Colonel Brooks who inherited this estate from his mother, Frances, only daughter and heiress of James Griffiths. Colonel Brooks' father was Chaplain to Dr. Smallwood, Bishop of St. Davids, and vicar of Llanarth'. Meyrick noted that the porch of the house was curiously ornamented. It would appear that Colonel Brooks left the estate to his cousin, the nephew of Frances Brooks, one John Brooks, formerly Residue Master and Auctioneer in the West Indies, described as a Captain of Cardiganshire Militia, living in 1797. He was High Sheriff in 1811. Some years before, in May 1797, John Brooks of Neuadd paid 18 guineas to the churchwardens of Llanllechid, Caernarfon, for the release to him of all the actions and orders in respect of a male bastard child born to Emma Evans of Whillan in the same parish on 17 March 1797. The old house was replaced at this time by a new one built alongside the old. The *Lucas Collection* in the National Library of Wales tells us that on 30 January 1810 John Brooks of

Noyadd, Esq., took out an insurance policy on the new mansion house of Noyadd and its contents'. In 1840 Samuel Lewis tells us that 'Noyadd Llanarth, anciently the seat of the family of Griffith, is now a spacious modern mansion, the residence of Lord Kensington'.

On 8 May 1978 Francis Jones visited the house then owned by a Mr. Ward, in company with Roger Clive-Powell, architect of Maesyfedw, Llanybydder and noted that 'the mansion is on top of a rise and in excellent condition and, furnished, had been used as an hotel and has now been sold. Near the entrance drive is a large old farmhouse, which may have been the original house, L-shaped with outhouses very close. It is ruinous and used as an outhouse. On an old enormous beam over a fireplace is cut the date 1754 and initials I.B.F. Close behind the present house is a very large garden, with remains of walling. As the arched entrance to it is on the side close to the present mansion it is not clear whether the garden belonged originally to the older house, or the newer one. The older house and buildings have been bought by a man, who with his wife and three children, have "opted out" and are attempting a "subsistence life" and now live in a caravan alongside. God help them! The mansion is probably late 18th century. Over a doorway at the rear, leading to a yard and domestic quarters, is an inscription '*Heb Dduw heb ddim'* (Without God, without all) and two shields, one shows a wolf walking and the other a castle and scaling ladders of Lloyd. The lettering and arms seem to be *circa* 1600, and were taken from the older home I think. The I.B.F. on the frame probably stands for John and Frances Brooks. In the old ruined house, the ceiling is partly gone and I could see in the bedroom at the pine-end a fireplace with some ornamental plasterwork around it, which, at a guess, is perhaps 17-18th century'.

Grid Ref: SN 4436 5802

Refs: Kitchin Map, 1754; Emanuel Bowen Map of South Wales, c. 1760; Colby Map, 1831; Carlisle, 1811; Meyrick, *Cardiganshire,* 1810 (edn. 1907) p. 236-7; NLW, Lucas Collection Nos. 1504-14, 4211; NLW, Morgan Richardson Deeds, ii, 403; Lewis *TDW,* 1840; PRO List 1727; Protheroe, C., VI; WWHR, iii, 86, 109; CRO, GGMS I (Tewdwr), fo. 45; *Oxford Book of Welsh Verse,* ed. T. Parry, 1976, p. 296.

NEUADD TRE-FAWR, Llandygwydd,
see NOYADD TREFAWR

NEUADD WILYM, Llangoedmor

Marked on *Colby's Map of 1831* and on modern OS maps adjacent to the main A484 road two miles east of Cardigan. The place name suggests a location of some antiquity dating back to Norman times or possibly before. It has been suggested that it may have been the home of Gwilym ap Gwrwared, one of the few Welshmen to win favour with the Saxon settlers of Ceredigion. The name Neuadd Wilym does not appear in the records until the 17th century when the property was linked with Penrallt, an estate in the same parish. Evan Jones a doctor, was living at Neuadd Wilym when he inherited the Dolwilym estate in Llanglydwen and assumed the name Protheroe. He died in 1795 in his 80th year. In the 19th century, Neuadd Wilym was the home of Griffith Griffiths (1762-1818), a Presbyterian minister at Llechryd where he also had a school. He died at the age of 56 and was succeeded by his son, Thomas Jeremy (1797-1871), known as *Tau Gimel*, a Unitarian minister and poet who spent some time in the USA. A new house had been built at Neuadd Wilym early in the 18th century which became the home of Thomas Morgan (1810-1879), a solicitor, whose family owned Plâs Aberporth and other property in Cardigan. Thomas married the daughter of his partner, Lewis Evans, and inherited the family property on his mother's death in 1867. His daughter, Jane Price, and his grandson, Morgan Price, both pre-deceased him and when he died in 1879 he devised his estate and the lucrative practice to his young partner, Charles Evan Richardson. Under the terms of the will Charles was to assume the Christian name of Davis and the surname Morgan. Charles Evan David Morgan-Richardson emerged as a young man of affluence and prestige among the familiar Tivyside county families. His great-grandfather, Arthur Richardson from Northern Ireland had settled at St. Davids when he became organist at the Cathedral in 1782. His three sons entered the church and Charles' father, the Rev. Thomas Richardson, became

head of the Cathedral school at St. Davids and married Jane Evan of Trefgarn Hall, Pembrokeshire. Charles was born in 1857 and was articled to Thomas Morgan at Chancery Lane, Cardigan, when he was 15 years old. When he came of age, he became a partner and following the death of Thomas Morgan he married Evelyn, younger daughter of Sir Henry Brownrigg, Bart, of Sandhill Park, Somerset. They lived at Neuadd Wilym where their son, Charles Lethbridge Ernest, was born in 1888 and a grand ballroom built two years later. He became a prominent member of the community; was Mayor of Cardigan three times, a JP, and a founder member of the United Counties Agricultural Society. On the 40 acres at Neuadd Wilym he bred shorthorn cattle, and he travelled widely to study farming practice. In his quest to expand his farming interests, he bought the 300 acre Rhysygilwen estate from John Vaughan Colby for £8,000 in 1904. He died in 1913 and his son, Charles in 1961. On the advice of the Lascalles, a Catholic family living at Pencraig, Llechryd, Neuadd Wilym was sold to Benedictine monks expelled from their monastery at Kerbeniat (Caer Benedict), Brittany, by the anti-cleric French government, for £4,060; a sale which became a crucial issue when Morgan-Richardson unsuccessfully fought the Tory cause in the 1906 election. The monks, 30 in number, with an average age of 24 and including several novices, disembarked at Llanelli and used a *gambo* and horse to transport their belongings 35 miles across country to Neuadd Wilym, which they renamed Caer Maria. One monk, Dom Simeon Kervennec born in 1845, learned Welsh in Brittany and the other monks followed his example and became accepted despite much early hostility from the locals. With the outbreak of the First World War most of the monks were conscripted into the Army as ambulance men and one brother was killed in action. The older monks left Caer Maria in 1916 and the property was sold in 1917. In due course, Henry Davies, his wife and family of nine children, bought Neuadd Wilym and moved there from Trefaes-fach, Beulah. Henry's sons, Ifan Davies JP and Dr. Lloyd Davies became well known in the Cardigan area and his grandson, Ieuan and Caroline, his wife, lived and farmed at Neuadd Wilym from 1962 to 1986. They bred horses and welcomed visiting pilgrims from far and wide.

In the cellar is an ancient well which gives a constant supply of clear, cold water. Two bells were used to call the monks to prayer at Caer Maria. One can now be heard at the Abbey of Landavennec in Brittany. The other is at the priory of French brethren in Haiti.

Grid Ref: SN 2039 4497

Refs: Colby Map, 1831; *Ceredigion,* 1952, p. 110; NLW, Morgan Richardson, Deeds, No. 1755; D. L. Baker-Jones, *Charles Evans Davies Morgan-Richardson, Ceredigion,* VIII, 2 (1977), pp. 47-80; S. Cunnane, Caroline Davies.

NOYADD TREFAWR, Llandygwydd

Situated in woodland north of Neuadd Cross on the old road from Cardigan to Newcastle Emlyn marked on *Kitchin's Map of 1754, Colby's Map of 1831* and on modern OS maps.

Located in an area steeped in antiquity. The prefix *Tref-* originally denoting 'family', later a 'township' along with the epithet *-fawr* is evidence of an important settlement dating perhaps to the fourth or fifth centuries. The element Neuadd or Noyadd meaning Hall and the presence of other ancient place-names in the immediate area – Hafod, Tre-cwm and Llan, along with the remains of an early chapel, further illustrate an ancient settlement. The first known occupant was Rhys Dafydd Llwyd, who bore the arms of Castell Hywel, and married Alson, daughter of Rhys ap Rhydderch ap Rhys, Lord of Tywyn, Ferwig parish. Dyddgu, their daughter and co-heiress married Thomas ap Harri ap Philip of Blaen Cuch, descendant of the famous Rhys Chwith, Esquire of the Body to King Edward I who traced to Cunedda

Wledig, Lord of Ceredigion. His son, Dafydd, adopted the surname Parry, signed for Dwnn in 1588 and was High Sheriff of Cardiganshire three times. He married firstly Elen, daughter of Lewes Dafydd Meredydd of Abernantbychan and then Maud, heiress of Llewelyn ap Dafydd of Blaen-pant, Llandygwydd. His son Dafydd Parry pre-deceased his father and it was another David, the eldest son of his brother, John of Doly-fonddu, Montgomeryshire and Mary, widow of John Pugh and daughter of Thomas Pryse of Gensor. Following David's marriage to Eliza-beth, heiress of Thomas Parry of Plâs Newydd, St. Dogmaels, and the purchases made by Dafydd Parry late in the 16th century, the Noy-add Trefawr estate was considerably enlarged and now included Forest, Cilgerran, the manor of St. Dogmaels including mills and the Abbey, lands in Ferwig, Clydau and Llanfyrnach parishes along with the tithes of Cenarth, Cilfowyr and Llangolman.

David (c. 1641-64) and Elizabeth had five children; David, High Sheriff of Cardiganshire in 1685 who died unmarried in 1711, and four daughters, Elizabeth, who married John Jones of Pantyderi, Mary, who died unmarried, Bridget who later married John Jones of Tyglyn Aeron, and Anne, who married her cousin, Stephen, son of John Parry of Pant Einon and grandson of the above John Parry of Doly-fonddu. Stephen, who lived at Rhydymendi before succeeding to Trefawr, was High Sheriff in 1720 and MP for Cardigan Boroughs from 1715 until his death, aged 49, in 1724. In the church at Llandygwydd is a monument to David Parry (d. 1711), John Parry (d. 1722) and Stephen Parry (d. 1724), of Noyadd, and part of the inscription reads 'Tis neither goodness, virtue, wealth, long pedigrees, nor orphan's tears, can rescue from the grave'.

Noyadd Trefawr passed to Stephen's nephew, David Parry, the only son of Susan Parry who had married William Parry of Nanhyfer. David lived at Trefawr and was High Sheriff in 1745 and married the 17 year-old Frances, heiress of Kedgwin Webley of Chancery Lane, London, with a portion of £4,000. David Parry died in 1753 and his widow spent much of her time at her childhood home in Gloucestershire with her daughter, also Frances. The widow survived her husband by 40 years and the heiress Frances, married the profligate Marmaduke Gwyn of Garth, Breconshire in 1768. There were no children and Marmaduke died in 1784. His widow died at Bath in 1815. She was the last of the ancient line of Parrys. She bequeathed the Trefawr estate to her second cousin, on her mother's side, Rear-Admiral William Henry Webley, a member of a Gloucestershire family with no previous connection with Wales. He took the name Parry in addition to his own and married Maria White (1776-1858) of Northfleet, Kent. Carlisle wrote in 1811 that 'Noyadd, Mrs. Gwynne's [is] in a dilapidated state' and Burke in his *Visitation of Seats* reported that 'the mansion was built in the time of Elizabeth . . .'.

William Henry Webley-Parry when Captain of the *Centaur* distinguished himself in an action with the Russian man o' war *Sewold* which he took in 15 minutes. The anchor in the Webley arms and the sword and anchor in each quartering were granted by George III in commemoration of the achievement. Although he spent much of his time away from Noyadd, William was responsible for the substantial rebuilding of the splendid Georgian mansion in 1820. Despite being appointed Commander of the Bath, a JP and a Deputy-Lieutenant of his adopted county, the Rear-Admiral was heavily in debt, mainly to Thomas Davies, Bridge House, Cardigan – 'Davies of the Bridge' – ship-owner, merchant, entrepreneur and money-lender, who later became master of Castle Green. William sold property and land in St. Dogmaels to pay for his new home and in 1828, from a yearly rental of £2,000, the debts of William and the Trefawr estate were £18,000. Davies took Webley-Parry to the Exchequer of Pleas to recover his money, and although David Davies, Thomas's son, was appointed a JP and served as High Sheriff as his father before him, the local gentry looked down on them as they were 'in trade'.

William Henry Webley-Parry (1803-53) succeeded to his father's debts when the former died in 1837. He married Angharad, (1807-53) daughter of David Saunders Davies of Pentre, Maenordeifi, who helped his son-in-law manage his debt-ridden estate. By 1839 Noyadd

Trefawr, whose rental in the early 17th century surpassed all others in the county, had shrunk to less than 1,000 acres in Llandygwydd parish. Reckless borrowing of money amounting to over £40,000 led to the sale of half the estate. William served his community well and when he died in 1853, their only child, David Kedgwin William Webley-Parry (1833-70), married Nina Catherine, daughter of the Count Demetrios de Palatine of Corfu in 1861. Their married life was brief. David died in 1870 and his widow in 1917. There were two daughters; Nina Catherine Angharad (1858-1954) and Williamina Mary Elizabeth who died in 1881 aged 11 years. Nina married Edward John, (1862-1918), son of Sir Pryse Pryse of Gogerddan in 1891. A Royal Licence allowed him to assume the name Parry and he was known as Sir Edward John Webley-Parry-Pryse, Bart, having succeeded his father to the Gogerddan estate in 1906, his elder brother having died in his father's lifetime. A former army Captain, he retired in 1893 and on his return to Noyadd Trefawr became High Sheriff of Cardiganshire in 1908 and was the Master of the Tivyside and Gogerddan Hounds. He infamously hunted the Tivyside hounds on the day of the funeral of Queen Victoria in 1901, allegedly declaring it was too good a scenting day to miss. Sir Edward died without issue in 1918, but his wife, Nina, carried on with her charitable work, for which she received an OBE in 1920, until her death aged 84 in 1954. With her death the names Parry, Webley and Pryse disappear from the chronicles of the Tivyside.

Francis Jones says 'I went to lunch at this house in November 1972. The owner Mr. Hayne, a retired army officer, later a colonial administrator, told me it was built about 1820 by Admiral W. H. Webley Parry, and showed me the architect's plan and an elevation picture of what the architect wanted it to be. It seems to have been built *de novo,* and although I went through the whole house from cellar to attic, there were very few antique features. There were very large floorboards here and there (e.g. in the inner or staircase hall) which clearly came from the earlier building. The owner told me that the old part of the house was the front part which included the drawing room, a hall and dining room; the inner wall connecting with the other rooms in the back part was very thick and *may* have once been an outside wall. Above the 'gothic' porch, which matches with the gable windows in the upper storey, is a shield, the crest of the Webley Parrys, viz, a lion *argent* couchant supporting with the right forepaw, an inescutcheon *azure* thereon a cross fitchy, a collar of leaves around the lion's neck, and an eastern crown on his head'.

The house was much modernised in the middle of the 19th century and a photograph taken in the time of Sir E. J. Webley Parry Pryse in *The Tivyside Photographic Souvenir: Pen y Lan,* by C. Allen, Tenby, shows a long house with a range of eight windows, two storeys, and an attic storey with six large attic windows, and a large 'gothic' porchway; with a wing running to the rear of the house. The *Landowners Return of 1873* shows D. K. W. Webley Parry as owning 2,105 acres 2 roods and 21 perches at £1,021 p.a. rental.

In 1983, under the name Neuadd Trefawr, the house was put up for sale. The Sale Catalogue described it thus: 'Sale consists of the mansion and an old farmhouse and outbuildings (map given and photograph of the front elevation). Ground storey and first floor, each with row of seven windows, and attic storey with six dormer windows. Entrance porch, centre, rising to first storey. Originally the first floor comprised five principal bedrooms, w.c., store-room. Second floor: three bedrooms, sitting room, kitchen and bathroom. The old farmhouse is a two storey building which has been partly renovated and has four good-sized ground floor rooms, one of which incorporates a splendid old *simme fawr* fireplace, and three first floor rooms, and this floor has an attractive gabled window facing north. Grounds around house total about 15 acres'.

Francis Jones revisited Noyadd Trefawr twice; in 1973 he noted that the house was in excellent condition, but by his last visit in May 1983 he wrote 'it is now in the hands of strangers of the drop-out type and the main building is deteriorating'. After many years of neglect the house is now in the hands of Mr. and Mrs. Christopher Mason-Watts who use the old name Noyadd Trefawr. They have restored the fabric of the building and retained its character.

Grid Ref: SN 2580 4625

Refs: WWHR, i, 13-14; NLW, Griffith Owen List (iv); Kitchin Map; Blome List, 1673; Meyrick, *Cardiganshire,* 186; Burke, *Visitation of Seats of Great Britain,* i (1852), 32, vol. I; *Contemporary Biographies of South Wales and Monmouthshire,* 1907, 155; NLW, Griffith Owen Deeds, No. 2333, 2337; PRO, Dale Castle MS., 20; NLW, Morgan Richardson Deeds, ii, 4, 96; C. Allen, *The Tivyside Photograph Souvenir: Pen y Lan,* Tenby [album in possession of Miss Gwynedd Taylor, Manorbier, 1975]; *Dwnn,* i, 29; NLW, Noyadd Trefawr Deeds, No. 460; Powis Castle Deeds, 17036; Horsfall-Turner, *Walks and Wanderings in Cardiganshire;* CRO, GGMS I (Tydwal Gloff), fo. 33; Landowners Return, 1873; CRO Sc; Francis Jones 'Noyadd Trefawr'; Peter Thomas, *Strangers from a Secret Land,* 1986, pp. 232-6.

OLMARCH (-FAWR), Llangybi

Marked on *Colby's Map of 1831* and on modern OS maps north-east of Llangybi between the A485 and the dismantled railway. Nearby are Olmarch-uchaf and -isaf.

Earliest found owner is David ap Owen of Olmarch (c. 1600), grandson of David ap Howell and son of Owen ap David. He married Elizabeth, daughter of Rees Llewelyn ap Rees of Llanwenog by Elen Vaughan of Penbryn. Thomas Jones (later Johnes), the younger son of James Jones of Dolau Cothi, was of Olmarch in 1666. On 10 August 1669 the *Bronwydd Deeds* tell us of an agreement between Thomas Jones of Olmarch, Esq., and Elizabeth his wife, Walter Lloyd of Llanfair Clydogau, Esq. and John Pugh of Mathafarn, Montgomeryshire, Esq., James Jones of Dolau Cothi, Esq. Thomas Powell of Llechwedd Dyrys, Esq., and John Lloyd of Ffosybleiddiaid, gent., to a covenant regarding the marriage of said Thomas and Elizabeth Jones, and to levy a fine on more than 100 properties in the parishes of Llanbadarn Odwyn, Betws Bledrws, Llanddewibrefi, Llanfair, Cellan, in the townships of Gorwydd, Prysag and Carfan.

The *Blome List* of 1673 tells us that Walter Lloyd, second son of David and Grace Lloyd of Crynfryn, Nantcwnlle, was of Olmarch, and the *PRO List* shows him, as living there in 1705. He married Anne, daughter of John Lloyd, and co-heiress of Ystrad Corrwg and Glangwili. David died before 1735 and had issue. The *Edwinsford Deeds* show Elizabeth Williams, widow, as also living at Olmarch in 1706. Walter and Elizabeth Lloyd had two sons and four daughters: John Lloyd, born on 7 July 1698, succeeded to Glangwili, Carmarthenshire his mother's home. He married Anne Philipps of Cwmgwili, the eldest daughter of Grismond Philipps. Thomas Lloyd, born on 29 January 1699, succeeded to Olmarch and married Grace . . . but died without issue and was buried in Llangybi. His will was dated 15 March 1738 and proved on 30 July 1739. Walter Lloyds' daughters were Anne, born on 14 June 1701, Grace-Anna born 3 August 1703, Jane born 17 June 1705, and Elizabeth born 6 December 1706. The *J. Francis Collection* tells us that David James of Tyglyn Aeron, High Sheriff of Cardiganshire in 1734, appointed Thomas Lloyd of Olmarch to be his Under-Sheriff. David James's seal showed a lion rampant between 10 roses, and crest: a lion rampant. Jane Lloyd of Olmarch married Rev. Arthur Laugharne, of Llanunwas, rector of Dinas and Prebendary of Carfai who died in 1753. They had one son, William Laugharne, and five daughters. In 1760 the Rev. Thomas of Olmarch also owned Clynmeherin in Llanwenog parish.

Grid Ref: SN 6260 5474

Refs: Colby Map, 1831; Blome List, 1673; PRO List, Edwinsford Deeds, 1852 & 2680; J. Francis Collection (Llanllawddog), No. 208; NLW, Bronwydd Deeds, No. 2299; WWHR, iii, 87.

ANT DAFYD, Llandyfriog

Pant Dafydd is marked on *Colby's Map of 1831* and modern OS maps as south-east of Llangunllo church and north-west of Bronwydd. The earliest found owners are the Brynes or Bruynes whose descendants lived in the house for many generations. Other Brynes lived at Ferwig, Troedyrhiw and Llanwnnen in the 17th century. On 22 July 1546 the *Coedmor Deeds* note that Thomas Bryne 'mawre' was a witness to a deed regarding Tir Dol-y-llan in the parish of Llanfihangel-ar-Arth. Thomas Bryne was the son of William Bryne, who in turn was the son of Hugh Bryne of Llanfynnonwen (Chirbury), in Shropshire, whose arms were: *or* a double-headed eagle displayed *sable.*

Thomas Bryne, described as of Penybuarth, Carmarthenshire, married Agnes, daughter of William ap Gwilym of Carmarthenshire. They had two sons, Rees ap Thomas, the heir born in 1563, Philip of Ffoshelig, Llandysul born in 1552, and a daughter, Janet, who married Rees Lloyd of Coedtren. Philip Bryne married Gwenllian Lloyd ab Evan ab Bedo Ddu of Lampeter. Tradition has it that Bronwydd was once located at Pant Dafydd and that the large oaks at Pant Dafydd marked the entrance to the mansion. Philip bought Bronwydd in 1562 and was living there in 1589. He had two sons, George Bryne of Pant Dafydd, surgeon, and Philip Bryne.

George married Mary, the daughter of Lewes David Meredydd of Abernantbychan. They had two children, John and Sage. John was of Llanfair Trelygen, and Sage, who married the Rev. Thomas Lloyd, MA, vicar of Llangeitho from whom descended the Lloyds of Bronwydd. George Bryne also had two natural sons by Catherine ferch Rhys ab Ifan Coch; Thomas Bryne of Henllan, and Philip Bryne. Thomas married Elizabeth ferch Ifan ab Rhys Gwilym, they had two sons Walter and John.

John Bryne described as 'of Llanfair helygen in Troedyraur' married Katherine, daughter of Owen ap Rees Lloyd of Llangoedmor. They had three sons, David, Harry and Edward, and two daughters Sage and Anne.

The *Bronwydd Deeds* state that on 20 October 1791, Thomas Lloyd of Bronwydd, leased Pant Dafydd to David John of the same parish.

Grid Ref: SN 3482 4370

Refs: PRO, Dale Castle MS., pp. 23-4 (93); CRO, GGMS, Calumptus ped. in Cardiganshire, 1667-7; NLW, Noyadd Trefawr Deeds, No. 153; Colby Map, 1831; NLW, Bronwydd Deeds, No. 1874, *Dwnn,* i, 17; NLW, Alcwyn Evans MS.; CRO, Coedmor Deeds;

PANT EYNON,
also known as PANT EINON, Beulah

Marked on *Colby's Map of 1831,* and on modern OS maps called Pant Einon, situated north-east of Bron-gwyn, west of the B4333 between Beulah and Cwm-cou. John Parry of Noyadd Trefawr, High Sheriff, who died in office in 1620 had a son, John Parry, of Dolyfonddu, Montgomeryshire, who died in 1651 and whose will was proved in 1652. His second son, also John, was described as of Pant Eynon, Bron-gwyn who married Margaret . . . They had two sons, Stephen and David, and one daughter, Susan. John Parry died in Dublin in 1722.

His son, Stephen Parry of Noyadd Trefawr, was High Sheriff in 1720 and an MP from 1721 until he died in 1725. He married his cousin, Anne Parry. His will was proved in the same year and he was buried at Llandygwydd. The second son, David Parry married Elizabeth daughter of Thomas Parry of St. Dogmaels [see Noyadd Trefawr]. The only daughter of John Parry, Susan Parry, alive in 1720, married William Parry of Nevern, later of Neuadd, who died in 1757.

The will of David Parry of Noyadd Trefawr names 'my uncle John Parry of Panteynon, gt.', and his son, Stephen Parry, who was the brother-in-law and cousin to the testator.

Grid Ref: SN 2927 4406

Ref: Colby Map, 1831.

PANTERLIS (Pantyrlys), Llandygwydd

Marked as Pant-yr-ilsa on *Colby's Map of 1831* and Pant-y-llys on modern OS maps half a mile north of Llandygwydd on the minor road to Neuadd Cross.

Meyrick states that the family descends from Llewelyn ap Ieuan Gwyn. Llewelyn lived in Llandygwydd in 1545, and bought Panterlis from Owain ap Jenkin and Elen William, his wife, as well as several other properties from others. Llewelyn's grand-daughter Jane, married John Lloyd of Hendre, in the parish of St. Dogmaels. They sold Panterlis to Thomas Griffith John who was a great-grandson of David ap Iwan Gwyn, who was a younger brother of the aforesaid Llewelyn. Thomas Griffith's great-grandson, David Jenkins, was seemingly the last of the line at Panterlis'.

John, the son of David ap Iwan Goch, brother of Llewelyn ab Ieuan Gwyn had a son, Griffith ap John, who traced to Elystan Glodrudd. Griffith married Jane, the daughter of Griffith ap Rosser, brother of David ap Rosser of Alltybwla in Llandygwydd. They had a son Thomas ap Griffith, alive in 1608, who bought Panterlys from the elder branch of the family, and settled there. He married Crusilla, daughter and co-heiress of Jenkin Thomas Llwyd of Rhosygilwen, the son of Thomas Lloyd ap Jenkin Llwyd of Clynfyw ap Owen of Pencelli and grandson of Jenkin Lloyd of Cemaes, by Margaret, daughter of Jenkin ab Owain John of Glynhenllan, Cilgerran. They had a son, Jenkin ap Thomas of Panterlis, alive in 1624, who married Mary, daughter and co-heiress of John ap Rhydderch of Penywenallt. They had two sons, Thomas and Griffith. The elder son, Thomas Jenkins succeeded to Panterlis. The younger son, Griffith ap Jenkins, described in 1649 as of Penrallt, Aberporth, bought Dyffryn, Blaenporth, which he purchased from the elder branch of the family. His son was Jenkin ap Griffith of Dyffryn, alive in 1675, who married Maud, daughter of John ap David ap Pentir. In 1700, their son Griffith, who adopted Jenkin as his surname, married Elen, daughter of Jenkin ap Griffith ap David ap Rhydderch of Cilbronnau, descended from Tydwal Gloff. In the same year Griffith Jenkin was High Constable of the Lower Division of the Hundred of Troed-yr-aur. He died in 1770. His son Jonathan Jenkin married Elizabeth, daughter of John Lewes of Tredefaid in 1738. Their son, Griffith Jenkin married Mary, daughter of John Morris of Bachendre near Boncath and they had five sons.

The aforesaid Thomas Jenkins married Lettice, daughter of Captain Edward Pryse of Eglwysig, Denbighshire. Their son was David Jenkins, who married Mary, eldest daughter of Morgan Howells of Penybeili. Their son, also David Jenkins was living in 1739 and owned the property in 1760. By 1810 the estate was the property of Morgan Jones, Esq., of Pen-y-lan, Llechryd, formerly of Cilwendeg, Maenordeifi. Panterlis was then let to tenants.

Grid Ref: SN 2412 4427

Refs: Meyrick, *Cardiganshire,* 1810, ed. 1907, p. 185; WWHR i, 53, iii, 79; NLW, Noyadd Trefawr Deeds No. 310; Colby Map, 1831; Nicholas, *County Families,* Vol. I, Cardiganshire; NLW, G.S. Cardiganshire, 5 Anne; CRO, GGMS, I (Gwynfardd); PRO, Dale Castle MS., p. 30 (115);

PANTERYROD, Llanarth

The home of the Thomas family, situated on the north bank of the Drywi, between Henfynyw and Llanina, near the coast and marked on *Colby's Map of 1831* as Pant yr erod. Panteryrod was part of the estate of Robert Lewis-Lloyd, son of Thomas and Anna (*née* Davis) formerly of Treforgan, Llangoedmor. They lived at Nantgwyllt in the Elan Valley five miles from Rhayader, before Birmingham Corporation built its reservoirs to take Welsh water to the Midlands. Robert also owned the Treforgan estate, in the right of his wife, and Wern Newydd, Llanarth, of which Panteryod was a part. When Lewis-Lloyd sold the estate, it was bought by Dr. Abraham Garrod Thomas, who was born at Panteryod in 1853. He was the son of Lewis Thomas (1815-1873) described as 'Teulu'r Adar' who married twice; firstly to Mary Thomas of Gilfachrhydie, by whom he had two sons, David Thomas, who had a son Griffith, and Griffith Thomas, born in 1845, who had two sons, Lewis and Derion.

By his second marriage to Jane (1821-91), he had five children, William, born in 1849, who had a son Lewis; John Aeron Thomas, born in 1850 and elected MP for Glamorgan in 1900, who had a son Gwilym Aeron Thomas, whose son John Aeron Thomas later lived at Mumbles, Swansea. Thomas died in infancy in 1852. The youngest son was Abraham Garrod Thomas (b. 1853).

An article in *Cymru* tells us that 'Dr. Garrod Thomas, was born 5 October 1853 at Panteryrod near Aberaeron, his parents were pillars of the Congregationalists at Llwyncelyn, went to school at Llwyncelyn and Pontshan. When about fourteen he went to school at Milford Haven, and one of his old masters there, the Rev. Caleb Gwion is still alive (1901). He first went to Glasgow where he stayed 1871-2, and then went to Edinburgh where he completed his course. He became MB and CM of Edinburgh, MRCS of England in 1876, and MD of Edinburgh in 1878. He studied afterwards at Berlin and Vienna. He settled at Newport, Monmouthshire, in 1877. In 1879 he married Elen, only child of R. H. Richards, native of Aberystwyth, a successful merchant at Newport. His nephew is Dr. T. Morrell Thomas MD, MS London, FRCS. He was a member of Newport Town Council for eight years, and resigned in 1897 owing to pressure of work. He was the first President of the Medical Society of Newport and the Shire. He was Physician of Newport Hospital and a JP of Newport Borough, and High Sheriff of Cardiganshire in 1901. When R. L. Lloyd sold his estate, Dr. Thomas bought his father's farm at Panteryrod, as well as Blaen-bedw, Cwm-bedw, Bargoed, Cilcert, and also several smallholdings in the area. He is tall. His brother, Aeron Thomas, became an MP'.

More information is provided by the *South Wales Historical Biographical Pictorial,* which tells us that Abraham Garrod Thomas was a JP and DL of County Monmouthshire and was a Liberal. Both of the above sources printed photographs of Dr. Thomas, who was knighted in 1912. By 1964, David John Davies had been farming at Panteryrod for almost 20 years. He was a founder-member of the Farmers' Union of Wales. By 1978 the house was owned by a Mr. Davies.

Grid Ref: SN 4326 6020

Refs: Colby Map, 1831; *South Wales, Historical, Biographical, Pictorial*, *Cymru,* ed. O. M. Edwards, vol. 20, 1901, pp. 83-84.

PANTGWYN, Llangoedmor

Marked on *Colby's Map of 1831* and on modern OS maps in woodland near the crossroads on the old B4570 road three miles east of Cardigan. Formerly the home of the Griffiths family. The *Noyadd Trefawr Deeds* tell us that David Griffiths, late of Noyadd Trefawr, was living at Pantgwyn on 7 August 1771. An elegy to Diana Griffiths of Pantgwyn by Ioan Siencyn of Cwm-du in 1790 mentions her grieving parents. Diana was

the 'daughter of an able man who lived at Cwm Conell and owned wide lands and was a member of the Church of England, but friendly to non-conformists'.

A year later Ioan was writing another elegy to her husband David Griffiths. Both are buried at Llandygwydd with their ancestors. David and Diana Griffiths left a son and heir Thomas Griffiths, MA, and three other children, David, William and Nell. The family was traced to *uchelwyr* formerly at Cawrens and Llwyndyrys.

The present house was built by George Woolgar Griffiths in the 1830's to replace the former home near the adjacent farm. He died in 1850 aged 56 and is buried at Llangoedmor where the east window of the church is dedicated to his memory. His wife, a Millingchamp from Plâs Llangoedmor, died in 1876.

Frances Elizabeth, elder daughter of Capt. Thomas Reynold Griffiths, of the Indian Army, who died in 1870, married Edwin John Moore Lascelles, eldest son of Rowley Lascelles of Pengraig, Llechryd, in 1885, and their son, Edwin Charles Griffiths, was born in 1890.

Until his death in 1912, Pantgwyn was the home of Col. J. R. Howell, a younger son of Glaspant in the valley of Cuch. He married well. His first wife, Sarah Hall, was the granddaughter of Admiral Lord Collingwood, and the Howells lived at Blaendyffryn, near Llandysul where their hospitality became legendary. When Sarah died, John Howell married 'Missie' Lewis of Llysnewydd and they moved to Pantgwyn. He became master of the Tivyside Hunt and chairman of Cardigan County Council. The entertaining continued. H. M. Vaughan recalls counting twenty cold dishes on the sideboard at Pantgwyn. Colonel Howell died in 1912 and 'Missie' some ten years later.

In 1926 William Phillips Jones, a surgeon, was living at Pantgwyn. His telephone number was Llechryd 3. He died in 1931.

A photograph of the house was published in *Photographs of South Wales* in 1871 by Charles Smith Allen, Tenby. Frances Jones visited the house on 14 May 1983. He tells us that the house was then occupied by Mr. Bedell-Smith, architect. The property was in a good state of repair. 'I enjoyed a glass of Malmsey.'

In 1988 Pantgwyn became the home of a local veterinary surgeon, Mr. and Mrs. Edward Jones and his family. Against the wall in the kitchen stands the largest oak dresser in Ceredigion.

Grid Ref: SN 2394 4596

Refs: Colby Map, 1831; Lewis, *TDW;* Blodau, *Dyfed,* 305, 316; NLW, Noyadd Trefawr Deeds, 219, 952; Mrs. L. Jones and Mr. K. Mills.

PANT-SEIRI (PANTSHERIFF), Tregaron

Situated two miles east of Tregaron, north of the mountain road on the bank of the Berwyn and marked on *Colby's Map of 1831.* Francis Jones wrote that the present house is comparatively modern but the outbuildings are earlier.

The Herberts were a younger branch of the Herberts of Hafod Uchdryd. Charles Herbert of Pant-y-seiri lived there between 1680-92. His son John was born in 1689. *The Book of Welsh Poems* by James Dwnn, found in a family home, bears the name 'Mr. Charles Herbert of Pantysheriff in the parish of Caron' and 'Cha Herbert, his Booke, 1692'. John's grandfather, David Herbert gent., married an Elizabeth . . . who was alive in 1654. They are mentioned in the *Cwrtmawr Papers* between 1663 and 1666. One of their daughters was Jane, who married Thomas David of Llanddewibrefi parish. The marriage was subject to a pre-nuptial settlement on 8 August 1666 regarding messuages called Brynamlwg and Gellie in Caron parish.

James, the son of David and Elizabeth Herbert, died in 1684. In Tregaron churchyard there was a headstone, inscribed 'Here lieth James Herbert of Pan Sheriff who died . . . 1684. G. E. Evans in *Ceredigion* gives us more detail and an intriguing story; 'There was formerly in Tregaron churchyard, a tombstone to James Herbert of Pan Sheriff who died in 1684, and the verse:

Remember man as thou goest bye,
So thou art now as e'en was I
Remember man that die thou must
And after come to judgement just.

A short time before his death James Herbert carried the gravestone himself, though very large and ponderous, by means of bands made of birch to the churchyard. The said stone is now, it is said, built into the interior of the southern wall of the chancel, but with the inscription turned inwards and the unhewn back of the stone to the front!'

However, according to the Rev. D. C. Rees in *Tregaron: Historical and Antiquarian* the story of the Herberts is told somewhat differently. 'Charles Herbert lived at Pant y seiri from 1680-92. His son, John, was born there in 1689. John Herbert who died in 1774 was a miller, presumably of Pentre, Tregaron: many stories are told of this family – Dafydd, John and James. The stories chiefly centre on Dafydd Coch Herbert, a redhead, who was enormously strong. Finding a monolith in the glen of Cwmberwyn, he decided to have it as his gravestone, and it was drawn by two yoke of oxen to Tregaron churchyard, and after his death placed over his grave. When the church was restored in 1879 a careless mason split the stone for building material, the larger portion was built into the south wall, adjacent to the vestry, so placed as to obliterate the inscription'. The brother, John Herbert, became involved in a lawsuit with William Williams of Pant Sheriff, which proved disastrous to John, both financially and mentally. In his later days he frequented the streets of Tregaron, either laughing maniacally and brandishing a sheaf of papers, or indulging in ecstatic jumps, under the impression that he had won the lawsuit. The other brother, James Herbert, engaged in a lawsuit with Mr. R. R. Price, steward of Ystrad-ffin. Price had a band of roughs at his command, and woe betide an unwelcome visitant to Ystradffin. A member of the Herbert family being in the neighbourhood of Ystrad-ffin, was set upon by Price's men. He galloped away for his life, gained on his pursuers but as he entered the confines of Cwmberwyn his gallant horse dropped dead under him'.

Following the lawsuit, the Williams family came to Pant Seiri. William Williams was the son of David Williams of Dol-goch, High Sheriff in 1725 and grandson of John Williams of Llanddewibrefi who had married Johan Price in 1661. His will was dated 20 August 1768. He had two sons, William (1698-1773), and Nathaniel.

William Williams, the elder son, who succeeded to Pant Seiri, had huge flocks and herds and was known as the 'King of the Mountains'. He was High Sheriff in 1750. He died on 31 January 1773 aged 75, and was buried at Llanddewi. William was succeeded by his brother, Nathaniel, a friend of John Wesley. Nathaniel was High Sheriff in 1775, married Elizabeth, daughter of John Jones of Diserth, Radnorshire, and they had a son, John Williams, later of Castle Hill, Llanilar and three daughters. When Nathaniel died in 1793 he was followed by his son, John, High Sheriff in 1801, who settled at Castle Hill. The family bore the arms: *azure* a chevron between 3 stags heads couped. By 1792 Rees Davies was the tenant at Pant Seiri.

Grid Ref: SN 7125 5912

Refs: Colby Map, 1831; NLW Castle Hill Docs., 690, 708-9, 711-13, 717; NLW, Cwrtmawr Deeds, Nos. 266, 277, 538, 568, 1485; The Revd. D. C. Rees, *Tregaron: Historical and Antiquarian,* 1936, pp. 55, 87-88; G. E. Evans, *Cardiganshire,* 1903, 101, 107-8; *Cymru*, Oct. 1901, pp. 222-3.

PANTSTREIMON, Llandysul

Situated a quarter of a mile north-east of Alltyrodyn mansion and marked on *Colby's Map of 1831* and on modern OS maps, equidistant between Rhydowen and Capel Dewi. 'This seat belonged anciently to the descendants of Cadifor ap Dinawal, Lord of Castle Howell.'

Thomas Fychan ap Howel ap Rhys ap Rhys Foel of Pantstreimon ap Rhys ap Rhydderch Lloyd had two sons, the second son and heir was named Thomas. Thomas married Gwerfyl, daughter of Rhydderch Evan Lloyd Evan Griffith foel. They had a son, Rhydderch, and a daughter, Angharad, who married Ieuan Lloyd of Llanfair Clydogau.

Rhydderch, aforesaid, had a son and heir, Thomas Fychan, who also had a son, Rhydderch Goch, whose son David Rhydderch Goch, married Jane, daughter and co-heiress of Rees Lloyd of Ffoshelyg. David had a son and heir, Rhydderch, and two natural sons; Owen, whose descendants were the Bowen of Bwlchbychan and Llanfair, and John, whose descendants were the Jones of Perthyberllan.

Rhydderch married Catherine, daughter of Morgan Rhys Jenkin of Llanbedr, by Jonet daughter of Morgan Ieuan Lloyd Llewelyn Gwilym Lloyd, and they had eight daughters who were all co-heiresses:

1. Maud married Rhys David Llewelyn Lloyd and had a son, David.
2. Jane, married David Lloyd Griffith Howel Rhys Howel David of Faerdref. Jane and her husband David remained at Pantstreimon.
3. Margaret, the third daughter married Hugh David Pugh of Neuadd, Llanarth.
4. Mary became the wife of David David Llewelyn Lloyd and their daughter Mary married Thomas Lewes of Gellidywyll in the parish of Cenarth. The marriage was the subject of a pre-nuptual settlement agreed on 20 January 1628/9.
5. Elizabeth, married George Thomas and had a son David.
6. Jonet married David Lloyd Thomas David Llewelyn Lloyd.
7. Gwenllian married Ieuan David Philip of Llechwedd-y-cwm and had a son Philip whose son was John of Cwm-y-Creigie.

8. The youngest daughter, Elen, married Jenkin Evan Howel of Troedyraur.

Meyrick states: 'Jane, daughter and coheiress of Rhydderch ap Dafydd married David Lloyd of Faerdre fawr, *iure uxoris*'. Meyrick records only two sons and one daughter but the Lloyd family records state that David and Jane Lloyd had four sons, Evan Lloyd of Faerdre, Thomas and Griffith of Cwm Meudwy and David, who received Pantstreimon. They also had five daughters, Mary, Catherine and Gwenllian who had issue, Elen and Elizabeth Jane.

Elen married David Thomas of Gelli faharen. They had a daughter, Jane, who married Henry Henry of Coed-y-foel, their son was David Henry, and their daughter, Gwenllian, married Thomas ap Thomas John ab Ieuan Thomas of Nantyrymenin and had two daughters Jane, who married Walter Einon and Margaret married the Rev. Samuel Williams vicar of Llandyfriog.

Meyrick states 'David Lloyd, *iure uxoris,* gave Pantstreimon to his youngest son, also David Lloyd and ever since, this estate has been annexed to Wern Newydd and is now (1810) in possession of Colonel Lloyd of Wern Newydd'.

The *Llandysul Tithe Map of 1841* gives Edward Price Lloyd as owner of Pantstreimon with Samuel Davies as tenant. The property at this time was of 234 acres.

Grid Ref: SN 4550 4467

Refs: Colby Map, 1831; WWHR, i, 18, 19, 49-50; Meyrick, *Cardiganshire,* 1810 (edn. 1907, pp. 197-8); CRO, GGMS I (Tydwal Gloff), pp. 25, 37; CRO, GGMS (Gwynfardd), p. 16; Lloyd Family Records (peds. p. 21); NLW, Noyadd Trefawr Deeds, No. 307; Llandysul Tithe Map, 1841.

PANT (Y) SWLLT, Llandisiliogogo

Situated north-west of Talgarreg on a minor road towards the A486 and marked on *Emanuel Bowen's Map of South Wales.* The first recorded occupier was Gruffydd, son of Rees ap Llewelyn ap Watkyn Gruffydd and his wife. They had a daughter, Lleucu, who married Rhys David of Glyn Adda, Llanllawddog in Carmarthenshire. Their daughter and heiress Elizabeth, married John Lewis of Blaen Cerdin and Dinas Cerdin and they had a son, David Lewis, who married twice; firstly to Sarah Evans, daughter of David

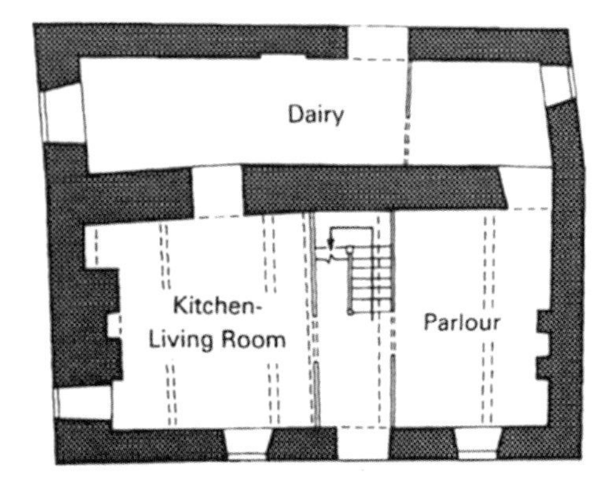

Evans, rector of Bangor Teifi, who died without issue, and secondly to Mary Evan, daughter of Edward Evan of Llwynyffynnon, Llangeler, Carmarthenshire.

Mary and David had a son, John, and daughter. John Lewis married a daughter of John Davies of Llwynpiod. Their son was a minor in 1755. John Griffiths, gent., was the owner-occupier of Pant-swllt in 1760. The farmhouse is an excellent example of the central-stairway houses which dominate the Cardiganshire countryside.

Prior to World War Two, the property was owned and farmed by John Lloyd and his wife. When they retired in 1945, Thomas Gilmor Davies, formerly a tenant at Blaen Cletwr, moved to Pant-swllt. He and Nansi, his wife, had returned from London where they, along with many other Cardis, owned a milk business and cafe. Mr. Davies was a County Councillor from 1958-1974 and was a founder-member of the Farmers' Union of Wales. His brother, W. Beynon Davies, became a respected and feared teacher at Ardwyn Grammar School in Aberystwyth and was the grandfather of Gwyn Jones, captain of the Welsh rugby team until his untimely injury. Thomas Gilmor Davies and his wife had nine children including Auronwy James of Penrhyn-coch and Llinos Devonald of Llandudoch. Upon his death in 1998, Pant-swllt is now farmed, complete with a renovated farm-house, by his son, Alun.

Grid Ref: SN 4200 5140

Refs: Emanuel Bowen Map of South Wales, c. 1760; PRO, Dale Castle MS., p. 26 (101); WWHR, i, 37; WWHR, iii, 84; Ex. Info. A. James and L. Devonald.

PANTYBETWS, Betws Ifan

A homestead situated near Betws Ifan church and marked on *Colby's Map of 1831* and modern OS maps eight miles north-east of Cardigan. G. E. Evans states, 'near this church is the farm of Pantybettws, formerly owned by a family named Griffiths, to whom several other farms in the neighbourhood also belonged'.

According to Dwnn, David Lloyd ap Griffiths of Pantybetws married Maud, the daughter of Philip ap Thomas ap Rhys ap Meredydd ap Owain, Arglwydd y Towy. The *Griffith Owen Deeds* state that on 4 July 1650 David Lloyd of Pantybetws, gent., granted 'three messuages called Llanborth, Tir Tre Dafydd, in Penbryn parish, Pantybetws in Betws Ifan parish, two cottages called Tir-y-brag and Tir Trero, as well as a water mill called Melin Llanborth, in Penbryn parish, to John Lewis of Penbryn, gent'.

Mathew Griffiths, a mercer, who was alive in 1671, the grandson of the Rev. Evan Griffith, (descended from Ievan Chwith of Caron), vicar of Cardigan, and Sibyl, daughter of James Lewis Thomas of Llanbadarn Fawr, and son of Abel Griffith, mercer of Cardigan, married Jane Lane of Bristol. Their son the Rev. Rees Griffith, of Pantybetws, was vicar of Penbryn from 1681 until he died in 1724. He married Mary Hughes of Penhill, Carmarthenshire and they had an enormously productive marriage, twenty-four children of whom at least five were sons. Abel, of Coedperthi and Llwynybrain dsp 1761; the Rev. Rice Griffith, who died in 1763, Mathew the third son, who succeeded to Pantybetws but died in 1769, unmarried, leaving a natural daughter, Mary, who married Edward Mainwaring Davies Howarth of Llandovery. The fourth son was the Rev. Walter Griffith who died without issue and the fifth son was William Griffiths who also died without issue 1750.

B. Williams writes in *Hanes Castell-newydd-yn-Emlyn* that in 1760, Abel Griffith, Esq., of Pantybetws 'also owned an ancient house in Cardigan where Caleb Lewis now lives: and that on inheriting Llwynybrain he went there to live'. Abel was a JP in 1740 and High Sheriff in 1758. In due course, his brother Mathew, of Llwynybrain owned Pantybetws. He died in 1769 without issue, but it was not until December 1785 that the house was offered for sale. The CRO *Aberglasney Documents* state that, 'among the properties of the late Mathew Griffith, Esq., to be sold by Order in Chancery was the capital messuages, farm and lands called Pantybetws now let on lease of three lives at £65 p.a.'.

By 1788 the house was owned by John Thomas who was a Churchwarden and in 1831 by Simon Davies. It was later owned by the Pryses of Gogerddan.

Grid Ref: SN 3037 4787

Refs: Colby Map, 1831; NLW, Griffith Owen Deeds, Box 51; G. E. Evans, *Cardiganshire,* 1903, 119; PRO List; CRO, Aberglasney Documents; B. Williams, *Hanes Castell-newydd-yn-Emlyn,* 1860, pp. 53-54; WWHR, iii, 81; *Dwnn,* i, 62; CRO, GGMS II (Adv. Pem.) fo. 231-2.

PANTYDEFAID, Llandysul

Located north of the A475 between Prengwyn and Rhydowen, marked on modern OS maps. The *Colby Map of 1831* names Ty Cwrdd Pant y defaid, a Unitarian meeting house. The suffix *defaid* is said to refer to the secret devotions of Roman Catholics in Tudor times.

David Thomas of Pantydefaid married Margaret, daughter of John David John of Pant-y-moch, the poet. According to the *Dale Castle Manuscripts* their daughter, Gwenllian married Thomas Lloyd David Rees of Camnant (who traced to Castle Hywel) and had a son and heir called David Thomas, alive between 1709 and 1739, later of Camnant. He married Mary, eldest daughter and co-heiress of John Davies of Y Fadfa, and had a son, Thomas David of Camnant and Pantydefaid. Thomas David married Elizabeth, daughter of Lewis Pugh of Ffwrneithin.

The National Library of Wales holds a deed showing that by 5 April 1762 John Jones of Pantydefaid, great-grandson and heir of John Jenkin of parish Llandysul, blacksmith, deceased, and John Lloyd of Coedlannau, parish Llanwenog, gent., another grandson of the said John Jenkins, were the residuary legatees and executors of said John Jenkins.

Grid Ref: SN 4313 4467

Refs: Colby Map, 1831; Meyrick, *Cardiganshire,* 200; PRO, Dale Castle MS., pp. 30, 114; WWHR, i, 52; AE 12356E; NLW, BRA. 898, No. 137.

PANTYRODYN, Betws Ifan

Marked on *Colby's Map of 1831* south-east of Betws Ifan and located on modern OS maps south of the minor road between Brongest and Beulah in the peaceful valley of the Medeni, which joins Afon Dulas south-east of Pantyrodin.

The house belonged to a branch of Lewes of Gernos. Benjamin Williams tells us that 'there was once a famous Plâs there, but now it is but a substantial farmhouse'.

Richard Lewes, fifth son of David Lewes of Gernos, married Eleanor, daughter and coheiress of David Lloyd of Glan Cletwr. He was living at Pantyrodin in 1627 when he 'entered into a bond with John ap Rees of Penbryn parish for £100 in observance of covenants in deeds of even date'. They had a son Nicholas, and a daughter, Jane, who married Rees Awbrey, son of John Awbrey and a daughter of Rees David Leia of Cymwil Elfed. Jane and Rees had two sons and one daughter: John Awbrey, the eldest son, of Carmarthen, attorney-at-law, Richard, a hatmaker at Aberarad near Newcastle Emlyn, who married in North Wales, and Anne, who married John James of Blaen-porth. John Awbrey, married Mary, daughter of Richard Thomas, Mayor of Carmarthen in 1635. They had two sons and two daughters; John Awbrey, was an attorney-at-law in London and was Clerk of the Introits in the Exchequer in 1730. He married the widow of Hugh Lloyd of Danyrallt, Carmarthenshire and died in 1759 without issue. The second son was the Rev. Thomas Awbrey, clerk. The daughters were Mary, who married John Oakley, and Jane who married twice, her second husband was Edward Davies, a lawyer.

Nicholas Lewes, son and heir of Richard and Eleanor Lewes, married Mary, daughter of Morris Morgan of Coed-llwyd, Clydau, Pembrokeshire. He was assessed at three hearths in 1672 and he was High Sheriff in 1675. He died before 1679, when his wife is described as a widow. His eldest daughter, Margaret, was married twice. Her first husband was David Morgan of Coed-llwyd, who died without issue and she married secondly, the Rev. John Parry of Llannerch Aeron, the rector of Troedyraur in 1704, and a JP in 1714. He became Archdeacon of Cardigan and died in 1727. John and Margaret Parry had two daughters, Lettice, who married Morgan Howel of Penbeili, Esq., High Sheriff in 1704, and Elizabeth, who married George Lloyd of Cwmgloyne, Pembrokeshire. The *Golden Grove Manuscripts* record that John and Margaret Parry also had a son, Lewis Parry, clerk, of Pantyrodin, who married Mary Parry, daughter and heiress of Stephen Parry. Lewis and Mary had a son, John Parry of Pantyrodin who married Anne, the daughter of Walter Lloyd of Ffynnon Bedr.

Pantyrodyn became part of the Llanerchaeron estate and was later let to tenants. The arms of the Rev. John Parry of Pantyrodin are on a stone on the outer wall of the chancel of Troedyraur church, but are now indistinct. They are as follows: first and fourth quarters, a lion rampant, a crescent on his shoulder; and the second and third quarters a lion rampant in a border indented. Above the shield is an open book with the verse Job XIX. v. 25 carved on it in Welsh.

The annual rental paid by tenants at Pantyrodyn was £60 in 1786 which rose to £100 in 1844. The farm and several other parts of the Llannerchaeron estate were sold in 1918 by Capt. T. P. Lewis to clear the debts of his father.

Grid Ref: SN 3103 4555

Refs: Colby Map, 1831; G. E. Evans, *Cardiganshire,* 1903, p. 72; PRO List; Meyrick, *Cardiganshire,* 1810, 2nd. Edn. 1907, p. 204; CRO, GGMS, II (Adv. Brec.), fo. 111; ibid (Gwyddno); Blome List, 1673; NLW, Morgan Richardson Deeds, i, 161, 162; NLW, Bronwydd Deeds, No. 2556; *Hanes Cas. newydd-Emlyn,* B. Williams, 1860, p. 54; Clark, *Generals of Glamorgan,* 1886, 347; NLW F. Green

Deeds, No. 25; Mair Lloyd Evans, *Llanerchaeron* (1996), pp. 64, 77.

PANT-YR-YNN, Llandysiliogogo

Located on modern OS maps south of Cwmtudu above a steep slope above afon Ffynnon Ddewi. Marked on *Emanuel Bowen's Map of South Wales*, c. 1760 as in the possession of Philipps, gent. In 1760 Daniel Shewen, gent., of Laugharne owned Pant-yr-ynn.

An anecdote told in New Quay concerns 'Shams' of Pant-yr-ynn. Shams was the local 'hard man', father of innumerable bastards, and go-between with smugglers for the infamous Sir Herbert Lloyd of Ffynnon Bedr. Having boasted of his activities in local hostelries, he became a liability to Sir Herbert who rode to Cwmtudu. Having caught Shams in the process of selling his wife to the smugglers, (wife selling being regarded as lawful in the 18th century), he had a make-shift gallows erected on the beach and Shams was ignominiously hanged.

Grid Ref: SN 3601 5688

Refs: Emanuel Bowen Map of South Wales, c. 1760; WWHR, iii, 85.

PANTYSGAWEN (PANTYSCAWEN), Llandysul

Marked on *Colby's Map of 1831* as Pantyscawen, south of Castell Hywel and east of the B4459 north of Pont-sian.

Ieuan ap Henry of Coedyfoel had a son, Ieuan ab Ieuan alias Coch-yr-aur of Pantyscawen, commonly called Ieuan Coch. He in turn had a son, Griffith ab Ieuan who married Angharad, daughter of John ab Ieuan Thomas of Nantyrymenin, and a daughter Angharad, who married Rees Thomas David of Llanfair-perthycynddyn. Their daughter and co-heiress Margaret, married Thomas David of Ffosesgob. Both were living in 1709. Their son, Rees Thomas established a line at Llanfair descending to William Thomas of Llanfair who died in 1880.

Grid Ref: SN 4437 4725

Refs: Colby Map, 1831; PRO, Dale Castle MS., p. 31 (115); WWHR, i, 52.

PARC MAWE, see FARDRE-FACH

PARC RHYDDERCH, Llanbadarn Odwyn

'Parc Rhydderch is one of those old houses in which the soul of a neighbourhood is laid away' wrote Ernest Rhys in *The South Wales Coast*. An old homestead built in the Vale of Aeron, south-west of Llangeitho, south of the main road from Talsarn to Llangeitho, where the Gwenffrwd flows under the road. Marked on *Colby's Map of 1831* and on modern OS maps. This was the home of the ancient family of Rhydderch, formerly of Glyn Aeron.

Gruffydd Foel (to Gwaethfoed, Lord of Cardigan who died in 1057), had a son, Ieuan, who married Elliw, the daughter of Maredudd ap Cadwgan Fantach. Ieuan swore fealty to the Black Prince in 1345 and Llewelyn Brydydd Hodnant dedicated a *cywydd* to him. His son, Ieuan Llwyd married Angharad, daughter of Rhisiart ab Einion ap Cynfrig of Buellt. He was Constable of Anhuniog and there is a poem dedicated to him by Casnodyn in *Llawysgrif Hendregadredd*, and an elegy *Caer Rhag Cenfigen,* written to his wife, Angharad, by Dafydd ap Gwilym.

They had a son, Rhydderch ap Ieuan Llwyd who was *'o Barc Rhydderch yn Glyn Aeron Esqe'*, from whom the Lloyds of Lloyd Jack descend, and who signed for the herald Dwnn. He held office in Mabwynion from 1386-90 and again between 1409 and 1442. He was Steward of Ceredigion in 1386 and Deputy of the Shire from 1388-9. In 1392-3 Rhydderch ap Ieuan Lloyd of Parc Rhydderch, Constable of Mabwynion in 1385-6, *bedellus* of same in 1386-7, obtained from Richard II a grant of the Lordship of Cellan and escheated lands owned by Tudor ap Grono who had died without heirs.

Horsfall-Turner tells us that 'the old homestead of Parc Rhydderch, below Llangeitho, was built by Rhydderch Llwyd, the reputed owner of *Llyfr Gwyn Rhydderch,* the original manuscript of *The Mabinogion and Welsh Romances*. Rhydderch ap Ieuan Llwyd lived to an old age and was probably married three times. His first wife was Marged, daughter of Gruffudd Gono ap Ieuan Fychan, who traced to Llawdden, and was long associated with the commotte of Perfedd. He then married Mawd, daughter of Sir William Clement, Lord of

Tregaron who held extensive lands in Genu'r Glyn. One of their sons, Phylip ap Rhydderch briefly supported Owain Glyndwr and lost his lands in the process. The other children of the marriage were, Siancyn, Tomas, Dafydd, Ieuan, Gwenllian and Marged. Rhydderch's third wife was Anne, daughter of Gwilym ap Philyp ap Elidir. It is thought that Dafydd Llwyd, son of Dafydd ap Rhydderch was the progenitor of the Gogerddan branch of the family. He was the son of Dafydd ap Rhydderch who was married to a lady from north Wales whose family held lands in north Cardiganshire. Ieuan ap Rhydderch, the poet, described as 'the epitome of the Welsh culture during the Middle Ages' boasted of his attainments in having detailed knowledge of the bible, grammar and civil law, French and the classics, harp playing, chess, swimming and riding.

A 'true coppie of an ancient memorable Treatise of Record touchinge the Progenie and Descent of the honourable Name and Family of Herberts', was signed by 'Ieuan ap Rhydderch ap Ieuan Lloyd, Esq.,' and the 'four chyffest men of skyll within the provynce of South Wallys'.

John ap Ieuan of Parc Rhydderch married Jane daughter of Ieuan Gwyn ap Thomas ap Hywel, sister of David Gwyn of Cefen Brechfa, who married Margaret Stedman. The *Golden Grove Manuscripts* state that John was the natural son of Ieuan. Their son Zaccheus married Rebecca, daughter of Ieuan of Llechwedd Deri who traced to Tydwal, and their son John married Judith daughter of a Jones of Gilfachberthog.

On 17 September 1556 a grant was made of a tenement and land called 'Tythyn Parke Rhydderchar Noyadd, in Llanbadarn Odyn' for £23.6.8. The parties to the bond were Jenkyn ap

David ap Owen of Nantcwnlle, and Morgan ap David ap Owen of the same, gent., and Rhydderch ap Dafydd Fain of Llanbadarn Odwyn, a yeoman.

A hundred years later, the house was the subject of a dispute. On 22 August 1656, the *Bronwydd Deeds* record that an affidavit was sworn by Sydney Ellis with reference to 'his title to a messuage called Parke Rudderch in Llanbadarn Odwyn, now in dispute'. John Zaccheus also laid claim to it in 1662. By 1697 Hugh Lloyd of Lloyd Jack, High Sheriff in the same year, was of the family of Parc Rhydderch.

Ernest Rhys wrote of: 'the great family of the Lloyds of Dyffryn Aeron. One built Parc Rhydderch in the thirteenth century. But ancient homes come to an end, and the last heiress of the race, Miss Lloyd of Cil-rhug (a seat not far from the older seat of the family at Cilpyll and Parc Rhydderch) was murdered by her serving man in 1792. However, as a matter of fact, many offshoots still do exist in the vale'.

Grid Ref: SN 6005 5887

Refs: Colby Map, 1831; Horsfall-Turner, *Wanderings,* 260; *Dwnn,* i, 15, 18, 27, 28, 45, 87; NLW, AE 12356E; O Pemb., IV, p. 483; NLW, Bronwydd Deeds, Nos. 1390, 2154, 2162, 7151; *Llawysgrif Hendregadredd;* CRO, GGMS III (Gwaethfoed), pp, 28, 34; Ernest Rhys, *The South Wales Coast,* 1911, pp. 361-2; *Ceredigion,* VII, No. 1 (1972), pp. 21-26; *NLWJ,* VIII No. 1 (1953), pp. 90-1.

PARC-Y-GORS, Llandygwydd

Located north-west of Noyadd Trefawr south of the minor road to Blaenannerch. Described as rather like an old vicarage, a photograph in *The Tivyside Photographic Souvenir* shows a square block of two storeys, with a ground floor veranda, an arched doorway in the centre and domestic buildings to the rear. The property was part of the Noyadd Trefawr estate and was used as a dower house. Mrs. Webley-Parry, on the death of her husband of Noyadd Trefawr, declined to live at Parc-y-gors and chose to rent Treforgan for the remaining 20 years of her life. Lewis states that, 'Park Gors and Dol, all within the parish, are handsome residences on a smaller scale'. W. O. Brigstocke formerly of Blaen-pant lived at Parc-y-gors in 1898.

Francis Jones writes that it was still inhabited

and in good condition when he visited it on 14 May 1983; 'the home of Mrs. Mitchley, an elderly lady who lives there alone'.

Parc-y-gors is now owned by her son, Christopher Mitchley, a veterinary surgeon, the grandson of a former Indian Army Colonel who married a daughter of Derw Mills, Pentre-cwrt, a volunteer nurse serving in India. Until recently the house was let to Mr. and Mrs. Julian Jones. It is currently tenanted by an organisation who offer holidays for under-privileged, inner-city children in a quiet rural location.

Grid Ref: SN 2488 4675

Refs: Colby Map, 1831; *The Tivyside Photographic Souvenir,* C. Allen, Tenby, c. 1860, (album in the possession of Miss Gwynedd Taylor, Manorbier, 1975); *Photographs in South Wales,* Charles Smith Allen; Lewis, *TDW,* 1840; BLG, 1898, i, 166.

PARC-Y-PRATT, St. Mary's Cardigan

About a mile south of Cardigan town bridge, and adjacent to the A487 (T) Cardigan-Eglwyswrw road. The earliest reference to the property is a deed of 1201. The earlier mansion stood in a grove to the north of the present residence. Near the earlier site stood a cottage in later days known as Hen Parc-y-pratt. According to *Pembs. Arch. Survey, 1896*, 'the old house stood some 300 yards below the present homestead, and was surrounded by trees, several of which still remain. There is nothing left of the mansion but some rough walling, and an out-house which has been converted into a cottage'. Little is known of the earliest owners, the Pratts, except that Geoffrey Pratt was living there in 1292, and that the family gave its name to the property. By the 15th century Elen Pratt heiress of Parc-y-pratt, married John Cole of St. Dogmaels, and had a son Philip Cole, who was followed by his sole daughter and heiress Janet Cole, who married Owain ap Rhys of Llystyn, 10th in descent from Einon Fawr o'r Coed in Cemaes who traced to Gwynfardd Dyfed, and eminent landowner of the county in medieval days . . .

Owain ap Rees had five sons, between whom their father's estate was divided by gavelkind. Gwilym who had Llystyn, Owain who had Llannerch-y-blaidd, James who had Henllys Isha, John who had Cryngae his mother's property, and Howell.

The Cole family also became owners of Llwyngwair in Nevern parish. Owain ap Rhys who married Janet, eventual heiress of Parc-y-pratt, was followed by his son Jenkin ap Owain, and he was succeeded by Thomas ap Jenkin. This Thomas married Elen, daughter of Howel Young ap Jenkin, and had a son and heir, David ap Thomas who enlisted in the army, served at Boulogne, and elsewhere in France in the reign of Henry VIII, and signed his pedigree for Dwnn on 21 January 1588. In 1559, Rice Fychan ap Rhydderch of 'St. Dogmaels vill', Esq., his wife Engharaud (Angharad), and Rhydderch ap Rhys Fychan of Selyham, gent., granted three pieces of land at Tir yrv hengoed, in Bridell, to David Thomas Jenkin ap Owen of Parc-y-pratt, gent. He was a much loved land-owner, interested in genealogy and antiquaries. Bards were welcome at Parc-y-pratt, and Sion Mawddog sang his elegy when he died at a very advanced age on 10 May 1601. By his wife, Janet, daughter of Sir James ab Owen ap William ab Owen of Pentre Ifan, he had three sons: Einion, vivens 1588; Nicholas, of Parc-y-pratt; the Rev. Nicholas David the younger, vicar of St. Dogmaels in 1601. The eldest son, Einion, married Margaret John of Trefaes-isa, 'and, as thei saye was devorsed and then married one Hugh Phe ap Ieuan Jenkin in the liff of her husband Eynon David, and had by him a son named David, and then she died, the said Eynon David surviving her' . . . so wrote her contemporary, George Owen of Henllys. Nicholas, the second son, entered the Church, became Vicar of St. Dogmaels, and according to George Owen, 'Parc-y-pratt the mansion house now of Nicholas David, cleric, second sonne to his ffather, David Thomas who in his tyme lyved and dyed in the love and likeinge of all his acquaintance, and who greathe beauwtified the place . . .'

Few references have been found of the David family afterwards, and it is clear that they had left Parc-y-pratt before the end of the first half of the 18th century; the post-nuptial references dated 25 September 1666, of Thomas Bowen, gent., of Cilgerran, and Ann David second daughter of Stephen David of Parc-y-pratt gent., mention some 23 properties settled, in the parishes of Cilgerran, Bridell, and Emlyn Is Cych.

The last reference to the family mentions William Morris of Parc-y-pratt, gent., living there in 1716. In 1760, Thomas Morris of Parc-y-pratt is listed as a parliamentary voter. The *Land Tax of 1786* states that Thomas Morris was the owner-occupier. In the period 1815-1875 the Jenkins family lived there, and in 1858 William Griffith George was the occupier. A manuscript of 1860 states, 'Parc-y-pratt was, during the last century and part of this in the possession of a family named Morris, the last of whom, dying without issue, left the estate to a cousin of his living in Bristol who resided for some time at Parc-y-pratt accompanied by a person named Sumner in whose favour he made his will. Sumner sold the estate to Thomas Davies, Esq., of the Bridge, Cardigan and ere he left the country erected a monumental stone in memory of his friend.'

In 1825 Thomas and Mary Makeig became the tenants of Parc-y-pratt having moved from Little Scotland in Llandygwydd. The Makeigs were an anceint Scottish family. Parc-y-pratt was then of 294 acres. Thomas and Mary took up residence when it was let by Letita, widow of Thomas Davies, who held it for her son, Thomas, a minor. Mary Anne, the third daughter of Thomas and Mary Makeig married Simon Davies, a surgeon from London at St. Dogmaels in 1829. Thomas Makeig IV died from gout in May 1838 at the age of 66. Mary left Parc-y-pratt for Canllefais a farm in Penparc and died there in 1858. Her daughter, Mary Anne died at Trefwtial in 1876. Another daughter married a James from Cardigan from whom the Makeig-James family descend. Henry Graham Partridge who extended the house, was owner-occupier of Parc-y-pratt from 1942. He was High Sheriff in 1971 and lived there and in Malta.

Grid Ref: SN 1725 4475

Refs: NLW, Mostyn MS., Nos.. 50 (c. 1592), No. 3033B and 5603; NLW, Bronwydd MS., No. 50, c. 1601-2; NLW, Eaton Evans and Williams Deeds, Nos. 49 & 1275; NLW, Noyadd Trefawr Deeds, No. 874; George Owen 'second book' 1269, and MS., 5603, fos. 84-5; CRO, Golden Grove Books (Adv. Pembs.) I, fo. 1239; PRO, Deeds MDX, 615, No. 1, C/A MSS., Wagner MS. 2; NLW, Griffith Owen Deeds; *Pembs. Arch. Svy,* 1896; *Dwnn,* i, 60; WWHR, II, p. 55; Nicholas, *County Families,* 1875 edn; *Ceredigion,* Vol. V, No. 2 (1965), pp. 209-28; ibid, Vol. VII, No. 2 (1973), pp. 189-206.

PEITHYLL, Llanbadarn Fawr

'Peithyll is a plain mansion', Nicholas tells us, 'chiefly noticeable for its investiture of modern farm buildings, adapted for an improved system of agriculture and rearing of stock'. Located on the banks of the Peithyll near to Capel Dewi east of the A4159 between Lovesgrove and Bow Street. It is near to Gogerddan with which it has always been associated. Marked on the 14th century *Rees Map* and on *Colby's Map of 1831.*

Gruffydd ap Rhys ap Tewdwr captured the castle at Peithyll in 1116.

The Pryses of Gogerddan were pioneers in the practices of agriculture and the very latest machinery and buildings were installed at both Gogerddan and Peithyll, the latter particularly having a reputation as a farm of note. Pryse Pryse of Gogerddan and Buscot Park, was MP for Cardigan Borough from 1818-49. He was born Pryse Loveden of Buscot Park, and took the additional surname Pryse in 1798. He had two sons; Sir Pryse Pryse of Gogerddan, a baronet by revived creation 28 July 1866, and Colonel Edward Lewis Pryse of Peithyll, the younger son, who was born in 1817. He became Lord Lieutenant of Cardiganshire and like his father was MP for Cardiganshire from 1857-68. He had served previously as a Captain in the 6th Dragoon Guards and rose to the rank of Colonel of the Royal Cardiganshire Militia. He died in 1888 without issue. When the Gogerddan estate was sold in 1948 Peithyll was bought by the tenant.

Grid Ref: SN 6313 8270

Refs: Rees, 14th Century Map; Colby Map, 1831; Nicholas, *County Families,* 1875, i, 207; *Ceredigion,* i, 1950, p. 40.

PEITHYLL or PEITHY, site unknown

Francis Jones places this house in Cardiganshire but does not give a location.

Walter, the younger son of Jenkin Lloyd ap David of Llanfair Clydogau made his home at Peithy. He married Joyce, daughter of Griffith Lloyd of Fforest, Carmarthenshire. They had four sons and two daughters: Griffith, Mathew, Morgan and Francis, (who married Catherine Williams, daughter of William Williams of Parc), Mary who married Rhys Evans of Llygadenwyn, Pencarreg, Carmarthenshire, and Lucy, who married twice; firstly William David of Dol-wen, and secondly, to James William Meredydd, an alehouse-keeper.

Francis, the youngest son of Walter and Joyce, and Catherine Lloyd had two sons; Jenkin Lloyd, DD, and Walter Lloyd of Llwyn-y-fedw who died without issue, and four daughters. One daughter married Ieuan David Hugh of Pencarreg, Carmarthenshire, and another married David Jones of Llansawel. Jane married John Evans of Talsarn, Cardiganshire, and another un-named daughter who married twice, firstly to William Price, the natural son of Sir James Price, knight, and secondly, Vicar Price of Caeo, Carmarthenshire.

Jenkin Lloyd, the heir, married Priscilla, daughter of Gilbert Jones by Miss Littleton. They had three sons, Walter Lloyd of London, sculptor, Middleton Lloyd and Thomas Lloyd, who died without issue. The two daughters were Bridget, who married William Williams, vicar of Carmarthen, and another daughter who married Jenkin Llwyd.

Refs: CRO, GGMS, III (Gwaethfoed), fo. 38.

PENBONTBREN,
Llanfihangel Genau'r-Glyn

Located north-east of Talybont in woodland on the banks of the Ceulan and marked on *Colby's Map of 1831* and modern OS maps. A sale catalogue gives the following description of the property: 'A three-storied, cube-shaped Georgian house comprising, on the ground floor, hall with Corinthian pillars, breakfast room (with corniced ceiling), drawing room (corniced ceiling) morning room, study, sun lounge, kitchen, bathroom, on the first floor – 8 bedrooms, bathroom, cloakroom. Second floor – 5 bedrooms, 2 bathrooms, 2 staircases. Cellars.'

G. E. Evans writes in *Cardiganshire* of 'the family of Griffiths who lived for many generations at Penbontbren'. Thomas Griffiths of Penbontbren, alive in 1650, had a son, Thomas, who married Ann, daughter of John West of London and Tre'rddol, Cardiganshire. Thomas died in 1694 and his son, Hugh, succeeded to his estates. Hugh married Susannah, daughter of Meredith Lloyd of Cwmbwa, Cardiganshire. They had three sons; John who succeeded, Cornelius and Charles. John Griffiths of Pentbontbren was a JP and served as High Sheriff in 1757. He had two sons, Thomas, and Charles Griffith who served as a Captain in the Royal Marines and who died in 1818. Thomas Griffith, married Jane, only child of Richard Philipps of Coedgain, Carmarthenshire on 10 December 1778. Their son, also Thomas (1786-1856), a surgeon at Chester, married twice. His first wife, Catherine Bond, died without issue. Thomas then married Elizabeth Margaret, co-heiress of William Boscawen and his wife, Anne, daughter of John Morley Trevor of Trefalun, near Wrexham.

The grandson of Thomas and Elizabeth, Trevor Griffith Boscawen, had two daughters; Enid Sophie, born in 1889 who married Sir Clement Wakefield Jones of Friends' Hall, Neston, Cheshire, and Vera Edith, who married Sir H. J. Delves Broughton, whose daughter Rosamund married Simon Fraser, 24th chief of Clan Fraser of Lovat in 1938.

Through the marriage of a daughter of Thomas Griffiths to William Jones, Prysgaga, in 1720, Penbontbren was occupied by a succession of the Jones family. William Jones was followed by another William who married firstly, Jane Watkin of Cynnull-mawr, Talybont, and then the widow of Lewis Morys, a notable scholar and bard, (Llewelyn Ddu o Fôn), who died in 1765. In 1787 William was living at Llandinam, Montgomeryshire, having formerly lived at Troed-y-rhiw, when he mortgaged properties in Elerch to the Rev. David

Ellis of Amlwch, Anglesey. William, the eldest son of the first marriage, married Mary, daughter of the Rev. William Tilsley of Llwyd-y-coed, Montgomeryshire, whose son, another William married Jane Tickell and later lived at Gwynfryn, Llangynfelyn. Their son, Basil, became Bishop of St. Davids. Lewis Jones (1793-1866), the second son of William and Mary, born at Penbontbren, was the grandson of William John of Hafodau, Llanbadarn-fawr. When a boy, he fell into the Leri near the house and save for his mother's prompt action, would have drowned. He attended Ystradmeurig school and later was appointed to the living of Almondbury in 1822. In 1830, he married Catherine Watkyn of Moel Cerni. Penbontbren was sold in 1801 by Charles Griffiths of the Royal Marines to the Carmarthen solicitor, Herbert Lloyd.

Grid Ref: SN 6609 8996

Refs: Colby Map, 1831; Meyrick, *Cardiganshire,* 323, 1810 (edn. 1907); WWHR, iii, 64; BLG NLW, Cwrtmawr Deeds 1721; G. E. Evans, *Cardiganshire,* 1903, 208; Horsfall-Turner, *Cardiganshire,* p. 61.

PENBRYN, Penbryn, see Dyffryn Hoffnant

PENBRYN, Llanbadarn Fawr

Situated north of the A44 (T) half a mile west of Goginan and marked on *Colby's Map of 1831.* Penbryn came to prominence in the 18th century when it became the house of Lewis Morris (Llewelyn Ddu o Fôn), the eldest of four brothers from Anglesey, three of whom became noted antiquaries and writers. Lewis Morris (1701-65), was a distinguished scholar, poet and cartographer. He was the first-born child of Morris ap Rhisiart (Pritchard), a cooper, and his wife, Margaret Owen, of Llanfihangel Tre'r Beirdd. Lewis became a self-taught surveyor and cartographer, and married Elizabeth Griffith, heiress of Ty-wriddyn, Rhoscolyn, in 1729 and they had three daughters. Elizabeth died before 1741. Lewis journeyed south in 1742 and was commissioned to survey Crown lands between the rivers Clarach and Rheidol. He was appointed Deputy-Steward of the Crown Manors in Cardiganshire. He became much involved in disputes with powerful landowners such as Herbert Lloyd, the Powells and the Vaughans, and was imprisoned for a period in Cardigan gaol. From 1746 Lewis Morris lived at Allt Fadog near Capel Dewi. Three years later he married Anne Lloyd, heiress to the small Penbryn estate at Goginan. They moved there in 1757. Anne gave birth to ten children of whom four died in infancy. Lewis served as a JP for Cardiganshire and on one of his visits to London helped his brother, Richard, to found the Honourable Society of Cymmrodorion in 1751: he died of the palsy in 1765, and in 1772 his widow, Anne, married William Jones, widower of Gwynfryn, near Tre'rddol in Llangynfelin. She died in 1785. A nephew, John Owen, son of Lewis's sister, Elen, a bard, harpist and writer, who died in Gibraltar in 1759, called his uncle Lewis, 'the Fat man of Cardiganshire'.

On 22 May 1787, William Morris, the fourth son (1758-1808), married Mary Anne Reynolds, heiress of the small estate of Blaennant, Llanfeigan, Breconshire. He republished his father's *Plans of Harbours* and died in 1808. Their son, Lewis Edward William Morris, was a solicitor and later became town clerk of Carmarthen. He bought Mount Pleasant, Llangynnor, Carmarthenshire, and rebuilt it. On completion he re-named it Penbryn after his old family home. His son, Sir Lewis Morris of Penbryn (Carmarthenshire), a friend of Oscar Wilde was called to the Bar, but is best remembered as a poet who wrote on themes of Welsh history. Vice-President of the University of Wales, Aberystwyth, he married Florence Julia Pollard in 1868. He died in 1907.

In recent years, Penbryn along with Ty-can, Abernant and Cwm Rheidol, was the property of Moses Griffiths, originally from Caernarfon, and Penbryn was occupied by Tom Williams and his family. Griffiths later sold the properties and the last, Penbryn, was bought by J. Vernon Howells of Penygreen, Llanidloes, with the Roberts family as tenants. In turn, the Roberts's purchased the property from Vernon Howells. Penbryn was the childhood home of the late Gwynfor Roberts of the National Library of Wales.

Grid Ref: SN 6838 8099

Refs: Colby Map, 1831; Tegwyn Jones, *Y Llew a i*

Deulu, 1982, & photograph on page 56; *Ceredigion,* X, No. 2 (1985), pp. 138-9; ex info G. Gruffydd, A. E. Jones.

PENGELLI, Llangwyryfon

Marked on *Colby's Map of 1831* and on modern OS maps south-east of Llangwyryfon on the minor road towards Trefenter.

Early in the 17th century, Morris Thomas ap Ieuan Lloyd married Catherine Owen. They had two sons, John Morris of Carrog and Owen Morris of Pengelli in 'Llanygrowdhon'. Owen married Mary, daughter of James David of Llanrhystud and their son, Morris ap Owen ap Morris married Margaret, daughter of David Richard David Parry (1640-94), of Rhod-mad, Llanilar and his wife, Anne, daughter of John Lloyd of Gilfachafael and Margaret, daughter of Stephen Parry of St. Dogmaels. They had six sons and one daughter, including Owen Morris of Pengelli. One of his sons was Richard Morrice of Treflys.

A descendant of Owen Morris was the Rev. Maurice Evans (1765-1831), later vicar of Llangeler. Born at Pengelli and educated at Ystradmeurig, Maurice Evans was received into Holy Orders at Abergwili in 1787 and spent some years in England. From 1810-20, Maurice was the parish priest at Tregaron where he was described as an effective preacher and the ideal parish priest. In 1820 he was appointed to Llangeler and also held the living of Penbryn. He was a JP and rebuilt the church at Llangeler in 1829. Maurice Evans died in 1831 aged 66 years. A tablet to his memory can be seen at Llangeler church. His son, William, curate of Christ Chapel, London, died at the Lodge, Llandysul in 1837 following a short illness, when he was 25 years old.

Grid Ref: SN 6027 7038

Refs: Colby Map, 1831; CRO, GGMS, III (Edwin).

PEN-GLAIS (Plâs), Llanbadarn Fawr

Formerly the home of the Richardes family, formerly Rhydderch, many of whom served their county as High Sheriffs and who owned an estate of twenty farms in the Rheidol valley. Marked on *Emanuel Bowen's Map of South Wales* c. 1760 as Penglais Fawr and *Colby's Map of 1831* as Penglais.

The earliest reference to a Richardes living at Penglais was to William in 1671. His son, Roderick, High Sheriff in 1699, had a son, also Roderick, who married Mary, daughter of John Lloyd of Mabws. Roderick, a Clerk in the Navy Office, London, retired to Pen-glais and built the new mansion there in 1770. He was High Sheriff in the same year.

His natural son, William, by Jane Welland, took the name Richardes and went to live at Pen-glais, where he died in 1787. He had two sons and left the estate to the eldest, Roderick Eardley Richardes. The younger son, William, had a son William Eardley Richardes later of Bryneithin born at Pen-glais in 1797, who was educated at Marlow and Woolwich Academy, appointed a JP and entered the Royal Artillery and fought as a lieutenant at Waterloo. He married Marianne Stephens, daughter of Hugh Stephens of Cascob, Radnorshire, JP and High Sheriff of that county. They had four sons and one daughter. The eldest son, Charles Richardes HEICS served in India and was awarded a medal for Lucknow and Delhi; he died without issue in 1867. The second son, William was a Captain of the 21st Horse and died in 1865 without issue. The third son Hugh Stephens Richardes served in India during the Mutiny and received a letter of thanks from the Queen. The fourth son, Frank Richardes followed his brothers into the Indian army and died without issue. The only daughter Frances Anne married the Rev. Charles Marriott Leir and they had one son. Frances died in 1910 and her husband in 1864.

The eldest son of Roderick and Mary Richardes, Roderick Eardley Richardes (1788-1854), was a spendthrift whose pecuniary difficulties often necessitated flight to Calais to escape debtors. Given to the use of 'blackguard low language' he was appointed a JP and served the office of High Sheriff in 1813. Following the severe beating of a rival with the assistance of his brother, he married Anne Corbetta Powell, daughter of Thomas Powell of Nanteos, much against the wishes of her mother. The pre-nuptial settlement was agreed on 20 October 1820, Anne's marriage portion of £5,000 was raised by a mortgage on the estate. In 1825, on a visit to Calais, Roderick, who regularly beat his wife, threw her out of the house in a psychopathic rage. Thereafter, Roderick lived mainly in Southampton, on an allowance of £640 a year and Anne took the unusual step of obtaining a Deed of Separation executed some years later in 1848. She continued to live at Pen-glais. They had, however, had six children, Alexander (1861-83), the heir, along with Roderick, Averina, Maria, Charles and Cornelius.

Alexander Richardes, with an allowance of £60 a year from his father, married Elizabeth . . . and served as a Captain in the Royal Cardigan Militia. The *Landowners Return of 1873* shows the estate to be of 1,610 acres, valued at £1,149. Alexander died in 1883, leaving two sons and four daughters. His sons were Eardley John, who died in his youth, and Roderick Clement Richardes. Roderick had a son who was killed in action in 1918. Roderick was the last of the male line to live at Pen-glais. He died in 1925 and the estate, which by then due to mismanagement and acute profligacy, consisted of little more than the home and gardens, Pen-glais farm and the Cae Melyn area of Aberystwyth, passed to a distant Warwickshire branch of the family. After World War Two and the threat of council housing on the estate, 200 acres was donated to the UCW Aberystwyth through the generosity of David Alban Davies, a wealthy London-Welsh businessman and benefactor.

The *plâs* became the official residence of the Principal of College and following extensive renovations under the direction of Sir Percy Thomas, the Principal, Ifor Evans, and his family moved in. The name of Rhys Evans, well-known to hymnologists, was immortalized following the composition of a haunting tune by his grandfather, W. J. Evans, to complement the words of Elfed, *Rho im yr hedd, na wyr y byd amdano.*

Grid Ref: SN5940 8220

Refs: Emanuel Bowen, Map of South Wales, c. 1760; Colby Map, 1831; Meyrick, *Cardiganshire,* 311; *Welsh Gazette,* 20th September 1925; Nicholas, *County Families,* 1875, p. 210; CRO, GGMS, I (Tydwal Gloff); NLW, Crosswood Deeds, p. 305; NLW, Cwrtmawr Deeds, 200; Landowners Return, 1873; PRO List; *Ceredigion,* vol. X, No. 1 (1984), pp. 97-103.

PENNAR (PENNARDD), Aberporth

The former Pennar-uchaf was located on the headland of Pencrib-bach, west of Aberporth, now occupied by the former RAE. Marked on *Colby's Map of 1831,* Pennarnewydd is situated a short distance away, near Parcllyn.

One of the many sons of Thomas Parry of Noyadd Trefawr was Ievan Thomas Parry of Pennardd in Aberporth. Ievan married a daughter and co-heiress of John William Philipps of Gelligati and had a five sons: Thomas the eldest, Rees, who had two natural sons, Ieuan and John; John who died without issue. David who had two sons, and Stephen Parry, who had a son David Stephen and a grandson, John David Stephen. Thomas Parry, the heir, married Maud, the daughter of David Ieuan Thomas Fain of Llanarth. They had two sons and two daughters. Ieuan Parry, the eldest, married the daughter and heiress of David Thomas of Treferedd, and David Parry who married Gwenllian and had two sons, Evan, a seaman, and Thomas. Jane Parry married Thomas John, a servant of David Parry of Noyadd Trefawr, Esq., in 1698, and Elizabeth Parry married James Rees of Trewern.

Francis Jones visited Aberporth churchyard in May 1978 and noted the following inscriptions:

1. Walter David Jones, MD, Member Royal College of Physicians. JP for the counties of Pembrokeshire and Cardiganshire. Deputy Lieutenant of Pembrokeshire. Born at Pennar, Aberporth on 28th June 1792. Died at Lancych 17th July 1869.

2. Anne, youngest daughter of Walter Jones of Llanio, Esq. and Letitia his wife, died at Pennar in this parish 11th April 1825, 67, to the inexpressible grief of her only son. She married first Rev. John Jones, BA, of Pennar, by whom she had one son: 2nd Howell Howell, Esq., of Penalltcych, Pembrokeshire, who died without issue.

3. Rev. John Jones, BA, of Pennar, Rector of Llanfairorllwyn and Perpetual Curate of Mount, erected by his widow in 1795. He died 28th February 1793, 46. Here also lies Cecilia daughter of George Price, Esq., of Pigeonsford, widow of Rev. David Jones rector of this parish, who lies interred in this church, and mother of

the above Rev. John Jones. She died on 22nd March 1788, aged 78. Also Elinor Mathias, daughter of Rev. David Jones and Cecilia his wife who died 19th July 1782.

Dr. Walter David Jones (1792-1869), was the grandson of Walter Jones of Llanio, Cardiganshire. His mother, Anne (1758-1825), married the Rev. John Jones (1757-1793), son of the Rev. David Jones, Rector of Aberporth, who was living at Pennar in 1760.

When Walter D. Jones inherited the property he modernized it and when he then inherited the Lancych estate in north Pembrokeshire he divided his time between the two properties. During the Rebecca riots, Dr. Jones incurred the wrath of the locals for his forthright views regarding the punishment of offenders. As a result some local men gathered at Pennar one night and putting pieces of an old iron pot in a gun as ammunition, shot at Dr. Jones through a window. The pieces of iron peppered the wooden panelling behind him in the drawing room and Mrs. Jones, 'an English woman unaccustomed to these riots' was in the room at the time. Thereafter he spent more time at Lancych where he died in 1869, leaving the estate of Lancych to his wife, Ann, for her life.

Grid Ref: SN 2450 5225

Refs: Colby Map, 1831; Modern OS maps; CRO, GGMS (Gwyddus), fo. 16; Lewis, *TDW;* Meyrick, *Cardiganshire;* WWHR, ii, 81. Francis Jones *Historic Pembrokeshire Houses and their Families,* 1996 (Brawdy Books).

PENRALLT, Aberporth

Located in woodland south of Aberporth off the B4333 between Blaenanwerch and the coast. Lewis in his *Travels* wrote 'The other seats are those of Penrallt, erected in 1813, a mansion in the Elizabethan style . . .'.

Griffith ap Jenkin of Panterlys, who traced to Elystan Glodrudd, settled at Dyffryn, Aberporth and purchased Penrallt in 1649. Jenkin ap David, lived at Dyffryn in 1675. His son Griffith was also of Dyffryn. In 1738 Griffith's son Jonathan married Elizabeth, daughter of John Lewis of Tredefaid. Jonathan died in 1781. His son, Griffith Jenkins married Mary of Bachendre, Pembrokeshire, the daughter of John Morris. It was their third son, Commander Thomas Jenkins, HEICS, who built the present house of Penrallt in 1814.

In 1806, Commander Jenkins married Jane, daughter of Thomas Morris of Bachendre and Trefigin. They had five sons, four of whom served in the armed forces; Major Thomas Jenkins of Trefigin, Captain Griffith Jenkins CB of the Indian Navy, Major-General John James Jenkins of the Indian Army and Lieutenant Alexander Jenkins of Penrallt of the Madras Staff Corps who lived at Penrallt in 1872 and married Mary, daughter of General Pinson of the Madras Army. They had five sons and a daughter. The youngest brother, James Jenkins became a vicar. The property is now an hotel.

Grid Ref: SN 2520 5038

Refs: Lewis, *TDW;* Colby Map, 1831; Nicholas, *County Families,* i, 197.

PENRALLT, Llangoedmor

Penrallt-uchaf is marked on *Kitchin's Map of 1754* and on *Colby's Map of 1831* east of Neuadd Wilym on the banks of the Arberth north of Llechryd. There is a Penrallt-isaf nearby.

John Powell of Penyrallt was High Sheriff in 1568. He was involved in the maintenance of a suit at law recorded in the *Col. Star Chamber Proc.* during the reign of Elizabeth. 'John Lewis of Llangranog versus John Birt, High Sheriff, John Powell, Lewis David and others, re. maintenance of a suit at law, perjury and sub-ornation, concerning the sale of a capital messuage called Plâs Pen Yr Allt alias Llety y Fidelon Wyre, messuages called Tyddyn Llechryd, Penyfelin Fach, Tir Fagwr ym mhen y Pant Llechryd, Tir Nant y Crefand, Tyddyn y Cei and Tir y Fron Goch in Llangoedmore and Llechryd and a water mill called Y Felin Fawr'.

The will of Christiana Jones of Pen-yr-allt, proved by her mother, Angharad Thomas, wife of Jones of Penrallt in 1699, bequeathed certain sums to relatives including £5 to her nephew, David Jones, the son of her brother, when he became of age. His brother, Thomas, who married Gwen Thomas, was High Sheriff in 1740 and later owned Llanio. His son, Walter, married Lettice Jones of Nantremenyn in 1746. Another son, David, who is said to have squandered his inheritance, was High Sheriff in

1724 and again in 1728. He died in 1763 and was buried at Llangoedmor. David was succeeded by his son John, who leased 'Penrallt, Tyddyn-y-wern, Cawrence-isaf alias Ffynnony gwyddil, and a hayfield called Parc Llyddan, all in Llangoedmor, and Nantcroy, Heol-y-cwm and Llainpant-y-gwyddau in Ferwig parish, to Rice Gwynn of Cardigan'.

Grid Ref: SN 2210 4510

Refs: Kitchin's Map, 1754; Colby Map, 1831; Meyrick, *Cardiganshire,* 121; WWHR, ii, 78; CRO, GGMS (Gwyddno); Edwards, *Col. Star Chambers Proc.,* 1929, p. 40.

PENRALLT FOCHNO, Llanfair-orllwyn

The house stands high on a slope, south of Penrhiw-llan on a plateau above a steep drop to the stream below which flows into the Teifi. Nearby in a small wooded dingle, is a very long stone trough having been hewn out of a rocky outcrop, where cattle were watered in former days. The house is nearly a mile from the road and is approached by a long drive with fine timber over rocky ground with a steep drop on one side. Marked as Penralltmachnog on *Colby's Map of 1831* it is a quarter of a mile east of Llanfair Orllwyn church.

Howel Fychan of Gilfachwen-Uchaf, married a daughter of Jenkin ap Rhydderch ap David Parc ap Ieuan Llwyd, who traced to Glyn Aeron. They had two sons, Rhys of Penrallt Fochno and David ap Howel Fychan, who married Nest, daughter and heiress of David ab Evan Llwyd of Gelli in Llanllwni, Carmarthenshire. They had two sons, David Lloyd of Gilfach-wen and Griffith Lloyd of Gelli Radlon in Llanllwni.

Rhys of Penrallt Fochno had a son and heir John, and a daughter Gwenllian, who married David Lloyd of Noyadd Trefawr, Llandygwydd from whom descend the Parry family. John Lloyd, son of Rhys, had a son Thomas Lloyd of Penrallt Fochno who married Elizabeth, daughter of David ap Thomas ap John of Cwmgwili. Their son, Rhys Lloyd, succeeded to the property and married Maud, daughter of David Lewis Morgan David of Cil-y-cwm, descended from Meurig Goch. Margaret, their daughter and heiress, married George Lewes of Nant-ddu in Llangrannog, son of Rhys Lewis ap Lewes David Meredydd of Abernantbychan. Of the nine children of the marriage, Rhys Lewes succeeded to Nant-ddu and married Miss Lewes of Coedmor, Elen married John Lewis of Emlyn Uwch-Cuch from Abernantbychan. By 1760 Thomas Lewes Esq., of Llwynewydd, Carmarthenshire, owned Penrallt Fachno. Nothing is known of the other children, David, James, Harri, Elizabeth, Bridget and Jane.

In 1978 Miss Frances Evans of Ty'ndomen, Tregaron wrote to Francis Jones, 'My great-grandmother (daughter of Penbeili) married the son of Penrallt Fochno. He was a tenant farmer and I was under the impression that his family had resided at Penrallt for many centuries, and indeed it is farmed at the moment by my cousin. There is a story that one of the family carried away the silver chalice from Llanfair Orllwyn and took it for safe custody to Penrallt when Cromwell's troops were in west Wales, and I believe it is still in use in Llanfair'.

Francis Jones visited Penrallt Fochno with Miss Evans in October 1978. 'The farm, some 400 acres, is owned by Mr. Ponsonby Lewes and let to Miss Evans' cousin who farms the land, the house being now empty. The house, which is comparatively modern, is in excellent condition. There is an impressive row of outbuildings. One of these, built at right angles down to the slope is of ancient construction as shown by three crucks and other roof timbers.'

Grid Ref: SN 3750 4080

Refs: Colby Map, 1831; NLW, Pen. 156; WWHR, i, 14, 35; PRO, Dale Castle MS., 20 (81 and 25 (100); NLW, 12356 E, 397; WWHR, iii, 83; Letter 18 March 1978 to Francis Jones from Miss Frances Evans, Ty'ndomen, Tregaron; CRO, GGMS I (Elystan), p. 34; *Dwnn,* i, 97;

PENRALLTYBIE (PENALLTGIBIE), Llandygwydd

A farm to the east of Blaen-pant, located near extensive woodland west of the B4590 between Pont Hirwern and Capel Tygwydd. Marked on *Colby's Map of 1831* as Pen-allt-y-bie. In Llandygwydd church is a monument to James Lewis, gent., of Penralltgybie 'descended from Owen ap Bradwen, Prince of North Wales, and for many years Coroner for the part of the county below Eiron [Aeron]', who died on 18th

March 1716, aged 65. The *Bronwydd Deeds* record on 31 May 1701 an assignment of messuages and lands called Blaen Braen and Tyr Pant y Bara, Tyr Abergavenny in Llangeler, Carmarthenshire and Tyr Aberdoyddwr in Llangynllo. The parties to the agreement were James Lewis of Penralltgybie, gent. and Thomas Lewis, his son and heir. In July of the same year letters of administration of Grace Lewis, late wife of James Lewis of Llandygwydd (died 1700), were granted to her natural son, Thomas Lewis.

By 1732 Penralltybie was owned by Brigstocke of Blaen-pant. The *Bronwydd Deeds* tell us that in 1855, Lewis Lloyd, farmer, was a tenant there.

Grid Ref: SN 2646 4425

Refs: Colby Map, 1831; NLW, Bronwydd Deeds, No, 2321-2; Carmarthenshire RO; Brigstocke Deeds Acc. 5991; CRO, GGMS, I (Tydwal Gloff).

PENRHIWGALED, Llanina

Marked on *Colby's Map of 1831* and on modern OS maps south-east of Llanarth off the A486 to New Quay a mile north-west of Synod Inn and above Cwm Penrhiwgaled, through which runs a stream that enters the sea at Llanina.

Evan Evans, gent., of Penrhiwgaled married Mary Davies, the second daughter of Thomas Davies and Elizabeth of Camnant, Llandysul. The marriage was subject to a pre-nuptial settlement agreed on 26 April 1774. They were married at Llandysul church and were subsequently buried there. Their eldest son and heir, David Evans, Esq., succeeded to the property. He married Jane Rowlands at St. Mary's Church, Cardigan after a pre-nuptial settlement had been agreed on 2 June 1808. David's will was dated 8 May 1834. He died on 16 June 1847 and his will was proved a month later. Both he and his wife Jane were buried at Llanina church. They had two sons and three daughters. The elder son, Evan Davies Evans later became the vicar of Mathry, Pembrokeshire. The younger son was Thomas Evans. Their daughters were Mary, who married the Rev. William Hughes of Ciliau Aeron, clerk, on 5 April 1839, Jane, a spinster and Elizabeth who died whilst a minor and was buried at Llanina.

The Rev. Evan Davies Evans married Mary Evans of Aberaeron at Henfynyw church on 31 August 1836. Although he was the vicar of Mathry he owned the Penrhiwgaled estate. He died in 1865 and his will was proved in the same year. He, too, was buried at Llanina. David Rowland Evans, the only son, succeeded to the property. His sister, Anna Jane, described as 'of Aberayron' celebrated her twenty-first birthday on 8 January 1869. David was married twice: firstly to Anne Rees of Llandysul, at St. David's Church, Merthyr Tydfil on 13 July 1861. Their marriage was short-lived for Anne died on 15 May 1865 and was buried at Llandysul. David remarried, almost exactly a year later. His bride was Matilda Reynolds of the Salutation Hotel, Haverfordwest and they were married at Prendergast on 3 May 1866. Theirs was also a short marriage for David died at New Quay on 19 April 1870. His will was dated 31 March 1870 and was proved at Carmarthen on 4 November. His widow was living at Picton Place, Haverfordwest, in 1904. She died in 1911. Edward Walter David Evans, later of Aberaeron, was the only son of the second marriage.

Grid Ref: SN 3995 5675

Refs: Colby Map, 1831.

PENRHIWPISTYLL, Llanllwchaearn

Lying on high ground above New Quay and marked on *Colby's Map of 1831* and on modern OS maps. Among early owners was Jenkin who had a daughter who married David ap Jenkyn ap Eynon ap Meredydd. Their son, Jenkin Beynon, married a daughter of Thomas Rees of Glyn Aeron. Also David Jenkin of Penrhiwpistyll married Ddyddgu, the daughter of Philip ap Meredith by a daughter of David Reed of Ffoshelyg. By 1760 Phillip David was the owner-occupier.

Grid Ref: SN 3921 5922

Refs: Colby Map, 1831; C/A Protheroe, C., VI; WWHR, iii, 85.

PENTRE(F) DU, Llandyfriog

Location unknown. The earliest known occupier is Rhydderch whose son Thomas had a son Rhys Thomas who married a daughter of James ap Rhys ap Morgan of Aberarthen by a daughter of Lewis David Meredydd of Abernantbychan. His daughter, Joan, married Rhys ap John of Llwyncadfor. Their descendant, David Rees married Angharad, daughter of Morgan Thomas Prydderch of Blaen-nant in Llandyfriog. They had a son, Richard David, later the vicar of Cenarth, and a daughter who married Evan Griffith (1655-1734), of Twrgwyn, Troed-yr-aur, author of *Halsingod* (popular religious songs). Richard David had a son, Methusalem David, of Llwyncadfor.

Refs: PRO, Dale Castle MS., p. 29 (110); WWHR, i. 47-8 (sn Llwyn Cadifor); CRO, GGMS, I (Elystan), fo. 33; ibid, GGMS (Gwynfardd), p. 15.

PENUWCH, Llanfihangel-y- Creuddyn

Francis Jones tell us that Penuwch is an area of high ground to the north-west of Llangeitho on the border with Nantcwnlle parish. The Parry family of Penuwch were descended from the Fychan family of Trawsgoed through the marriage of Jane, daughter of Richard Morris Fychan, with Harry Morris Goch in the 16th century. Their son, David ap Harry of Glennydd, who died in 1643, married Mary Morris. Their eight children included Morgan David Parry (c. 1650-1741) of Ty'nberllan, Llanilar, who married Margaret, daughter of James Parry of Penuwch and Ursula his wife, in 1674. Margaret's elder brother, Henry Parry (1665-1725) married Magdalen Lewis and they had seven children including Lewis Parry, who married his cousin, Elizabeth, daughter of David Morgan David Parry of Ty'nberllan. Their daughter, Dorothy, born in 1724 was regarded as a great beauty and her sister, Magdalen married Edward Griffiths, vicar of Llanfihangel-y-Creuddyn in 1757. The only son, James Parry (1726-99), was a lawyer. He married Jane Pugh (1747-1803), and their son, Lewis, married Sarah, the daughter of John Hopkin, agent of the Trawsgoed estate for 33 years. Lewis and Sarah had eight children. James Parry, a lawyer, died unmarried in 1802, and three other sons, George, Morris and John, entered the church. Lewis Parry then sold Penuwch. Morris Parry, vicar of Pennant, married a daughter of Capt. Abraham Peters. They also had eight children. The arms of the Parry family may be seen on a tombstone in Llanilar churchyard: *Argent* a lion rampant *sable*, claws and tip of his tail *gules*.

Grid Ref: SN 6538 7753

Refs: Colby Map, 1831; Meyrick, *Cardiganshire* (1808), 34; Jill Barber.

PENWERN HÎR, Ystrad Fflur

Marked on *Colby's Map of 1831* about one and a half miles north-west of Ystrad Fflur on the banks of Nant Lluest between Ffair-rhos and Pen-y-wern, Pontrhydfendigaid. John David of Penwern hîr by Strata Florida had a son David Jones of Betws who married Elizabeth, descended from David Lloyd of Llangybi and daughter and heiress of the Rev. Griffith David, clerk, by a daughter of Jenkin William Bowen of Pencarreg.

Grid Ref: SN 7489 6725

Refs: Colby Map, 1831; CRO, GGMS, III (Gwaethfoed), p. 36.

PENYBEILI, Llangynllo

Situated on the brow of a hill overlooking the Cwerchyr valley east of the B4334 between Penrhiw-pal and Aber-banc. The beili refers to an iron-age hill fort nearby. Francis Jones visited Penbeili in 1983. 'The old home is now ruined, roofs fallen in, parts of walls fallen, doors gone, windows gone, but some bits of glass still there; an old garden and orchard alongside. Parts of the Jacobean staircase are still there. There are two storeys and an attic storey. It is on a slope on the edge of a steep ravine. Behind the house is a spring and spout which runs down into the ravine. It was lived in during the second half of the 19th century.'

There is much disagreement regarding this pedigree. The first occupier of Penbeili was Morgan Howell, a man of some means, who according to tradition, tried to disrupt the puritan, Walter Craddock, when he was preaching in a field used by the locals as a playground. Morgan suffered an injury to his knee, became incapacitated and was converted to the puritan cause. He later ministered at

Cilgwyn, Caeronnen and Crug-y-maen. Howel Morgan Howell of Penbeili married Gwenllian, daughter of John ap Philip Lloyd of Dol-wyff, Llanwenog, and Maud, daughter of Gwion Lloyd of Llanfechan, son of Llewelyn Lloyd of Castell Hywel. Howell's will was proved at Carmarthen on 20 April 1646. He was succeeded at Penbeili by John Howell Morgan who married Elinor, daughter of John Lloyd, latterly of Llanllyr by Elinor, daughter of James Lewes of Abernantbychan, High Sheriff of Cardiganshire in 1589. His will was proved on 25 February 1667-8. Thomas Howell succeeded his father. He married Cecil, daughter of John Lewis of Gilfachwith. His brother, Oliver, married a widow, Mary Lloyd of Gwernmacwydd, daughter of Col. John Jones of Nanteos.

Thomas was followed by Morgan Howell, whose brother Walter, went into military service, and another brother, Francis, a doctor. Morgan Howell served the office of High Sheriff in 1704 and was appointed a JP in 1706. He married Lettice, the daughter and co-heiress of Nicholas Lewes of Pantyrodin by Gwenllian, daughter of Thomas Parry of Noyadd Trefawr. They had a son, John, and their eldest daughter, Mary, married David Jenkins of Panterlys in Llandygwydd. John Howell was twice married, firstly to Catherine, daughter of Captain John Lloyd of Gwernmacwydd, son of John Lloyd, and heiress of her uncle, Llewelyn Lloyd of Dolgrogws. John's second marriage was to Jane, daughter of John Lloyd of Cilgwyn. The *Cilgwyn Documents* tell us that a pre-nuptial settlement was agreed on 28 May, 1725 between 'Jane Lloyd (sister of John Lloyd of Cilgwyn and Thomas Lloyd of Coedmor) and John Howells of Penybayly, gent., Cardiganshire. The following messuages and lands were to be settled – Pen y Bayley Coch, Dole Make Llwyd, Pant Iago, Rhiw Voidw Blane Llan, Parke gwern Philley, in Llangunllo parish; Blane Llwarch, Brin Gwinn and Llether y Bystach, in Llangunllo and Llanver Orllwyn parishes; Gilvach Whieth, Ty Gwyn, Dole Wen and Gwern Rygan, in Llanver Orllwyn; Kellye Bychan and Cwrrws vawr in Llandisilio and Llandevriog'.

By his first marriage John Howells and

Major Francis Jones viewing Penybeili

Catherine had a daughter, Hesther who married John Parry of Gernos and Cwm Cynon, in 1739. He married secondly a daughter of Watkin of Gwndwn, Llangrannog. Hesther and John Parry had two sons and two daughters – Thomas Parry, eldest son who died an infant, Llewelyn, of Gernos, High Sheriff of Cardiganshire in 1773, Margaretta Eleanor, who married John Morgan of Cilpill, Nantcwnlle, and Catherine who died in infancy.

From his second marriage, John Howell and Jane had two sons and two daughters. Thomas Howells, born in 1728, educated at Merton, Oxford, was Rector of Llangynllo between 1763 and 1795. John Howell (1732-1801), educated at Jesus College, Oxford, succeeded his brother at Llangynllo until his death in 1801. Jane Howell married John Jones of Nantypele, New Quay in 1760 and Lettice married John Savage, officer of excise in Llandybie in 1754. When John Howell died in 1801, he devised the Penbeili estate to his niece, Grace, daughter of John and his sister, Jane Jones. Grace married John Davies of Llwyngorras, Nevern. Their son, John Howell Davies married Frances Thomas of Nantgarran. John sold part of the estate to Sir Thomas Lloyd of Bronwydd in 1849. He died two years later. In 1852 his widow Frances, sold the remainder of Penbeili to Thomas Lloyd. Thomas Howell Davies, son of John and Frances was rector of Llangynnllo from 1834-1870. As part of the Bronwydd estate, Penbeili was let to tenants until sold early in the 20th century. In 1978 when Francis Jones visited the farm with Mr. Thomas Lloyd he was well received by Mr. and Mrs. Jones, the owner-occupiers.

Grid Ref: SN 3635 4370

Refs: Colby Map, 1831; Meyrick, *Cardiganshire,* 201; NLW, Morgan Richardson Deeds, i, 210; ibid, Griffith Owen Collection; ibid, Bronwydd Deeds, 2796; BRA, Nos. 71 & 271; Ex. info Emrys Williams; ibid, 14th October 1978; ibid, 8718D, p. & 8723E; ibid, Cilgwyn Documents, Nos. 219-220; ibid, PRO List; ibid, Roy Evans Deeds, No. 5; WWHR, i, 7, 28; CRO, GGMS I (Tydwal Gloff), p. 25; ibid (Gwynfardd) p. 16.

PEN-Y-BONT, Tregaron

Now a farm of 250 acres on the edge of Cors Caron on the banks of the Teifi off the A485, towards Ty'rcelyn and marked on *Colby's Map of 1831* and modern OS maps. Nearby is Pont Einon, although the *Cambrian Register* stated in 1796 'that there were no mansions of note in this parish'.

The Rev. D. C. Rees tells us that Pen-y-bont was 'one of the largest farms in the neighbourhood'. Before 1650 Pen-y-bont was called Camer Uchaf; with Camer-isaf one hundred yards below it on the banks of the Teifi. Pen-y-bont was built early in the 17th century by the grandfather of Thomas Johnes of Hafod. The house was never the residence of the head of a gentry family, but of younger sons and estate agents. H. Lloyd-Johnes tells us that 'the present house, still in good condition, was built in the first half of the seventeenth century, probably on the site of an earlier building'. The house is of three storeys and contains sixteen rooms. On the ground floor are two large square rooms flanking a narrow entrance hall and a very large kitchen. On the first floor are a number of large bedrooms with good attics of the same size above. There is a broad staircase and a big cellar.

The Rev. Rees mentions a tradition in the area that one Einion, a Crusader, lived at Pen-y-bont. Edward Herbert lived there between 1654 and 1682. He was from a younger branch of the Herberts of Hafod. Edward Herbert died in February 1682 and John Herbert died there in 1695, aged 58. John's tombstone, carved entirely in Latin, may be seen in the churchyard at Tregaron.

In 1704, William Herbert of Hafod Uchdryd, died at the age of 47. His only child and heiress, Jane, was married to Thomas John of Llanfair Clydogau, and it was he who inherited Hafod following her death. When Thomas died in 1734, his estates passed to his cousin, Thomas Johnes of Pen-y-bont. He and his family moved to Llanfair Clydogau and Pen-y-bont was left to Jeremiah Lloyd of Mabws. Jeremiah married Alice Lloyd, daughter of Walter Lloyd MP of Foelallt, the sister of Sir Herbert Lloyd of Peterwell, and lived at Pen-y-bont from 1733-1750. He was agent to both the Peterwell and Llanfair Clydogau estates and Steward of the Manor of Lampeter. He later moved to Carmarthen and in 1763 was appointed Chamberlain and Chancellor of Carmarthen Circuit, a post he held till his death in 1781.

The next family at Pen-y-bont was that of John Jones, agent for the Llanfair and Hafod estates from 1766 to 1790 who was held to be a fine farmer He was alleged to have fleeced his employers and was dismissed in 1790. He died in 1819. His daughter married Mr. Davies of Glyn and their grandson was Peter Williams of Brenig View, Tregaron who died in 1926, aged 90.

Grid Ref: SN 6699 6110

Refs: Colby Map, 1831; Cwmm, Oct. 91, vol. 21, p. 272, illus.; Cambrian Register, 1796; H. Lloyd Jones, 'The Lesser County Houses of Cardiganshire', *Ceredigion,* vol. II, 1953, pp. 170-3; The Rev. D. C. Rees, Tregaron: *Historical and Antiquarian,* Llandysul, 1936, p. 54; PRO List.

PEN (Y) LAN, Llandygwydd

Located a mile east of Llechryd off the A484 overlooking the Teifi. Lewis in *TDW* in 1840 writes 'Penlan commands a rich and extensive prospect over the grounds on the opposite side of the river'. The first recorded occupier of Penlan were the Makeigs who had fled from Dumfries in Scotland in the 17th century at the time of the troubles and was a mercer. Prior to their time at Penlan, the family had lived at Little Scotland, Llandygwydd. Thomas Makeig who died there in 1766 aged 45, was a yeoman and mercer.

An Elegy to him, written by Ioan Siencyn, mentions his six children, Thomas, John, Jane, Margaret, Nell and Sara. He lived at Penylan where he held, as at Little Scotland, Parctwod and Pantyspyddaden, a lease granted for three lives by John Symmonds of Llanstinan. He bequeathed legacies totalling £650 including leases of Cardigan Island and a farm, Panterlys, adjacent to Penlau. Thomas and his wife, Margaret, had seven children, five girls and two boys. Mary married Josiah Evans and Jane married David Jones who rented Noyadd Trefawr for a time from the Parrys and who had made a fortune privateering during the Napoleonic Wars. Jane died at Parc-y-gors and David at Plâs Berllan, Maenordeifi. Margaret, the third daughter, married the Rev. William Jones, who for fifty years was the vicar of St. Dogmaels.

Later a branch of the family lived at Parc-y-pratt and when John Symmonds of Llanstinan faced financial difficulties, Penlan and the estate were sold. Meyrick notes, 'The present house was erected by Mr. Green, brother-in-law to Colonel Brigstocke of Blaen-pant, who bought this estate, which before had only a common farmhouse on it. It is now the property of Morgan Jones, Esq.'.

Morgan Jones was the only son of the Rev. John Jones, rector of Llanfyrnach, who bought the Penlan estate. The Jones's were a family of considerable wealth. This derived mainly from the Rev. Sutton Morgan, younger son of Jacob Morgan of Pen-gwern, Cenarth, rector of Cilgerran in 1730 and later a curate at St. Margaret's, Westminster. His wife, Ruth, was the sole heiress of her father, William Trench, who in 1713 had leased the Skerries, a rocky outlet off the north-west coast of Anglesey and built a lighthouse. Vessels passing within sight of the lighthouse paid one penny per ton weight of the ship to the lighthouse owner. In the 1830's the Government was anxious to buy out the interest of the Jones family which had passed to them following the death of French Morgan, only son of Ruth and Sutton. The settlement of 1841 amounted to £445,000 based on 22 years of the £20,000 income of 1820. With the death of his brother, Morgan in 1840, the Rev. John Jones became a very wealthy man, who owned estates and residences at Cilwendeg, Llwyn-bedw and Penylan. His son, Morgan, who married Helen Stewart of London as his first wife, and Sarah Goring Thomas as his second, spent a small fortune rebuilding Penlan to Edward Heycock's design in 1854. H. M. Vaughan recalls, 'I can remember Morgan Jones who when Master [of the Tivyside Hounds] built the mansion of Penlan near Llechryd, and close to his entrance gate erected the large kennels which served the Hunt for over fifty years'. Morgan was a frequent sufferer from gout, with his feet and hands swathed in bandages. He also owned the Llanmilo estate near Pendine and in 1873 was recorded as the owner of over 11,000 acres. Morgan's life was not without its excitement. The *NLW Morgan Richardson Papers* include correspondence from

1864-6, regarding a young widow, Mrs. Margaret McCord, with whom Morgan had formed an 'unfortunate connection' and he tried 'to buy her off'. The family retained the Llanmilo estate until 1941.

During the early years of the 20th century, Penlan was the home of Captain William Louis St. Julian Prioleau whose only daughter, Joyce, married George Stewart Berrington Davies of the Castle Green family in 1917.

Penlan was owned, after the Second World War by Major St. John Plevins and his wife, Tots, who are fondly remembered for their eccentric parties. In the 1970's Penlan became the home of His Honour Judge Gwyn Morris, QC (died 1982), and his wife, Lady Audrey, sister of the 21st Earl of Shrewsbury. Francis Jones visited Penlan at that time and was charmed by both the house and gardens. It was sold for £100,000 in 1979 and is now an independent day school.

Grid Ref: SN 2366 4380

Refs: Colby Map, 1831; Meyrick *Cardiganshire,* 1810 (edn. 1907), pp. 186, 355; *Blodan Dyfed,* p. 285; Carlisle, *TDW,* 1811; Lewis, *TDW,* 1840; Charles Smith Allen, *Photographs in South Wales,* 1871; C. Allen, *The Tivyside Photograph Souvenir, Pen y Lan;* H. M. Vaughan, *South Wales Squires,* 1926, p. 34;

Ceredigion; W. Davies, *General Views of the Agriculture and Domestic Economy of South Wales,* vol. I (1815), p. 150; Dwnn, *Heraldic Visitations* (1846); Llwyndyrus Deeds 16-17; M. E. Baylis in *Ceredigion.* Ex info P. Heneker.

PENYWENALLT, Llandygwydd

Marked on *Colby's Map of 1831* and on modern OS maps on the banks of the Teifi, between Cenarth and Cwm-cou, the birthplace of the antiquarian and author, Theophilus Evans (1693-1767). His grandfather, Evan Gruffydd Evans, nicknamed 'Captain Tory' was a Royalist who served as a captain in Charles I's army and 'for his King fought and bled' and was imprisoned in Cardigan by Cromwell. He was reputedly a man of great stature and strength. Resting on his hands and knees he once applied his back to the axle-tree of a cart laden with hay and lifted it. He could also throw a leaden plummet of five or six pounds in weight a distance of nearly 100 yards. He was the son of Gruffydd ap Ieuan Jenkins who 'died aged one hundred or more'.

Gruffydd's son, Charles, named after the unfortunate king, was married twice; firstly to a daughter of Gorslwyd, Blaen-porth, Cardiganshire, by whom he had four sons and three daughters, and secondly to Eleanor Beynon of Llangoedmor, widow, by whom he had a son, the great Theophilus.

Theophilus Evans (1693-1767), a cleric historian, was ordained priest in 1718 and served the Church in Breconshire for the rest of his life save from 1722-28 when he held the living of Llandyfriog. William, Pantycelyn, was his curate at Llanwrtyd Abergwesyn, but such was his hostility to Methodism, Theophilus refused to issue a certificate enabling him to take full orders and William resigned. Theophilus is said to have discovered the healing qualities of the springs at Llanwrtyd when he took the waters there in 1732, but he is chiefly remembered for the *Drych y Prif Oesoedd* published in 1716, which is regarded as a classic of Welsh literature. It is an entertaining account of the early history of Wales, full of colourful metaphor and robust in style. He married Alice, daughter of Morgan Bevan of Gelligaled, Glamorgan in 1728, and they had five children. His son-in-law, Hugh Jones was the father of Theophilus Jones, the author of *A History of Brecknockshire*, published in 1805, which is still regarded as the best of the old county histories and he succeeded Theophilus Evans at Llangammarch in 1763. The other children of Charles Evans and his first wife were; Josiah, whose daughter married Richard Pritchett (1709-72), clerk, of Richard's Castle, Worcestershire; Jonathan who went to America, and his brother John left school aged 19 and his father paid Samuel Godwyn of Bristol, a surgeon, £100 to take him as apprentice and £100 more towards expenses. John Evans left his master, eloped twice and went to sea against his father's will. He lived at Stepney, Middlesex and became a Master Mariner in 1724, married and his daughter and heiress, Sarah, whose will was dated 2 September 1793, married John Griffiths. They spent some time in America and lost land and possessions during the American War of Independence before returning to Penywenallt. John's will was dated 21 January and proved on 3 May 1791. His will mentions 'my brother-in-law Benjamin Evans, my sons, John and William, my eldest sister Mrs. Margaret Bazley and her children, Joseph and Margaret Robinson, Mrs. Margaret Bazley's two grandchildren the Misses de Hobes and (intriguingly) my unhappy sister Elizabeth Morgan'. Charles Evans's next son was Samuel, who was a private tutor in London in 1724, and who died unmarried.

Charles Evans' daughters were Sarah, Margaret and Charity. Sarah married Richard Pritchett of Narberth, a surgeon and they had two sons, Delabere (1713-1801), who was a sub-chantor of St. David's for 58 years and Richard, (1709-72) who was the rector of Bishop's Castle and who married his cousin, the

daughter of the aforesaid Josiah Evans. Margaret married Samuel Jones of Glaspant, and Charity married an Evans of Pont Einon.

John Griffiths of Penywenallt, was born in America and came to Penywenallt when he was 13. He became a Surgeon in the Royal Navy. He had seven brothers and two sisters: William, Ebenezer (who died before 1819, having married Harriet Marley), Thomas, Benjamin, Howel, Theophilus and Lewis. The sisters were Elizabeth and Anne.

John Griffiths was on half-pay in 1818 shortly before his death. His will was dated 2 October 1818 and was proved on 7 October 1819 by his mother. Penywenallt was sold c. 1840 to the Lloyd-Williams family of Glanyrafon and Trewern and let to tenants.

Penywenallt was the home of R. L. Jones (1888-1960), born at Ruel, Llandre, who was a noted farmer and land officer, breeder of pedigree dairy Shorthorns, President of the Shorthorn Society and a keen supporter of Young Farmers' clubs.

The house was damaged by fire in 1984 and demolished a year later.

Grid Ref: SN 2820 4160

Refs: Colby Map, 1831; Meyrick, *Cardiganshire,* 1810 (edn. 1907, p. 185); PRO, Dale Castle MS., p. 30; CRO, Aberglasney Documents, p. 57, 137-9; CRO, GGMS, II (Cadifor Fawr); Theophilus Jones, *A History of Brecknockshire,* 1805, ii, 246-8; Richard Philips, *Pob un a'i Gwys* 1970, pp., 36-52.

PEN-WERN, Llandygwydd

Marked on *Colby's Map of 1831* as Pen-y-Wern and on modern OS maps as Penwern-fawr on the minor road between Cenarth and Capel Tygwydd, north of Alltybwla. Philip Rhydderch Iorwerth of Pen-y-wern had a daughter Gwenllian Llwyd who married Rees Llewelyn ap Rhys ddu Sgwiar digri of Noyadd Trefawr in Llandygwydd, who traced to Tydwal Gloff. They had a son, Ieuan, who in turn had a son Rhydderch ap Rees of Pen-y-wern who married twice: firstly to Elen, daughter of David Lloyd Meredydd of Maenordeifi, Pembrokeshire and secondly to Nest, daughter of David Griffith Meredydd Thomas David of Cwm Hawen in Llangrannog. His descendant, Griffith Llwyd, married Gwenllian, the daughter of

Lewis John Vaughan of Pontfaen, Pembrokeshire. They had two sons and one daughter, Richard Llwyd of Maenordeifi married Gwenllian, daughter of Thomas David Wilcock; Sioned, who married Thomas Young of Tredrisi, Pembrokeshire in 1591, and David Lloyd, the younger son.

Other Lloyds of Pen-y-wern were John Lloyd, whose son Daniel Lewis Lloyd, born in 1844, was Bishop of Bangor in 1890. He bore the arms of Castell Hywel and died in 1899.

Pen-y-wern was home to Richard Jones, said to be of the same stock as Jones of Aberceiliog near Lampeter. He married Hesther, daughter of William Hughes, gent., of Hendy, Cilrhedyn, Carmarthenshire. Their son, William Jones, married Rachel, daughter of Thomas Thomas of Rhosychen, Trelech. Their eldest daughter married Methusalem Evans of Llangeler, gent. One of their sons was Rev. Thomas Evans of Nantyderry [now Nantyderi] House, Monmouthshire, rector of Goetre.

Grid Ref: SN 2660 4310

Refs: Colby Map, 1831; CRO, GGMS (Tydwal Gloff), fo. 33; *LD.,* i 162, Bookplate in NLW; *The Cambrian Journal,* 1864, 110.

PERTHCEREINT, Betws Ifan

Shown as Perth Cerynt on *Colby's Map of 1831,* and Beddgeraint on modern OS maps located south-east of Betws Ifan in woodland north of Brongest and near Alderbrook Hall [Gwernan].

Samuel Lewis tells us of Llongborth 'another place in this parish, thought by some to be that celebrated by Llywarch Hen as the field where Geraint ab Erbin, a Prince of Devon, was slain, with a vast number of his followers and who is supposed to have been interred on a farm in this parish, still called Porth Geraint; but others think that the place mentioned in the aged poet's elegy on the fall of Geraint was in Devon or Cornwall'.

G. E. Evans in *Cardiganshire* states 'about a mile and a half from distant [from Gwernant] is the mansion of Bedd Geraint (now let as a farm) which was at one time occupied by a family called Walters, of old descent'. The only representative now is Mrs. Mayhew, Aberglasney. Here was a tumulus which was opened about seventy years ago when a golden ring was found in it. No man's finger in the area was large enough to wear it. Antiquaries said it was 'as old, if not older, than the days of King Arthur'.

In 1734 Abel Griffiths of Pantybetws granted Pen-y-banc and Coedyperthi to a David John Walter of Penbryn parish by way of mortgage for £130. He later acquired the freehold of the properties mortgaged to him, for in 1748 David John Walter and Margaret, his wife, their

son, John David, and Frances, his wife, mortgaged Pen-y-banc and Coedyperthi to Miss Ann Beynon of Llwynderw.

David John Walter had two sons. The name of the elder, who died before 1748 is not known, but the younger brother, John, joined the Army before returning home following the death of his brother. John took the permanent surname of Walter and was owner of Perthceraint, Coedyperthi and Pen-y-banc; he is listed as owner-occupier of the former in 1760. John married well. His wife, Frances, was one of the 24 daughters of the Rev. Rees Griffiths of Pantybetws and his wife, Mary, of Llwyn-y-brain, who was descended from the Vaughans of Gelli Aur. Frances's portion was £100 and she and John Walter had a son, Abel and a daughter, Anne, who died unmarried. Abel became a tanner in Cynwyl Elfed and married there on 1 February 1780. His wife was Bridget, daughter of another tanner, Thomas Phillips of Pembroke. Following their marriage the couple returned to Perthceraint and Abel acquired further freeholds under the will of Angharad Thomas of Troedrhiwfelen, Aberporth. Following the death of Bridget, Abel built a residence on the banks of the Medeni known today as Glan Medeni. He died on 2 April 1841.

Abel and Bridget had five children. Jane and Thomas died in infancy. Frances died unmarried in 1851, aged 65, and Jane, also unmarried died in 1881, aged 89. John, born in 1788, became a lawyer in Newcastle Emlyn and inherited the Aberglasney estate in Carmarthenshire in 1824 from his uncle, Dr. Thomas Phillips, who retired from the East India Company and bought the Aberglasney estate from the Dyer family in 1804 for £10,500. John took the surname Philipps in addition to his own and became known as John Walters-Philipps. He married Anne Bowen of Waunifor with a pre-nuptial settlement dated 1 May 1817. They had four children. Their son, Thomas died in infancy and the three daughters married into the local gentry. With the death of Thomas, the male line of Walters of Perth-ceraint came to an end. Frances and Jane continued to live at Glan Medeni and engaged in good works throughout their lives. Jane, in particular, was an avid letter writer, poet and an enthusiastic supporter of good causes who built 'Capel Jane Walters' or the Watch Tower close to Glan Medeni and she is the only person buried there. She became devoted to Christ following an accident in which she fell off her donkey and during convalescence, 'the Lord spoke to her and changed her life'. The sisters became targets of Rebecca in 1843 when Glan Medeni was attacked but were unharmed. Jane's will, proved in 1881, left everything to her nieces. The annual rental return was £309 and her personal estate amounted to £2,530.

Grid Ref: SN 3140 4638

Refs: Colby Map, 1831; B. Williams (Gwynionydd); *Hanes Casnewydd-Emlyn* 1860, p. 56; Francis Jones, 'Walters of Perthgeraint,' *Ceredigion,* 1969, pp. 168-200; G. E. Evans, *Cardiganshire,* 1903, p. 271; S. Lewis, *TDW,* 1840, sn Penbryn parish.

PETERWELL (FFYNNON BEDR),
Lampeter

'The large old seat of Sir Herbert Lloyd, which is built close to the town exhibits a very striking appearance with its four great towers crowned with domes, in the middle of a well-planted enclosure; but it appears to have been long neglected and is now seldom inhabited. Of the house nothing now stands except some broken crumbling walls; but the avenue leading to it, still attracts the eye of the passing stranger.'

David Evans bought the land and built the first house there in Charles I's reign and founded the estate. He was the son of Ieuan Goch of Dolau Gwyrddon and Mary, daughter of John Lloyd Jenkin of Blaenburoth in Llangennech, Carmarthenshire. The Evans's were originally of Llechwedd Deri, descended from a natural son of Alltyrodin and traced to Cadifor ap Dinawal. According to E. B. Morris, David Evans fought at St. Fagans, Glamorgan, against his neighbours Sir Marmaduke Lloyd and his son Charles Lloyd of Maesyfelin. David had four sons: Thomas who succeeded, John, Rees and Erasmus and two daughters, Eleanor and Sarah. Thomas succeeded his father at Peterwell. In 1645 he was a Royalist; in January of that year he 'mustered the inhabitants of Llanbedr and charged them to be ready to assist the King against Parliament' In June 1645 he went with Colonel Gerard into the counties of Carmarthenshire and Cardiganshire against Pembroke that had declared for Parliament. Like so many men at the time he changed sides and became a Parliamentarian and served as a Captain of a troop of horse under the Committee of Safety. He was described by a contemporary as 'first a covenanter, then an eager advocate for the negative oath, afterwards most impetuous against a single person, especially the family of his Majestie, and endeavoured to incite men to take arms against General Monk. He was impatient without an office and tyrannical in one'.

Tradition has it that Thomas Evans and his son were employed by Cromwell as agents in Wales and in that way amassed much wealth. Thomas married Elizabeth, daughter of Ieuan Gwyn Fuchan of Moelifor and was High Sheriff in 1653. Their son, David Evans was a

Parliamentarian and the captain of a company of infantry under the Committee of Safety. He married Jane, daughter of William Herbert of Hafod Ychtryd. Daniel Evans, son of Thomas Evans married Mary, daughter of Morgan Herbert and had six children: Letitia, Mary, Jane, Elizabeth, Rebecca and Sarah. He was High Sheriff in 1691. Daniel rebuilt his grandfathers' house at Peterwell, using materials from the old mansion of Maesyfelin. He 'dyed in 1696 before twas finished' aged 49. He was the patron of Edwards Lhuys and was the last of the male line.

There is a memorial inscription to Daniel Evans in the chancel at Lampeter church. His widow Mary married secondly John Lloyd of Bwchllaethwen, Llangwynne who came to reside at Peterwell, where several of their children were born. His daughter, Eleanor, married Sir Thomas Stepney (died 1748). His daughter Elizabeth married Walter Lloyd of Foelallt [Voelallt] Llanfairclydogau, probably in 1713, and Walter then settled at Peterwell, which with Llechwedd Deri had already come to Elizabeth as co-heiress. Walter Lloyd was a lawyer and became Attorney General for Carmarthenshire, Cardiganshire and Pembrokeshire. He subscribed to *Laws of Hywel Dda* (Welsh and Latin). He was MP for County Cardiganshire from 1734-41, and was buried at Lampeter on 22nd February 1747; his wife had died in 1743. They had nine children: Mary 1714-20; Daniel and Walter who died young; John, born c. 1718 who succeeded to the estates; Anne 1719-46. She married Sir Lucius Christianus Lloyd, Bart, of Maesyfelin. Herbert born 1720, of whom more later; Elizabeth born 1721 who married John Adam of Whitland; Alice, born

1724 – married Jeremiah Lloyd of Mabws; Lastly Thomas, born 1725, who died young.

John Lloyd succeeded to the estates. He was MP for Cardigan from 1747 until his death in 1755. *The Annual Biography and Obituary for 1817* tells us that 'according to a memorandum furnished by a contemporary, he (Col. Johnes's father) was accustomed to entertain the Right Hon. Richard Rigby, Sir Charles Hanbury Williams and Mr. Fox, afterwards Lord Holland, together with Mr. Lloyd of Peterwell, for weeks together at his hospitable seat of Llanvair in Cardiganshire. They played cards during the evening for large sums and Messrs Fox and Rigby usually proved fortunate: thus the country gentlemen were cut up. However, both Mr. Lloyd and Mr. Johnes afterwards married heiresses and recovered. (Mr. Johnes' wife was a Miss Knight, portion £70,000)'.

John Lloyd married Elizabeth le Hoop [Heup], daughter of Sir Isaac le Hoop, a rich London banker; her dowry was £80,000. She was maid-of-honour to Queen Caroline. George III presented John and Elizabeth with a pair of gold wine-coolers, engraved with Royal arms, as a wedding present. Curiously, John Lloyd 'died of nerves' and was buried at Lampeter on 29 June 1755, without issue. His widow married George Montgomery and they too had no issue.

The last fabric at Peterwell, it is believed, was started by John Lloyd and one of the first things that Herbert did when he succeeded was to continue to rebuild Peterwell on a more spacious scale. The Rev. W. Edmunds tells us in 1860 'the large number of its windows, the flower-garden on the roof, the entrance steps of polished Portland stone, the artificial water on each side of the avenue, used to be frequent themes of evening conversation among the old people here'.

Herbert had succeeded his brother John not only to Peterwell, but also Llechwedd Deri and Foelallt, which last named his father had given him previously and where he resided for some time. He was married twice; firstly in 1742, aged 22 years, to Miss Bragge, of Essex whose portion was reputed to be £15,000. Sadly, she died five days after her infant daughter in Lampeter on 30 March 1743. Herbert married secondly Anne, daughter of William and Avarina Powell of Nanteos, the widow of Richard Stedman of Strata Florida. There is an inscription to her in Strata Florida church. There is, also, a chalice in the parish church of Lampeter, marked 'the gift of Mrs. Lloyd of Peterwell, 1751'.

In 1760 Herbert Lloyd presented an address from Cardigan Borough to King George III, who created him a Baron on 26 January 1763. Herbert was a very tall man, a feared and disliked tyrant, who ruled the area. He subscribed the princely sum of 2 guineas to the rebuilding of Cardigan church. Anne's life with Sir Herbert was inevitably unhappy. so she lived principally at Foelallt in Llanddewibrefi and on her death the Strata Florida estate passed to Powell of Nanteos. His tenure of Peterwell was from the first blighted by debt, power struggles, greed and avariciousness. Throughout his life Herbert Lloyd borrowed, took and stole. He had a violent temper, suffered badly from gout and was always in need of money and took badly to being crossed. One tale of him tells how he wanted to acquire a small farm near Felinsych, Pencarreg. Sir Herbert threatened the owner because he would not sell and demanded the farm. The farmer went to Mr. Vaughan Dolgwn, a man of authority in the district and told him of the threats. Mr. Vaughan then visited Peterwell and saw Sir Herbert. When Sir Herbert came into the drawing room, Vaughan locked the door and asked him what the blazes he meant by taking the farm. He drew a pistol from his pocket which he held to Sir Herbert's temple, saying that if he did not restore the farm he would kill him. Sir Herbert accordingly did as he was asked. This tale was told to G. E. Evans (author of *The House of Peterwell*), by John Davies aged 65 of Cefencoed, Blaencwrt, 21 August 1900, whose father had been a servant with Sir Herbert Vaughan.

According to tradition, Sir Herbert did not wait long before acquiring another smallholding, this one close to Peterwell, lying alongside his demesne and which blighted his view from the mansion. It belonged to Siôn (known as Shon), Philips who refused to sell. Sir Herbert was not to be stopped however, he is said to have ordered his servants to put a black ram down Shon's chimney. Next morning on a pretended search of the district, together with officers of the law, they found the ram in Shon's cottage. Sir Herbert called Shon to the mansion and told him that he would be hanged for sheep stealing unless he came to terms with Sir Herbert, and granted him the coveted field. Shon was arrested, and after a 'grotesquely unequal contest' was found guilty and was hanged in 1780.

Whilst Sir Herbert resided in London he had mortgaged Peterwell to Albany Wallis, a London attorney with a Welsh wife. Sir Herbert spent most of his adult life borrowing money and dodging his debtors. He had alienated all his friends, was involved in cattle rustling, and his erstwhile friends and acquaintance were determined that he should not stand another term at Westminster as MP when he came up for re-election in 1768. He was also plagued by ill health, particularly gout, compounded by the difficulties of travelling in rural Wales and his arduous duties as a magistrate. In 1769 an order was obtained to 'take, lead, drive, carry away and impound stock to settle debts' Unsuccessful in his attempts to be re-elected to parliament despite his machinations, impoverished and pursued by creditors, and no longer protected from them by his status as MP, Sir Herbert, facing ruin, after heavy losses at the gaming tables, committed suicide in London on 17 August 1769 by shooting himself through the temple. Strangely, all the newspapers of the day record a death from natural causes. Elisabeth Inglis-Jones explains this in *Peacocks in Paradise*, 'By dint of a good many lies, and the exchange of a good many guineas, a verdict of accidental death was obtained' He had signed his will on 13 August 1769, and he had reputedly married bigamously the following day a Mrs. Bacon, widow of Durham. A portrait of Sir Herbert and an armorial bookplate belonging to him was published in *Cymru*.

The property passed to his nephew, John Adams of Whitland, MP for Carmarthen Borough 1774-80, son of Sir Herbert's sister Elizabeth. He resided there for some time but ran through what was left of the already half-ruined estate. He attempted to clear encumbrances by selling Peterwell and it was offered to Thomas Johnes (later creator of Hafod). An account of the sale of Furniture at Peterwell, late property of John Adams, dated 24 September 1781 mentions the following rooms: 'Ground floor – Study, closet within the study, the common parlour, middle parlour, passage by the staircase, inner parlour, the hall, the parlours, drawing room, several rooms and passages, laundry, old laundry, the brewing kitchen, the unfinished room below stairs, kitchen, dairy, butler's pantry, cellar (wine), stable. Bedrooms – the green room above the stairs, Mr. Adams' room, closet, room adjoining Mr. Adams', little room above the nursery, nursery, Sir Herbert's room, closet, the garrets, blue and white room, pursage, red and white curtains room, Mr. Jenkins' room, Thomas Davies' room, servant's room, unfinished room, stewards room, servants hall, staircase' But the purchase of the estate was not completed. Thomas had pulled a great part of Peterwell down and its costly fittings were carried away or sold. As the poet of Castell Hywel wrote:

> *'cad main mayna Fesca'r tai*
> *'ll datod I wneud diottai*
> *ac wylo wnewch pan gweloch*
> *Flini 'I mur yn gafnan moch.'*

'Most of the great and the good were at, or were represented at, the sale as well as the "common classes" and among the more intriguing items sold were: 1 gun – £1.16.0. 1 Shot gun – 4.6d, 3 Blunderbuses – 15.0d, Dumb waiter- 9.0d, 1 gilded bedspread and curtain – 5.0.0., 2 old globes – 6.0d, 1 green japanned tea-chest – 6.6d, Old trumpery – 0.0.6d, Several pieces of paper – 0.6.10., 1 small boiler – £1.9.3. – bought by Mr Vaughan of Greengrove. 11½ old teaspoons and tongs and 1 Mahogany bottle-stand bought by the auctioneer – Mr William Cow. 1 coffee pot & stand & 6 gilt teaspoons and tongs – purchased by the Bishop of St. David's. 4 Bottle Stands & 1 Ink stand and glasses – purchased by Lady Mansell. 3 scallopped oyster shells – Mr Spurell. 1 Cross – John Evans. 1 Guggle or strainer – Mr Stewart. 1 Antiguggle – Dr Browne. 1 Pap boat – Mr Spurell and 1 pair of Holland sheets – 0.17.00 – Mr Thomas Williams.'

Albany Wallis, attorney of London, who held the original mortgage bought the Peterwell estate in 1776. Wallis did not reside there and the house decayed. He died in 1800 and left the bulk of his fortune to Lady Bailey of Pall Mall for life, the remainder to her son Colonel John Bailey, who took the name Wallis. Colonel Bailey Wallis served the office of High Sheriff for the county in 1806. He sold the Peterwell estate to Richard Hart-Davis, a partner in Harford Bank, Bristol, who improved the property by encouraging farming and planting. Entries from the *Vestry Book* quoted in George Eyre Evans' book *Lampeter* give interesting insights into Peterwell's history. 'Mr Rees Davies was the agent for the Peterwell estate in 1784 and on 12 April in that year he promised

Herbert Lloyd's bookplate

to pay Peterwell's taxes which amounted to £2.6.6.' In 1795, Evan Thomas, cooper, was to receive 10s. for destroying the crows (young and old if possible) in the rookery on Peterwell Farm, particularly in the Pigeons' home field. Bethan Phillips tells us in *Peterwell* 'The Harfords chose not to renovate it [Peterwell] . . . rather they erected a totally new residence at Falcondale, one mile away. So Peterwell was left to its memories and ghosts'.

On 28 May 1798, the parishioners consented to 'pay £1.10.0. for the carriage of stones from Peterwell, towards rebuilding John James the saddlers' house'. A poem was written by David Davis (1745-1827) entitled *Adfeolion Plas Ffynnon Bedr* (6 englyn) which was published in *The Oxford Book of Welsh Verse*.

Richard Hart-Davis was named as Lord of the Manor in 1812. In 1819 he lost his money and handed Peterwell over to John Scoundrett Harford of Blaise Castle, Bristol and his brother, A. G. Harford-Battersby.

G. E. Evans tells us in his booklet *The House of Peterwell* that 'owing to the Lampeter Parish church having been rebuilt on a slightly altered site to that on which the old church stood, the Peterwell Vault, in which Sir Herbert Lloyd was buried, is now outside the walls and not, as formerly, in the chancel. It has been disturbed more than once since the Baronet's interment. When the old church was taken down, the vault was opened and some bones, it is said, were taken out and carried in a girl's apron, to a hiding place in the town. They were found years afterwards in the loft of a house, the site of which is now occupied by the Castle Hotel. More recently too, the vault was accidentally opened when a grave adjacent to it was being dug. By the aid of a lighted taper let down into it, some of the coffins were distinctly visible. The battered black cloth with which they were originally covered being seen fluttering below the opening'.

In an essay written in Welsh by E. B. Morris the following story is told. 'In the house of the smith of the village [Llanwnen] we had the chance to see a clock that once ticked in the splendour and pride of the parlour of Sir Herbert Lloyd at Ffynnon Bedr. It continues to keep time and is likely to continue to do so for a long period. Carved on its face is "Thomas Taylor, Holbourne, 175(5)". Here is a list of its possessors – Sir Herbert Lloyd, Admiral Thomas of Llanfechan, David Price Thomas of Troedyrhiw and the present owner who bought it for three shillings at the sale of the last-named. Great sums have been offered for it since, but the smith will not part with it in a hurry.'

E. B. Morris comments 'Sir Herbert Lloyd's clock, owned by the smith of Llanwnen was exhibited to the Welsh Historical Society [Cambrensis] on their visit to Lampeter in 1878. It is now [1907] in possession of J. M. Edwards of Dol Wen, Lampeter, where I saw it a few months ago. Its face was cleaned and has Thomas Taylor in Holbourne on it and does not have the date as I described in 1905. Near my home, another old clock was kept and its face, 'tis said, made from the brass plate stolen from the coffin lid of Sir Herbert Lloyd after his obsequies and sold to a clock-maker in Lampeter'.

A photograph of the ruins of Peterwell was published in *Telyn Dewi* with two poems in Welsh: *Mawredd Ffynnon-Bedr* and *Cwymp Ffynnon-Bedr*. A fine avenue of lime trees still grows from the road to the mansion.

When the Peterwell estate was put up for sale by private contract at the Black Lion Inn in the town of Lampeter on 25th August 1807, it was a measure of the vastness of the estate (approximately 9,408 acres) that five days were set aside for the sale.

Refs: Colby Map, 1831; WWHR, i, 41-2; Carlisle, 1811; *Arch. Cam.*, 1860, p. 276; ibid, 1861, pp. 23-28, 156, 162-3, 315; ibid, 1878, p. 343; *Cymru,* 32, 1907, pp. 317-23; *Telyn Dewi* (Rev. David Davis), 1927, pp. 8, 9, 10, 11; Peterwell Sale Catalogue of 1781, lent by H. J. Lloyd Johnes; *Ceredigion,* 1, 1950-1, pp. 196-9; E. Inglis-Jones, 'Derry Ormond' *Ceredigion,* vol. II, No. 3, 1954; Giraldus (J. Rowlands), Ffynnon Bedr in Haul, 1863, pp. 236-7; Meyrick,, *Cardiganshire,* p. 222; Horsfall-Turner, *Wanderings,* pp. 232 & 240; Nicholas, *County Families,* i, 76; *Annual Biography and Obituary for 1817;* Rev. Williams Edmunds, 'Old Families of Lampeter', *Arch. Cam.,* 1860 (written in 1798); Rev. George Eyre Evans, *Lampeter – The House of Peterwell – An Old-Time Story,* 1905, pp. 192-239, & illust. of ruins; Vestry Book, quoted in George Eyre Evans, *Lampeter,* 1905, pp. 14, 102-5; W. Davies, *A General View of the Agriculture and Domestic Economy of South Wales,* 1814, vol. 1, p. 231; E. B. Morris, Essays (in Welsh & translated by Francis Jones), *Cymru,* March 1905, p. 177 & *Cymru,* June 1907, p. 323; J. T. Baker, *Tour,* 1803, p. 125; Phillips, *Tour,* 1805, p. 51; CRO, GGMS, I (Tydal Gloff); p. 28; State Papers; *Oxford Book of Welsh Verse,* ed T. Parry. 1976, p. 323; PRO List; NLW, Peterwell Estate Papers; Bethan Phillips, *Peterwell,* 1983 illust. pp. 21, 39, 40, 41, 118, 157, 208 & 223.

PIGEONSFORD (RHYDYCOLOMENNOD), Llangrannog

A neat mansion, formerly the seat of the family of Parry, a branch of Cwmcynon and Gernos. Marked on *Colby's Map of 1831* as Pigeonsford. A messuage formerly called Rhydyclomennod, Tythinhendraws, Pantycerig, Pantyquarrey, Pantdwfun and Tyrfywnowddy, but now known by the general name Pigeonsford.

David Parry was of Rhydycolomennod, (1577-1601), and George David Parry, his second son, was there in 1612. He was the second son of David Parry of Cwmeynon, in the parish of Llandisiliogogo who is mentioned as paying the subsidy levied by Queen Elizabeth in 1577 and in 1601. He married a daughter of Thomas ap Rhydderch ap William of Llanborth. His son Harry married Gwenllian the daughter and co-heiress of Thomas Morris of Bronhydden. Their son George Parry of Rhydglowen married Cisil, daughter of James Lewes of Cwm Hawen. Their daughter and heiress married James Lewes, descended from Bradwen. A pew of the Pigeonsford family dated 1674 was to be found in Llangrannog church.

When the family ceased to hold the property it became the home of the Price's. The earliest mention of a Price in the *Pigeonsford Deeds* is that of David Price of the parish of Llanarth, described as 'Clerk' in 1658. One of the bells in the church of Llangrannog bears the date 1682 and in the parish register that year is the entry of the baptism of William, son of David Price, Clerk 19 May 1682. His other children were David (b. 1686), John baptised 1689, Mary, Catherine baptised 1683, and Jane baptised 1685. William Price, gent., of Rhydcolomennod, married Bridget, the daughter of George Parry, grandson of George Parry of Cwmcynon. An inventory compiled on 21 September 1753 mentions the following rooms in the house – 'kitchen, dairy, room above the dairy, cellar, parlour, staircase, the white room above the parlour, the middle room, the room above the kitchen, closet, garret, stable, carthouse, barn and haggard, fold, the other fold and the mill'.

In a deed of 1739 William settled the portions of his daughters Mary, Elizabeth, Cisel, Jane and Bridget, and in the same deed he mentions two sons George and David. David the second son was born in 1723. He went to Jesus College Oxford, in 1742, and gained his BA in 1745. He took Holy orders in the church of Ireland. In 1746 Llangrannog was one of the places in Cardiganshire where there was one of the Circulatory and Catechetical Welsh schools. William Price wrote his will in 1751, and it was proved in 1753. He bequeathed to his 'four daughters now living, namely Mary, Cisel, Jane and Bridget the like sum of one shilling a piece,

and distributed the portion of his deceased daughter Elizabeth being £90 equally between Cisel, Jane and Bridget, and £20 to his daughter Jane'.

George Price, the eldest son, who succeeded his father in 1752 was High Sheriff in 1759. George, married Dorothea Bowen, the second daughter of James Bowen of Llwyngwair, Esq., dec. The bride's marriage portion was £500. The marriage was the subject of a pre-nuptial settlement agreed on 19 June 1762. By 1755 George Price was rebuilding the front part of the house and from this date it became known as Pigeonsford, being now thought too grand for the old Welsh name. He was made JP in 1767. His will was dated 8 June 1782; he died in 1786 and his will was proved on 5 October 1786. George and Dorothy had three children, Elizabeth Alicia (1763-1780), Bridgetta Dorothea born 1765, who married the Rev. Simson Lloyd of Bala, and George born 1768. When Elizabeth Alicia died in 1780, she was 'distinguished for her piety and beauty of character' and William Williams of Pantycelyn wrote an elegy on her, and there is a stone to her memory in the wall of the parish church above the Pigeonsford vault. Dorothy Price joined the Methodists and there is a traditional tale that she used to ride in a scarlet cloak to Penmorfa Chapel every Sunday. In her will dated 6 June 1789 she left a legacy of £10 to Twr-gwyn Chapel, and her gold watch to her son, George Price. Dorothea died in 1808.

In 1792 a conveyance from George Price of Pigeonsford, Esq., to George Bowen of Llwyngwair, Esq., was agreed. It included 'the messuage formerly called Rhydyclomennod, Tyrhinhendraws, Pantycerig, Pantyquarrey, Pantdwfun and Tyrfywnowddy, but now called by the general name of Pigeonsford'.

George Price succeeded his father aged 18. His father had left £700 to his daughters, and to his sister Bridget Jones of Trecregyn, an annuity of 40 shillings. In 1790 George Price was made JP, and in 1792 became a burgess of Cardigan and in 1797, Deputy Lieutenant, and in the same year as Captain of the 46th Foot he escorted the French prisoners from Fishguard to Whitehaven. In 1804 he was appointed Major in the Royal Clarence Volunteers, and 1808 Lieutenant-Colonel of the Royal Clarence Local Militia of the lower division of the county of Cardigan. In 1805 he married Elizabeth, daughter and co-heiress of Barrett Bowen Jordan, Esq., of Neeston. Pembrokeshire, and in 1806 his son George Bowen Jordan was born. To commemorate the birth he planted a walnut tree outside the drawing room window.

George Price was Mayor of Cardigan in 1808 and 1812. A reference in *The Church of Penbryn, its Connections and Associations* by D. Pryse Williams gives an account of a wreck on Penbryn Sands in 1816. It speaks of the loss of a French brig loaded with wines. 'A large body of the neighbouring peasantry assembled and (notwithstanding the praiseworthy efforts of Col. Price of Pigeonsford, and other gentlemen, with the assistance of the Custom-house officers), pillaged part of the cargo so immoderately that seven of them died.' Col. Price died in 1829, aged 61 and was succeeded by his only surviving child, George Bowen Jordan Price.

George Bowen Jordan Price of Pigeonsford, born in 1806 was educated at Shrewsbury and Emmanuel College, Cambridge where he took his MA. He was a great sportsman, especially fond of racing and built new stables at Pigeonsford in 1831. He was Mayor of

Cardigan in the same year. He married Ellen, daughter of Sir John Owen of Orielton, Pembrokeshire, in 1832, and was High Sheriff of Cardiganshire, JP and DL of the county. On succeeding to the property of his maternal aunt, Miss Hester Jordan, he took the surname of Jordan. He entered the Royal Pembroke Artillery Militia. His first wife Ellen died in 1856 and he married secondly, Eleanor Powell whose brother, Edward, afterwards succeeded to the Nanteos estate. Captain Jordan died after a short illness in 1881. *The Landowners Return of 1873* gives the estate of G. B. J. Jordan as 1,120 acres at a yearly rental of £568.

By his first wife Ellen, George Jordan had six children; George who died an infant. Another George died at Cheltenham aged 16. Barret Bowen Jordan who pre-deceased his father in 1878 leaving a widow and one son, Richard Price Jordan. Ellen who married Charles Webley Hope, RN. Elizabeth who married Morgan Jones of Penylan, and Angelina who died unmarried.

George Jordan was succeeded by his grandson, Richard, a minor. The house was let to tenants for many years and in 1908 the whole property was sold and the farms bought by the tenants.

The estate comprising lands in the parishes of Llangrannog, Llandisiliogogo, Penbryn and Blaenporth was advertised for sale by Captain Richard Price Jordan.

A picture postcard of Pigeonsford posted on 4 August 1902 to A. Abercrombie at Bombay House and owned by Ivor Llwyd of Carmarthen, showed a house of three storeys, ranges of three windows each, the upper storey has three dormer windows, an entrance on the ground floor alongside with a window beyond it and a window above that.

The catalogue describes the residence as 'a homely looking mansion in first-class condition – a great deal of money having recently been spent in improving and renovating throughout'. The demesne (62 acres) as follows – Ground Floor: the mansion is entered by two easy steps through an open porch having a door with the top panels of stained glass leading to the entrance, drawing room and dining room, with passages to butler's pantry, smoke room, kitchens etc., the main staircase springs from near the centre, rises on double flight, with easy rise and lighted by a handsome double-window, to a spacious landing; the domestic offices include butler's pantry, servants hall, lobby with corridor leading to rose garden, dairy, wash and boiler house, kiln house with apple room overhead, coal house with storehouse out, wine and beer cellars, two W.C.'s, ashpit etc. On the first floor: Seven bed and dressing rooms; leading from the main landing are two bedrooms, and dressing room; above these are three attics; a door shuts off the main landing from a corridor ending at the back stairs from which is reached three bedrooms, and a bedroom or nursery; a winding flight of stairs from the corridor leads to an upper corridor from which we enter five large bedrooms and a closet. In addition there were stables and farm buildings, near which are the ruins of the old kennels'.

The grounds were described thus: 'the residence has a walled garden through which runs the Cranog [sic] river. There is a drive and tennis courts. In front of the mansion is a clean green sward with azaleas, rhododendrons, laburnum, bay and other trees. To the left is the rose garden. The river Hawen runs through the demesne north of the house.'

The house was bought by Charles William Webley Hope (1864-1926), formerly of the Indian Civil Service, who had married Florence Lewes of Llanllyr in 1916. Charles was the son of Admiral Charles Webley Hope and Ellen Jordan of Pigeonsford who were married in 1861. His grandfather was also an Admiral, another Charles, a member of a prominent Scottish family and the first to settle in Wales following his marriage to Anne Webley-Parry of Neuadd Trefawr in 1826. When Charles William Webley Hope died in 1926, Pigeonsford became the country home of David Owen Evans, non-conformist barrister-at-law and industrialist born at Llanborth, Penbryn parish. He was educated at Llandovery College and Imperial College, London. From 1932 until 1945, D. O. Evans was Liberal MP for Cardiganshire and a close confidant of David Lloyd George who paid many visits to Pigeonsford.

It was in 1931 that Ifan (later Sir Ifan) ab Owen Edwards was staying with David Owen and Kate (née Morgan) Evans at Pigeonsford that his attention was drawn to Cefn-cwrt farm overlooking Cardigan Bay. It was on Cefn-cwrt land that Ifan ab Owen Edwards established *Gwersyll yr Urdd Llangrannog* (a youth camp) which has became a centre for thousands of Welsh youngsters, initially in the summer months, under the auspices of *Urdd Gobaith Cymru* (Welsh League of Youth), today the largest youth organisation in Europe.

The house has been extensively restored recently and is now headquarters and research centre of a charity devoted to the intellectual development of children. The walled garden is now a garden centre.

Grid Ref: SN 3258 5402

Refs: Colby Map, 1831; Meyrick, *Cardiganshire,* 1810, edn. 1907, p. 232; WWHR, iii, 84, 109; Evelyn Hope, *Llangranog and the Pigeonsford Family,* 1931, 28, pp. 3, 5, 11, 13, 16, 9-10, p. 19, 20, 21; CRO, GGMS; Burke, *LG,* 1850; CRO, GGMS, I (Tydwal Gloff); NLW, Morgan Richardson Deeds, ii, 398, 402; G. E. Evans, *Cardiganshire,* 1903, p. 78; Lewis, *TDW,* 1840; Landowners Return, 1873; CRO, P. Heneker.

PLÂS-CRUG, Llanbadarn Fawr

Not marked on any of the recognised maps, the remains of Plâs-Crug were demolished in 1967 to make way for a primary school. It stood at the far end of Plâs-Crug Avenue which is entered at Alexandra Road, Aberystwyth, near to the station. Meyrick writes, 'Plâs Crug, stands on a mound, hence its name, near the banks of the Rhyddol, in the centre of a large marsh, called for eminence, Morfa or the Marsh'.

In *Wanderings and Excursions in South Wales,* Thomas Roscoe tells us 'a mile from Aberystwyth, on the banks of the Rheidol, are the remains of an old fortified mansion, which the vulgar call Owen Glyndwr's Palace, but which was supposed to have been erected by the monks of Llanbadarn Fawr, the site of whose monastery was contiguous. It is believed to have been the residence of the early princes of Wales; for it is mentioned by the bard Eineon ap Gwgan, who flourished in 1244 in his ode on Llewelyn the Great:

'His spear flashes in the hand
accustomed to warlike deeds;
'It kills and puts his enemies to flight
by the palace of Rheido'.

It is believed by some that subterranean passages led from this monastery to the fortified mansion also mentioned, Plâs Crug and likewise to Aberystwyth Castle'.

Phillips also knew of this tale; he wrote of Plâs-Crug 'A square embattled tower still remains very perfect and there are other considerable fragments of the ruins of this fortified mansion which must have been very extensive. We were told of a subterraneous communication between this place and Llanbadarn Fawr, but no person could indicate its commencement or its termination'. The fortified medieval mansion was said to have been used by Owain Glyndwr during his seige of Aberystwyth Castle. In the 16th century it was the chief residence in the Manor of Llanbadarn Fawr. In 1588 it was called Crug-y-lliw and in 1667 Thomas Lloyd of Brynele and others granted a lease to Margaret Jones of 'Plâs y Crug', widow. By 1718, 'Plâs y Cryg' in Llanbadarn Fawr had become part of the Nanteos estate.

There is an engraving of Plâs-Crug by Henry Gastineau, c. 1830, and a photograph of the house, c. 1860, now in the NLW has been reproduced in *Arch. Cam.* It is interesting to note the changes that had been made in the structure in the intervening period.

Grid Ref: SN 5898 8108

Refs: Meyrick, *Cardiganshire,* 1810, edn., 1907, pp. 307, 308; NLW, Cwrtmawr Deeds, 125, 203, 1032; Phillips, *Tour,* 1805, p. 58; Dr. Ralph A. Griffiths, 'The Three Castles at Aberystwyth,' *Arch. Cam.,* vol. cxxvi (1977) pp. 74-87 & Pl. vi; *Dwnn,* i, 50; WWHR, i, 25; Blome List, 1673; Nicholas, *County Families,* I, 179; NLW, 12356E, 497; NLW,

Crosswood Deeds, p. 77; CRO, GGMS, I (Tydwal Gloff), fo. 29; Horsfall-Turner, *Wanderings,* 90; PRO, Dale Castle MS., 23 (91), 24 (96), sn Rhiwarthen; Thomas Roscoe, *Wanderings and Excursions in South Wales,* London, 1836, p. 7.

PLÂS-NEWYDD, St. Mary's, Cardigan

Built to replace an earlier residence on former St. Dogmaels Abbey land and situated in a superb position on the crest of a hill overlooking the Teifi estuary south of the river. Plâsnewydd was originally owned by the Lords of Tywyn who ruled over a vast area of Ceredigion from their domain on the north bank of the Teifi at the present-day Gwbert. Late in the 16th century, Margaret, daughter and heiress of Rhydderch ap Rhys Fychan (descended from Gwynfardd Dyfed), married Thomas ap Harry of Noyadd Trefawr and Blaen-pant and brought him Plâs-newydd as part of her dowry. Their son, Stephen Parry, settled at the property and was High Sheriff of Cardiganshire in 1629. His son, David, died heavily in debt in 1642 and was succeeded by his son, Stephen, who died unmarried and Plâs Newydd passed to his sister, Elizabeth, who married her cousin, David Parry, of Noyadd Trefawr, High Sheriff in 1684. Plâs-newydd was assessed at seven hearths in 1670. David Parry died a bachelor in 1711 and is buried at Llandygwydd.

Plâs-newydd was sold to the Lewes family of Penybenglog, on the Nyfer in Meline parish south of Eglwyswrw. Watkin Lewes (1740-1821) educated at Shrewsbury and Cambridge was called to the Court of Chancery in 1766. He married Rebecca, daughter of Thomas Popcyn of Forest, near Swansea and inherited extensive estates in Glamorgan and the parish of Rudbaxton, Pembrokeshire. Having failed on four occasions to become MP for Worcester, Watkin Lewes turned his attention to the City of London. He was appointed Sheriff in 1772 and was an alderman of the Lime Street ward. Lewes was knighted in 1773 and was Lord Mayor of London in 1780 and elected one of the four MP's for the City, a seat he held until 1796. A keen student of the history and literature of his native land, he followed Richard Morris as President of the Cymmrodorion. His latter years were full of difficulties. Having lost his money to fast women and slow horses he was imprisoned at the Coffee House on Ludgate Hill within the walls of the Fleet prison, where he died in July 1821.

The present Plâs-newydd, built by Sir Watkin before 1810, has two storeys and a basement. Fenton noted in 1811, 'on a pleasant eminence stands the new mansion . . . being a later creation of the countryman and old friend Sir Watkin Lewes as a temporary residence whenever he found leisure from City duties to visit his native country.' Watkin and Rebecca had an only daughter, Justina Bann Lewes, and the heir-at-law was described as Herbert Evans of Highmead. Plâs-newydd was bought by David James Esq., who was declared bankrupt in 1846 and the small estate was sold by public auction in Cardigan. 'Plâs Newydd', including two cottages and 25 acres, was bought by Captain George Bowen, shipwright and coxswain of the first Cardigan lifeboat launched in February 1850. Alterations to the house were carried out by George Bowen who died in 1902. His son, Albert, was captain of the *Arctic Stream*, the Clyde-built iron sailing ship which won a memorable race from Sydney to Rotterdam for the valuable prize of a bowl of pea-soup. In the 1930's and 40's, Plâs-newydd was owned by Philip Jones of the nearby Manian-fawr family. In 1950 it was bought by John Sambrook who farmed 30 acres and later built a bungalow on the site of the original house. When renovating an outhouse in Plâs-newydd, he uncovered a window inscribed with the words 'repaired in 1674'. In the 1980's

Arctic Stream

Mr. and Mrs. J. Gargaro excavated the previously concreted cellar built on bare rock and created a study and library. Plâs-newydd is now owned by Mr. and Mrs. Marlais Hughes.

Grid Ref: SN 4577 1638

Refs: CRO, John Francis Deeds; CRO, GGMS; PRO; LT List, 1786 and Deeds; Fenton, *Tour Pembrokeshire,* 1811, p. 282; Pritchard, *History of St. Dogmaels Abbey,* pp. 185-6; NLW, Great Sessions, Pembrokeshire Plea Rolls; NLW, Griffith Owen Deeds, No. 2594; Ex. Info. J. Gargaro; J. Sambrook; T. Bowen.

PORTH HOFIN, Blaenporth

The full name of Aberporth was formerly Aberporth-Hoddni with the variants Hofni, Howni or perhaps hofin. Circa 1400, Meredydd was of Porth Hofin. He bore the arms *azure* a sal coward *argent.* His daughter Agnes, described as daughter and heir of Porth Hofin, married Philip ap Rees ap Llewelyn of Neuadd Trefawr, ap Rhys Ddu Sqwiar digri. Their son, Lewis was of Llaethlliw and Llanychaearn.

Refs: CRO, GGMS, I (Tydwal Gloff).

PORTHYFFYNNON, Tregaron
see FOUNTAIN GATE

PORTHYNEUADD (PARC NEUADD), Ciliau Areon

Located on the A482 Aberaeron to Felin-fach road half a mile from Ciliau Aeron. Hugh Lloyd of Llwyd Jack married Ann Parry of Blaen-pant. They had a son John who had four sons: Hugh, John Lloyd of Breinog, Thomas Lloyd of Gwernfeilig and Griffith Lloyd.

Hugh Lloyd had two sons and three daughters: David Lloyd of Lloyd Jack (who died in 1743), Walter Lloyd who married Mary, daughter of Griffith Lewes of Porthyneuadd, they had a son, Hugh Lloyd, who succeeded to Lloyd Jack in 1743. He was still a minor in 1746; Mary who married Leonard Rice, Cissil married John Laugharne and Anne, who married Llewelyn Pugh (to Saer y Cwm). Most dates are lacking.

Grid Ref: SN 4945 5935

Refs: CRO, GGMS, III (Gwaethfoed), fo. 30.

HANDIR, Llangwyryfon

There are four farms named Rhandir in the Llangwyryfon area; Rhandir-hen, -uchaf, -isaf and Bwlchyrhandir. The *Law Codes of Hywel Dda* drawn up in the 10th century, laid down the pattern of the division of land. In principle, a *rhandir* (shareland) comprised of 312 acres and there were five *rhandiroedd* in each *gwestfa* (tribute), formerly render of food paid twice a year by freeman to the Lord, later the Chief Rent. Which Rhandir housed the Pryse family is a matter of conjecture. Evidence favours Rhandir-isaf which is located on the banks of the Wyre, half a mile from Llangwyryfon on the minor road towards Lledrod.

The earliest reference to Rhandir names Gwilym ap Rhys Llewelyn, great-grandson of Llewelyn Fychan, descended from Hywel Dda. His kinsman, Dafydd Llwyd, lived nearby at Aber-mad. His daughter, Tanglwst, married Dafydd Llwyd ap Richard, a younger son of Richard ap Rhys of Gogerddan and Elliw, his wife. Their son, John Pryce, married Sibil, daughter of Owen Phillips of Ystrad Dynny, Radnorshire and in turn, their son, Richard, married Catherine, daughter of Morgan Herbert of Hafod Uchdryd. Richard Pryse and Catherine had five children. The eldest son, John, living in 1691 became Coroner for the county and married Mary, daughter of Thomas Edwards of Henley, Shropshire. The second son, William, married Mary, daughter of William Morgan of Llanilar the widow of Morgan Evan. Their son, Edward married Ann, heiress of Stephen Lloyd of Cilfachau, Llanrhystud. Thomas Price (died 1702), the third son, married Mary Jenkins of Pantybarwn, nearby. They had two sons, Charles, who remained at Rhandir, Thomas and a daughter Anna Maria Sibyl. A daughter of Richard and Catherine married Rhys Lloyd of Lovesgrove.

John Pryse, who in 1672 paid tax on three hearths, and Mary, his wife, had six children. Richard married Hannah and lived in Donabate, Co. Dublin, and Catherine who died in London, Judith married John Lloyd of Cilrhug and Mary married Lewis Gwyn of Mynachty,

High Sheriff in 1702. Thomas Pryse became Gentleman of the Horse to Viscount Lisburne in 1698. Charles Pryse, Canon of St. David's and rector of Newport and Whitchurch, Pembrokeshire, died in November 1733 and is buried in St. Nicholas Church in Brecon. His wife was Elizabeth, niece of Thomas Watson, Bishop of St. David's. Her portion was £500 and the marriage agreement of 1691 settled the following properties for their use: 'Argoed, Pen-y-gaer, Tomen Argoed, Garth-fawr, Rhandir, Aberdeuddwr, Tyddyn y Cnwce, Tyddyn y fron, Gorslas, Llety Bongam, Bryn-chwith, Bryn rhosog, Cnwc-y-fran, Rhandir-hen, Penciog-uchaf and -isaf, Ty'nllwyn, Gelli-gorden-uchaf and -isaf, Ffynnon-wen, Cilcwm and Pwllydraenllwyn, all in the parish of Llangwyryfon and Hendre Rhys in Llanilar and Ty'nrhos, parish of Llanddeiniol'.

The bridegroom's grandmother, Catherine, was living at Argoed at that time. By 1705, Rhandir was owned by Richard Pryse, who lived in Co. Dublin with Hannah, his wife, who following her husband's death received an annuity of £20 charged on Rhandir. In 1749, their son, Edward and Elizabeth, his wife, sold the Rhandir estate, which comprised of the properties mentioned in the marriage settlement above, to William Williams (1698-1773), of Pantseiri, Tregaron, whose descendants later lived at Castle Hill, Llanilar. John Nathaniel Williams, (1793-1832), his great-nephew, and Sarah his wife, lived for a time at Rhandir-isaf during the renovations and extensions then taking place at Castle Hill following the move from Pantseiri at the beginning of the 19th century. In 1845 Stephen Edwards was the tenant of Rhandir-isaf, a holding of 99 acres. His neighbour at Rhandir-uchaf was David Davies, farming a holding of 188 acres. At Rhandir-hen, a farm of 72 acres, was William Williams, while David Edwards was the tenant of 163 acres at Argoed. In 1887 when local tenants wrote a letter to the Land Commissioners, David Thomas was the tenant of Rhandir-isaf, William Evans was at Rhandir-uchaf, William Rowlands at Rhandir-hen and Richard Phillipps was farming Argoed.

Grid Ref: SN 6055 7090

Refs: Colby Map, 1831; WWHR, i, 36, Meyrick *Cardiganshire,* p. 281; NLW, Crosswood Deeds, p. 93; Nicholas, *County Families,* 1875 ed., i, 195; PRO, Dale Castle MS., pp. 19, 26; WWHR, ii, 11; Castle Hill Collection Nos. 334-5, 342, 350-1, 353, 1453; Jones, *Brec.* iv. 191-2; NLW, Cwrtmawr Deeds, No. 38; CRO, GGMS III (Gwaethfoed); ibid, I (Tydwal Gloff), fo. 32; *Cardiganshire County History,* I, 1994 pp.351-364

RHIWARTHEN (-UCHAF), Llanfihangel-y-Creuddyn

The house is shown on modern OS maps south-west of Capel Bangor on the banks of the Rheidol and marked on *Colby's Map of 1831* which shows Rhiwarthen-isaf nearby. Rhiwarthen formerly belonged to Richard Lewis, and Elizabeth, his only daughter and heiress, the estate went to Morgan Lloyd on their marriage. Morgan was the son of Watkin Morgan, of Abertrinant, Llanfihangel-y-Creuddyn, who was the second son of Morgan David Lloyd of Glasgrug, a mile west of Rhiwarthen who traced to Cadifor ap Dinawal. Morgan's will was proved in 1641. He had a brother, Lewes, and a sister, Katherine, who married John Lloyd of Wern Newydd. On the death of Morgan Lloyd, his son, Thomas succeeded to Rhiwarthen. He married Elizabeth, daughter of Jenkin Vaughan of Caethle. Thomas was High Sheriff in 1661 and paid tax on six hearths in 1672. On 17 January 1675/6 Thomas Lloyd, Esq. gave a lease for 39 years of Pant Dafydd and Blaen Gwenllian in the parish of Llanfair Trelygen to Magdalen Lloyd of Bronwydd, widow. Thomas was succeeded by his son, Morgan, High Sheriff in 1713, who married Bridget, daughter of David Lloyd of Crynfryn, Nantcwnlle, whose grandfather, John Lloyd, had married Elizabeth, daughter of Watkin Morgan David Lloyd of Glascrug. Morgan Lloyd was succeeded by his son, also Morgan, who married Margaret, daughter of Thomas Pryse of Glanfrêd, Llanfihangel Genau'r Glyn.

Grid Ref: SN 6487 7967

Refs: Colby Map, 1831; Blome List, 1673; WWHR, i, 31-2; Meyrick, *Cardiganshire,* 311; PRO, Dale Castle MS., p. 24; NLW, Crosswood Deeds, p. 82; NLW, Bronwydd Deeds, No. 2206; NLW, Cards. G.S., papers, 1666-7.

RHIWBREN, Llanarth

Rhiwbren-fawr is marked on *Colby's Map of 1831* and on modern OS maps on a hill overlooking the Mydr and Felin Rhiwbren, east of Llanarth, south of Llanerchaeron and north-west of Dihewyd. Home of Jenkin ap Rees ap Hugh who signed his pedigree for the herald Dwnn on 27 July 1591 and more recently, the Herbert family.

Richard ap Evan and his brother, Rees Pugh were involved in litigation regarding Rhiwbren. Rees owned lands in Llanarth and died in 1676. His brother's son and heir, Watkin Rees, was heir-at-law of his uncle, Rees Pugh. He laid claim to the estate of Morgan Herbert. 'Watkin Rees petitioned that Rees Pugh of the parish of Llanarth, owned land in the parish of Llanarth and settled the same on himself for life and afterwards on Magdalen, his wife for her life, with remainders to their issue, and for want of such issue to the rightful heirs of said Rees Pugh for ever.' Rees Pugh had died over forty years before, without issue and then Magdalen, his wife, enjoyed the estate by virtue of settlement until she died about fourteen years before, having after the death of Rees Pugh married Morgan Herbert of Rhiwbren. They had a daughter, Margaret Herbert, who, Watkin Rees believed, had no right to the estate as heir-at-law to her said mother who had the estate only for life. The petitioner was the nearest living relation of Rees Pugh, who was his father's brother. Watkin Rees said that he 'lived for years past in Pembrokeshire more than twenty miles from the said estate and did not discover his right to the Rhiwbren estate until recently. He was in a poor and weak condition and wished to sue for the recovery of said lands'. The petition was allowed on 3 October 1715.

Morgan Herbert was the first of the Herberts to settle at Rhiwbren. He had married Catherine, the widow of Rees Pugh, mentioned above. Family records note that the petition of Watkin Rees for the recovery of Rhiwbren was unsuccessful. Morgan Herbert had been succeeded by his son, another Watkin, who died in 1696, while his elder brother, William, was disinherited due to his marriage, of which his parents disapproved. Another brother, Llewelyn, who died in 1720, had a natural son, Abraham, later of Teulur Adar and the youngest son, Charles, settled at Cwm-mawr, Llanybydder. Watkin was followed at Rhiwbren by Morgan Herbert, who married Anne, and their son, William, is said to have made two clandestine marriages, in 1744 to Margaret Williams and a year later to Hester Morgan, who bore children. William then married Judith Price of Blaenhownant, Penbryn parish. They had four children, William, Margaret, Bridget and David. William Herbert the eldest married Margaret Jones, born in 1793 and of their eight children the eldest, another William became a JP and died in 1815 aged 52 years. Three of their sons died in their thirties. David became a surgeon, Morgan was a solicitor in Lampeter and John Herbert of Ystrad died aged 34 years in 1832.

The Rev. David Herbert (1762-1835), youngest son of William and Judith, was educated at Wadham College, Oxford and became vicar of Llansanffraid in 1812. He married Mary Price of Felindre, Llanfihangel Ystrad and William, the eldest of their five children succeeded his father at Llansanffraid. His wife, Elizabeth, lived until after her 100th birthday. The second son, John, a brilliant scholar, was received into the church in 1828 and went to Ohio to teach at Kenyan College but died two years later. The Rev. William and Elizabeth Herbert had three sons. James, educated at Oxford became rector of Cilrhedyn, Carmarthenshire, David Herbert became vicar of Blaen-porth and a daughter, Frances, lived at Dolclychan until her death in 1895, when her brother sold the property to the parishioners of Llannon for £1,100. Another branch of the family of Herbert settled at Blaen Einon, Talgarreg. Jacob Herbert (1783-1813), later of Pant-glas married Martha Eynon who died in 1834 when a peregrine falcon pecked her in the eye. Their son, Owen, married as his second wife, Mary Hughes of Esgaireithin, Talgarreg, who died aged 109 years in 1879. A son of the first marriage to Margaret was John who became an analytical chemist and assayer of gold to the French and Mexican governments.

Rhiwbren was offered for sale on 15 July 1902. It was described as a total of 190 acres to be offered in four lots – the Dwelling house consisting of a parlour, sitting room, kitchen, dairy, 5 bedrooms, attic, outbuildings and 88 acres, Rhiwbren Mill with 21 acres, Pengribin a small holding of 20 acres and Penymorfa farm at 59 acres.

Grid Ref: SN 4705 5767

Refs: Colby Map, 1831; *Dwnn,* i, 53, 82; WWHR, ii, 86; NLW, Griffith Owen Deeds, No. 6166; CRO, GGMS, *Cardiganshire,* 2 James I; CRO, SC. 511.

RHOD-MAD, Llanilar

Marked on the *Rees Map* of the 14th century, on *Colby's Map of 1831* and on modern OS maps south-west of Llanilar adjacent to the B4576 road leading from Glan-mad towards Llangwyryfon. Richard David Parry (1609-64), was the first of the Parry family to settle at Rhodmad. He was the son of David ap Harry and Mary Morris of Glennydd, south of New Cross. David in turn was descended from Adda Fychan of Llanddwy through his father, Harry Morris Goch. Richard David Parry and his wife, Margaret, who died in 1679, had five children. The eldest son, David Richard David Parry (1640-94), married Anne, daughter of John Lloyd of Gilfachael, Llanrhystud and Margaret, daughter of Stephen Parry of Plasnewydd, St. Dogmaels, later of Noyadd Trefawr. They had seven children including James who moved to Gilfachafael having married Letitia, a daughter of Rhys Fychan of Glenydd, whose descendants include the Hughes of Allt-lwyd and the Williams family of Tynwern, Llanrhystud and later of Cwmcynfelin, Dolcletwr, Wallog and Tan-y-bwlch. A daughter, Margaret, married Morris ap Owen ap Morris in 1688 and their son, Owen, was the father of Richard Morrice of Treflys, Llangwyryton. The eldest son, Stephen Parry (1663-1739), remained at 'Rhodemaid' and married Magdalen, daughter of David Pugh who was descended from the Trawsgoed family. Their son, Richard (1690-1779), was the eldest of ten children. His brother, Stephen, became the vicar of Shrewsbury, and his sister, Gwen, born in 1694, married Griffith Jenkins, and their grandson was Theophilus Jones, who later lived at Rhod-mâd. Richard's son, John, married as his second wife, Elizabeth Parry of Llangwyryfon in 1757, and had three children.

Grid Ref: SN 5925 7425

Refs: 14th Century Rees Map; Colby Map, 1831; CRO, GGMS I (Tydwal Gloff), fo. 32; CRO, GGMS III, NLW, Cwrtmawr Deeds, 325; NLW, Morgan Richardson Deeds, ii, 449; WWHR, iii, 95.

RHOSCELLAN-FAWR, Llanfihangel Genau'r-glyn

Located in woodland off the B4572 towards Borth a mile from the Cross at Llangorwen. Rhoscellan-fach is a little to the south, and Wallog, overlooking Sarn Gynfelyn, is nearby.

The first known reference to the house is to John Vaughan of Rhoscellan who sold a cow in Machynlleth fair in 1532 for 34/-. The *NLW Cwrtmawr Deeds* tell us that on 7 September 1625 Watkin ap Richard alias Vaughan of Rhosgillan and David Vaughan of same place, son and heir apparent, gent. and Evan Griffith, David Lloyd of the parish of Llanbadarn Fawr, gent., were parties to a covenant to levy fines on messuages called 'Colyrog ucha and Bryn y fron in the parish of Llanfihangel Geneu'r Glyn'.

The Vaughans of Rhos Cellan were descended from the Lords of Tywyn, Ferwig parish. Rhydderch ap Rhys Meredydd descended from Gwynfardd Dyfed, married Margaret, the daughter and heiress of John Lloyd ap David ap Llewelyn ap David of Cefnmelgoed. His second son, Dafydd, who settled at Llangynfelyn, married Lowri daughter of Richard ap Rees ap Dafydd Llwyd of Gogerddan and their son Richard married Laura daughter of Richard Rees David Lloyd of Gogerddan. They had a son, Watkin who married Elen, daughter of Huw Prys ab Howell of Llanfendigaid, Meirionnydd. Watkin's son, David Fychan married a daughter of Thomas Wynn James of Llanbadarn Fawr and was the first of the family to live at Rhoscellan. Their son, John Fychan, married Jane, daughter of Lewis Evans of Brynbala, the neighbouring property. Their daughter and heiress, Mary, married George Jones, a brother of Col. John Jones of Nanteos. Meyrick tells us that the estate was 'now part of the property of Captain Powell of Nant Eos . . . the heiress of the original owners married George Jones, son of Edward Jones of Nant Eos: pedigree given'. Their son, John, succeeded and married a daughter of Lewis John of

Cefn-gwyn, Elerch. Their son, another George, was appointed JP in 1727 and is named as owner-occupier in 1760.

Before the end of the 18th century, Rhoscellan became part of the Cwmgynfelyn estate of Mathew Evans, whose family had resided at Cwmgynfelyn for many generations. Mathew Evans was a businessman in Aberystwyth and Mayor in 1734 and 1760. A daughter married Mathew Davies who also owned Wilcirog-uchaf and Wallog. A descendant, George Griffiths Williams lived at Rhoscellan in 1871 and was High Sheriff in 1876. In the early 20th century, Rhoscellan became the home of the Jones family formerly of Ruel, Llandre, who still live there.

Grid Ref: SN 5975 8550

Refs: Colby Map, 1831; Meyrick, *Cardiganshire,* 323; NLW, Cwrtmawr Deeds, Nos. 48, 331-2, 1005, 1365; PRO, Dale Castle MS., p. 23; CRO, GGMS (Gwynfardd); WWHR, i, 27.

RHOS-Y-RHIW, Llanfihangel-y-Creuddyn

Located north of Pont-rhyd-y-groes near to the B4343 towards Dol-gors and Devil's Bridge. On 24 July 1641 an assignment of a mortgage of a parcel of land called 'Tir Ysgenvaen in the township of Llanvarian in the parish of Llanbadarn fawr,' was agreed between 'William Herbert of Rhos- y-rhyw, gent and Thomas Powell of Llechwedd Dyrys in the parish of Llanbadarn Fawr'.

By 1760 William Ball was the owner occupier of Rhos-y-rhiw and four years earlier in 1756, John Ball Esq. is recorded as living at Abertrinant in the same parish. It was later the home of the Pughs of Abermad and Cymerau.

Grid Ref: SN 7405 7321

Refs: NLW, Cwrtmawr Deeds, No. 953; WWHR, iii, 96.

RHYDYMENDI, Llandygwydd

On modern OS Maps there is a Rhyd south-east of Llandygwydd church; a stream runs by it and joins the Teifi near Stradmore. Stephen Parry, High Sheriff in 1720, died without issue in 1724 and was buried at Llandygwydd, where there is a memorial inscription. He was the eldest son of David Parry of Noyadd Trefawr (High Sheriff in 1685) and was elected as MP for the county of Cardigan in 1721. The fortunes of Rhydymendi became merged with those of Noyadd Trefawr.

Grid Ref: SN 2510 4287

Refs: Modern OS Maps; Phillips, *Sheriffs of Cardiganshire.*

STRADMORE, Llandygwydd

The present Stradmore (Ystrad-mawr) lies above a steep-sided wooded slope overlooking the main A484 road between Llechryd and Cenarth. We are indebted to Miss T. Douglass for her research on Stradmore.

The original house was sited between the old turn-pike road and the river. The mansion lay to the south of the still existing walled garden and cottage, known as Stradmore Fach, in wide meadows, where the river Teifi describes a curve away from the road. A Sale Catalogue of 1833 describes it as a 'Picturesque Estate situated on the banks of the River Tivy celebrated for romantic beauty, and the finest Salmon Fishery in the World. The Estate comprises Stradmore House, Stradmore Hill, and 171a. 1r. 38p.' A map of the estate shows Stradmore Hill to be the modern Stradmore.

In 1610 the messuages called 'Stradmore Ucha and Issa' were settled on Phillip Lewes, gt., of Tremain and his wife, Gwenllian, daughter of John Thomas Parry of Manordeifi. Little more is known of the property until 1760 when David Thomas held the freehold. In 1766 *WWHR* tells us that Stradmore was part of the Symmonds of Llanstinan estates.

In 1784 Silvanus Nugent of Llechryd and Thomas Makeig of Penlan mortgaged Ddole, Stradmore and Pwllacka. Steele bought the estate of Stradmore Vale in 1801, from Taylor. He found it more convenient to be up near the turnpike road and away from the river, so he built/improved Ddol for himself before 1813 (probably around 1807). The house was tenanted by a Mr. Leslie who improved it, but had left by 1813. Mr. Steele sold the house to Dr. Shirreff. He also sold Ddol, although by 1924 it is back with Llwynduris estate. Later called Thorneville it had disappeared by 1891. Mr. Steele 'departs for drier climes or the graveyard'.

In 1835 Mr. Shirreff sold Stradmore House and and Stradmore Hill (since called Belvoir), to William Brigstocke of Blaenpant. Stradmore Hill described as a 'ferme ornee' in the sale catalogue – has a Gothic porch, a breakfast room, a drawing room with domed ceiling, a bedchamber. a dining room with domed ceiling, a library, a housekeeper's room, a store room and butler's pantry, a dairy with cheese room over and a cellar beneath, a good kitchen and scullery, and upstairs 4 principal bedchambers and 2 large bedchambers for domestics. It has 2 separate yards – one with stables, harness room, brew house, knife house, culm house, laundry with farm servants room over, a brick built barn, 5 piggeries, a dove house, a coal house, a grananry. A yard with cart lodge, malt kiln, team stable for 6 horses, an open loft over, cowhouse for 10 beasts with open loft over, a shed for young cattle, a poultry house and a range of enclosed sheds for carriages and agricultural implements.

In 1835 the estate of Stradmore Vale was sold by the family of Dr. Shirriff to William Owen Brigstocke of Blaenpant. Local folk history suggests that the owner of the house, riding to the wars, was informed that his wife was unfaithful. Riding back, and discovering it was true, he combined murder with arson. However, the truth is probably more prosaic and may reflect the Teifi's periodic tendency to flood. Brigstocke let Stradmore Hill to his brother-in-law Mr. Green – pulled down Stradmore mansion, and used the materials to improve Stradmore Hill and other Blaenpant Estate properties. The *Tithe Map of 1839* shows that Stradmore House has disappeared. The Brigstockes had one son and two daughters: William, Caroline and Sophia.

William Buck, was born in 1814. He matriculated from Balliol College, Oxford in 1835. He took a 99 year lease, from William Owen Brigstocke, of 'all that messuage tenement farm and lands called Stradmore Hill' in 1860. He became a busy lawyer, acting for many Tivyside families, and was High Sheriff in 1873. He died, unmarried and without issue, in 1880.

George Bevan Bowen lived at Stradmore from around 1894. *CRO/Trant/Box 189* shows him as Bowen of Stradmore joining a firm of Carmarthenshire Estate agents. He was also master of the Tivyside Hunt. He had left Stradmore by 1901. Sir John Lyn Thomas brought Stradmore. [See *Llwyndyrys.*] In 1892 he married Mary Rosina, only daughter of Edward Jenkins, of Cardiff. He commanded the Welsh Hospital in South Africa during the Boer war and was awarded the CB. In 1903 he became a JP and in 1907 was High Sheriff of Cardiganshire. He was colonel A.M.S. and Deputy Inspector of Military Orthopaedics, Western Command. He was awarded the CMG in 1917 and became KBE in 1919. He moved to Llwyndyrys in 1922.

Sir John sold the estate on 20 September 1924 (except Stradmore Gardens), to Levi Thomas Jones of Nantgwyn, Llanfairnantgwyn for £3,200. In that year he mortgaged Stradmore Hill for £2,000 to David Evans of Square Hall Mills, Drefach, Llangeller. In 1931 Levi Thomas Jones died. In his will he left monetary bequests to his other children and Stradmore to his son Griffith David Jones. His executors were Evan Owen Evans, Manager of Lloyds Bank, Newcastle Emlyn and Evan James of Parktwad, Llandygwydd. In June 1934 the mortgage was transferred from David Evans to E. O. Evans of Lloyds Bank. Mr. Griffith David Jones farmed the land as tenant until the war. E. O. Evans lived in the house, now known as Stradmore Mansion. In 1950 the farm was sold to Edgar Jones of Cilrhiwe, Lanfihangel Penbedw. E. O. Evans retained the mansion and 9 acres of woodland. He lived there until his death in 1953.

In 1954 Mr. and Mrs. Watkin Lewis, formerly of Bryn-chwith, Ponterwyd, bought the farm from their brother-in-law, Edgar Jones. The mansion house passed through several hands before, in 1994, Mr. and Mrs. Watcyn Lewis purchased the property, re-uniting the ownership of the farm and the mansion after 44 years. Stradmore Mansion is now used as holiday accommodation.

Grid Ref: SN 2495 4186

Refs: Colby Map, 1831; WWHR, iii, 79; WWHR, xiv, 232; Meyrick, *Cardiganshire,* 1807, (edn. 1907, p. 186); Lewis, *TDW,* 1840; J. G. Ward, *Principal Rivers of Wales,* 1813, pt. 1, 155; Carlisle, *TDW,* 1811; Castell Gorford Collec-tion, p. 205 (No. 308); NLW, Llwyndyrus Deeds, Nos. 26-7; NLW, Noyadd Trefawr Deeds, 135, 255; *Beauties of England and Wales;* G. E. Evans *Cardiganshire,* 1903, 255; Alcwyn Evans, Pedigrees in NLW, MS. 12357 E; Carmarthenshire RO, SC 492; Miss T. Douglass.

STRATA FLORIDA (YSTRAD FFLUR), Caron-Uwch-Clawdd

Situated west of Pontrhydfendigaid on the upper reaches of the Teifi adjoining the ruins of the Cistercian Abbey of Ystrad Fflur. The front of the Abbey farm, as it is now known, has not changed dramatically from the Buck engravings of 1741 which show a three-storeyed house with an attic storey with a line of four dormer windows, a fine ornamented porch doorway and a courtyard with iron rails. Following the Dissolution of the Monasteries, most of the Strata Florida Abbey estate in the Tregaron area was bought by Richard Devereux in 1547 and then leased to John Stedman, second son of John and Catherine Stedman of Staffordshire. He married Joan, daughter of John Lewis, also of Staffordshire, whose mother was descended from Gwaethfoed. Their son, John, was High Sheriff of Cardiganshire in 1581 and married Ann, the natural daughter of William Philipps of Pentypark, Pembrokeshire, who signed his pedigree for the herald Dwnn. John died in 1607. He was succeeded by another John. The *Griffith Owen List* also records 'John Stydman junior, known as John Moel (bald) of Ystradfflyr, who was born in 1550, and married Margaret, daughter and co-heiress of David Lloyd of Porth y Crwys, eldest son of John Llwyd of Blaen Towy'. John Stedman was High Sheriff of Cardiganshire in 1595 and 1608, when he is listed as of Ystrad-ffin and of Breconshire in 1610.

Meyrick tells us that 'the present mansion was erected by John Stedman, Esq., son of John Stedman of Staffordshire, Esq. from the ruins of the outbuildings belonging to the Abbey'. G. Eyre Evans wrote in 1903 'I lean to the idea that he [Richard Stedman but *recte* John] was the builder of the church, as he certainly was of the "Great House" in which he lived and within which I am now writing. Its earliest view shows the high-pitched dormer windows now gone, but the wondrously thick walls, the broad low tread flight of stairs with twisted balusters, the roomy attics, the great open chimney with fire on the hearth and the panels on part of the lower room with the mural painting above the moulded mantel; these still remain to bear witness to the former grandeur of the homestead. In all likelihood the present parlour, entrance hall and kitchen place formed originally one long hall, the existing partitions being but of thin wood and quite out of keeping with the walls and oaken beams which support the ceiling and upper rooms. Visitors often look at the dingy painting and wonder what it represents. Well, I have been rubbing up bits of it and hope some day to be able more fully to restore it. The scene portrayed is that of Youth's choice of Virtue or Vice. In the centre stands a boy on a dais, from which depends a scroll bearing a legend, which, to the best of my deciphering reads thus:

When Virtue and Vice
Youth doth woo,
Tis hard to say
Which way he'll go.

On either side of the lad are the standing figures of an aged and patriarchal-looking man, holding an open Bible in his hand and on the other the reclining effigy of Vice, represented with asinine ears and a mask in his right hand'.

John Stedman died in 1613. His son James, who married Catherine, daughter of Sir Richard Pryse of Gogerddan was High Sheriff in 1617. The inventory taken at the time of his death included 'sixteen beds in several chambers, tables long and square, with and without frames,

livery cupboards, joined stools, chairs, forms, trunks, chests, cupboards and carpets for long and square tables'.

In 1624 Sir John Price of Strata Florida was High Sheriff. Sir John, of Ystrad-ffin had married Catherine, widow of James Stedman who died during his year as High Sheriff. The family continued to supply the county with High Sheriffs; John Stedman in 1637, James Stedman in 1667 and Richard Stedman in 1693 and they made advantageous marriages. The Stedmans became linked with the most powerful and influential families in the country, including the Vaughans of Trawsgoed, the Pryses of Gogerddan and the Lloyds of Llanllyr. In 1672 Margaret Stedman of the parish of Deheuglawdd, widow of James Stedman and the daughter of Richard Owen of Rhiwsaeson, Montgomery, paid tax on eight hearths, an indication of the commodious size of the property.

Richard Stedman married Anne, the second daughter of William Powell of Nanteos. H. Lloyd-Johnes writes in *The Lesser Country Houses of Cardiganshire* that Richard was the last Stedman to own Strata Florida. 'He died intestate, without surviving issue and in 1747 administration was granted to his principal creditor Thomas Powell of Nanteos'. The widow married Sir Herbert Lloyd of Peterwell, but she resided at Foelallt till her death in 1778, aged 76. Strata Florida passed to the Powells and became part of the Sunny Hill Estate. The Cambrian Register noted that 'the abbey house was formerly a grand mansion, but is now a common farmhouse; the property belongs to Thomas Powell of Nanteos'.

In 1781 the *NLW Cwrtmawr Deeds* tell us that Thomas Powell of Nanteos granted a lease of The Abbey, Strata Florida, to Edward Evans of that address. By 1870 the Abbey demesne and lands were still part of the Tregaron estate of the Powells of Nanteos. Writing in 1953 H. Lloyd-Johnes observed that the house was by then a two-storeyed farmhouse, deprived of the top storey of the original. There is a view of the mansion and Abbey ruins in Nicholas's *County Families.*

Grid Ref: SN 7467 6569

Refs: Dwnn, i, 19, 79-80, 88; WWHR, i, 8-9; Blome List, 1673; Buck's Engravings; Meyrick, *Cardiganshire,* 1810, edn. 1907, p. 248; WWHR, iii, 98; WWHR, viii, 89. ff. Carlisle, 1811; *The Cambrian Register,* 1796, 388; Nicholas, *County Families,* ii, 169, 937, 1875 edn. *Arch. Cam.,* 1887, 290; PRO, Dale Castle MS.; Mont. Colln., vol. XXXXI, 1900, p. 73; NLW, Crosswood Deeds, pp. 142 & 1585; NLW, Griffith Owen List (iv); H. Lloyd-Johnes, *'The Lesser County Houses of Cardiganshire',* in *Ceredigion,* vol. II, 1953; G. Eyre Evans, *Cardiganshire, Aberystwyth,* 1903, 18; NLW, Cwrtmawr Deeds, No. 1585.

SUNNY HILL, Tregaron

A farmhouse situated in woodland just north-east of Tregaron off the road towards Pontrhydfendigaid and marked on *Colby's Map of 1831.* This house was originally called Camerwen. The present house was built about 200 years ago by the Rev. Daniel Jones, vicar of Tregaron from 1750 to 1784.

In 1775 Sunny Hill was described as a capital messuage called Camer otherwise Sunny Hill in the parish of Caron, part of the Powell of Nanteos estate and formerly part of the Strata Florida Abbey property. In 1778 a Mr. Jones lived there. Just over a hundred years later the demesne and lands of Sunny Hill still formed part of the Tregaron estate of the Powell family and in 1870 was occupied by a tenant William Williams. Cornelius Le Brun Powell, the younger son of W. T. R. Powell of Nanteos, was living at Sunny Hill in 1899. His son, Charles, took a keen interest in the agricultural activities of the area and lived at Glanbrenig. Cornelius died in 1917 aged 65 years and his wife Jessie Florence died aged 77 years in 1927. A photograph of Sunny Hill was published in *Cymru* in October 1901.

Refs: Colby Map, 1831; *Cymru,* October 1901, p. 268; NLW, Cwrtmawr Deeds, No. 1728.

TAI'N Y COED (TY'N-COED)
There is a Ty'n-coed near Capel Seion but the location is uncertain. Two deeds of the mid-17th century have survived. On 31 August 1666 David Lloyd of Tai'n y Coed, Cards, gent. mortgaged the messuage called 'Tythyn Rhyd y Velin vach and Tythyn Maes Hoell, a messuage, a water mill called y Velin Vach and a parcel of land called Llain or Tir Lan allt Morgan, all in the commote of Croythyn within the parish of Llanbadarn Vawr and a heretofore parcel of the grange of Trevaesmorva Vaughan to James Stedman of Ystrad Fflur for £200'.

On 12 August 1675 the *NLW Cwrtmawr Deeds* state that 'Benjamin Lewis of Kilgwyn, parish Myddfai, Carmarthenshire, gent., and Lettice his wife, as well as Mary Lloyd of Tay yn y Coed, Co. Cardiganshire, widow sold the messuages and land of David Lloyd, deceased husband of Mary Lloyd, and father of said Lettice, at Morfa Esgob in the parish of Llansanffraid, Cardiganshire to Thomas Powell of Llechwedd Dyrys'.

Refs: NLW, Cwrtmawr Deeds, No. 574, 63.

TALSARN, Trefilan
On a house in the village is inscribed 'M LL FB IE CARP' which suggests it to be the name of a Lloyd of Llanllyr as the builder and thus the house described here. Ieuan ap Gruffyd, traced to Blegywryd ap Dinawal married twice. His first wife was a daughter of Gruffydd Coch of Bodrychen by whom he had a son, Griffith of Penallt Gwerchydd who married Elen, daughter and co-heiress of Meredydd Thomas Llewelyn Owain descended from Rhys ap Tewdwr. From his second marriage to Margaret, daughter of Griffith Llewelyn Goch, he had two sons and a daughter, Dafydd, Ieuan and Angharad Llawarian. Dafydd is described as of Llwyndafydd, whose great-great grandson was Rhys ap Rhys of Talysarn who died without issue. Rhys was succeeded by his brother Morgan who had two sons, Thomas and Francis. Thomas Morgan, had a son John Thomas of Carmarthen, described as a scrivener and Francis Morgan who had a son, Thomas, and a daughter Mary. Thomas Francis of Llanddewibrefi had a son, John Thomas.

Grid Ref: SN 5447 5625

Refs: CRO, GGMS (Tydwal Gloff), I, 42.

TAN-Y-BWLCH, Llanychaearn
Located in woodland on the banks of the Ystrad below the original castle of Aberystwyth and marked on *Colby's Map of 1831* as a farm and occupied in 1760 by Richard Williams. By 1790 the house had passed to the Davies family of Crugiau. John Davies of Crugiau, agent to the Nanteos estate, married Jane, daughter of Richard Morris of Cyneiniog, in the Leri valley east of Tal-y-bont. Their third son was Lewis Davies (1777-1828) of Tanybwlch. In 1791 Lewis joined the 31st Regiment in which his brother, John, was a captain. He saw action on the continent, in the West Indies, in Spain with Sir John Moore and with great distinction at Salamanca in 1812. He rose swiftly through the ranks and became a full General in 1807. In 1800 he had married Jane, the daughter of Mathew Davies of Cwmcynfelin, High Sheriff of Cardiganshire in 1790 and had built the mansion at Tan-y-bwlch. General Davies died on 10 May 1828 and his wife in October 1840. They had three sons, John, later of Pen-bontbren, the Rev. Lewis Charles of Ynyshir and Mathew, who succeeded his father at Tan-y-bwlch was High Sheriff in 1847.

Mathew married Emma Davies of Twickenham. They had a son, Mathew Lewis Vaughan Davies, educated at Harrow, High Sheriff of Cardiganshire in 1875 and owner of an impoverished estate of 3,674 acres yielding a low annual rental of £947. In 1889, Mathew married the wealthy widow of Alexander Jenkins, of the Powell family which owned the Powell-Duffryn coal company. Her brother apparently went up in a balloon and was never heard of again! Mathew Vaughan Davies renovated Tan-y-bwlch and was the Tory who represented Cardiganshire for the Liberal cause from 1895 until he was elevated to the peerage as Lord Ystwyth in 1921 at the behest of Lloyd George who was looking for a safe Liberal seat for his Private Secretary, Ernest Evans. Lady

Ystwyth died in 1926 and her husband in 1935 at the age of 94. There were no children.

A story is told of Lord Ystwyth that when he was on his death-bed he created a great deal of noise and bother and his daughter who was attending to him said 'Father, die with dignity; remember you are a JP and Deputy-Lieutenant for Cardiganshire'.

Tan-y-bwlch was put up for sale in 1936. The Sale Catalogue describes the mansion: 'The residence was re-organised and conditioned fifty years ago and contains on Ground Floor – entrance hall, music and drawing rooms, dining room, morning room, boudoir, billiard room, smoke room, study, dressing room, w.c., bathroom and lavatory, housekeeper's room, servant's hall, pantry number 10, plate room, coal room, boot brushing and lamps room, housekeeper's pantry, butler's pantry, w.c. On First Floor – nine principal bedrooms (one with w.c. and wash basin), eight secondary bedrooms, dressing room, bathroom, w.c's., housemaid's pantry, linen cupboard. On Second Floor – six bedrooms and w.c. In Basement – wine and beer cellars, game larder. Outbuildings, coach-house and garage, saddle room, blacksmith's shop, tool shed, kennels, stabling (with seven bedrooms above), a cottage called Sea Cottage and 678 acres in Llanychaiarn and Aberystwyth parishes'.

In 1937 Cardiganshire County Council decided to buy Tan-y-bwlch for use as an isolation hospital, but the sale was not completed until 1946. It was soon in use following an epidemic of typhoid fever in July of that year. It became a convalescent home and later, the catering department of the Further Education College.

Grid Ref: SN 5810 7936

Refs: Colby Map, 1831; Lewis, *TDW,* 1840; WWHR, III, 94; Landowners Return, 1873; Phillips, *Sheriffs of Cardiganshire.* Ceredigion ex. info H. J. Lloyd Johnes, iii, pp. 261-2; ibid, v, pp 205-6.

TOWYN, see TYWYN

TRAWSGOED (CROSSWOOD), Llanafan

Located to the east of the B4340 and on the banks of the Ystwyth adjacent to the remains of a Roman fort. Marked on *Kitchin's Map of 1754.* For generations, the Vaughans were Lords Lieutenant, High Sheriffs and Members of Parliament for Cardiganshire – a family of much influence and patronage, including the remarkable and brilliant Sir John Vaughan, 1603-1674, Chief Justice of the Common Pleas. His son, John Vaughan was elevated to the Irish peerage in the late 18th century as the Earl of Lisburne.

From the early 13th century until 1947 it was the family seat of the Vaughans, Earls of Lisburne. The north wing, which may have formed the nucleus of an older building, was rebuilt in 1891, when four old beams bearing Biblical inscriptions were found under the kitchen plaster – assumed to have been taken from Strata Florida at the Dissolution.

In his book *County Families* Nicholas tells us: 'The house is an unpretentious edifice of some 250 years old, with a shallow entrance hall of the old style, with the massive table spread and the walls all round covered with valuable paintings of past members of the family. Additions have been made to the original structure, among which is a spacious library at the back, elaborately but chastely decorated, and containing a large collection of valuable books, many of them in the Italian and French languages. On this spot have the Vaughan family resided since the year 1200, through a long series of ages.'

The *Crosswood Deeds* state: 'Morris ap Richard, son of Richard ap Morris Vaughan viv. 1547, son of Morris Vaughan, married Elliw Howel, the daughter and heiress of Howell ap Jenkins ap Ieuan ap Rees.' The marriage was subject to a pre-nuptial settlement made on 10 June 1547. Morris ap Richard's father settled on him and his heirs two messuages of land and

land called 'the place at Trausgoed and the messuage of David Benlloid, in the parish of Llanavan and also all his lands in Llanfihangel Gelyndrod and other lands in Llanfihangel Gelyndrod and Llanbadarn Fawr'. Thus was founded the estates of Crosswood around the ancient family seat. The Vaughans signed for the herald Dwnn.

In 1601 the marriage of Edward Vaughan, was subject to a pre-nuptial settlement, when he married Lettis, one of the daughters of John Stedman, junior, of Strata Florida. Edward Vaughan was High Sheriff of Cardiganshire in 1619. By 1624, the pre-nuptial settlement of John Vaughan, eldest son and heir apparent of Edward Vaughan of Trowscoyd and Anne Stedman of Kilkenyn (widow of John Stedman gent., deceased) settled the capital messuage called Y Trowscoyd in Llanavan. Sir John and Edward Vaughan were living at Crosswood in 1673. A drawing of the house as it was in 1684 is given in Dinely's *Progress* and in Nicholas's *County Families.*

By 1802, the house became known as Crosswood Park and had suffered some neglect, Malkin's *South Wales* gives: 'Crosswood Park, the seat of the Honourable Colonel Vaughan, member for the borough of Cardigan, and brother to the Earl of Lisburne. This very ancient . . . For many years this venerable mansion has been altogether neglected, and has consequently fallen into decay. The late Lord Lisburne was so much attached to his beautiful seat in Devonshire, that he has never visited Crosswood Park, but for a short time, when county politics required his attendance . . . the house in the former instance, is set down in an obscure corner of the park, and though large, is laid out in a number of confined and inconvenient apartments. Colonel Vaughan is a very recent inhabitant; but as he informed me that he had taken sixteen hundred acres into his own hands, it is to be hoped the place will no longer be without a tenant, which only wants a judicious one, to render it a paradise . . .'. *County Families* shows an engraving of the exterior of the house at this time.

The estate prospered. The *Landowners Return, 1873,* gives the Earl of Lisburne, Crosswood, as having 42,666 acres at £10,579 p.a. The house was large, the park handsome, and the farm in the highest state of cultivation. The Earls of Lisburne were High Sheriffs in 1850, 1878 and 1889.

The original 17th century house had been much altered and in 1891 a vast French wing was added and an Ionic portico. In 1947 when the Vaughans had been at Crosswood for some 600 years, the house was sold for £50,000 and became the headquarters for the Agricultural Advisory Service for Wales and owned by the Ministry of Agriculture.

The Vaughan family retained the right of first refusal to the mansion and desmesne should the Government decide to sell. The right was exercised by the family through John Vaughan, younger son of the present Earl, who is a director of a limited company which purchased Trawsgoed in 1996.

Grid Ref: SN 6705 7305

Refs: Kitchin Map, 1754; *Dwnn,* i, 49-50; WWHR, i, 4-6; Dineley, *Progress,* fo. 246; Nicholas, *County Families,* 1872 & 1875; Lewis, *TDW;* Malkin, *South Wales,* 1804 pp. 379-80; ibid, vol. 2, p. 129 (1872); ibid, 1875; Crosswood by Giraldus, 1863, p. 49; Map of South Wales, c. 1760; NLW, Crosswood Deeds, p. 3; Ellis, Grwydro, *Ceredigion,* 1952; Steegman, II, *South Wales* (1962); Landowners Return, 1873; Howell and Beasley, 1977, p. 65. G. Morgan, *A Welsh House and its Family, The Vaughans of Trawsgoed* 1997.

TRE-FAES, Llanilar

Marked on *Colby's Map of 1831* and modern OS maps and located halfway between Llanilar and Llangwyryfon and reached by taking the B4536 from Glan-mad and then the minor road before Blaengader. The reference given is for the original settlement at what is now Tre-faes Isaf. Formerly the home of the Lewis and Philipps families. The 400 acre property, in addition to the adjacent Mynydd-mawr, was one of the smaller granges of the Abbey of Strata Florida. The original foundation, the gift of Gruffydd ap Cadwgan (d. 1192), possibly of Carrog, Llanddeiniol, was confirmed by a charter of Henry VI on 8 July 1426. In 1541 following the Dissolution it was valued at £6. In due course Tre-faes became part of the Nanteos estate and was let to tenants. By 1764 Tre-faes had been divided into two farms with Tre-faes Isaf occupied by Lewis David and Tre-faes Ucha by Edward Davies. The two farmsteads were located at what is now Tre-faes Isaf with an orchard dividing the two. Most of the land was made up of open fields, each of over 50 acres. A lease granted for three lives to Lewis Lewis in 1777 by the Nanteos estate stipulates 'to make and erect during the said term 30 perches of new mound properly planted with quickwood'. In 1760. Lewis Lewis, who was also a freeholder of Llethrmelin, Lledrod parish, married Mary, daughter of David Williams of Ty'n-wern, Llanrhystud and his wife Mary, daughter of Lewis Davies of Perthygwenyn. The Williams family, traced to Walter ap John, Lord of Ynys-wen, Carmarthenshire, who died in 1545, and includes among his descendants, Isaac Williams (1802-65) the Tractarian, who inspired the building of the church at Llangorwen and the Williams family of Cwmcynfelin. Jane Williams of Ty'n-wern married Thomas Jones of Brawdy, an ancestor of Francis Jones.

The Lewis Family of Tre-faes had connections with a young Methodist clergyman, Lewis Lewis, who died in 1764 aged 27 and who lived at Carrog, Llanddeiniol. He was the subject of elegies by Williams, Pantycelyn and Morgan Rhys. Lewis Lewis and his wife, Mary had three children. In 1793 the eldest, David, sold Llethrmelin, the family freeholding when he was living at Magpie Court, Aldersgate Street, London. His younger brother, Lewis, married Margaret, daughter of Humphrey Pugh of Pen-y-graig, Llanbadarn in 1790. Margaret's brother, Lewis Pugh, was the progenitor of the Pughs of Lovesgrove and later of Aber-mad, Llanychaearn. The Rev. John Lewis of Rhiw-goch who played a major role in the re-building of Llanrhystud church, was the eldest son of Lewis and Margaret Lewis. In 1826, he married Mary Anne Felix and their eldest son, Thomas, married Letitia Rogers in 1851 and from this union descend the Rogers Lewis of Abermeurig. In 1793 Mary Lewis of Tre-faes married Richard Philipps (1763-1831), reputed son of a Phillipps of Pentypark, Clarbeston Road. His elder brother, John, settled at Cefn-gwyn near Pennant and among his descendants was the Rev. D. I. Phillips Jones of Porthcawl, a notable preacher. Richard and Mary Phillips had four children. Ann married David Jenkins of Glangors, Llangwyryfon and Elizabeth married John Jones of Llwynddeiniol, Llanddeiniol parish. David (1810-1882), married twice and among his descendants is John Phillips James, a retired banker of Haverfordwest. John (1797-1860) the elder son, settled at Tre-faes Uchaf, built early in the 19th century at its present location and his brother, David, at Tre-faes Isaf when the Lewis family relinquished the tenancy in 1841. John Phillips was twice married. His second wife, Charlotte, (1814-1888) a strong character, read her bible nine times, each reading carefully recorded on the first page of Genesis in the family bible. Their son, Evan (1850-1928) a noted rower, was educated at Ystradmeurig and Jesus College, Oxford, and later farmed neighbouring Bryn-gwyn with his wife, Margaret (1867-1952), whose portion when they married in 1890, was £400. They had six children. Evan's brother, David (1848-94), was the father of Dr. Richard Phillips of Argoed, Llangwyryfon, a distinguished scientist and agriculturist whose expertise was utilised by successive governments in the promotion of farm husbandry. His sister Anne Jane, became the wife of T. Ifor Rees, son of the hymn writer, J. T Rees. The Phillipses lived at Tre-faes Uchaf until the 1970's, while Tre-faes Isaf is now owned by the Williams family.

Grid Ref: SN 6031 7331

Refs: Colby Map, 1831; *Ceredigion,* VII; NLW, Nanteos MSS., R45, Map 353; NLW, Phillips of Talybont, MSS.; NLW, Trefaes MSS.; NLW, Castle Hill MSS.; WWHR, iii; CASF, app. I, xiv.

TREFECHAN (THE LAWN),
St. Michael, Aberystwyth

Formerly located south of Aberystwyth across the Trefechan bridge and near the harbour. W. J. Lewis in *Born on a Perilous Rock* states, 'Around 1800, Trefechan was a hotch-potch of buildings of all kinds from the handsome 18th century structures of "The Green" and "The Lawn" to the narrow crowded little streets and courts . . . unfit for human habitation'.

The Wemyss family lived at The Lawn next door to David Roberts, the brewer. The family was originally from County Fife and a descendant, Col. James Wemyss of Southsea, Hampshire lost his right arm on board the *Bellerophon* at the Battle of Trafalgar. His eldest son Lieut.-General Thomas James Wemyss (1785-1860) was a distinguished officer who served in the 17th Regiment in the Peninsular War. He accompanied the Duke of Cambridge and commanded the Athlone District and was given a pension for wounds received. Thomas married Frances, only daughter and heiress of Herbert Pryse Ball of Lletherllestri, Carmarthenshire in 1819 and had four sons and five daughters. All four sons served in the military. David was an officer in the 78th Highlanders, Edward was of the 46th Regiment, Frederick of the 65th and Francis commanded the 3rd and 4th Battalions of the Duke of Wellington's West Riding Regiment until 1894. He was also one of HM Hon. Corps of Gentlemen-at-Arms. Of the daughters, Julia married Capt. T. R. Griffiths of Pantgwyn, Llangoedmor in 1861. The eldest son and heir, David Douglas Wemyss (1820-1889), married Harriet Letitia, daughter of George Murphy of Co. Louth and they had 13 children although five sons did not live beyond their teens. Following the death of their elder son, William Douglas, the second son, Walter Holmes, a lieutenant in the Derbyshire Regiment succeeded to Trefechan Green although it was his younger brother, John George Patrick Wemyss who remained in the area. He is described in 1891 as a 38-year-old innkeeper and jobmaster married to Maria Louisa with two infant daughters, Norah and Maria Louise and living at Trefechan. His mother, Harriet, his brother Frances, described as a Captain in the Mercantile Marine, and his sisters, Frances and Grace lived at Trefechan Green. The Green and The Lawn were later demolished to make way for the expansion of the Roberts Brewery and two fine 18th century houses were lost.

Grid Ref: SN 5826 8112

Refs: Colby Map, 1831; BLG 1898, ii, 1568; W. J. Lewis, *Built on a Perilous Rock.*

TREFILAN (CASTELL), Trefilan

Located in the hamlet of Trefilan opposite the church. Marked on *Colby's Map of 1831* and on modern OS maps as Castell Trefilan. A castle built by Maelgwn ap Rhys and completed by his son Maelgwn Fychan in 1233. In 1277-80 Trefilan was the seat of a *praepositus* on lands that had been given by Llewelyn Fawr during the wars against Edward I. Maelgwn Fychan was later imprisoned at Hereford. By 1277 the lands south of the Ystwyth were ruled by the brothers Gruffydd and Cynon ap Maredudd with the aid of their nephew, Owain. In 1672 John Evans of Trefilan, gent, paid tax on three hearths.

Grid Ref: SN 5488 5724

Refs: Colby Map, 1831; B of T, p. 323; *Arch. Cambs.,* p. 81 (1233-4); *Trans Cym,* 1895-6, 92, 95-6, 105-7, 131-2, 136; THSC.

TREFORGAN, Llangoedmor

A substantial mansion marked on *Colby's Map of 1831* and on modern OS maps off the old B4570 road two miles east of Cardigan and near St. Cynllo's well, which is said to have healing properties. This attractive mansion was built early in the 19th century.

At the beginning of the 18th century Lewis Turnor of Crug-mawr married Maud John of Treforgan who had inherited one-third of the estate by the will of her father. Another daughter had married David Bowen who is recorded as a freeholder of Treforgan in 1760.

Evan Davies of Cardigan, attorney, was builder of the present mansion of Treforgan at the beginning of the 19th century. He married Margaret, daughter of Archdeacon Benjamin Millingchamp, who had made his fortune in India, by Ann Gambold, grand-daughter of the publisher William Gambold. (See Plâs Llangoedmor.) Evan Davies died in 1832 and his wife on 11 December 1837. They had two daughters, Anne Eliza who married Thomas Lewis Lloyd of Nantgwyllt near Rhaeadr and Wern Newydd, Llanarth, and Jane Catherine, who is given as of Treforgan in 1832. Thomas Lewis Lloyd and his wife spent their winters at Treforgan. Whilst Anne travelled the sixty miles in a travelling-coach, her husband would ride from early morning utilising all known short-cuts and arrive at Treforgan late at night. For twenty years Maria Webley-Parry, formerly of Neuadd Trefawr, rented and lived at Treforgan in preference to Parc-y-gors, the dower-house of Neuadd.

A photograph in *The Tivyside Photographic Souvenir*, taken between 1860-70 shows a pleasing, square type of house, probably 18th century with two storeys, a pillared entrance, doorway with decorated fanlight. On one side is a wing of two storeys which is probably older than the main block.

Treforgan was later the home of Archdeacon William North, rector of Llan-goedmor (one time Professor of Latin at St. Davids, Lampeter) who died in 1893 at a great age. 'His household was conducted on very primitive lines. He farmed and his ancient clumsy cart-horses were used to draw the heavy chariot wherein he made his official visitations. . . . he also had a curious short-horn bull coloured purple and pink. It was said that he could write poetry in seven languages. He translated some Welsh poetry for the benefit of Carmen Sylva, Queen of Romania, when that literary potentate once attended the National Eisteddfod. Archdeacon North preached and conducted services in Welsh and English and his bi-lingual services were always at least two hours in length.

In *County Families* Nicholas tells us that Treforgan was the property of Evan Davies's great-grandson, Colonel Herbert Lloyd. In Llangoedmor church is a memorial to Col. George Evan Lloyd, CB, DSO, Duke of Wellington's West Riding Regiment, of Treforgan, who was killed at Rhenoster kop, Transvaal on 20 November 1900. He was the son of the Rev. Prebendary J. Rhys Lloyd RD, born at Bronwydd, rector of Troed-yr-aur and grandson of Thomas Lloyd of Nantgwyllt, a connection of Llangoedmor through his mother.

By 1901, Treforgan had become the home of Col. W. R. Picton Evans, formerly of the Priory, Cardigan, a well-known public servant in Cardiganshire, whose daughter, Cecil Elizabeth married Lieut. G. H. Finzel in Cape Town, South Africa in 1903. In 1912 it was owned by John Griffiths, formerly of Pantgwyn and in 1925, Brimley Jones and his daughter lived at Treforgan.

In 1994 Treforgan became the home of Mr. and Mrs. D. Shamtally. They have restored both the house and the surrounds, which includes a beautiful formal walled garden.

Grid Ref: SN 2012 4608

Refs: Colby Map, 1831; WWHR, iii, 78 & v, 112; Lewis *TDW*, 1840; *The Tivyside Photographic Souvenir Pen-y-Lan*, C. Allen, Tenby, 1871, in possession of Miss G. Taylor, 1975; Nicholas, *County Families*, i, 203; G. E. Evans, *Cardiganshire*, 1903, 266; NLW, Morgan Richardson, iii, 315; H. M. Vaughan, *South Wales Squires*, 1926, pp. 119-122.

TRE-GYBI (TYR Y GIBY, TIR GIGY, TREGIBY, TIR GIGY), St. Mary's, Cardigan

Now a farmhouse on the outskirts of Cardigan north of the road to Gwbert and marked on *Colby's Map of 1831*. Gilbert de Clare, the Norman Lord, was responsible for the founding of the Benedictine Priory at Cardigan. In 1165 Rhys ap Gruffydd confirmed the gift and its holdings included two carucates (240 acres) of land on the north side of the road towards Blaen-porth. Tyr y gyby was part of that gift. An early reference to Tyr y gybi is the marriage in 1490 of Joan, second daughter of William Warren of Cardigan, to Philip Richard of 'Tyr y gyby', son of Marion Gyby, a daughter of John Gyby from Anglesey.

Following the Dissolution, the Priory estate including Tyr y gyby passed to various owners who let the lands to tenants. Tyr y gyby became the seat of the Philipps's, later of the Priory, who were descended from Cadifor Fawr, Lord of Blaen-cuch. Early records note in December 1591 the assignment of a lease of a tenement called 'Terr u gybby' in the parish of Cardigan for the duration of the life of George Philipps of Cardigan town, gent. and James Lewis of Abernantbychan, Esq., at an annual rent of £3.6.8. George Philipps was the son of Einion Philipps, grandson of Thomas ap Philip of Cilsant, Llanwinio, later of Picton Castle, and Elizabeth Birt. George was High Sheriff in 1606.

On 28 June 1616, King James I by Letters Patent granted to George Philipps Esq. and his heirs for ever, the late Priory of Cardigan and the rectories and churches of 'Verwicke and Tremeyne' which had been exchanged by Sir William Cavendish, Kt., with King Edward. George had two sons, Hector, and James of 'Trigibby', Esq. an armiger (holder of arms), who donated two maces to the town of Cardigan in 1647. He was High Sheriff in 1649 and married Catherine Fowler (1631-64), who was known as 'Matchless Orinda', a daughter of a London merchant and one of the foremost poets of her age. She died at the age of 33 of the smallpox. The brothers were staunch Parliamentarians.

In 1643, James is described in the *Noyadd Trefawr Deeds* as 'son and heir of Hector Philipps late of Tir y Gibby'. Both James (1594-1675) and Hector, who died in 1693 represented Cardigan Boroughs and the county at Westminster. They were both active during the Civil War and are said to have sequestrated estates of royalists with excessive zeal. The brothers were also Commissioners for securing the place in 1655. Hector inherited the lands of his brother, James, but as he and his wife had an only daughter, the estate went to the Pryses of Gogerddan in 1744 who sold it to Thomas Johnes of Hafod Uchdryd. In 1760, Tir y Gibby was occupied by a tenant, Abel John, who also owned freeholds in Cardigan. In 1803 the trustees of the Priory estate which included the 'Mansion house called Tregibby, alias Gibby,' and exstensive holdings in Cardiganshire, gave instructions to sell the estate to discharge the debts of Thomas Johnes (see The Priory, Cardigan).

The farm was owned in 1890 by Dan Evans and the present occupiers are the Wilson family, exhibitors of Holstein cattle.

Grid Ref: SN 1825 4738

Refs: Colby Map, 1831; NLW, George Owen List (iv); Blome List, 1673; Meyrick, *Cardiganshire,* 206; WWHR, I, 14-15; PRO, Dale Castle MS., p. 22 (90); NLW, Crosswood Deeds, p. 298; NLW, GG & W, No. 1279; Deri Ormond Deeds No. 146-7. NLW, Noyadd Trefawr Deeds, Nos. 12, 14, 15, 34.

TRE-MAIN (Tremaen), Tremain

Situated three miles from Cardigan, the reference is for the parish church. The location of the house is unknown but the hamlet of Tremain is near the main A487 (T) road towards Blaenanerch and is marked on the 14th century *Rees Map.* Tre-prior and Tre Wtial are nearby.

In 1670/1 Mathew Griffith sued Thomas Phillipps of Tremayne, gent., 'for unjustly detaining cattle which were the property of the plaintiff'. In the same year Thomas Phillipps was taxed for three hearths and Gwenllian Phillipps for two hearths. Thomas had a son Phillip Thomas Phillip of Tremain and a daughter who married Evan ap Philip ap Meredydd. Phillip's daughter married Thomas Phillip of Gellifraith.

Grid Ref: SN 2368 4863

Refs: Dwnn, i, 33; PRO, Dale Castle MS., p. 25; Rees Map, 14th Century; NLW, Cards. GS 22 Charles II; Protheroe, C, IV; CRO, GGMS, I (Urien), 27-31; CRO, GGMS, I (Gwynfardd), p. 3.

TRE-PRIOR, Tremain

Located north of the main A487(T) road between Penparc and Tremain. The ancient occasional residence of the Benedictine Prior of Cardigan, situated north-west of Tremaen church and marked on *Colby's Map of 1831.*

Grid Ref: SN 2306 4880

Refs: Colby Map, 1831; Lewis, *TDW.*

TRE-WEN, Blaen-porth

Marked on *Colby's Map of 1831* as north of Blaen-porth parish church but not marked or named on modern OS maps. In 1760 the Rev. John Thomas, clerk of Tre-wen, was rector of the parish and kept a school at Llechryd. His son, the Rev. Thomas Thomas, later rector of Aberporth, was also born at Tre-wen but when he was nine years old the family removed to Henbant, Llandygwydd. He became curate to his father having been ordained at Gloucester. He later lived at Rhiwfelin, Aberporth. In 1816 he edited *Memoirs of Owen Glyndwr*. His literary notes on the genealogy of Welsh families were highly valued and he gave help to Carlisle and Lewis to produce their *Topographical Dictionaries*. He died in 1847, aged 81.

Grid Ref: SN 2670 4973

Refs: Colby Map, 1831; WWHR, III, 80, 1760; Horsfall-Turner, *Wanderings*; B. Williams, Enwogion, *Ceredigion,* pp. 231-2.

TREWIN(D)SOR, Llangoedmor

Situated in woodland south-east of Penparc and marked on *Colby's Map of 1831* as Trewinsor. Now known as Trewindsor.

The first recorded reference to this property is in 1613 when Lewis ap Rhys ap Meredudd married Isabel, the daughter of Thomas Llewelyn Owain of Tre-main. Their son, Philip ap Lewys ap Rhys ap Meredudd was of Trewynsor and signed his pedigree for the herald Dwnn. On 16 January 1689/90, Thomas Philipps of Trewinsor, parish of Llangoedmor, gent., granted to Thomas David of same parish, gent., and Thomas Philipps of Rhosygader in the parish of Aberporth, 'three closes of land and a house and parcel of land in Llangoedmor on trust (as to one of the closes) for grantor for life, remainder to his second son Jenkin Philipps of Trewinsor for life and his issue, with similar remainders to James Philipps the younger son of the said grantor'.

Jenkin Philipps was living at Trewinsor in 1728 with his wife Bridget and their eldest son Thomas Philipps. In 1760 David Philipps, Esq. described as of Cardigan owned Trewinsor. He was a JP in 1758. John Vaughan was of Trewinsor and was High Sheriff of Cardiganshire in 1788.

Trewinsor, at one time a holding of nearly 200 acres, was sold in 1913 to John and Elizabeth James, grandparents of Wil James, one-time owner of shire-horses and collector of iron ploughs, one of ten children born to David Thomas and Anne James.

In 1990, Wil James sold the farmhouse and 56 acres to Mr. and Mrs. David Lloyd Owen who are developing an equestrian centre at Trewindsor. The remaining 100 acres are let to neighbouring farmers.

Grid Ref: SN 2250 4720

Refs: Colby Map, 1831; *Dwnn,* i, 31, 33 (1613); NLW, Crosswood Deeds, pp. 159, 125; WWHR, III, 78; CRO, GGMS, I (Tydwal Gloff); Wil. James.

TREFWTIAL-FAWR, Tremain

Located south of Tremain on the banks of the Arberth. The messuage of 'Trevuttiall in Penbryn parish' was part of the Lewes of Abernantbychan estate and occupied by Evan David ap Rees who paid an annual rent of £2.10.0. Lewis tells us in *TDW* that it was the residence of a Miss Vaughan in 1840.

Grid Ref: SN 2371 4799

Refs: Colby Map, 1831; Lewis, *TDW.*

TROEDRHIWPENYD (TROEDRHIWFFENYD), Llandysul

Marked as Troed-rhiw-ffyned on *Colby's Map of 1831* and located on modern maps west of Pentre-llwyn towards Gorrig. The name takes us back to the catholic Middle Ages when it gave its name to an old track (foot of the Hill of Penance). The earliest recorded owner is Eleanor Thomas, widow. In her will, dated 17 September 1684, with a codicil added 18 September 1684, she left 'Cwm Hwplin otherwise Tyr Cwm Hwplin and Troedrhiwver in Llanfihangel ar arth, Carms. to Edward Price, eldest son of Evan Price of Llandysul parish and Mary his wife, grand-daughter of testator on condition he pays £100 to Richard Price, his brother'.

According to the CRO *Aberglasney Deeds,* Thomas Davies, gent., was living at Troedrhiwpenyd in 1709 having married Sarah Pryse, daughter of Evan Pryse, attorney of Rhydybenne. The marriage was the subject of a post-nuptial settlement agreed on 4 October 1709 and included the capital messuage and land called 'Tir Troedrhiwffenyd, messuages and land called Tir Dan y Coed, Tir y Pantygwyn and Tir y Darren fach, all in the parish of Llandysul. Messuages and land called

Tir yr hafod wnnog in Llandysiliogogo, Rhiwson and Baili Bedw in Llanwenog parish and Blaen Shedio in the parish of Llangeler'. In 1727 their daughter Mary married Daniel Bowen, youngest son of Waunifor was High Sheriff in 1740. They had four children: Thomas, an infant in 1739 and alive in 1768; John, who married Margaret, the daughter of Thomas Thomas of Maesycrugiau, Sina and Mary, who died unmarried.

It appears that the family had ceased to hold the property by 1750 for the *Carmarthenshire Deeds* tell us that Ellis Jones and Anne his wife 'were of Troedrhiwffenyd' in 1750 when they entered into an agreement for 'the release of all claims of John Evan and his wife Elinor, of Cilyblaidd'. By 1760 Troedrhiwpenyd was owned by Thomas Davies of Cilyblaidd. In 1761 Mary Davies of Troedrhiwpenyd gave a receipt to her uncle, Walter Jones, for £40 left to her under the terms of her grandfather's will. She was either the wife or the mother of David Davies who succeeded his father. David Davies died intestate in 1780. His widow, Bridget, was still of 'Troedrhiwfennyd' in June 1786 and her will was dated 8 February 1787. The Troedrhiwpenyd estate in the parishes of Llandysul, Llanwenog and Llandysiliogogo, was then partitioned between the co-heiresses, Gwenllian and Mary. Gwenllian married William Williams of Blaendyffryn, surgeon, in 1781 and Mary, married firstly James Lewis and secondly John Beynon of Newcastle Emlyn. William and Gwenllian Williams held Troedrhiwpenyd until their deaths, when the property reverted to Gwenllian's sister Mary, and her husband James Lewes, who was living at Troedrhiwpenyd when he wrote his will on 5 January 1792. He died soon afterwards as Mary was described as a widow on 21 November 1793 when the prenuptial settlement of Mary and her second husband John Beynon of Carmarthen, gent. was dated. John was a nephew of Anne Thomas of Llwynderw and under-Sheriff of the county when civil disturbances broke out due to food shortages and land enclosures. The *Llandysul Tithe Map of 1841* states that in that year Troedrhiwpenyd, then 85 acres, was owned by John Beynon and tenanted by Samuel Griffiths. John Beynon's will tells us that, apart from Troedrhiwpenyd, he owned land in Pantywyn, Llynddur, Dancoed Fach, Llain and Darrenfach. Mary Beynon's will dated 25 August 1795 states that the property was mortgaged and by 1845 had passed to Margaret Nicholl of Carmarthen. It became the property of Margaretta Bowen Davies, whose marriage to David Fryer Nicholl was the subject of a pre-nuptial agreement on 17 April 1838. In 1854 the estate was held by Walter Owen Price when Margaretta Bowen Nicholl died.

Grid Ref: SN 4094 4252

Refs: Colby Map, 1831; CRO, Aberglasney Collection; Carmarthenshire Deeds in Pembrokeshire RO; Llandysul Tithe Map, 1841.

TROEDYRAUR PLÂS,
Troed-yr-aur (Trefdoyr)

Located east of Beulah, north of the minor road towards Brongest and marked on *Colby's Map of 1831.* Called Y Plâs by local inhabitants. In *Cardiganshire*, Evans tells us 'The ancient name of Troed-yr-aur village was Llanfihangel Tref Deyrn – St. Michael of the Tref of the king or prince. According to tradition Owen ap Hywel Dda lived in this vale, on the banks of the river Ceri. In a field called Llys-wen on Cefn Maes-Mawr farm are some grass-coloured twmps: on the land of Dol-goch is a cottage called Cwrtygamil where Owen is said to have had a barracks for his soldiers and the bodies of these soldiers are said to have been buried in another field on Dol-goch land'. The house is situated about two miles west of the parish church, near Plâs Newydd and Crug Mawr remains, and is described by Carlisle as 'a beautiful seat and a spacious mansion'.

The first known occupier was Sion or John Bowen whose grandfather took the name Bowen from ab Owen. John Bowen is described as of Glynllebyng, the original name of the Plâs. He was a local bard and a collector of *halsingod*, simple religious poetry. He had a son, William, who married Rebecca, eldest daughter and co-heiress of Mr. Willy of Whitehouse. William was a JP in 1748 and served the office of High Sheriff for the county in 1755. They had three sons and four daughters. William's four daughters, Mary Anne, Rebecca, Hester and Elizabeth all remained unmarried.

Rebecca and Hester Bowen erected a memorial to their mother, Rebecca, who died in October 1791 aged 80 years, at Troed-yr-aur parish church. The eldest son, Thomas, inherited Troedyraur. The second son, John, became a barrister and married twice; firstly to Mary, youngest daughter of David Lloyd Morgan of Cardigan, secondly to Miss Hughes, heiress of Aberllolwyn, Llanychaearn. William, a doctor in Bath, married Miss Boycott of Shropshire, a sister of the Countess of Guildford. He died without issue.

The Rev. Thomas Bowen was born on 25 January 1757 and succeeded his mother at Troedyraur in 1793. He was rector of the parish church, a JP and Deputy Lieutenant of the county. He was married twice; firstly in 1792 to Sarah Malvina Vaulker of Hampton, Middlesex, and secondly, in 1802, he married Frances Norton also of Hampton. The marriage was the subject of a pre-nuptial settlement agreed on 18 June 1802. Thomas settled Glanllebyn, Blaen Pentrefi, Tir y Pant y Maer and Tir y Brundy in the parishes of Troed-yr-aur and Betws, Carmarthenshire. Frances settled a moiety of lands in Hatton, parish East Bedfont, Middlesex and sums of £2,000 and £3,600. In 1831, Thomas built a school for about 70 pupils and among its many grateful pupils was Benjamin Williams (*Gwynionydd)*. Lewis tells us in *TDW* that the Rev. Thomas Bowen 'has distinguished himself as an enlightened and successful agriculturist'. Meyrick adds that 'the seat of Rev. Thomas Bowen, a celebrated agriculturist and brother of John Bowen, Esq., of Cardigan Castle, is situated in a very pleasant vale'. The family bore the arms – *gules* a lion rampant regardant *or* crest: a nag's head bridled.

Under the terms of his will, Thomas Bowen was succeeded by James Bowen, second son of James Bowen of Llwyngwair. He was born in 1806 and became a JP, and a Deputy-Lieutenant of the county. In 1827 he married Dorothea, daughter of Richard David Griffith, vicar of Nevern. They had a son, William Rice Bowen, and three other children. A quiet, unassuming man, William rode out with the Tivyside Hunt and was a prominent breeder of cattle and horses. He also suffered a great deal from gout. He was High Sheriff in 1848 and

died in October 1872. The *Landowners Return of 1873* tells us that Dorothea Bowen of Troed-yr-aur held 1,022 acres, yielding £450 p.a.

The Tivyside Photographic Souvenir published two photographs of Plâs Troedyraur taken between 1860-71, one showing a large square house of admirable proportions, probably 18th century, with a 19th century veranda along one side and the other of a family group outside on the veranda.

Francis Jones visited Plâs Troedyraur in company with Major Lloyd-Johnes and the Rev. Towyn Jones on 17 October 1977 when the owner-occupier was D. A. Davies. The house was of two-storeys and on different levels, with large cellars and a walled garden. Francis Jones noted that on two of the fine, old outbuildings were tablets, one inscribed JBM 1734 and the other JBM 1737.

Grid Ref: SN 2980 4614

Refs: Colby Map, 1831; Carlisle, 1811; Lewis, *TDW*, 1840; C. Allen Smith, *The Tivyside Photographic Souvenir, Pen-y-Lan,* (Album in possession of Miss Gwynedd Taylor, Manorbier), 1975; Nicholas, *County Families,* i, 191; Meyrick, *Cardiganshire,* p. 204; B. Williams (Gwynionydd); *Hanes Casnewydd-Emlyn,* p. 58; BLG 1850; NLW, Morgan Richardson Deeds, No. 2074; Landowners Return, 1873; Evans, *Cardiganshire,* 1903, p. 269.

TROED-Y-RHIW, Llandyfriog

Marked but not named on modern OS maps, *Colby's Map of 1831* gives the location as across the valley from Bronwydd, north of Aber-banc. Thomas Bowen of Bwlchbychan in Llanwenog whose will was proved in 1716 had a son John, who married Jane, daughter of John Lewis of Troedyrhiw, Esq., formerly of Gernos. John was also the administrator to his brother,

Daniel, in 1713. He was John Lewis, the elder, and had two sons, John the younger, and the Rev. Erasmus Lewes of Lampeter, who died in 1745. John Lewes, the younger, of Gernos, married Margaret and had at least five children; Daniel Lewes of Gernos, the son and heir apparent in 1713, who married Lucy, daughter of Edward Jones of Llanina. The marriage was the subject of a pre-nuptial settlement on 1/2 April 1713. The second son, John Lewes of Gernos, viv. 1713, who had a son and heir apparent, David Lewes. Mary, the eldest daughter, married R. Morris of Carrog; they had a son John Morris of Carrog, Esq., in 1745. Margaret, who married Thomas Parry of Cwm Cynon, gent. Their son John married Heather Howells of Penybeili and had a son Llewellin Parry, later of Gernos.The youngest daughter, Elizabeth, married twice; firstly to John Phillipps who died in 1718, secondly to Lewis Lloyd of Gernos. By her second marriage Elizabeth had a son John Phillipps of Llwyn-on who died in 1762, and daughters Margaret, Elizabeth, Mary, and Sarah, who married Thomas Thomas of Maesycrugiau. They had a daughter, Margaret, who was also married twice; firstly to Thomas Bowen and secondly to the Rev. D. Williams of Maesycrugiau. They had a son, Thomas Bowen.

Grid Ref: SN 3500 4278

Refs: WWHR, I, 50; BL Bodleian MSS., Add C. 177-9; NLW, Morgan Richardson Deeds, i, 169 and 2697; Colby Map, 1831.

TROED-Y-RHIW (TAN-RHIW), Llanwenog

May be the house marked on modern OS maps as Tan-rhiw, located south of Brynllefrith on the banks of the Cledlyn. There is a tablet in the parish church to Elizabeth, wife of David Rice Thomas known as *'Yr hen Scweier Rice', Troedyrhiw, Cwrtnewydd'*. David Rice Thomas's grandson, the late A. R. T. Jones Esq., JP of Rhyd-y-fran, Cribyn is remembered by a lych-gate which was erected by his widow and son in 1935.

Grid Ref: SN 4880 4720

Refs: D. R. & Z. S. Davies, *Hanes Plwyf Llanwenog*, 1939, p. 39.

TYDDYN CAWRENS

see Cawrence (Carwens)

TYGLYN, Llanddewi Aberarth

Not to be confused with its neighbour Tyglyn Aeron, Tyglyn is located on the banks of the Aeron, a short mile from Ciliau Aeron immediately to the west of the minor road to Pennant. Marked on *Emanuel Bowen's Map,* c. 1760 and on *Colby's Map of 1831.* The first occupier of Tyglyn may have been Thomas ap Rhys, Cantor of Llandewibrefi, a cousin to Sir Rhys ap Thomas, Lord of Cilcennin, who owned the present Tyglyn Aeron and other properties in the area and it is thought Tyglyn itself. Rhys ap Cantor lived at Tyglyn in 1548 and was a lessee of Bronwenan, formerly a grange of Strata Florida Abbey. His son, Gruffydd, was charged in 1583 of making a false claim to a tenement with forty acres in Cilcennin, probably the New Mill, now part of Tyglyn Aeron. Gruffydd was succeeded by his son, David, who in 1583 mortgaged Tyglyn-uchaf, which included the present Ty'nffynnon with Blaenerddig, Cipyll-coch and Coed-gleision for £42 to Rhydderch ap Morgan Fychan. In 1619 he sold the properties to John Stedman of Plâs Cilcennin for £67. It remained part of the Trawsgoed estate until 1876 when it reverted to Tyglyn. In 1628 and deeply in debt, David Griffith sold Tyglyn to Llewelyn Thomas Parry, who built his mansion house at Tyglyn-isaf. Parry, whose mother, Dyddgu, was the heiress of Noyadd Trefawr, married Joan David of Clydau parish and having no issue, he left Tyglyn-isaf to his half-brother, John Parry of Tredefaid, Llantood. John, a full brother to Llewelyn, lived at Pentre, Maenordeifi and his second son, Llewllyn settled at Llanuwchaeron (Llanerchaeron). John Parry married Jane, daughter of Griffith David of Llanarth and their second daughter, Joan, who married Rhys Jones, succeeded to the estate. When he died in 1647, Rhys's personal property, valued at £288 included over 200 head of cattle, 14 horses and over 500 sheep. His will made provision for Elizabeth, his eldest daughter, by charging £500 on the Tyglyn property. Joan's second husband was the Rev. David James (1615-1682), a cousin of Rhys, her first husband. Her brother Henry, only son of Rhys Jones inherited the property when he was a young man. He married Mary, daughter of Hugh Lloyd of Lloyd Jack and was assessed at 6 hearths. In 1675 he disposed of a part of Tyglyn to William Hughes, a lawyer and a pupil of Henry Vaughan of Plâs Cilcennin. Hughes lived at Tyglyn until his death in 1712. John, the son of Henry Jones, married Bridget, daughter of David Parry of Noyadd Trefawr. They had seven children: five boys and two girls. John Jones (1696-1756), the eldest son married Mary, daughter of Dr. Morrice of Carrog, Llanddeinol and widow of William Hughes whose uncle, also William was the lawyer who died at Tyglyn. John and Mary lived for some time at Plâs Cilcennin and their son Henry (1721-1794) succeeded. Henry was educated at St. John's, Oxford and was High Sheriff of Cardiganshire in 1780. He married Jane Susanna (1718-1787) daughter of William Parry of Nevern and Plâs Newydd, St. Dogmaels. In his will, dated 1793, and proved in 1801 he wrote, 'Having laboured in my early life under various difficulties and incumbrances, I felt it my duty by the strictest care and economy to lighten those burdens as far as was consistent with necessary expenses (which some might have contributed to covetousness) . . . should my daughter die unmarried, I would not have the small estate sold or frittered away after her decease, or left to anybody who would be above residing upon it'. He left Tyglyn to his daughter, Susannah, and then to her issue, with remainder to his nephew, John Jones 'now at Eaton School', and then to the eldest son of David John Edwardes, with remainder to the Rev. Alban Thomas of Hampshire. In the event, Susannah, sole heiress married the aforementioned, Alban Thomas in 1797. Alban Thomas added Jones to his name and in 1805, following the death of their cousin, Lewis Gwynn of Mynachty, the couple inherited a life interest in the Mynachty estate as well as a fortune estimated to total £150,000 in gold and securities. Alban Thomas Jones (and under the terms of the Lewis's will), he took the additional surname Gwynn, obtained a private Act of Parliament and built the harbour and much of the framework of the present Aberaeron. When Alban died in 1819, Susannah, was allowed to

set aside the remaindermen under the terms of her father's will which stated 'my will for having the house and farm occupied is for the sake of improving the neighbourhood . . . In case that either of my remaindermen should ill-treat (my daughter) or should be likely to turn out an immoral man, she may . . . set aside such an one by her own will and testament, that my intention of doing good in the district should not be defeated'. Susannah left Tyglyn to Alban Thomas Davies (1803-1860), son of the Rev. Thomas Davies and Martha, a daughter of Martha Acton, the first wife of Alban Thomas Jones Gwynn.

The new owner of Tyglyn was a captain in the Hon. East India Company Service. He married Ann Wilson, the daughter of a colonel and their son, another Alban Thomas (1829-1870), was High Sheriff in 1868 but died without issue. He was succeeded by his brother, William John Davies, born in 1832, who returned from Australia with his wife, Florence Gadsby in 1873, to live at Tyglyn. They disposed of outlying parts of the estate. Their son, Francis Gadsby Davies was a major in the Suffolk Regiment and on his death, Tyglyn and the surrounding farms were inherited by his nephew, Reginald Davies, who was the owner in the late 1950's.

Grid Ref: SN 4989 5995

Refs: Meyrick, *Cardiganshire,* 1810, edn. 1907, p. 263; Landowners Return, 1873; NLW, Tyglyn Documents, No. 97; Emanuel Bowen, Map of South Wales; Turner, *Cardiganshire,* 110; Protheroe MS.; *Ceredigion,* viii, 2, pp. 224-36; British Library; Horsfall-Turner, *Wanderings,* p. 140;

TYGLYN AERON, Cilcennin

Located on the banks of the Aeron east of the minor road leading from Ciliau Aeron towards Pennant and marked on *Colby's Map of 1831* and on modern OS maps.

Known as Tyglyn Uchaf in the 18th century it included New Mill and Pantycnycau. The house has a long history. Sir Rhys ap Thomas, KG (1449-1525), Lord of the manor of Cilcennin inherited New Mill from his mother, Elizabeth, it formerly stood in the fields in front of Tyglyn Aeron. His grandson, Sir Rhys ap Gruffyd was betrayed by his brother-in-law, and the property reverted to the Crown who leased it to various individuals including Gruffydd Rhys (1530-1584), son of Rhys ap Gruffydd, whose cousin Gruffydd ap Rhys Cantor was the tenant of New Mill. In 1609 the Crown sold it to Salter and Williams, who in turn sold it to two London merchants, Bowyer and Cordell with David ap Gruffydd ap Rhys Cantor, the tenant of Tyglyn and Lewis ab Hugh occupying Plâs Ciliau Aeron. In 1625, both properties were sold to Llewelyn Thomas Parry, the fifth son of Thomas Parry of St. Dogmael's, who built a house at Tyglyn Aeron in 1620. Llewelyn's will was proved in 1635 and as he and his wife were childless, the property passed to his half-brother John Parry of Trede-faid, Llantood. Through the second marriage of John's daughter, Joan, to the Rev. David James, MA (Oxon.), Tyglyn Aeron passed to the James family of Pengwern, Cenarth. The Rev. David James, Rector of Cilrhedyn was succeeded by his son, Mathew, who lived at Cilfachau, Llanrhystud, and built Melin Tyglyn to replace the dilapidated New Mill. His son, David, married Ursula, daughter of John Lewis of Manorafon.

It was David James who built the first Tyglyn-uchaf between the present Tyglyn Lodge and Pont Newydd. He was High Sheriff in 1734 and was succeeded by his son, John (1711-1750), who married Elizabeth Lewis of Llwyngrawys. John died without issue and left Tyglyn-uchaf to his cousin, John Jones (1696-1756), High Sheriff in 1728. He was succeeded by his son, Henry (1721-1794) who died without issue. The estate then reverted to the James family in the person of John James, a merchant of Aberystwyth who married Anne, daughter of David Jenkins of Presteigne. Their daughter, Bridget, incurred the displeasure of her parents by marrying their groom and later, agent, David Rees of Clunglas, Cribyn. The newly-weds lived at Bontnewydd and had a large family and one of their descendants was the distinguished Timothy Rees, later Bishop of Llandaff. John James was followed by his eldest son, David, who married Mary, only daughter of Josiah Kinsley of Presteigne. David sold Tyglyn-uchaf to Alban Thomas Jones Gwynne (1751-1819), who re-named the house Tyglyn Aeron. His widow Susannah, finding the estate heavily encumbered, placed it in Chancery, by whose order it was sold by auction in 1824. The demesne only was bought for £4,099, by Thomas Winwood (1784-1838), a Bristol businessman whose fortune came from canal and railway enterprises. It was Thomas Winwood who built Tyglyn Aeron on its present site in 1825. The Winwood family had a grand seat at Willingford Manor, Somerset and a nephew, Thomas Henry Ricketts Winwood, MA, JP, born in 1852, sold Tyglyn Aeron in the 1880's to Price Lewes (1840-1911), a major in the Royal Artillery and the youngest son of Capt. John Lewes of Llanllyr. He married Florence Kinnear of Nova Scotia. In 1930 their son Col. Price Kinnear Lewes CMG, DSO, sold Tyglyn Aeron to Geoffrey Faber, a member of the distinguished London publishing house. The house was described in the Sale Catalogue comprising of: 'Ground floor – entrance hall with galleried staircase and parquet floor, drawing room, study, dining room, morning room, kitchen, scullery, larder, pantry, servant's hall, cloakroom and outside yard leading to dairy, larder, w.c. and workshop. On the first floor – approached by principal and secondary staircases, 11 bedrooms and dressing rooms, and two servants' bedrooms, and bathroom. Outbuildings included garage, stable, coach house, laundry, store and groom's room and a gardener's cottage called Glynaeron, a walled garden, greenhouses, vinery, tennis lawn. The grounds and demesne at this time amounted to 26 acres.' Tyglyn Aeron changed hands a further three times until bought by G. K. Wilton-Clark in the 1950's.

During the 1960's Tyglyn Aeron was converted into a nine bedroomed licensed country club with swimming pool as well as 20 chalets by Mr. J. Lynne and his wife. In June 1976 Tyglyn Aeron was again for sale.

In 1986 Lieut.-Col. J. J. Davies owned Tyglyn and with his wife wanted to develop the property for use as a holiday complex for the disabled, but failed to receive public grants. Tyglyn Aeron is now an hotel.

Grid Ref: SN 5024 5975

Refs: Colby Map, 1831; Nicholas, *County Families* (1872) & 1875 edn.; *Ceredigion,* vol. v, No. 1, 1964, & vol. iv, No. 2, p. 192; *BLG,* 1898, ii, 1617; *Dwnn,* i, 16; Lewis, *TDW,* 1840.

TY-LLWYD, Blaen-porth

Built in woodland about a mile south of Tan-y-groes off the minor road to Beulah and marked on the *Kitchin Map of 1754* and *Colby's Map of 1831.*

The seat of John Vaughan, Esq. the only surviving son of Edward Vaughan of Greengrove, the natural son of Dorothy, Countess of Lisburne. He bought it from John Bowen, Esq., of the Castle Green, Cardigan, attorney-at-law, who had purchased it from a freeholder. John Vaughan (1764-1845) married Jane (1765-1849), eldest daughter of Herbert Evans of Highmead at Llanwenog in 1788. Under the terms of the will of his great-uncle, David Lloyd of Brynog, John Vaughan took the additional name of Lloyd. John Vaughan Lloyd of Ty-llwyd served as High Sheriff for the county in 1821 and was a captain in the 47th Regiment. In *TDW,* Lewis describes Ty-llwyd, the property of John Vaughan Lloyd as 'having a chalybeate spring, the water of which is, however, but seldom used'.

Mary Ann Vaughan Lloyd, eldest daughter of John and Jane, married John Lewes, the younger son of Llanllyr. The pre-nuptial settlement was agreed on 5 May 1826. The *Llanllyr Deeds* record that on 24 May 1826 'Mary Anne Jane Vaughan of Tyllwyd, Cardiganshire, daughter of John Vaughan Lloyd of ditto, Esq. agreed with Price Lewes of Llysnewydd, Carmarthenshire, Esq. and Captain Edward Vaughan of the 98th Foot to a lease of possession of the remainder or reversion expectant upon the decease or other determination of the

estate of the said John Vaughan Lloyd in one fifth part of a messuage called Tyllwyd otherwise Tyrllwyd and in a messuage and land called Llainallt in the parishes of Blaenporth and Bettws Evan, a messuage called Bronyar otherwise Bronyarfawr in the parish of Blaen-porth; also the remainder or reversion expectant on death of said John Vaughan Lloyd and Jane his wife, in one-fifth of a moiety of the rectory, prebend church or chantry of Blaenporth'.

Mary Anne and John lived at Ty-llwyd until it was bought by Charles Arthur Prichard, who was married to Dorothea, Mary Anne's younger sister. In 1857 his only child, Dorothea Anne, born at Brynog in 1835 and grand-daughter of Colonel Vaughan, married Sidney Henry Jones-Parry, JP, High Sheriff in 1871, and a captain in the Madras Fusiliers, the son of Captain Jones-Parry RN of Llwyn-onn Hall, Wrexham. They had four children, two sons, Charles Arthur and Sidney Jones-Parry and four daughters. Dorothy, the eldest, who married Henry Fryer, Beata who married Henry Wood,

Mina and Blanche. A photograph published at this time in *South Wales* by Charles Smith Allen shows a two-storey house with an upper range of five windows. Dorothea Anne, the widow of S. H. Jones-Parry died on 30 January 1925 aged 96. Her son, Charles, was living in Philadelphia at the time of her death.

Francis Jones was invited to tea at the property in 1971 when it was the residence of Mrs. Jones-Parry, daughter-in-law to Sidney Jones-Parry. The house was large, in excellent condition and surrounded by trees. Mrs Jones-Parry was still at Ty-llwyd in 1975.

Grid Ref: SN 2865 4833

Refs: Kitchin Map, 1754; Colby Map, 1831; NLW, Griffith Owen Deeds; NLW, Crosswood Deeds, p. 287; Nicholas, *County Families,* i, 199; Charles Smith Allen, *South Wales;* Tredegar House, Tenby, 1871. (Album in possession of Miss Gwynedd Taylor, Manorbier), 1975; Lewis, *TDW,* 1840 and 1834; NLW, Llanllyr Deeds, No. 117, 119.

TY-MAWR, Cilcennin

The property is marked on *Colby's Map of 1831* south-west of Cilcennin and north of the Aeron a mile from Ciliau Aeron. Formerly called Tyddyn y Neuadd dan odre Gallt Cilcennin and reputed to have been part of an ancient tenement called Pen-graig.

Henry Vaughan of Plâs Cilcennin (1605-65), formerly of Trawsgoed, owned Tyddyn y Neuadd (Ty Mawr), which, in 1677, on his widow's death (Marie, nèe Stedman), devolved on Mary Vaughan, his youngest daughter, who married Morgan Herbert of Hafod Uchdryd (1634-87). Their son and heir, William Herbert of Hafod, 1657-1704, married Rebecca Hill of Shrewsbury and had a daughter, Jane, who was their sole heiress. Jane married Thomas Johnes of Llanfair Clydogau and pre-deceased him. He

married secondly Blanche Vaughan of Llanwern, but he died without issue in 1734, leaving Hafod to Thomas Johnes (1721-80), the son and heir of Thomas Johnes of Penybont, Tregaron, who died in 1751. In 1746 Thomas married Elizabeth Knight, daughter and heiress of Richard Knight of Croft Castle, Herefordshire. As Tyddyn y Neuadd was excluded from the Manuscript of 1746, it had probably been sold to John Hughes (1703-91) by this date. The *WWHR* records state that Ty-Mawr was owned and occupied in 1760 by John Hughes, gent, formerly of Narberth. He married twice. His first wife was Mary (1719-63), daughter of John Lewes, (1680-1742), of Carmarthen and Llanllyr and they came to live at Ty-Mawr, valued at £14 p.a. in 1750. After Mary died John Hughes married secondly, Mary Anne, the second daughter of Thomas Johnes, late of Dolaucothi, Esq., and sister of Thomas Johnes (1721-80), of Croft Castle and John Johnes of Dolaucothi. The marriage was the subject of a pre-nuptial settlement on 18 October 1773. John Hughes was High Sheriff in 1769 and died on 16 July 1791. Mary Anne's second brother, Captain John Johnes, had apparently borrowed money from her husband John and 'was not seemingly over-ready to repay it'.

Susan, John Hughes's daughter by his first marriage, was his sole heiress. She married Captain David Saunders in 1779. David (1727-1815) of the Hon. East India Company Service and of Glanrhydw, Llandyfaelog, the third son of David Saunders of Pentre, Maenordeifi. He was commander of the 499 ton ship *Grosvenor* carrying tea to England and was paid a salary of £10 a month. Their son and heir, Francis David Saunders (1786-1867) inherited Ty-Mawr. In 1853, he also inherited Glanrhydw on the death of his eldest brother. Francis David Saunders joined the 16th Regiment Madras N.L. Infantry as Ensign in 1803. He was promoted Captain in 1814 and retired in 1819. It is thought that it was he who built the present Ty-Mawr, in the 1820's. He served as High Sheriff for the county in 1842 and in 1845 he married Mary Anne (1819-93), daughter of the Rev. George Wade Green of Cwrt Henry, Llangathen.

William Francis David Saunders (1851-1910), inherited Ty-Mawr and Glanrhydw on the death of his elder brother in 1870. William married, but as he had no issue, the property passed to his eldest sister, Susannah Mary, born in 1847. In 1868 she had married W. Conrade Middleton Abadam of Middleton Hall, who was born in 1845. They had two daughters. In 1878 Susannah married secondly, Captain Frank Fiddes Rudman who died without issue in 1884. On her brother's death in 1910 Susannah assumed the name and arms of Saunders. Her second daughter, Geraldine Mabel, born in 1872, inherited her mother's properties at Ty-Mawr and Glanrhydw. In 1895 she married George (later Sir) Rice Pryse, of Gogerddan and as Lady Mabel Pryse-Saunders was the owner of Ty-Mawr in 1958. Her husband died in 1962 and the Gogerddan baronetcy became extinct.

The house was utilised as a private girl's school during the Second World War for pupils evacuated from Littlehampton, Sussex. After Susannah's death it was handed down by her sister, Mrs Elinor Briggs, to Peter Gwynne Hughes of Llwynbedw, Boncath, a farmer. The *Western Mail* wrote an article about the sale of the mansion in 1974 in which Peter Hughes stated that as a bachelor the house was too large for his needs and Ty-Mawr was sold to an Essex businessman, Donald Fisher. The eight-bedroomed Georgian house was advertised for sale again in 1983.

Grid Ref: SN 5135 5962

Refs: Colby Map, 1831; Nicholas, *County Families*, 1875, I, 190; WWHR, III, 94; CRO, JF (Ll) Deeds; NLW, Griffith Owen Deeds; *Western Mail,* 22 April 1974.

TY-MAWR, Trefilan

Located in Talsarn immediately west of the main road which leads through the village towards Trefilan and formerly called Talsarn Green. The first recorded occupiers were traced to the descendants of Ieuan Llwyd of Glyn Aeron. Morgan, a natural son of Dafydd ap Ieuan ap Philip had a son, Thomas, who married his cousin Joan and their son, Ievan, alive in 1609 married Mary, daughter of David Lloyd ap Hugh of Llwyd Jack. Their son and heir, Thomas Evans married firstly a daughter of Griffith Lewis and had two children, John and Bridget, and married secondly a daughter of John Hughes, a cleric from Bangor Teifi. John, married Jane, a daughter of Francis Lloyd of Llanfair Clydogau. Bridget married Lewis Richard of Ystrad and Samuel, the only child of the second marriage, married Sarah, daughter of Samuel Hughes of Allt-goch. In 1664 Bridget released to her brother John her claim to Llwyn-yr-iar in the parish of Trefilan.

John Evans and Jane, his wife, had seven children including Elizabeth, who married Rawleigh Lloyd, a younger son of Llanfechan. James, the eldest son, succeeded to Ty-mawr and married Anne, daughter of George Bowen of Crugbychan. On 30 January 1771, he was living in Westminster when he gave a lease of possession of 'Ty-mawr, Tyr y Gelli Gweni and Pant y Goras' in the parish of Trefilan, and a property in Lammas Street, Carmarthen to John Allen of Shrewsbury, clerk, agent for the purchaser, Daniel Stead. A Thomas Stead, gent., from Leominster is listed in 1760 as being the mortgagee of land in Trefilan. James Evans' brother, Thomas had a daughter, Dorothy, who married the Rev. William Hughes of Glanyr-afon, vicar of Llanilar, from whom the Hughes of Allt-lwyd descend.

In 1835, John Lewes of Llanllyr, late of 23rd Light Dragoons and a veteran of Waterloo, bought Ty-mawr, the Blue Bell, The Lamb and other properties in the village of Talsarn from William Preece of Leominster and John Bateman of Lincoln's Inn.

Ty-mawr was still owned by Capt. J. Hext Lewes of Llanllyr in 1975 when Francis Jones examined a doorway, on the lower floor, with 17th century decorative carving. In October 1978, during renovations at Ty-mawr, a great oak beam, 'as hard as iron', which supported the upper floor was uncovered. Inscribed on the beam were the letters I P and the date 1524. The letters could refer to Ieuan ap Philip, an early occupier of Ty-mawr.

Grid Ref: SN 5451 5636

Ref: NLW, Noyadd Trefawr Deeds, No. 261; ibid, Llanllys Deeds, Nos. 96-7; *Dwnn,* i, 15; WWHR, I, 49 and 40; Blome List, 1673; Meyrick *Cardiganshire,* 257 (ped. given); Burke, *LG,* 1850; Llanllyr Deeds, No. 96; PRO, Dale Castle MS., pp. 27, 104; *Dwnn,* i, 15; CRO, JF (dl) Deeds; NLW, Coleman Deeds, No. 102; ibid, Nos. 103, 129; CRO, GGMS

(Gwaethfoed); NLW, Dale Castle Deeds; *Dwnn,* i, 15; NLW, Cwrtmawr Deeds, No. 49; CRO, GGMS, I (Tydwal Gloff), fo. 24.

TY'N-LLWYN, Llanbadarn-y-Creuddyn

Situated near Devil's Bridge and marked on *Colby's Map of 1831.* Marked but not named on modern OS maps east of the village and is now an hotel and caravan park. The *Golden Grove Manuscripts* state that 'John Hughes was of Ty yn y llwyn in Llangrwiron [sic] and married Magdalen, daughter of Meredydd Llwyd, viv 1656, of Cwmbwa in Llanbadarn Fawr'. Thomas Hughes, gent., is described as owner-occupier of Tynllwyn in 1760. He died on 29 June 1781, aged 65. The property was still owned by Thomas Hughes's descendants in 1913.

Grid Ref: SN 7453 7712

Refs: Colby Map, 1831; CRO, GGMS, III (Gwaethfoed).

TYWYN (TOWYN), Ferwig

Located on the coast three miles from Cardigan overlooking the Teifi estuary near the Cliff Hotel in Gwbert and marked on *Colby's Map of 1831.* Formerly the home of a distinguished and powerful family, sponsors of medieval bards, whose descendants include the Vaughans of Penbryn, Rhoscellan, Morfa Bychan, Llanborth, Glanleri and many others. The family of Towyn traced to Gwynfardd Dyfed who lived in Cemaes and was a man of considerable wealth and the owner of vast estates. According to Meyrick the first edifice at Towyn was erected by Gwilym ab Einon, Constable of the Castle of Cardigan. The first of the family to settle at Towyn was Gwilym ap Einion Fawr o'r Coed ap Gwilym ap Gwrwared ap Cyhylyn. According to Edward Lhwyd, Gwilym 'slew the Irish that dwelt at Pritchert for firing the house of his foster-father . . . and got arms in France which he afterwards gave for his own viz: *gules* a chevron int: 3 delisses and in chief a lion rampant *or*'. Frances Jones writes that he found an old document giving the arms of the Lord of Iscoed as: *gules* a lion rampant bordered indented *or*'.

Gwilym was brought up at Waungelod, Ferwig parish, educated at Oxford and served at the King's Court. He became Constable of Cardigan Castle in 1326. Edward Lhywd maintains that Gwilym was the natural son of Owain ap Robert ap Einion Fawr o'r Coed by Lleucu, daughter of Gruffydd ap Llewelyn Fychan, Lord of Iscoed. The *Golden Grove Manuscripts* state that he was the son of Einion Fawr and Dido, daughter of Cadwgan Ddu, Lord of Aberporth. Einion Fychan married Joan, daughter of Llewelyn ap Owain who was descended from the Lord Rhys. Their only child, Einion Fychan married Joan, daughter and heiress of Stephen Langley, Lord of Coedmor. Their grandson, Meredudd ab Owen married Elliw, heiress of Morfa Bychan, whose father Rhys Ddu, Governor of Aberystwyth castle, was the father of Rhys ap Meredudd to whom Deio ab Ieuan Du wrote a *cywydd* in an attempt to broker an agreement in a dispute between Rhys and Gruffydd Fychan of Corsygedol and Deio as well as Lewis Glyn Cothi wrote elegies to Meredudd. Rhys imported fine wines from France, according to Dafydd Nanmor, who also sang to his son, Rhydderch and grandson, Rhys ap Rhydderch. The English translation of these odes are included in the *Oxford Book of Welsh Verse in English.*

Rhydderch ap Rhys, once fined £40 for allowing the escape of a prisoner in 1500, held many important posts including deputy-chamberlain of South Wales conveying cash to Prince Arthur in London. He married Margaret, daughter of John Llwyd of Cefnmelgoed. He later lived at Glanleri, Borth. He was succeeded at Tywyn by his son Rhys ap Rhydderch, who married Alson, daughter of Sir James ab Owen of Pentre Ifan, Co. Pembrokeshire. His brother, Rhys Fychan, took Vaughan as his surname and his descendants lived at Llan-borth and later at Dyffryn Hoffnant. John ap Rhys, the next generation to live at Tywyn, married Elizabeth, daughter of James ap Gruffydd ap Howell of Castell Maelgwn, Pembrokeshire, who became a fugitive on the Continent for 20 years and as a devout Catholic was opposed to the marriage of Henry VIII and Anne Boleyn. [See Francis Jones, *Treasury of Historic Pembrokeshire*, 1998, Brawdy Books.]

Two generations later Philip ap Rhys sold all the remaining Tywyn estates. His son, John, is described as a carpenter of Cardigan. Tywyn became part of the Noyadd Trefawr estate when Thomas Parry married Margaret, only daughter of Rhydderch ap Rhys Fychan then of St. Dogmael's. In 1646 their son Stephen received the manors of Tywyn, Clunyrymys, Heol y Gwyddel, Tir-bach in Ferwig and other properties in Llangoedmor which had been mortgaged to his father Thomas Parry. The will of Stephen Parry of Noyadd Trefawr dated November 1721 mentions the Tywyn estate which was then in his possession. In addition to various bequests he left the Ferwig estate to John Jones, the eldest son of Tyglyn, a relative by marriage. Tywyn and the Ferwig estate continued in the ownership of the Tyglyn family and was let to tenants. In 1808 Tywyn was described as 'merely a farmhouse', the property of A. T. J. Gwynn. Fifty years later Alban Thomas Davies of Tyglyn leased Tywyn farm to Lumley Edwards, who surrendered the lease in 1862. Mathiases and Davises were also tenants in the 18th and 19th centuries, including Joseph Davies, whose sons, David and Thomas were both sea-captains. There were many in the district who claimed descent from the Lords of Towyn, including Jenkin Morgan, bell-ringer and sexton at Llangrannog. In *Wanderings* Horsfall-Turner tells us 'about a century ago the small, Gothic, stone church of St. Cranog [Llangrannog] attracted large crowds to its services to hear the sermons of Peter Williams, its curate, and the attractive musical voice of the old *clochydd*. The sexton, Jenkin Morgan claimed a proud ancestry from the Lords of Tywyn and Llewelyn Vuchan of Emlyn. His son, David Jenkin Morgan, born in Llangrannog, became still more famous as a musician and composer, especially of Welsh hymns and he obtained important Eisteddfod prizes. He revolutionized the singing in many churches and died in 1844 at the very advanced age of 92'.

The *NLW Morgan Richardson Deeds* contain a map of 'Towyn Farm', circa 1894 and in his *Guide to Cardigan and District*, W. E. James tells us 'Towyn – once a celebrated mansion, now merely a farmhouse. Probably no part of the present house is over 200 years of age and it does not seem to have been built on the site of the former one'. Francis Jones visited the house in 1965 when it was the property of A. T. S. Gwynne of Tyglyn. Towyn farm today is owned and occupied by the Nicholas family.

Grid Ref: SN 1637 5005

Refs: Colby Map, 1831; *Dwnn,* i, 43, 55, 59, 61, 167; WWHR, i, 25-7, 55; *L. G. Cothi,* II. 283; Cywyddau, *Cymru,* pp. 49, 76, 77; PRO, Min. Acc. NLW, Bronwydd MS., 2 pedigrees c. 1700, fo. 94b; ibid, Noyadd Trefawr Deeds, Nos. 103, 106, 319, 466, 601-2, 1003; D. Hywel E. Roberts in *Ceredigion,* vii I, 1972, pp. 33-36; Horsfall-Turner, *Wanderings*, p. 136; *Oxford Book of Welsh Verse,* edn. 1972, pp. 144, 146-8; *Oxford Book of Welsh Verse in English,* Gwyn Jones, 1977, p. 60; W. E. Jones, *Guide to Cardigan and District,* 1899; Map of Towyn farm; NLW, Morgan Richardson Deeds; Bronwydd Volume of Pedigrees, c. 1700; *Gwyneddon* 3, pp. 186, 232; NLW, Tyglyn MSS. and Docs. No. 41; Francis Jones, *Treasury of Historic Pembrokeshire,* 1998, Brawdy Books, pp. 223-38.

EINOG, see Feinog

ALLOG, Llangorwen

Situated on the coast between Clarach and Borth and overlooking Sarn Cynfelin. In 1952 Ellis wrote of Wallog in *Crwydro Ceredigion* '. . . *Wallog, ty a saif mewn unigedd ac yn edrych allan dros y mor',* 'a house which stands in solitude'. Little is known of Wallog until 1760 when Richard John Morgan of Dolrhyddlan owned Gwallog. William Morris (1758-1802), son of the distinguished Lewis Morris by his second marriage to Anne Lloyd of Pen-byrn, Goginan, was of Wallog.

The NLW *Cwrtmawr Deeds* tell us that Anne Jane Morice, spinster, James Morice, gent., George Morice, gent., Thomas Richard Morice, gent., and William Hallen Morice, gent., all of Wallog and others entered into an agreement that a release should be made of sums of money which were the subject of a settlement dated 15 April 1834, by James Morice of Carrog, Llanddeiniol since deceased and in favour of his grandchildren. James Morice was of Wallog in 1848 and was a subscriber to Dwnn's *Heraldic Visitations*.

Late in the 19th century Wallog was the home of Col. George Griffiths Williams, eldest son of Mathew Davies Williams of Cymcynfelin and Susanna, heiress of Simon Griffiths of Cwmrhaeadr, Montgomeryshire. In 1873 he owned 1473 acres with an annual rental of £827. He was High Sheriff in 1876. George Griffiths Williams married Sarah Jane Checkland of Hawkswick, Herefordshire and their eldest son, George Checkland Williams was born in 1872. He served in the Worcester Regiment and married Jane, daughter of John Parry of Glanpaith. Among his possessions at Wallog was a bed which came to the Williams's through marriage from the Hughes of Mathafarn, Montgomeryshire, in which, it is claimed, Henry Tudor slept during his stay at Mathafarn on his long march to Bosworth Field in 1485. The Royal Coat of Arms was carved on the bed. Due to expensive litigation between members of the Cwmcynfelyn family, Wallog was sold in 1886 to Mr. Francis, a Clapham grocer and George Checkland Williams and his parents moved to Ffynnon Caradog between Bow Street and Aberystwyth.

Originally fishermen's cottages, the large house on the sea-shore was inherited in 1918 by Basil Parry Griffiths from his uncle, John Francis, a London businessman. Canon Parry Griffiths, who retired in 1927, lived at Wallog and looked after the property for his son. The Canon died in 1963 and left the property to his nephew, John Evershed, who now rears beef cattle on the estate of 400 acres which includes Rhoscellan-fawr (let to the Jones family, formerly of Ruel, Llandre), and Rhoscellan-fach. Mr. Evershed has built a bungalow, Llechwedd Melyn, on the property and his son, A. J. P. Evershed, lives at Wallog.

Grid Ref: SN 5905 8577

Refs: Colby Map, 1831; Meyrick, *Cardiganshire,* 375; BLG 1898, ii, 1603; Ellis, *Crwydro Ceredigion*, 1952, p. 15; WWHR, iii, 104; Dwnn, *Heraldic Visitations* (1846); NLW, Cwrtmawr Deeds, 50 & 1400; Landowners Return, 1873;

WAUN, Henllan

Described as 'the principal seat in this parish' by Meyrick and located near Henllan bridge but not named on modern OS maps. The earliest recorded occupier is James Lewes, a son of David Lewes of Dolhaidd, Mayor of Carmarthen in 1753, and his wife Elizabeth, daughter of George Bowen of Llwyngwair, Pembrokeshire. In 1724 James Lewes married Mary, daughter of Robert Lewis of Nantgwyllt and Posthuma Lloyd, his wife, formerly of Wern-newydd, Llanarth. James Lewes sold Waun to his kinsman, William Lewes of Llysnewydd. The pre-nuptial settlement of Grace, eldest daughter of James Williams of 'Wayne', gent., who married Methusalem Davies the younger, the eldest son of Richard Davies of Llanfair Helygen parish, was signed on 25 May 1732. In 1760 Henry Williams, gent., described as of Crickhowell is listed as owning Waun and two years later he was appointed a JP.

Meyrick wrote 'Wain is the principal seat in this parish and is now the property of William Lewes, Esq., of Llysnewydd, who bought it about thirty years ago of Mr. Rogers'.

Grid Ref: SN 3544 4020

Refs: Meyrick, *Cardiganshire,* 189; WWHR, iii, 82.

WAUNIFOR (GWAUNIFOR), Llandysul

In 1833 Lewis wrote, 'A genteel house, delightfully situated on the banks of the river Teifi and commanding from its park-like grounds a beautiful and picturesque view of the bridge of Llanfihangel-ar-Arth and the church of that parish'. Named as Gwaun Ifor on *Colby's Map of 1831,* the property is located south of Capel Dewi and east of Maesycrugiau.

The home of the descendants of Owen, natural son of David ap Rhydderch of Pantstreimon. Owen's son, Thomas ap Owen of Bwlchbychan was an Attorney in Sessions. His son, Francis Bowen was the father of Thomas Bowen who married a daughter of Lodwick Lewis of Brenhinlle. They had two sons and two daughters: Thomas Bowen, the eldest son of Bwlchbychan, married Jane, the daughter of David Lloyd of Alltyrodin. His will was proved in 1655. He had a younger brother John, and his sisters were Gwenllian, who married David Thomas alias Dai Mawr of Cwmbarry in Penbryn whose daughter Mary was in the service of James Lewes of Penralltybie in 1690. Another sister, unnamed, married David Lloyd of Bryn Hawg. Thomas Bowen and his wife, Jane, had two sons. The eldest, John of Bwlchbychan married Jane, daughter of John Lewis of Troed-y-rhiw, formerly of Gernos. The younger son, Daniel Bowen married Mary, daughter of Thomas Davies of Troedrhiw-ffenyd by Sarah Pryce. He was High Sheriff in 1741. They had two sons and two known daughters; Thomas, John, Mary and Sinai. John married Margaret, daughter and heiress of Thomas Thomas of Maesycrugiau. Mary was unmarried and Sinai married the Rev. David Jones, rector of Llangan, Glamorganshire in January 1771.

Thomas Bowen (1727-1805), the elder son, succeeded his father to Waunifor. He was a generous benefactor and erected Capel Waunifor for the Calvinistic Methodists on the land of Blaenborthin in 1760. He received inspiration from a sermon preached by Daniel Rowland of Llangeitho at Twr-gwyn. He was High Sheriff in 1778. In his will dated 1805 and proved on 27 February 1806, he laid down that it was to continue 'without interruption' for use by the Methodists. It was also used as a school and he lodged ministers at Waunifor. Thomas Bowen died on 14 October 1805, aged 78 and Jane on 29 November 1829, also aged 78. A memorial inscription erected by his son and heir, Daniel, can be found in Llanwenog church. Daniel (1777-1848), was educated at Castell Hywel and then at Oxford where he gained an MA. He took Holy Orders and became parson of Eglwys-wen in Pembrokeshire. He married Jane, daughter of John Lloyd of Gilfachwen, Pembrokeshire. He was then given the living of Llanllwni and Llanfihangel Rhos-y corn. As the church of Llanllwni was near Waunifor, Daniel Bowen paid curates to care for Eglwys-wen and Llanfihangel. Meyrick tells us 'the present owner of this place, the Rev. Daniel Bowen, resides here. His grandfather married the heiress, who was the daughter of Davis of Troedrhyw fennid and was the first to come to Waun Ifor. The Rev. Daniel Bowen is 9th in descent from Owen ap David ap Rhydderch Goch'. According to the *Llandysul Tithe Map of 1841,* Waunifor was of 186 acres. Daniel also owned sixteen other properties: Blaen Corthyn, Gallt-y-gof, Bryn Segur, Bryn Martin, Castell Martin, Gors-y-fran, Cefn Gwallter, Rhyd Caradog, Dan Capel, Fron Gon, Fynnonau, Fronfelen, Glanrhydypysgod, Maes-y-pwll and Pont Llwyni. These properties, with Waunifor totalled 1,052 acres. Daniel Bowen died in 1848, aged 71. In his will he gave £400 each to the parishes of Llanllwni, Llanwenog, Llandysul and Eglwys-wen, 'to be used towards the education of the poor'. He bequeathed gifts to the Bible Society and £12 for an annual scholarship to St. David's College, Lampeter.

The estate was left to his nephew, John Lloyd, eldest son of John Lloyd of Gilfach-wen and Jane, a sister of Daniel Bowen. John, in turn, gave the estate to his brother, the Rev. Charles Lloyd, vicar of Betws Bledrws. Charles, who married Frances, daughter of the Rev. George Wade Green of Cwrt Henry, died in 1867 and was succeeded by his eldest son, also Charles, born in 1850. He was educated at Marlborough and Oriel College, Oxford. Charles married Margaret, daughter of Alister Duncan Alexander Campbell of Argyll. He was High Sheriff in 1882 and the Waunifor estates, by now 1,951 acres with an annual rental of £839 passed to his eldest son and heir, Alister Campbell Bowen Lloyd, who was born in 1878. He became headmaster of Hill Crest School in Dorset.

By 1976 Waunifor had been adapted for the use of holiday-makers and an illustration and description was published in the Wales Tourist Board publication *Where To Stay in Wales.*

Grid Ref: SN 4601 4107

Refs: Colby Map, 1831; Lewis, *TDW,* 1833; *Where to Stay in Wales,* 1976, p. 178, illus; WWHR, iii, 109; Nicholas, *County Families,* i, 203; Landowners Return, 1873; W. J. Davies, *Hanes Plwyf Llandysul,* pp. 67-9, 97-99; CRO, GGMS I (Tydwal Gloff), fo. 37; Llandysul Parish Records, 1841.

WAUN-MEIRCH (GWAUN-MEIRCH), Llanddewi Aber-arth

Located east of Aberarth off the minor road towards Pennant. Named Gwernmeirch on *Colby's Map of 1831.* The home of a descendant of John Webley, Cwrtnewydd and his son, Dafydd, known as *Saer y Cwm.* His grandson, Evan, had six sons; Thomas the first of Cwrtnewydd, Lewis of Lan from whom descends Dr. Lewis Jones of Llansamlet, alive in 1939 and William of Ffwrneithin. The fourth son, John, lived at Nantremyn and Philip lived at Waunmeirch. Hugh, the youngest son, was of Blaenau Gwenog. Thereafter the records are silent.

Grid Ref: SN 4855 6377

Refs: W. J. Davies, *Hanes Plwyf Llanwenog,* 1939, p. 152.

WERN DDU, Llanbadarn Trefeglwys

Situated south-east of Pennant parish church and marked on *Colby's Map of 1831* and on modern OS maps. On 7 August 1755, Richard Lloyd of Wern ddu and Elinor his wife, daughter of David Evans of Cilcennin, a yeoman, gave a lease for a year to William Williams and Lewis Evans, yeoman, of the capital messuage and appurtenances called Wern-ddu in the occupation of Richard Lloyd, and other lands specified, so that a recovery might be suffered. In 1760, Richard Lloyd, junior, was owner-occupier of Wern ddu and Richard Lloyd, senior, owner-occupier of Tail glase.

Grid Ref: SN 5178 6279

Refs: Colby Map, 1831; NLW, Coleman Deeds, No. 145; WWHR, iii, 91.

WERN-DRIW, Llanddewibrefi

Marked on *Colby's Map of 1831* as Werndrew and located on modern OS maps, threequarters of a mile south-west of Llanddewibrefi. In the 17th and 18th centuries Werndriw was the home of a prominent Quaker family. The children of David George Jenkins, an Anglican, 'would not pull of their hats, nor go to church, but did sit together without any preaching'. John George Jenkins, the elder son, was the first to be buried at the cemetery at Werndriw in 1718. His younger brother Samuel became a Quaker minister for nine months before his early death at the age of 25 in 1712. Their sister, Ann, married Thomas Evans of Llanfihangel Rhydeithon, Radnorshire. Towards the end of the century, the children of John and Anne Jenkins of Wern-driw, all but one of whom predeceased their parents, were buried in the cemetery. The survivor, David Joel Jenkins, erected the memorial to his parents and siblings at Wern-driw.

Daniel Evans of Wern-driw and of Garth, son of Anne and Thomas Evans was buried at Wern-driw in 1790. He and his wife had two children, Daniel, later of neighbouring Troed-y-rhiw and William, owner of Garth on the banks of the Teifi.

Grid Ref: SN 6563 5479

Refs: Colby Map, 1831; The Rev. D. Benjamin Rees, *Hanes Plwyf Llanddewibrefi*, pp. 73-8; *TCAS,* vol. 1, Part 2, pp. 95-6.

WERNFEILIG (WERNFYLIG), Llanfihangel Ystrad

Located south of Temple Bar and east of the minor road to Cribyn. Home of the Lloyds, of Castell Hywel stock and descended from Cadifor ap Dinawal, with connections with the Llwyds of Llanllyr. The earliest recorded owner is Morgan Fychan, whose son, David Lloyd, had a son Morgan of Llanfihangel Ystrad who in 1609 married Elen, sole heiress of Rheinallt Meurig by his wife Elizabeth, daughter of Richard Pryse of Gogerddan. Morgan's son, John of Llanllyr, married Elen, daughter of James Lewis David Meredydd of Abernantbychan. They had three sons and three daughters: the eldest daughter, Lettice, remained unmarried, Jane married Oliver Lloyd of Ffosybleiddiaid. The youngest daughter Elinor, married John Lloyd of Penybeili, whose will was proved in 1668.

The eldest son, William, described as 'of Wernfylig', married Bridget, daughter of Sir Walter Lloyd of Llanfair Clydogau; they had a son Charles Lloyd who married Florence, the widow of Griffith Gwynn of Mynachty.

The second son, Thomas of Wernfeilig, married Lettice, daughter of Thomas Pryse of Glanfrêd. It was Thomas who bought Llanllyr back from Richard, Earl of Carbery. He and his wife had four daughters and co-heiresses. Elizabeth married John Lloyd of Ffosybleiddiaid, Bridget married Thomas Llwyd of Castell Hywel and Lettice married Edward Carew of London who was living in 1679. The fourth daughter, Jane was unmarried.

The third son of John and Elen Lloyd was Morgan who lived at Greengrove which his brother gave him. He was High Sheriff in 1675 and married Eleanor, daughter of Thomas Lloyd of Cilgwyn. Their daughter Jane married Sir Charles Lloyd of Maesyfelin. The will of David Lloyd of Ffosybleiddiaid dated 5 August 1714 mentions 'my messuage and land called Gwernfeilig in the parish of Llanfihangel Ystrad', so it is safe to assume that the property was his through his marriage to Elizabeth. In 1748 Vaughan Lloyd of Wernfeilig was appointed a JP but by 1767 it was part of the Peterwell estate and let to tenants. Following the death of Sir Herbert Lloyd the Wernfeilig estate was sold to an unknown buyer for £1,495. When it was sold again in 1807, Wernfeilig and Rhyd-y-gof, totalling 368 acres was tenanted by John Williams paying an annual rent of £94.10.0.

Grid Ref: SN 5368 5333

Refs: Colby Map, 1831; NLW, Castle Hill Documents, 506-7; Lloyd Pedigrees, Lloyd and Theakestone, p. 12 (peds.) & 56; CRO, GGMS, *Dwnn,* 156.

WERN NEWYDD (PLAS-Y-WERN), Llanarth

The house is marked on *Colby's Map of 1831* and marked but not named on modern OS maps is situated threequarters-of-a-mile north-west of Llanarth church and between Llanarth and New Quay.

'Wern (Newydd) is a quaint, interesting old house, but hidden away in a gloomy hollow. It has long been used as a farmhouse and the enterprising tenants supply tea and refreshment (for a consideration), to visitors from New Quay, who are duly impressed by the sight of the actual bed whereon the Tudor monarch rested his limbs' wrote H. M. Vaughan in his *South Wales Squires.* Vaughan was referring to

Henry Tudor who, according to tradition, spent a night at Wern on his long [slow, bedridden], march to Bosworth in August 1485.

In *Walks and Wanderings* Horsfall-Turner describes Wern Newydd thus: 'A closer view reveals the fact that it is indeed a somewhat unusual farmhouse and proclaims it as an old mansion. This is Wern Newydd where Henry Tudor (afterwards Henry VII) stayed for a night with Einon, son of David Lloyd, while on his march from Milford towards the field of Bosworth. Internally are spacious wainscoted rooms with ancient thick walls, wide entrance hall and broad oak staircase with twisted balusters, solid oak panelling and furnishings and capacious kitchen with cobbled floor and fire . . . The reputed bedroom in which the Earl slept, a small room for such a large mansion, is still shown and on the wall is affixed with inscription, *Hon yw ystafell lle y cysgodd Henry Iarll Richmond, gwedyn Harry y VII yn y flwyddyn 1485 gyda Einon ap Dafydd Llwyd, Esq., ar ei daith o Aberdaugleddau i'r frwydr enwog ar faes Bosworth yn yr hon y lladdwyd Richard y III a Henry a aeth oddiuno i Lundain ac a gafodd ei Goroni yn frenin Lloegr*. His reputed bedstead is in another room.' Included with this description is a sketch of the mansion captioned 'Wern' and a sketch of the said bedroom. An interesting account of Wern Newydd, with three sketches, exterior and interior can be found in the Cardiganshire Antiquarian Society magazine.

The home of the Lloyds, formerly of Faerdre, Llandysul, descended from Cadifor ap Dinawal. John Lloyd of Wern Newydd in Llanarth (to Tewdwr Mawr) married a daughter of Watkin Morgan of Abertrisant, Llanfihangel-y-creuddyn. Their son, also Watkin, married Frances, daughter of John Whittingham of

Littleham, Montgomeryshire. The house was commodious and assessed at five hearths in 1672. Watkin was High Sheriff in 1663 and his will was proved in 1685. He and Frances had seven children including David, born in 1667, John, who was unmarried in 1745 and Gwenllian who married James Griffiths of Neuadd, Llanarth, Esq. and their daughter Frances married Rev. James Brooks.

David Lloyd, Esq., the eldest son of Watkin and Frances, married Mary, daughter and heiress of Edward Price of Ystradffin, son of Richard Prys, attorney in Sessions. David Lloyd's will was proved in 1701. They had seven children including Watkin, the eldest, who died without issue, Edward, and David who married Mary, only daughter of John Phillipps of Cwmhawen and died at sea in 1700. Bridget married Morgan Lloyd of Glansefin and Postuma, married Robert Lewis of Nantgwyllt, Radnorshire and had a son, Thomas Lloyd.

Edward Lloyd, who by the death of his brother William, became the heir to Wern Newydd, married Anne, only daughter and heiress of Richard Stedman of Strata Florida, by Joan his first wife. The marriage was the subject of a pre-nuptial settlement agreed on 29 January 1718/19. Her portion was £3,000. Edward settled estates in Cardiganshire and Carmarthenshire on the marriage. He was the owner of properties in Llanarth, Llanina, Henfynyw, Llanllwchaearn, Llandysiliogogo, Llanfairorllwyn and Llandysul and several water corn mills, a tucking mill and cottages. He was High Sheriff in 1721, and died in London without issue in 1754, and was buried in Audley Chapel, Grosvenor Square. The estate passed to Richard Lloyd, the only surviving brother, who died in 1757 and then to his nephew Thomas, son of Robert and Postuma Lewis of Nantgwyllt who was born in March 1724/5. A memorial inscription in Llanarth church is dedicated to Richard Lloyd 'one of ye land surveyors of ye Port of London' by Mary, his wife. Thomas Lewis took the additional name of Lloyd. Thomas Lewis Lloyd bequeathed Wern to his nephew, David Edward Lewes, son of his sister Mary, wife of James Lewes of Waun, Henllan and Dol-haidd Uchaf. He also added the surname Lloyd to his name.

Wern Newydd was let to tenants and the Rev. William Hughes, MA (Cambridge), was born at the mansion in 1810. He succeeded his father, Rev. David Hughes, who died in 1836, aged 82, as rector of Ciliau Aeron in 1836. He lived later at the vicarage of Aber-arth and was Rural Dean. He died in 1867, aged 57. David Edward Lewes Lloyd died without issue in 1818 aged 67 years. He was buried at Penbryn and the Wern estate passed to his kinsman, Edward Pryse Lloyd of Glansefin (1786-1868), who married the daughter of Col. William Hughes of Tregibby. Edward was High Sheriff of Cardiganshire in 1825. His son and heir, Morgan Pryse Llwyd born in 1820, married Georgina Caroline, daughter of a Gwyn of Glan-bran in 1843. They had six sons and four daughters.

Edward Pryse Lloyd of Wern Newydd was High Sheriff in 1825. *Carmarthenshire Notes* tell us that in 1889 Wern Newydd 'was lately offered for sale at Aberayron'.

The Daily Mail of 2 November 1981 published an article with a photograph of Wern Newydd which gives modern interest to the house. In 1936 Alastair Graham, Oxford friend of Evelyn Waugh, the original Sebastian Flyte in *Brideshead Revisited*, settled at Wern mansion. 'He became well known for parties to which were invited friends like Waugh, Augustus John, Dylan Thomas and Clough Williams-Ellis. He sold up at Wern and moved to a cottage in Rock Street, New Quay, in 1958, where he still lived in 1981'.

In the 1980's the house, now called Plâs-y-Wern, was owned by Dr. Dylan Thomas, a doctor at Glangwili Hospital.

Grid Ref: SN4155 5847

Refs: Colby Map, 1831; Blome List, 1673; WWHR, i, 38-9; ibid, iii, 86; Meyrick, *Cardiganshire,* 1810, edn. 1907, pp. 235 & 237; Horsfall-Turner, *Wanderings,* pp. 113-116; D. J. Davies, *Llanarth,* 29; H. M. Vaughan, *South Wales Squires,* 1926, pp. 180-1; *TCAS,* No. 4, 914, illus., i, No. 2, 51 ff.; PRO, Dale Castle MSS., p. 26 (103); CRO, GGMS, Glasbrook, p. 33; *Carmarthenshire Notes* (ped. A. Mee), 1889, vol. 1, p. 160; Glansefin Colln. Nos. 2624 & 2621 (5th Aug. 1718); NLW, Hendrefelin Deeds, No. 189; *Arch. Cam.*, 1855, 145; ibid, 1865, 105; ibid, 1867, 239, 244; ibid, 1879, 183; *Daily Mail,* 2 Nov. 1981 & photograph; NLW, Trefaes Deeds.

WERVILBROOK (FFYNNON WERFIL), now known as Wervil Grange, Llangrannog

Located near Pentregat and clearly visible from the A487 (T). Marked on *Colby's Map of 1831* and on modern OS maps. Meyrick states that 'The mansion was built by the late Rev. David Turnor, who bequeathed it and about three hundred acres in which it stands, to his widow, Catherine, from whom it was purchased by his brother, the Rev. Lewis Turnor, in the year 1802. The family came to west Wales during the reign of Charles II and settled at Crugmor, on the outskirts of Cardigan in the parish of Llangoedmor. John Lewis Turnor married Maud John of Tre-forgan in the same parish. Lewis died in December 1753 and left his property to his son John also of Crugmor, who married, in June 1756, Margaret Gwyon of Ffynnon Coronau, Pembrokeshire, by whom he had five sons and six daughters. He died in June 1775. His second son, the Rev. David Turnor (1751-1799), purchased Wervilbrook from Thomas Jenkins of Coventry Street, Westminster, who had previously held a mortgage on the property. He married Catherine, daughter of William Haygarth, rector of Enham and Upton Grey in Hampshire.

The Rev. Turnor, in addition to his calling, was a prominent farmer and co-author with Thomas Lloyd of Bronwydd of *A General View of Agriculture in the County of Cardigan* published in 1794. He died on 7 March 1799 and was buried at Llangrannog. His wife Catherine died in 1802. Wervilbrook was bought by David's younger brother, Lewis Turnor (1757-1834), educated at Jesus College, Oxford, who followed his brother in pioneering agricultural practices and winning prizes for his produce. The third brother, John, joined the Navy at the age of 17 and fought against the French in the West Indies in 1783. In consequence of his capture of a French vessel he was awarded £12,000 as his share of the booty. When he died at Prince of Wales Island in January 1801, he was commanding *HMS Trident.*

Horsfall-Turner tells us that 'Wervilbrook is now being refaced consequent on further changes of owners'. This change of ownership is demonstrated by two Sale Catalogues for the Wervilbrook Estate at the Carmarthenshire Record Office; one dated 3 July 1896 which itemises the accommodation, including nine bedrooms and 277 acres of land held by the Misses Margaret and Mary Davies as yearly tenants, as well as Capel y Ffynnon, chapel, dwelling house and premises and part of Wervilbrook farm. The other catalogue dated 30 May 1922 describes the property as a 'residence with pleasure gardens, gardens, large orchard, paddock, fields, five-and-a-half acres of young plantation, altogether 77 acres; modern built mansion house, recently thoroughly renovated.

The property now caters for holidaymakers and is called Wervil Grange.

Grid Ref: SN 3487 5236

Refs: Colby Map, 1831; Meyrick, *Cardiganshire,* 1810, edn. 1907, p. 230; *The Cambrian,* 28 October 1809. Horsfall-Turner, *Wanderings,* 137; SC 429 & 669, CRO.

WSTRWS, Llandysiliogogo

Marked on *Colby's Map of 1831* opposite the entrance to a toll-house and on modern OS maps on the A486 towards Synod Inn, a little north of Capel Cynon. In 1774 the Rev. John Lewis Philipps of Llwyn-crwn, MA gave a lease of three lives of the messuage called Wstrws to Mary Rees, widow, at an annual rent of £24. Llewellin Parry, esq., of Gernos bought Wstrws in 1786 from the Rev. Philipps for £2,300. It included a corn mill called Gernos Mill, the fair and right of tolls of Capel Cynon Fair and a cottage called Maesllyn.

Later, Meredydd Lewes William Lloyd Price of Castell Pigyn, Abergwili, inherited Wstrws; he married Frances Margaret Lloyd of Gilfachwen, Llandysul, in 1879. Francis Jones wrote, 'I remember this interesting old house in the

1960's when travelling on my frequent visits to Aberystwyth and was saddened to see it progressively decaying so that by 1970 it was a gaunt, roofless ruin – this was deliberately done by the farmer-occupier. The old house was occupied when I first passed by in 1959. In the latter part of 1974 the last walls of the house were completely swept away and a new, ugly outhouse and yard now occupies part of the old site'.

Grid Ref: SN 3846 4990

Refs: Colby Map, 1831; NLW, Morgan Richardson Deeds, i, 189 & 194, 792-3.

YNYSGREIGIOG, Eglwys-fach

Situated on the west side of the main road between Tre'r ddol and Furnace overlooking the marshes of the Dyfi estuary. A very interesting old house dating from the early 17th century and a rare example of an early lateral-chimney house. Marked on *Colby's Map of 1831* and modern OS maps.

Ynysgreigiog has been associated with the Pryses of Gogerddan from the 16th century. Thomas Pryse of Glanfrêd, second son of John Pryse, High Sheriff in 1570, married Bridget, the daughter and heiress of John ap Griffith of Glanfrêd. They had a son, also Thomas, born in 1598, who married Elizabeth, daughter of John Parry of Noyadd Trefawr. He is described as of Ynysgreigiog in 1629 and of Glanfrêd from 1652. Their son, also Thomas, lived at Ynysgreigiog and married firstly, Susan the daughter and heiress of Richard Pugh of Dolyfonddu, and secondly, Jane Meridew, a widow from Shropshire.

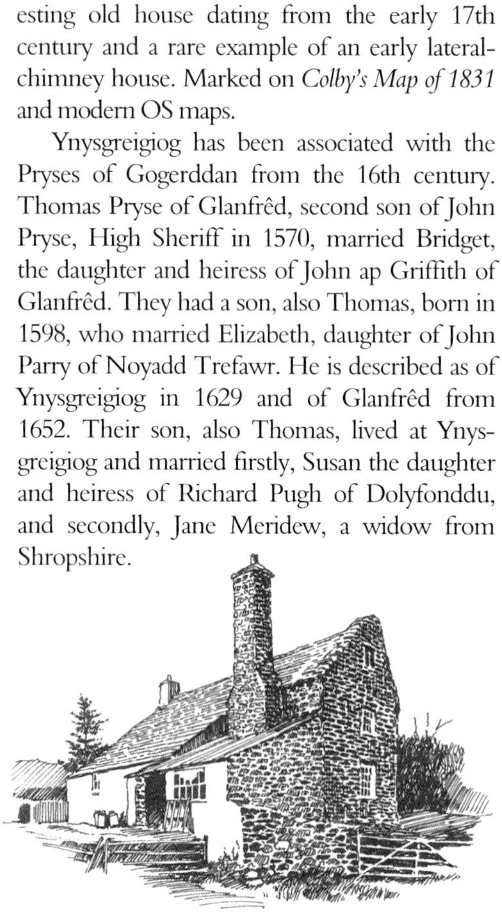

His brother, Richard, born in 1632, who married Mary, daughter of Richard James, lived at Ynysgreigiog. Their son, Thomas Pryse of Dôle inherited Gogerddan in 1720. In 1662, Thomas Pryce the younger, of Ynysgreigiog testified in a civil action that his father had got heavily into debt and borrowed £2,000 from his son. The son stated that he had Ynysgreigiog for life with remainder in fee at his father's death. The NLW *Cwrtmawr Deeds* relate that in 1676 a draft pre-nuptial settlement of Thomas Pryse, 'late of Ynys Grigog and now of Llanfread, Esq., and Thomas Pryse, the younger, his son and heir apparent and Margaret, eldest daughter of Lewis Owen of Peniarth, Merionethshire'. A Thomas Price of Ynysgreigiog was High Sheriff in 1681.

Grid Ref: SN 6730 9480

Refs: Colby Map, 1831; Blome List, 1673; NLW, Cwrtmawr Deeds, 1417; *Arch. Cam.* 1873, 107; L. Pugh MS.; PRO, Dale Castle MS.; CRO, GGMS I (Gwyddno), p. 4; Cawdor Colln. (add.) CRO; Cardigan County History, pp. 240, 259, Fig. 63.

YNYS-HIR, Eglwys-fach

A typical Welsh-type country house of two storeys, with a central porch block, and two storeys projecting in front and marked on *Colby's Map of 1831* and on modern OS maps and located in woodland near Eglwys-fach.

G. E. Evans tells us that 'the Lloyds lived at Ynyshir in the early 17th century David Lloyd of Ynyshir married Elizabeth, daughter of Griffith ab Ievan of Glanfrêd. David was appointed JP in 1640. The church of Eglwys-fach (known earlier as Llanfihangel Capel Edwin) was erected by their son, John Lloyd of Ynys-hir in 1623. Over the south window is inscribed HIC ECC' ERE'C PER JOHE LLOYD AN'O D'ni 1623'. The *L. P. Pugh Manuscript* states that 'formerly on the east pinnacle of the roof stood a curious sundial made of stone, on which were the arms of Lloyd, viz. a cross patonce between four martlets, and his initials and date AD 1623. On the east wall of the chancel were formerly emblazoned a painted coat of arms, quarterly. 1. *argent* a cross patonce *sable,* between four martlets *sable.* 2. a cher between three fleurs de lys. 3. Three boars' heads couped *sable.* 4. a lion rampant within a border engrailed. 5. a chevron between three roses. 6. a griffin rampant *sable*'.

A document from the early 17th century tells us that 'John Lloyd of Ynyshir, gent., was the complainant against Rowland Pugh and Rowland Owen, both JP's, Richard Owen, Thomas Oliver, Hugh ap Owen David, *et al,* with reference to the attempted murder of the complainant at Machynlleth in revenge for the murder of Edward Owen by the complainant's kinsmen at Llanbadarn Fawr'.

John Lloyd had a son, Thomas, of Ynys-hir who married Alice, daughter of Thomas Pryse of Glanfrêd. When Thomas Lloyd died, Alice married Thomas Knowles of Crugmor, Llangoedmor parish. He was a widower with a son, John. The marriage settlement was drawn up on 21 June 1671 as was the settlement upon the marriage of John Knowles, son and heir of Thomas and Dorothy, one of the daughters of Thomas Lloyd deceased, and Alice.

John Knowles was of Ynys-hir and is included in the *Blome List* of 1673. He was Mayor of Cardigan in 1693 and High Sheriff in 1698. Meyrick tells us that Ynys-hir 'is a large, old-fashioned house, belonging to the Lloyds and afterwards to the Knowles family. It then became the property of a Bowen of Upton in Pembrokeshire, Esq., by his marriage to Miss Knowles, the heiress. He left a daughter, who married a Skyrme of Pembrokeshire, Esq., who acquired it in her right and afterwards sold it to Mr. John Hughes the tenant. Mr. Hughes, about the year 1780, sold it to Matthew Davies, Esq., of Cwmcyfni [Cwmcynfelyn], High Sheriff in 1790, in whose possession it still continues'. It became the home of his brother, the Rev. Lewis Charles Davies.

Phillips's *Sheriffs of Cardiganshire*, tells us that in 1790, 'Matthew Davies of Ynys-hir bought the estate of Ynys-hir from Mr. Hughes about 1780. He married Jane, daughter of Roderick Richardes of Penglais and had two daughters who married General Lewis Davies of Tanybwlch and Issac Lloyd Williams of Cwmcynfelin, respectively and whose grandsons were Matthew L. Vaughan Davies of Tan-y-bwlch and George Griffiths Williams of Rhoscellan-fawr'.

With the break-up of the Cymcynfelin

estate towards the end of the 19th century, Ynys-hir was sold to Major James Barry Taunton, the eldest son of Joseph Taunton of Widney Manor, Knowle, Warwickshire. He was born in 1863 and educated at Shrewsbury School. In 1888 he married Priscilla Cheshire. They had three daughters. Major Taunton was a magistrate and High Sheriff of the county in 1903.

From 1921 to 1926, Ynys-hir was the home of Oliver Cross, a son of a Lancashire mill-owner, who had taken holidays at Borth. He was followed by William Mappin, a member of the Mappin & Webb jewellery family, who died in 1966. Most of the estate was sold to the Royal Society for the Protection of Birds for a reserve in 1970 and the house was converted into an hotel. Ynys-hir and 14 acres were bought in 1989 by Mr. and Mrs. R. Reen, and is now a luxury hotel, and whose guests have included royalty and prominent actors.

It is traditionally claimed that Queen Victoria made several clandestine visits to Ynys-hir and that she planted a Persian Ironwood in the grounds. The ghost which appears in the Degas room at the hotel, is said to be that of a young woman mistakenly accused of witchcraft in the 17th century and burnt at the stake.

Grid Ref: SN 6815 9575

Refs: Colby Map, 1831; WWHR, iii, 105; Blome List, 1673; Meyrick, *Cardiganshire,* 1810, edn. 1907, p. 323, also 1808, p. 461-2: see *Arch. Cam.,* 1917, 297-8. Edwards, *Col. Star Chamb.* 1929, p. 157; *Where To Stay in Wales,* 1976 (Wales Tourist Board), p. 52, illus.; NLW, Cwrtmawr Deeds, 1033, 1391; G. E. Evans, *Cardiganshire,* 1903, p. 61; Phillips, *Sheriffs of Cardiganshire;* NLW, P. Pugh MS.; Ex. Info. Mr. & Mrs. Reen.

YSBYTY CYNFYN, Ysbyty Cynfyn

The farm is situated between Devil's Bridge and Ponterwyd and marked on modern OS maps. Ysbyty Cynfyn church is marked on *Colby's Map of 1831* but not the house. The earliest reference is to Howel ap Ieuan Hir descended from Llewelyn Caplan who married Janet, daughter of Rhys Dafydd Meredudd of Llanfihangel Lledrod. His son, Philip ap Howel married Elliw, daughter and co-heiress of David Llwyd ap Morris Goch ap David ap Jenkin Llwyd of Creuddyn. Their son, Morgan Phillip Powel, living at Ysbyty Cynfyn in 1611, was party to several agreements and mortgages. He married Elizabeth, daughter of William ap Richard ap Rhys ap David Llwyd ap David ap Rhydderch ap Ieuan Lloyd. On 2 March 1640-1 David Phillip Powell and Walter Powell, both of Ysbyty Cynfyn were party to an agreement in respect of a grant in trust of two named messuages and a messuage and a mountain house, the latter called Y Lluest ym mlaen Ceunant, in the parish of Llanfihangel-y-Creuddyn. According to Dwnn, David Phillip Powell married Elizabeth, daughter of Edward ap John ap Ieuan Goch. Other pedigrees state that he married a daughter of John ap Edward of Nanteos. What is not disputed is that the Powells later of Llechwedd Dyrys and Nanteos, originated at Ysbyty Cynfyn.

Grid Ref: SN 7531 7909

Refs: Colby Map, 1831; *Dwnn,* i, 24; NLW, Cwrtmawr Deeds, Nos. 55, 315 & 726; G. Morgan *Cyfoeth y Cardi,* pp. 120-2.

YSTRAD, Llanfihangel Ystrad

A sale notice of 'the Llwyd Jack estate' in *The Cambrian* in 1804 describes 'an elegant modern-built dwelling house at Ystrad adjoining the Llwyd Jack demesne, with on the ground floor-two parlours, a dining room, kitchen, outward kitchen, servants' hall, laundry, dairy, pantry, cellar. On the first floor: five good bedchambers with dressing rooms; on the attic storey, bedrooms which will hold eight beds for servants. House lately erected for the residence of the proprietor of the said estate'.

Meyrick tells us that Ystrad House was 'late the residence of David Davies, Esq., and Anne, his wife, of Llwydsiac, in this parish, which stands close to the church and is a neat, respectable house'.

Early records note that in 1570 David Lloyd ap Morgan Fychan, gent., was of Llanfihangel Ystrad and by 1581 Rees David Ieuan Phillip was there. In his will, dated 19 January, 1806, David Davies mentions 'my mother Anne Davies of Aberystywth, my relation Henry Touchet (son of John Touchet of Milman St. County Middlesex, barrister), my relation Thomas Davies, (son of David Davies of Bristol, DL), my aunt Margaret Davies of The Turnstile in the town of Cardigan and in the event of my said realty vesting in the said Henry Touchet, he is to take the surname of Davies and to bear the arms and crest of the Davies's of Llwyd Jack'. Forty-one years later, in 1847, the opinion of J. Boyle of the Temple, barrister, was sought in a legal dispute. It was stated that 'Hugh Llwyd of Llwyd Jack, Esq., died before 1779, leaving wife Mary and daughters Anne and Mary, him surviving, and in possession of Ystrad and Llwyd Jack'. In 1779 the estate was divided between the widow and daughters and charged with annuities. The widow died soon after and the daughter, Anne, married John Davies and had no issue. She died intestate and her share was vested in her sister Anne, who mortgaged the property to Mr. Touchet Davies of Crickhowell, Breconshire, who had been in possession of the property for twenty-six years. In November 1822, Anne, by her will, bequeathed all her personalty to her niece, Mrs. Mary Ann Hyde, who considered herself entitled to the property, as she was first cousin to 'Pugh's wife'. It is said that Touchet Davies had felled enough timber on the estate to satisfy his principal and interest, exclusive of the rents received by him which amounted to £925.14.0. The outcome of this case is unknown.

Grid Ref: SN 5250 5625

Refs: Colby Map, 1831; Lewis, *TDW;* NLW, Griffith Owen Deeds; ibid, Coleman Deeds, Nos. 1461 & 1465, and pp. 13 & 16.

YSTRAD FFLUR, see STRATA FLORIDA

YSTRAD TEILO, Llanrhystud

Situated on the eastern fringe of Llanrhystud on the banks of the Wyre Fach and marked on *Colby's Map of 1831* and on modern OS maps. Meyrick tells us 'Now used as a parsonage house, it is the property of John Llwyd of Mabws . . . The first person who dwelt at Ystrad Teilo and probably erected the first edifice was Richard Llwyd, who married the daughter of Morgan Herbert of Hafod Ychtrid, in the sixteenth century'. Richard's father Ieuan Llwyd John of Llanbadarn Fawr was descended from Elystan Glodrudd and married Elen, daughter of John Pryse of Gogerddan.

Richard ap Ieuan Llwyd, High Sheriff in 1651, was the second son, but succeeded to Ystrad Teilo when his eldest brother David Lloyd, rector of Llangoedmor, died without issue and bequeathed him all his estates. Richard and his wife Gwenllian had a son and heir, Erasmus, who married Bridget, the daughter of David Lewes of Gernos by Mary, daughter of Sir John Lewes of Abernantbychan. Their son, Richard married Elizabeth, daughter of David Lloyd of Crynfryn in 1669. Her portion was £500. They had two sons and a daughter. The elder son, Erasmus succeeded his father and married Jane, the daughter of Thomas Pryse of Gogerddan and Margaret Owen of Peniarth, Merionethshire, and the widow of John Powell. The marriage settlement was agreed on 3 August 1702.

In 1672 Erasmus had paid tax on three hearths. His son Richard Lloyd, BA, a prominent Whig and MP for Cardigan boroughs from 1730-41, married Letitia, daughter of Edward Games of Tregaer, Breconshire. Their daughter and heiress, Anna Maria (1728-1786), married James Lloyd (1721-1800) of Ffosybleiddiaid on 4 June 1750.

Meyrick tells us that 'James Lloyd built a house in this parish, called Mabws and Ystrad Teilo has ever since been let to tenants'. James Lloyd died at Bath. John Lloyd succeeded and was of Ffosybleiddiaid and Mabws. He was born in 1753 and married Elinor, daughter of John Allen of Dale, Pembrokeshire, in 1776. John Lloyd was High Sheriff in 1803. Both he and his wife died in 1820. Their son, John Allen Lloyd married Eliza, daughter of Colonel Harry Bishop, the son of Sir Cecil Bishop and they had three sons, John, Harry and Richard.

In 1760 Owen Morrice was the tenant of Ystrad Teilo. He was followed by the Rev. Isaac Williams (1734-1811), who was instituted to the living of Llanrhystud in 1764 where he remained for the rest of his life. He was also vicar of Penbryn and Llanfihangel-y-creuddyn as well as acting as the Bishop's gamekeeper in the Lordship of Llanddewibrefi. He was the son of David Williams of Tyddynywyre-fach, Llanrhystud, who was descended from Walter ap John of Ynys-wen, Carmarthenshire. Prior to his tenancy of Ystrad Teilo, Isaac Williams lived at Mabws where he was engaged as private tutor to the Lloyd children. In 1769 he and his second wife, Anne Jones, married and moved to Ystrad Teilo where he lived in a style not unfamiliar to his landlord at Mabws. Isaac and his wife had five children; Isaac Lloyd (1771-1846), father of Isaac Williams, the famous Tractarian, Anne (1772-1838), Elizabeth (1776-1846), who married William Cobb Gilbertson and David. William, Isaac's son from the first marriage, died in 1799 aged 37. During the 19th century, Ystrad Teilo was occupied by various tenants. In the 1820's, William Sinnet, a native of Pembrokeshire and his wife, Margaret, farmed the 166 acres of Ystrad Teilo. Slightly deaf, William failed to master the Welsh language, but the Sinnet name has remained in the area to this day. William's son, John, became vicar of Bangor Teifi and one of his daughters married John Jones, who held the tenancy of Ystrad Teilo until the 1880's when the old house was demolished and the present house erected on the same site. A plan of the old house was drawn by E. T. Price, a local historian and reproduced in *Ceredigion* in 1975. In 1961 John D. P. Evans and his wife, Elspeth, moved to Ystrad Teilo.

Grid Ref: SN 5437 6979

Refs: Colby Map, 1831; Blome List, 1673; Meyrick, *Cardiganshire,* 1810 edn. 1907, p. 265-6; WWHR, iii, p. 93; PRO, Dale Castle MS., p. 27 (fo. 106); *TCAS,* vol. I, No. 4, p. 42; *Ceredigion,* vii, 3/4, 1974/5, pp. 332-4-9, D. Emrys Williams; NLW, Llanrhystyd Tithe Apportionment; *The Cambrian Register,* vol. 3, pp. 521-2; Lloyd Records and Pedigree (Davies & Theakstone) s.a.; NLW, Ffosybleiddiaid ped.; CRO, GGMS I (to Elystan Glodrudd); Ex info. J. Evans.

CARDIGANSHIRE DAYS, 1936-1945

by Hugh Charles Jones

The original idea for this book came to F.J. when we lived in Cardiganshire. Those years when he, his wife Ethel, and four children (of whom I am the eldest), were amongst the happiest and most exciting of our family life. They were also momentous times when a whirlwind of savagery devastated the world. It surprises me that my memories now dwell in the 30s of another century.

Whenever he heard an interesting story my father urged, 'Write it down, or it will be lost'. After he died, I surveyed his huge archives including the vast material and grand design for this and many more books. The challenge turned me from my own writing into publishing, aided by my capable and dear wife, Caroline.

As proper when hitching a wagon to a star, my words come after my father's. I hope they give an intimate postscript of social history. Also, that they create a human glimpse of the man behind F.J.'s pen. It is a tribute to the wonderfully happy years our family enjoyed in Cardiganshire. Glorious Arcadian times that we spent on the hills, river banks, beaches, villages and towns in this unforgettable, beautiful county.

It all started in 1936 when a tiny Austin car tackled the hills and sharp corners from Fishguard to Aberystwyth. On the traveller's left, after Aberaeron, Cardiganshire's azure bay sparkled. Ahead, the rippling blue green of the hills beckoned from the coastal road.

B. G. Charles and Francis Jones. Fellow pupils, colleagues and friends who became great Welsh historians.

So Francis Jones and his old school friend Bertie Charles, both in their early twenties, travelled for job interviews at the National Library of Wales. The Great Depression, the General Strike, the Jarrow march and the misery of mass unemployment darkened national life. B. G. Charles despite a brilliant university career was unemployed. F.J. had never left school. From sixth form he became a student teacher. He devoted school holidays and his spare time to historical researches – begun even before teenage years. He was an energetic young man of phenomenal memory, a gifted researcher, and an elegant writer in English and Welsh. He had already made a name for himself as a genealogist, historian and freelance writer. Bertie Charles had begun his remarkable study of Celtic place names, which now stands as a definitive classic on the subject. Sadly Dr. B. G. Charles, Uncle Bert to us, died aged 92 as this article was being written.

F.J. with children at Plas Broginin

The prospect for the young men of job security in the National Library of Wales, amongst its treasure trove of historical records, was dazzling. As tantalising as the Cardiganshire gold mines ahead had been for others on that same route centuries ago.

After their interviews, the nervous young men in their best suits were transformed. Their return journey was triumphant. They had both won jobs as Junior Archivists. F.J. was the first man without a University degree to get such a post. He rushed to his Haverfordwest cottage on Herman's Hill to tell my mother the good news. Happy anticipation must have filled our home as they planned their move to Cardiganshire.

Daddy knew the Pryses of Gogerddan, and rented Plas Broginin from them. In the ten years of formative life in the county I cannot recall even a fleeting instant of unhappiness. We were in rural isolation half a mile from the sparsely populated Penrhyncoch hamlet. Its people were mostly entirely Welsh speaking, shy and insular, for few travelled further than Aberystwyth. It was on the Pryse family estate, and their Gogerddan mansion a short distance away was to the villagers as Buckingham Palace was to Londoners. Cardiganshire in the thirties was thought to be at least fifty years behind the times. For us it was like being cocooned in a time warp of the 19th century. So started our Cardiganshire cadenza of delight.

It sounds incredible these days . . . My father cycled to work in Aberystwyth a 10-mile round trip. He left at the crack of dawn, bowled down through the village, up the hill to Ffynnon Caradog from where he tackled the awesomely long hill to the National Library. He did this two-way journey in all weathers, and I am told he was rarely late. His energy and ability quickly emerged shortly after his appointment. In 1938, *The Cambrian News* reported, 'At the National Library, Mr. Francis Jones gave a talk on *Three Cardiganshire Worthies of the Victorian Age*'. F.J. was also a Territorial Army officer, and often returned late after parades in the far off Drill Hall. I remember my mother lighting the Aladdin paraffin lamp and stoking the fire so that he returned to a welcome through winter gales and pouring rain.

On the crest of the rising ground behind the house a few evergreen pine trees stood like stately sentinels. I used to gaze at them fascinated by their form framed by blue sky. They gave me one of the sudden moments of beauty that a budding memory seizes upon. My father took me on my first visit to Gogerddan. Mouse-quiet, aged five or six I watched Daddy and Sir Lewes Pryse crouched over a long oak refractory table with carved bulbous legs. It overflowed with parchments, maps, family trees, scrolls, letters and diaries. The two men seemed like giant wizards to me then.

Plas Broginin

One rare sunny day when autumn tints were aflame, I was playing on the lawn. I heard a weird noise becoming louder and louder like an approaching devil's train. It was an

Elizabeth, Anne, Dedwydd and Hugh in the stream near Plas Broginin. Inset: 'water sprite' Anne.

unearthly jumble of deep baying, and a high peep-peep-peep of a ghostly horn. It came from behind the ridge facing our home. A red coated rider appeared as if by magic. Then a torrent of foxhounds in full cry poured down towards me. The silent countryside was instantly a tableau of colour and drama. It was the Gogerddan hounds, the oldest private pack of hounds in the UK, formed in 1600. That memory is beyond price to me.

After my sister, Anne, was born our remote home was too much for Mama with four small children. And maybe Daddy's bicycle had gone that puncture too far. We moved to Aberystwyth. Our new home, Glen Vista, was a steep gabled sort of Victorian-alpine whimsy in a secluded cliff-side terrace on the northern side of town. There were steep, gorse-yellow fields behind the house; over the little road a stream tumbled to the sea a short distance away through the sunken copse called the 'Dingle' From it a dawn chorus of birdsong often woke us. It was luxury after spartan life in Plas Broginin. Lamps and candles became redundant; we had electricity. My father's salary was then 2½ guineas a week, though he earned fees from newspaper and magazine articles along with his Territorial Army pay. I fancy that my mother's dowry helped smooth the way to a pleasant, but not extravagant, life. Glen Vista was rented. My parents didn't buy a car as Daddy liked to be driven so that he could view the countryside. He also started his broadcasting career, reading his scripts about Dyfed history in the BBC studio in Aberystwyth. My father had a roomy warm study soon piled high with his papers and lined with hundreds of books. Daddy's writing was of paramount importance in our indoor life. I fancy that along with potty training we were taught to be as quiet as mice when Daddy was writing. Or when Mama proof read for him. Yet she always found time for us children. My father was a complex, driven man with an enormous range of interests. I never knew anyone who managed to do so much. It seemed as if he could actually manufacture time at will. He was never in a great rush, in fact he always seemed to have time to cope with the unexpected. Being up before six he had put in at least two hours work before he went to his office. Often he'd write into the early hours too. His was a life of purpose, planning and a passion for perfection. Yet he was no pedantic dull dog. He delighted in witty repartee; the incongruous and the bizarre fascinated him. He loved funny stories, jokes, amusing limericks, ditties, and the ridiculous in human nature.

Daddy was short, slim, and athletic in movement. He had small dainty hands and feet, and had grey-blue eyes with a melodious baritone voice. He was a brilliant conversationalist of quick-witted perception and radiated a relaxed, easy confidence. Yet he always kept his innermost intentions and opinions to himself. Behind his charisma his mind calculated, analysed and made hidden judgements. He always carried a notebook and jotted down ideas and thoughts as they occurred to him.

Mama was a tiny trim figure, barely 5ft tall, with brown hair and eyes. She was vivacious, warm hearted, capable and energetic. At her Ladies College she had loved painting and music and was an excellent horsewoman. She came from a family of successful land-owning farmers of ancient Pembrokeshire stock. She was born and brought up at Llanrhian, a short distance away from Trevine where my father was born.

My younger brother Dedwydd, and my sisters Elizabeth and Anne and I now had Aberystwyth on our doorstep. Sometimes we heard the pounding thud of the ocean against the promenade wall, and the soughing rattle of pebbles as waves receded to gather for another foaming roar up the beach. The aroma of frying bacon and eggs from the kitchen speeded our dressing to another day of adventures. Now we had neighbours. Some even had cars, seeing them chugging about was as amazing to us as a rocket launch from Cape Canaveral is for today's children. We would rush out of our front garden to see those 20's and 30's models pass. Their spoked wheels with narrow tyres seemed fragile, like big prams. They had running boards, and some had dicky seats instead of boots. Their horns made tinny 'peep peep' noises, and they often left plumes of oily smoke behind them. Petrol was just a few pennies a gallon then. They were mostly small Austins, Morris and Fords. A brand new 10 h.p. A Ford then cost £150. Doubtless my parents could have afforded one, but Daddy wasn't interested. More rarely we saw statelier carriages, Armstrong Siddeleys, Rileys and even a rare Jaguar.

Aberystwyth was full of colour, the sea in all its moods, its sunsets and storms. The brightly painted hotels, guesthouses, students quarters, and cafes along the curving promenade. The pier jutting elegantly out over a rocky reef, the beach intersected by breakwaters sweeping into the sea, and to the eternal horizon beyond.

There was also the constant ebb and flow ashore of a human wave of students and holiday makers, all with their set times of wakes weeks and college terms. The outside world sent its ideas and fashions which the ancient town absorbed effortlessly, whilst the ruins of its castle looked benignly across the town and its quaint modern fancies. The promenade was a catwalk of thirties fashion. Young women wore low-hipped flapper dresses, their hair was bobbed and shingled under cloche hats. Single strapped buttoned shoes were the rage too, Greta Garbo set the style in perms and bright lipsticks for these chattering groups of young women. Their swains had short 'brillianteened,' plastered down hair, many with Douglas Fairbanks Jnr. mustachios and wore tight-fitting double-breasted suits and Gatsby type shoes. They smoked cigarettes through long holders and some wore straw boaters. We'd peer at them as they drank cocktails and flirted in hotel bars overlooking the sea. We sometimes heard strains of Jazz wafting out of the Bellevue and Queen's hotels on the front. George Formby and Gracie Fields were favourites then and 'The folks who live on the hill' was a hit of the moment. Fascist bands were roaring out patriotic music in Italy and Germany and there was talk of a phoney war.

Dearly loved by husband and children.
F.J.'s wife, Ethel, outside their Aberystwyth home during World War II.

"When the World was young."
Happy pre-War days in Cardiganshire
for Francis and Ethel Jones.

I was never in a hurry to get home in sunny weather, and I would meander along the promenade. It was two Pekinese dogs on a coupled leash that alerted me to a figure straight out of a fairy tale. An unearthly woman floated towards me. She wore a big floppy hat at a rakish angle, her unwaisted dress was a mass of softly rustling silk ribbons, diamonds glittered, and she wore shining dainty patent leather shoes. She had dark hair and big mascara'd eyes and her lips were painted scarlet. One gloved hand held the dogs' lead and the other a gay sun parasol, and she left behind her a delicate scent. Filled with excitement I rushed home and told my mother. 'She's a Countess,' my mother said. In fact she was the Countess Bacynska, also known less exotically, as Mrs. Ceredig Evans. Both she and her husband were writers.

Once I saw a strange mosquito-type craft, high in the sky and fluttering at heaven's doorstep it seemed. I was told it was a brand new invention, 'a gyro-copter.' In the outside world Armageddon stirred, Italian planes dropped poison gas on villages that once the Queen of Sheba had ruled, and they machine-gunned Abyssinian cavalry.

The promenade cavalcade included all generations. There were stately Midlands bourgeois men with ample waistcoated stomachs across which stretched heavy gold chains. Some wore stiff celluloid collars and had walrus moustaches, and diamond tie pins twinkled. Their well-upholstered wives were a flutter with bright silk dresses rippling with frills. Their hair was perm waved and topped with cartwheel hats with streamer ribbons. Other, younger, city men wore plus fours, diamond checked pullovers and big flat caps. It had not occurred to me before, but Aberystwyth's Welsh population was outnumbered by seasonal visitors and students from outside Wales for most of the year.

The next house down was divided into two flats. One tenant was a Mr. Abrahams, the first Jew I ever saw. He lived alone and seemed an exotic figure. Short and portly he wore a black coat and bowler hat in all weathers. He was bearded with long ringlets of hair about his ears. He never spoke to anybody. One day he vanished as suddenly as he had appeared. The other flat dweller was a pleasant young university student. We used to see him sometimes in his OTC uniform and talked to him. He kindly showed us his rifle, a Martini Henry I think it was. He told us it had last seen service in the Boer War. He vanished as suddenly as Mr. Abrahams, I often wonder if he survived the war.

Further down lived two old sisters, of 'independent means' as not having to work was called in those days. They took a liking to me and invited me to tea. Their house fascinated me, it was darkened by much large antique furniture and big Victorian oils and watercolours. They laid a large tea out on a decorative brass topped table which had dark teak legs ending in carved lions paws. Their father had been a tea planter in 'Injah' as they pronounced it. They were in their 70's and were old enough to have spoken to survivors of the Indian Mutiny and possibly the Black Hole of Calcutta.

One day some five or six new children arrived at school. They didn't speak much English as they were Jewish. They were pretty and had very good manners, and my favourite was called Ruth. I asked her one day what was it like to be Jewish, but her friends shook their heads at her and made shushing noises, so she never told me. The war was getting very close. They had fled from Nazi domination. They couldn't have got further away than Aberystwyth. There was only Ireland and Canada after that.

I was learning to read and write at North Road Primary School, and struggling to change my words and thoughts from Welsh into English. Daddy also taught me at home. At least he tried, but I was an obtuse student. We lived quite near to the school which stood in a long tree-lined avenue with brightly painted 1900s villas overlooking tennis courts.

Before the war when the global map was heavily red, and the sun never set on the British Empire, we had a visitor to our bay. It was a huge grey battleship, *HMS Resolution,* and although it stood a long way out it still seemed gigantic. It was dressed overall with bunting and flags over its killer cannons. Best of all it was fully lit up at night. It appeared overnight, and suddenly made the wide Cardiganshire bay seem smaller. The town was alive with sailors in tight blue jerseys and bell-bottomed trousers. Word soon got round to us children that it was lucky to touch a sailor's collar. We used to follow them and jump up, touch their collars and run away. There was a big dance for the visitors that night in the ballroom at the end of the pier. With my bedroom window open I heard the faint sound of music on the summer's night air. Then one morning the bay was empty and looking out at the waves where the leviathan had ridden at anchor we felt a sense of loss.

Running down to the beach one day I noticed that the bay's horizon was filled with tiny figures moving across it, little black crescent shapes diving and reappearing in an endless procession. It was the dolphins passing by.

One winter's night in 1938 a howling ferocious gale whipped up the sea and hit the town, tearing off chimneys, uprooting trees, and blowing off roof slates. All night long above the shrieking of the wind we heard the dull thump, thump of the sea pounding the promenade. Our house was sheltered, and being snug and warm we thought it was very exciting. Daybreak came and all able-bodied men went down to try and plug a gaping hole in the side of the promenade. Daddy took us down to see the action, the further we went down the hill the more pebbles, sand and seaweed there was which the sea had thrown up and over four-storied buildings. The sea wall was a breached ruin where rain soaked men formed a human chain, working urgently to rebuild the ramparts before the next high tide. The bay was a hissing boiling cauldron, and gusts of rain hammered the sea front. The streets ran with a mixture of rain, seawater, sand and pebbles. It was reckoned to be the worst storm to hit Aberystwyth for over a hundred years. We thought it was the most exciting event we'd seen in our young lives. A short distance from the devastation stood *The Queen's Hotel.* Its front windows were smashed and the furious waves had flooded the cellars. A young page boy swam through the cellars in the darkness to put out the boilers before they exploded. It was an incredible act of courage. A presentation was later made to this gallant youth to commemorate his bravery.

The lifeboat *Frederick Angus* was kept quite near to the slip-way which lead to the sea from the promenade. It had to be pulled through the streets to the slip by willing townspeople alerted by the wailing siren, in order to be launched. We often watched the launch.

My father once took my brother and me to his Regimental Boxing match in the Drill Hall. It was crowded and there were clouds of pipe and cigarette smoke. I couldn't see much of the contests. What I did see though were flashes of white bodied men with cropped hair flailing at each other, gobs of blood flying through the air, and roaring spectators with gaping mouths, popping eyes and a tremendous amount of coarse shouting. All rather frightening to small boys. My father bought us boxing gloves, and used to get my brother and me to fight each other. It upset my mother so my brother and I agreed that we wouldn't hit each other hard. We would flail away, which seemed to satisfy my father.

Daddy had a friend called Kenneth Bristow; he was a tall slim man with glasses and a mop of tousled hair. He was always smiling and giving us piggyback rides I remember. He had a long rowing boat, and once took us out a short way from the shore and then dived into the clear, still, sea. Down he went, down and down. It seemed to last forever, and we were much relieved when he came up at the other side of the boat. My father and he decided to row to Ireland. My mother was deeply upset, however Daddy persisted. So one day we all helped to pack the boat with provisions. Lots of round cake tins with food my mother had prepared, as well as my father's big service revolver. Must be pirates around, I thought. We watched them row out of sight. Then we went home, my mother crying silently from time to time, we children were quiet, and huddled round her holding her hand. A few days later we got a telegram from North Wales. It was from my father, and he was coming home by train.

In Aberystwyth town near the church where I was a choirboy, there was a pub with a stable yard. I don't know who discovered the pony in it and the red eyed handyman who worked there. However, my mother came to an arrangement with him in the yard which smelled of the manure heap and the beery smell of the bars. He was to lead the pony with me astride for an hour or so for money which was soon spent on beer, for the man always smelled of it. My enthusiasm for riding became an obsession after a while, so my mother decided it was time to buy me a pony. We went out to a hill village to see a horse dealer who was reputed to be the illegitimate son of a local land-owning squire. We settled upon a black pony complete with saddle and bridle, reassured by the many loud phrases in English and Welsh regarding its suitability and countless virtues. The animal, Betty by name, was delivered to us and put in our milkman's orchard up the small valley from our house. I spent a sleepless night at the thought of riding my very own pony and got up very early to catch her. Complete with a bowl of oats and a bridle I thrilled to the approach of my pony. As she snuffled for the feed I grasped her firmly by the forelock. With effortless expertise she swung her head from left to right. Still hanging on I described an arc with my feet high off the ground, at the end of which I sailed through the air to be thrown against an apple tree trunk, landing winded in the dewy grass. My mother finally came

The bucking pony. H.C.J. with Betty.

A lesson in manners.
H.C.J.'s mother sorts out the wild pony.

up to help me. I can't remember how on earth we finally caught her, but the pony became my partner in many escapades.

There were three cinemas in the town, The Forum, The Coliseum and The Pier; admission cost 1s. 3d., 9d. or 6d. My brother and I used to go to see the adventures of Flash Gordon and the Lone Ranger on Saturday mornings. We soon found that the trick was to get there early, to get seats that weren't broken. A broken seat really spoiled the experience. During the holidays my brother and I decided that we'd go to the evening performance. My mother said 'No.' We persisted, she was adamant. We mutinied and told her that we had saved enough money and that we'd go anyway. 'No you won't,' she said. We edged to the door. She still said 'No'. We walked down the path, and said from the gate, 'we ARE going'. We walked briskly down the road. Then our steps slowed. We stopped, turned and went back home. My mother opened the door; she'd been watching us from the bay window. She said, 'I knew you'd come back. Now have some cake and milk before you go to bed'.

My brother and I being rather cherubic (in looks anyway), were pressed into service for a local Christmas pantomime. We were to be, in one scene, little sailors, and in another, part of a pack of rats. Rehearsals were held in the great gothic Queen's Hotel. As the performance day drew closer our costumes, made from blackout material, were finished by my mother, and we arrived at the venue. I became fascinated by an enormous fire extinguisher, red and pointed in shape with a round brass plunger. I don't know what impelled me so very slyly to push that plunger home. With a whooshing sound foam appeared everywhere and spattered children, rats and pirates who shrieked in rising terror as the extinguisher emptied itself inexorably. The adults, startled by the pandemonium, rushed in, to be immediately covered in the foam storm. They added their own hysteria to ours as they searched for the deadly flames which surely was the cause of the drama. As foam and panic abated I realised for the first time in my life that there was potential for big, big trouble. Each budding star was questioned with dreadful directness 'Did you do it?' In a shameful split second I lied with conviction, 'No' I said. To give my denial more authority, I repeated it in Welsh. When I got home with foam-spattered costume I told my mother the truth. She put her hand over her mouth and went away for awhile.

There was a blacksmith's forge in Aberystwyth. Its entrance was in a horseshoe shape. I loved going there. The dark interior, the glowing fire, and the cheerful brothers who hammered the iron shoes were great company, being full of humour and horse talk. I told them once that I needed a pair of spurs to get more speed out of my pony. There was such kindness in that forge that the next time I visited a pair of smart spurs was produced for me. I took them home to polish the straps before riding out to introduce speed aids to Betty. The golf course up the road would do very nicely I thought, and I rode glancing down to admire the silver glinting heels that I'd acquired. On the green turf I rammed home the spurs. We careered headlong at full gallop. I dug them in again. This time Betty, whose astonishment had turned to rage, stopped dead. With unbelievable ferocity she bucked, squealed and threw me and my legs got tangled up with the reins. In her wild flight she trampled me and I can still see in my mind's eye, the girthed belly above me, and the glint of her iron hooves. When she tired of kicking me about I sorted myself out and caught her and we walked home slowly with the spurs in my pocket. I then pleaded a headache, and went up to my room to examine the red swollen bruises on my body.

When the war came I was disappointed that Betty and I were not asked to lead a death-or-glory charge against the enemy. She was then out on the hillside behind our house with a few younger companions. Betty, perhaps also infected with war fever, decided to break out and lead her chums down to town on night patrol. In the darkness they used the wide promenade as a nocturnal racecourse. The effect of the ringing, galloping hooves on the slumbering townsfolk was as dramatic as if Prussian cavalry had arrived intent on slaughter, rape and pillage. Blackout regulations worked in the animals' favour, as no one dared to produce a torch, in case it brought down the venom of the German Luftwaffe. Living out of the town we were still fast asleep, as in the early dawn policemen and furious townsfolk cornered the ponies. By breakfast they had been identified, and by lunchtime my mother's respectable name was on a shaming charge sheet in the Police station.

Looking back I think that the fine of five shillings my mother received was quite lenient really. Possibly because it was her first offence. But she was mortified to see her name reported in the *Cambrian Times.*

One of my riding companions was called Daphne, she was tall and had long golden plaits. I fell in love with her and she with me. We enjoyed many happy days in the mountains thrilled by our innocent affection. We wrote to each other in the term time as she lived in far away England, where I had never been. A place I'd never heard of called Bognor Regis. She sent me letters that were scented, and if I smell that fragrance even today I instantly recognise it.

I was grooming my pony in our back yard, and thought how very amusing it would be for my mother, who was in the front garden, to come in and see the pony in the kitchen. So I coaxed the animal in. Things went very wrong. The pony's greed didn't desert her in the strange confines of the kitchen. She stuck her head into a bowl of flour on the table. One snort and the room was filled with a mini snowstorm. This startled her, and my mother rushed in to get the frenzied animal out of the wreckage. She was never allowed in the house again.

We used to run down the shale cliff to the beach like mountain goats. One day my cliff-leaping antics attracted the attention of a old lady. As children we were never warned against strangers, and I have no recollection of children being abused. So when I was asked to sit down on a bench with a stranger I did. The woman told me all about the pleasures of Scouting. I must have met her again, because I still have a hand-written copy of the Cub's prayer 'As a cub I will always do my best, etc.' Inspired, I joined the local cub pack and waited for my uniform which was a green jersey, cap, neck scarf held together with a woggle and green garters. I was thrilled to see my mother sew the Welsh dragon on the sleeves. The meetings were great fun, as were the camps for we had excellent teachers. Some time during my scouting career I took my scholarship exam for boarding school. During the anxious weeks waiting for the results I was part of a parade through the town with units from the army, Air Force, St. John Ambulance, the Salvation Army Band and Territorials. Marching through the town with enormous seriousness and oblivious of my insignificance, I felt a tap on my shoulder. I saw my mother alongside me. 'You passed the exam,' she said, her face glowing with happiness. In my mind I was then the star turn of that parade through Aberystwyth.

In those perfect days of my childhood near to the sea, my brother and I soon learned to swim. We started by kicking our heels in the shallows, as we got more confident we went further out. Then just a little further. The transition to actually swimming a few strokes was quick. I loved the sea so much that I would skip breakfast to be in the water. I would stay in until I shivered and my teeth chattered until my jaws ached.

One morning I woke to the sun streaming into my bedroom. I knew what I wanted to do more than anything. The tide should be just right, I decided to dive off the end of the wooden breakwater into the sea. Breakfast could wait. Within moments I was out of the house and running down the terrace. I saw Cardiganshire Bay stretching out to a hazy horizon under an azure sky. I was so full of eagerness that racing downhill my heels tapped at my buttocks; I felt that if I took a big jump I could leap far out into the blue bay.

On the deserted beach I quickly changed and clambered up the last upright post of the breakwater. I wanted to savour the moment. Instead of diving in instantly I looked far out to sea. The far bay was empty of ships, my eyes travelled from the clear blue sea, I looked down into the water below me. Behind me the sleepy town was silent. The mirror calm sea lapped like sighs. I saw through the clear water to the sand and pebbles. I was enthralled. I dived, and still remember the hubbling, bubbling waters drumming at my ears; I still have the vision of the sand and the coloured pebbles. Why does nature make such moments unforgettable? I have dived in many seas since, but this particular experience I can never forget. The memory of it is pure, poignant nostalgia.

During those days the wireless become a command post for information in our home. For we children it was the music we loved, George Formby's ukulele and ragtime jazz, and classical music. My parents listened intently to war talk, and with some relief to the news of Chamberlain's 'Peace in our Time'.

About this time momentous things happened under distant waves. The submarine HMS *Thetis* sank with her crew outside Liverpool. Desperate efforts were made to raise her but she slipped back to the bottom. There were two survivors, and the tragedy cast a horrified gloom in the UK. Other submarine crews were in serious training as U-boats of the resurgent German navy took to the sea.

We had became expert at catching little fish in rock pools, so raised our sights to big fat trout. A few miles off the cliff path there lay little Clarach bay where a river runs into the sea. In its lower reaches there were trout pools. One sunny day, we set out fishing as my father did. My mother put our lunch into my father's big angling bag. With rods on our shoulders my brother and I tramped off. The river was deserted and we fished various pools. Then to our dismay we were joined by an adult angler, an Englishman at that, who asked us where the best spots were. In an instant silent conspiracy we pointed at a pool we had previously decided was useless. Amiably he set up there, a few hundred yards away. To our dismay he soon pulled out a fine fish, then another. Outraged and disgusted we decided to have lunch. I discovered that in the bumpy walk the maggot tin lid had come off and there were squirming maggots everywhere. So we picked the maggots out to eat our sandwiches. My brother was munching away andI was maggot removing, when the man came over to show us his fine catch and to thank us for our generosity in putting him onto a good thing. He stopped, stared at the sandwich in my hand, and asked me what I was doing. 'Getting the maggots out of my sandwich', I said. He left silently. We told Mama all about it when we got home. She said that it didn't matter that we hadn't caught any fish. We'd brought home the best fisherman's story she'd ever heard. We were always careful of the maggot tin after that.

Being a university town there were always lots of young men trying to impress girls on the beach. I saw one upside-down walking on his hands. Very dramatic it was too. Even more spell-binding I saw loose change falling from his pockets into the soft sand. I waited, and when they left, I swiftly took the money. I soon became expert at handstands. So when I saw a mixed group on the beach I would walk on my hands. Sure enough some young man would do the same. But as a way of making steady money it was hard work. I had to do it before the men got into swimming trunks. Sometimes they'd have no money, or worse would pick it up and put it back in their pockets. Then I went home where happiness had nothing to do with money.

War years

My father was in the Territorial Army so we often saw him in uniform. On one parade he marched with his regiment through the town. My mother and I were standing in the crowd when they marched by. As my father passed, Mama reached out and touched his shoulder. But he didn't react at all, just stared to his front, no doubt filled with dreams of military glory like Alexander or Napoleon. I thought it strange that he didn't say hello or smile. Then it was time to say goodbye. My father in his best uniform, creased trousers, and with shining badges and buttons; my mother in her smartest clothes, we children clean and tidy. We all went down to the railway station. My first sight was of the huge green glistening steam engine hissing out smoke in the dark Victorian station. My mother clung very close to my father, and the platform was full of other soldiers' families saying goodbye. Then with a great hissing and chuffing the train drew away. All we saw were waving khaki arms getting smaller through the wisps of smoke, as they left for the darker fog of war. My mother was silent as we went home in the winter's gloom. She didn't cry in front of us. Throughout the long war not once did she let us see that she was worried or sad.

'Give us the child until he's seven, and we'll show you the man', say the Jesuits. When Daddy went away I was about eight years old, his influence on me was profoundly permanent. Being polite, table manners, neatness, respect for elders, family loyalties, saying my prayers nightly – all became second nature to me then. My parents taught me a love of animals, to ride, swim, shoot, draw, to listen to music. They kindled my imagination in a love for literature. We had family expeditions in the countryside and along the coast when they pointed out the beauty of nature to us. At our fireside we heard legends and family stories. I absorbed the parental example of having purpose in life. Daddy at his desk, Mama, knitting, sewing, proof-reading, playing the piano, writing letters and planning the structure of our family life. As I get older, my parents seem to grow wiser in retrospect. They are gone now, but their precepts still form the rock from which I weather life's storms.

War clouds gather. Territorial soldiers march through Aberystwyth. Sailors and police line the route. F.J. is in line with second tree.

In 1940 Aberystwyth was full of young men in uniform. The town was full of activity, lots of men drilling, loading lorries and a great deal of shouting and the noise of hobnailed boots on the promenade.

There were pilot cadets from Canada, Australia and New Zealand in blue uniforms and forage caps with white flashes, and soldiers in khaki with all sorts of regimental badges on their berets. Yet in spite of all of many strangers I never heard of any serious crimes. In fact law breaking in Aberystwyth was rare. One of the reasons for this was that the magistrates stood for no nonsense. For example a gang of boys who robbed vending machines on the pier got four strokes of the birch. An uninsured car driver received a three-year ban. The police were hot on gambling too, arresting a group of lads playing pitch and toss. They were fined £2 each, a great sum for them no doubt. Stern Victorian justice reigned. The suggestion of having women in the police, even for the duration of the war was smartly rejected by the Council as 'outrageous'.

We got food parcels in the war, chiefly from America and Australia. Many convoys had run the gauntlet of bombs and torpedoes to get to Great Britain. Lots of the foods were in powdered form. A story went round that a family got a battered parcel with a tin containing grey powder. This was thought to be a composite grain for soup. The family didn't really like it, but being Cardiganshire farmers, who are notoriously frugal, they persevered. A month or two later they got a letter from Australia. It said that it was hoped that they had received the ashes of Great Uncle Evan, and would they scatter them over the farmland where he had been brought up. I suppose it was another of the Chinese whispers that go round in wartime, like the one about Russian soldiers with snow on their boots being seen in Scotland.

The Aberystwyth promenade stood some 14 to 20 feet above the beach. When the sea was rough the waves would rush in and pound at the walls sending up great torrents of water onto the promenade. It was great fun to wait till the sea receded, run forward, and then back again when the next wave hit. Without doubt the most thrilling exploit was to jump down to the beach in one spot and run round the end corner before the breakers got you. Some onlookers would applaud us; others threatened to tell our parents, or even the police. I suppose I would have forgotten these exploits, but as it was wartime some keen young officer decided to toughen up his men. They tried to do what we had done, but they didn't take their heavy equipment into account, and some soldiers were drowned. I didn't see the incident, but for a long time afterwards I always thought of them when I passed the spot. They were training for a commando raid on St. Nazaire I think.

Leaflets were delivered to our home telling us how to help to win the war. To kick the Hun where it hurt we should 'Dig for Victory' and grow food we were told. My brother and I consulted Mama who got some young lettuce plants. We then carefully dug a little plot in our top garden behind the house. Then we watered them. All day we returned with a watering can and fussed over them. By evening there was no sign of growth, and we worried that they might die overnight. So we put up our tent and settled down for the lettuce guard. It got darker, and we relieved the boredom by stealing apples from a neighbour's orchard as the sun set. We got cold and had tummy aches too from green apples so we went indoors to our beds. The following morning we rushed back to our vegetable plot. The lettuces just lay on the earth looking waterlogged, yellow, and dead. So we made another plan to defeat the Germans with our spades. We went up the hill to where the cliffs were really high, dressed up in every item of military style gear we had. A forage cap of my fathers, water bottles, and toy guns. We found a spot with a good view of the bay. We spent hours digging a shallow trench from which we would repel the enemy who would surely land in the cove some 200 ft below. We were resting on our backs listening to the gorse popping, and watching the white clouds in the clear blue sky when a tall army officer appeared. He seemed very old to us. He had glasses and a red nose which blended nicely with the acres of First World War medal ribbons on his chest. He tried to be kind to us and pointed out that our trench was in the wrong place. On the way home for food, my brother and I decided that digging for victory was too difficult and unrewarding, that we'd find different ways of destroying Hitler at some other time. German tank machine gunners were annihilating the Polish Cavalry at the time.

My father was overseas. All the news we had from him in Africa, Italy and so on came in blue Forces airmail letters which were crammed with tiny writing. There were long intervals between these letters when he was in action. My mother showed me something strange about one letter. My father wrote asking after friends she had never heard of. She solved the puzzle by writing down the initials of these names, and found she had a code account of where he had been. I was, as the eldest son, sworn to secrecy.

One night we saw a flickering glare down the coastline. The next day we heard that it was the oil refinery at Milford Haven which the Germans had bombed. Little war dangers came to Aberystwyth, though once there was a great deal of siren howling and whistle blowing and we were told to stay indoors. We heard a dull booming roar out at sea, a German mine had been exploded. We searched in vain for pieces of shrapnel; some of the University windows were blown out.

The total blackout meant our windows were completely curtained in case a small chink of light could signal a German bomber in from the night sky to kill us all. My mother worked hard on the blackout as it was known. We had a bay window in our sitting room, and one dark winter's night I wriggled under the curtains, and then stared for a long time at the sparkling stars. One bright group fascinated me. Later I asked my mother about them. She took me outside and said, 'I call them the frying pan' Whenever I see the Great Bear constellation I think of her.

My mother had the four of us to feed and keep, and war fever came into her kitchen. A great Appeal was launched, and she had to part with her prized aluminium saucepans, they were thrown onto a lorry and driven off to England to make weapons to obliterate Germans. We were luckier than some of our neighbours, who lost their iron railings to patriotism, and gates went too. We thought that the railings were to be made into special spears.

One afternoon when we had an aunt staying with us my mother said 'Get your best clothes on. When the others have gone to bed, I've got a surprise for you.' My mother dressed up too. She took me by the hand and we walked down the hill and along the promenade to the *Seagull* cafe. There we had a cup of tea then we walked home. I know now that those outings were important to her. Her husband being away at war, the only way she could get out among all the young soldiers, airmen and students in the town was by bringing her small son with her as a squire and to show that she was a married woman.

My mother was visited by an evacuee billeting officer. Then three completely strange children arrived in our house. They were evacuees from Liverpool. Some of the 14,200 scheduled for evacuation to Cardiganshire. We couldn't understand a word they spoke. They took all our toys. They grabbed all the food they were given, and took ours too. The only things they had that they shared with us were fleas. They turned the dining table into a shambles. They adapted to the freedom of the country only too soon, and my mother was constantly searching for them. Mama must have appealed to the billeting officer and the children went to other homes. They were sad to go, and came back to see us from time to time.

I once heard on the wireless an account of a battle in North Africa when an artillery regiment held an advance by the Panzers at a place called Beja. Later when my mother was decoding a letter from my father the name Beja was mentioned. I told her 'There's been a battle there, and Daddy was in it'. True enough it was, and my father was mentioned in despatches and received a special medal for the action.

As the war went on toys became scarce, we were lucky, we didn't need many. We had our fishing tackle and ponies, we swam and used to go long distances exploring. We climbed the cliff rocks round the corner from the breakwater where Mama and adults couldn't stop us. We progressively climbed higher and higher on our secret outings. We decided we needed a rope to climb the final stretch, up over an overhang to get to the top cliff path. So before our next assault we borrowed my mother's clothes line. We got a pal to wait at the top; he was to throw the line down to us so we could clamber the last lap hanging onto the rope. Everything worked perfectly. After the long climb I grabbed the line and hauled myself up. When I cleared the overhang with an enormous drop to the rocks below me I noticed that the rope was fraying where it cleared the final ledge. No monkey ever went up a stick as fast as I moved then. I stared at the fraying rope with strange clarity of mind, I remember a feeling of urgency but no panic. It's a feeling I've had many times since, but that was the first time. We never told anybody about this. It stayed in the secret world of children from which even the kindest parents are excluded.

Throughout the war nobody of importance visited Aberystwyth, it was after all a rural backwater. In the outside world it was the time of the Blitz and Battle of Britain. One exception was Lady Baden-Powell, whose husband had founded the Boy Scout movement. We cubs took part in the grand parade, after which we went to a big chapel for a service. The order was given after a final line-up to break ranks and approach Lady Baden-Powell and her staff. I remember they all had enormous busts that seemed to cast a shadow over their thin legs. I wondered how they remained upright. I didn't speak to her.

My mother called us children to a family conference one day. It was to do with food rationing. Sugar to be precise. She explained we had a choice. No sugar in tea meant we could have jam. Sugar in tea meant no jam. Jam today won the day easily by a unanimous vote. Living in Wales, even in the war there was never a shortage of milk for our tea. It was delivered to our house by a horse and milk float early in the mornings. So my memories of daybreak are of cocks crowing in the distance and the clip clop of the milkman's horse and his cry of milk'o.

My brother Dedwydd and I went away to public school. Our adventurous freedom ended abruptly. Those schooldays were not the happiest of my life. I was homesick and lived for the holidays. Few of my fellow boarders had fathers in the armed forces, most seemed to be in reserved occupations. My sisters, Elizabeth and Anne, went to St. Padern's Convent school in Aberystwyth.

My father meanwhile took part in three sea-borne landings. North Africa, Sicily and then the carnage of Salerno. His regiment fought a desperate winter campaign with the retreating Germans up to the slaughter of the battle of Monte Cassino. He still managed to write sporadically, and his blue airmail letters stamped 'Passed by the censor' came through the Glen Vista letterbox.

My brother and I were home on holiday when our grandmother visited, as usual laden with butter, eggs, ham etc. from the farms of our Pembrokeshire relatives. When we saw her off home on the train she said, 'I have the strangest feeling that Francis is back in England'.

Mama answered a knock on the door the next day. A slim brown faced man in uniform stood there. She fell into Daddy's arms. After over four years he had come home. Within days he was back in his study going through his papers. He had been second in command of his regiment and in line for promotion to Colonel. He was suddenly pulled out from the front line and posted to the War Office as a Staff Officer to help with writing the official history of the War.

So our one parent family days ended. Daddy then went to London which was being pounded by the savagery of the dying Third Reich. Flying bombs called doodlebugs crashed into the capital hourly. My father decided we would move to Roch Castle in Pembrokeshire which Lord St. Davids lent us. Our Cardiganshire idyll ended. The big blue Pickfords van loaded up. Suddenly our old home was echoing and empty. We children cried. I traced my name on the lorry's dusty tail gate. I wanted to see it when we arrived. I wanted to remember it was the last thing I did in Cardiganshire. I recall it now as if it were yesterday.

Gogerddan

The Author when a young follower of the Gogerddan Foxhounds.

Shortly after Daddy left for war I rode my pony in a gymkhana at Gogerddan. Sir Lewes and Lady Pryse, knowing my father was on active service, sought me out. They took me into the great mansion for tea. She was a glamorous figure, slim, blue eyed, vivacious. He was short, stocky, with a grey moustache and had great charm. They had only recently been married. Swiftly they put me at ease, talking of horses and the bore of having to go to school. We laughed a lot and they invited me to stay whenever I wished, and to ride and hunt there to my heart's content. It was an invitation I eagerly accepted as we were living in Aberystwyth then. Later, living in Pembrokeshire and then London and the Cotswolds, I returned like a Cardie homing pigeon to the Pryses.

Gogerddan had been the heart of a virtual kingdom in mid Wales for over 500 years. The Pryse family fortunes consisted at one time of gold and lead mines in the area, as well as over 33,000 acres in the county. They owned further acreage in Pembrokeshire, Merionethshire and Breconshire, another estate in Gloucestershire, a London town house and even a Scottish island.

I used to ride through the wrought iron gates past the tall lodge with its dormer windows and leaded panes. Up a long curved drive with iron railings to my left, and the right hand side was a mass of flowering multi-coloured rhododendrons. I came round the final curve, to my left was a sweep of parkland running up to vast deciduous woods. On the right was an enormous circular lawn bordered by a gravel path, behind which stood the largest house I'd ever seen. Its partially ivy covered facade must have stretched some 300 yards and it was three stories high and painted white. There were some thirty large windows, and ten huge chimney stacks. To the far right of this glorious place a humpback bridge crossed a stream, and because Gogerddan was set in a hollow, the hills behind framed the building with a solid background mass of trees. there was always birdsong. In its heyday it needed a staff of 85 servants to run the house, the kennels and the stables. Then there were the gardens, formal and vegetable, and the gardeners, and there was a team of builders and carpenters fully employed maintaining the whole estate. There was even a private steeplechase course near the lodge gates. A stone age burial ground was found when that was constructed.

All around was many millennia of continuous human history and a rare way of life. So when I went off to boarding school I wrote to them and asked if I could come and stay. We had moved to Pembrokeshire by then and lived at Roch, the gaunt old castle, which none of us liked.

I set off by GWR steam engine to Aberystwyth and Gogerddan for the first trip away from home on my own. I was met at the station by a very likeable Irishman called O'Donnell, who was the professional huntsman. He was a superior type of hunt servant, came from a good family, but had no money and had turned his sport into his livelihood. He lived with his very pretty wife in the lodge. He had a green Bentley and he drove me to Gogerddan with the hood down. I hadn't been in many cars, so it was exciting with the wind blowing my hair about and the roar of the engine. The Pryses were as kind and welcoming to me as if I'd been a Prince of the Blood, sadly they were childless.

The great hall at Gogerddan had a huge polished refectory table in the middle of it, with gloves, riding whips, papers and a big silver salver with claw feet on it. Facing me were two enormous Van Dyck portraits of Pryse ancestors, on the right there was a Georgian writing desk surmounted with oil paintings of hunting scenes. There were dogs everywhere, dachshunds, retrievers and some very active terriers. In front of me, and to left and right there were doors leading to the endless recesses of the mansion. I wasn't to know it at the time, but I was in a complete time capsule, nothing much had changed there for many hundreds of years, the last face-lift took place in the 1850s, and the furniture and pictures had been there a great deal longer.

After supper served by a dour old butler, Lady Pryse showed me to my bedroom, up the broad stairs to a large landing, then to a decorated glass door. When we opened it my candle flickered in the draught; we went down a long corridor, then through another glass door to my room which overlooked the front lawn. I was left to unpack alone with my silver candlestick and a box of matches. My bedroom was a typical Georgian bachelor bedroom. It contained a tall cheval mirror, a tallboy, a chest of drawers with another mirror, there were combs, brushes, scissors and stud boxes laid out An elegant wash stand stood complete with water jug, bowl and soap dish all marked with the Pryse coat of arms. There were delicate watercolours of Italy, and a print facsimile of Charles I's death warrant above a very long high bed. It was hard to get to sleep on this my first night away from home. I don't know when there was a child in the house last. Certainly it was over sixty years ago since Sir Lewes was my age.

I was awoken by the sound of gravel hitting my window. Dear heaven, I'd overslept. I drew the curtains. On horseback and leading another horse saddled up was O'Donnell. I dressed at speed and flew downstairs past the housekeeper, out of the door and into the saddle, unwashed unbreakfasted. What a way to start my stay. One moment fast asleep, the next on a horse rubbing the sleep out of my eyes. Then down to the kennels, and out for hound exercise with about twenty couple of eager rough coated Welsh foxhounds.

Lady Pryse and I rode in front with two whips flanking the pack as we rode up through Penrhyncoch village, where most of the men and women had worked for the estate as had their fathers before them. I saw a sight that didn't strike me as unusual then. An old woman in a sparkling clean pinafore came to her cottage door and curtsied as we passed. All the men tipped their caps, and the older ones removed them altogether. Altogether quite a royal progress. The village was at one time owned entirely by the Pryse family, along with many more in Wales. Most of the men would have been trained on the estate farms, on the rivers, in the gold and lead mines and various other big houses owned by the family. Most of them would have never seen the world outside Cardiganshire, many of them only knew a few words of English. You could spot the exceptions who had travelled. They wore 1914-18 war ribbons even on their working clothes, as well as their old regimental badges on their broad leather belts.

When we got back I noticed a big bay horse in the paddock next to the kennels, unusually he had a docked tail. I was told that he was Sir Lewes's favourite hunter, and that he'd gone to the First Great War as an officer's charger. They'd both survived a very different sport than foxhunting. His name was *Sportsman*.

There were living quarters for single grooms above the stable range, and at the end of it was the coach house which I explored. It was packed with dainty governess carts and a brougham, but

I loved the big coach, it was padded inside in faded red buttoned upholstery, there were wide tooled leather straps to open the windows. There was a metal retractable step outside, and painted coats of arms on the leather panelled doors. Although the coach house was gloomy I could see the old leather tack with brass ornaments, and the horse collars all hanging on the walls.

The chief groom and lord of the stables was short and bandy-legged. He loved the horses and knew his business backwards. Gogerddan was the only place he had ever worked, man and boy. He turned the horses out superbly, in spite of being short staffed with all the young men away in the war. His name was Will Rowlands. He told me about one of the Gogerddan ghosts. Back in the 1700s there had been a great party, and two hot blooded young squires fell to quarrelling, and they fought a duel with swords by candle light on the lawn outside the house. One was killed. His body was taken into the big hall and laid on the refectory table, before a coach took him away to his home. Will told me that the noise of a ghostly coach had often been heard crunching on the gravelled drive in the early hours of the morning. Will could speak good English. He had a pretty house full of children near a ford in the woods.

One morning, Marjorie was teaching me how to crack a hunting whip. This was essential when hunting on the hills. Not only for controlling the hounds, but also for keeping in touch, for the noise of a properly cracked whip carries a long way. Will hurried up 'My Lady' he said 'Please to come to the stables, the new horse is very odd'. We rushed down to see a very pretty chestnut mare in the yard held by O'Donnell. Every new horse had to be used to having a whip cracked from its back before it could go out hunting. Will cracked a whip. Immediately the mare reared up and pawed the air. She showed no fear whatsoever. She was called *Gin and Tonic*, she'd been bought from a horse dealer who didn't let on that she'd come from a circus. I don't know how on earth Will cured her of her tricks, but his magic certainly worked, and I often hunted her. I never forgot *Gin and Tonic*, nor indeed how to crack a whip. Once a Texan challenged me to crack his 15 ft long bull whip. It had a short handle, and was very thick tailing down to its end. It was heavy too. The Texan was over 6 ft tall, I am about 5 ft 5 in. weighing about 10 stone. After the first swing which was hard, the lash developed a momentum of its own, then I flipped it, and felt the power snaking down, there was an enormous detonation. 'Jesus Christ in the mawning' said the Texan. Thank you Gogerddan.

The speed machine of the Gogerddan stables was *Dusky*, a black thoroughbred. He knew only one gait – flat out. How on earth he didn't kill himself and Ceredig Davies, the huntsman who usually rode him is a mystery. I longed to ride *Dusky*, even dreaming about it. My chance came at Talybont show where I rode him in the open jumping. Before the start he got into a complete lather of excitement, then refused to move. Humphrey ap Evans of Lovesgrove thwacked *Dusky's* rump with a tree branch with impressive results. The tricky course needed controlled riding but Dusky and I flew round as if his tail was on fire. We destroyed every fence. However, it was agreed it had been the fastest round ever seen at Talybont. We got great applause. A few years later I was at school in London. A fellow pupil said accusingly said, 'I saw you ride at Talybont'. I shied away from him nearly as fast as *Dusky* galloped.

We didn't see Sir Lewis down at the stables often, he spent full days at his desk, and had a procession of land agents, lawyers and the like to see. However, one New Year's Day we took hounds to a meet traditionally held at *The Black Lion* in nearby Bow Street. It was a popular event and people came in throngs from the whole district. I looked at the crowds from the back of a tearaway pony called *Brandy*. Sir Lewes Pryse Baronet, Master of Foxhounds sat on his horse, red coated, and looking every inch the squire of tradition which he was. Lady Pryse rode her favourite hunter, a grey called *Mary*. Sir Lewes finished his port and produced a leather pouch from his breeches pocket. A silence fell on the children standing grouped in the front of the crowd. Then Sir Lewes produced handfuls of silver and threw it at them. The children pushed, fought, jostled and trampled. Still the coins rained down. The crowd entered into the fun of it, and yelled encouragement. There's nothing in the world like an excited Welsh crowd. This had been a traditional event for many years, and Sir Lewes's father had possibly been doing it when Wellington was Prime Minister. Probably he divided humanity into two classes, the equestrians and the pedestrians. Even in those days not so many people rode for sport. My mother, grandmother, pretty well the whole family had ridden all their lives. They used horses as cars are used today, some for work, some for sport. My paternal grandfather was a horse master cum gaucho on his uncle's ranch in South America. Not that it did him much good, poor man. He arrived back in Wales a cripple. When it was cold he used to put his poncho cape on, and tell me tales of fighting Indians, the civil wars he'd been in, he'd show me his bullet scars and great gouge marks from a cougar that nearly killed him. He told me of the haunting beauty of the Patagonian plains and of the Andes mountains. I remember too the look in his eyes as he told me of his adventures, distant, gazing inwards. He gave me his old gun belt, and I have it still.

The name Bow Street and the event turned my pony into a right little runner, for that New Year's Day she just kept bolting. She put me down three times, and then bolted straight through hounds. This is the ultimate sin, and quite rightly we were sent home to the stables. It was a long lonely ride back, and as Will took the reins from me he said 'It's her feed I'll cut Master Hugh' I thought bitterly, 'It's her throat that needs cutting.' Thousands of hounds had passed through those kennels over the centuries, at some time bloodhounds were introduced into the pack, and this accounted for the very musical quality when hounds were hunting in full cry. Not only when hunting. I'd sometimes go to the kennels and howl like a banshee. In no time the whole pack would be at it, and the haunting chorus would be heard from miles and miles away. I even did it one night and they went on for hours. Better than a concert really. There were legends too. Will told me that once hounds had attacked and eaten a kennel man. 'Honest to God there wasn't no piece of him left.' I believed him too.

Another great house and estate lay to the south of Aberystwyth, owned by a branch of the Pryse family. It was called Nanteos and its chatelaine was a widow in her late seventies. Mrs. Powell known as Missey, was Sir Lewes Pryse's sister. Lady Pryse took me to tea there a few times. We'd go through the lodge gates into a long wooded meandering drive which suddenly opened out. My first impression was of a lake with swans and other waterfowl swimming among the big water lilies. Then the drive curved to the left through parkland dotted with oak trees. The big square house stood with a wooded hill behind it overlooking the idyllic beauty of the parkland setting which had inspired many poets and artists. Missey was a small vivacious woman with her family's facility of finding amusement in the smallest things. She used an ear trumpet being slightly deaf, and I was encouraged to try to blow it like a hunting horn. There were also some nuns gliding about the place. Nobody knew how they had come to be there, but they acted as guardians to a chalice reputed to be the Holy Grail. It was just a small wooden bowl, but with a silver rim on it. This had been put on because pilgrims bit pieces out of it to take away as holy relics.

My most unforgettable visit to Nanteos was not of a spiritual nature, but it was most certainly in the line of a long tradition. It was for the Hunt Breakfast, and really started at the Boxing Day meet of the Gogerddan hounds held at *The Gogerddan Arms* on the outskirts of Aberystwyth. This meet was a big attraction for townsfolk and hill farmers alike. Down from the hills came an astonishing collection of horses and riders, more like moss troopers. Many were mounted on shaggy Welsh ponies usually used for sheep herding. Then there were bigger cob types straight from the cart as I could see from the collar marks on their necks. Then there were the lighter racing ponies normally used for flapping races, (banned by the Jockey Club of course), as well as a few more conventional hunting horses. So, all sizes, all colours, and all ages we jostled around the hounds in the rain in a great steaming close-packed circle. The riders were turned out in an extraordinary variety of clothes. There was one grey-bearded old man in a complete dark suit, with a white muffler at his throat, a trilby on his head. His hobnailed brown boots nearly reached the ground from his shaggy little pony. Some had risen to the occasion with a pair of riding breeches, but wore gum boots, or old brown gaiters into which they slipped their sticks. A few had bowler hats, normally used, I'm sure, for funerals. Most of the horses were unused to being in a crowd, and there was a lot of kicking and cursing going on as we swirled about trying to keep some sort of order. But the man who attracted the most attention of all was dressed in the conventional English hunting kit. Black coat, polished top boots, all crowned by a shiny top hat. He attracted as much attention as King Kong would have sitting on Nelson's column. He was young Captain Humphrey ap Evans of Lovesgrove, home on leave to recuperate from wounds. He had won a Military Cross, the family had a history of military bravery, his grandfather was General Evans, VC.

So we of this motley cavalcade hunted rather casually towards Nanteos, the enthusiasm wasn't for the chase that day, it was all centred on the great banquet to come. After an hour or so we were hunting in the estate woods and I looked around. I was practically alone with hounds. The entire field of followers had legged it down the drive to Nanteos and its waiting hospitality.

When I arrived there I rode into to the big stable yard, past the Powell family hearse with its shafts resting on the cobbles. I went to stable my pony, but all the boxes were jam packed with steaming, snorting, kicking horses. I finally put her in a feed room to share it with a cart horse and another pony.

The house itself was a scene of cheerful chaos. The corridors to the dining room were packed with damp horsemen some trying to get to the food, and some having eaten trying to get out. All were clutching beer glasses, there was a reek of ale, damp clothes and tobacco. Above it all a great babble of Welsh I was passed from hand to hand to a seat in the large and square panelled dining room with its long bay windows and every available table was loaded with food with no trace of wartime restrictions.

There were great hams, lines of cold chickens, the odd turkey, shoulders of lamb, pickles, chutney, and everywhere great jugs of beer and wine bottles. Early on an attempt had been made to serve soup, that was abandoned being quite impossible in the scrum. I remember the clatter of knives and forks, the loud toasts, the tremendous good humour, the laughter and the sheer tumult of it all. When we left and rode down the drive on that winter afternoon I saw riders reeling and singing in the saddle. Most of them had long miles of riding home in the dark, but my goodness they'd had a great day out look you.

It had all been unforgettable. We all felt the happier to have shared the goodwill and generosity of that old sporting family. Turning our backs on that lovely mansion and in pointing our horse's heads away, none of us knew we were leaving the last hunt breakfast that was held at Nanteos.

There were so many sports for me at Gogerddan, I used to visit the gun room, and admire all the beautiful weapons; braces of Purdy and Holland and Holland shot guns, old flintlocks, big game rifles, some of these weapons were in leather brass bound cases, there was even a huge old punt gun. From all these, a little 4.10 shotgun was selected for me. I got a long stern lecture about safety starting 'Never, never point a gun at anyone, never bring a loaded gun into the house, always unload a gun whenever going over a fence or crossing a stream'. I got a short course from the butler on how to clean a gun. He also showed me the game diary where the day's bag was recorded, rabbits, hares, pigeon, duck, snipe and so on – it went back to 1780. Around me were thousands and thousands of wooded acres to shoot over.

As far as I could walk, and a great deal further I had the right of the squire's dominion to shoot wherever I pleased. To be honest I never bagged much. Once I shot a jay, and when I saw it lying on the ground just a little pile of bright feathers I was quite upset at what I'd done, although jays do act as sentinels of the wild and eat the eggs of other birds. When I first went on my lonely shooting expeditions the gun dogs would come along. Later, the dachshunds, the terriers and a few old hound bitches joined in. So I had a mixed pack of odd canines. What with the hounds casting about, the terriers and the dachshunds yapping away as we penetrated the deep wild woods, no wonder I never shot much, except the odd idle rabbit. Then my assistants would eat it. I did once shoot a buzzard, they were plentiful and killed lambs, so they were fair game. It was still alive when I reached it on its back flapping its wings and clenching its talons. It looked me full in the face with its tawny wild eyes. I never shot another.

Rabbits. Now they were a different matter. They had the impudence to come on the front lawn and eat the border flowers and dig holes in the cultured sward. Seeing an easy target for once I ignored the rules and loaded my gun in the house, I gently raised the window frame. Then in the early morning, and in my pyjamas, I fired. And missed. A furious housekeeper reached me before the smoke cleared away. There was a big row 'Shooting on Sunday. You've brought disgrace on the house' and so on. Later Sir Lewis said 'No, not on Sundays boy' then with a smile 'anyway, let them come a bit closer before you fire'.

Oh it was a lovely thing to be alone in those woods with my collection of dogs and hounds. Apart from the companionship, they had a very practical use too. They would know the way home when I got lost, which happened more than once.

A little river rang along the back of Gogerddan. Once a fishing competition was organised, and Lady Pryse and I were allotted stretches of this little river, I was upstream of the other competitors. I nipped down to the stables and got a tin full of red juicy worms from the manure heap. Then I got to work with my rod. Soon I had my first trout, then another and another. It was easy, I was thrilled and soon had an impressive catch all laid out on the grass ready to be photographed. My rivals had I suppose about four fish between them. They all admired my catch. I was asked 'What fly were you using?' 'No flies,' I said 'just worms.'

All hell let loose, I was scolded, sworn at, and scorned for using low common poaching techniques while all the others had been using gentlemanly flies. Hardly any trout had got past me to the genteel competitors downstream. My photograph was taken anyway, I was also given some flies, everybody laughed. The tale spread like wildfire through the stables and up to the village. A day later I went for a ride, 'No worms left then?' said O'Donnell.

A few days before I was due back at school after one of my Gogerddan holidays, some English friends were also returning to their

"The cheating angler at Gogerddan."

own school. They would pass the drive gates en route. Lady Pryse and I decided to hold them up, so we saddled up a couple of horses. Then dressed up as highwaymen using velvet curtains as cloaks, wearing her big cartwheel summer hats and black masks, we armed ourselves with shotguns and Horse Guard sabres. We lay in ambush near the lodge gates. A car in those petrol rationed days was a fairly rare event. We heard the engine, and then I spotted it, 'Here comes the black car' I said and we rode out into the road. 'Stand and deliver!' we yelled. We looked down at an ashen-faced farmer with his terrified wife on their way home and definitely minding their own business. 'Oh Lady what a fright to see ghosts,' said the farmer's wife. Traditionally to separate a Cardiganshire farmer from his cash requires an Act of God aided by the hordes of Genghis Khan, but I reckon they'd have stumped up there and then.

I was at Gogerddan when the famous sporting and animal artist, Lionel Edwards, came to paint the portraits of the rough haired Welsh hounds which were rare those days. I remember a tallish man with glasses wearing a Sherlock Holmes-type coat with a cape. I also remember him throwing down sketches he wasn't satisfied with on the dirty kennel floor. If only I'd kept them; they'd be worth a pretty penny these days. However I doubt any artist could have captured the dangers of our hunting days. Quite often hounds would run foxes to the cliff tops, and hounds running on scent alone wouldn't see the danger until it was too late. This happened on the craggy mountains and the slopes of Plynlimon too. They would also be bitten by adders in the marshes by Borth. Then there were the railway lines, we used to lose a few there as well. Sometimes we'd hunt until darkness came, because hounds were so far ahead, running on the mountains hard on a fox. They would usually come back to the place where we met. We never knew for sure what had happened to those who didn't come back. Many's the time we'd be out with a hunting horn till the early hours of the morning looking for them. Once I was galloping on a mountain slope when I saw a depression in the ground with some collapsed posts around it. Ceredig, the Huntsman, shouted over at me 'Now you look out for those old mine shafts.' I was of course too young, and excited to feel any fear whatsoever.

However I did sometimes feel fear in the great house, but only at night. I used to go to bed clutching my candlestick with white knuckled hand. When I opened the first door into the long passage to my room lined with family portraits, I could see myself as a ghostly figure reflected in the far glass door through which I had to pass to get to my bedroom. It was eerie walking towards that reflection, especially if there was a winter's storm raging outside. I learned to be careful in opening and closing the doors, because once the draught blew out my candle. I was left in the darkness feeling for the right end of the matches to relight the candle. Once I got to the bedroom with my heart pounding away, I don't know why but I forced myself to go back all the way to the big landing to repeat the whole business. I suppose I was trying to exorcise the fear but it didn't work.

There was a bedroom on one corner of the house known as the Blue Room, it had lovely views to the formal gardens and down to the little river below. I decided I'd love to sleep there in the ancient four-poster bed with its hanging curtains and I was delighted when I got permission. I settled down in the comfortable bed and I could hear the trickle of the stream. For the very first time in my life, I heard the trilling of a nightingale cutting melodiously through the night air. Later a horrendous nightmare jolted me out of my sleep. I dreamed that writhing tendrils came at me from under the bed and were choking the life out of me. I spent the rest of the darkness rigid with fear and shock, afraid even to move. At breakfast I told Lady Pryse about it all. 'Oh dear' she said, 'Lew's mother died on that bed after she set fire to it with her candle.'

The rest of the house was a constant delight to me. When it rained heavily I loved spending time in the glass domed library. There were many thousands of books there. So I pored through bound volumes of *Punch,* I read endlessly; adventure books by Jules Verne, Whyte, Melville, Rider Haggard. I studied illustrated books on wild animals, travels abroad, Italian architecture, ancient illustrated children's books and even older books where the s's were spelled with double ffs. Then there were toys, surviving favourites of generations of children, lead soldiers in hundreds, cast off bits of fancy dress, early Victorian mechanical toys and so on. I even discovered an electricity machine in a box with faded grubby instructions. If I held the two wire-connected metal grips and turned the machine's handle very quickly I could give myself tingling shocks up my arms. I also found bygone dance cards, souvenirs from great dances and hunt balls held in the house. They had tassels and little pencils hanging from them and inside there were lists of waltzes and polkas, sometimes with partners' names written in them. What memories must have lingered in that vast room, and then just one small boy rummaging through the deserted keepsakes. I still have an old Hunt Ball card, and two broken lead toy racehorses with jockeys. Certainly I was one of the last, if not the last child to play and read there in the silence haunted with past romances and gaiety. The rooms above, which I never bothered to explore, were disused and dusty, and had been once crowded servants quarters. In my time at Gogerddan, the only living in servants were the old butler and his wife, who acted as housekeeper. The cook and the cleaners came in from the villages, and all of them had been trained in their youth in the large servants' hall. I discovered yellowing notices posted about the house in various work places. In capital letters they were headed 'Rules For The Servants Hall at Gogerddan'. This is how they read:

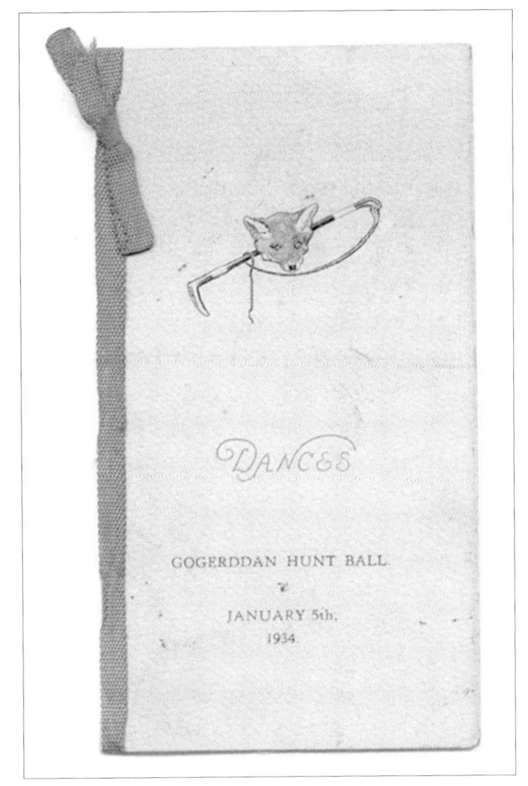

A relic of a romantic past.
Gogerddan Hunt Ball dance card, 1934.

'First. No Followers to be allowed.

Second. Breakfast at Nine o'clock, and everything to be cleared away by Ten.

Third. Dinner at One, and the Hall to be cleared by Two.

Fourth. The Under Stable Boy to come in when the Bell rings, to sweep up the Hall and lay the Cloth.

Fifth. Supper at Nine.

Sixth. No Person to set down to dinner in a Jacket or Stable Dress.

Seventh. No Person will be allowed Breakfast, Dinner, or Supper, if not at the Table in proper time, unless a sufficient reason for their absence is given to the Housekeeper.

Eighth. The Coachman to see that the drinking Utensils are cleared away after each meal – the Table wiped down, and the Hall left tidy – and in the absence of the Coachman, the next eldest Stableman.

Ninth. No Shoes or Guns to be cleaned in the Hall.

Tenth. No Smoking to be allowed.

Eleventh. Every one who from absence on Business may take their meal after the rest of the Family is to clear everything away after them, and in case of Failure, to be brought back by the Butler to do so.'

If I could add a twelfth commandment it would be 'If God gives you a choice to be a member of the Pryse family. Take it.'

The church that the family had built was maybe a couple of miles away in the village of Penrhyncoch. I suppose the family could have sited it near to the mansion, but the stables and the kennels were there, after all the Pryses hunted, shot and fished six days a week. It must have been a question of priorities. When we went to services, we arrived on the dot of eleven. Everybody else was in their seats and we walked up to the squire's family pews, then and only then, did the service begin. I remember being fascinated by all the family memorial plaques on the church walls They seemed to have altered and changed the surnames as they married into other great families. There was a Webley-Parry-Pryse, Saunders-Pryse, Rice-Price, a Pryse-Pryse, and all these double and triple barrelled names had the Pryse coat of arms above them. I suppose in the family's hey-day most of the staff would go to church as well, in addition to any visitors and their servants. What a cavalcade of social strata it must have been. Of course even the appointment of the vicar would have been in the squire's gift.

The village gossips must have had a field day in the churchyard after the services. Even in my time it took an age to get down to the wicket gate there were so many people to greet. There were lovely houses dotted along that church route. They used to be occupied by the estate executive class you might say. They were the estate land agent, the timber manager, the chief gamekeeper, the huntsman, the chief water bailiff, the master builder and so on. An old estate tenant told me that everybody ate really well in his day, so I suppose that all the fishing and shooting were not only a sport, but a necessity too. The mansion employed at least fifteen staff in the kitchen alone at one stage. They provided hundreds of meals every day, year in, year out. I remember seeing an enormous collection of books in the main kitchen full of hand-written recipes that must have been tested and tried down through the ages. I assume there were also recipes brought from the other great houses the family owned such as Buscot Park, as well as the London house. Across the road from Gogerddan's kitchens was a huge walled kitchen garden, it could have been three or four acres in all. It was overlooked by a handsome Georgian house where the head gardener probably once lived.

The gold and lead mines back in the hills must have given up a pretty good harvest to support the family in such splendour. Even the wedding rings worn by the British Royal family to this day came from Welsh gold mines.

Sometimes in the evenings we'd listen to gramophone records. My favourites from Lady Pryse's gramophone collection were arias sung by Gigli, Tauber and Caruso. I was allowed to choose the records on condition I wound up the gramophone. Now whenever I hear say 'O Sole Mio', or German lieder I go straight back in time to that extraordinary house echoing beautiful evocative music through empty corridors.

The Chinese drawing room was the biggest formal drawing room in the house. It was rarely used but I loved to slip in and admire the lovely things in it. Every generation had added to Gogerddan in their life time. They might have been hard living sportsmen, but they were certainly not bucolic barbarians. Used to the best of everything and mostly being well travelled and cosmopolitan, so the Chinese drawing room had a quality of elegance. The wallpaper was hand-painted in soft colours, flowers and birds featured in it. I was fascinated by a great ivory ball under a glass dome on a stand. I could see through the fretwork to another ball inside it, then another, and another. All round the room there were portraits of the family in hunting clothes and various uniforms. There were Dutch landscapes there too, as well as miniatures and delicate watercolours, maybe souvenirs from the Grand Tour. The graceful mahogany, elm and rosewood furniture glistened from years and years of hand polishing. One day, when I was alone in the house, some friends of the Pryse's called, so I ordered tea and we all sat in the Chinese drawing room and I acted the host. I was maybe 11 years old at the time.

Behind the green baize door in the hall were the butler's pantry, the huge kitchen, the sculleries, the larders, the gun room – they stretched all along the back of the house. I remember a huge walk-in safe, off the butler's pantry, and seeing stacks of silver in great piles and all the polishing materials laid out. There were groups of exquisite silver dining table ornaments of foxes, horses, peacocks, elephants and so on. I remember too the lovely delicately painted china we used to eat off, all marked with the family crest; also the delicate fruit knives and forks with exquisite painted porcelain handles.

Even going to the lavatory in Gogerddan was unforgettable. The one I used near my bedroom was a revelation. On entering one mounted steps leading up to the lavatory itself, which had a huge, dark, hardwood seat. There was a pump handle to pull up to flush it.

When I stayed at Gogerddan I didn't know that the whole estate was in decline accelerated by death duties. Cardiganshire and Gogerddan were so remote from the outside world that the estate had become like an independent kingdom. I was so lucky, I saw only kindness, happiness and adventure in it. But the outside world was inexorably moving in on the bastion created over so many years of continuity.

On my last holiday there Sir Lewis Pryse had taken to his bed. When it was time for me to go back to school, I went up to his bedroom. He was supported by masses of pillows so that he could see the parkland and up to the rising woodlands where the buzzards and pigeons flew. He

A lawn meet at Gogerddan in Victorian times.

was dying of cancer. His last act to me, like his first, was of thoughtful kindness. He produced a ten shilling note for me from under the pillows. 'Here's a tip for you to spend in the tuck shop' he said. I remember his hand brown spotted with age. My last sight of him was lying back on the pillows; from under his wispy white hair his eyes twinkled at me. A few weeks later at school I read in the paper that he was dead. His memory became part of the magic of my childhood. Centuries of family life in Gogerddan slipped away. I was one of the last to see it. I clearly recall my father and Sir Lewes Pryse crouched over papers, my father gathering information now contained in this book.

Sitting on the rocky peak of Dinas Mountain above my home I sometimes gaze at the Cardiganshire hills. Images of Gogerddan often come to mind: the bustling stables; the torrent of foxhounds pouring from the kennels; the echoes of Italian opera, and the flickering candle when I went to bed. The Pryses, with their humour and kindness, smile at me again. The images of the Cardiganshire countryside return so vividly; I ride once more with the ghosts of Gogerddan's long-dead squires.

The Pryse family crests

Sir Lewes Lovedon Pryse, MFH,
outside Gogerddan in his prime.

A CARDIGANSHIRE CHARACTER

Marjorie Pryse was simply one of the most fascinating and fabulous people I ever knew. I visited her and husband, from school, after my army days, after I married, when I returned from overseas work. Our friendship spanned over fifty years. I'm told that most people are forgotten half a century after their death. I decided to write this hoping that maybe she will be remembered by those who follow me.

Cardiganshire history abounds with colourful personalities. Plas Gogerddan produced its fair share. Marjorie Pryse stands in her own right as a legend. Her background was a mystery, and may never be known. She was the adopted daughter of Mr. and Mrs. David Howells of Cwm Mansion near Aberystwyth. Mr. Howells had emerged from obscurity as a draper's apprentice to build a hugely successful business empire which included Howells Store. Rumour was rife about Marjorie's parentage; that her mother was a washerwoman, that her father was the Prince of Wales, and such like. Whoever they were, they certainly produced a remarkable person. She was born on December 22nd, 1907.

She went to the exclusive St. Paul's school in London. It still upholds its long tradition of producing brilliant students, women of formidable character. It consistently appears in the UK's league of top schools. Among her school friends were the film star Celia Johnson, and the fabulous society beauties, the Goddard sisters – daughters of the grim Lord Chief Justice Goddard, the 'hanging judge'. Marjorie excelled at music, continuing her studies at a Paris conservatoire. She had ample income from the Howells fortune and she threw herself enthusiastically into the milieu of the continental music world; becoming in effect a concert 'groupie', travelling to concert halls, music conservatoires, and opera houses. She lived in Poland, Hungary, France and Italy. Her vivacity and beauty ensured her a picturesque, bohemian life among musicians and high society as she toured Europe in her smart Jaguar car. She told me that she and 'Rad' a famous Polish pianist went to Verdi's funeral in Italy, and how, as the coffin passed through huge crowds they spontaneously burst into an aria from one of his operas.

The late Lady Marjorie Pryse, MFH . . . 'She hunted in the remotest of areas and grew to know them as few others had, or even would.'

When her adopted parents died she came into a considerable fortune. Apart from music, her other passion was for riding to hounds. Whenever in Cardiganshire she hunted with the Gogerddan Foxhounds. She captivated the Master, Sir Lewes Pryse and he made her Joint

Master in 1930. He and Marjorie married in November 1938, immediately after Sir Lewes's divorce. Ceredig Davies, their huntsman, was a witness. Sir Lewes was born in 1864, and was then 74 years old; Marjorie was 32 years old. Estate tenants bought a large solid silver figure of a running fox and presented it to them, along with a silver salver with the Pryse coat of arms inscribed on it. Marjorie told me that at the presentation, an old man who spoke English with difficulty, addressed the assembled company ending with, 'We all 'opes you gets an "hair" soon.' Sadly that was not to be. Certainly their age difference was no barrier to a happy, busy and active life, they were rarely out of each other's company, riding, shooting hunting and fishing together. They often took holidays on their Scottish island, and at home Marjorie ran an efficient household, helped with estate management, and ran the kennels and stables.

Gogerddan became full of gaiety, dances, shooting parties, and the country house weekends so popular since early Victorian times. Both Marjorie and Lewes had a shared, wicked sense of humour. They constantly played practical jokes, usually on each other. I was a small boy when I first met them and it was the beginning of a friendship which lasted until their deaths. And what a helter skelter, roller coaster of fun it was. They had eight years of happiness together before Sir Lewes died in 1946. The estate and title, along with hefty death duties went to his brother.

Marjorie then moved to Ffynnon Caradog, set on the side of a wooded hill facing down to Gogerddan, the Penrhyncoch valley and distant hills. It was part of the Pryse estate and it became her dower house. Though much smaller than Gogerddan, it was a gentry house with kennels for the hounds, ranges of stables, a coach house, barns and outbuildings. Pretty gardens lay in front, with a grass tennis court and a croquet lawn. High above, near the house, were 40 acres of mixed woodland with rhododendron-flanked rides, enchanting little paths and glades extending to the hilltop. Behind that lay Cwm Mansion. Her childhood there had not been particularly happy and she told me the reason; it is a confidence I will not break.

Marjorie had a tenanted home farm where she kept her herd of Jersey cattle, and the flock of black Shetland sheep she and Lew had brought down from Scotland. Ffynnon Caradog was now packed with antique furniture from Gogerddan, and that which she had inherited from Cwm. *Objets d'art,* paintings, elegant carpets, silver, rare old books and fine furniture from handsome oak of great age to dainty Georgian pieces filled the house to its attics. They even overflowed into the coach house. The dining room was so cluttered with the trappings of the old life it was a squeeze to get round the dining table.

Marjorie was sole Master of Hounds and, though in a smaller establishment, she led the old life. But alone. She had an allowance from the Pryse estate but of her own fortune, it seems only a small portion remained. Whether it had gone in an effort to keep Gogerddan afloat I do not know. Certainly she continued to fund hounds. She was always generous and trusting. She never charged a hunt subscription, had no hunt secretary, never held a hunt ball again, or a Point-to-Point. So the hunt did not (as is usual), produce any revenue for upkeep. She stood the cost herself and continued the unbroken breeding line of the pack which Sir Richard Pryse had started in 1600. It was the oldest private pack of foxhounds in Great Britain, covering a territory of 408 square miles. Much of which is described by Bailey's *Hunt Directory* as 'unsafe to hunt'. My own experiences confirmed this. It was, and is, one of nature's assault courses, dangerous to riders, horses and hounds. But a wonderful challenge and hauntingly beautiful country.

Marjorie continued the life of a *grande dame* with open-handed hospitality. She had a housekeeper, cleaning staff, grooms and farm servants. To many she appeared imperious, only being used to command. She still controlled a big establishment, and many livelihoods depended on her but she no longer had her beloved husband to turn to for help and advice. She was soon avidly courted, men had various (and hidden) motives for marrying her. As a life, it was not entirely beer and skittles. Now in her forties, she was still highly attractive, it was inevitable she should have a retinue of admirers. To my knowledge she rejected at least four persistent marriage proposals. All from rich men, and one famous and titled. Though as the years passed she had relationships, and not a few either, she never remarried though, or even considered it. On another occasion when we were laughing about some lovelorn admirer of hers, she said 'You know I ought to put notches on my bed post. One for each lover'. I said that she would need a telegraph pole for the job. It started a running joke which lasted for years.

Marjorie and I were prone to sudden high-spirited escapades. She once dared me to jump a five-barred gate in the yard. To her surprise, and mine, I succeeded. I even did it wearing riding boots once. She used to get me to do it to amuse guests.

One of her friends I got to know really well was Guy Wayte, a thoroughly amusing swell from the exclusive Quorn Hunt. He drove a beautiful silver Bentley. Marjorie, my wife and I were all going to Aberystwyth. She said 'I do wish I had a mascot on the car like Guy'. I said, 'I'll be the mascot'. 'I dare you,' replied Marjorie. So I sat on the Land Rover bonnet all the way to Aberystwyth. Marjorie and my wife jeered and tooted the horn at me all the way. I remember still the looks of surprise on oncoming driver's faces.

Years before the Breathalyser was thought of, Marjorie and I were leaving the Bellvue Hotel in Aberystwyth after a pretty liquid lunch. Outside the back bar was a Salvation Army band with a small group of hymn singers. One passage instantly fascinated us. When it came round we roared it out; it ended 'And save the poor drunkard's soul'. A collection box was smartly stuck under our noses, and helpless with laughter we gave generously. We shared a remarkably similar humour, and used to egg each other on crying with laughter till our ribs ached from it. From such silly little things too, and always spontaneous.

One summer evening as we chatted over drinks, sitting on the lawn looking out over the Gogerddan valley to the far off hills. I remember too seeing the smoke and sparks coming from a passing GWR steam engine chugging to Bow Street station, she said wistfully, 'You know Hugh, whenever I look back at my life now, my thoughts always return to Lew". She kept his desk, with a framed picture of him in hunting dress on it, alongside the great silver fox. They were her dearest possessions.

She was an accomplished hostess, cosmopolitan, witty and unselfconscious. She had a fund of amusing gossip about an amazing number of people, and a store of jokes she heard from Lewes. I saw her in various stressful situations, with difficult horses and wilful hounds but she never swore, though she was indifferent to hearing bad language from others. She might have been a horsewoman, but she never rode a 'high horse'. Her animals and the Cardiganshire countryside were her entire life. She hunted in the remotest areas and grew to know them as few others had, or ever will. Rural life with its inexorable seasonal tasks with animals claimed her life utterly, and she never saw the Continent of her youth again. I only ever recall her leaving Ffynnon Caradog once. She visited us in London, and I drove her to a wedding reception at the Savoy Hotel. It had been a big job to get her ready. My parents and I spent hours getting dog hairs off her smart clothes.

Over the years a tremendous procession of animal life was centred in her home. Hounds often more than twenty couple, four or five horses, the sheep, cattle, chickens, ducks, there were even a few goats in the yard, which used to infuriate me by jumping on my car roof. She also loved dachshunds; Lew had given her Betty-Boo-Boos, her favourite. She bred from her and at one time had a pack of thirteen. There were other house dogs, yapping hunt terriers, a collie or two and old retired hounds. They soon found their way into the house, even to her bedroom. From time to time she'd take in an orphan fox cub, and once a badger she named Brock who savaged my ankles and ruined my shoes. When Brock was nearly full grown we returned him to the wild. The following day his body was found near the tennis court. Marjorie reckoned he had been set upon by another badger who didn't like the smell of humans on the poor waif. The smell in the house with the animals traipsing through, became pretty fearsome. Too much for anybody to do housework there for long. I got used to it but Marjorie had a big turnover of servants. At first when she could afford to pay well, they were pretty good. As she had to perforce pay less, she got less reliable people. They became a procession of idlers, drunks, thieves and deadbeats, it became a sort of clearinghouse for lost souls. Cardiganshire was the end of the line for many of them.

Then death duties finally did for Gogerddan and the baronetcy became extinct. The house was sold, as was much of the land. Marjorie was now dependent on her allowance from the remnants of the Gogerddan Trust. Of her own fortune I suspect little now remained. Offered a chance to buy Ffynnon Caradog for £4,000 she turned it down. I now realise she just didn't have the money.

The hounds and other animals took a lot of feeding. Many farmers, some, who had been tenants, still followed the old practice of giving dead animals to the kennels. I often collected the carcasses from far off hill farms. Dead sheep, I remember, smelt particularly ghastly. I often drove with all the windows open and my head stuck out, gasping for fresh air. Collecting them in the winter rain with terriers worrying at the carcasses in the back are nostril-wrinkling memories.

Marjorie was now setting to and dissecting the carcasses herself. Over time she discovered a new skill. She became curious about the animals' inner workings. With her innate intelligence she grew knowledgeable. So much so that veterinary surgeons used to consult her on animal post mortems. She took to selling hides for some extra money. Working for the BBC at the time, I thought she'd make an excellent TV documentary. So Fyfe Robinson interviewed about her life. It was a great success, viewers nation wide were riveted to see this titled lady disembowelling a cow, and chopping up the carcass whilst talking about Rossini's overtures. As a passing moment of fame it was fun, but her finances were still run down. She never had television or even central heating. When her horses died she could not replace them. She now hunted hounds on foot. This required exceptional stamina for walking long hours in all weathers over hard, unrelenting country in winter. Through in her fifties, and then in her sixties, she soldiered on. The cry of the Gogerddan hounds still echoed in their Cardiganshire country.

As hounds snuffled round carcasses in the yard, so did human vultures alight at Ffynnon Caradog. Door knocking 'dealers' swindled and cajoled her out of her antiques and valuables. Being as startlingly naïve in business as she was about housework, the parasites feasted on her. She was given just a few pounds for rare heirlooms when she was desperate for money for essentials like car tax, electricity or telephone bills, and feed for the animals. She ate and drank sparingly those days, eating slowly and carefully, she always had a very small appetite for food. Marjorie was in a perilous state when I visited her in the 1980's. All her fine belongings had vanished. The family trust was unable to help; the Fund was running dry. There were too many

Caroline Charles-Jones and Marjorie Pryse at Ffynnon Caradog.

beneficiaries. At one stage there had been three Lady Pryses' receiving allowances. Legal fees and administration costs were draining the estate. She had managed though to hang on to Lew's desk and alongside his picture she put some of my son, Alexander's, drawings of horses. She also followed another of my sons' progress with great pleasure. I had named him Gareth Francis Hugh, the same initials as the Gogerddan Fox Hounds. He became a successful steeplechase jockey and at one stage, he, with the initials GFH sailed over Becher's Brook with the leaders. His artist brother, also an amateur jump jockey, recently rode the winner of the Foxhunters' Cup at both Aintree and Cheltenham. A rare achievement, rarer still it leaves me as the only man living to have two sons complete the Grand National course. For the moment anyway. I had encouraged my sons to ride and hunt from an early age, just as Sir Lewes and Lady Pryse had encouraged me when my father was away at war. They gave me some of the Gogerddan sporting spirit and I passed it on to my children.

Times being very bad, Marjorie and I concocted a plan. I was then hunting with fashionable English packs in the Cotswolds where I lived. Marjorie appointed me joint Master of the Gogerddan hounds. My task was to find a rich man to become another joint Master to help carry the cost of running the pack properly. With the status of a 'Joint' I was entitled to hunt with any pack as a visiting guest Master. She gave me Lew's old hunt buttons, and his pink evening tail coat. Most touchingly she asked me never to forget I was representing the old Gogerddan tradition, and that I was the only man to wear the button outside Wales for many a long year from 1982-85. I did my very best, and hunted with some 16 different packs in England, Scotland and Wales. I ended up in hospital twice through hunting accidents, but it was the greatest fun. I did meet several people interested in having MFH after their names. However they thought Cardiganshire too far from the social world, and the country too rough to gallop across, having no neatly prepared jumps to leap. There was no social status in being Master of an obscure Welsh pack. One sporting millionaire, a publisher, commented 'It's just too far from anywhere, and I can't even pronounce the name'.

Adversity never changed Marjorie's essential nature. I never heard her complain or whine about her changed circumstances. Hunting falls had given her a bad back and she was often in pain, yet she soldiered stoically on, with a handful of hounds. Old friends died, she lost touch with others, and fair weather friends turned their backs on her. Being adopted, she didn't know if she had any blood relatives, though several impostors turned up to try to swindle her out of her supposed wealth. To the outside world she appeared to be just an eccentric old woman. Even so, when I took her out for a meal her old vivacity returned, her eyes twinkled and we were soon sharing jokes. By now she was easily the oldest serving Master of Foxhounds in the UK. It is a record never likely to be beaten. She was now wrinkled, weather beaten and white haired, she was bowed, but not yet beaten. She no longer had her car, her home was a smelly shambles, the roof leaked, the walls ran with water, and the broken window frames rotten. Dressed in rags and smelling of carcasses, she now begged for lifts on the road in horrible weather. I wonder how many old acquaintances, old estate tenants, and those who had hunted with her in the old days passed

The 'Lady' out in all weathers, the longest-serving MFH, a record never likely to be equalled.

Joint Master H. C.-J. with the Jed Hunt in Scotland.

this broken-down old woman without a thought.

Caroline and I often visited Marjorie in her decline. One lasting memory was of the three of us sitting on the bank chatting in the summer sun. In the yard below hound puppies frolicked about in the skeletal rib cage of some large animal.

I called on her again when I returned from more travels. She told me that she had accepted a lift from a stranger. He had attacked her savagely and thrown her on to the roadside and left her for dead. After a short spell in hospital she had discharged herself to get back to her animals. Her courage was only equalled by her outstanding tenacity. Her story was deeply upsetting, so I tried to help her financially. However I lacked the means to make any great difference. I bought her a van in Cirencester and had the initials GFH put on the side. I asked Marjorie to meet me for lunch at *The Black Lion* in Bow Street. When she came in, she said 'Hello Hugh. Do you know, I've just seen the strangest thing. There's a van outside with the initials GFH on it'. I said, 'It's yours'.

It gave her a new lease of life for some time. Then finally garage mechanics declined to repair it because of the appalling smell of carcasses in it.

Marjorie's birthday and mine were only days apart. We always telephoned and sent cards with ribald messages on them. One year she told me she was now housed in a small cottage at Bont Goch, it was probably amongst the last of the properties once owned by the fabulous Pryse estate. I turned up with a bottle of her favourite sherry. She was now in her eighties and for once she was muted and complained of being cold. I gave her my coat. Even then she still had plans for building a small kennels there; of the Gogerddan foxhounds, I saw only one old hound. She had been burgled and her precious silver box and even the silver frame round Lew's picture had gone too. Doubtless to some thieves kitchen to be melted down into an anonymous ingot.

A week or so later she was taken to hospital suffering from malnutrition and hypothermia. Thanks to her mental and physical toughness, and with excellent care she quickly recovered. It was strange to see her in bed, in a ward, but we were soon laughing at the old days. She could no longer manage to live on her own and was sent to an old people's home in Bow Street, the village once owned by the Pryses. It was not far away from the children's sports ground that she and Lew had given to the village to mark their marriage. She was now a mile or so away from Gogerddan mansion where she had once reigned. Now, for the first time in her long life she didn't have any animals around her. She seemed at the end of the line, at the bottom of the heap.

Was she downcast? Not one little bit. I think her new circumstances were a cross between boarding school routine and country house living. Instead of servants she had nurses to care for her. They were a wonderfully kind lot too, and spoilt her. In a way she was their star resident. I travelled up from Pembrokeshire where I now lived, and took her out for car trips. We visited the old haunts where she had hunted with her husband and I had trailed after them on my pony. We sat viewing the countryside and I played operatic tapes of her favourite arias. My cousin,

Aerwyn Charles, is a renowned opera singer. We visited Marjorie and he gave an impromptu concert. It was a revelation when the silent old folk huddled in their chairs, became animated and clapped for encores. Marjorie was thrilled. Her best friend there was a Mrs. Maxwell Davies. She told me once, 'Lady Pryse told me that you are like a son to her'. I am moved nearly to tears whenever I think of that.

Once we were setting off on a car trip on a lovely autumn day. She said, 'You know I felt so happy walking in the sun this morning that I gave a little hop, skip and a jump. Yes, I can still jump a little'. It was the last time we were together. She was suddenly taken seriously ill, and an emergency operation was advised. This she refused adamantly. Knowing her I think she recognised that her time had come. She died alone shortly afterwards. I was told she was unconscious, and she was gone before I could see her.

The last of the titled Pryses was buried with her beloved husband at Penrhyncoch church in 1993. I attended the melancholy service. I left with the strangest feeling that something important was missing. A few days later I returned to her grave. The churchyard was empty. As is traditional I blew the 'Gone Away' on my hunting horn over her grave. She would have wanted that.

At the wicket gate I looked back at the mound of fresh earth. I said 'Goodbye Marjorie'.

Following Gogerddan's sporting legacy . . .

Right: Artist Alexander Charles-Jones barging through to win the Foxhunters Cup, Aintree, 1999.

Below: Gareth Charles Jones "GFH" (No. 24) taking Bechers Brook, Grand National, 1986.

BIBLIOGRAPHY

(with Abbreviations)

Primary Sources

CARMARTHEN RECORD OFFICE
Aberglasney Collection
ACC : Local History Survey
: 271
: 284
: 4836, Annals of Edwinsford, Clovelly & Hawthornden
Barnsfield Collection
Brigstocke Collection
Bryn Myrddin Collection
Carmarthenshire Antiquarian Society Scrapbooks
Cawdor Golden Grove Books I, II & III [G.G.B.]
Charities Records
Cilycwm Parish Registers [p.r.]
Clyngwynne Collection
Cwmgwili Collection
Derwydd Collection
Dynevor Collection
Electoral Registers
Glasbrook Collection
John Francis Collection, Sale Catalogues
Landowners Return 1873
Museum Collection
Plas Llanstephan Collection
Protheroe-Beynon Collection
Quarter Sessions Order Books
Tithe Maps [t.m.] and Schedules [t.s.] for Cardiganshire

NATIONAL LIBRARY OF WALES, ABERYSTWYTH
Aberglasney Deeds
NLW MSS.
Alcwyn Evans Manuscripts
British Records Association Deeds
Brigstocke Collection
Bronwydd Deeds and Documents
Castell Gorfod Collection
Church in Wales Records
Cilgwyn Deeds and Documents; Manuscript Volumes
Coleman Deeds
Crosswood Deeds
Cwmgwilli Manuscripts and Documents
Cwrtmawr Deeds
Dale Castle Pedigree Book
Derry Ormond Deeds and Documents
Dolaucothi Manuscripts and Papers; Correspondence
Dynevor Deeds and Documents
Edwinsford Deeds and Collection
Francis Green Deeds and Documents
George Eyre Evans Manuscripts and Deeds
Glansevin Collection
Great Sessions Records
G. E. Owen Collection
Highmead Estate Papers
D. T. M. Jones Collection
Llancych Deeds and Documents
Llanllyr Deeds and Documents
Llanstephan Manuscripts
Llwyndyrus Deeds and Documents
Llwyngair Deeds and Documents
Llysnewydd Deeds and Documents
Maesgwynne Deeds
Morgan Richardson Deeds and Documents
Neuadd-Fawr Deeds and Documents
Neville, Druce and Co.
Industrial Records and other Documents
Noyadd Trefawr Deeds
Owen and Colby Manuscripts, Deeds and Documents
Picton Castle Collection
Spence-Colby Manuscripts and Documents
Thomas (Saundersfoot) Deeds and Documents
Trewern Deeds
Tucker Manuscript NLW 10871B

GLAMORGAN RECORD OFFICE
Cardiff Central Library Collection

HAVERFORDWEST PUBLIC LIBRARY
Francis Green Manuscripts

PEMBROKESHIRE RECORD OFFICE
Court Papers
Henllan Deeds
Lewis and James Papers [D/LJ]
Lloyd-Phillips Papers [D/LP]
Price and Kelway Papers [D/PK]
Saunders-Davies Collection
Trenewydd Collection

COLLEGE OF ARMS MANUSCRIPTS
Fellows Visitations

PUBLIC RECORD OFFICE
Chancery Proceedings, Ser. 11 420/40
Chancery, Mitford, CO 603/25
Exchequer Accounts

BRITISH MUSEUM
Egerton Manuscripts
Wood Manuscripts

BODLEIAN LIBRARY
Bodleian Manuscript Add. C177
Harleian Manuscript 6823

Printed Primary Sources and Secondary Sources

Allen, Charles Smith, *Photographs in South Wales,* 1871.
Allen, Charles Smith, *The History of South Wales and Monmouthshire* (illustrated). Vols. I and II, Tenby, 1891. [Allen, S., *Wales and Mon.*]

B. Williams, *Hanes Castell Newydd yn Emlyn,* 1860.
Baker-Jones D.L., *Cardiganshire* 1977.
Baker-Jones D.L., *Charles Evans Davies Morgan-Richardson,* 1977.
Baker-Jones D. L., *Princelings, Privilege and Power,* 1999.
Barber, J. T., *A Tour through South Wales and Monmouthshire,* London, 1803.
Beazely, E. and Howell, P., *The Companion Guide to South Wales,* 1977.
Bonsall Henry, *Records of the House of Bonsall,* 1903.
Borrow, George, *Wild Wales, its People, Language and Scenery,* London, 1862.
Bowen E. G., *The History of Llanbadarn Fawr,* 1979.
Bridgeman, G. T. O., *History of the Princes of South Wales,* Wigan, 1876.
Burke, *A Genealogical and Heraldic History of the Landed Gentry of Great Britain and Ireland.* [Burke, *L. G., B.L.G.*]
Burke, *A Genealogical and Heraldic History of the Peerage and Baronetage,* 36th edn. 1874.
Burke, *A Visitation of Seats and Arms of the Noblemen and Gentlemen of Great Britain and Ireland.*
Burke, John and Bernard, John, *A Genealogical and Heraldic History of the Extinct and Dormant Baronetcies of England* 1st. edn. 1838.

Cardiganshire County History, Vols. 1 & 3.
Carlisle, *Contemporary Biographies,* 1907.
Carlisle, Nicholas, *A Topographical Dictionary of the Dominion of Wales,* London, 1811. [Carlisle, *TDW.*]
Carmarthenshire Studies: Essays presented to Major Francis Jones, ed. T. Barnes and N. Yates, Carmarthen, 1974. [*Carms. Studies.*]
Clark, G. T., *Limbus Patrum Morganiae et Glamorganiae etc,* London, 1886. [Clark, *Glamorgan Genealogies*].
Cledlyn Davies, D. R. & L. S., *Hanes Llanwenog,* 1939.

David, E. Awelrydd, *Guide to Laugharne and Pendine,* Carmarthen, 1904.
Davies D. J., *Llannarth.*
Davies J., *Herberts of Hafod*, 1946.
Davies John, *Annuls and Pedigrees of the Lloyds and Edwards of Crynfryn and other Families.*
Davies John, *Display of Heraldry,* 1709.
Davies W. J. *Hanes Plwyf Llandysul,* 1896.
Davies W. J. *Hanes Plwyf Llanwenog,* 1929.
Davies, E. M. *The Story of Llandyfeilog Parish,* Carmarthen, 1953.
Davies, Walter, *A General View of the Agriculture and Domestic Economy of South Wales,* Vols. I and II, London, 1814.
Davies, William, 'Gwylym Teilo', *Treathawd ar Caio ai' Hynafiaethau,* Caernarfon, 1862.
Debrett, John, *Peerage of England, Scotland and Ireland,* 1st edn., London, 1802.
Dictionary of National Biography, 63 vols., London 1885-1900; reprinted Oxford, 1921-22. [*DNB.*]
Dictionary of Welsh Biography down to 1940, Cymmrodorion Society, London, 1959. [*DWB.*]
Dineley, Thomas, *The Account of the Official Progress of the First Duke of Beaufort through Wales, 1684,* ed. R. W. Banks, London, 1888.
Donovan, E, *Descriptive Excursion through Wales and Monmouthshire,* London, 1804.
Dwnn, *Heraldic Visitations,* see Meyrick, Samuel Rush.

Ellis T. L., *John Humphrey Davies,* 1963.
Ellis, *Crwydro Ceredigion,* 1952.
Evans D. J., *Hanes Capel Seion,* 1935.
Evans, George Eyre, *Cardiganshire,* 1860.
Evans, George Eyre, *Lampeter,* Aberystwyth, 1905.
Evans, George Eyre, *Lloyd Letters 1754-1786,* 1908.
Evans, J., *Letters written during a tour through South Wales,* 1804.
Exchequer *proceedings (equity) concerning Wales, Henry VIII – Elizabeth,* ed. Emyr Gwynne Jones, Cardiff, 1939.

Fenton, R., *An Historical Tour Through Pembrokeshire,* Brecknock, 1903.
Fenton, R., *Tours in Wales, 1804-1813,* ed. J. Fisher, Cambrian Archaeological Association, London, 1917.

Griffith, R. E., *Urdd'Gobaith Cymru,* 1971.
Griffiths, Dr. R. A., *The Three Castles at Aberystwyth.*
Griffiths, Ralph A., *The Principality of Wales in the Later Middle Ages, the Structure and Personnel of Government, I, South Wales 1277-1536,* Cardiff, 1972,
Gwaith Lewis Glyn Cothi, ed. J. Jones & W. Davies, Cymmrodorion Record Society, London, 1837.

Hext Lewis J., *Ceredigion,* 1971.
Hilling, J., *The Historic Architecture of Wales,* Cardiff, 1976.
Hope Evelyn, *Llangranog and the Pigeonsford Family,* 1931.
Horsfall-Turner, *Wanderings through South Wales.*
Hughes John, *Methodistiaeth Cymru II Gwrecan,* 1854.

Isaac, Evan, *Coelion Cymru,* Aberystwyth, 1938.

James, D. H., *A Guide to Llanybydder,* 1908.
James, John Lloyd, *Hanes eglwys Glandwr o'r cychwynaid,* Merthyr Tydfil, 1902.
James, W. E., *Guide to Cardigan & District,* 1899.
Jenkins, David, *The Pryse Family of Gogerddan.*
Jenkins, David, *Bro Dafydd ap Gwilym,* 1992.
John Piper Architectural Press, *Buildings and Prospects,* 1948.

Jones, Daniel E., *Hanes Plwyf Llangeler a Phenboyr,* Llandysul, 1899.

Jones, David, *Hanes y Bedyddwyr yn Neheubarth Cymru,* Caerfyrddin, 1839.

Jones, Francis, *An Approach to Welsh Genealogy,* 1948.

Jones, Francis, *God Bless the Prince of Wales,* Carmarthen, 1969.

Jones, Francis, *Historic Carmarthenshire Homes and their Families,* 1998.

Jones, Francis, *Historic Houses of Pembrokeshire and their Families,* 1997.

Jones, J. Islan, *Ymofynydd.*

Jones, Tegwyn, *Y Llew a'i Deulu,* 1982.

Jones, Theophilus, *History of the County of Brecknock,* Vol. I, 1805; Vol. II, 1809; rept., Brecon, 1908.

Jones, T. Gwynn, *Welsh Folklore and Folk Custom,* London, 1930.

Leland's Itinerary in England and Wales, ed. Lucy Toulmin Smith, Vols. 1-5, Centaur Press, London, 1964.

Lewes, Evelyn, *Out with the Cambrians,* 1933.

Lewis, W. J., *Atlas Hanesyddol,* 1955.

Lewis, W. J., *Born on a Perilous Rock,* 1980.

Lewis, Samuel, *A Topographical Dictionary of Wales,* Vols. I & II, London, 1833, 4th edn., 1849. [Lewis, *TDW.*]

Lhuyd, E., *Parochialia, Archaeologia Cambrensis,* supplement, 1909-11.

Lipscomb, George, *Journey into South Wales,* London, 1802.

Lloyd, J. E., *A History of Wales from the earliest times to the Edwardian Conquest,* Vols. I & II, London, 1911, 3rd ed., 1939.

Lloyd, Thomas, *The Lost Houses of Wales,* SAVE, London, 1986.

Lloyd-Johnes, H., *The Lesser Country Houses of Cardiganshire,* 1953.

Malkin, Benjamin Heath, *The Scenery, Antiquities and Bibliography of South Wales,* Vol. II, 2nd ed., London, 1807.

Meyrick, *Cardiganshire,* 1810 edn., 1907.

Meyrick, Samuel Rush (ed.), *Heraldic Visitations of Wales* (by Lewys Dwnn), Vols. I & II, Llandovery, 1846.

Morgan David, *Hanes Llangeitho,* 1859.

Morgan Gerald, *A Welsh Home and its Family, The Vaughans of Trawsgoed,* 1997.

Morgan Gerald, *Cyfoeth y Cardi,* 1995.

Morris, J., *Hanes Methodistiaeth Sir Gaerfyrddin,* Dolgellau, 1911.

Morris, John Edward, *The Welsh Wars of Edward I: a contribution to medieval military history,* Oxford, 1901.

Murray, *Handbook of South Wales,* 1860.

Nicholas, Thomas, *Annals and Antiquities of the Counties and County Families of Wales,* Vols. I & II, London, 1872.

Osborne-Jones, D. G., *Edward Richardes of Ystrad Meurig,* 1934.

Parry, Thomas, (ed.), *The Oxford Book of Welsh Verse,* Oxford, 1962.

Peate, Iorwerth, *The Welsh House,* 1943.

Philips, Richard, (ed.), *Pob un a'i Gwys,* 1970.

Phillips, Bethan, *Peterwell. The History of a Mansion and its Infamous Squire,* 1983.

Phillips, *Dyn ai Wieiddiau,* 1975.

Phillips, *Sheriffs of Cardiganshire.*

Pike, W. T. (ed.), *Contemporary Biographies of South Wales and Monmouthshire,* Brighton, 1907.

Poole, Edwin, *The Illustrated History and Biography of Brecknockshire,* Brecknock, 1886.

Price, Fred S., *History of Caio,* Swansea, 1898.

Rees, D., *Hanes Plwyf Llanddewibrefi,* 1984.

Rees, D., *Tregaron: Historical & Antiquarian,* 1936.

Rees, Thomas, *The Beauties of England and Wales, South Wales,* Vol. XVIII, London, 1815.

Rees, Vyvian, *South West Wales, A Shell Guide,* new ed., 1976.

Rhys Ernest, *The South Wales Coast,* 1911.

Roberts, Gomer Morgan, *Hanes Plwyf Llandybïe,* Caerdydd, 1939.

Roberts, Gomer Morgan, *Y pêr ganiedydd* (Pantycelyn), Cyf. I, Aberystwyth, 1958.

Roscoe Thomas, *Wanderings and Excursions in South Wales,* 1854.

Rowlands, John (Giraldus), *Carmarthenshire Monumental Inscriptions,* Cheltenham, 1864. [*Carms. Monuments.*]

Rowlands, John (Giraldus), *Historical Notes on the Counties of Glamorgan, Carmarthen and Cardigan,* Cardiff, 1866.

Royal Commission on Ancient and Historical Monuments in Wales, *An Inventory of the Ancient Monuments in Wales and Monmouthshire, Vol. V, Carmarthenshire,* London, 1917. [R.C.A.M. (Carms)].

Sampson Aylwin, *Aberteifi,* 1971.

Skryne, Henry, *Two successive tours throughout the whole of Wales,* London, 1798.

Smith, Peter, *Houses of the Welsh Countryside,* London, 1975.

South Wales, *Historical, Bibliographical, Pictorial,* 1908.

Squibb, G. D., *The High Court of Chivalry,* Oxford, 1959.

Steegman, J., *A Survey of Portraits in Welsh Houses,* Vol. II: South Wales, Cardiff, 1962.

Teilo, Gwilym – see Davies, William.

Theakston, Lady E. Lloyd, and Davies, John, *Some Family Records and Pedigrees of the Lloyds,* Oxford, 1913.

Thompson, *Journeys of Sir Richard Hoare 1793-1810.*

Treherne, George G. T., *Eglwys Cymmin Epitaphs,* Carmarthen, 1920.

Vaughan, H. M., *The South Wales Squires,* London, 1926.

Wales, Historical, Biographical and Pictorial, Privately Published, London, 1908.

Walford, Edward, *County Families of the United Kingdom,* London, 1865.

Who's Who in Wales 1921.

Wilkins, Charles, *Tales and Sketches of Wales,* 1879.
Williams, B., *Enwogion, Ceredigion.*
Williams Glanmor, Prof. Sir, *Wales and the Reign of Queen Bess.*
Williams, E. Rolland, *Elizabethan Wales.*
Williams, W. R. (ed.), *Old Wales,* Vol. III, Talybont, 1907.
Williams-Drummond, F. D., *Annals of Edwinsford, Clovelly and Hawthornden,* Rhydedwyn, 1924.
Wood, J., *The Principal Rivers of Wales,* 1813.

Journals and Periodicals

Anglo-Welsh Review
Archaeologica Cambrensis, London, 1846. [*Arch. Camb.*]
Cambrian Tourist, edn. 1814
Cambrian Traveller's Guide 1813
County Quest
Country Life
History Review
Trafnodion Cymdeithas Bedyddwyr Cymru.
The Cambrian Journal
The Cambrian (Newspaper)
The Cambrian Register
The Carmarthen Journal (Newspaper)
The Carmarthen Times (Newspaper).
Transactions of the Carmarthenshire Antiquarians Society and Field Club, Vols. 1-29, 1905-1939. [TCASFC]
The Carmarthenshire Antiquary, Vols. 1, 1941. [*Carms. Antiq.*]
An Index to the Transactions of 'the Carmarthenshire Antiquarian Society, 1905-1977, compiled by Andrew Green, Carmarthen, 1981. [CAS *Index.*]
The Carmarthenshire Historian
Transactions of the Cardiganshire Antiquarian Society, Ceredigion
Journal of the Historical Society of The Church in Wales
Transactions of the Honourable Society of Cymmrodorion. [*Trans. Cymmrodor.*]
The European Magazine
Journal of the National Library of Wales
Neath Antiquarian Society Transactions
The Pembrokeshire Historian
The Red Dragon
Journal of the Royal Welsh Agricultural Society
The South Wales Daily News (Newspaper)
West Wales Historical Records. [WWHR.]
Where to Stay in Wales 1976
The Western Mail (Newspaper)

BIBLIOGRAPHICAL ABBREVIATIONS

Add. MS.	Additional manuscripts
Arch. Cam.	Archaeologia Cambrensis
BL	British Library
BM	British Museum
Burke, *LG*, 1850	*Burke's Landed Gentry,* 1850 edn.
C/A	College of Arms, London
Carms. RO	Carmarthenshire Record Office
Carms. Studies 1974	Carmarthenshire Studies, presented to Major Francis Jones, ed. T. Barnes and N. Yates, Carmarthen, 1974
Chancery Proc	Chancery Proceedings
DNB	*Dictionary of National Biography,* 63 vols., Ldn. 1885-1900, reprinted Oxford 1921-22
DWB	*Dictionary of Welsh Biography down to 1940,* London, 1959
Dwnn	*Heraldic Visitations* see Meyrick, Samuel Rush
Fenton Tour Pembs.	*An Historical Tour through Pembrokeshire,* Richard Fenton. 1811
Fo.	Folio
GGMS	Golden Grove Manuscripts
ibid	See last reference
JWBS	*Journal Welsh Bibliographical Society*
L.T.	Land Tax lists
Laws Little England	Laws, *Little England beyond Wales,* edn. 1888
Lewis, *TDW*	Lewis Samuel, *A Topographical Dictionary of Wales.* Vols. 1 & 2, London 1833, 4th Edn
MSS	Manuscripts
NLW	National Library of Wales
NLWJ	National Library of Wales Journal
PRO	Public Record Office
Papers of G.S.	Great Sessions
Pembs. RO	Pembrokeshire Record Office
Pembs. Hist.	The Pembrokeshire Historian
Protheroe	Protheroe Beynon Collection
S.C. (JF) 1988	John Francis Sale Catalogues
Steegman, *Portraits*	*A Survey of Portraits in Welsh Houses,* Vol. II, J. Steegman, Cardiff 1962
Thos. Lloyd, *Lost Houses*	T. Lloyd, *The Lost Houses of Wales,* SAVE London 1986
Trans Cymmrodor	Transactions of the Honourable Society of Cymmrodorion
TCAC	Transactions of the Cardiganshire Antiquarian Society
V.L.	Voter's Lists
WWHR	West Wales Historical Records

GLOSSARY OF USEFUL TERMS

BOVATE: Area an ox can plough in a season.

CARUCATE: 64 acres. See PLOUGHLAND.

CORVISER: Shoemaker.

CUSTOS ROTOLORUM: Keeper of Records (of secular or eccesiastical Court).

DEMESNE: Land retained by the lord of the manor for his own use and upon which tenants give free labour as part of their obligations in return for their holdings.

DSP: Died without issue.

ENCIENTE: with child.

GAVELKIND: Equal succession to land of all heirs.

HUSBANDMAN: Tenant farmer.

INTER ALIA: Among others.

MESNE: Subordinate lord holding estate from superior feudal lord.

MESSUAGE: Dwelling house with outbuildings and land assigned to its use.

OXLAND: 8 acres but variable from place to place.

PLOUGHLAND: The amount of land that could be ploughed in a year. It varied from 60-180 acres from place to place.

PORTREEVE; Chief officer of town or borough

PRAEPOSITUS: Chief or Commander.

PROTONOTARY: Chief clerk or registrar in a law court.

STANG: Measure of land, a quarter of a Welsh acre.

SUIT OF COURT: Obligation to attend the lord's court.

TOWNRED: Township or cluster of homesteads.

IURE UXORIS: In right of his wife.

VIDE: See.

YEAR: Given as 1748/9 for example. The year is written in this way to denote dates between 1 January and 24 March in the years from 1582 to 1752. In 1582 the Gregorian Calendar was introduced in Catholic Europe by Pope Gregory XIII to replace the old Julian Calendar. Britain did not change until 1752 when the start of the official year was moved from 25 March to 1 January. For example 9 February 1715 in Europe is written as 9 February 1714/5 in Britain.

INDEX

A

Adams:
Foelallt Y 108
Peterwell 239
Adda Fychan of Llanddwy
178, 187, 249
Creuddyn 71
Llandwy 159
Allen:
Alltyrodyn 21
Gwastod 141
Axford: Nantybenglog (isaf) 203

B

Bailey Wallis:
Alltycordde 18-19
Llan-borth 157
Peterwell 240
Ball:
Abertrinant 13
Grogwynion
(Pengrogwynion) 140
Rhos-y-rhiw 250
Beadnel: Llanfair Clydogau 163
Bedell-Smith: Pantgwyn 214
Benedictines:
Cardigan, the Priory 40
Tre-gybi (Tyr y giby,
Tir gigy, Tregiby,
Tir gigy) 259
Tre-prior 260
Bevan:
Cawrence (Tyddyn
Cawrwens) 48
Llwyn-y-groes 189
Bevan Bwl Aur 205
Cryngoed 75-6
Beynon:
Adpar Hill 14
Dyffryn 98
Laethlliw 157
Troedrhiwpenyd
(Troedrhiwffenyd) 262
Birt:
Llangoedmor(e) 169
Llwyndyrys 183-4
Bledri of Cilsant 37
Blegwryd ap Dinawal 82, 182, 254
Bliss: Nanteos 202
Bonsall:
Cwmcynfelyn 77
Fronfraith 110-11
Glanrheidol 132
Bowen:
Bwlchbychan 36
Esgair Tanglwst 103
Plas-newydd 245
Treforgan 258
Waunifor (Gwaunifor) 272-3
Ynys-hir 279
Bowen of Crugbychan:
Crugbychan 71-2
Morfa Bychan 196
Bowen of Troedyraur and
Cardigan Priory:
Cardigan, the Priory 40
Castle Green 44
Gwernan(t) 142
Stradmore 251
Troedyraur Plâs 262-3
Ty-llwyd 267
Bradwen 122
Brathwaite: Cilgwyn 59-60
Bredow: Cymerau 86
Brenchley: Glaneirw 127-8
Briggs: Mynachty 199
Brigstocke:
Abernantbychan
(Plâs Glynarthen) 9
Blaen-pant 25-6
Carrog 42
Emlyn Cottage 102
Glanhelyg 129
Henbant Fawr,
Llandygwydd 150
Parc-y-Gors 220
Penralltybie
(Penalltgibie) 229
Stradmore 251
Brochwel Ysgythrog 34, 158
Brooks:
Neuadd Llan(n)arth 205-6
Browning: Glan Medeni 131
Bryne (Brein, Bruyn, Brwyn):
Bronwydd 29
Ffoshelyg 113
Llanfair Trelygen 164
Llanffynnon-wen 167
Pant Dafyd 211
Buck: Stradmore 251
Burgess:
Birchgrove (Alltfedw) 22
Bushell:
Lodge Park (Bodfrigan) 155

C

Cadifor ap Dinawal,
Lord of Castell Hywel 12, 27,
34, 36, 45, 53, 61, 81, 91,
100, 132, 145, 157, 176,
178, 188, 190, 194, 215,
237, 247, 274, 275
Cadifor Fawr,
Lord of Blaen-cuch 259
Cadwgan Grach
of Carrog 115, 154, 170
Camden, Earl of *see* Pratt
Carbery, Earl of: Llanllyr 174
Castell Hywel, Lords of
39, 151, 153, 178, 217
see also Cadifor ap Dinawal,
Lord of Castell Hywel
Castle: Capel Cynon 39
Cawdor, Lord: Glanfrêd 128-9
Cayo Evans: Glandenis 127
Ceredig,
Lord of Ceredigion 72
Chambers: Hafod 149
Charles: Coed-y-foel 70
Cistercians:
Llanllyr 173
see also Strata Florida

Clement
family of Tregaron 70, 188
Clermont: Coedmor(e) 64
Cole: Parc-y-Pratt 221
Collwyn ap Tangno 185
Cosens: Cwmcynfelyn 77
Craig: Maenoreifed 191
Crawley-Bovey:
Birchgrove (Alltfedw) 22
Cross: Ynys-hir 279
Cuff: Llangoedmor(e) 169
Cunedda Wledig,
Lord of Ceredigion 207-8

D

Dafis: Castell Hywel 46
Dafydd ap Gwilym:
Brogynin Plâs 28
Dol-goch, Troed-yr-aur 95
Dafydd ab Ieuan 78, 118
Llwyndafydd 182
Dafydd ap Thomas Fychan:
Llanwenog 176
Daniel(s):
Allt-ddu 16
Cwrt Mawr 83-4
Cyfoeth y Brenin 86
Ffwrneithin 117
David(s):
Cil-fforch 54
Coedyperthi 71
Dyffryn Saith 102
Ffosesgob 112
Garthfrefi 118
Gilfachafael 122
Parc-y-Pratt 221-2
Penrhiwpistyll 229
Pentre(f) du 230
Penwern hîr 230
Tre-faes 257
David ap Ieuan (ab Ievan)
see Dafydd ab Ieuan
David ap Owen:
Olmarch (-fawr) 210
David ap Rhydderch ap Ievan
Lloyd of Glyn Aeron 37
David of CilyGwyddyl:
Cilygwyddyl 63
Davies:
Aber-mad 6
Abermeurig 7
Alltycordde 18
Blaenau Gwenog 23
Blaen-nant 25
Blaenythan 27
Brynllefrith 34
Brynog 35
Caerllygest 38
Camnant 39
Carrog 43
Castle Green 44
Cefn Gwallter 49
Cwm Einon 78
Cwm ul (Cwm yl) 83
Cwrt Mawr 84-5
Dolaugwyrddion 91-2
Dolcletwr 94
Dyffryn Bern 99
Fadfa Y (Fadfay) 103-4
Faerdre-fach 104-5
Ffosesgob 112-13
Ffosrhydygaled 114
Gelli faharen 119
Gellifraith 120
Glandulais 127
Glanrhoca 132
Glynaeron (Glyn uchaf) 134
Hafod 149
Henbant-fawr,
Llandysul 151
Hendre Phylip 152
Llan-borth 158
Llanfechan
(Llanvaughan) 166
Llanina 172
Llwyncadfor 182
Llwyn-coed 182
Llwyngaru 185
Neuadd Wilym 207
Panteryrod 213
Pant-seiri (Pantsheriff) 215
Pantstreimon 216
Pantybetws 217
Pant (y) swllt 216-17
Parc-y-Pratt 222
Penybeili 231
Rhandir 247
Tan-y-bwlch 254-5
Tre-faes 257
Tre-forgan 258
Troedrhiwpenyd
(Troedrhiwffenyd)
261-2
Troedyraur Plâs 263
Tyglyn Aeron 267
Tywyn (Towyn) 271
Wervilbrook
(Ffynnon Wervil) 277
Ystrad 280
see also Lloyd Davies;
Saunders Davies
Davies of Aberceri and
Nantgwylan Aberceri 3
Nantgwylan 200
Davies of Cwmcynfelyn:
Cwmcynfelyn 77
Ynys-hir 279
Davies of Llangoedmor:
Castle Green 44
Llangoedmor(e) 169
Davies of Lloyd Jack:
Llanfechan 166
Lloyd Jack
(Llwyd Siac) 180-1
Davies of Tyglyn:
Tyglyn, Llanddewi
Aberarth 265
Tywyn (Towyn) 271
Davies-Evans: Highmead 154
Davis:
Castell Hywel 46
see also Hart Davies
de Clare 43, 86, 259
Cardigan, the Priory 40
de Hoghton: Hafod 148
Devereux
Hafod 145
Morfa-mawr 196
Mynachty 197
Strata Florida 252
Dudley: Llanllyr 173

E

Ednyfed Fychan 3, 107
Edward(s):
Bryneithin 33
Cae Madoc(g) 38
Lovesgrove 156
Navy Hall 204
Tywyn (Towyn) 271
Edwarde-Gwynne:
Glanleri 130
Edwardes:
Abermeurig 7
Dyffryn Llynod 101
Edwyn ap Owen ap
Hywel Dda 187
Einion: Pen-y-bont 232
Elystan Glodrudd 50, 53, 54,
98, 122, 123, 181, 212, 227
Enoch: Aberarthen 1
Evan:
Aberarthen 1
Cefngarthfrefy 48
Llwyn-coed 182

Moelfryn 194
Evans:
Abercarfan 2
Aberllolwyn 4
Aber-mad 6
Aberporth Plâs 11
Allt-ddu 16
Allt-goch 17
Alltycordde 18
Blaenau Gwenog 23
Blaenpistyll 26
Camnant 39
Cardigan, the Priory 41
Castell Hywel 46
Castell Nadolig 47
Castle Green 44
Cwm ul (Cwm yl) 83
Cwrt Mawr 85
Cwrtnewydd 85
Dolaugwyrddion 91
Dol-wlff 97
Esgair-wen, Llandysul 103
Gilfach-wen isaf 123
Glan nant-y-Cou 131
Gwarcoed Einon 140
Highmead 153-4
Lovesgrove 156
Llaethlliw 157
Llanfechan (Llanvaughan) 166
Llanio-fawr 173
Llwynhywel 187
Moel Ifor 195
Nantremenyn 203
Pen-glais 226
Penrhiwgaled 229
Penywenallt 234-5
Pigeonsford (Rhydycolomennod) 243-4
Stradmore 252
Strata Florida 253
Trefilan (Castell) 258
Treforgan 259
Tre-gybi (Tyr y giby, Tir gigy, Tregiby, Tir gigy) 260
Ty-mawr, Trefilan 269
Ystrad Teilo 281
see also Cayo Evans; Pugh Evans
Evans of Capel Gwnda:
Capel Gwnda 39-40
Gwernan(t) 142
Llwyndyrys 184
Evans of Cwmcynfelyn:
Cwmcynfelyn 77
Rhoscellan-fawr 250
Evans of Peterwell:
Falcondale 105-6
Llechwedd Deri 176-7
Llechwedd-y-cwm 178
Peterwell 237
Evans of Wern-driw and Garth:
Garthfrefi 118
Wern-driw 274
Evershed: Wallog 272

F

Farn: Lovesgrove 157
Fforest: Faerdre-fach 104
Fisher:
Ty-Mawr, Cilcennin 269
Fitzwilliams:
Adpar Hill 14-16
Cilgwyn 60
Emlyn Cottage 102
Folk: Cardigan Town 41
Ford(e) Hughes
Aberceri 3
Gwernan(t) 143
Nantgwylan 200
Forester: Dol(e) 91
Francis: Wallog 272
Fraser: Llanfair 161
Fryer: Lodge Park (Bodfrigan) 155
Fychan
Hafod 145
Penrallt Fochno 228
see also Adda Fychan; Vaughan

G

Gabler: Glanhelyg 129
Gardiner:
Birchgrove (Alltfedw) 22
Gargaro: Plas-newydd 245
Gataker: Aber-mad 5
Gee: Llanllyr 176
George:
Cawrence (Tyddyn Cawrwens) 48
Llangoedmor(e) 169
Llwyngrawys 186-7
Parc-y-Pratt 222
Gevers: Glanfrêd 129
Gibb: Hendre Felin 152
Gilbertson: Dolcletwr 93-4
Goose:
Nantybenglog (isaf) 203
Goronwy Goch, Lord of Llangathen 141, 142
Gough:
Ffoshelyg 114
Graham:
Wern Newydd (Plas-y-wern) 276
Green:
Dyffryn Llynod 101
Pen(y)lan 233
Stradmore 251
Griffith:
Brynele 34
Cardigan, the Priory 41
Cilbronnau 50
Coedyperthi 71
Llancynfelin 159
Llangybi 169
Llwyndyrys 184
Maesyfelin 192
Tyglyn, Llanddewi Aberarth 264
Griffith, Lord of Castell Odwyn 47
Griffith Foel
see Gruffydd Foel of Glyn Aeron
Griffiths:
Aberbrwynen 1-2
Castle Green 44
Cawrence (Tyddyn Cawrwens) 47-8
Cwmnewidion 82
Dol(e) 90
Dolau gwartheg 91
Dolcletwr 94
Glanleri 130
Gwynfryn 145
Llwyndyrys 183, 184-5
Neuadd Llan(n)arth 205-6
Neuadd Wilym 206
Pantgwyn 213
Pantybetws 217
Pant (y) swllt 216
Penbontbren 223-4
Penbryn 224
Penywenallt 235
Treforgan 259
Troedrhiwpenyd (Troedrhiwffenyd) 262
Wallog 272
Griffiths of Dol-wen, Llanwenog:
Abercarfan 2
Dol-wen 96

Grono Goch of Llangathen 53
Gruffydd (family):
Nantceiro 199
Gruffydd 47
Gruffydd ap Henry
ap Ieuan ap Philip ap
Rhydderch of Glyn
Aeron: Llanllyr 173
Gruffydd Foel of Glyn Aeron
61, 134, 141, 219
Gruffydd of Mynachty 63
Gruffydd,
son of Rees ap Llewelyn
ap Watkin Gruffydd:
Pant (y) swllt 216
Gunton: Mabws 191
Gwaethfoyd,
Lord of Cardigan 7, 38, 48,
61, 76, 109, 133, 135,
161, 169, 176, 219
Gwilym ab Einon:
Tywyn (Towyn) 270
Gwilym ap Gwrwared:
Neuadd Wilym 206
Gwilym ap Rhys Whith
of Cefn Garth yr enni 48
Gwilym ap Seisyllt,
Lord of Abernantbychan 8
Gwilym Griffith Goch Rhys
Rydderch 100
Gwrwared 99
Gwyddno 172
Gwyn(n)(e):
Cardigan Town 41
Cefn Brechfa 48
Cilcert 53
Cil-fforch 53-4
Cilpyll 61
Glennydd 133
Gwernan(t) 142
Llanina 170
Moel Ifor 194-5
Morfa-mawr 196
Penrallt, Llangoedmor 228
Tywyn (Towyn) 271
see also Thomas Jones
Gwynn(e)
Gwyn(n) of Cwmtydy:
Cwm Hawen 79
Cwmtudu (Cwm Tydu) 82
Gwyn(n)(e) of Mynachty
Llanerchaeron 160
Mynachty 197-9
Gwynfardd Dyfed 1, 22, 71, 80,
157, 245, 270

H

Hall:
Adpar Hill 14
Cilgwyn 60
Gilfach-wen uchaf 125
Harford:
Dyffryn Hoffnant 100
Falcondale 106
Llan-borth 158
Peterwell 240
Harry: Coedyperthi 71
Hart Davis:
Cardigan, the Priory 41
Llan-borth 157, 158
Peterwell 240
Hayes: Lodge Park
(Bodfrigan) 155
Hayne: Noyadd Trefawr 209
Heneker: Glanhelyg 129-30
Henry: Coed-y-foel 70
Herbert:
Cwmberwyn 76
Cwmnewidion 82
Greengrove 139
Henbant Fawr 150
Hendre-Felin 152
Moelfryn 193-4
Moel Ifor 194
Rhiwbren 248
Rhos-y-rhiw 250
Herbert of Hafod 193
Dol-y-gors 97-8
Hafod 145-6
Pant-seiri
(Pantsheriff) 214-15
Pen-y-bont 232
Ty-Mawr, Cilcennin 268
Holtam: Glanhelyg 130
Hope: Glanhelyg 129
Horsman: Castell Hywel 46
Howard de Walden,
Baron: Llanina 172
Howell(s):
Cwmcynfelyn 77
Llwyncadfor 182
Pantgwyn 214
Penbryn 224
Penybeili 230-1
Hugh(es):
Aberllolwyn 3-4
Allt-goch 16-17
Allt-lwyd 17
Birchgrove (Alltfedw) 22
Brynllefrith 34
Cilcennin 52
Crugmor 73
Feinog (Veinog) 106-7
Glanrheidol 131-2
Llwyngaru 185
Nantgwylan 200
Plas-newydd 246
Ty-mawr, Cilcennin
268, 269
Ty'n-llwyn 270
Wern Newydd
(Plas-y-Wern) 276
Ynys-hir 279
see also Ford(e) Hughes
Hughes of Castell du and
Neuadd-fawr:
Castell du 43
Neuadd-fawr 204-5
Hughes of Morfa Bychan:
Aberllolwyn 3-4
Morfa Bychan 196
Hughes of Tyglyn:
Hendre-Felin 152
Tyglyn,
Llanddewi Aberarth 265
Hywel Dda 246

I

Ieuan, of Dolfawr: Dol-fawr 94
Ieuan ab Griffith:
Glynaeron (Glyn uchaf) 134
Ieuan ap Henry: Coed-y-foel 70
Ieuan ab Ieuan alias Coch-y-aur:
Coed-y-foel 70
Pantysgawen 219
Ieuan ap Ieuan ap Howel:
Ffosesgob 112
Ieuan ap Thomas ap Griffith:
Abercefail 2
Ieuan Ddu:
Beili (Bayly) 22
Cefngarthfrefy 48
Ievan ap Ievan Fychan:
Cefnmelgoed 49
Ievan Rees Fychan:
Cefnmabws 49
Ifor ap Cadafor
ap Gwaethfoed 47
IGER: Gogerddan Plâs 135
Inglis-Jones:
Deri Ormond 87-9
Foelallt Y 109
Iorwerth: Pen-wern 235

J

James:
Brynllys 34
Cilcennin 53
Cilfachau 53
Gwern-y-medd 143
Llwyn-Iorwerth 187
Nantybenglog (isaf) 203
Navy Hall 204
Plas-newydd 245
Trewin(d)sor 261
Tyglyn Aeron 266
Jawetz:
Cwrt Mawr 85
Jeffreys:
Glandyfi 127
Jenkin ap Rees ap Hugh:
Rhiwbren 248
Jenkin(s):
Allt-ddu 16
Capel Cynon 39
Carrog 42
Castell Nadolig 47
Cwmtudu (Cwm Tydu) 82
Dolychennog 97
Dyffryn 98
Dyffryn Bern 99
Dyffryn Llynod 100-1
Dyffryn Paith 101
Glynmeherin 134-5
Lovesgrove 156
Panterlis (Pantyrlys) 212
Parc-y-Pratt 222
Penrallt, Aberporth 227
Penrhiwpistyll 229
Wern-driw 274
Jenkins of Blaen-pant:
Alltybwla 18
Blaen-pant 25
Henbant Fawr, Llandygwydd 150
Jenkins of Cilbronnau:
Cardigan, the Priory 41
Cilbronnau 50-1
Jervis: Bryneithin 33
John:
Abercarfan 2
Aber-mad 4
Alltycordde 19
Camnant 39
Gilfach-wen uchaf 125
Llwynhywel 187
Nantremenyn 202-3
Pant Dafyd 211
Treforgan 258
Tre-gybi (Tyr y giby, Tir Gigy, Tregiby, Tir gigy) 260
John ap Richard of Blaen-tren 37
John(e)s
Cwmnewidion 82
Dyffryn Hoffnant 99
Pen-y-bont 232
see also Jones
Johnes of Croft Castle:
Foelallt Y 108
Johnes of Dolaucothi:
Aber-mad 5
Olmarch (-fawr) 210
Johnes of Hafod:
Abertrinant 13
Hafod 145-8
Peterwell 239
Tre-gybi (Tyr y giby, Tir gigy, Tregiby, Tir gigy) 260
Johnes of Llanfair Clydogau:
Cardigan, the Priory 40
Dol-y-gors 98
Llanfair Clydogau 161-3
Jones:
Abercarfan 2
Argoed Hall 21
Brogynin Plâs 28
Brynele 33
Brynllefrith 34
Castle Green 44
Cefnmelgoed 50
Cilcennin 52
Cilpyll 61
Coedlannau 64
Coedmor, Llanddewibrefi 70
Coed-y-Parc 71
Crynfryn 75
Cwm ul (Cwm yl) 83
Cwrtnewydd 85
Danyfforest 87
Dolaugwyrddion 92
Dolcletwr 93
Dol-goch, Troed-yr-aur 95
Dol-wlff 97
Dyffryn Llynod 101
Faerdre-fach 104-5
Fountain Gate (Porthyffynon) 109-10
Fronwen 111
Gelli faharen 119
Gilfach Berthog 122
Glandenis 126
Glanleri 130
Glynaeron (Glyn uchaf) 134
Gwastod 141
Hafodau 150
Henbant-fawr, Llandysul 51
Llanio-fawr 172-3
Llwyngaru (Llwyn y gary) 185
Llwyn-Rhys 188-9
Mynachty 199
Nantremenyn 203
Nantybenglog (isaf) 203
Navy Hall 204
Neuadd-fawr 205
Neuadd Wilym 206
Pantgwyn 214
Pant y defaid 218
Parc-y-gors 221
Pennar (Pennardd) 226-7
Penrallt, Llangoedmor 227-8
Pen-wern 235
Penybeili 231
Pen-y-bont 232
Penywenallt 235
Plâs-Crug 244
Plas-newydd 245
Rhoscellan-fawr 250
Stradmore 251
Sunny Hill 253
Treforgan 259
Troedrhiwpenyd (Troedrhiwffenyd) 262
Troed-y-rhiw (Tan-rhiw), Llanwenog 264
Tyglyn, Llanddewi Aberarth 264-5
Tyglyn Aeron 266
see also Johnes; Parry-Jones
Jones of Brysgaga
Brysgaga (Prysgaga) 35-6
Penbontbren 223-4
Jones of Deri Ormond
Deri Ormond 87-9
Foelallt Y 108
Glanfrêd 129
Jones of Gwynfryn:
Castell Du 43
Gwynfryn 144-5
Jones of Nanteos:
Llanina 170-1
Nanteos 200-1
Rhoscellan-fawr 249-50
Jones of Llwyn-y-groes and Neuadd-fawr:
Castell Du 43
Llwyn-y-groes 189
Neuadd-fawr 204

Jones of Pen(y)lan:
Panterlis (Pantyrlys) 212
Pen(y)lan 233
Jones-Parry: Ty-llwyd 267-8
Jordan: Pigeonsford
(Rhydycolomennod) 243

K

Keller: Argoed Hall 21
Kensington, Lord:
Neuadd Llan(n)arth 206
Kidd: Llanfair 161
Knolles: Crugmor 73
Knowles: Ynys-hir 279

L

Langley: Coedmor(e) 64
Langton: Abernantbychan
(Plâs Glynarthen) 9
Lansdowne, Marquess of:
Cardigan, the Priory 40, 41
Laugharne: Alltybwla 18
Leigh: Brongest 28
Leslie: Stradmore 251
Lewes:
Alltycordde 18
Cilfachau 53
Crugmor 73
Cwm Hawen 79
Cwm ul (Cwm yl) 83
Ffosybontpren 117
Gwastod 141
Nant-ddu 200
Penrallt Fochno 228
Plas-newydd 245
Stradmore 250
Tyglyn Aeron 266
Lewes (Lewis) of
Abernantbychan and
Coedmore:
Aber-mad 5
Abernantbychan
(Plâs Glynarthen) 8-9
Castell Nadolig 47
Coedmor(e) 64-6
Coedyperthi 71
Glandulais 127
Gwern-y-medd 143
Trefwtial-fawr 261
Lewes (Lewis) of Gernos:
Gernos 120-1
Pantyrodyn 218
Troed-y-rhiw,
Llandyfriog 263-4
Lewes (Lewis) of Llanerchaeron:
Faerdref-fawr, Y 105
Lan-las 155
Llanerchaeron 159-60
Pantyrodyn 218
Lewes (Lewis) of Llanllyr:
Llanllyr 175-6
Llwyndyrys 185
Ty-llwyd 267
Ty-mawr, Trefilan 269
Lewes of Waun:
Waun 272
Wern Newydd
(Plas-y-Wern) 276
Lewes-Lloyd *see* Lewis-Lloyd
Lewis:
Castell Hywel 46
Coed-mawr 64
Coed-y-Parc 71
Cwm Hyar 80
Dinas Cerdin 89-90
Dolcletwr 93
Dyffryn Llynod 101
Fronwen 111
Gilfach-chwith 122
Glynaeron (Glyn uchaf) 134
Henbant Fawr,
Llandygwydd 150
Lan-las 154-5
Laethlliw 157
Llanllyr 175
Nantybenglog (isaf) 203
Penralltybie
(Penralltgibie) 228-9
Rhiwarthen (-uchaf) 247
Stradmore 251-2
Tre-faes 256-7
see also Rogers Lewis
Lewis of Allt Fadog
and Cefn-gwyn:
Allt Fadog 16
Cefn-gwyn 49
Lewis of Blaencerdin:
Blaencerdin 23
Pant (y) swllt 216
Lewis of Llwyngrawys:
Gwern-y-medd 143
Llwyngrawys 186
Lewis ap Hugh: Ciliau Aeron 53
Lewis (Lewes)-Lloyd:
Panteryrod 212
Treforgan 258
Wern Newydd
(Plas-y-Wern) 276
Lisburne, Lord
see Vaughan of Trawsgoed
Longcroft:
Gilfachreda 122
Llanina 170-2
Lort Phillips: Glanarberth 126
Loxdale:
Castle Hill 45
Llwynhywel 187
Lynne: Tyglyn Aeron 267

LL

Llawdden,
prepositus of Commote of
Perfedd 195
Llewelyn ap Cadwgan of Carrog
194
Llewelyn ap Gwilym Fychan,
Lord of Cardigan: Dol-goch,
Troed-yr-aur 95
Llewelyn ap Ieuan Gwyn:
Panterlis (Pantyrlys) 212
Llewelyn Caplan
of Dyffryn Aeron 177, 280
Llewelyn Dafydd ap Rhydderch
197
Lloyd:
Aberllolwyn 3
Abertrinant 13
Alltybeili 17-18
Berth-Rhys 22
Blaencerdin 23
Blaenythan 27
Brynllefrith 34
Brysgaga (Prysgaga) 35-6
Bwlch-mawr 37
Cardigan, the Priory 40
Cefn-coed 48
Cilfachau 53
Ciliau Aeron 53
Cil-rhug 61-3
Coedlannau 63-4
Coed-y-foel 70
Cwmbwa 76
Cwmtudu (Cwm Tydu) 82
Dolcletwr 93
Dol-wen 96
Dol-wlff 96-7
Fountain Gate
(Porthyffynon) 110
Fronfraith 110
Ffoshelyg 113-14
Glan-y-wern 133
Gwern-y-medd 143
Henbant Fawr,
Llandygwydd 150
Henblas 151

Lovesgrove 156
Llan-borth 157-8
Llandysul 159
Llanfair Clydogau 161-2
Llanfechan
(Llanvaughan) 164-6
Llangoedmor(e) 167-8
Llwyngaru
(Llwyn y gary) 185
Llwynrhydowen 188
Llwyn yr Heol 189
Maesbangor 192
Navy Hall 204
Pant (y) swllt 216
Penbontbren 224
Penrallt Fochno 228
Penralltybie
(Penallygibie) 229
Pen-wern 235
Rhiwarthen (-uchaf) 247
Tai'n y coed 254
Wern ddu 274
Ynys-hir 278-9
see also Vaughan Lloyd
Lloyd of Aberbrwynen:
Aberbrwynen 1
Gwastod 141
Lloyd of Aber-mad:
Aber-mad 4-5
Morfa Bychan 195-6
Lloyd of Alltyrodyn and Castell Hywel 113, 159, 164, 188, 189, 207, 274
Alltyrodyn 19-21
Blaendyffryn 23-4
Caerau 38
Castell Hywel 45-6
Dyffryn Cletwr 99
Ffosesgob 112
Gellifraith 120
Gilfach-wen isaf 122-3
Henbant-fawr, Llandysul 151
Llanfairperthycyndyn 163
see also Lloyd of Maesyfelin; Lloyd of Llanllyr
Lloyd of Bronwydd 73
Aberceri 2-3
Abertrinant 13
Bronwydd 29-32
Brynele 33
Deri Ormond 87
Glan-y-wern 133
Lodge Park (Bodfrigan) 155
Pant Dafyd 211
Penybeili 231
Lloyd of Cilgwyn, Gilfach-wen and Coedmore:
Cawrence
(Tyddyn Cawrwens) 48
Cilgwyn 54-60
Coedmor(e) 64, 66-70
Gilfach-wen uchaf 123-5
Gwernan(t) 141-2
Llanina 170, 171
Waunifor (Gwaunifor) 273
Lloyd of Cilrhiwe:
Aberarthen 1
Lloyd of Crynfryn:
Crynfryn 73-5
Deri Ormond 87
Olmarch(-fawr) 210
Lloyd of Danyfforest:
Danyfforest 87
Llangybi 169
Lloyd of Faerdre(f) 37
Bryn-Hawg
(Bryndahawg) 34
Cwm Meudwy 81
Faerdref-fawr, Y 105
Pantstreimon 216
Wern Newydd
(Plas-y-Wern) 275-6
Lloyd of Foelallt and Peterwell:
Foelallt Y 107-8
Llan-borth 157-8
Llechwedd Deri 177
Maesyfelin 192-3
Peterwell 237-41
Wernfeilig (Wernfylig) 275
Lloyd of Ffosybleiddiaid 151
Ffosybleiddiaid 115-17
Llangoedmor(e) 167-8
Mabws 190-1
Morfa Bychan 196
Wernfeilig (Wernfylig) 275
Ystrad Teilo 281
Lloyd of Glynaeron and Parc Rhydderch 173
Cilpyll 60-1
Glynaeron (Glyn uchaf) 134
Parc Rhydderch 219-20
Lloyd of Lacques:
Dolaugwyrddion 91-3
Lloyd of Llanfair Clydogau:
Peithyll (or Peithy) 223
see also Lloyd of Danyfforest
Lloyd of Llanllyr 138
Brynog (Braenog) 35
Cil-fforch 53-4
Dol-fawr 94
Llanllyr 173-5
Talsarn 254
Lloyd (Llwyd) of Lloyd Jack:
Brynog (Braenog) 35
Lloyd Jack
(Llwyd Siac) 179-80
Parc Rhydderch 219-20
Porthyneuadd 246
Ystrad 280
Lloyd of Mabws:
Ffosrhyygaled 114
Llangoedmor(e) 167
Mabws 190
Pen-y-bont 232
Ystrad Teilo 281
Lloyd of Maesyfelin 96
Coed-y-Parc 71
Maesyfelin 192-3
Lloyd of Trawsgoed:
Abermagwr 6
Lloyd of Wernfeilig:
Greengrove 138-9
Wenfeilig 274-5
Lloyd of Wern Newydd and Nantgwyllt:
Gilfachreda 122
Treforgan 258-9
Wern Newydd
(Plas-y-Wern) 275-6
see also Lewis (Lewes)-Lloyd
Lloyd Davies:
Alltyrodyn 20-1
Blaendyffryn 23-4
Glancletwr 126
Lloyd-Phillips
Ffosybleiddiaid 117
Mabws 190-1
Lloyd Price:
Aberporth Plâs 11
Cwm Hyar 80
Wstrws 277-8
Lloyd-Williams:
Birchgrove (Alltfedw) 22
Brynele 34
Gwernan(t) 141, 142-3
Llwyn yr Heol 189
Lloyd-Williams of Glanyrafon:
Glanyrafon 132-3
Penywenallt 235
Llwyd:
Abertrinant 12-13
Blaencerdin 23
Blaenhoffnant 24
Blaen-y-rhaw 27
Castell Hywel 46
Coed-Llys 64
Gernos 121

Glancletwr 126
Mabws 190
Maesbangor 192
Morfa Bychan 195
Nant ddu 200
Noyadd Trefawr 207
Parc Rhydderch 219-20
Pen-wern 235
Ystrad 280
see also Lloyd
Llwyd of Cemaes 27
Llwyd of Mabws
see Lloyd of Mabws

M

Macdonald: Llanfechan 166
Madoc Danwr 76
Maelgwn ap Rhys:
Trefilan (Castell) 258
Makeig:
Parc-y-Pratt 222
Pen(y)lan 232-3
Stradmore 250
Mappin: Ynys-hir 279
Martin: Allt-goch 17
Mason-Watts: Noyadd Trefawr 210
Mathias: Tywyn (Towyn) 271
Maurice: Llanina 172
Meredith:
Cilbronnau 50
Ffosybleiddiaid 117
Meredydd:
Castell Nadolig 47
Porth Hofin 246
Meredydd ab Owen:
Faerdre-fach 104
Meurig, grandson of Rhys Fychan ap Rhys Mechyll ap Rhys Grug 120
Meurig Goch: Crynfryn 73
Meurig Goch of Cil-y-cwm 41
Miles: Cardigan, the Priory 41
Millingchamp:
Llangoedmor(e) 168-9
Mitchell: Aberporth Plâs 10
Mitchley: Parc-y-Gors 221
Moethy: Castell Odwyn 47
Morgan:
Aberporth Plâs 10-11
Camnant 39
Cilpyll 61
Coedyperthi 71
Cwmbwa 76
Cwmnewidion 81-2
Dol-goch, Troed-yr-aur 95
Fronfraith 110
Ffosrhydygaled 114
Glanfrêd 129
Llan-borth 157-8
Llysfaen 189
Nantceiro 199
Nantybenglog (isaf) 203
Neuadd Wilym 206-7
Talsarn 254
Wallog 271
Morgan Dafydd Goch:
Dolaugwyrrddion 91
Morgan-Richardson:
Aberporth Plâs 11
Cilbronnau 51
Neuadd Wilym 206-7
Morice: Wallog 271-2
Morrice: Ystrad Teilo 281
Morris:
Aberbrywynen 1
Allt Fadog 16
Blaendyffryn 23
Carrog 42
Morfa Bychan 195
Parc-y-Pratt 222
Penbryn 224
Pengelli 225
Pen(y)lan 233
Wallog 271
Mortimer:
Castell Cefel 43
Cilbronnau 50
Coedmor(e) 64-5
Morydd,
King of Ceredigion 23, 89
Murton: Crynfryn 73
Musgrave: Llanina 170
Musty: Lodge Park (Bodfrigan) 155
Myddleton: Lodge Park (Bodfrigan) 155

N

National Geological Survey:
Bryneithin 33
Newcastle, Duke of:
Hafod 145, 148
Newland: Llanfair 161
Nicholas: Tywyn (Towyn) 271
Nicholl:
Toedrhiwpenyd (Troedrhiwffenyd) 262
Nicholls: Gwernan(t) 143
North: Treforgan 259
Novelli:
Aberystwyth Castle House 13
Nugent:
Dol(e) 90-1

O

Oliver:
Gelli faharen 119
Owen (family):
Abernantbychan (Plâs Gynarthen) 9
Gwern-y-medd 143
Trewin(d)sor 261
Owen 47
Owen ap Bradwen, Prince of North Wales 8, 79, 228
Owen (Owain) ap Hywel Dda 4, 262
Owen (Owain), natural son of David ap Rhydderch of Pantstreimon 272
Bwlchbychan 36

P

Parrott: Aber-mad 6
Parry:
Allt-goch 16
Blaen-pant 25
Cefn-gwyn 49
Cilcert 53
Cwmtudu (Cwm Tydu) 82
Dolychennog 97
Dyffryn Paith 101-2
Esgair-graig 102
Ffynnon llefrith 118
Gilfachafael 122
Glan-paith 131
Lan-las 154
Llanerchaeron 160
Llanllyr 174
Llidiardau 178-9
Llwynhywel 187
Pantyrodyn 218
Penuwch 230
Plas-newydd 245
Tyglyn, Llanddewi Aberarth 264
Tyglyn Aeron 266
see also Jones-Parry, Webley-Parry
Parry of Cwm Cynon and Gernos 182-3
Cwm Cynon 78
Gernos 121

Pigeonsford
(Rhydycolomennod)
241
Wstrws 277
Parry of Glennydd 134, 178
Glennydd 133-4
Rhod-mad 249
Parry of Noyadd Trefawr:
Cilgwyn 58
Gwenan(t) 142
Noyadd Trefawr 208
Pant Eynon 211
Pennar (Pennardd) 226
Rhydymendi 250
Tywyn (Towyn) 271
Parry-Jones: Esgair-Graig 102
Partridge: Parc-y-Pratt 222
Paynter: Hafod 146
Philip: Ferwig, Y 107
Philipps:
Cilbronnau 51
Cilcennin 52
Pant-yr-ynn 219
Tre-faes 256-7
Trewin(d)sor 261
Wstrws 277
Philipp(s) of Cardigan Priory:
Cardigan, the Priory 40
Tre-gybi (Tyr y giby,
Tirgigy, Tregiby,
Tir gigy) 259-60
Philipps of Dol-haidd 27
Cwm Hawen 79-80
Moel Ifor 194-5
Philipps of Pentypark 151
Cilcennin 52
Phillip(s):
Aberporth Plâs 10
Blaenythan 27
Gellifraith 120
Gwynfryn 145
Lan-las 155
Llechwedd-y-cwm 178
Moel Ifor 194-5
Nant-y-llan 204
Tre-faes 257
Tre-main 260
see also Lloyd-Phillips;
Lort Phillips
Phillipp(s):
Cwm Hawen 79-80
Rhandir 247
Tre-main 260
Phylip ap Rhydderch ab Ieuan
Llwyd of Glyn Aeron 196
Plevins: Pen(y)lan 233
Pocock: Nanteos 202
Powell:
Penrallt, Llangoedmor 227
Ysbyty Cynfyn 280
Powell of Llechwedd Dyrys and
Nanteos:
Aberbrwynen 1
Aberpyllu 12
Alltybeili 18
Birchgrove (Alltfedw) 22
Dyffryn Paith 101
Fountain Gate 110
Glan-y-wern 133
Lovesgrove 156
Llanddwy 159
Llangybi 169
Llechwedd Dyrys 177-8
Nanteos 200-2
Plâs-Crug 244
Rhoscellan-fawr 249
Strata Florida 253
Sunny Hill 253
Tai'n y coed 254
Tre-faes 256-7
Pratt (including Earl of Camden):
Maesbangor 192
Parc-y-Pratt 221
Preignald: Aberbrwynen 1
Price:
Aberbrwynen 1
Aberystwyth Castle House 13
Blaendyffryn 23
Blaenhoffant 24
Cilcennin 52
Cwmcynfelyn 77-8
Dolaugwrddion 93
Pigeonsford
(Rhydycolomennod)
241-3
Rhandir 246-7
Strata Florida 253
Troedrhiwpenyd
(Troedrhiwffenyd)
261-2
see also Lloyd Price; Pryse
Prichard: Ty-llwyd 267
Prioleau: Pen(y)lan 233
Pritchard:
Cardigan, the Priory 41
Probert: Blaenpistyll 26
Protheroe:
Neuadd Wilym 206
Prydderch: Blaen-nant 24-5
Pryderi, son of Pwyll 153
Pryse:
Cefnmelgoed 49
Glan-y-wern 133
Rhandir 246-7
see also Price;
Webley-Parry-Pryse
Pryse of Gogerddan:
Abernantbychan
(Plâs Glynarthen) 9
Brysgaga (Prysgaga) 36
Bwlchbychan 36-7
Cardigan, the Priory 40
Cwmcynfelyn 77
Glanfrêd 128
Gogerddan Plâs 135-8
Grogwynion 140
Lodge Park (Bodfrigan) 155
Pantybetws 217
Peithyll 222
Tre-gybi (Tyr y giby,
Tir gigy, Tregiby,
Tir gigy) 260
Ty-Mawr, Cilcennin 269
Ynysgreigiog 278
Pryse-Saunders:
Ty-Mawr, Cilcennin 269
Pugh:
Abermagwr 6
Cefnmelgoed 50
Coedmor, Henfynw 70
Cwrt Mawr 83
Ffwrneithin 117
Llidiardau 179
Rhiwbren 248
Pugh of Aber-mad and Cymerau:
Aber-mad 4, 5-6
Cymerau 86
Rhos-y-rhiw 250
Pugh of Rhos-y-rhiw:
Cwmnewidion 82
Pugh Evans:
Abermad 5-6
Lovesgrove 156

R

Rattray: Llidiardau 179
Read: Ffoshelyg 113
Reen:Ynys-hir 279
Rees:
Blaen-nant 24-5
Brysgaga (Prysgaga) 36
Crugbychan 72
Fadfa Y (Fadfay) 103
Llet(t)y Meurig 178
Lloyd Jack 181
Pentre(f) du 230
Wstrws 277

Rees ap David Llewelyn Lloyd:
Gwarcoed Einon 140
Rees ap Jenkins: Capel Dewi 39
Rees ap Philip ap Rees 42
Rennie: Hafod 149
Rhydderch (family) 135
Allt-goch 17
Glynaeron (Glyn uchaf) 134
Parc Rhydderch 219-20
Rhydderch 141
Pentre(f) du 230
Rhydderch ab Ieuan Llwyd of
Parc Rhydderch 7, 135
Rhydderch ap Ievan Lloyd:
Cefnmelgoed 49
Rhydderch ap Rhys,
Lord of Towyn:
Glanleri 130
Twyn (Towyn) 270
Rhydderch ap Tewdwr 105
Rhys ap Griffith, Sir,
Lord of Llansadwrn 107
Rhys ap Gruffydd: Fronwen 111
Rhys ap Gruffydd (Rhys Ddu):
Morfa Bychan 195
Rhys ap Rhydderch,
Lord of Towyn 99
Llan-borth 157
Tywyn (Towyn) 270
Rhys ap Robert 71
Castell Bigyn 43
Rhys ap Thomas, Sir:
Tyglyn Aeron 266
Rhys Chwith 72, 207
Rhys ddu, y Sgweier Digri 157,
194, 235
Rhys y Crugbychan,
Lord of Caerwedros 71
Rice: Blaenhoffnant 24
Richard:
Henblas 151
Tre-gybi (Tyr y gigy,
Tirgigy, Tregiby,
Tir gigy) 259
Richardes:
Bryneithin 32-3
Pen-glais (Plâs) 225-6
Richards:
Aberbrwynen 1
Brogynin Plâs 28
Carrog 42
Dyffryn Paith 101
Ffosybleiddiaid 117
Glanleri 130
Roberts:
Aberllolwyn 4
Aber-mad 6
Penbryn 224
Trefechan
(The Lawn) 257-8
Rogers:
Abermeurig 7
Brynele 33-4
Gelli 118-19
Llwyn-Rhys 188-9
Waun 272
Rogers Lewis: Abermeurig 7-8
Rowland(s):
Argoed Hall 21
Garthfrefi 118
Rhandir 247

S

Sackville: Llanllyr 173
Sambrook: Plas-newydd 245
Saunders:
Cwm Hawen 79
Cwm ul (Cwm yl) 83
Moel Ifor 195
Nant-ddu 200
Ty-Mawr, Cilcennin 268-9
Saunders Davies:
Blaenythan 27
Moel Ifor 195
Savin:
Aberystwyth Castle House
13-14
Scott: Aberbrwynen 1
Selyf, King of Dyfed 29, 73
Shamtally: Treforgan 259
Shewen: Pant-yr-ynn 219
Sibbold: Foelallt Y 108
Sinnet: Ystrad Teilo 281
Sion ap Gruffydd ab Ieuan ap
Siencyn: Glanfrêd 128
Skyrme:
Allt-goch 17
Ynys-hir 279
Smith:
Falcondale 106
Foelallt Y 108
Smiths Crisps family:
Ffosrhydygaled 114
Smyth: Aber-mad 6
Spence-Jones:
Maeroreifed 191
Spurrell: Glandyfi 127
Stalbow: Llidiardau 179
Stedman:
Cilcennin 51
Strata Florida 252-3
Tyglyn,
Llanddewi Aberarth 264
Steele
Dol(e) 91
Stradmore 250-1
Stephens: Aberporth Plâs 12
Stewart: Alltyrodyn 21
Strachey: Dol(e) 91
Stradling: Cwmnewidion 81
Strata Florida Abbey
Aber-mad 4
Hafod 145
Morfa Bychan 195
Morfa-mawr 196
Mynachty 197
Strata Florida
(Ystrad Fflur) 252
Tre-faes 256
Sumner:
Llanllyr 175
Parc-y-Pratt 222
Symmonds of Llanstinan:
Pen(y)lan 233
Stradmore 250
Symmons: Llwyndyrys 183, 184
Symmons-Jones: Mynachty 199

T

Talley Abbey:
Faerdre-fach 104
Faerdre-fawr 105
Tarrant: Hafod 149
Taunton: Ynys-hir 279
Taylor:
Aberystwyth Castle House
13
Dol(e) 91
Stradmore 250-1
Tewdwr Mawr 37, 70, 81, 203
Thomas:
Aberceri 2-3
Aber-mad 5
Abernantbychan
(Plâs Glynarthen) 9
Aberporth Plâs 11
Blaendyffryn 24
Cilrhyg 63
Coedyperthi 71
Cwmbarry (Cwm Bern) 79
Cwmcynfelyn 78
Cwm Hyar 81
Cwm Meudwy 81
Cwrtnewydd 85
Dyffryn Bern 99
Dyffryn Llynod 100

Ffosesgob 112
Ffoshelyg 114
Gelli faharen 119
Gilfach-wen uchaf 125
Llanfair 161
Llanfairperthycyndyn 163-4
Llanfechan
(Llanvaughan) 164-6
Llwyndyrys 185
Llwyngrawys 185-6
Llwyn-Iorwerth 187
Mynachty 198
Nantremenyn 202
Panteryrod 212-13
Pantybetws 217
Pantydefaid 217
Pantysgawen 219
Rhandir 247
Stradmore 250, 251
Tre-wen 260-1
Troedrhiwpenyd
(Troedrhiwffenyd) 261
Troed-y-rhiw (Tan-rhiw),
Llanwenog 264
Wern Newydd
(Plas-y-Wern) 276
see also Thomas Jones
Gwynne
Thomas of Fadfa:
Camnant 39
Fadfa Y (Fadfay) 104
Thomas of Olmarch:
Glynmeherin 134
Olmarch(-fawr) 210
Thomas ap Rhys:
Tyglyn,
Llanddewi Aberarth 264
Thomas Jones
see Thomas Jones Gwynne
Thomas Jones Gwynn(e)
Blaencerdin 23
Mynachty 197-9
Tyglyn,
Llanddewi Aberarth 265
Tyglyn Aeron 266
Tywyn (Towyn) 271
Tindall: Crugbychan 72
Touchet Davies: Ystrad 280
Touchett:
Lloyd Jack (Llwyd Siac) 181
Towyn, Lords of 4, 102, 249
Ferwig, Y 107
Plas-newydd 245
Tywyn (Towyn) 270-1
see also Rhydderch ap Rhys;
Rhys ap Rhydderch
Trahaearn:
Cwmbarry 79
Tredwell: Aberllolwyn 4
Turnor (Turner):
Crugmor 72, 73
Treforgan 258
Wervilbrook
(Ffynnon Wervil) 277
Tydal ap Rhodri Mawr 181
Tydwal Gloff 53, 78, 83, 118, 23,
181, 235

U

Uchtryd of Tegeingl 4
University of Wales Aberystwyth:
Aberystwyth Castle House
14
Penglais (Plâs) 226

V

Vaughan 270
Alltycordde 18
Dyffryn Hoffnant 99-100
Glanleri 130
Llet(t)y Meurig 178
Rhoscellan-fawr 249
Trefwtial-fawr 261
Trewin(d)sor 261
Vaughan of Greengrove:
Brynog 35
Greengrove 138-9
Llangoedmor(e) 168-9
Vaughan of Hengwrt:
Lovesgrove 156
Vaughan of Trawsgoed
(including Lord Lisburne) 230
Aber-mad 5
Aberpyllu 12
Allt-ddu 16
Birchgrove (Alltfedw) 22
Cilcennin 52
Creuddyn 71
Cwmnewidion 81-2
Ffosybleiddiaid 117
Glennydd 133-4
Trawsgoed
(Crosswood) 255-6
Tyglyn,
Llanddewi Aberarth 264
Ty-Mawr, Cilcennin 268
Vaughan Lloyd:
Greengrove 139-40
Ty-llwyd 267-8

W

Waddingham: Hafod 145, 149
Wade: Coedmor(e) 66
Wagner:
Aberporth Plâs 10, 11
Maenoreifed 191
Wallis:
Cardigan, the Priory 40
Coed-llys 64
Dyffryn Hoffnant 100
Peterwell 239, 240
see also Bailey Wallis
Walters:
Glan Medeni 131
Perthcereint 236
Ward:
Neuadd Llan(n)arth 206
Watkin(s)
Brysgaga (Prysgaga) 36
Cynnull-mawr 86
Gwndwn 143-4
Webb: Aberceri 3
Webb (Webley):
Cwrtnewydd 85
Waun-meirch 274
Webley Hope:
Pigeonsford
(Rhydycolomennod)
243
Webley-Parry:
Glanhelyg 129
Noyadd Trefawr 208-9
Parc-y-Gors 220
Treforgan 259
Webley-Parry-Pryse:
Gogerddan Plâs 137
Noyadd Trefawr 209
Welley: Llwyndyrys 183
Wemyss:
Trefechan (The Lawn)
257-8
Whittaker: Llanina 172
William: Allt Fadog 16
Williams:
Abernantbychan
(Plâs Glynarthen) 9
Argoed Hall 21
Blaendyffryn 23
Bwlchnewydd 37
Carrog 42
Cilcennin 52
Cynnull-mawr 86
Dol-goch, Tregaron 95
Dyffryn Saith 102
Faerdre-fach 104

Falcondale 106
Foelallt Y 107
Ffosesgob 112
Ffwrneithin 117
Henblas 151
Llechwedd Deri 177
Penbryn 224
Rhoscellan-fawr 250
Sunny Hill 253
Tan-y-bwlch 254
Tre-faes 257
Troedrhiwpenyd
(Troedrhiwffenyd) 262
Waun 272
Wernfeilig (Wernfylig) 275
Ystrad Teilo 281
see also Lloyd-Williams
Williams of Cwmcynfelyn:
Cwmcynfelyn 77
Lodge Park (Bodfrigan) 155
Wallog 272
Williams of Pant-seiri
and Castle Hill:
Castle Hill 45
Pant-seiri
(Pantsheriff) 214-15
Rhandir 247
Wilson:
Argoed Hall 21
Cawrence (Tyddyn
Cawrwens) 48
Tre-gybi (Tyr y giby,
Tir gigy, Tregiby,
Tir gigy) 260
Wilton-Clark:
Tyglyn Aeron 267
Winwood:
Tyglyn Aeron 266
Wogan:
Dol-wlff 97
Llwyndyrys 183, 184
Woods:
Castle Green 44
Wyn:
Dyffryn Llynod 101

Y

Ystrad Fflur Abbey
see Strata Florida

THE FRANCIS JONES ARCHIVES
and Websites

NOTA BENE

Although the county name has reverted to Ceredigion we have used the name 'Cardiganshire' as this book is sold throughout the world where Welsh is not spoken. Regarding the contentious matter of Welsh place-name spellings, we have referred to those listed by the University of Wales Press in *A Gazetteer of Welsh Place-Names*. However, where this could lead to confusion or an inability to find the village or house on modern OS maps, we have used popular spellings. In the spelling of place-names in deeds and documents of past centuries, we have used the spellings current at that time where possible so that readers can follow the evolution of Welsh spelling through the centuries.

WELSH HISTORICAL SOCIETIES

Notice to all researchers of Welsh history

The National Library of Wales is a vast treasure house of Welsh records.

We highly recommend their efficient and supremely helpful staff and up-to-date facilities for any imaginable facet of past Welsh historical records.

The National Library of Wales

Aberystwyth, Ceredigion, Wales SY23 3BU

Telephone: 01970 632800 Fax: 01970 615709

www.llgc.org.uk e-mail: holi@llgc.org.uk

Carmarthenshire Antiquarian Society

Membership Secretary: Mrs E. Dale Jones

Telephone: 01267 232085

The London Pembrokeshire Society

Hon. Secretary: David Morris

Telephone: 0208 6731767

Ceredigion Antiquarian Society

Membership Secretary: Gwyn Davies

Telephone: 01970 625818

Pembrokeshire Historical Society

Hon. Secretary: Mrs A. Eastham

Telephone: 01348 873316

THE WELSH HISTORIC GARDENS TRUST

This charitable trust was formed ten years ago to raise the profile of the historic parks and gardens of Wales and to play a role in their preservation and restoration. At that time the future for gardens in Wales looked all too bleak. Many had fallen victim to insensitive planning, lack of money or sheer indifference. Things are rather different today. There is a great deal of interest in visiting gardens of all descriptions and learning about their history. But the dangers have not gone away. If the gardens that people love to visit are to be preserved for their children and their children's children, an organisation dedicated to fostering knowledge and an informed understanding of this great national heritage is still essential.

If you would like to join the Welsh Historic Gardens Trust, please contact:

The Membership Secretary,
Peter Williams,
Llangunnor House, Crickadarn,
Builth Wells,
Powys LD8 3PJ
Telephone / Fax: 01982 560 288